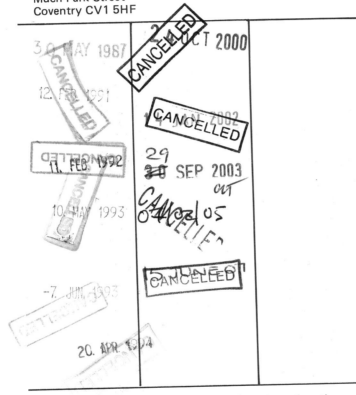

Computer Technology and the Law

John T. Soma
Associate Professor of Law
University of Denver
College of Law

SHEPARD'S/McGRAW-HILL
P.O. Box 1235
Colorado Springs, CO 80901

McGRAW-HILL BOOK COMPANY

New York ● St. Louis ● San Francisco ● Colorado Springs
Auckland ● Bogota ● Hamburg ● Johannesburg ● London
Madrid ● Mexico ● Montreal ● New Delhi ● Panama ● Paris
São Paulo ● Singapore ● Sydney ● Tokyo ● Toronto

Copyright © 1983 by McGraw-Hill, Inc. All rights reserved. Printed in the
United States of America. No part of this publication may be reproduced,
stored in a retrieval system, or transmitted, in any form or by any means,
electronic, mechanical, photocopying, recording or otherwise, without the prior
written permission of Shepard's/McGraw-Hill.

345678910   SHCU   892109876

Library of Congress Cataloging in Publication Data
Soma, John T.
    Computer technology and the law.
    Includes index.
    1. Computers—Law and legislation—United States.
I. Title.
KF390.5.C6S65   1983   343.73'0999   83-9430
                             347.303999

ISBN 0-07-059642-5

To Mom and Dad

Acknowledgments

Due to the kind efforts of Dean John Murphy I was privileged in the Spring of 1979 to teach as an Adjunct Professor, a Computers and Law Seminar at St. John's University College of Law, Queens, New York. This seminar, and an annual Computers and Law Seminar at the University of Denver College of Law in 1980 through 1983 formed the basis of this lawyer's handbook on Computer Law. Numerous students in this yearly seminar have aided enormously in generating ideas and doing extensive research for the author.

At the University of Denver College of Law, the author wishes to acknowledge the extensive assistance and support of several individuals. Gary L. Alexander was of invaluable assistance in providing a great deal of researching, editing, and citing assistance, and, in large measure, many sections of the book bear his excellent input. Lorna C. Youngs also deserves extremely high praise for her assistance in numerous areas of the text including drafting, researching, and editing. Elizabeth B. Emmons and James R. Young contributed extensively to the text as well. Paul J. Zylstra, Richard A. Wehmhoefer, and Andrea R. Stern also aided greatly to portions of the book.

Richard G. Macklin, Debra L. Shoemaker, Kyra E. Jenner, and Carter B. Foulds, Richard S. Dash, Rodney D. Peterson, Scott D. McCoppin, Jan F. Suzukawa, Kurt W. Petty, John D. Molloy, Eugene C. Cavaliere, David L. Leach, Deborah M. Minnich, Dennis J. Wolford, Don A. Childears, Alisun L. Smith, Patrick Seferovich, Robert J. Sherman and Eileen Wilhelm also aided the author in numerous areas of the writing, reviewing, and editing of the text.

Peter B. Maggs, Professor of Law, University of Illinois, College of Law, reviewed the entire text and made numerous and extremely helpful suggestions. Peter served on the author's Ph.D. Dissertation Committee, and assisted the author in many areas throughout the development of the text. Louis Emmons, a friend of the author's since childhood, first suggested the writing of the book after reviewing several Continuing Legal Education and Association for Computing Machinery (ACM) seminar materials.

The author also wishes to thank David Williams, at Shepard's/McGraw-Hill for his helpful editing suggestions and comments.

Most importantly, the author wishes to thank Anne M. Aamodt for her tireless efforts in typing the vast majority of the initial text and numerous drafts. Gloria D. Shonrock also assisted in typing one of the chapters and thanks are due to her.

Finally, I am most indebted to my parents for their encouragement and support during the entire writing of this book.

Contents

6 A Legal and Technical Assessment of the Effect of Computers on Individual Privacy

Emergent Role of Computers in Society

1

§1.01   Introduction—The Computational Perspective

The concept of a computer is scarcely a century old, and modern electronic computation has existed for only a few decades.[1] The computer, however, has already become a standard fixture in American business and is rapidly being introduced into the home.[2] Just as our economic and social lives are increasing-

---

[1] See generally N. Metropolis, A History of Computing in the Twentieth Century (1980); Reid-Green, *A Short History of Computing,* 3 Byte 84 (1978); J. Bernstein, The Analytical Engine: Computers, Past Present and Future (1964); P. Morrison & E. Morrison, Charles Babbage and His Calculating Engines (1961).

[2] See Gampert, *Home Input: the Computer Moves from the Corporation to Your Living Room,* Wall St J, Feb 4, 1977, at 1; Moses, *The Home Computer in Your Future,* 75 Graduate

ly touched by the computer, legal relations between and among business, households, and governments are also being affected. Indeed, a new field called "computer law" is developing.[3] As computer law passes through its infancy and into maturity, the field may even divide into subspecialties. In the extreme case, we may even see the creation of a computer court in the not-too-distant future. Whatever happens, the computer will not go away—it is here to stay, and society will surely be altered by its presence.[4]

While not all businesses have computers, and while not all consumers have them in their homes, home and business have long since been invaded by this new computational technology.[5] Electronic calculators, capable of solving percentages and square roots, have been on the desks and in the pockets of American consumers for several years.[6] The operation of dishwashers, TV games, and microwave ovens has been governed by microcomputers for nearly a decade. Social security checks, income tax data, driver's license information, and personal financial records are now being transmitted and stored by computer and telecommunications facilities.[7] Schools at all levels use computers,[8]

Women 42 (July/Aug, 1981), *reprinted in* The Computer Age, (M. Dertouzos & J. Moses ed); *Soon: a Computer in Every Home?* US News & World Rep, Nov 21, 1977, at 77; *The Personal Computer Strives to Come of Age,* Economist (London), May 19, 1979, at 101.

[3] See Bigelow, *Introduction - Symposium Computers In Law Society,* 1977 Wash ULQ 397; Brooks, *Profession Must Nurture Growth of Computer Law,* Legal Times of Wash, May 25, 1981, at 12, col 1.

[4] See R. Amara, *Toward Understanding the Social Impact of Computers* (1974) (Rept R-29) (Inst for the Future); Leepson, *The Computer Age,* Editorial Research Rep, Feb 13, 1981, at 107; W. Ware, Computers in Society's Future (1971) (P-4684) (Rand Corp); Man and Computer for Higher Education (M. Marois ed 1972).

[5] See Raghavan, *Chipping Away: Demand Continues to Increase as Cheaper Technology Brings the Computer Within Reach of More Businesses and Homes,* 4 Singapore Bus 17 (June 1980).

[6] See generally *Tiny Computers that Speed Business Decisions,* Bus Week, Jan 10, 1977, at 40.

[7] See generally Note, *Social Security May Go Cashless; Direct Deposit of Checks Via Computers,* Bus Week, Nov 16, 1974, at 35.

[8] See generally J. Baker, Computers in the Curriculum (1976); Spence, *Using the Computer to Teach: A New and Simple Approach,* 19 Electronics & Power 284 (July 1973); *Instructional Uses of the Computer,* 41 Am J Phys 914 (July 1973); Koch, *Basic Facts About Using the Computer in Instruction,* 38 Educ Dig 28 (Mar 1973); Kreyche, *New Gatherers: Computers in the College,* 101 Intellect 235 (Jan 1973); David, *The Little Red School House and the Big Black Box,* 19 Computers & Automation 15 (Dec 1970); Ferguson, *Computer Assistance for Individualizing Instruction,* 19 Computers & Automation 27 (Mar 1970); May, *A Landmark Year for Computers in High Schools,* 19 Computers & Automation 26 (July 1970); Computers in Instruction: Their Future for Higher Education (R. Levien ed 1971); J. Rockart & M. Morton, Computers and the Learning Process in Higher Education (1975); Statewide Computing Systems: Coordinating Academic Computer Planning (C. Mosmann ed 1974); *As Computers Start to Transform Schools: Classrooms without Books or Teachers?* US News & World Rep, Jan 8, 1979, at 39; *Electronic Brains in Classrooms (pocket calculators and mini-computers),* US News & World Rep, Jan 13, 1975, at 30; Willey, *Nine Ways for Small and Middle-size School Districts to Make Computers Pay Off,* 160 Am School Bd J 35 (Aug 1973); Peters, *Could Computers be Doing and Saving a Lot More for Your School*

as do governments.[9] Nonprofit institutions such as churches, foundations, libraries, and unions all keep records, store information, and transmit data by computer.[10] The transportation and public utilities industries schedule, issue orders, and bill via computer.[11] Many grocery stores now use computerized

---

District? 161 Am School Bd J 41 (May 1974); Vinsonhaler & Moon, *Information Systems Applications in Education,* in Annual Review of Information Science and Technology 277 (1973); Staff of House Comm on Science and Technology Subcomm on Domestic and Internal Sci Planning Analysis and Coop, 95th Cong, 2d Sess, Computers and the Learning Society (Comm Print 1978).

[9] See generally Council of State Governments, State Legislative Electronic Data Processing Applications (1970); Keston, *Information Systems in Urban Government,* 20 Computers & Automation 21 (Sept 1971); C. Smith, Coordination and Control of Computer Technology in State Government: Constraints and Strategies, DPA Thesis, University of Southern California (1970) (University Microfilms Order No 71-21, 498); Weiner, *Systems Analysis for Municipalities,* Mun Fin 151 (May 1971); Orchanian, *Effective Use of Computers in Government,* 1 Rutgers J Computers & L 98 (Spring 1970); Cook, *Computer Systems in the Federal Government,* 11 Printing & Pub 7 (July 1970); Fisch, *City Hall's Approaching Revolution in Service Delivery: Programming Municipal Facilities,* 18 Mgmt Controls 251 (Dec 1971); *Chief Executives, Local Government, and Computers,* 13 Nation's Cities 17 (Oct 1975); K. Kraemer & J. King, Computers, Power, and Urban Management: What Every Local Executive Should Know (1976); Anochie, *Using Minicomputers in Local Government,* 10 Mgmt Info Serv Rep 1 (Aug 1978); Anochie, *Computers and Small Local Governments,* 10 Mgmt Info Serv Rep 1 (Feb 1978) (No 2A); *The Computer Boom,* 59 Pub Mgmt 2 (Dec 1977); Simolin, *Information, Computers and Local Government: an Administrator's Guide,* 10 Mgmt Info Serv Rep 1 (Feb 1978) (No 2B); Dutton & Kramer, *Technology and Urban Management: The Power Payoffs of Computing,* 9 Admin & Socy 305 (1977); Nielsen & LoCascio, *Computer-assisted Planning in the Public Sector,* 10 Mgmt Adviser 34 (May/June 1972); Rowan, *Information Systems Technology in State Government,* 44 State Govt 113 (Spring 1971); Cheetham, *Progress with Computers,* Munic & Pub Serv J May 21, 1971, at 717; Maschino & Emmer, *An Automated Information System for Local Government,* 19 Mgmt Controls 257 (Nov 1972); *How City Departments Use Computers & Communications Equipment,* 12 Nation's Cities 26 (Oct 1974); *Computers in Local Government,* 7 Governmental Fin 3 (Aug 1977); Allen & Rosa, *Integrating the Management of a Big City,* 25 Mgmt Focus 14 (May/June 1978); Perlman, *Computer System Facilitates Comprehensive Planning by Washington, DC Local Officials,* 35 J Housing 351 (July 1978); Weiser, *Testimony for the Defense - A Case for Computers,* 4 Socio-Econ Plan Sciences 407 (Dec 1970).

[10] See generally Davis, *Illustrative Computer Programming for Libraries,* in Contributions in Librarianship and Information Science (1974); S. Swihart & B. Hefley, Computer Systems in the Library: A Handbook for Managers and Designers (1973); Salton, *Computers & Libraries,* Lib J, Oct 15, 1971, at 3277; McKenzie, *Automation and Labor Law,* 4 USFL Rev 229 (April 1970); The Impact of Computers on Collective Bargaining (A. Slegel ed 1969).

[11] See generally Matt, *An Effective Tool for the Optimization of Distribution Systems,* 5 Long Range Plan 48 (Dec 1972); Mylton & Walker, *Computer Models in Planning Container Terminals,* 58 Dock & Harbour Authority 4835 (April 1978); *Computer Service for Port and Waterway Management,* 52 Dock & Harbour Authority 431 (Feb 1972); *In the Interest of Efficiency,* 62 Pacific Bus 35 (Nov/Dec 1972); W. Norman, The Impact of Computer Technology on Road Transport Planning (1969); Ballou, *Computer Methods in Transportation-Distribution,* 16 Trans J 72 (Winter 1976); Windus, *A National Freight Car Information System,* 30 Traffic Q 23-29 (Jan 1976); Boswick, *Computer Systems Impact on Railways,* 36 Chartered Inst Tran J 179 (Jan 1975); Jones, *Using Computers Southern Style (Southern Railway System),* 26 Atlanta Econ R 6 (Nov/Dec 1976); *Data Communications System Keeps Short-Haul Trucking Firm Competitive,* 22 Infosystems 43 (1975); Matsui & Nukui, *Railway*

label-reading devices at the checkout counter to register prices, control inventory, and facilitate reordering.[12] Some recent model automobiles even contain a computerized device which sparks, mixes fuel with air, and controls combustion, all in conjunction with speed and flywheel revolutions.[13] Assembly lines in modern factories use robots which are run and monitored by computers to accomplish a variety of tasks in the production of intermediate inputs (such as steel and aluminum) and final outputs (such as autos and appliances).[14] Com-

---

Freight Information System, 22 Computers & Automation 22 (Sept 1973); D'Anna, *Transportation Information System (Western Electric),* 21 Computers & Automation 14 (Sept 1972); Nordling, *Analysis of Common Carrier Tariff Rates,* 17 Datamation 28 (May 1971); Boyd, *The Computer Revolution—And the Railroads,* 20 Computers & Automation 25-27 (Feb 1971); Petrash, *Computers Installed in American Railroads,* 20 Computers & Automation 19 (Nov 1971); Gluck, Heissenbuttel & Hillman, *Model Railroading Simulation May Make Commuters Love the LIR,* 2 Computer Decisions 32 (Aug 1970); *Traffic Control System,* 16 Datamation 222 (May 1970); Plowman, *Computer and Synthetic Freight Rates,* 38 ICC Prac J 57 (Nov/Dec 1970); United Nations Econ Comm for Europe, Symposium on the Application of Operational Research Methods in Solving the Economic Problems of Planning and Operating Large Electric Power Systems and on the Use of Computers for that Purpose. (Varna, Bulgaria, May 25-27, 1970) (Sales no: E.70II.E/Mim.23) (E/ECE/EP/56); Sager & Wood, *Electric Utility Corporate Models,* Pub Util Fort, Aug 3, 1972, at 30; Brown & Black, *Gas Measuring Computer Eliminates Winter Overruns,* 202 Pipelines & Gas J 20 (July 1975); *Power Company Uses Computer to Control Energy Flow,* Pub Util Fort, July 31, 1975, at 63; Glavitsch, *Computer Control of Electric-Power Systems,* 239 Scientific Am 34 (Nov 1974); Humpage, *Structure of Multinode-Power-System Dynamic-Analysis Methods,* 120 Inst EE Proc 853 (Aug 1973); White, *Magnetic Tape for Measurement of Energy Use (Public Service Electric and Gas, Newark, NJ),* Pub Util Fort, Aug 2, 1973, at 19.

[12] See generally Note, *Automated Supermarket,* 219 Nation 518 (1974); Note, *Coming Soon: Computerized Checkout Counters,* Changing Times, Feb 1975, at 53; Note, *Grocery Checkout by Computer-What it Means to Shoppers,* US News & World Rep, Dec 30, 1974, at 56; *News: 'Unmanned' Supermarkets,* US News & World Rep, Nov 3, 1975, at 90; Moyer & Seitz, *The Marketing Implications of Automated Store Checkouts Impact of Point-of-Sale Systems on Consumers, on Mass Distributors, on Smaller Retailers, and Manufacturers, and on Marketing Researchers,* 40 Bus Q 68 (Spring 1975); *Cash Drawers that 'Talk Computer',* Bus Week, Aug 29, 1970, at 66-7; *The Superregisters: Computer Terminals Replace Cash Registers,* Wall St J, Nov 20, 1972, at 1, Bauldreay, *Mark Reading,* 16 Datamation 34 (Oct 1970) (optical mark reading technology).

[13] See generally Witkin, *Computerized Chrysler Engine Planned to Save Fuel in 76 Car,* NY Times, Apr 11, 1975, at 1, col 1; Note, *Computer Monitoring Shaves Fuel Use,* Aviation W & Space Tech, Dec 9, 1974, at 30.

[14] See generally *Computers in Manufacturing,* 24 Infosystems 35 (1977); Cook, *Computer-Managed Parts Manufacture,* 229 Scientific Am 22 (Feb 1975); Cole, *Automotive Industry and the Computer Industry: Common Language, Common Future,* 22 Computers & Automation 8 (Oct 1973); Suchecki, *Digital Computer in Process Control,* Textile Industries 87 (1973); Anderson, *Programmable Automation: The Bright Future of Computers in Manufacturing,* 18 Datamation 46 (Dec 1972); Soden, *Planning For the Computer Services Spin-out,* 50 Harv Bus Rev 69 (1972); *Robots to Take Over in Factories,* 14 Ind Res 31 (Nov 1972); *Robots: Progress Depends on Computer Technology,* Kredietbank W Bul, June 5, 1981, at 1-5; *Now Minicomputers Run Machine Tools,* Bus Week, Aug 12, 1972, at 120; *Minicomputers That Run the Factory,* Bus Week, Dec 8, 1973, at 68-73; *Ford's Computer Changes Models on the Fly,* Bus Week, July 28, 1973, at 30B; Gold, *Factors Stimulating Technological Progress in Japanese*

putational technology is a persuasive influence on every aspect of everyday life, and will continue to grow in importance in our society.

Socio-Economic Functions and Effects of Computers

§1.02   Technology and Economic Activity

Economic activity occurs whenever technology is applied to society's resource base. Economic institutions, however, must impose technology onto resources to create economic production and distribution. Economic choices and resource allocations cannot be made unless there is some human interaction in conjunction with technology. The story of economic life is largely the story of human intervention through the mechanism of *social institutions*—ways of doing things—which are continually adjusting to technological change. Society is in a constant state of flux because technology is continually advancing, sometimes at a snail's pace and sometimes at breakneck speed. Changes in technology cause social, economic, legal, and political impacts on values and established patterns of living.[15] Most societies acquire their values from the cultural epochs through which they have traveled, which means that economic behavior is past-binding. Whenever technology jumps ahead, institutional drag and cultural lag tend to impede the full application of new-found technology to both physical and human resources.[16] As a result, an economy often fails to live up to its potential because of human reluctance, habit, and custom, which refuse to allow new ideas to be applied to their fullest. The adoption process for new technology may take decades, or at least until the general public becomes willing to utilize a scientific achievement.

§1.03   —Computational Technology: Economic and Social Activity

The computer in modern society touches the economic and social relations

---

Industries: The Case of Computerization in Steel, 18 QR Econ & Bus 7-21 (Winter 1978); *How Computers Keep GM (General Motors Corporation)'s Materials Flowing,* Bus Week, May 19, 1973, at 14D; Manufacturing Management System: New Challenges and Profit Opportunities (F. Gruenberger ed 1974); Computer Technology for Textiles (1979) (a compilation of twenty-six articles from the October 1969 and March 1970 issues of *Textile Industries*).

[15] See generally Tayiss & Burbank, *Implications of Computer Technology* (1971) (Harvard Univ Program on Tech and Society, Research Rev no 7); George, Computers, Science and Society (1970).

[16] See generally Foster & Gluck, *Impact of Antitrust and Regulatory Actions on the Progress of Technology,* 18 Research Mgmt 7 (July 1975).

of nearly every citizen.[17] Computers increase productivity in an energy-scarce world and shift employment away from certain mechanized assembly lines toward the electronics industries which develop and produce computers and computer-oriented products. Computational technology will, in the short run, widen the cultural gap between the beneficiaries and nonbeneficiaries of computer technology. In the long run, the impact on society will undoubtedly be favorable as the computer brings an increasing amount of education and training to those segments of society which traditionally have had insufficient knowledge and understanding of the world around them.[18] The computer will also alter the relationships between property owners, and will compound some of the legal problems concerning property rights. It is the uniqueness of the computer in relation to traditional modes of living which will cause institutional adjustments to the technology of the computer. The computer is a unique technological phenomenon which in the decades ahead will undoubtedly experience additional advancements.[19] The economic and legal characteristics of computational technology largely govern the direction this technology, and the institutional adjustments to it, will take. It is the interrelations between technology and traditional legal areas which have given rise to the newly emerged field of computer law.

Technical Aspects of Computational Technology

§1.04   Transforming Information Into Machine Readable Data

One justification for a separate field of computer law necessarily flows from the technological basis of the computer itself. This section provides a brief introduction to computational technology. Readers who are either uninterested in the more technical aspects of computers or who are already familiar with basic computer technology may wish to proceed to **§1.07.**

Before a computer can process data, the information to be processed must

---

[17] *See generally* Spencer, Computers in Society: the Wheres, Whys, and Hows of Computer Use (1974); *The Computer and American Society,* Am Phil Soc Proc, Oct 17, 1977, at 339; *The Computer in Our Lives,* 27 Infosystems 40 (Jan 1980); *Computers Rush into Your Daily Life,* US News & World Rep, Nov 5, 1973, at 45; and Herman, *Manpower Implications of Computer Control in Manufacturing,* 93 Mo Labor Rev 3 (Oct 1970).

[18] *See generally* Kleinfield, *Help Wanted,* Wall St J May 12, 1977, at 40; Bumstead, *Opening up High Technology Careers to Women (as computer workers),* 25 Occupational Outlook Q 26-31 (Summer 1981); Bur of Labor Statis, Computer Manpower Outlook (Critchlow ed 1974) (Bul No 1826); and Org Econ Comp & Development, Training Policies for Computer Manpower and Users (1975) (OECD information studies No 9).

[19] See Doan, *A New—and Bigger—Computer Explosion,* US News & World Rep, April 20, 1981 at 62-4; *Coming: Another Revolution in Use of Computers,* US News & World Rep, July 19, 1976, at 54; Kamrany, *Technology: Measuring the Socioeconomic Impact of Manufacturing Automation,* 8 Socio-Econ Plan Sci 281 (Oct 1974).

be converted into machine readable form. Historically, key punches were the primary means to convert information into machine readable form. More recently, key-to-tape and key-to-disk systems have been in use in which information is key stroked into machine readable form and then stored on either tape or disk before being processed by the computer. Optical character recognition (OCR) is another method by which printed information is read by a computer-driven device and converted directly from printed information into machine readable data. As the cost to store and process machine readable data continues to decline, information is rapidly being converted into machine readable form (e.g., invoices for billing and inventory control information), and that information, once in machine readable form, is being stored in computer systems (e.g., history of airline reservations).

§1.05 —Hardware Components of a Computer System

There are five functional hardware components of computer systems: input, control, logic, memory, and output. Input hardware usually consists of key punches, key-to-tape, key-to-disk, optical character recognition (OCR), paper and ink tape readers, and on-line data collection devices such as terminals and process control equipment. The control and logic components make up what is generally called the central processing unit (CPU). Most control and logic functions are performed within the CPU. The control and logic functions, and the main memory, which is either directly attached to or located in the CPU, perform most of the data manipulation including the basic addition, subtraction, multiplication, and division functions.

Memory comes in many forms: tape devices, disk drives, memory based on integrated circuitry, magnetic drum, and magnetic strip memory. Typically, tape drives are used to store machine readable data which can logically be organized and processed in sequence. Examples of sequential machine readable data are employee payroll checks processed either by social security number or in alphabetical order, or billing for life insurance premiums. Disk drives are more expensive than tape drives (per machine readable data stored), but store data in such a manner that all machine readable data are quickly retrievable on a random basis. Consequently, inventory control data and airline reservation data, both constantly changing, are examples of machine readable data typically stored on disk drives. Core memory (small doughnut-shaped magnets) was traditionally used extensively as main memory in the CPU. In the 1980s, however, most main memory is composed of integrated circuits. Core memory and memory based on integrated circuit technology is instantaneously accessible on a random basis, and consequently, is the fastest memory in terms of accessibility. Main memory, however, is also the most expensive memory. Bubble memory is a newer type of memory which is somewhat comparable to very fast disk memory and relatively slower main memory composed of integrated circuits.[20] Magnetic drum and magnetic strip memory are also generally comparable to or faster than disk drive memory in access time, but are slower than main memory based on integrated circuit technology.

Output hardware is often integrated with input hardware. The final results of processing by the CPU may be stored on disk or tape drives, and simultaneously routed to a line printer or cathode ray tube (CRT) for review by the individuals using the computer system. A telecommunications controller can be quite small or can effectively be a huge computer controlling all of the thousands of terminals in, for example, an airline reservation system. As computers increasingly communicate with each other, telecommunication becomes more important.

§1.06 —Software Components of a Computer System

Software consists of a set of coded instructions which detail the steps needed to process data. The three major categories of software are system software, application software, and documentation. System software, also referred to as the operating system, is a set of generalized instructions for any practical use to which the computer might be put and is designed to provide the control and logic functions for a particular central processing unit (CPU). While the CPU actually does the data manipulation, it is the system software that tells the CPU what operations are required, how to perform them, and instructs the CPU to retrieve and send information between the peripheral devices and the CPU. Application software, on the other hand, is a very special set of coded instructions designed to perform a specific task or achieve a specific goal. By way of illustration, the system software tells the CPU how to perform the addition function, but it is the application software that specifies the appropriate numbers to be added. As with the various hardware components, most software is compatible with only a limited amount of hardware. Documentation is simply the literature, instructions, operating manuals, and technical information which detail the characteristics of either the hardware, the system, or application software. The definition of documentation generally includes the training and instruction provided by the vendor to the customer.

Rapid technological change and the component nature of computer systems have given rise to an industry structure in which only a few manufacturers actually produce all the components of a computer system. These large system vendors can afford the huge research and development costs necessary to maintain technological parity with competitors. Numerous smaller firms have arisen which provide only a portion of computer systems' components. These smaller vendors survive by concentrating on a limited product line which is plug-compatible with the components of system vendors.

---

20 *The Poor Man's Magnetic Bubble Memory,* Bus Week, April 29, 1972, at 80.

Computers and the Law

§1.07 The Origin of Computer Law

Computer law has recently become a reality. Not only are there specific courses on computer law in several law schools, but several textbooks and many journal articles have been published on the subject.[21] Computer law even has its own professional journal.[22] Indeed, specialized computer lawyers have the serious task of protecting both clients and employers from themselves and others in their everyday use of the computer.[23]

The computer is only one innovation in a long line of significant inventions and developments since the beginning of the 1900s. Indeed, as Jewkes and his co-authors have discribed, the twentieth century has witnessed the innovation of more than 50 scientific breakthroughs.[24] Among them are the ball-point pen, the safety razor, bakelite, xerography, the disc brake, the automatic transmission, and the jet engine. But why is there an emerging legal field called computer law, and not one called "jet engine law" or "ball-point pen law?" What is there about the computer, its applications, and its benefits which cause it to be singled out for special treatment, and to be in the unique position of having its very own area of law?

Perhaps the reason for this separateness is that the computer was perfected when it was—in the middle-to-latter part of the twentieth century when other technologies were abounding. In the mid-1950s, advancing technology and other complementary developments spawned giant corporations, multinationals, and economies of scale. To be properly managed, the modern large-scale enterprise, requires knowledge, specialization, organization, and planning.[25] Vast quantities of information must be processed rapidly and stored efficiently. As large-sized firms began to employ the computer to accomplish these information-processing objectives, the computer not only assumed an increasing number of business functions, but it became integrated into the economy.

The computer has permeated every corner of the economic system, and in so doing has become involved in nearly every aspect of business enterprise. Inventories are controlled and reordered by computer;[26] employees' work

---

[21] See G. Bender, Computer Law: Evidence and Procedure (1973).

[22] The Computer Law Journal.

[23] See C. Morrison, *Computer Suits Spur Specialty,* Nat LJ, Mar 29, 1982, at 1.

[24] Jewkes, Sawers & Stillerman, The Sources of Invention (1968).

[25] J. Galbraith, The New Industrial State (1968).

[26] See generally Brewster, *Controlling Inventory: On-Line Computer Systems,* 45 The CPA 35 (Sept 1975); Joss, *Data Collection Speeds Retail-Store Inventory,* 2 Computer Decisions 29 (March 1970); Perlman, *Materials Handling: New Market for Computer Control,* 16 Datamation 133 (May 1970); Simone, *Production and Inventory Control,* 11 Data Systems News 20 (Oct 1970); Bailey, *Dynamic Programming Approach to the Analysis of Different Costing Methods in Accounting for Inventories,* 48 Accounting R 560 (July 1973); Hess & Waters, *Inventory Control and Stores Management,* 6 Soc Research Ad J 37 (Winter 1975); Moore

time is monitored by computer;[27] and their paychecks are printed by computer.[28] Customers' orders and accounts are handled by the computer.[29] Computer simulations aid in developing corporate planning strategies;[30] capital budgeting and investment alternatives are evaluated by computer analyses.[31] Financial and accounting data such as working capital, revenues, costs, and profit are calculated and recorded by computer.[32] Personnel records are com-

---

& Fearon, *Computer-assisted Decision-making in Purchasing*, 9 J Purchasing 5 (Nov 1973); Moore & Fearon, *Computer Operating and Management-reporting Systems in Purchasing*, 9 J Purchasing 13 (Aug 1973); Bonge, *Purchasing Managers and the Introduction of Computers* 8 J Purchasing 25 (May 1972); Fearon & Moore, *Why Haven't Computers Been Used More Effectively in Purchasing?*, 10 Purchasing & Materials Mgt 30 (Aug 1974); Campanella & Fearon, *An Integrated Computer Materials Management System*, 6 J Purchasing 5 (Aug 1970); Timbers, *Status of Computer Developoment Activity in Purchasing*, 6 J Purchasing 45 (Nov 1970); Monczka, *Time-shared Information Systems for Purchasing and Materials Management*, 7 J Purchasing 15 (May 1971).

[27] See *Real Time System Keeps Employee Time Real*, 22 Infosystems 62 (Sept 1975); Sprigg, *Controlling Direct Labor Costs Through Performance Reporting*, Cost & Mgmt 49 (March-April, 1975).

[28] See *Checkless Payrolls Are Here*, Industry Week, July 14, 1975, at 55; *Checkless Payroll Saving Hospital Dollars & Time*, 20 Computers & Automation 50 (Oct 1971); but see White, *The Case for a Checkful Society*, 16 Bus Automation 46 (Aug 1969).

[29] See generally Klein, *Computerizing Accounts Receivables*, 77 Fin Mgmt 30 (Aug 1975); *A Checklist for Computerizing Accounts Receivable*, 6 Pract Acct 45 (1973); and Smith, *Automation Collections*, Credit & Fin Mgmt, May 1975, at 10.

[30] See generally Sokolik, *A Strategy for Planning*, 26 Mich State U Bus Topics 57 (Spring 1978); Hammond, *Do's and Don'ts of Computer Models for Planning*, 52 Harv Bus Rev 110 (Mar/Apr 1974); Rupil, *How to Improve Profits Through Simulation*, 55 Mgmt Accounting 16 (Nov 1973); Stone, *Computer Simulation in Financial Accounting*, 48 Acct Rev 398 (Apr 1973); Jutila & Sass, *Uses of Computers for Corporate Strategy Development*, 10 Data Mgmt 73 (Sept 1972); Hodge, *Business Simulation and Modelling*, 3 Modern Data 1982 (May 1970); Ockene, *Losing Business? Simulation Makes it Easier to See Why*, 2 Computer Decisions 37 (March 1970); Naylor, *The Future of Corporate Planning Models*, 24 Managerial Plan 1 (Mar/Apr 1976); Naylor & Mansfield, *The Design of Computer-based Planning and Modeling Systems*, 10 Long Range Plan 16 (Feb 1977); Boulden, *Computerized Corporate Planning*, 3 Long Range Plan 2 (June 1971); Boulden & McLean, *An Executive's Guide to Computer-based Planning*, 17 Col Mgmt 58 (Fall 1974); Wagner, *Enhancing Creativity in Strategic Planning Through Computer Systems*, 28 Managerial Plan 10 (July/Aug 1979); Luecke, *Computer Models: 'Black Box' or Management-oriented*, 10 Mgmt Adviser 17 (Jan/Feb 1973).

[31] See generally Hardy, *Computer Investment Systems: What They Are, How They Work*, 64 Banking 50 (Oct 1971); Blasch, *Computer Models for Investment Analysis*, 20 Mgmt Controls 272 (Dec 1973); Ziskind & Boldin, *A Computer Simulation Model for Investment Portfolio Management*, 2 Fin Mgmt 23 (Autumn 1973); Gerrity, *Design of Man-machine Decision Systems: an Application to Portfolio Management*, 12 Sloan Mgmt Rev 59 (Winter 1971); *'Managing' ROI on Business Contracts through Simulation*, 10 Mgmt Adviser 28 (Jan/Feb 1973); Carter, *A Simulation Approach to Investment Decision*, 13 Cal Mgmt R 18 (Summer 1971); Joines, *Computerized General Ledger and Budgetary Accounting System*, Gov Fin, May 1976, at 26; Murphy, *A Computer Model Approach to Budgeting*, 56 Mgmt Acct 34 (June 1975); Vansant & Stenis, *Estimating Provides the Scale for Budget Control: Computerized Cost Estimating System*, Architectural Record, Oct 1974, at 69; Sawhney, *Time-sharing Systems in Financial Planning*, 3 Fin Plan Today 346 (Jan 1980); Forrester, *Simplified Financial Modelling Via Time Sharing*, 139 J Accountancy 39 (March 1975).

[32] See generally Hardowy, *Computerized Financial Reporting Systems-How & Why*, 101 Can

puterized,[33] as are stockholder data, stock transfers, and dividend payments.[34] Even government reports and income tax data are computer-created.[35] In short, computer law exists because of the computer's use as a business tool and its interaction with the large-scale enterprise in modern capitalism.[36]

As the computer assumes additional business functions in personnel, marketing, purchasing, manufacturing, accounting, and finance, the number of information relationships tends to increase geometrically rather than arithmetically. This tendency occurs because data on customers, suppliers, em-

---

Chartered Accountant 26 (July 1972); Rands, *Using Computers in Small Company Cash Management*, 4 Acct & Bus Research 251 (Autumn 1974); Kick, *A Profit-planning and Control System (PPCS) for the Small Firm*, 14 J Small Bus Mgmt 8 (Oct 1976).

[33] See Juvigny, *Data-handling and the Protection of Workers' Rights*, 114 Internat Labour R 247 (Nov/Dec 1976); Taft & Reisman, *On a Computer-aided Systems Approach to Personnel Administration*, 5 Socio-Econ Plan Sciences 547 (Dec 1971); Cheek, *Personnel Computer Systems: Solutions in Search of a Problem*, 14 Bus Horizons 69 (Aug 1971); Tomeski & Lazarus, *The Computer and the Personnel Department*, 16 Bus Horizons 61 (June 1973).

[34] See generally Schorr, *Automated Deals*, Wall St J Oct 3, 1978, at 1; Note, *New Kind of Stock Market*, US News & World Rep Dec 23, 1974, at 65; Blumenthal, *The Development of the Central Market System: Revolution-One Step at a Time*, 3 Rutgers J Computers & L 232 (1974); *When Computers Come to Stock Exchanges*, US News & World Rep, April 9, 1979, at 80; Bowlin, Dukes & Ford, *The Computer, Broker of the Future: A Speculative Forecast*, 20 Computers & Automation 8 (April 1971); *Computer Revolution at Dun & Bradstreet*, Bus Week Aug 27, 1979, at 72-76; Schussel & May, *Wall Street Automation: A Primer*, 16 Datamation 109 (April 1970); *Wall Street Automation: A Plan for Survival*, 11 Data Systems News 8 (March 1970) (Part 1); 26 (April 1970) (Part 2).

[35] See generally Jacobs, *Ever Wonder How Tax Accountants Do All those Returns? Simple, they just turn them over to some expert-namely, to a computer*, Wall St J, April 5, 1979, at 1; *Computer Prepared Returns*, 11 Taxn for Acct 284 (Nov 1973); *Preparation of Returns by Computer*, 9 Taxn for Acct 286 (Nov 1972); Woodfin, *Should Your Company's Taxmen Be Using Computer Time-sharing?* 17 Price Waterhouse Rev 22 (Summer/Autumn 1972); Woodfin, *Time-shared Computer Useage in the Corporate Tax Department*, 23 Tax Exec 519 (April 1971); Woodfin, *Modelling Corporate Taxes Using Computer Time-sharing*, 27 Tax Exec 127 (Jan 1975) 241 (April 1975); Meyers, *How to Computerize Corporate Tax Operations*, 30 Tax Exec 17 (Oct 1977); Duff & Henry, *Computer-aided Management*, 9 Mgmt Decision 204 (Winter 1971); Ross, *Computers: Their Uses and Misuses: Some Do's and Don'ts for Management*, 15 Bus Horizons 55 (April 1972); N. Foy, Computer Management: A Common Sense Approach (1972); Carroll & Watson, *The Computer's Impact upon Management*, 23 Managerial Plan 5 (May/June 1975); Karp, *Management in the Computer Age*, 8 Data Management 24 (Dec 1970); Terrence & Uretsky, *Computers in Management: Some Insights Into the State of the Revolution*, 5 Mgmt Datamatics 55 (1976); Krauss, Computer-based Management Information Systems (1970); Kaufman, *On Understanding the Computer and the Problem of Executive Decision-making in its Alien Technological Environment*, 11 Conference Bd Rec 52 (Oct 1974); Jones, *At Last: Real Computer Power for Decision Makers*, 48 Bus Rev 75 (Sept 1970); G. Chacko, Computer-aided Decision Making (1972); L. Albrecht, Organization and Management of Information Processing Systems (1973).

[36] See generally Ernst, *Management, The Computer, and Society*, 20 Computers and Automation 8 (Sept 1971); G. Brabb, Computers and Information Systems in Business (1976); *The Future of Computers in Business Organizations*, 1 J Contemporary Bus 1 (Spring 1972); Cerullo, *Maximizing Computer Utilization in Business*, 9 Baylor Bus Studies 23 (Feb/Apr 1978).

ployees, and stockholders are being computerized. As data and information about persons are stored, processed, analyzed, and divulged, a firm's exposure to risk increases. In addition to problems of privacy concerning the collection of data, the storage of information on devices connected to telecommunications facilities creates a security problem in maintaining the privacy of the information. All this, in turn, has the potential—indeed the reality—of touching the major areas of law—tort, contract, property, and criminal law—and others. Increased use of the computer will undoubtedly add to an already overcrowded court system with additional contract, tort, criminal, and property disputes which must be resolved.

§1.08 The Computer-Legal Interface

The widespread use of the computer in modern society, given all the interdependencies both inside and outside of business, guarantees that *computers and the law* problems will arise. Indeed, there are few substantive areas of the law which remain untouched by the computerization of advanced societies. Even procedural and evidentiary areas are touched by this technological innovation.[37]

Basically, the computer can be involved at two different levels of legal situations. First, the legal action could arise without the computer. There is little difference between an action for damages because a computer failed or because a drill press failed. Both are machine devices relied on in a production process. Secondly, the legal action could not have arisen without the computer. Some unique features of the computer can give rise to a cause of action (such as when a computer program is converted and used by the tortfeasor to invade someone's privacy). A brief look at some basic areas of law highlights the *computer and the law* interface.

Tort Law

Personal wrong and civil liability can occur in conjunction with any device (such as any of the significant inventions of the twentieth century).[38] The owner of a Polaroid Land Camera, for example, could commit actionable invasion of privacy with it, and so could the owner of a long-playing record. Consider computer wrongs from the standpoint of intentional and negligent torts. Electronic components may fail without anyone's fault, or failure may be due to negligent design, assembly, or instructions for use. The faulty construction of a computer software package which sends multiple collection letters to the same client may form the basis for a tort claim of outrageous conduct or

---

[37] Nelson, *The Impact of Computers on the Legal Profession*, 30 Baylor Law Rev 829 (Fall 1978); Bigelow, *The Use of Computers in the Law*, 7 L & Computer Tech 16 (1974); Bigelow, *Footnotes to the Use of Computers in the Law*, 8 L & Computer Tech 99 (1975); D. Bender, Computer Law: Evidence and Procedure (1973).

[38] W. Jewkes, Sawers & R. Stillerman, The Sources of Invention (1976).

infliction of mental distress. Intentional computer torts may involve conversion, misrepresentation, defamation, interference with business relations, and wrongful reliance.

Consider a representative case in this area. In the late 1960s, Swarens purchased an automobile through a credit arrangement with a dealer who sold the debt instrument to Ford Motor Credit Company. Swarens made adequate payments on time, but these payments were not properly credited to his computerized account at Ford Credit. Collection agents visited Swarens twice, at which times he showed them canceled checks to prove he was not in default. On the third collection visit, Swarens showed the agents his shotgun. Later, the collection agents repossessed the car from a parking lot. Swarens sued for the market value of the car and punitive damages. The trial and appellate courts held for Swarens.[39]

Contract Law

Several legal issues of a contractual nature arise because of the computer. Not only are computer hardware and software contracted for between vendor and vendee, but computer users may also contract with others for the sale of computer-related services of one kind or another. In either instance, disputes ending in lawsuits can occur. Breaches of the explicit terms of an agreement, however, are only part of the contractual problems which can arise. Far more prevalent are *alleged* breaches of express and implied warranties for computers and accompanying applications software. In one case, IBM sued Catamore Enterprises for nonpayment of rent and service charges due from Catamore's use of data processing equipment owned by IBM. Catamore counterclaimed for breach of contract based on a theory of warranty. The First Circuit held that the parties to a systems-engineering contract can shorten, by agreement, the prevailing state statute of limitations. Catamore's counterclaim was therefore held to be void even though it came within the jurisdiction's statute of limitations.[40]

Whenever the use of a computer in a business becomes so routine that invoices and payments are not checked carefully before encoding and processing, costly mistakes can occur. In *State Farm v Bockhorst*, the defendant's automobile insurance policy had lapsed prior to his having an accident.[41] Immediately thereafter, Bockhorst mailed a check to cover the premium to his agent, and told his agent about the accident. The agent called the regional office to inquire whether the mailing of the check would reinstate the policy so that the accident would be covered. The check arrived at the regional office, was processed, and a notice issued reinstating the policy as of 12:01 a.m. of the date of the accident. The company paid a claim against the policy, discov-

---

[39] Ford Motor Credit Co v Swarens, 447 SW2d 53 (1969).
[40] IBM Corp v Catamore Enterprises, Inc, 548 F2d 1065 (1st Cir 1976).
[41] State Farm Mutual v Bockhorst, 453 F2d 533 (10th Cir 1972).

ered the mistake, and sued Bockhorst for the amount of the claim. The Tenth Circuit held that the company could not recover because no fraud was shown.

Patent-Copyright-Trade Secret Law

One of the biggest issues in computer law is whether computer software and firmware can be protected by patent law. An item of computer hardware is obviously a tangible device and can be patented if original, unique, and practical.[42] A computer program, however, may involve mathematical and statistical formulas, and thus may not be eligible for patent protection.[43] The concept that mathematical and statistical formulas are unpatentable has been applied to computer programs. Benson and Tabbot applied for a patent on a procedure that converted binary-coded decimal numbers into pure binary numbers for any type of digital computer. The Patent Board rejected the application, as did the Patent Appeals Board. The United States Court of Customs and Patent Appeals (CCPA) reversed, and granted a patent. The Supreme Court reversed the CCPA and held that a computer program which was merely a mathematical formula could not be patented.[44] In *Diehr,* however, the Court, in a five to four decision, held that a computer program which was part of a patent application, and which was contained in frameware, could be patented.[45]

Antitrust and Trade Regulation Law

A fourth area of computer law where significant litigation has occurred is antitrust and trade regulation. One important concept in antitrust law is the *relevant product market.* The advent of the computer, with its many components, has compounded the problem of the relevant product market. In *Telex v IBM,* the central issue was the proper antitrust market definition for plug-compatible peripheral devices for computer systems. At issue was whether plaintiff's device was in the same market as defendant's. The Tenth Circuit held that two goods do not have to be identical to be economic substitutes (hence IBM's, Telex's, and other firms' devices were in the same product market).[46] The Ninth Circuit, however, in *Greyhound v IBM,* held that because the leasing and sale of computers are made to different types of customers, a jury could reasonably conclude that there are two relevant product markets (the sale market and the lease market) rather than one for antitrust purposes.[47] The complexity of computerization has even led one district court judge to rule that a large computer antitrust case should be retried without a jury. In *ILC v IBM,*

---

[42] 35 USC §101 describes patent protection as covering "any new and useful process, machine, manufacture, or composition of matter. . . ."

[43] Gottschalk v Benson, 409 US 63 (1972).

[44] *Id.*

[45] Diamond v Diehr, 450 US 175 (1981).

[46] Telex Corp v IBM Corp, 510 F2d 894 (10th Cir 1975).

[47] Greyhound Computer Corp v IBM Corp, 559 F2d 488 (9th Cir 1977).

Judge Conti declared a mistrial following a jury deadlock.[48] Because the issues regarding relevant product market, predatory pricing, and monopoly power were so complex, these issues were considered to be generally "beyond the ability and competency of any jury to understand and decide rationally."[49] As a result, in this type of situation, the trial judge may become the fact finder.

Computer Crime

Not only have the courts begun to try ever-increasing numbers of civil cases involving computers, but a rising number of criminal cases have also been heard. Generally, computer crime involves the theft of computer software or the theft of computer time. There have also been several instances of breaking into the computer system of a financial institution and transferring funds from one account into the account of the felon. Criminal law is also relevant whenever someone robs or burglarizes a store which sells computer hardware and software. Indeed, this illegal activity may well increase as small home computers become increasingly popular. Piracy of copyrighted computer software used on home computers will also undoubtedly increase.

In one criminal computer case, Ward, an employee of UCC, a computer service company in Palo Alto, California, used his employer's computer access code to convert a program to his own use by calling up a customer's computer and charging the bill to his employer. The printout of a source deck for a program subject to legal protection as a trade secret was found in Ward's home after a search warrant was obtained. The court held that the computer program was indeed a trade secret and had been illegally stolen. Even though the program was not tangible property, evidence of it in a printout showing a value in excess of the statutory minimum enabled the court to convict Ward of felony theft rather than a misdemeanor.[50]

In another case, computers were alleged to have affected the accused criminal's rights. Mackey was hitchhiking and was routinely stopped by the police for identification. The identification computer check through the National Crime Information Center showed an outstanding warrant on Mackey. Consequently, he was booked and searched. An illegal firearm was discovered for which he was arrested. The computer crime check was erroneous and therefore Mackey argued that the evidence (the illegal firearm) was illegally seized. The United States District Court for the District of Nevada agreed with Mackey's defense and suppressed the evidence.[51]

---

[48] ILC Peripherals Leasing Corp v IBM Corp, 458 F Supp 423 (ND Cal 1978).

[49] *Id* 425.

[50] Ward v Superior Court, 3 Computer L Serv Rep 206 (1972).

[51] United States v Mackey, 387 F Supp 1121 (Nev 1975).

§1.09   Overview of Topics Covered

The balance of this book consists of eight substantive chapters, a glossary, and an index. The goal is to present most of the major legal issues involved in computer usage.

Chapter 2

The initial plunge into the waters of computer law is in the murky area of *Legal Protection of Proprietary Software*. Given that hardware is tangible and thus patentable, whereas software is not tangible, the question arises as to whether software can be protected by the laws of patents, copyrights and trade secrets.

Software legal protection, however, is in a state of flux. There are several alternative approaches to solving the protection problem depending on the goals of management. The advice a lawyer gives a computer client who seeks an effective software legal protection program is based on the ever-changing relative strengths of patent, copyright, and trade secret legal principles. A methodology to aid the attorney in selecting the appropriate legal procedures to be used will be presented in this chapter.

Chapter 3

The heart of the business economy is the use of contracts—voluntary agreements between parties to perform promises. At any given moment in our advanced industrialized economy, millions of individual binding agreements among firms, employees, suppliers, customers, and governments are in force. In this chapter, "Contracting for Computer Services," both the legal and economic aspects of computer procurement agreements are examined. Negotiating the agreement as well as problems in living with the negotiated agreement are also reviewed. Hardware and software are obviously contractable items and it is imperative that the computer user become familiar with unique contract principles which have evolved in the field. Differences between lease contracts and purchase contracts are discussed, as well as prevalent computer contract disputes. Recommended contract clauses are also analyzed.

Chapter 4

The computer industry is big business. Consequently, it is appropriate to consider "Computer-Related Antitrust Considerations." The effect of antitrust laws on computer manufacturing and sales, as well as problems of refusals to deal, tie-in sales, requirements contracts, and pooling will be examined. The antitrust litigation history, including allegations of antitrust violations by intentional bundling together software and hardware and software lock-in, will also be analyzed. Mergers, predatory pricing, price discrimination, false and misleading advertising, monopolizing, and unfair business practices as applied to the computer arena will be reviewed as well.

Chapter 5

The American economy has been characterized by certain regulated industries for nearly a century. Communications has been regulated since 1934. With the growth of computer telecommunications, a chapter on "The Communications Regulatory Environment in the 1980s" is appropriate. Despite the deregulation efforts in transportation, the fields of communications and power continue to be regulated by various levels of governmental agencies. Although the computer industry is not regulated per se, telecommunications lines are in widespread use to enable one computer to talk to another. Telecommunications for computer purposes will undoubtedly continue to be regulated in some fashion in the future. Indeed, as high-speed computers become more common, an increasing amount of telecommunications will be required. An interface exists between a regulated and a nonregulated industry which possesses unique characteristics, and which yields unique interlegal relationships. The 1982 AT&T consent decree to restructure AT&T will also have a dramatic impact on these relations. The legal rules from the regulated areas, as well as their impact on the unregulated computer industry, will be examined.

Chapter 6

In "Privacy and Computer Data Banks," the real possibilities of invasions into the quiet area of one's personal life are considered. The raison d'etre for computer operations is to process information, the vital ingredient for managerial decision making. Data from consumers, workers, governments, and other firms are not only processed by one company both individually and collectively, but are stored for retrieval and future use. Often, data are shared among business firms. In a dynamic economy, the status of individual economic units changes over time so that what was true yesterday may not be true today or tomorrow. Not only do problems of confidentiality arise whenever computerized information is shared (and thereby publicized), but problems of inaccuracy (within confidentiality) occur when false and misleading information is communicated.

Specific threats to individual privacy in a computerized world are reviewed. Possible misuse of information held in computers is covered, followed by an analysis of statutory and case law on privacy. Specifically, federal statutory developments including the Fair Credit Reporting Act (1978), Privacy Act (1974), Federal Reports Act (1976), and the Right to Financial Privacy Act (1978) are reviewed, followed by a brief look at what other countries have done to deal with threats to privacy and to protect privacy.

Chapter 7

Not only are computer-legal problems encountered on the civil side, but the subject of "Computer Crime" is also a growing area of law. Generally, there are three aspects of computer-criminal activity: theft of software, computer time, and noncomputer resources (i.e., money, goods, etc.). Inadequate security, including inadequate physical facilities for housing computer hardware and software, has caused computer users to be susceptible to breaking and entering by thieves who want to gain information about software or access to goods and services managed with the aid of a computer. There have been instances of illegal computer-facility usage, similar to the ways some criminals have stolen telephones, electricity, and cable-TV services. In addition, thieves have broken computer codes to learn access numbers so that vast sums of money can be transferred out of one account and into the thief's account. Present computer criminal laws at the state and federal level, as well as future expected developments, will be analyzed.

Chapter 8

Futurists have speculated about the "checkless society" for more than 20 years. The computer has already made it a reality for certain kinds of transactions. This chapter, on "Banking—Electronic Funds Transfer Systems," not only outlines many electronic funds transfer (EFT) uses, but identifies some of the legal and economic problems which arise when using EFT. The United States has a dual commercial banking system: state-chartered banks exist alongside nationally chartered banks. Both entities carry on commercial banking operations in similar ways. In 1927 the McFadden Act was passed to equalize competition between national and state banks. The McFadden Act allows national banks to establish branches in a state if the state permits state-chartered banks to branch. In 1974, the Comptroller of the Currency ruled that national banks could set up customer-bank communications terminals (CBCT) within a specified distance from the head office of a given national bank. As a result, the computer and EFT would have essentially created branch banking via the CBCT system. After extensive litigation on this subject, the Comptroller withdrew the opinion. These EFT issues will be examined, as well as the future amalgamation of all financial services through EFT. Various antitrust aspects of EFT will also be reviewed.

Chapter 9

The world has become increasingly interdependent. Foreign trade among nations continues to prosper as both transportation and communications facilities are perfected. This last chapter—"International—Import/Export of High Technology Items,"—considers foreign trade not only in computers but in other high technology electronic products as well. As scientific information is imported and exported via computer products, political considerations are involved in the trade of electronic and other information as are economic considerations of protectionism and the business cycle. There is an interface between international trade restrictions on the one hand, and protection of scientific advancements, (such as hardware and software) on the other. The application of antidumping laws to hardware and software are considered, along with other types of tariff restrictions which are applicable to international trade in computers. Export and re-export penalties for dealing with communist countries are also examined.

Chapter 10

A final chapter briefly looks at the future interactions of each of these computer related legal areas. As each of these computer law areas continues to change at an arithmetic rate, due to the ever constant forward press of computational technology, the interaction of these areas causes a geometric rate of change in the totality of computer law.

Software Protection

2

§2.01   Definition of Software and Hardware

The burgeoning computer industry, with its full complement of unique legal problems has, until very recently, seen its grievances addressed solely by existing legal principles which were formulated in times that never anticipated the impact computers would make on the world and in the law. The widespread recognition that computational technology is causing increasingly more convoluted extensions of *traditional* laws to be used to resolve computational-legal disputes, is hastening the emergence of a specific body of computer law. One of these areas that has received fairly extensive judicial and legislative attention is software protection. In spite of this heightened focus on software protection, intellectual property law protecting computer programs is a topic characterized by many unanswered questions.

The software segment of the computer industry is the fastest growing segment of the entire computer industry. The trend is toward software costs becoming a major percentage of total system costs, and consequently the legal status of software is increasingly more important. The legal structure surrounding software has not, however, kept pace with the technological changes occurring within the computer industry. Although there is voluminous material on the legal protection of software, no definitive legal principles have emerged concerning the procedures used to protect software.[1]

Rapid software development is essential for the continued growth of the computer industry. Today, software packages are commonly sold for thousands of dollars.[2] In addition, there are now large numbers of identical computers available on which these software packages can be used. Large social gains exist if these software packages can be used on all machines rather than having a similar software package independently developed for each computer. Consequently, some type of legal mechanism is essential to provide software developers with a means to protect their intellectual products. Once appropriate legal protection is provided, the developers of software will be more willing to sell their products, and thus wasteful duplication of effort can be avoided. By providing a viable method to protect software, public policy will therefore foster the commercial development of software.

In order to fully understand the complexities of providing software with sufficient legal protection, it is necessary to understand some of the computer terminology involved.[3] Hardware and software mean different things to differ-

---

[1] See, e g, George Washington University, Computers in Law Institute, The Law of Software (1968 & 1969). For a bibliography on software protection see 7 Rutgers J Computers, Tech & L 393 (1980).

[2] With the introduction of microcomputers, the price of software packages after development has dropped to between $15-300. The purchaser generally receives an operating system, adequate documentation, and a reasonable amount of technical support. The purchase price typicaly represents one-fifth to one-tenth of the total cost to develop an equivalent package. Head & Linik, *Software Package Acquisition,* 14 Datamation 24 (1968).

[3] An entirely different concern is found in the area of firmware protection. For a

ent people. The problem of the definition of these terms has been a major stumbling block in the resolution of the protection dispute. Hardware and software are the two general components of modern computer systems. The hardware of a computer system has been defined with little trouble. The concept of hardware as "the machinery that is built to store and execute patterns and processes"[4] is easily grasped by most people. Another definition describes hardware as "[E]lectronic or electromechanical components, instruments, or systems."[5] Hardware is thus a machine, a part of a machine, or a group of machines which does things to information, and thus constitutes the framework within which functions take place.

An acceptable definition for software is more difficult to grasp and also more controversial. As the capacity and capabilities of computer systems have grown, so too has the complexity of software. A simplistic definition of software is that software is the computer program which runs the hardware and manipulates the information inside the hardware. Even though hardware has been defined as the physical machine, this is not to imply that software has no physical manifestation. Software has a physical nature that is usually exhibited in one of three locations: it is an arrangement of specific patterns of magnetic pulses either in the main memory of a computer, on tapes, or on disks.[6] The uses for these arrangements of magnetic pulses are even more varied than the locations of the pulses, and it is those uses of software which are its actual definition.

Definition of a Computer Program

The first digital computer, ENIAC,[7] was able to electronically store data (numbers, etc.) inside the machine, but the processing of the data was controlled by a board containing wires which could be arranged so as to intercon-

---

discussion of firmware, and of its protection status, see Ruckman, *Firmware Patents Can be Firm*, IEEE Spectrum 35-40 (Aug 1980). See also Schmidt, *Legal Proprietory Interest in Computer Programs: The American Experience*, 21 Jurimetrics J 345, 359 (1981); Pierson, Bates, *Copyright Protection for Firmware: An International View*, 4 Hastings Intl & Comp L Rev 473 (1981); Ramey *Patentability of Software and Firmware*, 3 Pat & Trademark Rev 147 (1980); Pokotilow, *Microchip Programs: Copyrightable Programs?* 5 Pa LJ 3 (1981); Ross, *Patentability of Computer "Firmware"*, 59 J Pat Off Socy 731 (1977); *To Insure Patent on Software, Make it Reusable Hardware*, Electronic News, Jan 18, 1970, at 48.

Firmware is software which has been imbedded in hardware, i.e., the software program can be embodied in the silicon chip. For a good discussion of the economics of software development, see Frank, *The New Software Economics*, Computerworld (1979), at 17.

[4] Gagliardi, *Software: What is it*, 8 APLAQJ 233 (1980). See generally *Law Research Service, Inc v General Automation, Inc*, 5 Computer L Serv R 220, 223 (1974); *Computer Sciences Corp v Comm of Internal Revenue*, 5 Computer L Serv R 786 (1974).

[5] 61 Proc IEEE (Proceedings of the International Electrical Engineering) 1636 (Nov 1973).

[6] Gagliardi, *supra* note 4, at 234.

[7] ENIAC stands for Electronic Numerical Integrator And Calculator.

nect various internal circuits. Therefore, the machine was rewired for each different type of processing. With EDVAC,[8] the next digital computer, the wires were replaced by electronic circuits designed so that they could only be on (1) or off (0). The *on* state of the circuit was equivalent to a wire being plugged in, and the *off* state was the equivalent of the absence of a wire. The setting of these circuits could be done by *reading* punched cards, thus the machine could be *rewired* by reading a different deck of cards. The process of deciding how to wire the ENIAC or how to punch the cards for EDVAC was called *programming.*

As new computers developed, this primitive method of setting the 1s and 0s was replaced by a symbolic form of defining the machine *instructions,* i.e., ADD instead of 100111001. This language was called assembler language, and a program called an *assembler* was developed to translate the ADD to the equivalent 1s and 0s. As development continued, *high level* languages, such as FORTRAN, COBOL, or BASIC, and more complex programs, called compilers were developed. A compiler translates a high level program called a source program into assembler language, which is then processed by an assembler into 1s and 0s, called the object program. The programmer however, may not be aware of the intermediate assembler step. The compiler and assembler together translate a source program from a high level language into the object program consisting of 1s and 0s which essentially *rewires* the computer to process data in order to achieve certain results.

Programming is the process of defining how to process data, and then encoding this process (or algorithm) into the high level language source program. The program is a set of very precise instructions, which have been translated from the algorithm to tell the computer how to process the data. At any given stage, the *program* may be an algorithm, a source program, an assembler program, or an object program. The technical and legal question becomes which of these—the algorithm, source codes, assembler programs, or object programs, or what combination of them—is the *real* program and therefore entitled to legal protection?

Types of Software

Various types of software perform various functions in a computer system. These functions include system software, utilities, applications software, and turnkey systems. System software is used to perform basic functions within the computer and to provide the basic building blocks for creating new software. Systems software includes applications in compilers, telecommunications systems, and the other basic systems involved in operating a computer. Utility software is used, in a typical application, as a text editor. Applications software is used to get results from the information in the hardware. This type of software is often user-generated instead of manufacturer-generated. Applications software is designed with a specific methodology and intended result in

---

[8] EDVAC stands for Electronic Discrete Variable Automatic Computer.

mind, and is designed to work under certain specific conditions. Also, applications software may be created by the manufacturer or some other software producer in the form of packages, often used to handle tasks such as payroll accounting or order processing in commercial applications. Turnkey systems are a conglomerate of the other three types of software, and are highly complex. A standard type of turnkey system is the common airline reservation system.[9] A definition of software, based on the uses of software, is that software is "a computer program plus associated documentation. . . ."[10] The documentation would include any flow charts, printouts, or instructions for the use of the computer program.

Computer systems are made up of hardware (machines) and software (which controls the machines). Protection of computer hardware inventions, including printers, memory systems, central processors, and the like, is available through the United States patent system.[11] The protection of computer software, however, has been a subject of controversy for nearly two decades. The proponents of software protection seek adequate compensation for their labor and investment in the research and development of software. The opponents of software protection warn of the danger of granting limited monopolies, and advocate the importance of a free exchange of ideas in the marketplace. This chapter will consider the traditional methods which software owners have used to protect their proprietary interests in computer software: patent law,[12] copyright law,[13] and trade secret protection.[14] As will be evident, none of these methods has provided software owners with the full scope of protection they desire.[15] This chapter will then examine the unique problems of the computer

---

[9] Gagliardi, *supra* note 4, at 236-38.

[10] Advisory Group of Non-Governmental Experts on the Protection of Computer Programs, WIPO AGCP/NGO/II/3, Mar 17, 1975, at 5, §13. The 1980 Copyright Act Amendments defined computer program as "a set of statements or instructions to be used directly or indirectly in a computer in order to bring about a certain result." Pub L No 96-517, 94 Stat 3028, 17 USC §101.

[11] 35 USC §101; see also **§2.02.**

[12] See **§§2.02-2.05.**

[13] See **§§2.06-2.10.**

[14] See **§§2.11-2.15.**

[15] Ogden, *Protection of Computer Software—A Hard Problem*, 26 Drake L Rev 180 (1976). For a discussion of software protection in general, see Root, *Protecting Computer Software in the 80's: Practical Guidelines for Evolving Needs*, 8 Rutgers Computer & Tech LJ 205 (1981); Maggs, *Computer Programs as the Object of Intellectual Property in the United States of America*, 30 Am J Comp L 251 (1982); Pope, *Protection of Proprietary Interests in Computer Software*, 30 Ala L Rev 527 (1979); Rilee, *The Protection of Property Rights in Computer Software*, 19 Pub Ent Advert & Allied Fields LQ 265 (1981); Rose, *Protection of Intellectual Property in Computers and Computer Programs: Recent Developments*, 9 Pepperdine L Rev 547 (1982); Selinger, *Protection of Proprietary Software: Evolving Needs for Legal Protection in the Modern Day Business*, 45 Tex BJ 11 (1982); Zammit, *Computers, Software and the Law*, 68 ABAJ 970 (1982); Cohen, *Computer Programs—Does the Law Provide Adequate Protective Mechanism?*, 56 Am LJ 219 (1982); Pressman, *A Guide to Software Protection*, Legal Times of Washington (Nov 17, 1980); Hoffman, The Software Legal Book (1981); Ebel &

industry and will conclude with an examination of some of the proposed alternatives to the traditional methods of software protection.

Patent Protection

§2.02   Generally

The protection of inventions is subject to federal patent law as established in the Constitution of the United States. Proprietary protection is found pursuant to congressional power to "promote the progress of science and the useful arts by securing for limited times to authors and inventors the exclusive rights to their respective writings and discoveries."[16] This protection covers "any new and useful process, machine, manufacture, or composition of matter, or any new and useful improvement thereof. . . ."[17] While patent law does provide protection to the investor of an article falling under one of the listed catagories, it does not provide the inventor with an unlimited monopoly. Patent law "gives the inventor only the right to exclude others from manufacturing, using, or selling the patented article for a finite period of time."[18]

Patent law provides the owner/creator of an invention with protection for a period ranging from 14 to 17 years. Design patents, those granted for inventions of, among other things, the ornamental aspects of machines, are limited to 14 years. Utility patents, granted for the invention of and processes used to make machines, products, and compositions, and plant patents, granted for the invention or creation of new varieties of plants, are grants of protection for up to 17 years.[19] The protection provided by these patents prohibits the unauthorized use, manufacture, and sale[20] of a patented invention, not merely an

---

Aston, *A Field Guide to Intellectual Property,* 9 Colo Law 25 (1980); Ducker, *Liability for Computer Software,* 26 Bus L 1081 (1971); Goldberg, *Legal Protection of EDP Software,* 5 L & Computer Tech 97 (1972); Popper, *Technology & Programming—Is It a Problem in Definition?,* 5 APLAQJ 13 (1977); Lahore, *Computers and the Law: The Protection of Intellectual Property,* 9 Fed L Rev 15 (1978); Pfeifer, *Legal Protection of Computer Software: An Update,* 5 Orange County BJ 226 (1978); Melville, *Legal Protection of Software,* 119 New LJ 1169 (1969); *Computer Program Protection: The Need to Legislate a Solution,* 54 Cornell L Rev 586 (1969); *Legal Protection for Computer Software,* 18 Computers & Automation 12 (1969); *The Process Right: A Negative Opinion,* 2 Modern Data 92 (1969); McFarlane, *Legal Protection of Computer Programs,* 1970 J Bus L 204 (1970).

[16] US Const art I, §8.

[17] 35 USC §101.

[18] Rupert, *The Relationship of Patent Law to Antitrust Law,* 49 Antitrust LJ 755 (1980). See also Jacobs, *Computer Technology (Hardware and Software): Some Legal Implications for Antitrust, Copyrights and Patents,* 1 Rutgers J Computers & L 50-69 (1970); Note, *Patentability of Computer Programs,* 27 U Miami L Rev 494 (1973). See also §§4.15, 4.16.

[19] Safran, *What Non-Patent Attorneys Should Know About Patents,* 28 Prac Law 60 (1982).

[20] 35 USC §271.

unauthorized copying.[21]

Those who oppose the extension of software protection via patent law cite several reasons, including the burdens which, arguably, would fall upon the Patent Office and the courts hearing patent cases. Those burdens, it is argued, would arise due to the massive quantity of software which is produced each year. If each item of software were patentable, the Patent Office would have to search each existing software patent in order to satisfy the other requirements of patentability.[22] With the proliferation of software, the increased number of software searches would lead to an increased burden for the courts as more software patents became more vulnerable to attack on the basis of alleged infringements of prior software patents.[23] Another reason cited by the opponents of increased patent protection of software is the possible lack of technical knowledge on the part of judges, which would make them at least partially unqualified to hear complex computer software patent cases. A final reason often cited by opponents to expanded protection is the potential increase in the saleability and versatility of software if the free exchange of information were encouraged.[24]

The Supreme Court has traditionally considered software to be beyond the scope of patent protection.[25] An inspection of the historical treatment of computer software and patent law is valuable nonetheless due to the recent Court cases which, in effect, reflect the decision in an earlier appellate court case from the late 1960s.[26] This historical inspection will be followed by an analysis of *Diamond v Diehr*[27] and *Diamond v Bradley*,[28] and of future developments in the area of patent law and computer software.[29]

§2.03   Patent Case Law Prior to *Diehr* and *Bradley*

While §101 of the Patent Act of 1952 (Patent Act) states that patentable items include "any new and useful process, machine, manufacture, or composi-

---

[21] *See* Copyright Law, 17 USC §101. See also **§§2.06-2.10.**

[22] Note, *Gottschalk v Benson - The Supreme Court Takes a Hard Line on Software,* 47 St John's L Rev 635, 649 n 85 (1973). See also Note, *Patentability of Computer Programs: Gottschalk v Benson, 93 S Ct 253 (1972),* 27 U Miami L Rev 494 (1973); *Gottschalk v Benson: A Bright Light with a Dim Future,* 28 Baylor L Rev 187 (1976); Freed, *Protection of Proprietary Programs in Light of Benson and Talbot,* 13 Jurimetrics J 139 (1973); Note, *Patent Law-Computer Programs-Unpatentable Mental Process-Gottschalk v Benson,* 14 BC Ind & Com L Rev 1050 (1973).

[23] Lautsch, *Computers and the University Attorney: An Overview of Computer Law on Campus,* 5 JC&U 217 (1979).

[24] *Id.* See also Note, *Gottschalk v Benson supra* note 22.

[25] See **§2.03.**

[26] *Id.*

[27] 450 US 175, 101 S Ct 1048 (1981). See **§2.04.**

[28] 450 US 175, 101 S Ct 1495 (1981). See **§2.04.**

[29] See **§2.05.**

tion of matter, or any new and useful improvement thereof,"[30] §102 of the Patent Act requires that the subject matter be novel and §103 limits patentability if the differences between the new invention and the existing technology are "such that the subject matter as a whole would have been obvious at the time the invention was made to a person having ordinary skill in the art."[31]

Three elements must be present for an object to be considered patentable: (1) it must be the *proper subject matter;* (2) it must involve *novelty;* and (3) it must be *nonobvious.* The Patent and Trademark Office (PTO) has consistently turned down every application for a patent on a computer program. The Court of Customs and Patent Appeals (CCPA) has, however, consistently fought for software patents, even in the face of opposition from the Supreme Court.[32] The new Court of Appeals for the Federal Circuit has taken over the CCPA and has stated that it will follow the precedents of the CCPA in its decisions. The Supreme Court has continually reversed the CCPA while maintaining that programs were not, per se, unpatentable, and, in fact, has urged Congress to resolve the issue.[33] In 1964, the PTO stated that programs were not patentable because they were "creations in the area of thought,"[34] and in 1965 the President's Commission on the Patent System was formed to suggest revisions to the Patent Act.[35] The commission recommended that programs not be given patent protection.[36] Legislation implementing this recommendation was not passed by Congress.[37] By 1968, the PTO had officially declared that programs were not patentable,[38] but in 1969 the CCPA ruled that the PTO was in error. The court allowed patents in two program cases[39] by relying on traditional aspects of patent law as applied to computer software.

Software patent applications are generally claimed under one of two theories. The first type of claim is based on the program as an *apparatus.* Here, the apparatus is like a machine, which is statutorily eligible for patent protection. The program controls the computer, and together the program and the com-

---

[30] 35 USC §101.

[31] 35 USC §§102, 103. See also Comments, *Patent Law—Patentable Subject Matter—Computer Software,* 24 NYL Sch L Rev 975 (1979); Comment, *Patentability of Computer Software: The Nonobvious Issue,* 62 Iowa L Rev 615 (1976); Davis, *Computer Programs and Subject Matter Patentability,* 6 Rutgers J Computers & L 1 (1977).

[32] Gemignani, *Legal Protection for Computer Software: The View From '79',* 7 Rutgers J Computers, Tech & L 269 (1979); but see **§2.04;** see also Hamburg, *Inventions Relating to Computers or Use Thereof Again Being Considered by U S Supreme Court,* 78 Pat & Trademark Rev 518 (1980).

[33] Gotschalk v Benson, 409 US 63, 73 (1972).

[34] Gemignani, *supra* note 32, at 295.

[35] Exec Order No 11215, 30 Fed Reg 4661 (1965).

[36] *The President's Commission on the Patent System* 13 (1966), *reprinted in* S Rep No 5, 90th Cong, 1st sess.

[37] Gemignani, *supra* note 32, at 295.

[38] *Id* 296.

[39] *In re* Prater, 415 F2d 1393 (CCPA 1969), *In re* Bernhart, 417 F2d 1395 (CCPA 1969).

puter create a special and unique machine.[40] The apparatus claim has been upheld by the CCPA, and in fact the court has stated that "if a machine is programmed in a certain new and unobvious way, it is physically different from the machine without that program. . . ."[41] The apparatus theory, although upheld by the CCPA, does not offer unlimited protection. Under §101 of the Patent Act, the patent protection is extended to the program, but "not to the idea underlying the program."[42]

The second claim theory is that the program is a *process*, an entity which is also eligible for patent protection under §101 of the Patent Act. This theory supposes that the process is controlled by the program, much as the machine under the apparatus theory.[43] A process is defined as a:

> mode of treatment of certain materials to produce a given result. It is an act, or a series of acts, performed upon the subject matter to be trans- formed and reduced to a different state or thing.[44]

The program must control a process which is new and useful and, if certain other restrictions are fulfilled, the patent for a process offers more protection than that for an apparatus. The process patent, however, is more difficult to obtain than the apparatus patent.[45] Full disclosure in the specification of the claim "as to enable any person skilled in the art . . . to make and use the same" is required by §112 of the Patent Act.[46] Not only must this full disclosure be made, but the process also must satisfy the requirements of the *mental steps doctrine.*

Mental Steps Doctrine

In several early cases, the Court held that a newly discovered scientific truth or mathematical expression could not be patented, but that "a novel and useful structure created with the aid of knowledge of scientific truth may be."[47] From this line of cases, and other cases related to the field of electronics, the Court

---

[40] Evans, *Computer Program Classification: A Limitation on Program Patentability as a Process,* 53 Or L Rev 501, 511-12 (1974). See also Koller & Moshman, *Patent Protection for Computer Software: Implications for the Industry,* 12 Idea 1106 (1968).

[41] 417 F2d at 1399. *See In re* Foster, 438 F2d 1011 (CCPA 1971).

[42] Evans, *supra* note 40, at 514.

[43] *Id* 512.

[44] *Id* 514 n 102, citing Cochrane v Deener, 94 US 780, 788 (1876).

[45] *Id* 515.

[46] 35 USC §112. See also Scott, *Failure to Disclose Computer Program Invalidates Patent,* The Scott Report, Oct 1982, at 1.

[47] Mackay Co v Radio Corp, 306 US 86 (1938). See also Blumental & Riter, *Statutory or Non-Statutory?: Analysis of the Patentability of Computer Related Inventions,* 62 J Pat Off Socy 454 (1980); Longhofer, *Patentability of Computer Programs,* 34 Baylor L Rev 125 (1982); and Soltysinski, *Computer Programs and Patent Law: A Comparative Study,* 3 Rutgers J Computers & L 1 (1973).

developed the mental steps doctrine.[48] In brief, the mental steps doctrine means that if an idea can be totally carried out by the human mind without the aid of a mechanical device, then the idea is unpatentable. Applied to computer programs, the result is devastating because most software can, at least theoretically, be performed solely by the human mind. If some steps are physical and some mental, the novelty and nonobviousness of the process must not be contained solely in the mental steps. If the novelty and nonobviousness are contained in at least one of the physical steps, the patent may be allowed.[49]

Software Patent Case Law

In *In re Prater* the PTO rejected Prater's process claim based on the mental steps doctrine, but the CCPA ruled that a patent claim could not be "precluded by the mere fact that the process could alternatively be carried out by mental steps."[50] *In re Bernhart* offered a different situation. In that the program involved no mental steps, which made the machine, and the program, patentable.[51] *Bernhart,* however, failed to qualify for a patent, but on other grounds. The CCPA ruled on several other cases concerning process claims, including *In re Mahoney*[52] and *In re Musgrave.*[53] In *Musgrave* the CCPA first established the *technological arts* test.[54]

Through a series of cases, the CCPA attempted to distinguish computer programs that provided some physical change on materials from programs that did not physically affect materials.[55] Based on this distinction, the CCPA separated computer programs performing some physical act on materials from the mental steps doctrine and upheld several patents on computer programs. While the PTO and CCPA were distinguishing types of computer programs, the President's Commission on the Patent System concluded that the Patent Office lacked adequate methods and facilities for classifying computer programs, and thus recommended against a patent policy that would allow the

---

[48] *See, e.g.,* Cochrane v Deener, 94 US 780 (1876); O'Reilly v Morse, 56 US (15 How) 62 (1853). See also Woodcock, *Mental Steps and Computer Programs,* 52 J Pat Off Socy 275 (1970).

[49] *In re* Abrams, 188 F2d 165 (CCPA 1951). See also Flewellen, *An Anomaly in the Patent System: The Uncertain Status of Computer Software,* 8 Rutgers J Computers, Tech & L 273, 286, 289 (1981).

[50] 415 F2d 1378, 1389 (CCPA 1968), *affd in part & revd in part,* 415 F2d 1393 (CCPA 1969).

[51] 417 F2d 1395 (CCPA 1969).

[52] 421 F2d 742 (CCPA 1970).

[53] 431 F2d 882 (CCPA 1970).

[54] This test was not dependent on the novelty of the process, but was based on whether or not the process fell under the definition of §101 as a technological art. *See In re* McIlroy, 442 F2d 1397 (CCPA 1971); *In re* Toma, 575 F2d 872 (CCPA 1978).

[55] See Note, *Patent Law-Computer Programs-Unpatentable Mental Process-Gotschalk v Benson,* 14 BC Ind & Com L Rev 1050 (1973); Comment, *Patent Law-Computer Programs for Processing Data With a Digital Computer Cannot Be Patented Under Present United States Laws,* 4 Loy U Chi LJ 560 (1973).

patentability of computer software.[56]

In 1972, the Supreme Court attempted to clarify this confused situation by deciding *Gottschalk v Benson*.[57] Writing for a unanimous Court, with three Justices abstaining, Justice Douglas held that the program was not patentable under the existing patent laws. Based on the settled principle that ideas are not patentable, the Court reasoned that granting a patent for converting binary coded decimals (BCD) to binary numerals with the aid of a digital computer would in effect be a patent on the algorithm embodied in the computer program, because the use of the algorithm on a digital computer would be the only practical method of implementation.[58] The Court described an algorithm as "a procedure for solving a given type of mathematical problem."[59] The principal concern of the Court was that the patent would give a monopoly on the algorithm, which would give a monopoly on a mathematical formula.[60] The Court stated that "phenomena of nature, though just discovered, mental processes, and abstract intellectual concepts are not patentable as they are the basic tools of scientific and technological work."[61] Justice Douglas, however, stressed that the decision was limited only to invalidating the overly-broad claim of patenting a mathematical algorithm, and that the decision was not an invalidation of all computer programs. Further, the Court requested that Congress investigate and act in this area.[62] One possible interpretation of *Benson* is to read the opinion narrowly and conclude that mathematical algorithms are

---

[56] *The President's Commission on Patent System, supra* note 36, at 21. See also Evans, *supra* note 40 (proposal for a software selection scheme to decide which computer programs should be patented).

[57] 409 US 63 (1972). Gary Benson and Arthur Talbot filed an application with the Patent Office in 1963 seeking a patent on a method of converting binary coded decimal (BCD) numerals into pure binary numerals through the use of a mathematical algorithm. Although this process could be performed mentally with the aid of pen and pencil, the algorithm enabled one to program a computer to do the same conversion with large savings in manpower and time. The Patent Office refused to issue the patent on the grounds that the subject matter of the invention was not within any of the statutory classes of patentable inventions. Reasoning that the application was within the mental steps doctrine, the Patent Office ruled that the claims were outside the statutory class of patentable material. On appeal, the CCPA reversed the Patent Office decision, and held that the patent application claims were within the statutory classification of patentable inventions. *In re* Benson, 441 F2d (CCPA 1971).

[58] In binary coded decimal (BCD) notation, four binary bits are used to represent a decimal number. Thus 0001 represents 1, 0010 represents 2 . . . and 1001 represents 9. The combinations 1010 through 1111 are not used in the BCD method. To represent the number 743, the combinations 0111 (7), 0100 (4), and 0011 (3), would be used and these require 12 binary bits. In pure binary notation, all combinations of bits are used. Thus, 743 becomes 1011100111 which only requires 10 bits. Pure binary numbers are more compact whereas BCD numbers are easier to convert to decimal numbers.

[59] 409 US at 65. See also *Invention is Algorithm and Not Patentable,* 5 Computer L Serv Rep 518 (1976).

[60] 409 US 68.

[61] *Id* 67.

[62] *Id* 73.

not constitutionally patentable. Thus, the patenting of software is still permitted. A broad reading of *Benson,* however, indicates that all software is unpatentable.[63]

The CCPA has validated patents for computer programs that adequately describe the program and that do not relate to a purely mathematical algorithm.[64] The legal support for issuance of these patents, however, is based on cases before *Benson,* which distinguished computer programs from the mental steps doctrine.[65] While the *Benson* decision has been interpreted by the PTO as creating a *point of novelty* test,[66] the decision has not affected apparatus patents, the mental steps doctrine, all process patents, or previously issued process patents.[67] The CCPA has continued to find statutorily permissible patents for programs, provided the claims combine apparatus and process components.[68]

The CCPA had several opportunities to interpret the Supreme Court's *Benson* decision. In *In re Chatfield,*[69] the court emphasized the possibility of valid program patents by determining that the patentability of a process was not determined by its form as a program.[70] In *In re Freeman,*[71] the CCPA continued its narrow reading of *Benson* and found no algorithm, thus reversing the PTO and allowing the patent. In *Freeman,* the CCPA suggested a two-step analysis to determine if a claim was being made for nonstatutory subject matter.

> First, it must be determined whether the claim directly or indirectly recites an "algorithm" in the *Benson* sense of that term, for a claim which fails even to recite an algorithm clearly cannot wholly preempt an algorithm. Second, the claim must be further analyzed to ascertain whether in its entirety it wholly preempts that algorithm.[72]

---

[63] Comment, *supra* note 55.

[64] *See, e. g., In re* Bradstradter, 484 F2d 1395 (CCPA 1973); and *In re* Doyle, 482 F2d 1385 (CCPA 1973).

[65] *See In re* Musgrave, 431 F2d 882 (CCPA 1970); *In re* Mahony, 421 F2d 742 (CCPA 1970); *In re* Bernhart, 417 F2d 1395 (CCPA 1969); *In re* Prater, 415 F2d 1393 (CCPA 1969).

[66] See Note, *The Patentability of Computer Software - Parker v Flook,* 1979 Wis L Rev 867, 872.

[67] Evans, *supra* note 40, at 517-18.

[68] *See In re* Comstock, 178 USPQ 616 (CCPA 1973); *In re* Knowlton, 178 USPQ 486 (CCPA 1973).

[69] 545 F2d 152 (CCPA 1976), *cert denied,* 434 US 875 (1977).

[70] 545 F2d at 155; *See also In re* Richman, 563 F2d 1026 (CCPA 1977).

[71] 573 F2d 1237 (CCPA 1978).

[72] 573 F2d at 1245. *In re* Walter, 618 F2d 758 (CCPA), restated the second step of the Freeman test as follows:

> If the mathematical algorithm is implemented in a specific manner to define structural relationships between the physical elements of the claim (in apparatus claims) or to refine or limit the claim's steps (in process claims), the claim is statutory subject matter. If, however, the mathematical algorithm is merely pre-

In *Freeman,* the first test was unsatisfied (there was no algorithm) and the second test was not considered. In *In re Deutsch,*[73] however, even though an algorithm was present, the court found that the invention as a whole had not preempted any algorithm.[74]

The Supreme Court also had opportunities to review its *Benson* decision. In *Dann v Johnston,*[75] the Court rejected the patent claim on grounds of obviousness, but stated that *Benson* was a *limited* decision. As in *Benson,* the *Johnston* decision mentioned the concept of a *mental process* and found that computer programs which derive their "utility from mathematical algorithms general in nature and not confined or limited to a particular apparatus or end use are particularly vulnerable [to rejection of their patent application]."[76] In 1978, the Supreme Court held, in *Parker v Flook,*[77] that the claim, considered as a whole, was not "new and useful." The entire process, not merely the algorithm, was to be inspected. The Court stated that:

> the novelty of the mathematical algorithm is not a determining factor at all. Whether the algorithm was in fact known or unknown at the time of the claimed invention, as one of the "basic tools of scientific and technological work," . . . it is treated as though it were a familiar part of the prior art.[78]

In *Flook,* the only new feature of the invention was the algorithm in one of the three parts of the invention. Because the Supreme Court had decided that the algorithm was, as a law of nature, already known, and because the other two parts of the *Flook* procedure were known, the Court ruled that the invention was not patentable.[79] The conclusions of the Court left program patents in a

---

sented and solved by the claimed invention and is not applied in any manner to the physical elements or process steps, no amount of post-solution activity nor limited field of use will render the claim statutory.

See D. Davidson, Computer Software Protection, at 19 (1982). Davidson has suggested that to avoid the Freeman-Walter test, the patent should be described in terms of apparatus (the hardwired version of software) and later use the doctrine of equivalents to prevent software versions of the apparatus from being manufactured and sold. Davidson, at 24-25.

[73] 553 F2d 689 (CCPA 1977).

[74] 553 F2d at 693.

[75] 425 US 219 (1976). See also *Dann v Johnston: Program Patentability Postponed,* 1976 Det CL Rev 663.

[76] Schmidt, *Legal Proprietory Interests in Computer Programs: The American Experience,* 21 Jurimetrics J 345, 357 (1981).

[77] 437 US 584 (1978). See also Note, *supra* note 65.

[78] 437 US at 594.

[79] See Flewellen, *supra* note 49, at 293; Gorenstein, *Dual Standard of Patentability: A New Look at the Computer Issue,* 62 J Pat Off Socy 96 (1980); Novick & Wallenstein, *The Algorithm and Computer Software Patentability: A Scientific View of a Legal Problem,* 7 Rutgers J Computer, Tech & L 313 (1980); Rinkerman, *Computer Program Patentability,* 1 Computer L Rev 20 (1982).

position where, for a process patent, the entire process, assuming that the algorithm is already common knowledge, had to be both new and useful.

§2.04   The *Diehr* and *Bradley* Decisions

After the Supreme Court decisions in *Gottschalk v Benson*[80] and *Parker v Flook*,[81] the Court of Customs and Patent Appeals (CCPA) continued to over-rule the Patent Trademark Office (PTO) when it refused to find statutory justification for software patents. In both *In re Diehr*[82] and *In re Bradley*,[83] the PTO rulings that the claims in the patent applications were not statutorily acceptable under §101 of the Patent Act of 1952[84] were reversed by the CCPA. In *In re Bradley* the court utilized its two part *Freeman* test[85] and found that no algorithm was present,[86] totally ignoring the *Flook* test established by the Supreme Court. The same reasoning was applied in *In re Diehr* and in both cases the Supreme Court granted *certiorari*.[87]

Diamond v Diehr[88] has been called a fundamental shift in interpreting §101.[89] While the Court did sustain the CCPA's decision that Diehr's invention qualified for a patent under §101 of the Patent Act, the Court also rejected the *Freeman* test and used an original test.[90] This *Diehr* test may be the most important result of the longstanding dispute between the CCPA and the PTO. At last, the manufacturer of software may have a single precedent to work

---

[80] 409 US 63 (1972).

[81] 437 US 584 (1978).

[82] 602 F2d 982 (CCPA 1974).

[83] 600 F2d 807 (CCPA 1979).

[84] 35 USC §101; *see also In re* Sherwood, 613 F2d 809 (CCPA 1980).

[85] See **§2.03.**

[86] Gemignani, *Should Algorithms be Patentable*, 22 Jurimetrics J 326, 328 (1982).

[87] Kayton, *Update of Legal Protection of Computer Software Via Patents*, APLAQJ 1980 273, 274 (1980). See also Note, *Computer Program Patentability—The CCPA Refuse to Follow the Lead of the Supreme Court in Parker v Flook*, 58 NCL Rev 319 (1980).

[88] 450 US 175 (1981). See Sprowl, *A Review of Niblett's Legal Protection of Computer Programs and Diamond v Diehr and Some Thoughts on Patenting Computer Programs*, 1981 Am B Found Research J 559; Blumenthal, *Supreme Court Sets Guidelines for Patentability of Computer Related Inventions - Diamond v Diehr*, 63 J Pat Off Socy 117 (1981); Greenlee, *New Criteria for Patentable Subject Matter*, 47 Brooklyn L Rev 43 (1980); Lockhart & McGarry, *Patent Eligibility of Computer Implemented Inventions in the Wake of Diehr*, 59 U Det J Urb L 63 (1981); Richter, *The Subject Matter Analysis For Computer Related Processes: A Matter of Characterizations*, 27 Loy L Rev 1140 (1981).

[89] Schmidt, *Legal Proprietary Interest in Computer Programs: The American Experience*, 21 Jurimetrics J 345, 358 (1981).

[90] Flewellen, *An Anomoly in the Patent System: The Uncertain Status of Computer Software*, 8 Rutgers J Computers, Tech, & L 273, 297-98 (1981). See Hamburg, *US Supreme Court Affirm CCPA in Two Cases According Patent Protection to Inventions Relating to Computers*, 79 Pat & Trademark Rev 211 (1981).

under in the area of program patents.[91]

Diehr's invention was a process to cure rubber objects with continuous monitoring of the temperature in the mold. The temperature and time, plus other relevant variables, were entered into a computer which applied the variables to a well-known equation used to determine curing time. The computer then determined the exact length of time needed to cure the rubber and automatically opened the mold at the correct time.[92] The industry had been unable to obtain accurate cures because, until Diehr's development, the temperature in the mold press could not be accurately measured thus making it difficult to calculate the proper cure time. Because temperature was an uncontrollable variable, cure times were often either over or underestimated, resulting in either over or undercuring the rubber. Diehr's process involved constant measurement of the temperature inside the mold. These temperature measurements were then fed into the computer which constantly recalculated the cure time and signaled the press to open at the correct time.

The Court distinguished *Diehr* from *Flook* by noting that Diehr's invention involved more than just the use of an algorithm. The *process* in *Diehr* was what Diehr wanted to patent, not just the formula. For this reason, the Court used its new test and inspected the claim as a whole, rejecting the *Flook* test and finding that Diehr's claim was statutorily valid under §101 of the Patent Act.[93] As stated by the Court, although Diehr's process included a well-known mathematical equation, it was not the use of that equation which Diehr sought to prevent, but rather "to foreclose from others the use of the equation in conjunction with all of the other steps in their claimed process". These steps included the constant recalculating of the appropriate cure time through the use of formula and digital computer. The test adopted by the Court is very similar to the *Freeman* test used by the CCPA. Under the *Freeman* test, Diehr's invention would (as evidenced by the decision of the CCPA) be considered statutory material. An algorithm *was* present, but the effect of a patent would only limit public usage of the algorithm in that situation which involved Diehr's entire process. Therefore, the second part of the *Freeman* test would not invalidate the invention. The Court's test that when a claim recites a "mathematical formula (or scientific principle or phenomenon of nature), an inquiry must be made into whether the claim is seeking patent protection for that formula in the abstract," also allows the same result.[94] The Court did comment on its test by limiting nonpatentable material to the algorithm itself, standing independently, and by adding that the other parts of the process must be significant.[95]

The minority in *Diehr* claimed that the facts of *Diehr* were indistinguishable from those in *Flook* and, applying the *Flook* test, concluded that Diehr's inven-

---

[91] Flewellen, *supra* note 90, at 298.

[92] Nimtz, *Diamond v Diehr: A Turning Point,* 8 Rutgers J Computers, Tech & L 267, 268 (1981).

[93] *Id* 269. See also Kern, *Washington Tackles the Software Problem,* BYTE 128, 136 (1981).

[94] Diamond v Diehr, 450 US 175, 101 S Ct 1048, 1058 (1981).

[95] Nimtz, *supra* note 92, at 269.

tion could not fall under §101.[96] Part of the dissent was a scathing attack on the majority opinion as trivializing "the holding in *Flook,* the principle that underlies *Benson,* and the settled line of authority reviewed in those opinions."[97] Justice Stevens, writing for the four dissenters, felt that the majority had both misread the patent claim and had misapplied the law. The strong dissent in *Diehr,* taken with the result in *Diamond v Bradley*[98] where Justice Burger removed himself from the case thereby resulting in the Court affirming the CCPA on a 4-4 split, leaves the new test of *Diehr* on tenuous ground. It has been suggested that the Court adopted the *Freeman* test from the CCPA in order to clarify the requirements of a patentable process under §101.[99] At present, however, software manufacturers must struggle with the Supreme Court's *Diehr* test, the possible application of the CCPA *Freeman* test by the new Court of Appeals of the Federal Circuit and the possible application of the *Flook* test by the PTO. Only time, and additional clarification by the Court, will clear the fog from the issue of the patentability of computer software processes.

§2.05   The Future of Patent Protection

Patent law protects only inventions which are a new and useful process, machine, manufacture, or composition of matter, or any new and useful improvement thereof. A patent grants the patentee a negative property right, giving the patent holder the exclusive right to control the use, manufacture, and sale of the invention. A patent serves an important public purpose in encouraging inventors to disseminate their inventions by guaranteeing their proprietary rights for a limited period. The grant of a patent on information otherwise available to the public domain however, impinges upon the public's wealth of knowledge, and must be granted only where deserved. The three elements of patentability—novelty, usefulness and nonobviousness—therefore, are strictly construed, and operate both to deny a claim's patentability at the application stage, and to invalidate patents already granted, in instances where invalidity is asserted as a defense in an infringement suit.

The most difficult element to prove, nonobviousness, requires that the differences (advancements) between the subject matter to be patented and the prior art must be a product of some special inventiveness, and not obvious to a person having ordinary skill in the relevant art at the time of the invention. Judicial hindsight has made nonobviousness a formidable barrier to overcome in obtaining patent protection. Novelty is dependent upon the existing prior

---

[96] Flewellen, *An Anomaly in the Patent System: The Uncertain Status of Computer Software,* 8 Rutgers J Computers, Tech & L 273, 301 (1981).

[97] Schmidt, *supra* note 89, at 358-59.

[98] Flewellen, *supra* note 96, at 300.

[99] *Id* 303.

art; and usefulness, as a standard, takes its definition from prevailing social values. In addition to the legal burden that the proving of these three elements imposes on a patent seeker, the process is drawn out and time consuming.

On the practical side, a strong deterrent exists to the use of patents to protect software. The minimum cost of legal fees in obtaining a patent is several thousand dollars with many patent applications costing considerably more due to their controversial nature. In addition, the gestation period for a patent application averages three years, and thus, if a patent is finally disapproved, the developer of a program will be left in the same position as before the beginning of the patent application procedure. A patent application remains confidential unless a patent is issued. Many patents are invalidated in infringement suits.[100] Patent disclosure standards are also quite high.[101] Once a patent is declared invalid in an infringement suit, its contents are known. Trade secret protection, therefore, is no longer available.[102] The net result of these difficulties is that the choice of patent protection for software is not particularly inviting.[103] Despite the excitement generated by the *Diamond v Diehr*[104] decision, seeking computer software protection through the patent laws will generally remain a risky venture until the conflicting theories being applied by the Supreme Court, the new Federal Circuit Court of Appeals and the Patent Office are resolved.

---

[100] Approximately 100,000 patent applications are annually filed, of which two-thirds result in the issuance of patents. The overall issuance level is approximately 60 to 70%. Great variation in patent issuance percentages exists between the circuit courts of appeals; the new Court of Appeals for the Federal Circuit will prevent this. (Interview with Stanley Schlosser, Office of Legislation and International Affairs, Patent Office, US Department of Commerce, Washington, D C July 1975.

[101] *See In re* Doyle, 482 F2d 1285 (CCPA 1973) (mere disclosure of computer program flow chart was ruled insufficient disclosure).

[102] See Dobyns & Block, *Adequate Disclosure of Computers and Programs in Patent Specifications,* 56 J Pat Off Socy 574 (1974).

[103] Some software has a useful life of less than three years before it is technologically obsolete. Therefore, going through the patenting process for such short-lived software is pointless. The Canadian government has issued a patent on a computer program. See Computerworld, Aug 7, 1974, at 1. See generally Falk & Popper, *Computer Programs and Nonstatutory Subject Matter in Canada,* 4 Computer L Serv §9-4, art 2 (1975) (if any foreign government upholds a patent on a computer program, the patent may be valid in the United States under various patent treaties); S. Ladas, Patents, Trademarks, and Related Rights: National and International Protection (1975); American Bar Association, Section of Patent, Trademark, and Copyright Law, 1974 Committee Report; Myrick & Sprowl, *Patent Law for Programmed Computers and Programmed Life Forms,* 68 ABAJ 920 (1982); Moskowitz, *The Patentability of Software Related Inventions After Diehr and Bradley,* 63 J Pat Off Socy 222 (1981); Prasinos, *Worldwide Protection of Computer Programs by Copyright,* 4 Rutgers J Computers & L 42 (1974).

[104] 450 US 175, 101 S Ct 1048 (1981).

Copyright Protection

§2.06 Generally

Although the Copyright Office stated that it doubted that computer programs were capable of registration, it began accepting programs for copyright in 1964 in accordance with its policy of resolving doubtful issues in favor of registration whenever possible.[105] The registerability question has been resolved by the 1976 Copyright Act,[106] the Committee Report to the House of Representatives, and the 1980 Copyright Act Amendment.[107] In addition, the Commission on New Technological Uses of Copyrighted Works (CONTU)[108] prepared an amendment to the 1976 Copyright Act that unambiguously declared programs subject to copyright.[109] To be copyrightable, however, the program must still be an *original work of authorship* fixed in a tangible medium from which it can "be perceived, reproduced, or otherwise communicated, either directly or with the aid of a machine or device."[110] The degree of originality required is minimal.[111] Copyright protects the intellectual work product as a form of expression, as opposed to the idea which is being expressed.[112] It protects a writing or expression by an author from copying by another, but it does not protect against another's use of the ideas contained in the expression.[113] This distinction between the idea and its form is of real significance to the protection of computer software, because a copyrighted

---

[105] 11 Bull Copyright Socy 361 (1964). See Samuels, *Copyright and the New Communications Technologies,* 25 NYL Sch L Rev 905 (1980). See also **§4.19.**

[106] 17 USC §§101-810. See also Pataki, *Copyright Protection for Computer Programs Under the 1976 Copyright Act,* 52 Ind LJ 503 (1977).

[107] H Rep No 1476, 94th Cong, 2d Sess 54 (1976); Copyright Act Amendments of 1980, Pub L No 96-517, 94 Stat 3028, as codified 17 USC §101, 117.

[108] National Commission on the New Technological Uses of Copyrighted Works, Final Report, July 31, 1978 [hereinafter cited as *CONTU*]. See also Koenig, *Software Copyright: The Conflict Within CONTU,* 27 Bull Copyright Socy of USA 340 (1980); Freed, *Software Protection: Introductory Observations on the Study Sponsored by the National Commission on New Technological Uses of Copyrighted Works,* 18 Jurimetrics J 352 (1978); Holmes, *CONTU to Recommend Copyright for Programs,* Computerworld, Jan 12, 1978 *Software Protection Survey,* 18 Jurimetrics J 354 (1978). at 5; and Miller, *The CONTU Software Protection Survey,* 18 Jurimetrics J 345 (1978).

[109] 17 USC §101. *See also* Perle, *Copyright and New Technology,* 25 Bull Copyright Socy 250 (1978).

[110] 17 USC §102(a).

[111] 17 USC §103(a).

It should be noted that programs created for video games and computer assisted instruction are essentially similar to traditional writing while other programs which control a mechanical process are simple engineering solutions to technical problems. Still other programs fall within these two poles.

[112] Pataki, *supra* note 106, at 508. *See also* Mayer v Stern, 347 US 201 (1954).

[113] Baker v Selden, 101 US 99, 105 (1879). See Pierce, *Copyright Protection for Computer Programs,* 47 Tenn L Rev 787 (1980).

program is not protected against another's independent development of an identical program.

Consider for example a newly designed computer system which controls the fuel flow in a typical automobile engine (as an alternative to traditional methods of carburation or fuel injection) by monitoring factors such as the speed (m.p.h.) and velocity of the vehicle, the speed of the engine (r.p.m.), and the atmospheric air pressure (altitude). The inventor of the system, X, could copyright the computer program for the control system, thereby protecting the proprietary interest, and then sell the program to General Motors, making a legitimate profit.

A problem arises, however, when the ailing Chrysler Corporation purchases a General Motors vehicle containing this new fuel control system and subsequently *discovers* the same or effectively similar fuel control program for their line of vehicles.[114] Under the Copyright Act, Chrysler's implementation of the fuel control system would not be an infringement on X's copyright, so long as the Chrysler fuel control program was developed independently.[115] Copyright will protect only an author's particular expression of an idea, it will not prohibit others from using the idea itself. The protection afforded by copyright is, therefore, limited and incomplete, unlike patent protection which is a grant to its owner of a monopoly on use of the invention's embodiment of the idea itself.[116]

The problem is that computer programs are not predominantly *writings* or expressions that need to be protected from unauthorized *copying,* which is the primary purpose of the copyright law. Rather, they are generally more akin to *inventions* or discoveries of novel methods of applying technology to accomplish various tasks. What needs to be afforded legal protection is the process or method contained in the software, not the copying of the actual written program.

This particular dilemma has prompted several commentators to suggest combining copyright and patent protections as an alternative form of protecting computer software.[117] A monopoly on the written portion of a program would be granted by copyright, while use of the program's underlying idea would be protected by patent, provided the idea is sufficiently inventive[118] and

---

[114] This could be a legitimate subsequent independent discovery, or a discovery by improper means, such as decoding or reverse engineering.

[115] Or at least so long as Chrysler, who will bear the burden of proof, can present some evidence that its program was not wrongfully obtained. Once it has discovered the program, this burden will not be difficult to bear.

[116] Ogden, *Protection of Computer Software-A Hard Problem,* 26 Drake L Rev 180, 194 (1976). *See also* Baker v Selden, 101 US 99 (1879).

[117] Ogden, *supra* note 116, at 197. See also Maggs, *Some Problems of Legal Protections of Programs for Microcomputer Control Systems,* 1979 U Ill L Forum 453, 468; Galbi, *Proposal for New Legislation to Protect Computer Programming,* 17 Bull Copyright Socy 280 (1970).

[118] That is, it must meet the criteria of novelty, utility, and nonobviousness under 35 USC §§101-103.

is not so basic as to be considered a fundamental law of nature.[119]

§2.07   Copyright Act of 1976

In the past, there was considerable confusion as to whether computer programs were the proper subject matter for copyright protection. In 1964, the Copyright Office framed the two basic questions that had to be resolved regarding the registerability of computer programs:

1.   Whether a program as such is the "writing of an author" and thus copyrightable

2.   Whether a reproduction of the program in a form actually used to operate or be "read" by a machine is a "copy" that can be accepted for copyright registration[120]

Consistent with its policy of resolving copyright issues in favor of registration whenever possible, the Copyright Office decided to accept registration of computer programs as books for the time being,[121] while awaiting congressional revision of the Copyright Act.[122]

The National Commission on New Technological Uses of Copyrighted Works (CONTU) was established by Public Law 93-573 Title II, which was signed into law by President Ford in December, 1974.[123]

> This Commission was created to assist the President and Congress in developing a national policy for both protecting the rights of copyright owners and ensuring public access to copyrighted works when they are used in computer and machine duplication systems, bearing in mind the public and consumer interest.[124]

Since CONTU was established to create several policies, four subcommittees were formed, one each to study photocopying, computer software, computer data bases, and computer-created works.[125]

As a foundation for its recommendations, CONTU discussed the short history of computers and concluded that:

---

[119] Parker v Flook, 437 US 584, 98 S Ct 2522, 57 L Ed 2d 451 (1978).

[120] *Copyright Registration for Computer Programs - Announcement From the Copyright Office,* 11 Bull Copyright Socy 361 (1964).

[121] *Id.*

[122] Copyright Act of 1909, 35 Stat 1075 (codified as amended 17 USC §§1-215 (1978).

[123] National Commission on the New Technological Uses of Copyrighted Works, Final Report, July 31, 1978, at 105 [hereinafter cited as CONTU].

[124] *Id* 3.

[125] *Id* 6.

the need for protecting the form of expression chosen by the author of a computer program had grown proportionally with two related current trends. Computers have become less cumbersome and expensive . . . while, at the same time, programs have become less and less frequently written to comply with the requirements imposed by a single purpose machine.[126]

CONTU concluded that while there was little need to protect the rigid brass wheel of a nineteenth century music box because the cost of reproduction approached the cost of producing the original, the cost of copying a reel of magnetic tape was so small as compared to the cost of the original program contained on the tape that "legal as well as physical protection for the information is a necessary incentive if such information is to be created and disseminated."[127] Because the cost of developing programs is far greater than the duplication cost, CONTU concluded that programs would be disseminated only if:

1. The creator may recover all of his costs plus a fair profit on the first sale of the work, thus leaving the creator unconcerned about the later publication of the work

2. The creator may spread his costs over multiple copies of the work with some form of protection against unauthorized duplication of the work

3. The creator's costs are borne by another, for example, when the government or a foundation offers prizes or awards

4. The creator is indifferent to cost and donates the work to the public[128]

CONTU determined that since possibility number 2 is most likely, some form of protection is necessary to encourage the creation of computer programs in a creative market and it further determined that "the continued availability of copyright protection for computer programs is desirable"[129] although it was not unanimous in selecting copyright as the form of protection.[130]

The software subcommittee identified several principles which guided its recommendation to the full commission:

1. Encouraging the broad dissemination of works of authorship such as computer programs

2. Enabling authors to recover their costs from the distribution of their wares

---

[126] *Id* 10.

[127] *Id.*

[128] *Id* 11.

[129] *Id.*

[130] *Id. See* Commissioner Hersey's dissent at 27.

3.   Protecting such works against misappropriation[131]

The recommendation of CONTU was that: §101 of the 1976 Copyright Act be amended to allow for computer programs to be copyrighted, that §117 be "repealed to indicate that all computer uses of copyrighted programs are potential infringements," and that §117 be "redrafted to authorize rightful possessors of copies of computer programs to use or adapt these copies for their own purposes."[132]

The Copyright Act, as amended by Congress in 1976, does not single out computer programs as a category of works subject to copyright protection, but the language used by Congress to define *literary works* under the amended statute is clearly intended to include computer programs:

> "Literary works" are works, other than audiovisual works, expressed in words, numbers, or other verbal or numerical symbols of indicia, regardless of the nature of the material objects, such as books, periodicals, manuscripts, phonorecords, film, tape, disks, or cards, in which they are embodied.[133]

The report of the House Committee on the Judiciary explicitly stated that the statute was intended to cover computer programs to the extent that they "incorporate authorship in the programmer's expression of original ideas, as distinguished from the ideas themselves".[134]

As the title implies, the Copyright Act prohibits the unauthorized copying of another's work for the statutory period, which in 1976 was revised from 28 years to ". . . a term consisting of the life of the author and fifty years after the authors death."[135] The 1976 Copyright Act and the 1980 Copyright Act Amendments,[136] therefore, resolved the question of whether computer programs are proper subject matter for copyright protection. The question remains as to the nature and scope of protection afforded to computer software under the Copyright Act. The unique problems of the computer software industry, however, will not be resolved by copyright protection alone.

It is important to note that the process of loading the program into the computer includes making a copy and would be an infringement. The CONTU recommendation would allow this use without infringement. Furthermore, since creating a copy for archival purposes in order to guard against destruc-

---

[131] Keplinger, *Computer Intellectual Property Claims: Computer Software and Data Base Protection,* 1977 Wash ULQ 462. See CONTU, *supra* note 120, at 12 for the final guidelines.

[132] Pope & Pope, *Protection of Proprietary Interests in Computer Software,* 30 Ala L Rev 548 (1979).

[133] 17 USC §101.

[134] HR Rep No 1476, 94th Cong, 2d Sess 54, *reprinted in* 1976 US Code Cong & Ad News 6089, 6097.

[135] 17 USC §302(a).

[136] Pub L No 96-517, 94 Stat 3028, (as amended 17 USC §§101, 117).

tion or damage (i.e., back-up copy) is essential in the computer industry, the CONTU recommendation allowed this type of copyright by the rightful possessor.[137] CONTU went beyond this, however, and allowed a program to be *modified* by the rightful possessor without infringing because there exists a:

> lack of complete standardization among programming languages and hardware in the computer industry, [and therefore] one who rightfully acquires a copy of a program frequently cannot use it without adapting it to that limited extent which will allow its use in the possessor's computer.[138]

CONTU included in this right the conversion of a program from one higher level language to another as well as the right to add features not present at the time of acquisition.[139] The right of adaptation could not be "conveyed to others along with the licensed or owned program without the express authorization of the owner,"[140] therefore, the adapter could not sell the adapted program.

In keeping with the spirit of the copyright law not to protect ideas, CONTU ignored the problems associated with misappropriation of the algorithm, "since monopolization of the process or algorithm embodied in a program is antithetical to the basic principles of copyright."[141] Professor Nimmer in his concurrance, was concerned about how far the copyright law was being extended and stated that:

> if literary works are to be so broadly construed, the Copyright Act becomes a general misappropriation law, applicable as well in what has traditionally been regarded as the patent arena, and, indeed, also in other areas to which neither copyright nor patent law has previously extended.[142]

According to Professor Nimmer the protection for programs should be limited to those programs which *produced* copyrightable results such as a program in a legal information retrieval system that produces an enumeration of cases on a given topic, that would be copyrightable, but not extended protection to programs such as those which control the heating and air conditioning of a

---

[137] CONTU, *supra* note 123, at 12. It is generally true that the process of loading the program into the computer includes making a copy. In unusual circumstances, when a program is loaded into a volatile memory, and no other copy is made, then there is probably not a "copy" under the copyright laws, because it is not fixed pursuant to 17 USC §101.

[138] CONTU, *supra* note 123, at 73. See also Silverman, *The New Copyright Act: An Overview of the New Law,* 1977 Pat L Ann 363.

[139] *Id.*

[140] *Id.*

[141] Keplinger, *supra* note 131, at 463.

[142] CONTU, *supra* note 123, at 26.

building. Professor Nimmer was also concerned that CONTU's recommendation "poses a serious constitutional issue in that it is arguable that such an approach stretches the meaning of *authors* and *writings* as used in the Copyright Clause of the Constitution beyond the breaking point."[143]

In his dissent, Commissioner Hersey argued "that copyright is an inappropriate, as well as unnecessary, way of protecting the useable forms of computer programs."[144] Commissioner Hersey felt that the existing Copyright Act already protected programs while they are in the early stages of development where they exist in a written form,

> but the program itself, in its mature and useable form, is a machine-control element, a mechanical device, which on constitutional grounds and for reasons of social policy ought not be copyrighted.[145]

Commissioner Hersey felt that since computer programs, in their mature phase (i.e., object programs) are addressed to machines and have no purpose beyond being engaged in a computer to perform mechanical work, they should not be subject to copyright since "admitting these devices to copyright would mark the first time copyright had ever covered a means of communication, not with the human mind and senses, but with machines."[146]

Commissioner Hersey felt that the argument that computer programs were just like ordinary printed lists of instructions for mechanical work did not hold up beyond a certain point because:

> in the case of computer programs, *the instructions themselves eventually become an essential part of the machinery that produces the results.* They may become (in chip or hardware form) a permanent part of the actual machinery; or they may become interchangeable parts, or tools, insertable into and removable from the machine.[147]

According to Commissioner Hersey, when the program was running (i.e., controlling the machine) it "enters into the computer's mechanical process."[148] Hersey summarized by stating: "printed instructions explain *how* to do something; programs are *able* to do it."[149] Concerned about the CONTU recommendation of allowing adaptations to facilitate use because the protection would remain in effect for an underlying idea, Hersey felt that this "may well have opened the way for covert protection, in the name of copyright, of

---

[143] *Id.* See also Hilde, *Can a Computer be an "Author" or an Inventor,* 51 J Pat Off Socy 318 (1969).

[144] CONTU, *supra* note 123, at 27.

[145] *Id.*

[146] *Id* at 28.

[147] *Id.* The emphasis is that of Commissioner Hersey.

[148] *Id.*

[149] *Id.* The emphasis is that of Commissioner Hersey.

the underlying mechanical idea or ideas of a program, rather than that of its original means of expression."[150] Finally, Commissioner Hersey recommended that copyright protection not be extended "to a computer program in the form in which it is capable of being used to control computer operations."[151]

§2.08   The Copyright Act Amendments of 1980

The United States Copyright Office has maintained a policy of accepting computer programs for registration since 1964, but that practice was not legitimized by statute until the new Copyright Act of 1976 (Copyright Act)[152] became effective on January 1, 1978. Under the Copyright Act, the creator of an original work of authorship fixed in a tangible form, may be afforded the exclusive right to control its reproduction, performance, display, and any preparation of derivative works. A copyright "offers little protection against the incorporation of the program concepts into another form. Similar programs using the same mathematical concepts do not constitute a copyright infringement."[153] Only the representation of an idea is protected, not the idea. This limitation is clearly delineated in §102 of the Copyright Act, stating:

> In no case does copyright protection for an original work of authorship extend to any idea, procedure, process, system, method of operation, concept, principle, or discovery, regardless of the form in which it is described, explained, illustrated, or embodied in such work.[154]

Notwithstanding this limitation, the parameters of protection afforded to a copyrighted computer program have just recently been detailed in the copyright laws. Until the language of the statute is given contours and meaning by judicial interpretation, the complete scope of copyright coverage for software is indeterminable.

The amendment represents a major change in the position of copyright laws toward computer software, and indeed resulted from congressional recognition of the need for an in-depth examination of how the copyright law should apply to computer programs and data bases. Although an appropriately thorough study was not possible before the enactment of the 1976 Copyright Act, Congress provided in §117 of the 1976 Copyright Act that, as to the issue of computer copyright, prior law, in whatever form it took, would control until further federal legislation was adopted.[155] Congress then created the National Commission on New Technological Uses of Copyrighted Works (CONTU) to

---

[150] *Id* at 34.

[151] *Id* at 37.

[152] Pub L No 94-553, 90 Stat 2541-2598 (as codified 17 USC §§101-810).

[153] 14 Akron L Rev 85, 85, 94 (1980).

[154] 17 USC §102(b).

[155] Copyright Act Amendments of 1980, Pub L No 96-517, 94 Stat 3028, as amended 17 USC §117.

recommend the necessary additional legislation. Three recommendations relating to software protection were made by CONTU and each was signed into law December 12, 1980. Section 117, with its mandate to maintain the status quo, was repealed. The Definitions section, §101, was amended to include the following:

> A "computer program" is a set of statements or instructions to be used directly or indirectly in a computer in order to bring about a certain result.[156]

By virtue of the addition of this definition, a *computer program* which is embodied in a tangible medium of expression is an appropriate candidate for copyright protection.[157] Finally, a new and totally different §117 was adopted, creating a right in the owner of a copy of a computer program to "make or authorize the making of another copy or adaptation" of the program as long as it is essential for archival purposes or for use on a different machine. These noninfringing copies and the copy from which they were made may be leased, sold, or otherwise transferred, but only with the authorization of the copyright owner. This section grants rights to both the copyright holder and any authorized owners of copies. It gives the lawful users of copyrighted computer programs the right to adapt them to their own needs and equipment, and it gives the copyright owner the ultimate authority to check the spread of these adaptations and copies.

It is strongly arguable that the new §117 will result in the formal abandonment of the eye-readability standard for eligibility for copyright protection. Introduced in the 1908 case of *White-Smith Publishing Co v Apollo,* the standard required that an infringing copy be an intelligible notation that could be seen and read.[158] The court in *White* found the copying of a song by means of a perforated piano roll was not an infringement. Under the Copyright Act, a copy now is considered to be infringing if the work embodied therein is capable of being reproduced, perceived, or communicated by means of a machine or device.[159]

---

[156] 17 USC §101.

[157] There is the constitutional issue as to whether or not a computer program which performs a purely mechanical function is a "writing of an author" and, thus is constitutionally eligible for copyright protection. *Trade Secrets v Copyright Protection,* Information Systems News, May 13, 1981, at 4. See also Stern, *Software Piracy and the Copyright Laws,* Computer Design 209, (Nov 1981); Scott, *New Legislation to Strengthen Software Copyright Protection,* Scott Report, Nov 1982, at 2.

[158] 209 US 1 (1908).

[159] Data Cash Systems v JS & A Group, Inc, 480 F Supp 1063 (ND Ill 1979), *affd,* 628 F2d 1038 (7th Cir 1980). It is clear that an object code which can be converted into a visual display meant for humans (as in a video game) is protectable. While it can be argued that any object code can be disassembled, the disassembled version may be viewed as a description of a code rather than as a display of the code. As Stern has argued, a computer could use pattern recognition and artificial intelligence to write a description of a chair, but that does not make a chair copyrightable.

The demise of the requirement of visual perceptibility in an infringement action has extended copyright protection to the object code of a program. An object code is the copy or adaptation of the original program which is translated into machine readable form. Recognition that this version of a program can no longer be recreated without being classified *a copy* within the meaning of the Copyright Act, and hence infringing if not authorized, greatly increases the developer's property rights. The fundamental principal in copyright law, that ideas are not protected, remains a stumbling block to obtaining comprehensive proprietary exclusivity.

§2.09 Copyright Case Law

The question arises as to the adequacy of using copyright protection and also as to just which form of the *program* is protected under copyright. As of January 1, 1977, only 1,205 programs had been registered; 971 of these came from two large hardware manufacturers, IBM and Burroughs.[160] It is estimated that over 1,000,000 programs are developed each year.[161] This data, being before the flood of copyrighted mass market micro computer software, may not accurately indicate interest in using copyright protection.

Two aspects of copyright law would also seem to make copyright of protection undesirable. First, the Copyright Act, as amended in 1980 requires that an infringer actually copy another program. If the programmer develops the same program independently, without access to the copyrighted program, there is no infringement. The Supreme Court has stated that some *actual appropriation* of language is necessary for infringement to exist.[162] In addition, the plaintiff must prove that the copy has a *substantial similarity* to the original work.[163] Proving access alone is, quite often, a formidable task.

The second undesirable aspect of copyright protection is that copyright will not protect the algorithm which is the underlying concept used in writing the program.[164] If another person obtains the original program and gains knowledge of the algorithm, the software writer would be free to write a program, using the same algorithm, without infringing the copyrighted program. This fact pattern is a particularly prevalent problem in a world where programmers are in great demand, and thus are often changing jobs every two to five years. If a programmer goes to work for a competitor, the programmer is able to write a new program based on the algorithm learned on the previous job.[165]

The question of what is protected by copyright was first answered by Judge

---

[160] National Commission on the New Technological Uses of Copyrighted Works, Final Report, July 31, 1978, at 34. [Hereinafter cited as CONTU].

[161] *Id.*

[162] Baker v Selden, 101 US 99 (1880).

[163] Gross v Seligman, 212 F 930 (2d Cir 1914).

[164] 17 USC §102(b).

[165] This problem can be dealt with by the use of employment agreements. See §2.12.

Flaum in *Data Cash Systems, Inc v JS & A Group, Inc.*[166] This action for copyright infringement and unfair competition was brought by Data Cash Systems, Inc., the creator of a computer program (CompuChess) against J.S.&A Group, Inc., for allegedly reproducing, importing, distributing, selling, marketing, and advertising copies of the program.[167] Data Cash hired a consultant to develop a program which allowed the computer to play chess at six different levels of difficulty. All copies of the source program contained copyright notices and the consultant assigned the copyright to Data Cash. After compilation, the object program was placed in read only memory (ROM) which "was then installed in the computer as part of its circuitry."[168] No copyright notice appeared anywhere on the ROM, the CompuChess itself, its packing, or its accompanying literature.[169] Defendants stipulated that the program in their machine was identical to the one in CompuChess, although they did not know how the ROM was manufactured. J.S.&A. Group, Inc., apparently purchased the programmed ROM from a supplier. The court *assumed* direct copying of the ROM since the two ROMs were identical, but under the 1909 Copyright Act[170] "a 'copy' must be in the form which others can see and read"[171] and therefore, the copying of the ROM did not infringe the copyright of the source program. Judge Flaum went on to say however, that "the 1976 Act applies to computer programs in their flowchart, source and assembly phases, but not in their object phase."[172] The judge compared this to cases holding that a completed building is not a copy of the architectural plans upon which the building is based.[173] The court also compared the defendants' copying to *White-Smith Music Publishing Co v Apollo Co*[174] in which the Supreme Court held that a perforated roll of music used with player pianos was not a copy of the musical composition recorded thereon. A copy of the source program (or flow chart or assembly source) would be another technical writing and would be protected just as a copy of the architectural plans of a building would be protected. On appeal, the Seventh Circuit Court of Appeals upheld the district court, but based its decision on the fact that no copyright notice appeared on the ROM, CompuChess, or its packaging, and that under the 1909 Act the absence of copyright notice was fatal.[175]

In a case directly contrary to *Data Cash*, the United States District Court for

---

[166] Data Cash, 628 F2d at 1038.

[167] *Id* 1065.

[168] *Id* 1066.

[169] *Id* 1066.

[170] The Copyright Act did not apply. §117 of the Copyright Act states that the Copyright Act does not afford to the owner of copyright in a work any greater or lesser rights . . . than that afforded to works under the law . . . in effect on December 31, 1977.

[171] 480 F Supp 1063, at 1068.

[172] *Id* 1067 n 4, 1068.

[173] Id 1068.

[174] 209 US 1 (1908).

[175] Data Cash, *supra* note 166. *See* 37 CFR §201.20(g).

the Northern District of California held in *Tandy Corp v Personal Micro Computers, Inc* that a computer program was a work of authorship subject to copyright and that a silicon chip upon which the program is fixed the "tangible medium of expression" which will subject the program so fixed to copyright laws.[176] Tandy was the first case to hold that a program with purely mechanical functions, such as handling keyboard input, was an appropriate subject for copyright. The Tandy Corporation had developed a program for one of its home computers, which would translate information placed in the computer into machine language. This program was imprinted on a silicon chip which was permanently wired into the computer. The defendants claimed that this type of information storage, called "read only memory" (ROM), was not copyrightable because the ROM chips are not "copies" of the computer program. The court stressed that the definition of "fixed" within the copyright laws was all inclusive and thus, the imprinting of a program on a silicon chip which permits the computer to read the program and act on its instructions falls easily within the ambit of a fixed, tangible medium of expression. In addition, the court noted that it might be shown that the defendants made a copy of the chip containing the imput/output ROM by making a readable printout of the program an thus violated the copyright law. Some commentators disagree with the court's reasoning that the imprinting of a program on a chip that corresponds to the 1s and 0s of the object code which can be easily read by a computer complies with the statutory definition that a copy must be able to be perceived, reproduced, and otherwise communicated.[177] It is arguable that a series of 1s and 0s is intelligible to humans because there are seasoned programmers who understand these 1s and 0s. In addition, it has been suggested that it is erroneous to speak of a machine as *reading* or *understanding* object code in that computers:

> do not read books or understand them in the same sense as a person

---

[176] Tandy Corp v Personal Micro Computers, Inc, 524 F Supp 171 (ND Cal 1981).

[177] Stern, *Copying ROMS: Right or Wrong,* Computer Design, Feb 1982, at 131, 132. The Copyright Office will accept object code without any assurances as to copyrightability if it is submitted with the corresponding source code. Source code is given preference over object code in all cases. When object code is submitted by itself, it will be accepted under the rule of doubt, but only if accompanied by a notarized letter assuring the Copyright Office that there is copyrightable ownership. *See* 37 CFR §202.20(vii), which requires that the first and last 25 pages of the source code must be submitted. This would permit developers to omit the trade secret aspects of the program from these submitted pages and place them in the middle sections of the program. However, under "the rule of doubt" the registration certificate issued by the Copyright Office does not provide evidence of copyright validity. The rule of doubt has been criticized because many materials which are deposited with the Copyright Office such as books in foreign languages, code books and source codes are not readably understandable by examiners yet are not subject to the rule of doubt. The copyright holder on object code is thus at a disadvantage in an infringement action in both burden of proof and in obtaining a preliminary injunction. See 1 Software Protection 16 (Feb/Mar 1983).

does. Yet, the court's reasoning assumes this to be true and that "perception" by a machine or "communication" to a machine is covered by the statute. This is highly questionable, and possibly wrong.[178]

To speak of a machine reading is to use a metaphor which fails to properly describe the machine's limitations. Another argument against the *Tandy* court's interpretation is that the transformation of source code to object code is dissimilar to a language translation because "some statements in the source program may not have counterparts in the object code, while some portions of the object code version may not have counterparts in the source program."[179] This transformation from source to object code is generally reversible.

In *Apple Computer, Inc v Franklin Computer Corp,* the court held that a ROM *might* not be copyrightable using reasoning similar to *Data Cash.* At issue in the case were fourteen programs expressed in object code which was imprinted in a ROM or enscribed on floppy disks. The defendant Franklin had designed a computer which was "Apple-compatible". Apple contended that by so doing, Franklin had stolen the logic and structure of their system. Franklin argued that, in order to create a system which could run Apple-compatible software, it was necessary to create a similar operating system structure. Also, Franklin argued that object code imprinted in a ROM or enscribed on a floppy disk was not "fixed" according to §101, and thus not copyrightable. After an extensive discussion of the law, the judge denied the motion for a preliminary injunction based on the fact that Apple could not sustain its burden of showing a reasonable possiblity of success on the merits so as to sustain the issuance of a preliminary injunction against Franklin for copyright infringement.[180] In *Williams Electronics, Inc v Artic International, Inc,* the Third Circuit Court of Appeals held that there was *fixation* in both the attract and play mode of a video game because the new images created by the video game in each mode were identical to earlier ones and, thus, the developer had a right to protection for the audiovisual embodiment of the work.[181] The court also noted that the definition of *copy* in §101 of the Copyright Act was meant to be broad enough to make computer programs copyrightable. To do otherwise "would afford an unlimited loophole by which infringement of a computer program is limited to copying of the computer program text but not to duplication of a computer

---

[178] Stern, *supra* note 177, at 132. See Note, *Computer Programs: Does the Copyright Law Apply?,* 5 Artists' Rights & Labor Relations 66 (1980); Boorstyn & Fliesler, *Copyrights, Computers and Confusion,* 56 Cal St BJ 148 (1981); Stern, *ROMS in Search of a Remedy: Can They Find It?,* 1 Computer L Rev 4 (1982).

[179] Stern, *supra* note 177, at 132.

[180] Apple Computer, Inc v Franklin Computer Corp, 545 F Supp 812 (ED Pa 1982). Apple is appealing this decision. The Association of Data Processing Service Organizations (ADAPSO) has filed an *amicus* brief which is excerpted at 1 Software Protection 2 (Feb/Mar 1983).

[181] Williams Elects, Inc v Artic Intl, Inc, 685 F2d 870 (3d Cir 1982).

program fixed on a silicon chip."[182] In *GCA Corp v Chance,* the court held that because the object code is the decryption of the copyrighted source code, the two should be treated as one work and, therefore, the Copyright Act protects both the source and object codes.[183]

In *Synercom Technology, Inc v University Computing Co,*[184] a suit was brought for copyright infringement of instruction manuals and input formats used with a computer program designed to solve engineering problems incident to the analysis of structures.[185] There was no claim of copyright of the actual program involved since it had been developed earlier by IBM, modified by McDonnell Automation, and further modified by plaintiff. In fact, defendant's program was independently developed.[186] Synercom had invested over $100,000 in writing the instructional manual and by the time defendant entered the market with its competitive program, Synercom had achieved considerable success in training customers to use the input formats to its program. Although Synercom had based its manual on an earlier version published by McDonnell Automation, which made no claim to proprietary rights, the court found "that at least 70% of the prose found in Synercom's manuals is indeed original to Synercom."[187] That manual, therefore, was protected by copyright. The court went on to find that the defendant had infringed the copyright of the instruction manual and granted injunctive relief. In deciding the issue of copyright of the input formats, the court focused on the question of whether the defendant "plagiarized Synercom's idea or its expression." If the idea is contained in the sequence and ordering of data, there was no infringement. If, however, the sequencing and ordering of data was an expression, it "follows that FDI's preprocessor program infringed."[188] The court concluded that formats are *not* proper subjects for copyright protection and there was no infringement.

§2.10   The Future of Copyright Protection

Although the Copyright Act of 1976 and its 1980 amendments expressly make copyright protection available to a computer program, the nature of a copyright itself dictates against comprehensive coverage of all aspects of a program that may be of value to the owner. Specifically, the methodology underlying a particular program, *i.e.,* why and how the program was written the way it was to instruct the computer in achieving a certain result, might be

---

[182] *Id* 877.

[183] GCA Corp v Chance, No C-82-1062 (ND Cal July 19, 1982); 24 Patent, Trademark & Copyright J (BNA) 574 (Oct 7, 1982).

[184] 462 F Supp 1003 (1978).

[185] Input formats are the arrangement of data which is *read in* by the program. See Reznick, *Synercom Technology, Inc v University Computing Co: Copyright Protection for Computer Formats and the Idea/Expression Dichotomy,* 8 Rutgers J Computers, Tech & L 65 (1980).

[186] 462 F Supp 1003 (1978).

[187] *Id* 1010; the court later stated that 79% was original.

[188] *Id* 1013.

classified as the underlying idea and hence not copyrightable. A copyright only protects the expression of an idea from exact or near-exact copies. Thus, when focusing on the question of whether the right to the methodology used in developing a program can be preserved exclusively in the proprietor, it is necessary to examine other theories in intellectual property which are potentially capable of accomplishing this task. To date, software has been afforded an uncertain protection through a patchwork of copyright, trade secret, tort, and contract law. One of the most serious dilemmas currently confronting software proprietors is whether the federal copyright law, now specifically applicable to software, will preempt protection afforded under the state and common law. The preemption issue arises from §301 of the Copyright Act, which essentially establishes federal law as the exclusive purveyor of rights and remedies for copyrightable works.[189] If so, and if, as is highly likely, the methodology underlying a particular piece of software is classified as an idea and is refused copyright protection, there may be no legal theory available to prevent its unrestricted absorption into the public domain.

Fortunately, a more favorable interpretation, and the one prevailing among the commentators, suggests that federal preemption will operate to deny the injured party redress under state law only where the same or similar interests would find protection in a copyright infringement suit. Except where the grant of state protection for a properly copyrightable work is co-extensive with that provided under the federal statute, trade secret as well as other common law theories of unfair competition predicated upon contract and tort law can be used to protect an idea. Finally, as a very tenuous alternative means of protecting software methodology, the *Diamond v Diehr*[190] decision in 1981 has opened the door for software patentability. Although a valid patent is the only statutorily available means of obtaining an exclusive right to an idea, the procurement of a software patent is a risky endeavor. It is exceedingly difficult to satisfy the three legal requirements for a valid issuance, and it is both time-consuming and expensive.

Trade Secret Protection

§2.11   Generally

A viable third alternative to protect computer software for many firms is the use of trade secret law. Just as copyright law originated in the common law of each state, the origin of trade secret law can also be found in the common law of each state.[191] Judicial recognition of trade secret law has a long history. In

---

[189] 17 USC §301. See generally *Avco Corp v Precision Air Parts, Inc,* 496 DTCJ A-1 (MD Ala 1980).

[190] 450 US 175, 101 SCt 1048 (1981).

[191] *See* Uniform Trade Secrets Act, 14 ULA 537 (1979). *The Restatement of Torts* defines

Board of Trade of Chicago v Christie Grain & Stock Co, Justice Holmes stated that "the plaintiff has the right to keep the work which it has done, or paid for doing, to itself. The fact that others might do similar work, if they might, does not authorize them to steal plaintiff's."[192] In a later case, however, Justice Holmes pointed out that it is not the subject matter per se that gains for itself the status of trade secret, but rather "the primary fact that the law makes some requirements of good faith. . . . The property may be denied, but the confidence cannot be."[193]

State courts have held that a trade secret must meet four major requirements: appropriateness of subject matter, secrecy, novelty, and economic value.[194] Appropriateness of subject matter has three broad subcategories of protectable information: (1) patentable and unpatentable inventions along with the know-how associated with these inventions (e.g., secret processes, patterns, and compounds); (2) abstract ideas of a commercial or industrial nature (e.g., advertising plans and schemes for media presentation) and (3) other sorts of information that are not novel, but which are of value to the owner (e.g., customer lists, discount codes, and supply sources).[195]

The second requirement, secrecy, is rather vague and has at least two interpretations: internal and external secrecy.[196] The distinction between internal and external secrecy is basically one between in-house secrecy (which involves the steps taken by the owner of the secret to prevent its disclosure by those in contractual relationships with the owner) and industry-wide secrecy (which involves the knowledge of the subject matter among those outside of the owner's control). When the secrecy requirement is mentioned by courts, they typically are referring to internal secrecy. The secrecy requirement is not absolute. Some disclosures are permissible, but the disclosures are limited to persons who enter into confidential relationships with the owner of the trade

---

a trade secret as: "any formula, device, or compilation of information which is used in one's business, and which gives him an opportunity to obtain an advantage over competitors who do not know or use it." Restatement of Torts §757, comment (b) (1939). See also Bender, *Trade Secret Protection of Computer Software,* 38 Geo Wash L Rev 909 (1970). Some commentators have suggested an interesting combination of trade secret and copyright to protect software. Copyright registration is not needed for protection, although it is needed to sue for infringement. If the secret is registered within five years of publication, registration is prima facie evidence of the validity of the copyright and makes available statutory damages and attorney's fees. Marton, *Copyright in the 1980's: Fifth Anniversary of the Revised Law,* 30 Fed B News & J 39, 42 (1983).

[192] 198 US 236, 250 (1905). See also Ellis, Trade Secrets §12 (1953).

[193] Dupont Power Co v Masland, 244 US 100, 102 (1917).

[194] See Wessel, *Legal Protection of Computer Programs,* 43 Harv Bus Rev 97 (1965). Several of these requirements are discussed in Kewanee Oil Co v Bicron Corp, 416 US 470 (1974).

[195] Turner, The Law of Trade Secrets 12 (1962).

[196] *See* BF Goodrich Co v Wohlgemuth, 117 Ohio App 463 (Ct App 1963); Kaumagraph Co v Stampagraph Co, 235 NY 1 (1923); National Tube Co v Eastern Tube Co, 3 Ohio CC (NS) 459 (Cir Ct 1902), *affd* 69 Ohio St 560, 70 NE 1127 (1903).

secret.[197] As long as all parties maintain the secrecy, the independent discovery of the information by others does not destroy its protectable status. If the secret is revealed by dissemination of the product containing it, the trade secret is no longer protected.[198]

The third requirement, novelty, is not as stringent as its counterpart under patent law.[199] The novelty concept in trade secret law, however, is more discriminating than the originality concept under copyright laws.[200] The fourth requirement, which deals with economic value, focuses on factors as the value of the information, the amount of effort expended in obtaining the trade secret, and the difficulty of acquiring or reacquiring the trade secret.[201]

Computer programs clearly satisfy the first requirement of appropriateness of subject matter. Those programs that are in the developmental stage are not as safe as completed programs, but "as the idea becomes more detailed and moved toward implementation, it is more likely to be regarded as qualified for trade secret protection."[202] Mere documentation and data in the form of programs will probably fall into the least protectable class. In order to insure fulfillment of the secrecy requirement, special care must be taken by the owner both in the case of maintaining in-house secrecy and in the case of selective proliferation of the program. The owner should ensure limited access to the program and all relevant documents should be stamped as secret or confidential. In the case of a sale or rental of a program package, the owner should contract with the vendee to insure that disclosures are limited and closely controlled to protect the trade secret status of the program package.[203] Very

---

[197] Morris, *Protecting Proprietary Rights of Computer Programs: The Need for New Legislative Protection,* 21 Cath Univ L Rev 181 (1970). *See also* Dupont Powder Corp v Masland, 244 US 100 (1917); General Aniline & Film Corp v Frantz, 50 Misc 2d 994, 274 NYS2d 634, (Sup Ct 1966); Cincinnati Bell Foundry Co v Dodds, 10 Ohio Dec Reprint 154 (Super Ct 1887).

[198] *See* Wesley-Jessen, Inc v Reynolds, 182 Patent, Trademark & Copyright J (BNA) A-2 (June 13, 1974) (trade secret no longer a trade secret if embodied in a product which is then sold and examined with reverse engineering techniques). See also Oppenheim, Cases of Unfair Trade Practices 237 (2d ed 1965).

[199] WR Grace & Co, v Hargadine, 392 F2d 9 (6th Cir 1968) (comparison of patent and trade secret novelty requirement).

[200] Alfred Bell & Co v Catalda Fine Arts, Inc, 191 F2d 99 (2d Cir 1951) (example of copyright novelty). The degree of novelty will also enter into the determination of damages awarded by the courts. See Bender, *supra* note 191.

[201] In a few instances, heavy reliance on this fourth requirement has resulted in lowering of the requisite secrecy and novelty standards. Ellis, *supra* note 192, at §14.

[202] Irizarry y Puente v Harvard College, 248 F2d 799 (1st Cir), *cert denied,* 356 US 947 (1957); *See also* Hamilton Natl Bank v Belt, 210 F2d 706 (DC Cir 1953).

[203] Various methods are available to facilitate the maintenance of secrecy including:
1. Only allowing the transfer of object code
2. Limiting the amount of documentation transferred with the package
3. Establishing a licensing system on an individual installation basis
4. Contractural provisions to limit the grantee or licensee in proliferation of the program from the installation site

little has been written on the novelty requirement of computer programs for trade secret protection due to the limited case law dealing specifically with trade secret protection of computer software. It would appear, however, that if a program involves many complicated sub-routines, the novelty requirement would be satisfied.

For the fourth requirement, the greater the value of the program, the wider the scope of protection afforded by the law of trade secrets.[204] Consequently, the owner should establish a detailed log for each use of the program to provide tangible evidence of its value. Establishing the actual development costs of the program is also an important element in insuring common law protection.[205]

The *Restatement of Torts* outlines the protection given by trade secret law. Generally a person is liable for the use or disclosure of another's trade secret when the person either discovers the secret by improper means, or breaks a confidence for that purpose. Further, an individual is liable, if with full knowledge of the facts the individual learns the secret from a third party. Finally, if disclosure is accidentally made to an individual, the individual is not liable for use of the secret until informed of the mistaken disclosure. Thereafter, the individual is liable if the person continues to use the trade secret.[206]

§2.12   Employment Agreements

The arrival of the computer age has created new internal security problems in the workplace. The speed and efficiency of computers, the easy access to large volumes of information that they provide, and the competitive value of newly-developed computer hardware and software all present risks as well as profits to business.

Employers have long used employment agreements of various types to protect the confidentiality of information obtained and products developed during the course of employment, and to minimize competition from departing employees. The rapid growth and change of the computer industry adds a new dimension to the employment relationship with which the old legal solutions may be unable to cope.

A common method to protect computer software is the use of restrictive contractual agreements between the owner of the trade secret and all others with whom the owner deals. The two distinct categories of such contractual

---

[204] The deposit of a copyrighted work, under 37 CFR 202.20, may be deemed an act inconsistent with maintaining a trade secret. Also, secrecy could be lost by release of the work under the Freedom of Information Act. *See* 5 USC §552(e); 17 USC §701(d); D. Davidson, Computer Software Protection, at 66-7 (1982). Ellis, *supra* note 192, at §14.

[205] Wessel, *supra* note 194, at 100-01.

[206] See generally Restatement of Torts §757 (1939). Although Restatement 2d of Torts omits these provisions on trade secrets, courts have continued to rely on these rules on the basis of *stare decisis.*

agreements are employee and nonemployee contracts. Clauses in employee contacts requiring nondisclosure both during employment and after employment are commonly used. Another device commonly used in employee contracts is the noncompetition clause.[207] Employment agreements appear in two basic forms: the agreement not to disclose confidential information, and the covenant not to compete, or post-employment restraint. Both are intended to restrain the employee from using knowledge gained during employment in later competition with the employer.

The confidentiality agreement normally acknowledges the proprietary nature of customer lists, manufacturing or other business processes, product information, and inventions, and provides that the employee will not, during or after the employment, divulge that confidential information. The agreement usually further provides that the employee assign all rights to any inventions and processes developed during employment to the company. The covenant not to compete restrains the employee from engaging in work that directly competes with the employer after termination. These covenants are generally enforceable to the extent that they are: (1) not contrary to public policy or the public interest; (2) not unnecessarily injurious to the employee; and (3) limited to restrictions reasonably necessary to protect the goodwill and business of the employer.[208]

Employee Confidentiality

The employee problem should be dealt with when the employee is hired by requiring the new employee to sign a nondisclosure agreement. Care must be taken to ensure that the employee is given consideration for signing the agreement. The employee should also agree not to take anything of a confidential nature when the employee changes jobs.[209] Nondisclosure provisions should also be included in all lease or license agreements with customers. These customer agreements should restrict the number of copies these customers can make.

---

[207] These clauses simply limit an employee from competing with the employer for a definite time period and within a specified geographic area once the employee terminates the relationship with the employer. Courts have applied a rule of reason to both time and geographic limitations. The reasonableness of the time period in restrictive agreements will vary between jurisdictions, and may vary depending on the type of position held by the employee. See Klein, *The Technical Trade Secret Quadrangle: A Survey*, 55 NWUL Rev 437 (1960). Traditionally, geographic limitations have been viewed as the competitive region of the employer, but the software industry is national in scope, and thus, national territorial limitations should be valid. 10 Cavitch, Business Organization §234.02 (1974). See Krendl & Krendl, *Noncompetition Covenants in Colorado: A Statutory Solution?*, 52 Den LJ 499 (1975). It should be noted that California, a major center for the computing industry, has a strong public policy against enforcing most covenants not to compete. Briody, *Employment Agreements Not to Compete in California*, 47 J Calif State Bar 318 (1972). See also §§3.11, 3.14.

[208] Denny v Roth, 296 SW2d 944 (Tex Civ App 1956).

[209] Bender, *Trade Secret Software Protection*, 5 APLAQJ 49, 53 (1977).

Several cases involving disloyal employees have been decided. One question arises, however, concerning how the trade secret is removed. Is appropriation by memory within the scope of protection? This is important since most programmers who develop or perform extensive maintenance on a program necessarily commit the algorithm and a significant part of the program structure and code to memory. These programmers, therefore could easily reproduce it for another employer. Although not a case involving computer programs, a court addressed this issue in *AH Emery Co v Marcan Products Co*,[210] where plaintiff's former employee drafted blueprints of a hydraulic load cell from memory. The trial court found that "it is as much a breach of confidence for an employee to reproduce his employer's drawings from memory as to copy them directly."[211] A similar situation occurred in *Sperry Rand Corp v Rothlien*[212] where defendant alleged that the drawings of specifications of a silicon alloy junction transistor had been reproduced from memory. The court stated that the theft may have been by memory, but "it does not matter whether a copy of a Sperry drawing came out in a defendants' hand or in his head. His duty of fidelity to his employer remains the same."[213]

In *Republic Systems & Programming, Inc v Computer Assistance, Inc*, the plaintiff faced the consequences of having no employment contract with its employees.[214] Republic was in the business of *contract programming*, that is, writing programs for someone else under contract. Republic's branch manager for its Chestire, Connecticut office, Andrew Vignola, like the rest of Republic's employees had no employment contract. Vignola, unhappy with his work situation, decided to form his own company, and as soon as the incorporation papers were prepared submitted his resignation to Republic by mail on Friday, after work. Immediately, he contacted his former co-workers and induced 20 of the 25 of them to join his new company. Soon they began contacting their former customers. Republic sued Vignola for breach of fiduciary duty and misappropriation of trade secrets, in this case, customer lists. The court dismissed Republic's claim, stating that because there was no employment contract, his employment terminated when he mailed his resignation and after that time he had no obligation to Republic and also was free to hire Republic's employees and solicit Republic's customers.[215] The customer lists did not qualify as trade secrets because some of the customers were listed in advertising brochures as representative customers and "efforts to keep the names of the remainder secret were meager at best."[216]

The result was different, however, in *Structural Dynamics Research Corp v Engi-*

---

[210] 268 F Supp 289 (SDNY 1967), *affd* 389 F2d 11 (2d Cir), *cert denied*, 393 US 835 (1968).

[211] 268 F Supp at 300.

[212] 241 F Supp 549 (D Conn 1964).

[213] *Id* 563.

[214] 322 F Supp 619 (D Conn 1970).

[215] *Id.*

[216] *Id* 628.

neering Mechanics Research Corp,[217] where three employees of Structural Dynamics (SDRC) left the company and formed Engineering Mechanics Research Corp (EMRC). The EMRC employees then developed a program very similar to the one being developed by SDRC. One of the three had done considerable research at SDRC on a computer program for the analysis of mechanical structures involving curved surfaces. Prior to the research, programs doing this analysis could only work with straight-sided surfaces such as triangles and rectangles. The court found the two programs similar, with the basic difference between them being that the EMRC program was more fully developed.[218] The court stated that "the relationship giving rise to a duty [not to disclose] is not necessarily dependent on contract; it may be based on agency principles or on specific dealings between parties in which a situation of trust arises and out of which sought-to-be-protected knowledge is acquired."[219] The court distinguished between two ways of acquiring the information: (1) where the employee learns about it in the course of the employment in a relationship of confidence, and (2) where the subject matter of the trade secret is created by the employee during the employment. In the first case, a duty not to use or disclose the information arises, whereas in the second case,

> no duty arises since the employee may then have an interest in the subject matter at least equal to that of his employer. . . . In such a case, absent an express contractual obligation by the employee not to use or disclose such confidential information acquired during his employment . . . he is free to use or disclose it. . . .[220]

All three individuals had entered into an Employee Patent and Confidential Information Agreement with SDRC in which they agreed not to divulge or use any privileged or confidential information, trade secret, or other proprietary information. The court found that "while the defendants used their own experience, skill and knowledge, this was commingled with the confidential information taken from SDRC,"[221] and awarded SDRC damages.[222]

§2.13 Nonemployment Agreements

When dealing with customers, a contract is even more important than when dealing with employees, for a confidential relationship is not likely to be implied. The customer should agree "not to disclose the software (including documentation) to third parties, and moreover, to take affirmative steps to

---

[217] 401 F Supp 1102 (ED Mich 1975).

[218] *Id* 1109.

[219] *Id* 1111.

[220] *Id.*

[221] *Id* 1120.

[222] *See* Cybertek Computer Prods, Inc v Whitfield, 203 USPQ 1020 (1977) for a similar result.

avoid any such disclosure."[223] Trade secrets between competing companies is another area where software trade secrets have been upheld. In *Com-Share Inc v Computer Complex Inc*[224] two companies were in the business of selling computer time on a *time sharing* basis where different customers can use the computer system concurrently and pay only for the actual time they use the computer system. The companies had entered into a "Technical Exchange Agreement" where the "plaintiff supplied to defendant, in confidence, . . . information, training, knowledge, documents, tapes, tangible things and other technology developed by plaintiff."[225] The agreement specified that the parties "agreed not to lease, sell or otherwise divulge to any third party interest, without prior written consent of the other, any and all systems software developments supplied to it by the other"[226] and to further safeguard the information. The agreement also provided:

> Notwithstanding the expiration or termination of this agreement, the limitations set forth . . . shall continue for a period of 24 months after such expiration or termination.[227]

The parties terminated the agreement after three and one half years by mutual agreement. Nine months later, the defendant announced plans to sell substantially all of its assets and the goodwill related to its computer time sharing operations to a third party who was a competitor of the plaintiff. The plaintiff then filed a motion for preliminary and permanent equitable relief. The court found that while "defendant may have made certain technical changes in software supplied to it . . . the defendant did not alter the unique principles, engineering, logic, and coherence developed by plaintiff."[228] The court also found that "the utmost caution was used by plaintiff in protecting the secrecy of this software."[229] Defendant argued that because the transfer of software had already started and "the omelet cannot be unscrambled" that it would have been illusory for plaintiff to obtain an injunction. The court responded that it was "not persuaded that modern technology has withered the strong right arm of equity",[230] and issued the preliminary injunction. In *Com-Share,* the initial relationship between the parties was friendly so each was aware of the other party and each was aware that a potential conflict might arise in the future, thus the technical exchange agreement provided the confidential relationship which was the basis for protection.

---

[223] Bender, *Trade Secret Software Protection,* 5 APLAQJ 49, 53 (1977). See also §3.15.
[224] 338 F Supp 1229 (ED Mich 1971), *affd,* 458 F2d 1341 (1972).
[225] 338 F Supp at 1231.
[226] *Id* 1232.
[227] *Id.*
[228] *Id* 1234.
[229] *Id.*
[230] *Id* 1239.

In *Ward v Superior Court*,[231] no such relationship existed, but criminal law became the basis for protection. Defendant Ward was an employee of UCC, a computer service company, who obtained the customer number and site code of a customer of a competing service company, ISD, as well as ISD's unlisted computer telephone number. Using the customer number and site code, he was able, by telephone, to log onto ISD's computer. Once logged on, he had access to the computer's memory and was able to copy a program from that memory onto the UCC computer. The value of the program was $5000, and Ward was charged with grand theft and theft of a trade secret. The California Penal Code, §499(c) provided that every:

> person is guilty of theft who, with intent to deprive or withhold from the owner thereof the control of a trade secret . . . does any of the following: (1) Steals, takes, or carries away any article representing a trade secret . . . (2) Having unlawfully obtained access to the article, without authority makes or causes to be made a copy of any article representing a trade secret.[232]

The court found that the definition of *article* required that it be tangible,[233] and further found that the electrical impulses transmitted over the telephone were not tangible.[234] The court, however, found that there was probable cause that the defendant made a copy of the program "through the use of the UCC computer and thereafter carried that copy from the UCC computer to his office at UCC, thus providing the asportation requirement."[235] Although this opinion deals only with a motion to dismiss and a demurrer to the information, defendant reportedly pleaded guilty to theft of trade secrets and was sentenced to a fine of $5000 and three years probation.[236]

Joint Venture Agreements

In addition to disloyal employees, customers, and competitors, trade secrets must also be guarded in joint ventures. *University Computing Co v Lykes-Youngstown Corp*[237] involved a joint venture, a disloyal employee, and the bribing of a customer. Lykes and UCC entered into a written agreement to create a new corporation which was to offer computer services in an area neither company was currently servicing. The president of the new corporation, Oliver Shinn, was formerly vice-president of sales for UCC. Before the corporation was actually formed, the companies had a disagreement and Lykes formed a whol-

---

[231] Ward v Superior Court, 3 Computer L Serv Rep 206 (Cal Super 1972).

[232] *Id* 208.

[233] *Id.*

[234] *Id.*

[235] *Id* 209.

[236] Bender, *supra* note 223, at 63.

[237] 504 F2d 518 (1974).

ly-owned subsidiary, Lykes-Youngstown Computer Services Corp (LYCSC), with Shinn as its president, which began to market a program that had been developed by UCC. LYCSC obtained the program by bribing an employee of a UCC customer.[238]

The court found that Lykes had breached its joint venture agreement by unilaterally terminating the joint venture corporation. The court also found that the program was a trade secret, that the trade secret had been wrongfully appropriated, and that Lykes, Shinn, and the bribed customer employee would share liability. The court also upheld the trial court's charge to the jury that the following factors should be considered by them in arriving at the proper damages for the defendants' misappropriation of the program:

1. The development costs incurred by the plaintiff

2. The fees paid by customers of the plaintiff who utilized the system on a service bureau basis

3. The prices at which the system was leased or sold by the plaintiff for restrictive use

4. The sale price placed on the system by the defendants

5. Expert testimony as to what would constitute a reasonable royalty for the rights to unrestricted use of the system[239]

Nonemployee contracts present more difficult problems. If owners choose to lease their programs on a nonexclusive basis, the lessees will acquire only the right to use the programs while title remains with the lessors. On the other hand, if the developer chooses to sell the software, full title and exclusive rights will be transferred to the vendee. A transaction similar to the outright sale of software is a contract for development of a program. In this relationship, title may reside in either party to the contract, and therefore, the division of rights should be clarified before execution of the contract.[240]

On the civil side, the owner of a trade secret may obtain injunctive relief to prevent an appropriator from either using the secret or from disclosing the secret to a third party.[241] If the secret has already been disclosed to a third party or used by the appropriator, the owner may seek damages resulting from the disclosure or from the profits accrued by the use of the trade secret.[242]

---

[238] *Id* 529.

[239] *Id* 539.

[240] Often a vendor/developer will issue a license for nonexclusive use of the computer software. In exchange for a license fee, the vendee received the object code, while the source code is placed in escrow.

[241] *See* Kewanee Oil Co v Bicron Corp, 416 US 470 (1974); Schulenburg v Signatrol, Inc, 33 Ill 2d 379 (1965), *cert denied*, 383 US 959 (1966) (although an injunction is a drastic remedy, it may be granted in appropriate instances). See also *Software, Statutes, and Stare Decisis*, 13 How LJ 420 (1967).

[242] Morris, *Protecting Proprietary Rights of Computer Programs: The Need for New Legislative Protection*, 21 Cath Univ L Rev 181 (1970).

The use of state criminal sanctions is a relatively new aspect of trade secrets protection.[243] Two methods of providing such sanctions presently exist: criminal prosecution for software theft, if the stolen information is in such a form as to fit the relevant language of the existing statute; and specific criminal sanctions for misappropriation of trade secrets.[244] At the federal level, no express trade secret statutes exist. There are however, statutes that prohibit the transportation and sale or receipt of stolen goods, wares, merchandise, securities, or money.[245] It is still not settled whether the theft of computer programs falls under the federal statutes.[246] Further, no protection exists under these statutes against appropriation by memory.[247]

Overall, trade secret protection of software is a viable alternative for private industry. Theft of trade secret protected software (and hardware) has been ruled a violation of Oklahoma trade secret law.[248] Although trade secret protection has serious limitations, it currently appears to be the best alternative for private firms in protecting their software.[249]

§2.14 Preemption of Trade Secret Protection

One of the appealing traits of trade secrecy is that the enterprise controls its own legal destiny through the seriousness of the efforts directed at securing confidentiality of the information. Conduct the courts look to as indicative of intent to maintain a trade secret includes: whether action was taken to limit the extent of knowledge of the secret information inside the business, as well as outside, and whether the use of the protective measures taken were maximized or only illusory. The *Restatement of Torts* details three other indicia of the existence of a trade secret: (1) the value of the information to the business and its competitors, (2) the development costs, and (3) the ease or difficulty by

---

[243] Many states have passed computer crime statutes. See Sokolik, *Computer Crime-The Need for Deterrent Legislation,* 2 Computer LJ 353 (1980); Volgyes, *The Investigation, Prosecution, and Prevention of Computer Crime: A State-of-the-Art Review,* 2 Computer LJ 385 (1980); *Survey, White Collar Crime: Computer Crime,* Am Crim L Rev 370 (1980). Trade secret theft continues in the computer industry. See, e.g., Curtis, *Theft of Secrets Continue,* 48 Electronics 63 (1975); Hammer, *IBM-Tightens Reins on Trade Secrets; Pledges Fight on Lawsuits,* NY Times, Apr 30, 1974, at 57.

[244] *See* Hancock v Texas, 402 SW2d 906 (Tex Crim App 1966).

[245] 18 USC §§2314, 2315.

[246] In several cases the courts have held that the act of transporting photostatic copies of the stolen information (not computer programs) violated federal statutes. See, e.g., United States v Greenwald, 479 F2d 320 (6th Cir 1973), *cert denied,* 414 US 854 (1973); United States v Bottone, 365 F2d 389 (2d Cir), *cert denied,* 385 US 974 (1966); United States v Lester, 282 F2d 750 (3d Cir 1960), *cert denied,* 364 US 937 (1961).

[247] 365 F2d 389 (court commented that 15 USC §2314 would not apply to the theft of trade secrets by memory).

[248] Telex, Corp v Intl Busines Machs Corp, 367 F Supp 258 (ND Okla 1973), *revd on other grounds,* 510 F2d 894 (10th Cir 1975).

[249] 367 F Supp at 258.

which the trade secret may be properly acquired or duplicated.[250]

The last item expresses one of the most severe shortcomings in the degree of protection trade secrecy confers upon software. The owner of a trade secret has legal recourse only to prevent someone from using or disclosing the secret where there has been a breach of confidence, a discovery through improper means, or where the secret was learned through a third party who obtained it improperly or through a breach of confidence. Trade secrecy offers no protection against independent development of computer software, or against obtaining it lawfully through reverse engineering.[251] Although trade secret law does provide a means of protecting the methodology underlying a computer program, it is not airtight even if no one besides the developer has access, since independent origin is not proscribed. The risk is magnified by licensing, especially where the licensee might ultimately arrange for public distribution in some form, as there is then a correlative rise in the number of opportunities for reverse engineering attempts.

The other major drawback to reliance on trade secret protection for software methodology is the possibility, seemingly remote, of federal preemption. Section 301 of the Copyright Act of 1976 (Copyright Act) states that any work of authorship fixed in a tangible medium, which falls within one of the categories of copyrightable subject matter (i.e., literary works, dramatic works, and motion pictures), is governed exclusively by the Copyright Act.[252] No person is entitled to any Copyright Act right or any equivalent right in the work under common or state law. The preemption provision further states that: (1) it does not annul or limit the rights or remedies granted by common law or state statute where the subject matter is not copyrightable as detailed in §102 and §103; (2) where the course of action arose before the effective date of the Copyright Act, or (3) where the alleged wrongdoing encroaches upon any rights which are the same as, or equivalent to, those protected in the Copyright Act, as delineated in §106.

Although the issue of possible preemption has been targeted as troublesome, and is the focus of much speculation, a close reading of the statute would indicate that the two sources of protection can coexist so as long as the plaintiff is not seeking to enforce the same or a substantially equivalent right under state law as would be provided under federal copyright protection. In instances of overlap, federal law prevails. This interpretation would allow the idea or methodology behind even a copyrighted computer program protection under the auspices of trade secret law. Section 301(b) abrogates only the existence of a state or common law remedy where the subject of the suit is within the scope of properly copyrightable material, as set forth in §102. Section 102, however, specifically excludes ideas, processes, concepts, etc. from protection. As to methodology, a trade secret would not be the same as

---

[250] Restatement of Torts, §757, comment b.

[251] Wydick, *Trade Secrets: Federal Pre-emption in Light of Goldstein and Kewanee*, 55 J Pat Off Socy 736, 739 (1973).

[252] 17 USC §301.

or equivalent to a copyright, therefore, the owner can use trade secret protection concurrently with copyright protection, where the respective elements of each are met, to obtain redress against unauthorized use of the idea behind a piece of software and the way it is expressed.

There is a series of Supreme Court decisions interpreting a similar conflict between state trade secret law and patent law that lends credence to the conclusion that state trade secret law and federal copyright law may conflict. The first two of these cases, *Sears, Roebuck & Co v Stiffel Co*,[253] and *Compco Corp v Day Bright Lighting, Inc*,[254] involved patented lighting fixtures. An action was brought to restrain unauthorized use under both the federal patent laws and the state unfair competition laws. The lower courts invalidated the patents but upheld the unfair competition claims. The Court reversed, holding that to grant plaintiff's invention "patent like protection under state law when no federal patent was warranted, would be to give greater protection than federal patent law provided."[255] Although neither of these cases involved a trade secret, the prevailing view was that, because such protection was grounded in state law, its scope would also be restricted.

In *Goldstein v California*,[256] the Court upheld a California criminal statute aimed at phonograph record piracy, reasoning first that the Constitution did not expressly confer federal exclusivity in the area of copyright protection, and second, that the state criminal statute at issue did not conflict with the federal scheme. The Court's decision in *Kewanee Oil Co v Bicron Corp*,[257] finally clarified the contours of trade secret protection as it interfaces with federal patent law. The Court stated that "the patent policy of encouraging invention is not disturbed by the existence of another form of incentive to invention. In this respect the two systems [patent and trade secret law] are not and never would be in conflict."[258]

The most recent Supreme Court statement defining the extent of federal preemption came in *Aronson v Quick Point Pencil Co*,[259] where it was held that federal patent law does not preempt state contract law. In *Aronson*, a contract action enforcing payment of royalties was allowed. Read together, this series of cases affirms the existence of a judicial trend in recognizing the right of the states in many instances to continue to provide protection for intellectual property independently of federal law.

---

[253] 376 U S 225 (1964).

[254] 376 U S 234 (1964).

[255] Note, *The Protection of Property Rights in Computer Software*, 14 Akron L Rev 85, 99 (1980).

[256] 412 U S 546 (1972).

[257] 416 U S 470 (1974).

[258] *Id* 484.

[259] 440 U S 257 (1978).

§2.15   The Future of Trade Secrets Protection

While trade secrets seem to offer the protection desired for computer programs, there are several problems involved. Because trade secret law is state
law, it can vary significantly from jurisdiction to jurisdiction. The elements of
secrecy and novelty mentioned earlier must be considered. If a program is not
carefully guarded, usually at great expense, courts will not find it to be a trade
secret.[260] Once secrecy is lost, regardless of *how* it is lost, there is no protection
for the program. If no novelty is found, most courts will not find a true trade
secret, or award damages if the program is appropriated. The ordinary program (e.g. standard accounting or payroll programs), although quite valuable
and marketable, would seem to have no protection under trade secrets since
most of the industry is aware of how to write this type of program. Because
trade secrecy is more expensive,

> users must cover the sellers expenses associated with maintaining a se-
> cure system through increased prices. Their freedom to do business in
> an unencumbered way is reduced, since they may need to enter into
> elaborate nondisclosure contracts with employees and third parties who
> have access to the secrets and to limit that access to a very small number
> of people. Since secrets are by definition known to only a few people,
> there is necessarily a reduced flow of information in the marketplace,
> which hinders the ability of potential buyers to make comparisons and
> hence leads to higher prices.[261]

Reverse engineering is an acceptable way of discovering trade secrets. Programs, therefore, are very vulnerable to the process of disassembly which is the
reverse of the assembly process described earlier.[262] Although the disassembly
process is more difficult and not as precise as assembly, it is quite common,
especially in the new microcomputer marketplace.

Trade secrets seem to be more effective in the large, commercial programming environment where *program support* (i.e. vendor supplied maintenance) is
more important, and totally ineffective in the small microcomputer *hobbyist*
marketplace where obtaining *free* software from a friend seems to increase the
excitement of owning the microcomputer. Somewhere between these two markets, the protection decreases from good to adequate to ineffective.

---

[260] In Telex v IBM, 367 F Supp 258 (ND Okla 1975), IBM had to show that a
diagnostic program had been kept secret by looking up the source code and only
distributing the object code.

[261] National Commission on the New Technological Uses of Copyrighted Works,
Final Report, July 31, 1978, at 17.

[262] See **§2.01.**

Suggested Legal Approach to Software Protection

§2.16   Generally

Copyright protection extends, at most, to the source and assembly phases of the program. Yet, that part which is usually misappropriated by computer users, the object program, in two instances, has been found to be not copyrightable. Patent protection is only available if the program is part of an apparatus and, therefore, most programs would not be covered. Trade secret law protects most software, but it is questionable as to how practical this protection is, given that the small vendor or consultant must disclose most of the *secret* in order to sell the product. As cumbersome as it seems to be, trade secret protection is, at present, the most reliable protection available.

Copyright would provide good protection for a literal copy, but since object code is readable only by a machine, it is extremely difficult to show substantial similarity as defined by copyright law in object code. Also, detection of any software copyright infringement is very hard. Patent protection provides its own set of problems along with detection and proof of infringement. Search of prior art which is under third party trade secret protection and the standard to be used for obviousness are both difficult issues. If patent or copyright protection were made available to software, trade secret protection or this new method of software protection might preempt existing trade secret laws.

§2.17   Foreign Perspectives

One possible compromise that would allow software to be patentable yet limit the amount of protection afforded would be to adopt the petty patent structure available in the Federal Republic of Germany (FRG).[263] The FRG patent system has two types of patents: the formal patent law (*Patentgesetz*) and the petty patent structure (*Gebrauchsmustergesetz*).[264] The petty patent system functions as an auxiliary or supporting branch of the regular patent system and allows inventions which have a lower standard of inventiveness than inventions eligible for the formal patents to receive a lesser patent.[265] In the FRG system the *nonobviousness* standard is bifurcated, allowing a much more flexible approach than is available in the United States system.

The length of protection afforded by the petty patent in the FRG is less than the formal patent and consists of a three year term renewable for an additional

---

[263] National Commission on the New Technological Uses of Copyrighted Works, Final Report, July 31, 1978, at 37.

[264] *Petty Patents in the Federal Republic of Germany: A Solution to the Problem of Software Protection?* 8 SWUL Rev 888 (1976).

[265] *Id.*

three years.[266] This length of protection would be much too short under the United States patent system where one to three years are required just to obtain the patent. The FRG also has a shorter method of processing patent applications, and the FRG grants patents after an abbreviated registration procedure, which consists mainly of examining the application to determine that: (1) it does not contain omissions; (2) the document is signed; (3) the application does not contradict the substantive requirements on its face; and (4) the application describes the invention with clarity and in definite terms.[267] The validity of any patent can be challenged through cancellation proceedings.[268] This alternative of patent protection, if applied to computer software, would solve the problems of searching prior art, obviousness, and would allow patent protection for software without burdening the patent office, and without restricting the computer software industry.

In 1972, the Japanese Ministry of International Trade and Industry proposed a sui generis system of software protection, and in 1976, the Japanese Agency for Cultural Affairs issued a report on the adequacy of copyright law.[269] The first Japanese decision on the subject matter was decided in December of 1982 in the case of *Taito v ING Enterprise* which awarded 540,000 yen damages for copying a read only memory (ROM) program of a video game.[270] Given the present advancement of the Japanese software industry to the cutting edge of software technology, future software protection disputes in Japan can be expected.

In his dissenting opinion to the subcommittee report to CONTU (but not included in his dissent to the final report), Commissioner Hersey recommended a hybrid system of software protection that has aspects of both copyright protection and patent protection.[271] An act to implement this proposal was prepared for Commissioner Hersey.[272] This act would establish a Registry of Computer Software within the Department of Commerce. Owners of software could obtain protection by attaching notice to their software and registering it. The protection would extend for 10 years and would seem to have protection mechanisms very similar to copyright. The only apparent difference between their new protection mechanism and copyright is the extention of protection to the idea or algorithm, although this model would exclude "any element of computer software which is merely the embodiment of a mathematical relationship or scientific principal."[273] This method would provide good protection, but it is unclear what the cost of this protection would be. A

---

[266] *Id* 889.

[267] *Id* 893.

[268] *Id* 894.

[269] 5 Copyright Management No 12, Dec 1982, at 8.

[270] *Id.*

[271] Pope & Pope, *Protection of Proprietary Interests in Computer Software*, 30 Ala L Rev 548, 551 (1979).

[272] *Id* app A, at 584.

[273] *Id* §3(b).

search, such as is performed in a patent application, could be performed or infringement might be left entirely to the courts. Either the FRG petty patent system or Commissioner Hersey's Registry of Computer Software proposal could provide adequate software protection for those who expend their efforts to create software.

§2.18   A Two Step Matrix Approach to Protect Software

In the development stage of software, trade secret law provides the best protection when precautions are taken to carefully document software development.[274] In the marketing stage, the type of protection available may differ according to the type of software.

Protection of Operating Systems

Generally, copyright protection is a viable method to protect operating system software. As operating systems are gradually incorporated into firmware, protection may be obtained from either patent or trade secret law, although it is extremely difficult to maintain the secrecy requirement of trade secret if firmware is sold as a mass market product. Because standardization is important in telecommunications, copyright can also be used to protect network/communications software. Database software may be protected under trade secret while micro- and mini- database software is probably best protected by copyright, given the large distribution of mini- and micro- database software. Some database managers may be patented in the future, given developments in firmware and hardware database managers.

Protection of Language Translators

Language translators consist of the assemblers and compilers which transform high level programs into machine readable form. Today, copyright and some trade secret protection is utilized. In very limited circumstances where a new assembler or compiler is novel and nonobvious, patent protection is viable, given the shift of assemblers and compilers into firmware.

Protection of Application Software

Application software can be divided between business application software and mass market software. The major problem with business application software is that it usually fails the nonobviousness and novelty tests of patent protection. Copyright protection is also a problem because competitors can easily use the ideas contained in business software. Most licensors of business application software, consequently, have turned to trade secret protection by making sure that their software is designated proprietary in the license agree-

---

[274] Wessel, *supra* note 194.

ment. In contrast to business applications, mass market software cannot use trade secret protection because of the impossible task of keeping secret the proprietary nature of software available to thousands of users. Patent protection is also generally unavailable because of the obvious and novel patent requirements. Copyright protection, therefore, is the only viable method available for mass marketed software.

Protection of Firmware

All three methods of protection are available to protect firmware. If the firmware is novel and not obvious, patent protection is a viable option. If the firmware is not novel and is nonobvious, copyright protection is viable in the software mass market area, systems software, and language translators, while in the business application area, trade secret protection is probably the best approach.

Given the complex interrelationships between the three types of software protection and the various major types of software, a two part matrix analysis of the present choices of legal protection and a second two part matrix of future legal software protection provides a view of the expected evolutionary process of software protection. The selection of software types is based not only on technological considerations, but also enconomic factors such as marketing and development costs. Some firmware, for example, is presently being marketed in the software mass market. Some operating system software is presently being mentioned as likely future firmware. These two matrixes, therefore, are designed only as a guide in assisting attorneys and software developers, marketers, and users in choosing the appropriate legal protection. Given the everchanging computational technology and the gradual changes in the three legal protection methods, the line between present and future is indistinct.

Present Software Protection Matrix

Types of Software	Development Stage			Use Marketing Stage		
	Patent	Copy	T/S	Patent	Copy	T/S
1. OPERATING SYSTEM						
a. Data base Managers		*	X		X	Possible
b. Network/ Communications/ Software		*	X		X	Possible
2. LANGUAGE TRANSLATORS						
a. Assemblers		*	X		X	
b. Compilers		*	X		X	
3. APPLICATION SOFTWARE						
a. Business Application		*	X			X
b. Mass Market Application		*	X		X	
4. FIRMWARE		*	X	Possible	Most Likely	Possible

* Source code is automatically protected by federal copyright laws as soon as it is written.

Future Software Protection Matrix
[Late 1980's and 1990's]

Types of Software	Development Stage			Use/Marketing Stage		
	Patent	Copy	T/S	Patent	Copy	T/S
1. OPERATING SYSTEM						
a. Data Base Managers		*	X	Possible	X	Possible
b. Network/ Communications Software		*	X	Possible	X	Possible
2. LANGUAGE TRANSLATORS						
a. Assemblers		*	X	Possible	X	
b. Compilers		*	X	Possible	X	
3. APPLICATION SOFTWARE						
a. Business Application		*	X	Possible Limited Areas		X
b. Mass Market Application		*	X	Possible	X	
4. FIRMWARE		*	X	Possible	X	Possible

---

* Source code is automatically protected by federal copyright laws as soon as it is written.

Computer Contracts

3

§3.01   Introduction

The subject of computer contracts is likely to be one of the first areas of difficulty to confront the potential user of computers. From an economic perspective, contracting for computational resources represents a substantial and continuing investment.[1] From a legal perspective, the absence of a com-

---

[1] There is a wealth of written material to aid business and technical decisionmakers in determining the effects of computer acquisitions. For an earlier article discussing the cycles involved in data processing growth see Gibson & Nolan, *Managing the Four Stages of EDP Growth,* 52 Harv Bus Rev 76-88 (1974). Purchasing guidebooks are now becoming available. In the microcomputer area, see, e.g., W Skees, Before You Invest In a Small Computer (1982). For a sample computer contract, see Warren, Markuson & Glickman, 3 Warren's Forms of Agreements, Ch 15, §84-86 (1983).

puter contract is a poor business practice, and may invite litigation, although signing a standard form contract may present a similar risk because vendor contracts eliminate most user's rights and remedies.[2] This chapter is intended to serve as an introduction to computer contracting issues. Contracting for computers has been the subject of numerous books and articles covering both practical and legal aspects of contract negotiation and performance.[3] A single chapter on this subject, consequently, is not enough space in which to discuss, exhaustively, all computer contracting issues. The objective of this chapter, therefore, is to give the reader a basic appreciation of the issues and areas of potential problems, along with a reasoned approach for avoiding most of the computer contracting pitfalls and difficulties that may be encountered.

Contract Issues

§3.02   The Hardware Market

Computer hardware can generally be grouped into three major categories: mainframes, minicomputers, and microcomputers. The performance of computers in all three categories is constantly improving, while costs continue to decline. Acquisition of computer mainframes is a lengthy process, and can involve many individuals on both sides of the negotiations. A large corporation may budget millions of dollars each year for the acquisition of additional mainframes, in which case a division within the data processing department is given the exclusive task of acquiring new hardware and software. Minicomputers are similar to mainframe computers, except that minicomputers are generally less powerful and less expensive than mainframe computers. Minicomputers may be either: (1) sold as a complete computer system called a turnkey system, with the system supplier providing hardware, systems software, and application software as a package; or (2) sold with basic hardware central processing unit (CPU, main-memory, disk memory, keyboard, and cathode-ray tube), and some type of operating system, with application software being sold separately. The acquisition process for minicomputers, therefore, is generally not as complex as that for acquiring mainframe computers. Microcomputers are generally sold at the retail level, and the negotiation process, as well as the contract itself, is minimal compared to the acquisition process for mainframe computers or minicomputers.

---

[2] Douglas, *Some Ideas on the Computer and the Law,* 2 Tex S U L Rev 20, 43 (1971). Some observers believe that an extensive legal document containing detailed contract provisions is economically impracticable. See Merian, System Vendors and Duty of Care: Mini-Micro Systems 166 (1981).

[3] In an informal survey of computer users, Douglas found that only 30% of computer users obtained legal advice before signing a contract for computer products and services. See Douglas, *Some Ideas on the Computer and the Law,* 2 Tex SUL Rev 20, 43 (1971).

§3.03   The Software Market

Basically, there are two markets for software. One is the commercial business market which generally consists of medium and large-sized corporations. In this traditional market, software is licensed, and can therefore be controlled by contract. The price of software sold in this commercial business market is usually high because the software packages are large and have only a limited distribution. This software is usually sold on an individual basis, and may be installed and maintained by the software vendor. The second market is the mass consumer market for software for use with the small micro or personal computers. This market, born in 1975 with the development of the MITS *Altair* computer, is characterized by high volume sales and mass distribution through mail order and local retail stores. These products are marketed by advertising in magazines devoted to this industry and by displaying them on dealers' shelves. The price is often less than 10 per cent of the cost of comparable software for a larger computer.[4] Software in the mass market requires almost no installation, and is characteristically more reliable than software in the commercial market.

In the traditional market, the software supplier may act as a consultant, providing free advice on how to solve particular problems related to the software, training on how to use the software, and even customizing the software to a customer's particular application. For software vendors, maintenance and support must be provided to the user just as hardware vendors provide similar services.

In the mass market, the sales price is too low for a vendor to be able to provide much advice, training, or customizing. A well-written and attractive sales brochure must catch the purchaser's attention, and provide enough information for the purchaser to determine if the software will solve the problem. Good documentation is essential in this market, as is error-free software. Reliable software, as in the traditional market, is not enough. Support is provided (if at all) by answering telephone inquiries usually at one central location in the United States. One interesting aspect of this market is the Detroit approach where new versions of the software are periodically provided with new features and capabilities. This result stems more from the expanding nature of the market than from some conscious marketing approach. Due to the limited legal protection which copyrights provide, in the future, the offering of mid-life enhancements at a low price to all purchasers who legally purchased earlier versions of the software will become a common marketing technique.[5]

---

[4] During early 1983 a compiler for the FORTRAN language for a Digital Equipment Corporation (DEC) PDP-11 minicomputer sold for approximately $6,800 whereas a FORTRAN compiler for a Radio Shack TRS 80-II sold for approximately $295.

[5] See **ch 2** for a full discussion of software legal protection. IBM, in the late 1980s and early 1970s, applied this continuous enhancement approach to marketing its peripheral disk and tape drives to the point that many industry observes called them *planned mid-life kickers*. The mid-life product enhancements made competition by the

One subdivision of the traditional software market is the time sharing and service bureau market. Service bureaus provide three computer services to customers: (1) processing data and providing reports for customers; (2) renting computer time (similar to the way cars are rented); and (3) providing access to a computer via telephone through the use of computer terminals. Service bureaus may also provide custom programming and training to their customers. For a further discussion of service bureaus, see **§3.15.**

Another subdivision of the traditional market is the custom development of software, sometimes called contract programming. In contract programming, the developer acts as a consultant, defining the problem and then solving it for the customer. The work may be done at the customer's site or at the developer's site with programs being transferred at the completion of the project.

Software suppliers, therefore, must usually offer three items:

1. Advice, including systems analysis and design (in effect, telling the customer what is needed and selling a software package to fit that need)

2. Training the customer on the system beyond that which was stipulated and paid for in the contract

3. Custom programming of software to make the software capable of handling a particular business application[6]

§3.04 The Software Life Cycle

Before discussing details of the various computer contracts, the life cycle of software (designing, developing, and using software) will be reviewed. Software must be designed, much like hardware. Software design requires specialized knowledge and skills, and a large project requires considerable managing and control to be completed within a reasonable time and cost. After software is written and *debugged,* it must be maintained over the life of the product. Software maintenance, unlike hardware maintenance, consists of changing the characteristics of the program, and usually requires an effort similar to the initial design process.[7]

The development phase of a software product consists of:

---

peripheral plug-compatible manufacturers (PCMs) more difficult because the IBM product was always changing, and thus the window of time during which there would be profitability for a PCM competitor for a specific product was very short. See **ch 4** for a discussion of the antitrust implications of this type of marketing practice. See **§3.14** for a further discussion of custom development.

[6] Although customizing software may be held to a minimum, at least some customizing is almost always required in the commercial market. See Proceedings, 1980 Computer Law Association West Coast Conference.

[7] For example, tax programs usually have to be updated each year to reflect new tax laws and revisions to the existing tax law. This effort is both labor intensive and costly.

1. The system requirement phase where the basic outlines of what the system must do are defined

2. The software requirements phase where it is determined how many programs will be needed in the system and what functions each program will perform

3. The preliminary design phase where it is determined how each program will be subdivided into smaller *subprograms* so that the program can be constructed logically

4. The detailed design phase which determines the *algorithm* to be used in each subprogram

5. The coding phase which consists of writing the program in one of the computer languages (e.g., FORTRAN, COBOL, BASIC)

6. The testing phase which links all the programs of the package together and ensures that the entire package performs as expected

The maintenance phase, which may well consume most of the resources and time spent on the program, completes the life cycle of the software. Software is constantly maintained and updated until it is replaced.

§3.05   Systems Approach to Contracting

Many potential first time computer users will not have had substantial experience in acquiring, evaluating, or using computer systems.[8] Contracting for computer hardware, software, and services involves legal, financial, and technical questions of considerable complexity. To ensure that important (and expensive) decisions are made through informed choice, rather than by chance, or worse, under the influence of irrelevant or perhaps negative factors, a potential user should undertake the acquisition process using a system approach. There are basically two means of accomplishing this: hiring a consultant who has specialized knowledge and experience, or putting together an acquisition team.

The first step in either process is to evaluate the resources and expertise which are available within the organization. A consultant can aid in resolving some or most of the esoteric issues, but consultants cannot have as clear an understanding of the client's operations as the employees of the client. An evaluation and negotiation team, therefore, should at minimum consist of the client's attorney, accountant or other financial expert, tax advisor, key data processing personnel, and senior management. This team should have as its primary responsibility during the pre-acquisition period the evaluation of the user's needs in relation to data processing issues. A timetable, an agenda, goals, and performance standards for the acquisition process should also be

---

[8] See Proceedings, 1980 Computer Law Association West Coast Conference, at 21.

formulated during this period.[9]

§3.06 Request for Proposal

When acquiring expensive and complex equipment or services, the wisest course of action is to obtain comparable and competitive ideas for meeting the user's computing needs from a variety of vendors. Ideally, this procedure, known as a request for proposal (RFP), will allow both user and vendor expertise to combine in developing a plan for acquiring hardware, software, or computer services which best suits the needs of the user. For a smaller acquisition, the same principles used in a formal RFP can be used on an informal basis.[10] The RFP contains a statement of the user's computational problem to be solved, an invitation to vendors to suggest solutions, and a description of the procedure and standards by which the proposals will be evaluated. A well-thought out RFP can be the most important step in obtaining a satifactory result. A poorly-written RFP is, at best, a waste of time, and at worst it may produce disaster by failing to direct the thinking and design efforts of the bidding vendors and the user. The first step in formulating an RFP is to assemble the acquisition team. The next step is for the team to outline the known parameters of the task ahead, particularly important are timing and financial considerations. The third step is to evaluate present and future computational needs. The decision to *get into* computers will have an effect on all aspects of a business, and whatever choices are made will require a long-term commitment to those computational resources acquired or contracted for. Evaluating present and future computational needs is the phase where independent consultants can be most helpful. A good RFP must tell potential bidders what tasks must be done by the system as first installed as well as those anticipated changes which may affect the capabilities, expansion possibilities, and suitability of whatever system is acquired.[11]

§3.07 Application of the Uniform Commercial Code to Computer Transactions

Section 2-102 of the Uniform Commercial Code (UCC) defines the scope of

---

[9] See generally Cheney, *Selecting, Acquiring, and Coping With Your First Computer,* 17 J Small Bus Mgmt 43 (1979).

[10] The informal acquisition process, just like a formal RFP, would include appropriate negotiations and contract provisions for delivery dates, performance specifications for hardware and software, and acceptance procedures.

[11] See generally Brandon & Segelstein, Data Processing Contracts: Structure, Contents, and Negotiations 13-19 (1976); Harris, Complex Contract Issues In The Acquisition of Hardware and Software 3 (1982) Computer Law Institute University of Southern California Law Center pt VII (1982).

Article 2 as applying to "transactions in goods."[12] *Goods* are defined in the UCC as "all things (including specially-manufactured goods) which are movable at the time of identification to the contract. . . ."[13] Clearly, this includes computer hardware,[14] and most courts have construed it to include combinations of hardware and software, e.g., where a system including hardware and software is sold.[15] Acquiring a software program copy by purchasing programs "presents the clearest case of an identified good. Such a software purchase is strikingly analogous to a purchase of record albums or tapes. A record buyer wants music, but buys the record. A software buyer wants a computer program but buys [the media containing the program]."[16]

Although sales are clearly subject to the UCC, leases may not be, and the applicabilty of the UCC may depend on the particular circumstances surrounding the transaction.[17] The economic effect of most commercial leases is to place the lessee in the position of a purchaser, paying the equivalent of the full purchase price, plus interest, during the initial lease term. The lease, in effect, is treated as a financing vehicle. This type of lease will often be governed by the UCC.[18] The UCC is less likely to be applied where there is no option to purchase at the end of the lease.[19] Transactions involving software frequently contemplate that the vendor will provide certain services, including custom programming. Where the contract is essentially one for service, and any goods provided are only incidental to the much larger service aspects, the UCC may not apply, or may apply only to the sales portion of a mixed contract.[20] Where the transaction is essentially a sale of *goods* in the form of a computer program,

---

[12] Certain provisions of the UCC e.g., 2-204, 2-205, 2-206 only apply to the sale of goods rather than transactions in goods. See §8.19 for a discussion of the effect of electronic fund transfer systems on the UCC.

[13] UCC 2-105(1).

[14] United States v. Wegematic Corp, 1 Computer L Serv Rep 341 (SDNY 1959), *affd*, 360 F2d 674 (2d Cir 1966).

[15] *See* Carl Beasley Ford Inc v. Burroughs Corp, 361 F Supp 325 (ED Pa 1973), *affd*, 493 F2d 1400 (3d Cir 1974); Chatlos Sys Inc v National Cash Register Corp, 479 F Supp 738 (DNJ 1979) *affd*, 670 F2d 1304 (3d Cir 1982).
One commentator has proposed defining the *transport* copy of the program, i.e., the magnetic tape or disc delivered to the user, as the moveable thing identified in the contract so as to satisfy the strictures of the UCC. See Note, *Computer Programs as Goods Under the UCC,* 77 Mich L Rev 1149 (1979).

[16] *Id* 1155.

[17] See, e.g. Chandler, *Computer Transactions: Potential Liability of Computer Users and Vendors,* 1977 Wash ULQ 405.

[18] Chatlos Sys, Inc v National Cash Register Corp, 479 F Supp 738 (DNJ 1979), *affd*, 670 F2d 1304 (3d Cir 1982).

[19] OJ&C Co v General Hospital Leasing, Inc 578 SW 2d 877 (Tex Civ App 1979); see Note, *Computers Programs as Goods Under the UCC,* 77 Mich L Rev 1149, 1157 (1979); Newmark v Gimbels, Inc, 120 NJ Super 279, 245 A2d 11 (1968), *affd*, 54 NJ 585, 258 A2d 967 (1969); Computer Servicemasters Inc v Beacon Mfg Co, 328 F Supp 653 (DSC 1970), *affd*, 443 F2d 906 (4th Cir 1971).

[20] UCC 2-102.

however, incidental *service* aspects of the contract will not remove the sale from the purview of the UCC.[21] Gray areas in the applicability of the UCC to software contracts are new versions of a program and custom-developed software. Often, the software contract provides that the vendor will furnish new releases or versions of the program to the user at some relatively nominal cost. The issue is whether each new release establishes a service contract, or whether each new release is a separate good.[22] In the case of custom software, ambiguity results because the actual programming is clearly a service, while the software delivered to the user as a result of the custom programming effort would normally be considered a good. The best analysis of the custom software issue may be to treat the programs as specially-manufactured goods under §2-105(1) of the UCC.[23] In the event of litigation, the applicability of the provisions of the UCC to a computer-related contract can have important consequences in the areas of performance, warranties and disclaimers, and statutes of limitation. It is worth noting, however, that many provisions of the UCC are applicable "unless otherwise agreed."[24] The parties, and particularly the vendor, will often insist on contract terms that limit, or eliminate altogether, otherwise applicable rules of the UCC. On the other hand, the parties to a custom software contract may agree to have the UCC apply to the contract.[25]

§3.08 Computer Contract Problems

One problem in the computer industry is the inability of the vendor and the vendee to maintain an arms length relationship. The theoretical model of two parties with equal knowledge and equal bargaining strength often does not exist when the vendor is selling to a smaller business because more systems analysis and design is needed than with a larger vendee. A software supplier, for example, may offer advice as to what a small business customer needs. Due to the close relationship between the vendor and small business, the vendor cannot rely on the contractual limitations in the software purchase or lease contract which are based on not knowing the "particular purpose for which the goods are required."[26] Thus, contractual provisions for warranty disclaimers, liability limitations, and integration and merger clauses may not be legally binding.

A second problem is customer ignorance and indifference. This problem

---

[21] Delivery, installation, and start-up are the most commonly-provided services which may be found to be *incidental* to a sale of computer software. Moreover, service bureau data-processing contracts, which consist almost exclusively of services, are not governed by the UCC.

[22] See generally Note, *Computer Programs as Goods Under the UCC*, 77 Mich LR 1149 (1979).

[23] See generally Zammit, *Contracting for Computer Products*, 22 Jurimetrics J 337 (1982).

[24] UCC 1-102(3).

[25] UCC 1-102, comments.

[26] UCC 2-315 (warranty of fitness for a particular purpose).

derives from a customer either not knowing how to use computers, or refusing to train personnel on the use of a particular software package. The customer expects the supplier to rectify any problem which arises with the system, including improper use of the software by the customer.

There is also the ever present problem of personnel shortages. For at least the last 15 years, and forecasted to continue through the 1980s, trained programmers have been a scarce resource.[27] As a result, the customer quite often does not have the talent necessary to keep the software working.

Overselling or *puffing* is another problem which often occurs.[28] When a prospective customer asks "will the system do *x,y,z*," if it is at all conceivable that the system could perform the desired function, the salesperson will be very tempted to say "yes, it will do that function with no problem." The customer who relies heavily on this particular function may discover that the system is not capable of performing in the expected manner.[29] Given the problems of losing the traditional arms length relationship between vendor and vendee, widespread ignorance on the part of vendees, chronic programmer shortages, and puffing of hardware and software, the commercial computer contract becomes a natural focus of attention.

§3.09 General Contract Provisions and Commercial Computer Contracts—Warranties

One of the most important legal issues in commercial contracts is the disclaimer of warranties. Ordinarily, the vendor will be deemed to have made a number of warranties (most will be express warranties), either through its sales brochures, published specification sheets, representations made by the vendor's sales personnel during the course of the negotiations, or created by demonstrations to the customer of sample software. In addition, the vendor will be assumed to have made a warranty of title to the software being marketed.[30] Typically, in form contracts, the vendor will disclaim all warranties, express or implied, and substitute in lieu of these warranties a provision stating

---

[27] See generally Bernacchi, Davidson, & Grogan, *Computer System Procurement,* 30 Emory LJ 395 (1981).

[28] See generally, Proceedings, 1980 Computer Law Association, West Coast Conference, at 99; See also **§3.19.**

[29] This problem can be solved by a comprehensive statement in the request for proposal (RFP) quite specifically detailing, the user's requirements, both present and future. If the vendor incorporates the RFP requirements language into the bid, the vendor may be liable for breach of contract when the system does not perform the agreed upon functions.

See Napasco Intl, Inc v Tymshare, Inc, 556 F Supp 654 (ED La 1983), wherein a computer services company's breach of contract for installation of an on-line computer system was not done in bad faith under Louisiana law, because both parties worked delegently toward implementing the system.

[30] UCC 2-313 (warranty of title).

that the only recourse to the customer for problems in the system is repair or replacement of malfunctioning items.[31] This provision is of questionable value in commercial contracts because the customer will ordinarily execute a maintenance agreement which will provide the same services as would be provided by the limited warranty.[32] The best method of avoiding the effect of a disclaimer of warranties is to attach, or incorporate by reference in the final agreement, as many of the preliminary documents or statements which could be the basis of express warranties, and to insist that all substantial documents which describe the commitments of the parties (including the functional specifications) be made an express part of the agreement.[33]

There are two implied warranties: the implied warranty of merchantability;[34] and the implied warranty of fitness for a particular purpose.[35] Although often confused, there are clear differences between the scope of these two warranties.[36] The implied warranty of merchantability arises in the context of a sales contract in which the seller is a *merchant*.[37] This implied warranty is often said to be an implied warranty of fitness for *ordinary* purposes because it implies an obligation on the part of the merchant to ensure that the goods will be fit for the ordinary purposes for which the goods are sold.

The implied warranty of fitness for a particular purpose is narrower, but more relevant to computer system procurement. The warranty of fitness for a particular purpose arises only if the vendor, at the time of contracting, has reason to know the particular purpose for which the goods are required, and that the buyer relied on the seller's skill or judgment to select or furnish suitable goods.[38] This is a fairly common situation in the context of computer software procurement, especially where the vendor is dealing with an unsophisticated customer, or where the vendor makes a review and study of the needs of the customer and provides a detailed proposal on how to meet those needs.

The clause disclaiming implied warranties will generally be upheld and interpreted literally, provided it satisfies the formal requirements of the Uniform Commercial Code.[39] The implied warranty of merchantability and the implied warranty of fitness for a particular purpose may be disclaimed by a disclaimer which is conspicuous, mentions *merchantability* (in order to exclude

---

[31] Chatlos Sys, Inc v National Cash Register Corp, 479 F Supp 738, (DNJ 1979), *affd*, 670 F2d 1304 (3d Cir 1982).

[32] 1981 University of Southern California Computer Law Institute ch X, at 23.

[33] *Id.*

[34] UCC 2-314.

[35] UCC 2-315.

[36] See generally Chandler, *Computer Transactions: Potential Liability of Computer Users and Vendors,* 1977 Wash ULQ 405.

[37] Under UCC 2-104, *merchant* is defined as a person who deals in goods or holds himself out as having special knowledge or skill.

[38] See generally Zammit, *Contracting for Computer Products,* 22 Jurimetrics J 337 (1982).

[39] UCC 2-316.

the warranty of merchantability), and is in writing (in order to exclude the warranty of fitness for a particular purpose).[40] This disclaimer language should always be placed in a separate paragraph, in large, contrasting type. The limitation of liability clause as usually found in vendors' standard form contracts is an exclusion of liability for consequential damages, and limits other liabilities.[41] This limitation of liability clause typically limits the vendor's liability for damages in the event of a breach in one of two ways: by placing a flat ceiling on liability, usually the amount paid by the customer under the contract; or by excluding indirect, special, or consequential damages. These clauses are generally upheld unless they are contrary to public policy, or are unconscionable.[42]

The integration or merger clause is another clause usually found in a vendor contract. This clause integrates all the prior commitments into the final contract being signed. During the course of negotiations between the vendee and the vendor, the vendor's sales personnel typically will have made a wide range of representations as to the capabilities of the vendor's hardware and software, and how these capabilities will fulfill the customer's needs. The vendor will usually have provided brochures and specification sheets, written proposals with detailed information, additional letters and memoranda on specific issues, demonstrations of the hardware and software, and a variety of oral representations regarding both the capabilities of the hardware and software, and the commitments of the vendor for installation, maintenance, and services. These representations, demonstrations, statements, and documents can be the basis for warranties and commitments made by the vendor, and can be relied upon by the user.[43] The vendor's standard contract, however, almost invariably has a clause which provides that there are no understandings or agreements between the parties except as specified in the contract, and that the vendor has no obligations except as expressly set forth in the written contract. These *merger* or *integration* clauses are generally held to be valid, and the courts enforce these clauses for two reasons: where the negotiations were extensive, and the discussions included drafts of the contract, a merger clause prevents an earlier draft from being brought in and introduced as evidence contrary to the final agreement; and any unauthorized or overinflated representations (puffing made by the vendors sales representative) will not bind the vendor.

In *Carl Beasley Ford v Burroughs Corp,* however, the court allowed the submis-

---

[40] WR Weaver Co v Burroughs Corp, 580 SW2d 76 (Tex Civ App 1979).

[41] See generally Raysman, *Warranty Disclaimer in the Data Processing Contract,* 6 Rutgers Comp & Tech LJ 265 (1978).

[42] Investors Premium Corp v Burroughs Corp, 389 F Supp 39 (DSC 1974). See also Niehaus, *Unconscionability and the Fundamental Breach Doctrine In Computer Contracts,* 57 Notre Dame Law 547 1982); Plunkett, UCC Section 2-719 As Applied to Computer Contracts—Unconscionable Exclusions of Remedy, 14 Conn L Rev 77 (1981).

[43] UCC 2-313. A vendor may create a specific document intended as part of the basis for the parties' overall understanding of their commitments. Although this type of document is more common in hardware contracts then in software contracts, it is sometimes found in major system software contracts.

sion to the jury of evidence that an oral contract for programming services existed.[44] The court emphasized that there was no mention of services in the form contract, and that the vendor's representatives had been specifically instructed to rely upon oral agreements for programming and not to incorporate any provisions regarding programming into the contracts for the sale of the equipment.[45] A court may be inclined to allow parole evidence where it is written and consistent with the document purported to be the final and complete agreement. In *W.R. Weaver Co v Burroughs Corp,* the court held that an integration clause in the form agreement was not conclusive on the issue of whether the form contract contained all understandings and commitments of the parties because the vendor had previously provided the customer a "written statement of installation conditions" which contained many of the specific conditions of the procurement.[46] The best approach for the user is to insist that all sales brochures, functional specifications, or any other vendor literature be incorporated into the agreement, making the merger clause virtually irrelevant. In *IBM v Catamore,* oral agreements which were not included in the language of the final written agreements were held to be barred by the integration clause of the written agreement. The effect of the integration clause therefore has been mixed: in *Carl Beasly Ford,* the integration clause was rejected; in *IBM v Catamore,* the integration clause was accepted; and in *WR Weaver,* the court allowed parole evidence to expand and clarify the effect of the integration clause.[47]

§3.10 —Other Contract Clauses

A clause outlining the parties' proprietary rights is very important in commercial contracts. Key software may be the *crown jewels* of a software vendor.[48] Its value is probably best preserved by delivering only the object code to the customer and keeping the source code with the vendor.[49] Three problems arise, however, where only object code is provided to the customer and where the particular software package is essential to the user's business: (1) the user may wish to have the source code to avoid having to rely on the software vendor for support and maintenance should the system not perform as expect-

---

[44] 361 F Supp 325, 332 (ED Pa 1973).

[45] See Zammit, *supra* note 38.

[46] *See* WR Weaver Co v Burroughs, 580 SW2d 76, 78 (Tex Civ App 1979).

[47] Carl Beasley Ford, Inc v Burroughs Corp, 361 F Supp 325 (ED Pa 1973); IBM v Catamore Enters, Inc, 548 F2d 1065 (1976); WR Weaver Co v Burroughs, 580 SW2d 76 (Tex Civ App 1979).

[48] See generally Milquin, *Protecting and Licensing Software,* 1982 US Cal L Center Computer L Inst §I.

[49] See Bernacchi & Larsen, Data Processing Contracts and the Law 74, 79 (1974). Withholding source code is perhaps the best form of protection in the commercial setting, but another common method is withholding maintenance from those users who did not buy the system from the original vendor.

ed; (2) the vendor may go bankrupt; or (3) auditors may need to have access to the source code in order to audit the customers' accounts. The bankruptcy problem may be satisfied by *source code escrow*, with the software vendor depositing the source code with a trustee (typically a bank).[50] In the event the vendor goes out of business, the trustee is authorized to distribute the software to all the vendor's existing customers, usually at nominal reproduction costs. If the software is under trade secret protection, then a confidential information clause must be included in the contract, and the clause should specify that the customer and all employees of the customer who have access to the software will sign a confidentiality agreement.[51]

The contract should always define the operating environment for the software. The vendor should be very careful to specifiy the exact hardware and software which the customer must provide in order for the product to function properly. Without this operating environment clause, the customer may not know what is required, or may be misled into thinking that the product can be run on any system which the customer already has or may acquire in the future. The multiple system use clause is designed to prevent the customer from using the software on more than one computer which the customer may own. In the alternative, the multiple system use clause should provide for additional payment (typically at a percentage of the price for the first use) if the software is used on more than one system. In addition, an assignment clause should be included to prevent assignment of the software rights.

Training and support should at least be mentioned, if not covered completely, in the software contract. Some vendors provide no training, whereas other vendors provide classes which the customer can pay to attend.[52] Maintenance response time (the maximum time within which the vendor must respond to a customer problem), should be included in the contract. While the response time to a software problem can be significantly longer than the response time to a hardware problem, the vendor should be willing either to commit to a specific time, or at least to acknowledge the problem and to start working with the customer to solve it. Some maintenace contracts now contain a clause which reduces the maintenance fee paid by the customer as the mean time between failures (MTBF) increases, or as the terminal response time decreases to agreed upon limits, thereby causing the maintenance personnel to act as quickly as possible in attempting to repair the system. Other contract clauses provide a bonus if the MTBF or terminal response time reaches specified levels.

Most vendor contracts provide an acceptance clause which covers the testing period that the customer will have during which to test the software once it is installed. This period is often variable in length, although it is usually limited

---

[50] See Gilburn, *Source Code Escrows: Meaningful Solution or Inadequate Protection?*, Computer Negotiations Rep, issue no 6, at 4-8.

[51] See Hoffman, *Computer Contracts—A Lawyers Primer*, NY St BJ 472 (1979).

[52] Chatlos Sys, Inc v National Cash Register Corp, 479 F Supp 738 (DNJ 1979), *affd*, 670 F2d 1304 (3rd Cir 1982).

to a maximum of 20 days or one month. This clause will usually provide that the customer may continue the testing period (up to the limit) until the time when the customer starts using the software for production work, at which time the testing period ceases, the license period begins, and the system is assumed to be acceptable. Seldom does a customer provide adequate acceptance criteria, and even if provided, the software is usually not tested against the criteria.[53] Moreover, problems may not be found for months after production has begun, long after the testing period has ended.

The customer should be careful when relying upon preinstallation demonstrations or experimental periods because, if the demonstrations, experiments, or tests prove unsatisfactory, the customer must act quickly to preserve its rights. In *Investors Premium Corp v Burroughs Corp,* the buyer had attended two demonstrations of the operation of the computer and had entered into a conditional one year lease terminable at will if the computer did not perform to the customer's satisfaction.[54] The customer eventually converted the lease into a purchase, and then purchased a second computer of the same type. The demonstration and the one-year experimental use lease influenced the *Investors* court to conclude that the buyer had not relied on certain alleged oral warranties made prior to the lease, but had, instead, bargained for an experimental test period and had been satisfied with the results. The buyer, consequently, was bound by the express terms of the final written sales agreement.

The termination clause in commercial market contracts should provide all the terms under which the agreement will be concluded. In a license agreement, a termination clause should provide for destruction of the software and all *backup* copies, or for return of the software to the vendor, and an agreement that the customer will cease use of the software. In most situations, however, termination is not a viable user remedy, because where most, if not all, of the users records are machine-oriented, transition to another vendor's software or replacement with an upgrade of the existing software may be unacceptable. Termination should be an option, but not the exclusive remedy.

§3.11 Marketers/Developers Software Contracts

The marketers/developers software contract deals with products which are developed but not yet marketed, and with the relationship between the firm which will market the product and the person or firm who developed the product. These contracts are negotiable, and the negotiating team should be multi-disciplined, consisting of technical, legal, business, and financial members to ensure that the contract meets the parties' business needs as well as being legally sufficient.[55] Technical personnel must be involved for several reasons:

---

[53] *See* Hoffman, *supra* note 51.

[54] Investors Premium Corp v Burroughs Corp, 389 F Supp 39 (DSC 1974).

[55] See Hollman & Burnacchi, Forming and Financing High Technology *Ventures,* 1982 US Calif L Center Computer L Inst., §X, at 1 *et seq.*

1. To assist in developing the functional specification, or in interpreting the specification if the product already has one
2. To review all the *deliverables*
3. To test the product
4. To perform any conversion needed if the product is to be marketed on a machine different from the one on which it was developed
5. To evaluate any training available on the product or to define the training needed if none is available
6. To ensure compatibility with the system for which the product is intended
7. To evaluate response times for marketability
8. To ensure that the documentation is adequate
9. To ensure that the programs are documented to a sufficient degree that the product is maintainable if the marketing organization is accepting responsibility for maintenance

There are generally three different types of developers: single individuals; two or more developers; and corporations or associations.[56] The single individual who has not licensed the product, has not used another organization's equipment in developing it, has not received help from anyone else, did not hire consultants, and developed the documentation and a training program, is an ideal person who does not exist in the real world. There are, however, many individual developers, particularly in the microcomputer market, who can perform most of these functions. Where there are two or more individual developers, agreements between them are necessary, unless they have already formed a partnership or corporation. In this situation, development and marketing must be structured to cover the possibility that these two *friends* may not always remain friendly, and in the future, may forever part company. This contingency must be covered because if they do part company, the marketer must be able to continue marketing the product, secure in the knowledge that all rights are protected.

With the third type of developer, the marketer must make sure either that confidentiality agreements have been acquired from all the persons (the corporation and its employees, independent contractors, and consultants) involved in the development, and that they have all signed covenants not to compete. A problem may exist where these people were only brought in for a small part of the project, and no agreements of any type were obtained. The marketer may have to find these people, and possibly compensate them so that they do not attempt to compete with the marketer by introducing a similar product.

The product definition is a critical part of the contract, and should include the scope of the product, as the developer intended it, and the market for

---

[56] *Id* at 9-13, 73-76.

which the developer intended the product. The most important part of the product definition is the product specification, which includes what the product is capable of doing, how the product will perform, the hardware requirements for running the program, and what additional software must be provided by the user in order to run the program. The product specification should also include either definitions of, or procedures for determining, the current *state* of the product.[57] It is also important to define the documentation, e.g., a user's guide, which must be included with the system. If the marketer is acquiring the source code, a maintenance manual of some type is needed so that the maintenance programmers can understand what the developer created. If the product is not yet developed, the contract should include provisions for progress reports and interim copies of the program.

The payment terms are obviously very important. If the product is small, a fixed price may be appropriate. If the product is large and the developer has commited a considerable amount of resources to its development, a royalty payment on each sale is desirable from the developer's point of view, and also desirable from the marketer's standpoint because it allows the marketer to avoid an initial large cash outlay for an unproven product. Another alternative is the use of a lump sum payment on delivery, with a smaller royalty payment to follow with each sale. This allows a developer to recoup some of its investment quickly, and to receive the income generated by each sale. The payment terms should also cover whether maintenance fees are to be shared between the marketer and developer, and what the ratio is to be if they are shared. From the marketer's point of view, it is better for the developer to share the market risks, with payment only by royalties, so that if the product is a *bomb*, the marketer is at least partially covered.[58]

A delivery and acceptance clause is also very important in this type of contract. The method of delivery should be specified, and the items to be delivered should be explicitly defined—object code, source code, documentation, etc. The marketer must have a good acceptance test to ensure that all items are received in the appropriate condition. A good acceptance test, however, is very difficult to create, because any software large enough to be worth marketing will be complex enough to require considerable effort in testing. While some problems are to be expected, these problems should be cured in a short amount of time and before any marketing is done, particularly if the product is going into the mass market. A good acceptance test incorporates the agreed upon functional specifications. The most powerful form of an acceptance clause is a test to the satisfaction of the marketer, which allows for rescission

---

[57] Key questions include the status of the product: (1) development; (2) design (has the product been designed, but not yet programmed); (3) program (has the product been programmed, but not tested; (4) testing (has the product been tested, but not documented); and (5) documentation (has the program been documented, but the documentation was done so long ago it is now out of date).

[58] See generally Gilburne, *Structuring and Negotiating Software Development Contracts*, 1981 USC Computer L Inst, §X.

if the marketer decides after testing that the product is not marketable at a profit. Termination, however, is not a satisfactory remedy for the marketer in this instance, because a fair amount of resources for evaluating the product and its market will have already been expended. The marketer should negotiate the strongest standard of compliance that the developer will agree to. Substantial compliance is usually sufficient, with the exception of problems which can be expected to be corrected by normal installation, maintenance, and software support. The marketer should be aware that acceptance testing is a dynamic process, and that the system may work well for a while only to fail later. A warranty period, therefore, should be specified in which to resolve problems that may arise later. Any payments should be conditioned on satisfactorily completing the acceptance test.[59]

The marketing rights acquired must be clearly specified including:

1. The extent of the legal rights which each party has
2. The responsibility of training either the marketer's personnel or the customer's personnel
3. The extent of marketing assistance provided by the developer for special or difficult customers
4. The areas where the product will be marketed
5. Who has the responsibility for, and legal rights to any enhancements
6. Who has the responsibility for maintenance[60]

The marketer should insist on warranty of title and on indemnification, but a vendor/developer will not agree to indemnify a marketer against all claims that could ever arise under any circumstances. The most that the marketer can expect is a provision calling for indemnification of the marketer for infringement of proprietary rights. Confidentiality is another important clause because if the developer tells someone else what was done to create the program, the marketer may soon face competition. The developer, therefore, should be bound not to disclose the product. The developer will probably want a similar clause from the marketer as well. A nonsolicitation of employees clause should also be included as both sides will want such a clause to ensure that neither hires any *key* employees away from the other.

A termination clause should be included, particularly in the event that the products fails to qualify, and the marketer wants to return the product to the developer. The marketer must make sure that it does not give up the right to market other products which are identical or similar, and the developer will

---

[59] See generally Gilburne & David, *Structuring Agreements for Vertical Distribution of Hardware and Software*, 1982 USC Computer L Inst §IX.

[60] See generally Brandan, *Checklists* in Practicing Law Institute, Computer Law: Purchasing, Leasing, Licensing Hardware, Software and Services 217-43 (Brooks ed 1980) (excellent treatment of checklists to be used in computer contracts). Also see **§2.12** for a discussion of employment agreements.

want to make sure that the marketer does not steal its ideas and create a competing product. These agreements must be executed in advance, because once problems develop, agreements are extremely hard to obtain. A termination clause should also include rights to future fees paid by customers where there has been partial marketing of the product. Another clause which the marketer generally wants is the right to market any future products which the developer may create. This future products clause is also a good way to handle competition because the developer of an existing system may add several enhancements, and call it a new system, thereby creating needless litigation to determine if the *new* product is, in fact, new.

§3.12   Contracts for Mass Marketing of Software

There are several differences between the mass software market and the traditional market.[61] The most important difference is the volume of the software sold. The traditional market is based on individual selling and one-to-one relationships between buyers and sellers. The mass market, however, is based on the distribution and sale of large numbers of units, both of hardware and software. This high volume allows the selling price to be substantially less than a comparable product sold in the traditional market. Another distinction of the mass market is the wide distribution of the software in this market which makes it difficult to sell and maintain this software in the same manner as in the traditional market. Due to the high volume and wide distribution, the investment of the developer per unit sold is small compared to the traditional market. There is also a lower profit margin in this market.

Due to differences between the mass market and the traditional market, there is virtually no leverage in the mass market, on the part of either party, and, therefore, no negotiation in the sale of products in this mass market. Wide distribution also results in less control over the product by the seller. The developer usually has no contact with the buyer, and may not even know the name and address of the buyer, or the type and characteristics of the microcomputer that the software product is to be run on, contrary to the traditional market. The developer has little control over the product once it reaches the mass market.

There is a wide range of expertise among users in the mass market, which can cause significant problems in making a piece of software work properly. The traditional market, due to its structure, its business approach, and its marketing methods, is based on the assumption of user sophistication and technical expertise. In the mass market, however, users may be completely naive, or they may be technical professionals buying software for their personal computers.

The marketing techniques in the mass market typify the consumer marketing

---

[61] See generally Bylinsky, *The Computer Stores Have Arrived,* Fortune, Apr 24, 1978, at 52. See **§8.12.**

approach.[62] In the traditional market, software products are generally market-ed directly by the manufacturer to the end user, with close marketing and sales support, and post sale support. In the mass software market, however, close dealings are uncommon. There are three major forms of distributing software in the mass market.[63] One is through computer stores owned and operated by local independent retailers. These computer stores, in addition to selling soft-ware, also sell computers, peripheral products, paper supplies, and entire customized computer systems, depending on the expertise and capability of the particular store. These retailers sell hardware and software of one or more manufacturers. Quite often retailers will employ programmers and system integration experts to complete custom systems for their buyers. Some manu-facturers, notably Tandy Corporation, have direct outlets for their products. These operations specialize in their own company products, and their intent is to reduce the support cost per sale on items with a lower profit margin. In this type of outlet the end user is dealing directly with the manufacturer, and contractual issues are more like those in the commercial data processing mar-ket.

The second major distribution outlet in this market is through program publishers who function much like their counterparts in the book publishing business. These publishers acquire programs from independent authors, document and package these programs on suitable magnetic media, and dis-tribute them through various marketing channels, typically through magazine advertisements. The program publisher effectively insulates the developer from the end user.[64] It is quite likely that the buyer of a published program will never know who created the original, and the buyer will not be a party to any direct contractual relationships with the original developer. Another form of distribution is through mail order sales by the program developer. It is easy to advertise a program for sale in magazines. Given the low advertising rates, typically one to two thousand dollars for a full page advertisement, that is a common distribution method, particularly for widely-distributed programs such as computer games.

Whether contracts are even feasible in the retail market involves a number of considerations unique to this market. There is rarely a contract. If there is a contract, the contract is generally only between the developer and the mar-keter, and not between the marketer and the user.[65] When there is a contract in the retail sale, it often is simply handed out by the retail sales clerk, and it is expected that it will be executed, on the honor system. Retailers often have little interest in making anyone sign anything. In the mail order business, the seller often does not even attempt to give the buyer a contract. Many compa-

[62] See *Discovering a Vast Potential Market*, Bus Week, Dec 1, 1980, at 91.

[63] See generally Brooks & Brewer, Special Problems In The Mass Distribution of Hardware, Software and Firmware, 1982 US Cal Computer Inst, §II.

[64] See generally Libes, Random Rumors, Byte, May 1982 at 388, col I.

[65] *See* Brooks, *supra* note 63.

nies in the industry provide a service whereby the buyer calls a telephone number, gives a credit card number, requests the product, and it is sent.

Large volume transactions present another problem. The number of computer and computer-related products now being advertised, sold, and delivered effectively precludes the development of close relationships between buyers and sellers. High volume, low prices, and low profit margins prevent many small-sized vendors from dealing closely with any but a few of their customers.

The lack of privity in this market presents yet another bar to the feasability of contracts.[66] The marketing methods and distribution channels limit any privity between the developer and the customer. The essential elements of a contract are consideration and mutuality of consent. Mutuality implies a common understanding by the parties to a contract of the substance of the contract, and of the terms and conditions which the parties have agreed to through a process of bargaining and negotiation. Because vendors and users often do not even see one another, let alone negotiate a meaningful contract to govern their business and legal relationships, mutuality of understanding is uncommon in the mass market. Typically, an agreement is displayed on an outer binder or on a paper included in the binder, so that a user can read the terms of the agreement before opening the *shrink wrap* containing the software. Somewhere in the agreement will be a provision that opening the package constitutes acceptance of the terms of the contract. There is some question as to whether this type of unilateral agreement is enforceable. A final reason for questioning the feasibility of contracts in this market is that very little money is at stake in any given transaction.

§3.13   —Contract Contents

In spite of several drawbacks, license agreements are commonly used in the mass market to protect software, and very few products are sold without some form of license agreement.[67] The primary purpose of a license agreement is to protect the developer or seller against illegal piracy. Traditional trade secret licenses are not feasible in this market. Due to the wide distribution, the software is not secret, and there is also the practical problem of getting the retail agreements signed.

The main reason for any contractual relationship in this market is for the purpose of disclaiming warranties. There is some doubt that the sale of software in this market constitutes the sale of goods to consumers. The UCC defines consumer goods as "those goods which are used or bought for use

---

[66] See generally Comment, *Consumer Warranty Law In California Under the Uniform Commercial Code and Song - Beverly and Magnuson - Moss Warranty Acts,* 26 UCLAL Rev 583 (1979). See §2.18.

[67] See also §3.12. For a conflicting view of contracting in the personal computer field, see McGonagle & McClain, *Negotiating Computer Contracts,* 2 Popular Computing 126 (1983).

primarily for personal, family, or household purposes."[68] The Magnuson-Moss Warranty Act defines the term consumer product as "any tangible personal property which is distributed in commerce, and which is normally used for personal, family or household purposes."[69] The Federal Trade Commission has promulgated regulations which state that a product is to be deemed a consumer product if its use for personal, family, or household purposes is not uncommon.[70] The fact that some systems are purchased for professional or industrial use probably does not affect the consumer nature of the product.[71]

The UCC provides several warranties which are applicable to consumer transactions. Under the UCC, a contract for sale carries with it, unless expressly excluded or modified by "specific language or by circumstances," a warranty of good and clear title.[72] The warranty is basic and is taken seriously by the courts. Since *pirated* programs are unfortunately common in the mass market, the warranty of title carries with it an important restriction, in that a buyer, having accepted the tender of goods, must "within a reasonable time after he discovers, or should have discovered any breach, notify the seller of breach or be barred from any remedy."[73] This provision may have far-reaching effects in that it is unlikely that a buyer will discover that the program is pirated until the buyer contacts the original developer for maintenance, and only then discovers that the purchase was not from a legitimate dealer. In those instances where the buyer can see by the packaging, or lack of it, or from other indications that the program is likely a *bootlegged* copy, there is little doubt as to whether the buyer "should have discovered" the breach in the warranty of title.

The seller of goods in either a commercial or consumer context can create express warranties in three ways: (1) by affirmation of fact or promise which relates to the goods and becomes part of the basis of the bargain;[74] (2) by "description of the goods which is made part of the basis of the bargain;"[75] or (3) by any "sample or model which is made part of the basis of the bargain" and which sample or model creates a warranty that the "whole of the goods" will conform thereto. These UCC provisions are particularly applicable to the mass market. Where products are sold in retail stores, it is common for buyers to rely on demonstrations and even hands-on use of a system in retail showrooms as the basis of their decision to buy a particular product.

---

[68] UCC 9-109(1).

[69] 15 USC §2301(1), *et seq.*

[70] 16 CFR §7001(a).

[71] See generally Smith, *The Magnuson-Moss Warranty Act: Turning the Tables on Caveat Emptor*, 13 Cal W Reserve L Rev 391 (1977).

[72] UCC 2-312(1).

[73] It is the *buyer's* responsibility to notify the seller at the time of a breach; however, the breach may not be discovered until sometime later, e.g., when maintenance is needed. UCC 2-607(3)(a).

[74] UCC 2-313(1)(a).

[75] UCC 2-313(1)(c), and 2-313(2).

The two warranties which the seller will attempt to disclaim are the warranty of merchantability and the warranty of fitness for a particular purpose. These two warranties will often be disclaimed in large bold face print on the documentation provided with the program. Merchantability may be difficult to prove in the mass microcomputer market. A program would seem to be merchantable if it conforms to the reasonable expectations of users of similar programs running on similar machines. With the variety of programs, computers, and users in this market, it might be difficult to show what these expectations were or whether they were satisfied.

Another aspect of warranty disclaimers in the mass market is the Magnuson-Moss Warranty Act, which applies to all consumer transactions.[76] The definition of consumer product in the Magnuson-Moss Warranty Act leaves open the question of whether the statute applies to software. The definition of a consumer product turns on the notion of *tangibility,* and the courts have struggled with the tangibility of computer programs for some time.[77] There is little question that the media upon which the programs are distributed comes under the Magnuson-Moss Warranty Act (programs are magnetically recorded on the distribution media, typically diskettes). It can be argued, however, that as to product warranties, the intellectual content of a program recorded on a diskette is no more tangible personal property than is the intellectual content of a book, and therefore, would probably be considered intangible. Regardless, vendors would be wise to consider this statute when marketing their software, primarily in relation to warranties. The Magnuson-Moss Warranty Act does not require anyone in the chain of distribution to give any product warranties, but does specifically prohibit modifications or disclaimers of implied warranties where a supplier makes a written warranty or enters into a service contract for the product within 90 days of sale.[78] Under the Magnuson-Moss Warranty Act, every written warranty given on any consumer product "actually costing the consumer more than five dollars" must "fully and conspicuously disclose" its terms and conditions "in the simple and readily understood language."[79] Every written warranty under the statute must be conspicuously designated as either a *full* [statement of duration] or a *limited* warranty.[80] A written warranty may be designated a full warranty if it meets the federal minimum standards for warranties as set forth in §2304(a) of the Magnuson-Moss Warranty Act.[81] Any warranty that does not meet these requirements must be designated as a

---

[76] Brooks & Brewer, Special Problems In The Mass Distribution of Hardware, Software and Firmware, 1982 US Calif Computer L Inst II-91 to II-122 (this article contains an excellent section by section discussion of the Magnuson-Moss Warranty Act.)

[77] *Id* II-93.

[78] 15 USC §2308(a).

[79] *Id* §2302(a).

[80] Since the Magnuson-Moss Warranty Act was passed, the regulations promulgated for this provision have increased the consumer cost threshold to 15 dollars. *See* 16 CFR §701.2 (this threshold of $15.00 excludes tax).

[81] See Comment, *Consumers Warranty Law in California Under the* Commercial Code and

limited warranty under the act.[82]

§3.14 Custom Development of Software

The custom development of a software system by a vendor for a user often creates more problems than the sale of existing software.[83] In a custom software contract, the parties are attempting to define exactly what is being purchased even though neither one may know. Often the user has only a general idea of what is needed, and is willing to leave the details to the vendor. With this type of arrangement, therefore, it is difficult to determine what is being purchased, and it is even more difficult to determine when the transaction is complete.

The nature of software development is responsible for most of the problems. Software development is not only a very labor intensive process, but in over 90 per cent of the cases of custom development, a totally new *system* must be created. Because of variations in vendor expertise in solving the particular problem and because time and cost estimating for any labor intensive undertaking is, at best, an uncertain science, estimates of time and cost vary greatly from vendor to vendor. The most important factor in the estimate is the quality of the user's request for proposal (RFP), the definition of the project as the user sees it.[84] If the RFP is complete and detailed, a vendor is better able to make an accurate estimate, and is more likely to meet that estimate and to deliver the product on time.

A vendor's standard form agreement is usually an open-ended time and materials commitment, calling for the user to pay the vendor its standard hourly rates for the time spent by its employees on the project, and to reimburse the vendor for all materials utilized in the course of the project. The user, of course, wants a fixed time and fixed price. Given these starting positions, these contracts are negotiable, and the user, therefore, should enlist a multidisciplined team to negotiate these contracts.

A major risk involved with a fixed price and time contract is the risk of vendor bankruptcy, which may be significant when contracting with a smaller vendor.[85] A good rule of thumb is that a software development project will take twice as long, and cost twice as much, as the original estimate. To obtain the product, the user may be forced to switch to a time and materials contract if

---

the Song - Beverly and Magnuson-Moss Warranty Acts, 26 UCLAL Rev 583, 662-67 (1979).

[82] *See* 16 CFR §700.7(b).

[83] See Brandon & Segelstein, Data Processing Contracts: Structure, Contents, and Negotiations, ch 8 (1976). The chapter includes a discussion of performance requirements, changes, termination procedures, security, access and confidentiality, and timesharing contracts.

[84] See **§3.06.**

[85] Brandon & Segelstein, *supra* note 83, at 125. (Item I "Vendor Bankruptcy" is cited as a major concern in software development contracts).

the vendor is facing bankruptcy. The risk of delay in receiving the product is significant for the same reasons. Another significant risk is the *90 percent complete* syndrome, where the system reaches a stage of near completion, but changes occur so frequently that the system is never completed.

The best assurance for a successful contract is a complete and adequate RFP which is included in the contract and which contains the functional specifications, a definition of the project stages, the progress reports and deliverables which must be completed for each stage, and a definition of the documentation which must be provided. The functional specifications should include a definition and example of all inputs, all outputs, all reports, all data files, and a description of the algorithm if it is unique to the industry or system.[86] Progress reports should be verified by examining the deliverables for completeness. The deliverables of each stage should be so well defined that a new vendor, if necessary, could complete the project. Documentation standards are necessary if the system will be maintained by the user's organization.

If the vendor will utilize the user's equipment and facilities for the development project, the contract should stipulate the maximum resources which the developer may consume, such as memory usage, peripheral device usage, processor time maximums, amount of printing available per day, and any other restrictions necessary to prevent the vendor from disrupting the user's normal business activities. If the vendor does the work at the user's business, the amount of space, furniture, etc., that will be made available should be specified along with building access and security procedures. The contract should also state the maximum amount of staff participation which the vendor can expect at each stage of the project.

A guarantee that the system being developed is original to the vendor should be included to avoid any problems with proprietary rights, as well as a clause stating that the user will not be held liable for any infringement that occurs. The user should have complete ownership of all source and object code created as part of the development, and should have unlimited access to any software which will be used in the system, even if not developed specifically for it. A noncompetition clause for a reasonable geographic area and reasonable time should also be made part of the contract. A confidentiality clause should be present to cover all information supplied by the user, and this clause should have an extended time period and definite geographic limits.[87]

The payment terms should be conditioned on receipt of deliverables at each stage of the development. Progress payments are necessary, because projects often extend over a long period, and it is unlikely that any software developer would be willing to wait until the end of a long (and expensive) project to

---

[86] *Id* 127-31. (Extensive checklist and samples of project deliverables).

[87] A typical confidentiality clause with a vendor would include a provision clearly stating that the user's duty to maintain secrecy about the vendor's trade secrets is conditioned on the vendor's silence about the user's business operations. Such a clause is particularly useful when the object of the contract is proprietary software. See also §§2.12, 2.13, 2.15.

recoup its costs. The percentage payment due at each stage should be specified in the contract. A certain percentage of each payment, however, should be held back until the deliverable is quality checked. The progress payments should equal the costs incurred by the vendor so that the vendor makes no profit unless the project is completed. In a fixed time and cost contract, this might create a problem because determining exactly what the vendor's costs are at a given stage is complicated by the fact that work progress is continuous with no clear break or cutoff point. The vendor might also resist divulging its costs. A better approach may be to pay up to 70 percent of the total in progress payments, retaining the balance for payment at total completion. In addition to progress payments, the right to cancel at any stage is highly desirable for the user. Very definite and objective criteria, however, are necessary if such a right is to be acceptable to the vendor and enforceable by the courts.

A clause not to solicit employees of either party for a period of time is desirable, particularly from the vendor's point of view. This prevents the user from luring key personnel away from the vendor, and promotes a better working relationship between the two parties. Delivery and acceptance is perhaps the most important clause of the contract. If the functional specifications and project definition have been given proper attention, this clause should simply state that the product is accepted when it meets the functional specifications, as tested by the user. This may sound easy, but in practice, acceptable testing is often difficult with a large system. The contract should stipulate the source of test data for the acceptance test, and should also state which party is responsible for creating this test data. The test data should be created by the user and verified by the vendor. After successfully running the test data, the system should be accepted, but a small percentage of the payment should be withheld until the warranty period is complete.

§3.15 Time Sharing and Service Bureau Contracts

Service bureaus supply computer services in the form of batch processing where input data is delivered to the service bureau and reports picked up some time later (or these reports may be obtained from interactive computers via terminals).[88] Batch processing can be subdivided into manual delivery systems where data and reports are delivered and picked up by messenger, and remote job entry systems where data is transmitted to the service bureau over telephone lines, processed in batch mode, and reports are delivered to the user via telephone and printed at the user's place of business. The software aspects of the service bureau contract are essentially the same for both types of processing. Most of the software-related clauses in the service bureau contract will focus more on the data than the actual software.[89] Since most of these contracts

---

[88] See generally Practicing Law Institute, Computer Law: Purchasing, Leasing, and Licensing Hardware, Software and Services (1980). See also §2.13.

[89] Id 249-62.

are for data processing needs essential to the user's business, the accuracy of results should be clearly specified. The complexity of data processing makes it impossible for the service bureau to guarantee 100 percent results. A service bureau, however, should be willing to provide a reasonable guarantee, and should also provide a procedure for error notification and correction.

Data protection is essential to the contract. While the user is generally responsible for the accuracy of the original data, the service bureau must provide means for ensuring that data is not changed, lost, or destroyed. In addition, the contract should provide means for allocating responsibility in case of loss, with costs being distributed or allocated to one party based on the reason for loss. The data must also be kept confidential by the service bureau, which should be willing to provide security measures to prevent disclosure to other customers, to destroy intermediate files to prevent inadvertant disclosure, and to destroy carbons removed from multiple copy paper.

Ownership of programs should be covered in the contract. The contract should acknowledge that programs developed by the customer remain the property of the customer at all times. The customer should retain ownership of programs developed by the service bureau at the expense of the customer. One sticky area is ownership of modifications where the programs are modified for the benefit of both parties. The contract should provide a procedure for determining who owns the modifications when this occurs. The customer should retain the rights of access to the programs at any time, specifically after termination of the contract.

The right to audit without notice should be included in the contract to provide: for audit of the programs being used by the customer; and for audit of the physical security of the service bureau. The termination clause should include specific references to data and program ownership how and when this information will be delivered to the customer, and should state that all other copies will be destroyed by the service bureau. For the customer who will become dependent on the service bureau to run its business, the right to a long cancellation notice provision, six months or longer, should be provided to allow the customer to find another bureau to perform the work. A short termination notice period, even if it is reciprocal, is not usually satisfactory to the parties.

Additional Legal Concerns

§3.16   Computer Tort Theory

The law of torts as applied to computer-related issues is only now beginning to emerge. At the present time, most computer torts amount to no more than technologically advanced versions of already-familiar causes of action, e.g., fraud and misrepresentation, invasion of privacy, and negligence. As computational technology becomes more prevalent, entirely new causes of action can be expected. These new causes of action will reflect the process by which the law seeks to adapt to constantly changing social, economic, and political realities.

The technological character of the computer is such that a computer is not an inherently dangerous machine. The only direct physical injuries which are likely to be suffered by a computer user result from potential fire and electrical hazards, and possibly from contact with the peripheral equipment's moving parts. There has been some speculation on possible radiation hazards associated with cathode ray tubes (CRT). Cases of physical injury have been reported, but these are rare, and in general are easily analyzed using traditional tort principles as the plaintiffs' injuries do not involve the technological basis of computers.[90]

Aside from computer torts related to physical injury, two areas of computer tort law are developing. Computers and their related equipment are specialized machines, purchased with a view towards performing certain tasks such as information-handling or process control. Consequently, the two areas of potential computer torts involve economic injuries caused by the failure of the computer system to perform as expected, or by its failure to perform at all. These conflicts can be genereally divided into the categories of vendor/user disputes, and user/third party computer failures.

§3.17   —Vendor-User Conflicts

In the realm of computer contracts, disputes between equipment and service vendors and their customers are common occurrences.[91] The theories of recovery closely parallel contract theories. Warranty disclaimers, integration clauses, and limitations of remedies for breach are usually found in computer contracts. These contract clauses, together with a possibility that the user may suffer losses which a court may subsequently decide were not sufficiently within the contemplation of the parties at the time of the contract, place the user in the position where the best, or perhaps only, recovery can be obtained by framing the cause of action in tort.[92]

§3.18   —Fraud and Misrepresentation

Tortious misrepresentation may be the most successful theory of recovery for a disappointed consumer of computer products and services.[93] Most of a computer user's unsatisfied expectations were created by the statements, rep-

---

[90] In Watts v IBM, 341 F Supp 760 (ED Wis 1972), the machine operator injured a finger due to a malfunction of the computer. The plaintiff's third party action in tort was sustained in spite of an earlier dismissal of her workmen's compensation claim.

[91] See generally Gilburne & David, Structuring Agreements for Vertical Distribution of Hardware and Software, 1982 US Cal Computer L Inst, §XI A.

[92] See Zammit, *Contracting For Computer Products,* 22 Jurimetrics J 337, 350 (1982).

[93] *Id* 352.

resentations, and other non-contractual promises made by a vendor's sales personnel during the selection of a computer system or product. Sales agents, who exhibit an understandable reluctance towards telling a prospective customer that the proffered system cannot realistically be expected to perform miracles, may make commitments during the negotiation process which are, at best, overly-optimistic. This understandable but unfortunate tendancy is made worse, from a user's point of view, when these commitments and representations are incorporated in oral agreements or in *side-letter* agreements, but excluded from the final contract. Warranty disclaimers and the parol evidence rule will ordinarily prevent a user from successfully asserting contractual claims based on these representations against a vendor. Thus, the disgruntled user may be forced to proceed against a vendor for extra-contractual promises by framing the complaint as a tort action grounded in misrepresentation.[94] If victorious, a plaintiff can recover all of its damages, regardless of any contractual limitations of liability. Additionally, a successful plaintiff may be able to recover punitive damages.[95]

Courts have imposed liability for negligent and even innocent misrepresentation, as well as for intentional fraud.[96] It has been argued that permitting a disappointed purchaser to recover on a theory of nonintentional misrepresentation effectively nullifies those provisions of the Uniform Commercial Code which permit disclaimers of warranties.[97] To be actionable as intentional misrepresentation (common-law fraud), there must be an intentionally false statement of material fact which the plaintiff reasonably relied on to its detriment.[98] Mere predictions, opinions, or other *sales talk* concerning the performance or capabilities of a system will not be held to have given rise to a viable cause of

---

[94] *See, e.g.,* Centronics Fin v El Conquistador, 573 F2d 779 (2d Cir 1978). Some courts have refused to allow plaintiffs to avoid contractual limitations of liability merely by casting their complaints in terms of misrepresentation. *See, e.g.,* Investors Premium v Burroughs, 389 F Supp 39 (DSC 1974); Westfield Chem v Burroughs, 6 Computer L Serv Rep 438, 21 UCC Rep 1293 (Mass Super Ct 1977). These cases generally involve some failure of the plaintiff's proof. To the extent that the plaintiff is unable to plead and prove all of the necessary elements of a case of tortious misrepresentation, the result in these cases is unassailable. No contractual limitation of liability is capable of shielding a culpable defendant where all of the elements of the plaintiff's misrepresentation case are proved. See generally Chandler, *Computer Transactions: Potential Liability of Computer Users and Vendors,* 1977 Wash ULG 405.

[95] *E.g.,* Glovatorium v NCR, 684 F2d 658 (9th Cir 1982) ($2 million); Hall Affiliates v Burroughs, No CV-79-001536 (Ala Cir Ct June 12 1981)($91,000).

[96] *See, e.g.,* Lovebright Diamond v Nixdorf Computer, No 78-4585 (SDNY Oct 9, 1979) (common-law fraud); Teamsters Sec Fund v Sperry Rand, 6 Computer L Serv Rep 951 (ND Cal 1977) (common-law fraud); Badger Bearing v Burroughs, 444 F Supp 919 (ED Wis 1977), *affd mem,* 588 F2d 838 (7th Cir 1978) (common-law fraud) (negligence) Rozny v Marnul, 43 Ill 2d 54, 250 NE2d 656 (1969) (negligence); Miller v Dames, 198 Cal App 2d 305, 18 Cal Rep 13 (1961) (negligence); Strand v Librascope, 197 F Supp (ED Mich 1961) (negligence); Clements Autos v Service Bureau, 444 F2d 169 (8th Cir 1971) (innocent misrepresentation).

[97] See Zammit, *Contracting for Computer Products,* 22 Jurimetrics J, 337, 354 (1982).

[98] *Id* 354.

action. Nor will a plaintiff be able to demonstrate the requisite reasonable reliance when the contract contains explicit statements of fact incompatible with the alleged misrepresentation.[99] In *Clement Auto Co v Service Bureau Corp,* the court held that an electronic data processing company was liabile in fraud for misrepresentation it had made to a customer that the proposed data processing system would, when fully implemented, be capable of supplying the company with information needed for more effective inventory control.[100] The court further stated that a general disclaimer clause will not negate the buyer's reliance on false representations. The court looked to the state of computer technology, noting that each of the disputed matters was susceptible of knowledge, and concluded that the inequality of knowledge between the parties rendered the plaintiff's reliance on the misrepresentation justified.[101]

A similar case arose where a plaintiff, the purchaser of a computer from the defendant vendor, alleged that the defendant had fraudulently misrepresented that the machine in question was suitable for service bureau data processing.[102] The defendant had also allegedly agreed to refer enough customers so that the plaintiff would require no sales force. One of the plaintiff's purchasing officers, who knew even before the sale that the system in question had a relatively slow print-out rate, claimed that it relied on the representations of the defendant that the role of printing was unimportant, and that the machine was otherwise suitable for plaintiff's purposes. As to the slowness of the printing rate, the court held that the plaintiff had no right to rely on the representation as to the adequacy. Stating that while a prospective purchaser may rely on a misrepresentation of facts peculiarly within a vendor's knowledge, it may not do so after it knows of a defect. Even assuming that the misrepresentation had occurred, plaintiff's agent (the purchasing officer) was in as good a position as the defendant to foresee the effect of a slow printer on its business.[103]

---

[99] *See, e.g.,* Shivers v Sweda, 146 Ga App 758, 247 SE2d 576 (1978); Teamsters Sec Fund v Sperry Rand, 6 Computer L Serv Rep 951 (ND Cal 1977); Badger Bearing v Burroughs, 444 F Supp 919 (ED Wis 1977), *affd mem,* 588 F2d 838 (7th Cir 1978).

The basic rationale of this line of cases is the lack of reasonable reliance upon what should obviously have been dismissed as mere *puffing.*

[100] Clements Auto v Service Bureau, 298 F Supp 115, *affd,* 444 F2d 169, 179 (8th Cir 1971)

[101] The courts often look to the degree of knowledge possessed by the parties to determine the extent and reasonableness of reliance. In Strand v Librascope, Inc, the court stated that:

> in the rapidly advancing field of computer technology, a manufacturer often possesses technical information known only to him, and where a third party reasonably relies on the manufacturer's superior knowledge, the manufacturer must disclose the state of development of his new product when necessary to prevent unwarranted inferences.

197 F Supp 743, 745 (ED Mich 1961).

[102] Fruits Indus Research Found v National Cash Register Co, 406 F2d 546 (9th Cir 1969).

[103] *Id.*

§3.19   Negligence

While it would be advantageous to users if they could always frame their dissatisfaction with the performance of their computers in terms of tortious vendor conduct, this is not always possible.[104] Mere negligence on the vendor's part may not be enough to avoid the terms of the contract regarding limitation of liability. Courts have held that negligent performance of a contract makes one liable in damages for breach of the contract, but not for the tort of negligence. As a result, a negligence theory is more likely to be successful when the plaintiff is not a party to a vendor/vendee contract.[105]

§3.20   Computer Malpractice

If programmers are viewed by the courts as professionals, courts may take the next step and hold them to a higher standard of care, such as doctors or lawyers. In the past, programming services were generally sought only by fairly sophisticated business customers. These services were viewed as being provided by persons who did not fulfill the traditional tests of professionalism.[106] As the demand for programming services has expanded, skilled programmers and systems analysts have increasingly been involved in relationships with users that bear a resemblance to the more traditional professions. The interest shown by commentators in a professional malpractice theory of recovery for negligent performance of computing-related contracts has not spread to the courts. The few reported cases have either rejected or ignored the malpractice theory. It is possible, however, that as the mass market for hardware and software expands, a computer professional malpractice theory may become more acceptable.[107]

§3.21   Negligent Overreliance on the Computer

Because of the efficiency of computers in handling large volumes of information and in performing repetitive tasks, many businesses use computers to handle the bulk of their record keeping. As with any large and complex system, errors do occur. It has become fashionable to blame billing errors on the creditor's computer, even though such errors are not (ordinarily) the result of any failure by the machine. Assuming that the computer's hardware and software are functioning correctly, the computer system will do only that which it

---

[104] See generally Nycum, *Computer Abuses Raise New Legal Problems*, 61 ABA J 444 (1975).

[105] See generally Gilburne & David, Structuring Agreements for Vertical Distribution of Hardware and Software, 1982 U S C Computer L Inst §XIA.

[106] See Zammit, *Contracting for Computer Products*, 22 Jurimetrics J 337, 351-52 (1982). See also Bigelow & Saltzberg, Computer L Newsletter, July 1980.

[107] See generally Gemignani, Product Liability and Software, 8 Rutgers Computer & Tech LJ 173 (1981).

is programmed to do. Most failures of computer recordkeeping systems can be attributed to operator error at some point in the process. The courts are increasingly concluding that no matter what the source of the computer errors, overreliance on the product of data processing systems can be a source of liability for negligence.[108]

An example of overreliance on a computer resulting in liability in common law negligence occurred in *Ford Motor Credit Co v Swarens.*[109] Swarens purchased an automobile on credit through the Ford Motor Company. He paid his monthly charges in full and on time, and when an error occurred, collection agents came to visit Swarens who then exhibited his cancelled checks. This visit was followed by a second one, at which time Swarens again showed the agents his cancelled checks. On the third visit, however, Mr. Swarens showed the collection agents his shotgun. Ford first seized, and then sold the automobile, at which point Swarens brought suit for compensatory and punitive damages. Addressing Ford's defense, the court stated that:

> Ford explains that this whole incident occurred because of a mistake by a computer. Men feed data to a computer and men interpret the answer the computer spews forth. In this computerized age, the law must require that men in the use of computerized data regard those with whom they are dealing as more important than a perforation on a card. Trust in the infallibility of a computer is hardly a defense, when the opportunity to avoid the error is as apparent and repeated as was here presented.[110]

Clearly, a computer user has a duty to act reasonably in relying upon computer-generated information. It is less clear, however, just how this duty can be applied in everyday commerce. No legislature has seen fit to impose an obligation on computer users to inject human judgment between computer output and the public, and it is unlikely that such a requirement would be either practical or beneficial.[111] As the *Swarens* case indicates, the courts will not hesitate to impose a duty of human intervention when it would be unreasonable to fail to use human judgment.[112] If a computer user either knows or

---

[108] See generally Chandler, Computer Transactions: Potential Liability of Computer Users and Vendors, 1977 Wash ULQ 405, 414-415.

[109] Ford Motor Credit Co v Swarens, 447 SW2d 533 (Ky 1969).

[110] *Id* 535. On a similar theme, the Court of Appeals for the Tenth Circuit has stated that "holding a company responsible for the actions of its computers does not exhibit a distaste for modern business practice. . . . A computer operates only in accordance with the information and directions supplied by its human programmers. If the computer does not think like a man, it is man's fault." State Farm Mutual Ins Co v Bockhorst, 453 F2d 533 (10th Cir 1972) (involving reinstatement of an insurance policy).

[111] See Wessel, *Computer Services and the Law,* 18 Bus Automation 79 (1970).

[112] *See* Ford Motor Credit Co v Hitchcock, 116 Ga App 563, 158 SE2d 468 (1967); Price v Ford Motor Credit Co, 5 Computer L Serv Rep 956 (Mo 1975). Another interesting case in a similar vein is Palance v Columbia Gas Co, 342 F Supp 241 (1972) (alleged violations of the fourth amendment to the United States Constitution and of 42 USC § 1983, as a result of faulty computer billing procedures in connection with

should have known of a possible machine error, the user must take reasonable action by way of human intervention, or be held liable for any harm that results.

A more difficult problem arises where the computer errs, malfunctions, or fails outright, and the failure results in immediate damage through the instrumentalities the computer controls. The potential for injury in such cases is far greater than in the computer recordkeeping arena of commerce and government.[113] For example, computers control dangerous industrial processes, provide essential data to the air traffic control system, and even form a vital link in our national defense. The potential for disaster has been explored in hypothetical terms by several writers.[114] Real life has provided several examples of computer-originated near catastrophe.[115] Computer error may already have come close to causing World War III.[116] In view of the enormous harm which may result, total reliance on computers probably does not constitute an exercise of reasonable care.

§3.22 Arbitration in the Computer Contracting Context

Arbitration is "the oldest known method of settlement of disputes between men."[117] Yet, commercial arbitration existed with little support from the legal system until the period immediately following World War I,[118] and labor arbitration had no statutory authority until after World War II.[119] The common law rule was that an agreement to arbitrate could be revoked at any time. Written agreements to arbitrate were "neither more nor less enforceable" than

---

utility bills. Interestingly, at least part of the problem stemmed from improper programming).

[113] Many recordkeeping errors are, eventually, relatively easy to correct, even if maddening to the unfortunate victim.

[114] See Nycum, *Liability for Malfunction of a Computer Program,* Rutgers J Computers, Tech & L 1 (1979).

[115] Near-misses have included potential mid-air collisions by aircraft, *CPU Fails, Two Jets Nearly Collide,* Computerworld, Nov 12, 1979, at 1; and nuclear power plant accidents *Computer Error Closes Nuke Plants,* Indianapolis Star, Mar 16, 1979, at 1. A computer error contributed to critical fuel waste during Skylab's reentry, which could have been disastrous if the satellite had landed in a populous area. See *NASA Jumbles Skylab Flight Data,* Computerworld, July 9, 1979, at 1.

[116] *U S Aides Recount Moments of False Missile Alert,* NY Times, Dec 16, 1979, §1, at 25; See also *Norad System Goofs, Calls Missile Alert,* Computerworld, Nov 19, 1979, at 1.

[117] McAmis v Panhandle Pipeline Co, 23 Lab Arb Rep 570, 574 (Kan Ct App 1954). See also Lazarus, Resolving Business Disputes (1965).

[118] Bernstein, Private Dispute Settlements: Cases and Materials on Arbitration (1968).

[119] An excellent overview of labor-management arbitration and collective bargaining agreements and a history of the development of both can be found in Elkouri & Elkouri, How Arbitration Works (3d ed 1973). For a survey of collective bargaining agreements formed without including an arbitration clause, *see* Mason, *Collective Bargaining Agreements Without Arbitration Clauses,* 7 U Dayton L Rev 387 (1982).

oral agreements.[120] Some courts refused to enforce arbitration agreements because "insofar as they were deemed to oust the courts of jurisdiction [the agreements] were against public policy and illegal."[121] It should be noted that while arbitration is no longer "an unwanted stepchild" to the courts, some courts still are not disposed to uphold agreements to arbitrate disputes in areas where a strong public policy exists.[122] This reluctance has been overcome by statute in some areas, and has been reinforced in others.[123]

Arbitration can be seen as an attempt to set standards for the contract that will be invoked when disputes arise.[124] It provides for arbitration procedures for the resolution of the dispute outside of the judicial process, and places great emphasis on the realities of the relationship of the parties, the expectations of the parties, the standards that are peculiar to the industry in which the dispute occurs, and on achieving a just result.[125]

§3.23 —Prerequisites to Arbitration

Before arbitration may be initiated, the parties must reach an agreement on the standards and procedures which will be used in deciding disputes arising under the contract. The arbitration agreement may be one of two kinds: a future dispute arbitration clause placed into the contract before formation; or the submission of an existing dispute to arbitration prior to resorting to litigation.[126]

§3.24 —The Burroughs Model Clause and the American Arbitration Association Clause

The American Arbitration Association suggests that an arbitration clause to cover disputes which may arise under a contract for computer hardware and services should contain the following language:

STANDARD ARBITRATION CLAUSE

Any controversy or claim arising out of or relating to this contract, or the breach thereof, shall be settled by arbitration in accordance with the

---

[120] Bernstein, *supra* note 118, at 69.

[121] Wales v State Farm Mut Auto Ins Co, 38 Colo App 360, 559 P2d 255 (1970).

[122] 9 USC §1 *et seq.*

[123] The American Arbitration Association resulted from a combination of the Arbitration Society of America and the Arbitrators Foundation. See Kellor, American Arbitration (1948). For the text of the Uniform Arbitration Act, see 7 ULA 4-82 (1978).

[124] Arbitration differs from mediation which is merely an agreement to seek assistance in reaching a settlement, and is not binding on either party.

[125] Bernstein, *supra* note 118, at 3.

[126] American Arbitration Association, A Businessman's Guide to Commercial Arbitration 4 (1962).

Rules of the American Arbitration Association, and judgment upon the award rendered by the Arbitrator(s) may be entered in any Court having jurisdiction thereof.[127]

The Burroughs Corporation uses an arbitration clause which includes several of these elements.[128] The clause[129] states clearly and unambiguously the procedures which will govern the arbitration, including: (1) the locale of the arbitrator; (2) the number of arbitrators;[130] (3) how they will be selected; (4) the qualifications the arbitrators must have; (5) and how soon after the demand for arbitration the selection process for the arbitrators should begin. Provision should also be made for all costs and fees connected with the arbitration, and if and where judgment may be entered on the arbitrators' decision.[131]

§3.25 —Procedures and Practice

If the parties have made specific agreements regarding the procedures for arbitration, they should strictly adhere to the procedures as outlined. Many commercial contract arbitration clauses, however, merely reference American Arbitration Association (AAA) rules and procedures. When an arbitrable controversy exists, one party initiates the process by serving a Demand for Arbitration on the other party listing the parties involved, the nature of the dispute,

---

[127] American Arbitration Association, Commercial Arbitration Rules of the American Arbitration Association (as amended and adopted Nov 1, 1973).

[128] The following is a copy of the arbitration clause which Burroughs uses in its computer contracts.

ARBITRATION CLAUSE

Any controversy or claim arising out of or relating to this Agreement, as well as any extension or modification thereof, shall be settled by arbitration, conducted on a confidential basis, under the then current commercial Arbitration Rules of the American Arbitration Association ("the Association") strictly in accordance with the terms of this Agreement and the substantive law of the Commonwealth of Pennsylvania. The arbitration shall be held at the regional office of the Association located closest to the principal place of business of the Customer and conducted by three arbitrators, at least one of whom shall be chosen from a panel of persons knowledgeable in data processing and business information systems and one of whom shall be an attorney. Judgement upon the award rendered by the arbitrators may be entered and enforced in any court of competent jurisdiction. Neither party shall institute a proceeding hereunder unless at least sixty (60) days prior thereto such party shall have furnished to the other written notice by registered mail of its intent to do so. If notice is issued it should be addressed to its "General Counsel". Neither party shall be precluded hereby from seeking provisional remedies in the courts of any jurisdiction including, but not limited to, temporary restraining orders and preliminary injunctions, to protect its rights and interests, but such shall not be sought as a means to avoid or stay arbitration.

[129] Uniform Arbitration Act §1, 7 ULA 4 (1978) Commercial Arbitration Rules §1.

[130] Generally, there is a single arbitrator unless the parties otherwise agree. 9 USC §5.

[131] Friedman, Checklist for Commercial Arbitration, 37 Arbitration J 10, 11 (1982).

the amount involved, and the remedy sought. Two copies of this demand are filed with the AAA if the parties have agreed to an AAA appointed arbitrator.[132] If the parties have previously agreed to arbitrate, and one party refuses to arbitrate, the willing party may apply for a court order compelling arbitration.[133] Likewise, if a party to an arbitrable controversy brings a judicial action, the other party may obtain a stay, or, in some instances, a dismissal of the judicial action and force arbitration.[134]

Once the demand has been served, the next step is the selection of the panel of arbitrators.[135] A good arbitration clause will settle the number and method of selecting arbitrators. This selection clause should also state what qualities the individual arbitrators should have: "general competency, no possible bias, specialized knowledge, energy and character."[136] In a particularly complex case, the parties may desire to select a *super panel*,[137] which would consist of persons who were highly skilled and knowledgeable.[138] Arbitration hearings are conducted at a time and place convenient to both parties and are very informal. Arbitrators are not required to follow either the rules of evidence, or the rules of civil procedure.[139] Parties may be represented by counsel at the hearings.[140] No record is made of the hearing unless specifically requested by one party, in which case that party is required to pay all costs of creating the

---

[132] CAR §7 (1973).

[133] 9 USC §4.

[134] 9 USC §3.

[135] If the dispute is referred to the American Arbitration Association, a *tribunal clerk* is appointed to handle all scheduling and other administrative matters. The tribunal clerk also prepares a list of potential arbitrators, and sends a copy of the list and a brief biography of each potential arbitrator to each party. Each party has seven days to cross off the names of arbitrators to which they object, and to number the remaining candidates in order of preference. A date for the hearing is usually scheduled within two months of the services of the demand for arbitration. Note that the arbitration will not necessarily be held within two months since the arbitrator is required by AAA §12 to grant reasonable requests for continuance. See Brown, *Some Practical Thoughts on Arbitration*, 6 Litigation 8, 10 (1980). Parties may at any time agree upon arbitrators outside of the AAA procedures. Roth, *Choosing an Arbitration Panel*, 6 Litigation 13 (1980).

[136] Roth, *supra* note 135.

[137] *Id.*

[138] Arbitrators in commercial arbitration are rarely paid by the parties. Instead, if AAA arbitrators are used, the AAA charges an administrative fee and the AAA pays the arbitrators. §50 of the Commerical Arbitration Rules (1973), specifies that members of the National Panel of Arbitrators serve "without fee" in commercial arbitrations. The National Panel of Arbitrators is a listing of experts in several hundred different fields maintained by the AAA. This has the advantage of eliminating the necessity of the parties having any contact with the arbitrator prior to the hearing and the potential for bias that might result from such contact.
CAR §12 (1973).

[139] They must however, hear all material evidence. Refusal of an arbitrator to hear material evidence may constitute grounds for vacating the arbitrator's award. 9 USC §10(c); UAA §12(a)(4).

[140] CAR §21 (1973).

record.[141] There is no burden of proof. Instead, each side attempts to convince the arbitrator of the correctness of its position.[142] Under AAA rules, the arbitrator has 30 days from the close of the hearing to render a final decision. The Commercial Arbitration Rules (CAR) are silent on the appealability of arbitrator's award.[143] The AAA provides that a court may *vacate* an arbitrator's award only where:

1. The award was procured by corruption, fraud, or other undue means

2. There was evident partiality by an arbitrator appointed as a neutral,[144] or corruption or misconduct prejudicing the rights of any party

3. The arbitrator exceeded his or her powers

4. The arbitrator refused to grant a continuance for good cause, refused to hear evidence material to the controversy, or conducted the hearing so as to prejudice substantially the rights of the party

5. There was no arbitration agreement and the party or parties did not participate in the arbitration hearing without raising the objection[145]

The award may be *modified* by the court where:

1. There was a miscalculation of figures or a mistake in description of a person, thing, or property[146]

---

[141] CAR §22 (1973).

[142] Discovery is generally not available in arbitration proceedings. There is a continuing debate over when it should be allowed and whether discovery would aid in streamlining procedures even further in the arbitration process. See generally Willenken, *Discovery in Aid of Arbitration,* 6 Litigation 16 (1980).

[143] The appealability of arbitrators' awards depends to a large degree on whether the arbitration is binding or nonbinding. Nonbinding arbitration is, by definition, appealable to the courts because any determination made is not binding on the parties. Most nonbinding arbitration agreements contain a clause which specifically allows either party recourse to the judicial system de novo. For an examination of the effects of nonbinding arbitration see Lind & Shapard, Evaluation of Court-Annexed Arbitration in Three Federal District Courts (1981) (a publication resulting from a study funded by the Federal Judicial Center). The result of binding arbitration is usually a judgment entered in a court of competent jurisdiction by the successful party.

[144] The neutrality of arbitrators has been the subject of much debate. CAR §18 requires a person who has been appointed as a neutral arbitrator to disclose any circumstances likely to affect his or her impartiality, including any bias or any financial or personal interest in the result of the arbitration or any past or present relationship with the parties or their counsel. The courts have indicated, however, that disclosure is no longer required when a non-neutral arbitrator has been appointed and agreed upon by the parties. See Kim, Unconscionability of Presumptively Biased Arbitration Clauses Within Contracts of Adhesion, 70 Cal L Rev 1014 (1982). *See generally* Fredrico v Frick, 3 Cal App 3d 872, 84 Cal Rptr 74 (2d Dist 1970); Graham v Sissor-Tail, Inc, 28 Cal 3d 807, 623 P2d 165 (1981) (per curiam).

[145] 9 USC §10(c); UAA §12(a)(4).

[146] 9 USC §11(a); UAA §13(a)(1).

2. The award was on a matter not subject to arbitration[147]

3. The award is imperfect in form[148]

§3.26 —Streamling Arbitration Procedures

Some commentators have attempted to streamline the arbitration process, which can become quite lengthy when attempting to resolve large or complex issues.[149] In some complex cases, arbitration in the form of a *mini-trial* has been successful. A six-week schedule of limited discovery was followed by a two-day mini-trial at which each side presented its *best case* through two, top-management representatives. After the mini-trial, the parties met, and with an assessment of the other party's position in mind, attempted to resolve the dispute.[150]

Another approach allowed the arbitration panel to actively participate in the hearing process. Arbitrators held a procedural conference in advance of an evidentiary hearing to set ground rules, to specify what evidence had to be exchanged, and to arrange and schedule longer hearing days. By requiring parties to exchange documents, to depose witnesses wherever possible, and prepare charts, graphs, and summaries, hearing time was significantly reduced. At the close of the period for discovery, each party submits a brief summarizing all evidence they wish to present at the evidentiary hearing.[151]

§3.27 —Arbitration versus Litigation

Some commentators have stated that the debate in the data processing industry over the use of arbitration clauses in contracts is the result of a lack of understanding of the arbitration process.[152] Arbitration has several advantages over litigation. The costs of litigation, both in money and in time, are generally higher than the expense of arbitration.[153] In the computer industry,

---

[147] 9 USC §11(b); UAA §13(a)(2).

[148] 9 USC §11(c); UAA §13(a)(3). See generally Friedman, *Correcting Arbitrator Error,* 33 Arbitration J 9 (1978).

[149] Sandver, Blaine and Wagner, *Time and Cost Savings Through Expedited Arbitration Procedures,* 36 Arbitration J 11 (1981). One system developed by the steel industry has been applied to situations where the same matter comes up for arbitration on a regular basis. In contrast to many other streamlined procedures, the steel industry plan is designed to handle arbitration of issues that are not novel, not contractually significant, and not complex. See generally Fisher, *Arbitration: The Steel Industry Experiment,* 95 Monthly Lab Rev 7 (1972).

[150] Olson, *Dispute Resolution: An Alternative for Large Case Litigation,* 6 Litigation 22 (1980).

[151] See Poppleton, *The Arbitrator's Role in Expediting the Large and Complex Commercial Case,* 36 Arbitration J 6 (1981).

[152] Bernacchi & Larsen, Data Processing Contracts and the Law 215 (1974).

[153] In a recent case, the parties estimated that more than 110 days would be needed to hear all the evidence on claims, counter-claims, and defenses in a complex patent

technological changes can revolutionize aspects of the industry in a very short time. The faster a dispute can be settled, therefore, the better the position of both parties. Furthermore, the informal setting of arbitration allows the parties to maintain continuity in their business relationship, a spirit of goodwill, and evidences a desire to maintain a positive working environment. Informality and the resulting cooperation are especially important where a vendor is the only source of hardware components or software, and the other party to the dispute needs these computational resources to remain in business. Arbitration also affords privacy to the parties involved in the dispute. Records of the arbitration proceedings are released to the public, but proprietary software and trade secrets are not divulged, and thus retain their legal protection.[154] Another distinct advantage of arbitration over litigation is that there are few jurisdictional problems. Parties to a dispute may meet with the arbitrator at a place and time convenient to everyone involved in the dispute and thereby avoid transportation costs. The most persuasive reason for arbitration in the data processing industry is that it allows parties to select arbitrators who are knowledgeable in all aspects of the contract in dispute, and who have the technical background and sophistication which is lacking in many judges and almost all juries.[155]

Despite the distinct advantages of arbitration, many businesses are still reluctant to use arbitration. In a recent survey of 51 companies who had been issued patents (some of which were in computer-related fields), only 25 per cent had used arbitration to settle patent disputes. Most of those surveyed were willing to use arbitration in disputes where the amounts were less than $100,000.[156]

Arbitration can be a very useful tool in the context of the computer industry because it provides for the quick resolution of disputed issues by persons

---

suit. It was estimated that more than two years would be spent before a decision would be reached via the judicial system. Arbitrators, using a streamlined procedure, reduced the hearing time to nine extended days (8 am to 6 pm), and reached a decision less than eight months after the arbitrators were selected. See Poppleton, *The Arbitrator's Role in Expediting the Large and Complex Commercial Case,* 36 Arbitration J 6 (1981).

[154] On August 27, 1982, a new voluntary arbitration statute came into effect. It allows parties to a patent dispute to agree to arbitration of the dispute. Prior to the passage of the law, codified as 35 USC §294, agreements to arbitrate some aspects of disputes arising under patent licenses were enforceable by the courts. Traditionally, courts had been reluctant to allow arbitration of disputes concerning patent validity or infringement to escape judicial review, partly because of the complexity of the issues. *See* Zip Mfg Co v Pep Mfg Co, 44 F2d 184, (D Del 1930).

[155] The disadvantage of *expert* arbitrators is that they may not be totally impartial and will bring some of the biases of their expertise in the industry to the arbitration process.

[156] PTC Research Report: *Alternatives to Court Litigation in Intellectual Property Disputes* 22 IDEA 271 (1981). The companies surveyed chose *lower cost* as the most favored reason to take the arbitration route. *Speedy resolution* was the second favored reason. Many of those surveyed noted that they would prefer mediation (assistance of a neutral party in reaching a settlement) to arbitration (which they considered binding and not subject to any judicial review).

familiar with the industry while maintaining goodwill and business relations. Arbitration clauses should be narrowly drawn, and should specifically state the wishes of the parties as to when arbitration will be used and how the arbitration panel will be formed. Parties who are considering arbitration clauses must be sure to include all necessary provisions since courts will not overturn the decision of an arbitrator except in a few circumstances.[157]

Taxation

§3.28   Introduction

The following short discussion of federal and state taxation issues involved in computer contracts is intended as a springboard for further research into computer contract tax issues.[158] The overriding concern in examining computer contract tax issues, just as in other business equipment acquisitions, is the essential role which tax planning plays. The user's acquisition team, therefore, should have either a tax specialist assigned to it, or ready access to competent tax advisors to ensure that the computer acquisition fits into the user's overall tax and financial plan.[159]

§3.29   Federal Tax Considerations

Numerous federal tax considerations must be reviewed in the computer acquisition process. Four of the major federal tax considerations are: (1) the Investment Tax Credit (ITC); (2) depreciation procedures under the Accelerated Cost Recovery System (ACRS); (3) equipment leasing under the Economic Recovery Tax Act of 1981 (ERTA); and (4) the Research and Development (R&D) incremental tax credit procedures also under ERTA.

Investment Tax Credit

The ITC is governed by §§38 and 46-50 of the 1954 Internal Revenue Act. The ITC applies to tangible personal property which is defined as "any tangible property except land and improvements thereto. . . ."[160] Most computer hardware, therefore, is eligible for the ITC. If hardware and software are bundled as a single acquisition item (i.e., wihout separately stated prices for the hardware and software), the ITC will generally be available for the entire

---

[157] See generally Murray, *Claims for Damage and Submission to Arbitration Clauses as Traps for Lethargic Businessmen*, 87 Com L J 359 (1982).

[158] For a thorough, recent tax analysis, see, e.g., Bigelow, *The Computer and the Tax Collector*, 30 Emory LJ 357 (1981).

[159] See generally Bernacchi, *Selected Tax Problems*, in Brooks, Computer Law (1980).

[160] Economic Recovery Tax Act, Pub L No 97-34, 95 Stat 172 (1981); IRC §§38(a), IRC §§46-48; 48(a)(1)(A); Treas Reg 1.48-1(c).

acquisition.[161] In a combined hardware and software acquisition with the resulting tangible aspects of the combined hardware and software, state and local personal property taxes on the software may become a major concern.[162] If software is acquired separately from the hardware, it probably will not qualify for the ITC. The maximum ITC credit is 10 per cent, and for equipment with a useful life of seven years or more, 100 per cent of the full 10 per cent credit is available.[163] Since 1981, the ITC has been liberalized by using the more rapid recovery period provided by the Accelerated Cost Recovery System (ACRS), rather than basing the amount of the allowable ITC on the useful life of the asset.[164] There is no dollar limit on the total ITC for new property. For used property, the ITC may be claimed up to $125,000 for qualifying used property.[165] There are, however, limits on the amount of income tax liability which may be offset by the total ITC.[166] Timing of the acquisition of an asset eligible for the ITC is critical, because ITC is a lump sum credit based on the user's taxable year.

Accelerated Cost Recovery System

ERTA established a new depreciation procedure called the Accelerated Cost Recovery System (ACRS), to replace the earlier accelerated depreciation procedures, for property placed in service after December 31, 1980. ACRS provides a significantly shorter time period to depreciate assets without regard to the useful life of the asset.[167] Most personal property, and thus almost all computer equipment (and software bundled with the acquisition of hardware) will qualify for the five year write-off period.[168] An important consideration under ACRS is that the entire cost of the depreciable property is recovered under the prescribed statutory period, and thus the salvage value of the equipment is not used to reduce the basis upon which the ACRS is computed.[169]

Tax preference rules continue, and thus the excess of the ACRS over straight line cost recovery on leased personal property continues to be a tax preference. In the transfer of computer assets to new corporations and transfers of computer assets to controlled corporations, taxable gain may be recognized to

---

[161] Rev Rul 71-177, 1971-1 CB 5.

[162] If the purchase is bundled, under most state sales tax statutes, (which tax tangible personal property), the whole purchase price will be taxed, rather than just the hardware portion. In exceptional cases taxpayers have persuaded a court to unbundle the purchase and tax only the value of the hardware. *E.g.* DC v Universal Computer Assoc, 465 F2d 615 (DC Cir 1971), Honeywell, Inc v County of Maricopa, 118 Ariz 171, 575 P2d 801 (1977).

[163] IRC §§46(a)(2), 46(c)(2).

[164] IRC §46(c)(7).

[165] IRC §48(c)(2)(A).

[166] IRC §46(a)(3).

[167] IRC §168(c)(2). Property is classed as either 3-, 5-, 10-, or 15-year property.

[168] IRC §168(c)(2)(8).

[169] IRC §168(b)(1).

the transferor if the adjusted basis of the computer assets is less than the amount of liabilities to which the assets are subject plus any other liabilities assumed by the transferor in the transaction.[170] Timing of the computer acquisition is critical because the tax year the computer equipment is placed in service is the year ACRS begins, regardless of the date within that year when the computer equipment was actually acquired. The ACRS tables have a half year of depreciation figured into the rates for the first year of cost recovery.[171]

Taxes and Equipment Leasing

Under ERTA, tax benefits may be transferred from potential lessees to corporate lessors if certain guidelines are followed: (1) the lessor and lessee both elect to treat the lessor as owner of the computer equipment; (2) the lessor is a corporation, but neither a Sub-chapter S corporation nor a personal holding company; (3) the lessor maintains an *at risk* investment of 10 per cent of the adjusted basis of the computer property; (4) the term of the lease cannot exceed 90 per cent of the useful life of the computer equipment; and (5) the computer property must be leased within three months of acquisition.[172] If the user's acquisition team decides that leasing is a more attractive alternative than an outright purchase, careful consideration of all tax implications must be made to ensure that the expected leasing tax benefits are actually realized.

R & D Expense Tax Credit

ERTA also permits a 25 per cent tax credit for the excess of *qualified research expenses* in a given taxable year over the average annual amount of these expenses in a defined *base period*.[173] The net effect is that the software developer, if properly qualified, obtains the benefit of the normal expense deduction for the R&D expenditures as well as this additional tax credit. *Qualified* research expenses include certain in-house costs, plus contracted for research.[174] Research performed outside of the United States, in the social sciences and humanities, and research funded with another person or any governmental entity does not qualify for the credit.[175] Under the R&D tax credit, expenses must be incurred in *carrying on* a trade or busines rather than *in connection with* a trade or business.[176] This carrying on a trade or business requirement will generally limit the R&D credit to actual users of the software R&D, effectively denying the credit to most tax oriented R&D limited partnerships. An R&D

---

[170] IRC §1245(a)(2)(E).

[171] IRC §168(b)(3)(B)(1), 168(b)(3)(B)(1)(iii).

[172] IRC §168(F)(8)(A).

[173] IRC §44F(a).

[174] IRC §44F(b)(2), 44F(b)(2).

[175] IRC §44F(d).

[176] See Hollman & Bernacchi, *Forming And Financing High Technology Ventures*, 1982 USC Computer L Inst §X; and *Is High Tech Getting Low Priority?* Bus Week, Mar 7, 1983, at 112.

limited partnership however, can use only the R&D credit against income resulting from the R&D expenditure.[177]

§3.30   State and Local Taxation

Because taxation at the state and local level has generally been limited to tangible personal property, hardware and firmware fall under state and local taxing schemes.[178] Software, however, due to its intangible nature, is a more difficult issue. Several states have battled over the definition of software as either tangible or intangible personal property.[179] Other states have shifted to a sales tax approach for all software sold separately from hardware.[180] The user's acquisition team should pay close attention to state and local taxes when considering:

1. Local applicable tax laws

2. Bundling hardware and software for ACRS and ITC purposes and the resulting state and local tangible personal property tax exposure

3. Multi-state acquisitions of one original software package and duplicate copies at reduced rates for other locations in other states

4. Consider refund claim procedures in states where the state or local taxing authorities are found after taxes are paid, to have exceeded either constitutional or legislative taxing authority

The user's acquisition team should carefully consider the interplay between federal, state, and local taxes. The interrelationship between tax considerations, and various lease versus purchase alternatives should also be reviewed as well as the overall tax effect the computer acquisition will have on the user's operation.[181]

---

[177] IRC §44F(g)(1)(8).

[178] There is no debate about the sales and property taxability of hardware.

[179] The landmark decision is Commerce Union Bank v Tidwell, 538 SW2d 405 (Tenn 1976), (holding that software is intangible).

[180] E.g., South Carolina, by regulation, expressly taxes the sale of both canned and custom software. Bigelow, Computer L Serv, App §§2-3 2d, SC No 2 (1975). California and Colorado, by regulation, expressly tax the sale of canned software, and the sale of custom software if it is transmitted to the customer in the form of cards, tapes, disks, drums, or optical character recognition (OCR) sheets, but not if just coded (nonmagnetic) on paper, requiring manual entry. Computer L Serv App 2-3 2d, Cal No 1 (1972); Computer L Serv App 2-3 2d, Colo No 2.

[181] An excellent introductory discussion of the tax aspects of leasing arrangements may be found in Contino, *The Leasing of Computer Equipment,* 1982 US Cal Computer L Inst, §VIII.

§3.31   Leasing Versus Purchase

The choice of an acquisition method should not be left to chance, nor should a choice be made without a full consideration of the consequences and alternatives.[182] The two basic options, to purchase or to lease, both have legal, economic, and tax consequences, and the vast number of permutations of each assures that a user will be able to arrange an acquisition which meets its needs.[183]

§3.32   Leasing

The computer industry has historically relied on relatively short-term rental agreements, largely because of the risk of technological and economic obsolescence.[184] Advances in largescale integration of electronic components in the last 10 years have revolutionized computer hardware, and there is every reason to expect equally remarkable advances in the near future.

In a true rental situation, and even in some lease-purchase agreements, the lessor absorbs most of the risk of obsolescence. In a *true* lease, the lessee obtains the use of the equipment for a specific period in return for its periodic payments. Title to the computer remains with the lessor who takes back the equipment at the expiration of the term. The main advantages to the lessee are the possibility of smaller periodic payments, particularly when dealing with non-manufacturing vendors, and minimization of the risk of obsolescence due to either changing data-processing requirements or technological evolution. One disadvantage for the lessee is the inability to use ownership tax credits which may be available, although this factor may be balanced out by the ability to treat the lease payments as an expense of doing business.

A commonly encountered leasing arrangement is the lease-purchase, or *leveraged* lease. In this type of arrangement, the parties contemplate that the lessee will acquire actual ownership of the computer at some point during the relationship. The main advantage for the lessee is the ability to obtain, in effect, 100 per cent financing of the transaction. Leveraged leasing is not without disadvantages, however, as the lessee purchaser is assuming the risk of obsolescence, and is also being tied into a system that may have limited capability for expansion.

In general, all types of leasing arrangements share the advantage of being

---

[182] Among the more common arrangements are those where:
1. Title passes to the *lessee* at the beginning of the term, and a lien is retained by the lessor for security against nonpayment
2. Title passes to lessee after completion of the term with no additional payment
3. Title passes to lessee after completion of the term and payment of some additional amount. Usually the *package option* price is so low the lessee would be foolish *not* to exercise the option

[183] See Eastway & High, *Lease or Buy?* New LJ, July 28, 1979, at 4.

[184] See generally Alexander Grant & Co, Computer Leasing (1980).

somewhat more flexible than outright purchases.[185] Furthermore, maintenance is usually included in a lease agreement, which simplifies that concern. Lease agreements can usually be negotiated with *bug-out* or *walk away* options, if a user is concerned about the suitability, present or future, or possible obsolescence, of the hardware. Leases can often be structured to allow for the acquisition of additional equipment under the same basic financing agreement, which may be a benefit to a user whose data processing requirements are expected to change during the term of the lease. A user should carefully consider the various leasing alternatives from both a financial and a tax viewpoint. Leasing can be a particularly advantageous alternative to purchasing, but only if it fully addresses the user's needs and expectations.

§3.33   Purchasing

The outright purchase of computer hardware may be preferable for some users. Total costs may be lower in the long run, although operating capital will probably be tied-up to a greater extent than under a lease arrangement. Users with substantial cash reserves or for whom the tax benefits of ownership are particularly attractive may find the purchase of a computer to be a profitable investment.

There is the possibility that some or all of a user's software may be compatible with several machines. This capability enhances the flexibility of the user's position with respect to upgrading in the future, and improves the resale value of a used computer.

A used computer system may be quite advantageous for some users. A used system will generally have most of the *kinks* wrung out, and subsequent purchasers may be able to obtain accurate information about the system's capabilities and drawbacks from the former owner. A used system may be dramatically lower priced in terms of initial investment than a newly-manufactured computer of similar configuration. The possibility of higher maintenance costs, however, should not be overlooked.

Purchasing a computer system may afford the user greater flexibility in adding or eliminating equipment or software options, and provides a kind of *walk away* option (selling the system) which may be difficult to negotiate into leasing or lease-purchase arrangements. Purchasing also eliminates one potential pitfall in leasing or lease-purchase arrangements, which is the risk that the lessor will default on any loan involved in the lessor's initial acquisition of the computer. Should such a default occur, the third-party creditor may attempt to repossess the equipment. The possibility of such a default is one factor which the user must consider in evaluating acquisition alternatives. Finally, because of the additional complexities of many lease agreements, purchasing is often a simpler transaction, and from a tax standpoint, adequate documenta-

---

[185] *Id.*

tion of the purchase can be effected more easily.[186]

Insurance

§3.34   Introduction

There are foreseeable and substantial risks involved in the use of electronic data processing equipment in the course of business operations which range from invasion of privacy to contributing to actual business failure. Management must be cognizant of these risks, and provide for adequate resolution of these problems. Preventive measures to reduce risk must be instigated and adequate security provided, even though all risks cannot be controlled. The balance between the risk of economic loss, and the cost to prevent economic loss is called risk management. One option for risk management is insurance, that can help a computer user to minimize the risk of economic loss. The first step in risk management is to indentify and estimate the severity and frequency of all foreseeable risks. The process of identifying economic risk of loss can include discussions with the vendor, insurance agents, and a review of computer trade associations' literature.[187]

Once all foreseeable risks of economic loss have been identified, loss prevention techniques should be utilized in order to minimize those risks. Simple management efficiency in proper storage of files and in security procedures can effect a safer environment for the computer system. Strict adherence to simple precautionary procedures creates a smoother-running, as well as a better protected, computer system. The user should be primarily responsible for designing and implementing loss prevention techniques because the user is most familiar with the daily operations of the computer system. Insurance provides the most significant of the risk management options beyond loss prevention techniques. The insurance industry, aware of the demand for coverage in the electronic data processing area, is moving quickly to fill the void where risk is at an unacceptable level, yet too costly for the user to alleviate. New standard and tailor-made policies are constantly being developed and marketed.

§3.35   Types of Coverage

Once the need for insurance is recognized, the first problem is to secure a policy that effectively meets the user's needs. A policy can be as comprehensive as the user either requires or desires. Coverage by insurance takes several

---

[186] Burroughs Corporation v Barry, 380 F2d 427 (8th Cir 1967) (an early case dealing with problems of distinguishing a *lease* from a *purchase.*)

[187] See generally F Barrett, Attorney's Guide to Insurance and Risk Mangement (1978).

forms, from the general (comprehensive) to the specific (electronic data processing). Comprehensive, or *general liability* insurance, simply covers the damage caused to others (third parties) by the insured. This coverage includes damage to persons or property. There is a distinction between *tangible* and *intangible* property as determined by the individual insurer. Certain computer processes are considered intangible, and therefore are not covered by a comprehensive policy. It is wise to check each step in a computer process with the insurer to see what is covered and what is not.

Most data processing policies available on the market today have been developed primarily for businesses using data processing systems rather than for the manufacturer (or lessor) of computers. Data processing users can now buy electronic data processing (EDP) insurance to cover the areas of greatest potential for loss. EDP insurance covers damage to computers, including repair and replacement costs. This is similar to insurance which covers personal and office property, but it is generally less expensive to exclude computer equipment from personal/office property insurance, and purchase a separate EDP policy. Intangible computer data presents a problem in terms of coverage. But as data is made more tangible via loss prevention technologies (special storage procedures, *etc.*), coverage of these items is possible. The use of loss prevention techniques when insuring computer data may be an express condition precedent to insurance coverage.[188]

Most EDP policies exclude war, government seizure, and nuclear risks as is standard for the entire insurance industry. Certain EDP policies specifically exclude infidelity or any dishonest act, and inefficient or negligent handling of the insured property on the part of the insured's employees or agents, or others to whom the property may be entrusted.[189] EDP policies also require specific identification of all equipment and component parts related to the processing unit. A schedule must be obtained of the units to be covered, and an important item for users to note is whether coverage is sometimes required to be provided for equipment which is rented, leased, or otherwise within the legal responsibility of the insured. Coverage can be modified when the insured increases or decreases its inventory of equipment, and serves the insurer with adequate notice.

Products liability and business interruption are two additional areas in which insurance is available to the user. The familiar tort concept of products liability is complicated by the question of whether a computer software program constitutes a *product* (the damage of which would be damage to property, hence covered). This question of definition and resulting coverage, remains unan-

---

[188] Couch on Insurance §§7:18 (2d 1959).

[189] The risk of injury from incompetent or disatisfied operators is substantial. One author has stated in this regard that "human error has natural disaster capability which beats intentional abuse." Edwards, *Security and the New Technologies,* Banker, Oct 1979, at 41.

swered.[190] Business interruption caused by the use of electronic data processing is a relatively new area, and determining risk is very difficult. The risk can be broken down in various ways, however, each risk category entails a value judgment.

Electronic data processing can cause loss if there is an interruption of the operation. Interruptions can be as short as a few picoseconds, or long enough to be measured in minutes, hours, or even days. Different users can absorb an interruption better than others, depending on the importance of immediate response to each data processing environment. A significant interruption of a user's data processing capability may cause bankruptcy or otherwise jeopardize the continuation of the user's business. Business interruption insurance provides a sum certain in the event of a risk (named in the policy) occurring and causing damage to property. The coverage is intended to sustain the business through this crisis, but is generally not provided for a long period of time. Even relatively small companies can now obtain insurance coverage on their computer systems and computer programs. Small business coverage provides for continued normal operations in the event of computer hardware and software failure or damage.

Another type of risk is the disclosure of sensitive information, which includes disclosures of credit information. Corruption of data being processed can have far-reaching effects and can influence a user's confidence in the information that results from the computer processing. The loss of previously gathered data means that the effort and expense of processing the data has been wasted and represents a financial loss to the user. The user, processor, or service bureau that has lost control of the data could, in certain circumstances, be held liable for an invasion of privacy which the disclosure might have caused.

There is a significant time interval between the signing of a contract for acquisition of a data processing system, and the acceptance of the system by the user as fully meeting the functional specifications and requirements. This time window has the potential for exposing the user to a great deal of risk as the new system is implemented. Very few users adequately address the problem of determining risk of loss or damage to the equipment before acceptance in the purchase contract. The allocation of this risk is relatively simple. By including a clause in the contract that specifies who has the risk of loss and for what time frame, the user can insure the continued operation of the business.

Insurance companies take a very keen interest in the security measures in force at the insured's site because these measures play a significant role in determining certain types of risk. Computer security has been said to be the combination of human and machine monitoring intended to prevent unauthorized activity. A computer security system must prevent or detect an almost infinite number of schemes, as varied as imaginable. Computer-related crimes

---

[190] The UCC definition of what constitutes a *good* (§1-102 (1980)) may be of some use when litigation arises in this context. See generally Johnson, *Liability Security Need Seen,* Computerworld, Dec 6, 1982, at 83 (the premiums for a typical $1 million E & O (errors-and-omission) policy cost between $10,000-15,000).

cut across the entire spectrum of human activity. The security risks which are present in a user's data processing operation are a key factor in determining what precautionary methods to institute. A user must make a decision as to the amount of risk which needs to be covered by insurance. To do this effectively requires extensive knowledge of the problems associated with data processing security. Computer security is a new area, which may account for the lack of management awareness of security requirements. Factors that should be considered include:

1. Access to terminals and access codes

2. Probability that unauthorized acts can be perpetrated

3. Countermeasures, e.g., limiting physical access and screening of personnel

4. Contingency measures, e.g., remote location and immediate back-up capability

5. Monitoring and review procedures

It benefits each user to embark on a stringent security risk recognition program, and then develop some type of prevention program. A comprehensive risk avoidance program, combined with insurance, should minimize the risk of loss in a user's data processing operations.

§3.36 Errors and Omissions

Data processing errors and omissions (E & O) insurance policies are generally designed to provide coverage for data processing service organizations that perform data processing functions for other businesses. This insurance covers these firms' risks of loss from error, malfunction, or mistake. These companies may reduce their liability to customers through contractual provisions, but some responsibility must remain. An E & O policy is, in effect, professional liability insurance providing a specialized and limited type of coverage. Compared to general comprehensive insurance, E & O insurance is designed to insure members of a particular professional group by limiting the liability which may arise out of special risks such as negligence, omissions, mistakes, and errors inherent in the practice of the profession.[191] E & O policies frequently overlap with another policy, completed operations, which covers faulty workmanship discovered after the insured leaves the claimant's site. It would be wise for the user to check these two policies, and to guarantee that the same coverage is not being paid for twice. E & O coverage can be tailored to fit individual user needs through the use of definitions and exclusions. The need to match the coverage purchased with the coverage which is required is critical and cannot be overstressed.

---

[191] Grieb v Citizens Casualty Co, 313 Wis 2d 552, 148 NW2d 103 (1967), *citing* Couch.

E & O policies covering data processing present a problem as to the discovery of the error (timely claims are impossible if the discovery was made *after* termination of the policy). Some solutions to the timely claim problem are: (1) self-insurance; (2) purchasing an extended discovery endorsement to supplement the policy; (3) purchasing a policy which includes an extended discovery period; or (4) purchasing a new policy (after the first expires) which covers *prior acts.* Some E & O policies contain exclusions as to occurrences taking place, for example, more than 10 days after discovery of the error. The purpose of these exclusions is to prevent the employer from profiting by its own failure to act. The problem of indemnity in the E & O policies area is extremely complex.[192]

§3.37   Areas of Dispute

Problems with insurance typically arise when a claim is made. The insurance company may send the user a reservation of rights letter, outlining the company's obligations should a lawsuit ensue. Generally, claims based on intentional torts or seeking punitive damages are not covered by insurance policies. The third-party plaintiff's attorney will often use these intentional tort and punitive damage claims to attempt to procure a settlement. The insured usually places itself in the hands of the insurer, relying on the company's *good faith* duty to defend. The insured, however, is free to retain counsel in regard to the non-covered claims. Insurance companies, in turn, may ask for a declaratory judgment concerning their liabilities on the policy. This action for a declaratory judgment satisfies their good faith duty to defend.[193]

Other problems related to the filing of a claim with the insurer are retrospection, aggregate limit, and consent to settle. Retrospection involves the difficulty of pinpointing (for claim purposes) exactly when the negligent act that caused the damage occurred. This problem can be solved by purchasing a *prior acts* coverage policy which covers these contingencies. The problem of aggregate limit is merely that the insurance policy will cover only a certain specific time period, for a specific amount of money. If the user is concerned about the aggregate limit, there are several options to obtain adequate coverage. One of these options is an *umbrella policy* which, as its name implies, covers the user's other policies, and makes up the difference if one of them should exceed its aggregate limit (providing, of course, that the umbrella policy's own aggregate limit is not thereby exceeded). Consent to settle simply means the user's right to consent to any settlement by the insurance company. If the user does not agree to the settlement, the case will go to trial. Generally, however, the user's consent will be asked for as a matter of course.

---

[192] 13A Couch on Insurance 48:166 (2d rev ed 1982), I Woods, The Insurance Aspects of Computer Litigation (1979). See also 16 Couch on Insurance 62:184 (2d rev ed 1983).

[193] American Employers Ins Co v Goble Aircraft Sp, 131 NYS2d 393 (1954).

A possible area of dispute when the user and the user's insurer go to court is the duty of the insurance defense attorney. Although retained as an employee of the insurer, the insurance defense attorney owes an absolute fiduciary duty to the insured, i.e., the user.[194] Third party claims present an interesting twist to the good faith criterion. Under the *Royal Globe Ins Co v Superior Court* doctrine, third party claimant may sue the insurer of the user under the Unfair Insurance Practices Act, for not effectuating "prompt, fair, and equitable settlements" of claims in which the liability has become "reasonably clear."[195] *Royal Globe* was an example of *bad faith* by the insurer, in which the court held that where the insurer operates in bad faith against the third party claimant, the third party claimant may sue the insurer directly for punitive damages.[196]

Federal Leasing Inc v Underwriters at Lloyds, which briefly discusses the use of insurance in the computer field, stands as a classic example of how to use insurance to minimize a risk.[197] The parties contracted for insurance designed to insure against the risk that early terminations of a computer lease would occasion losses not recoverable through remarketing.[198] In 1977, a massive change in the computer market, caused by IBM's introduction of the Series 3000 and the discounting of earlier models, triggered an unprecedented number of lease terminations by customers of Federal. The circumstances typified the "very risks covered by the indemnity insurance policies."[199] Federal's losses totaled $23 million whereas Lloyd's had collected premiums of only $3.75 million.

Insurance, then, is an important area to consider when contracting for computer products and services.[200] Continuing concern should be focused on risk

---

[194] *Id.*

[195] Royal Globe Ins Co v Superior Ct, 23 Cal 3d 880, 153 Cal Rep 842 (1979). Several states have enacted Unfair Insurance Trade Practices Act. Cal Ins Code §790 *et seq* (West 1972).

[196] See generally Wagenseil, *Royal Globe: Reasonably Unclear Liability for Insurers,* 678 Ins LJ 376 (1979).

[197] 487 F Supp 1248 (D Md 1980).

[198] Federal purchased computers from manufacturers, and marketed them through lease and conditional sales contracts, borrowing the initial purchase money from investors, and then assigning to the investor part of the lease payments. While the lease was for a term of several years, the user could terminate earlier and without penalty merely by giving notice.

[199] Federal Leasing Inc v Underwriters at Lloyds, 487 F Supp 1248 (D Md 1980).

[200] A recent addition to insurance coverage is one put out by St. Paul called the St. Paul Mini-Computer Policy. It is designed to insure the small computer components that are being used in a regular office setting (not housed in special computer rooms). The policy provides broad *all risks* coverage in three areas:
1. Data processing equipment—the hardware owned by the insured or for which the insured is legally responsible
2. Data, media, and computer programs—covers direct physical loss or damage to data, media, and computer programs
3. Extra expense—coverage for continuing normal operation of the insured's busi-

management by all computer users.[201]

Negotiating Strategies

§3.38   Introduction

Among the concerns of the user's acquisition team should be the negotiating strategies which the team should follow, as well as the awareness of different vendor marketing traits and ploys commonly used in the computer industry. The following brief discussion is designed to acquaint the acquisition team with basic negotiating strategies and vendor-user marketing ploys.

§3.39   Macro-Negotiating Strategies

User Acquisition Team Leader's Control

Probably the most important negotiating concept is for the user to maintain control over the negotiating process. A single negotiating leader for the user's acquisition team should be responsible for initiating each meeting with the vendor as well as taking minutes of the meeting. All discussions, correspondence, and contract drafts should be coordinated through the acquisition team leader. If possible, the acquisition team should draft the initial acquisition contract. Many vendors, however, have standard form contracts which they will insist on using as the initial contract negotiation starting point.

Acquisition Team Membership

The acquisition team should consist of high-level management to ensure that the vendor realizes the importance that the user places on the computer acquisition. Having the user's decision-makers involved in the negotiation process can also accelerate the contract negotiations because the "*authority to act,*" whether it be agreeing on minor points of dispute or resolving the major issues in dispute, is at all times present. High-level user management involvement will also ensure that the vendor has equal decision-making authority on its marketing-negotiating team. This user and vendor decisionmaking authority could range from the data processing manager and a regional vendor sales manager in a relatively small computer acquisition to several senior vice-

---

ness in the event of damage or destruction of the data processing equipment, data, or media
There is no coverage for program supportive documentation such as flow charts, record formats, or narrative descriptions.

[201] See generally Greene, Risk and Insurace (3d ed 1973); C Williams, Jr & R Heins, Risk Managment and Insurance (3d ed 1976).

presidents representing the user, and the vendor's national marketing managers in a large computer acquisiton.

§3.40   Micro-Negotiating Strategies

Sunshine and Storms

In their text, Brandon and Segelstein recommend that negotiating sessions alternate between very easy sessions concerning areas where the user and vendor can easily agree, to sessions where there are major points of dispute. [202] This balance between easy and hard negotiating sessions will aid in building a solid business relationship between the user and vendor over the term of the contract, and will also minimize the possibility of a total breakdown of the negotiations, e.g., one party walking out of the negotiations.

Issue Balancing

The user's negotiation team should be prepared to establish a priority list of the points to be negotiated before the beginning of negotiations.[203] The acquisition team leader should be prepared to argue forcefully for key issues which the user wants, and also be ready to concede on key issues which the vendor cannot concede on. If an issue is equally important to user and vendor, but no agreement can initially be reached, the issue should be put aside temporarily. To keep the negotiation process moving, other points can then be negotiated while a major stumbling block type of issue can be individually analyzed by user and vendor. After separate analysis, the stumbling block issue can be raised again in an attempt to resolve the issue.

Impasse Points

The user acquisition team should be prepared to suspend all negotiations temporarily if there is a major disagreement on many key issues. A temporary suspension will allow both sides to reconsider their positions, and also to provide a cooling-off period during which the entire acquisition process can be reviewed to determine if further negotiations would be fruitful.[204]

Good Guy—Bad Guy Scenario

The user's acquisition team leader, as well as the vendor's team leader, will many times be perceived by the opposing team as the negative factor in the negotiation process. A second team member for the user and vendor acquisition teams should be available to soothe tempers or suggest alternatives when

---

[202] Brandon & Segelstein, Data Processing Contracts: *Structures, Contents, and Negotiations* 36 (1976).

[203] *See* generally, Bellow & Moulton, The Lawyering Process: Negotiation (1981).

[204] Zartman & Berman, The Practical Negotiator 69-80 (1982).

negotiations became emotionally *hot*.[205] The user's acquisition team leader, however, should remain in control.[206]

§3.41   Vendor Contract Ploys

Form Contracts—Nothing Else Written

Some vendors attempt to manipulate personal relationships between the vendor's marketing staff and other key members of the user's staff as an excuse to use the vendor's standard form contract and not memorialize in writing additional agreements between user and vendor that should be included in the writing. Auer and Harris state that a vendor uses the three "*R's*" of selling—rapport, rationale, and relationship—to prevent agreements outside of the form contract from being included in the final contract.[207] The most vivid example of the problems that result when personal relationships form the foundation of a computer acquisition is when user and vendor personnel move on to other jobs or retire.[208] The remaining personnel are then left with a one-sided vendor contract.

Vendors will also often downplay the importance of the contract by not even mentioning the contract until all technical concerns have been discussed, and then suggest in a casual way that the *final paper work* is all that is left to finalize the user-vendor agreement.[209] Some vendors will even go so far as to delay in returning a copy of the signed contract to the user. This technique makes it difficult for the user to understand the final agreement, and equally difficult for the user's attorney to analyze the agreement in the event of subsequent disputes.

Changes Must Receive Corporate Approval

This common vendor negotiating tactic is quite easy for vendor marketing representatives to utilize successfully due to the surface reasonableness of the statement that the standard form contract cannot be changed without higher corporate vendor approval. Vendors particularly like this tactic because:

1. It forces the user to justify the user's negotiating position
2. It allows the vendor to hide behind the general concept that this is the way to do business in the industry

---

[205] See Walton & McKersie, A Behavioral Theory of Labor Negotiations 249-67 (1965).

[206] Brandon & Segelstein, *supra*, note 202, at 35.

[207] Auer & Harris, Computer Contract Negotiations 12 (1976).

[208] Walton & McKersie, A Behavioral Theory of Labor Negotiations 234-39 (1965).

[209] See generally Kennedy, Benson, & McMillan, Managing Negotiations 99-110 (1982).

3. It adds credibility to the vendor's concern for a speedy conclusion of the negotiating process

4. The ploy forces the user to disclose all of its requests for changes to the standard form contract at the beginning of the acquisition negotiations, and it becomes difficult for the user to later on request additional changes

5. The tactic allows the vendor representatives the option of appearing to have limited authority, thereby allowing the vendor to probe the user's true bargaining position with several counter-offers from the vendor's *corporate management,* while not disclosing the actual vendor position[210]

The user's acquisition team should realize that the *corporate approval for any changes* tactic is just a vendor ploy for unsophisticated users. The user's acquisition team should refuse any oral or *side letter* agreements which will not be included in the contract, but which are offered by the vendor's marketing representatives as alternatives to obtaining vendor corporate approval of changes in the vendor's standard form contract. The user's acquisition team should also clearly state at the outset of the negotiations, or even before the negotiations are begun, that various clauses in the standard form contract will be subject to negotiations. Taking a hard line on the vendor changes requiring the *corporate approval* tactic will aid in:

1. Increasing the responsibility level of vendor representatives who already have authority to change the standard vendor contract

2. Determining who on the vendor side has true authority

3. Ensuring the validity of changes approved at the vendor corporate level, which will in turn assure the vendor's performance of the contract[211]

§3.42 Vendor Price Ploys

Our Best Price

The vendor will attempt to convince the user that the offered price is the vendor's best price, leading to the implication that the vendor is at its bottom level of profitability. Price negotiations and negotiations over soft dollar concessions, such as maintenance and documentation, consequently appear to be futile. To support a vendor assertion of a best price, the user should obtain a *most favored nation* clause from the vendor concerning price and other key contract clauses.[212] Unless there are similar users with which the vendor has also included a most favored nation clause in the contract, this may be more of a contracting ploy for the user to use against the vendor. If there are many

---

[210] Auer & Harris, *supra* note 207, at 25-27.

[211] Illich, The Art and Skill of Succcessful Negotiation 89-93 (1973).

[212] A most favored nation clause forces the vendor to give the previously contracting user any terms which are given to a later contracting user.

users who have acquired similar computer products and services from the vendor, a most favored nations clause is an effective method of insuring that the vendor is really quoting its best price.[213]

The Proverbial Impending Price Increase

This vendor marketing ploy follows the classic pattern of an announced price increase effective at a future specified date. The vendor hopes this will result in a large volume of users scrambling to sign contracts before the price increase becomes effective. A related ploy is for vendors to tell their most favored customers of an impending price increase and ask the customers to sign various types of price protection contracts without negotiating either price or other terms of the contracts. The easiest way to avoid these price increase ploys is to require a full review and approval of all computer contracts on a deliberately paced schedule.[214]

The General Services Administration Will Not Let Us

This tactic is used by a computer vendor as a method to end negotiations on a particular issue by simply stating that the General Services Administration (GSA) will not permit any of the user's proposals for changes. The federal government is claimed to be the vendor's biggest customer, and consequently terms of the GSA contract can not be varied by the vendor in its negotiations with nongovernmental users. This tactic is sadly successful in many instances because users do not take the time to learn what is contained in the GSA contract. Generally, contracts between the vendor and the government are computed by a separate vendor marketing division. Vendor representatives outside of this specialized governmental division may not even know the terms and conditions of the GSA contract. A good user response to this GSA ploy is to ask for a copy of the GSA contract. If the vendor does have a problem with a GSA contract provisions, such as a GSA *most favored nations* clause, the user's acquisition team can suggest ways to make its acquisition differ from that which the vendor is marketing to the federal government under the GSA contract terms. Many GSA vendor concerns may be real. The user acquisition team must be willing to exert enough pressure on the vendor to force the real GSA problems out onto the negotiating table so that the true GSA concerns can be resolved.[215]

Trade-In Credit Tactic

This vendor tactic attempts to settle any user concerns that the user is being locked into a particular product. The vendor will offer trade-in credits on old computer products for newer products from the vendor. Naturally, the trade-

---

[213] Auer & Harris, Computer Contract Negotiations 14-16.

[214] *Id.* 17-19.

[215] *Id* 33-36.

ins are only valid for equipment sold by the same vendor. The user's acquisition team should carefully analyze any vendor contract clauses which use vague terms to define the conditions under which trade-ins will follow the then existing *vendor trade-in policies.* Specific percentages or trade-in formulas should be included in the final contract. When negotiating for new computer products which will upgrade existing computer products, the user's acquisition team should separate any vendor discounts from the previously agreed upon trade-in credits. If necessary, the user should even consider selling, if possible, the older equipment in the open market, and thus obtain the full price from the buyer and contract commissions from the vendor, without regard to any linkage between trade-in credits on old equipment and discounts on new equipment.[216]

Setting a Precedent

This vendor tactic relies on the vendor's perception that the user has little information on other contracts between the vendor and other users. The *setting a precedent* ploy, therefore, is based on user ignorance, and can be used by the vendor in many different situations. The user's acquisition team should try to obtain a list of all of the vendor's alleged concessions. If the vendor will not supply a list of concessions, the user can attempt to obtain some of this information from other users, or from various computer contracting report services.[217] The user can also insist on a *most favored nations* clause. Any side letter agreements by the vendor should only be considered as acceptable alternatives to the user if they are formally included in the contract. Thus problems resulting from integration clauses in the final contract may be avoided.

§3.43 Other Negotiating Concerns

As with any negotiated contract, there are numerous negotiating strategies and tactics which can be used by vendors and users. In brief, some additional tactics include: (1) *here is everything you need* to solve all of your data processing needs; (2) *just try our new system* in which a trial period is set, and only if the user *likes* the computer products or services will the vendor negotiate the terms of the contract; (3) the key or *hot button* tactic in which the vendor agrees to provide key items which the user really wants, and then quickly glosses over the rest of the standard form contract provisions; and (4) *we did not figure the deal this new way* in which the vendor states that any last minute changes in the standard form contract or other requests will cause the entire negotiations

---

[216] *Id* 27-30.

[217] One such computer contracting loose leaf service is published by Sunscape International, Inc of Orlando, Florida and is entitled CN Report: Computer Contract Resource Service. Sunscape also publishes a newsletter entitled Computer Negotiations Report which contains information regarding long-term vendor strategies.

process to begin anew. There are obviously as many variations to these negotiating tactics and ploys as there are vendors and users.[218] The important point is for the user's acquition team to be aware of these negotiating tactics and ploys, and to be ready to respond in a timely and unified fashion against them.

Conclusion

§3.44   Remarks

This chapter on computer contracts has reviewed a wide range of legal-economic concerns which a computer user must address in the acquisition of computational resources. The most important step in the acquisition process is to assemble an acquisition team to prepare a complete request for proposal (RFP). Various members of the acquisition team will logically be concerned with their relative speciality areas, *e.g.,* the data processing manager with technical computer requirements, the financial representative with leasing or purchase concerns, the legal representative with the various contract clauses, and the tax advisor with tax issues. The primary responsibility of the acquisition team leader is to ensure that all of the team members perform their respective jobs in a timely and integrated manner. Users should also be advised, as well as each of the acquisition team members, that no computational acquisition is perfect. The rapid rate of technological improvement dictates that any acquisition will be technologically dated in a few years or even a few months. The important point, however, is that firms need computational resources, and thus decisions on actual products and services must be made. It is also important to note that computational resource acquisition decisions have major and long term impacts on the user. These acquisition decisions, therefore, should be made in an orderly and thoughtful manner.

---

[218] Fisher & Ury, Getting to YES: Negotiating Without Giving In 134-50 (1981).

Antitrust Considerations in the Computer Industry

4

§4.21   Amount Charged for license

§4.01   Generally

The computer industry has witnessed a plethora of antitrust litigation. One reason is that developments in computer technology foster natural monopolies.[1] For example, when a vendor develops a new product, a natural monopoly is created which exists until competitors are able either to reverse engineer or to develop comparable or compatibile products. Antitrust violations also may arise when an innovator, instead of creating a new product, changes an existing design solely to frustrate competition. The nature of computer equipment is another factor which has precipitated antitrust litigation.[2] The term *computer* frequently is used to refer to one unit, but in fact, a computer consists of interconnected components, all of which are necessary to process information. An understanding of the functions of these components elucidates the reason why the computer industry has been a breeding ground for antitrust litigation.

Computer components are divided into two broad categories, hardware and software, and each category is further divided into several subcategories.

Hardware consists of five functional components: input, memory, control, logic, and output.[3] Control, logic and some portions of memory comprise the central processing unit (CPU). Input, output, and memory functions are performed by various devices generally known as peripheral devices. Peripheral devices are connected to the CPU at a point which is referred to as an interface or *shared boundary*. The shared boundary is created by a complex electrical plug.

Not every peripheral device, however, is plug-compatible with every CPU.[4] Manufacturers of both CPUs and peripheral devices design their components

---

[1] *See* Telex Corp v IBM Corp, 367 F Supp 258, 271-73 (ND Okla 1973), for a discussion of the growth of the computer industry. For a discussion of computer developments from the 1940s through the 1970s, *see* Honeywell, Inc v Sperry Rand Corp, 1974-1 Trade Cas (CCH) ¶74874 (D Minn Oct 19, 1973). For a discussion of antitrust enforcement during the computer industry's expansion in the national market, see Kirkpatrick, *Antitrust Enforcement in the Seventies*, 30 Cath UL Rev 431 (1981).

[2] See generally Jacobs, *Computer Technology (Hardware and Software): Some Legal Implications for Antitrust, Copyrights and Patents*, 1 Rutgers J Computers & L 50 (1970).

[3] See C. Sippl & C. Sippl, Computer Dictionary and Handbook 202 (2d ed 1972).
The function of each sub-category has been stated as: the function of input is to get instructions and data, prepared in some computer-readable form into the computer. Storage (memory) retains the data and instructions so entered, as well as the intermediate and final results of processing. Control directs the whole process, in accordance with pre-determined instructions kept in storage. Logic performs the arithmetic and logical operations. Output disgorges the requisite information in accordance with instructions.

[4] See generally G. Davis Computer Data Processing (1969); Frost, *IBM Plug-to-Plug Peripheral Devices*, 16 Datamation 24 (1970); Menkhaus, *Terminals: Pipelines to Computer Power*, 17 Bus Automation 48 (1978). See also Slutsker, The Peripherals Proliferation: Technological Advances and Productivity Gains Spur Funding of Computer Peripherals Startups Despite the Country's Recession, Venture 58-60 (1980). A generally-ac-

to be compatible with one another, but not all manufacturers produce both CPUs and peripherals. Those manufacturers who do not produce all parts of a computer must be sensitive to technological changes within the industry in order for their components to remain plug-compatible with the components of other vendors. Computational innovations require these manufacturers to alter the designs of their products to reflect the design changes of other manufacturers.

Software is a set of coded instructions which detail the steps necessary for data processing.[5] Software is divided into three subcategories: systems software, application software, and documentation. Systems software is a set of generalized instructions designed to provide the control and logic functions for a particular type of CPU and all of the peripherals attached to the CPU. While the CPU actually manipulates the data, it is the systems software that gives the CPU instructions, as well as retrieval and input information to and from the peripheral devices.[6]

Application software is a set of coded instructions designed to perform a specific task or goal.[7] For example, systems software may tell the CPU how to add, but it is application software that specifies what numbers are to be added together. As with the various hardware components, most application software only works on one specific hardware configuration. Documentation is the operating manual or instructions which explain the characteristics of either the hardware, or the systems or application software. Documentation may also include training and instruction provided by the vendor to the customer.

Rapid technological changes and the sophisticated design of computer components have shaped an industry in which few manufacturers actually produce all the parts of a computer. Large vendors are able to absorb the research and development costs necessary to maintain technological parity with competitors, while smaller vendors, who provide only a portion of computer components, survive by concentrating on developing a limited product line which is plug-compatible with the components of full-system vendors.[8]

---

cepted definition of a plug compatible product is a device which can be used in place of another device without substantial electronic, mechanical or programming modifications and without significant change in the operation of the computer system.

[5] 458 F Supp at 428. See generally Software Industry Analysis, in Computer Yearbook 98 (1972). See also Bender, Computer Law: Evidence and Procedure §§2.02-2.06 (1980); Stern, *Restricting Customers' Use of Software to Particular Computers - Proprietor's Right or Competitive House?*, 1 Computer L Rep 194 (1982) [hereinafter cited as Stern].

[6] The Supreme Court of Tennessee has stated that systems software controls the hardware, and is fundamental and necessary to its functioning. Commerce Union Bank v Tidwell, 538 SW2d 405, 406 (Tenn 1976).

[7] *Id.* The court distinguished applications software as that which "instruct the central processing unit of the computer to perform the fundamental computations, comparisons, and sequential steps required to take incoming information and compute the desired output." See also Note, *Sales and Use Tax of Computer Software - Is Software Tangible Personal Property?*, 27 Wayne L Rev 1503, 1508 (1981).

[8] *See* Honeywell, Inc v Sperry Rand Corp, 1974-1 Trade Cas (CCH) ¶74874, at 95933 (D Minn Oct 19, 1973).

This Chapter will discuss the major antitrust developments in the computer industry. In the course of the chapter, computers will be considered in one of three classes: mainframes, minicomputers, or microcomputers.[9]

Mainframe computers were the first developed, and are the largest, fastest, and the most expensive of the three types. Mainframes are general purpose computers, designed to perform multiple tasks and to "handle a wide variety of problems."[10] Minicomputers, introduced in 1963 by Digital Equipment Corporation, are essentially the same as mainframes, but incorporate technological advances which allow for smaller and cheaper computers.[11] Minicomputers are also general purpose computers, but they cannot process data as rapidly as mainframes. The newest class of computers, microcomputers, are less expensive, smaller, and slower than the other two classes of computers, although microcomputers can also be considered general purpose computers.

The antitrust litigation for each class of computers will be discussed separately. Antitrust considerations in the patent and copyright areas will also be reviewed.

Mainframes

§4.02   Bundling

A tying arrangement or bundling is illegal under the Sherman or Clayton Acts if the following four general conditions are found to exist:

> First, there must be more than a minimum market effect—a requirement to be derived from the specific language of the Clayton Act and from the Sherman Act requirement that there must be a restraint of trade. Second, there must be two products and not merely the sale of a single product—a requirement derived from the nature of a tie itself. Third, there must in fact be tying—as distinguished from the simple sale of both the tying and tied products. Fourth, there must be no showing of justification.[12]

---

[9] Mainframes, minicomputers, and microcomputers are constantly changing, and as further developments increase their sophistication, these three classifications may be redefined. Therefore, when making any comparisons between or among computer systems within each of these broad classes, this chapter is using those classifications currently recognized in the computer industry.

[10] See generally Ratchford & Ford, *A Study of Prices and Market Shares in the Computer Mainframe Industry*, 49 J Bus 194 (1976). *But cf* Brock, *A Study of Prices and Market Shares in the Computer Mainframe Industry*, 52 J Bus 119 (1979).

[11] Davis, *A Fresh View of Mini and Microcomputers*, Computer Design, May 1974. See also Epstein & Bessel, *Minicomputers are Made of This*, 2 Computer Decisions 10 (Aug 1970); *Mini-Menagerie: A Survey of the Minicomputer Field*, 2 Computer Decisions 20 (Aug 1970).

[12] Frost, *Tying Clauses and Package Licensing*, 28 U Pitt L Rev 207 (1966). See also Pantages, *A Look at Unbundling*, 15 Datamation 85 (1969).

The major antitrust case involving bundling was decided prior to the development of modern electronic computers. In 1932, the United States brought suit against International Business Machines Corp. (IBM) and Remington Rand, alleging that the leasing contracts of the two companies violated §3 of the Clayton Act.[13] The allegations were based on an agreement between IBM, who controlled 81 per cent of the market for tabulating cards, and Remington Rand, who controlled the remaining 19 per cent, to include a clause in their tabulating machine leases that prevented the lessee from purchasing punch cards from any one other than the lessor.[14] If this clause was breached, the lease was terminated.

IBM claimed that the clause was consistent with its patent rights, and that the tying arrangement was necessary to protect its goodwill. The Supreme Court dismissed both claims, and, commenting on the protection of goodwill allegation, stated that there was:

> [N]o contention that others than appellant cannot meet these requirements (quality of the cards). . . . [t]he suggestion that without the tying clause an adequate supply of cards would not be forthcoming from competitive sources is not supported by the evidence. [The] Appellant is not prevented from proclaiming the virtues of its own cards or warning against the danger of using, in its machines, cards which do not conform to the necessary specifications, or even from making its leases conditional upon the use of cards which conform to them. For aught that appears such measures would protect its good will, without the creation of monopoly or resort to the suppression of competition.[15]

The judgment entered against IBM proved significant in two ways. The decree pointed toward practices that later haunted IBM in other, computer oriented antitrust suits. The judgment also became a public record that could

---

[13] United States v IBM Corp, 13 F Supp 11 (SDNY 1935), *affd*, 298 US 131 (1936). §3 of the Clayton Act, 15 USC §14 states that:
> It shall be . . . unlawful for any person engaged in commerce, in the course of such commerce, to lease . . . machinery . . . whether patented or unpatented, for use, . . . within the United States, . . . on the condition . . . that the leasee shall not use . . . goods, wares, merchandise, . . . supplies or other commodities of a competitor or competitors of the lessor, . . . where the effect of such lease, . . . or such condition, . . . may be to substantially lessen competition or tend to create a monopoly in any line of commerce.

[14] 298 US at 136.

[15] *Id* 139-40. The Court sounded an important theme that later became the standard for evaluating a tying arrangement; a tying arrangement is not justified if there are other, less restrictive, means of achieving the same goal. The Court stated that:
> [W]e can perceive no tenable basis for an exception in favor of a condition whose substantial benefit to the lessor is the elimination of business competition and the creation of monopoly, rather than the protection of its goodwill, and where it does not appear that the latter can not be achieved by methods which do not tend to monopoly and are not otherwise unlawful.

be used against IBM to illustrate a history of *bad acts.* This in effect opened up a line of attack on IBM similar to that used against Alcoa in *United States v Aluminum Co of America.*[16] IBM was again sued by the United States in 1952 for alleged violations of §§1 and 2 of the Sherman Act.[17] The government challenged IBM's business practices in its tabulating machines and electronic data processing equipment divisions.[18] This 1952 suit charged that IBM owned 90 per cent of the tabulating machines in use, and sold 90 per cent of the tabulating cards used in the United States. The complaint was directed at IBM's policy of leasing rather than selling its equipment. IBM's actions, particularly its lease policy, were alleged to constitute monopolization. The consent decree entered in 1956 substantiated the government's contentions that IBM's lease practices, along with its market share, had permitted IBM to tie the sale of its cards to the leasing of its tabulating machines.[19]

The consent decree required IBM to change its marketing policy. IBM was ordered to sell its machines at terms not substantially more advantageous to IBM than the terms and conditions of its lease.[20] IBM was also required to aid in the development of a used machine market,[21] and to provide technical training, at nondiscriminatory rates, to any person (other than another manufacturer) who was engaged in or who intended to engage in the business of repairing IBM's equipment.[22] IBM also was instructed to create a separate subsidiary to handle all of IBM's service bureau business.[23] The decree further directed IBM to grant a nonexclusive patent license to those who requested it,[24] and to provide those licensees with IBM's technical information.[25] The decree applied to IBM's electronic data processing equipment, but as noted earlier, IBM's pre-computer marketing practices affected its activities in the developing market for modern computers.

§4.03   *United States v IBM*

Thirteen years after the 1956 consent decree, on January 17, 1969, the

---

[16] United States v Aluminum Co of Am, 148 F2d 416 (2d Cir 1945).

[17] United States v IBM, 1 Computer L Serv Rep (Callaghan) 41 (1956); Biglow, *United States v IBM, 1969-1973,* 5 Computer L Serv (Callaghan) §7-1, art 6 (1974).

[18] IBM did not deliver its first general purpose computer until three years after the government filed its complaint. The consent decree, however, included IBM's electronic data processing equipment.

[19] United States v IBM, 1956 Trade Cas (CCH) ¶68245 (SDNY 1956).

[20] *Id* at ¶71123; Art IV of the Consent Decree.

[21] *Id* at ¶71123; Art V.

[22] *Id* at ¶71126; Art IX.

[23] *Id* at ¶71125-6; Art VIII.

[24] *Id* at ¶71127-8; Art XI.

[25] *Id* at ¶71129-30; Art XIV.

Department of Justice (DOJ) filed a civil antitrust suit against IBM.[26] In its complaint the government alleged that IBM, commencing in or about 1961, had monopolized and attempted to monopolize the market for general purpose electronic digital computers in violation of §2 of the Sherman Act.[27] The complaint charged that IBM had maintained a pricing policy under which hardware, software, and related support were sold at a single price.[28] The government again alleged that IBM was employing illegal bundling tactics. Other allegations included IBM's use of software support and related facilities to preclude competition, premature announcements of new products and introduction of new products at low-profit margins to restrain entry, and domination of the educational market by discriminatory allowances for educational institutions.[29] The suit sought to enjoin IBM from further activity in any of the alleged practices. In addition to injunctive relief the government sought such "divorcement, divestiture and reorganization" of IBM as might be appropriate to restore competition in the market for general purpose digital computer. The government amended its complaint on January 14, 1975 to provide that the attempt to monopolize and the monopolization had continued to the date of the amended complaint. The market was stated to be "general purpose digital computer *systems.*" (emphasis in original) The product market was further broadened to include certain "peripherals equipment" submarkets. Finally, the amended complaint charged that IBM's pricing and marketing policies had created a lease-oriented environment that raised barriers to entry or expansion in the relevant market and submarkets.[30]

After 13 years of judicial battling, and nearly six years after the trial began, in 1982 the suit was dropped. The dismissal was called an "unconditional surrender" by a partner of the New York firm of Cravath, Swaine & Moore, which directed IBM's defense.[31] William F. Baxter, Assistant Attorney General in charge of the Antitrust Division of the Department of Justice, announced that his review of the case "convinced him that the costs of continuation, weighed against the government's likelihood of success and the potential benefits to be obtained, warranted dismissal."[32]

Baxter's conclusions contradicted those of four different administrations, including two Democratic and two Republican presidents. In addition, five previous assistant attorneys general in charge of the Antitrust Division had

---

[26] United States v IBM Corp, No 69 Civ 200 (SDNY Jan 17, 1969).

[27] General purpose computers are defined as computers with general commercial applications which are offered for sale or lease in standard model configurations. See generally Bigelow, *United States v IBM, 1969-1973,* 5 Computer L Serv (Callaghan) §7-1, arts 6, 2 (1974).

[28] *Id* at 2-3.

[29] *Id.*

[30] *See* United States v IBM Corp, 618 F2d 923, 925 n 1 (2d Cir 1980).

[31] *IBM's Antitrust Troubles Are Not Finished Yet,* Bus Week, Jan 25, 1982, at 24.

[32] See Trade Reg Rep (CCH), No 524 (Jan 11, 1982) (text of Department of Justice Release of Jan 8, 1982).

each reviewed and found merit in the case. Baxter found several flaws in a suit which had generated over 100,000 pages of testimony, 2,500 depositions, 66 million pages of documents, and created work for some 300 lawyers.[33] Among the suit's alleged fatal errors was an allegation by the government not that IBM had achieved a monopoly position illegally, but that IBM had maintained a monopoly by ceans of illegal actions against competitors. The alleged so-called *bad acts* concerned "computer systems that are not included within the market IBM was alleged to have monopolized."[34] Baxter said the most convincing episode was against Control Data Corp., which settled with IBM. Bad acts were also committed against peripheral companies, most of whom sued IBM and lost.[35]

According to Baxter, even if the government had won, injunctions or structural reorganizations would have been inappropriate. Baxter believed that it would be impossible to fashion injunctions that would be meaningful outside of the exact circumstances under which the suit arose, and thus injunctions to prevent similar conduct could only have been drafted in the specific context in which the alleged violations occurred, which was some 13 years before. It was also feared that the injunctive measures would merely parrot the antitrust laws already in effect. Baxter said that other "conduct concerning manufacturers of IBM-compatible products might theoretically be ameliorated by injunctions. It was likely, however, that such injunctions would be either so general as to be easily circumvented, or so stringent as to retard innovation in this technologically dynamic industry."[36]

Structural relief also was deemed unacceptable because it would be "totally disproportionate to the nature and scope of the violations. . . . Moreover, despite years of effort, no structural relief proposal has been identified that would inject new competition into the industry while retaining the efficiencies necessary to create viable successor companies."[37] After the dismissal of the IBM case, Baxter stated that "a company that is large and has a large market share is free, should be free, to go on competing aggressively, to keeping its prices down, to capturing an even larger market share if it can. None of these

---

[33] Dun's Business Month, Feb 1982, at 13-14. The Government's direct case lasted for almost three years, ending on April 6, 1978. IBM's defense began on that date and continued. Thirteen years had elapsed since the filing of the initial complaint, pre-trial depositions had commenced some ten years ago, and more than six years of trial time had been consumed. 618 F2d at 925. Before trial, IBM deposed all of the government's witnesses. Between 1975 and 1977 during trial, IBM deposed or redeposed twenty four of the government's trial witnesses. By 1980 IBM had taken some 160 depositions of government agencies and non-parties, and the government had answered some 500,000 requests for admissions made by IBM. *Id* 933.

[34] *Government: New Review Showed Victory Over IBM Unlikely,* Econ News, Jan 11, 1982, at 6.

[35] *Id.*

[36] *Id.*

[37] *Id.*

things violate Section 2."[38]

Most of IBM's competitors in the mainframe and peripherals markets agreed that the dismissal of the suit would not unleash dramatic changes in IBM's business practices.[39] In fact, many competitors contended that IBM had been aggressively "cutting prices and entering new markets with bareknuckle abandon," especially in the final stages of the suit.[40] As an example of this attitude, David Martin, executive vice president of National Advanced Systems, an IBM-compatible equipment vendor, said that "by the mid-70s, IBM took the gloves off, and the suit per se did not affect their business." According to Martin, IBM had been extremely aggressive for several years and would continue to be the price leader in the industry.[41] Officials of companies selling plug-compatible central processing units (CPUs) agreed that IBM had not been intimidated to discontinue its aggressive sales in its mainframe market.[42]

The Computer and Communications Industry Association, however, maintained that the suit, while active, had restrained IBM, permitting the formation and success of new companies during that period. The association contended that the dismissal of the suit quashed hopes of some meaningful disclosure of IBM interface specifications.[43] The Computer and Communications Industry Association was not the only critic of the suit's dismissal. Lewis Bernstein, former chief of the special litigation section of the Antitrust Division, said the case did have merit, and delays in the litigation were the result of IBM's "strategy to avoid a judicial determination of the case on the merits."[44]

The House Subcommittee on Monopolies and Commercial Law investigated the dismissal of the suit. Committee Chairman Peter W. Rodino, Jr. urged the review because "if violations had occurred, vindication of the antitrust laws and the public interest require that some remedial action be taken, even if the major structural relief originally sought by the government is no longer appropriate."[45] Rodino specifically wanted the committee to investigate the propriety of dismissing the suit without opportunity for public review. The Antitrust Procedures and Penalties Act (the Tunney Act) mandates public comment on the settlement of antitrust suits by consent judgments, but not by dis-

---

[38] 525 Trade Reg Rep (CCH), No 525, at 9 (Jan 18, 1982).

[39] *More Aggressive IBM Expected by Competitors,* Electronic News, Jan 18, 1982. See also Note, *Sales and Use Tax of Computer Software—Is Software Tangible Personal Property?,* 27 Wayne L Rev 1503, at 1504, n 10. It was reported that in the first nine months of 1980 IBM's total sales were $18,407,670,000. Assuming a 12.5% growth rate . . . sales in 1983 should be nearly $35 billion. *Information Still On the Leading Edge of Growth,* Bus Week, Jan 12, 1981, at 60.

[40] *Life after Litigation at IBM and AT&T,* Fortune, Feb 8, 1982, at 59.

[41] Electronic News, Jan 18, 1982, at 4.

[42] *Id.* (Comments from Joseph Krug, president of Cambex, and Steven J. Ippolito, president of IPL Systems).

[43] *Id.*

[44] Trade Reg Rep (CCH) No 549, at 6 (July 6, 1982) (Mr. Bernstein's comments were made before the House Subcommittee on Monopolies and Commercial Law).

[45] Trade Reg Rep (CCH) No 525, at 8 (Jan 18, 1982).

missals.[46] Rodino, who acknowledged that the Tunney Act probably was not designed to cover dismissals, said DOJ's "abrupt action may violate the spirit, if not the letter of the Act."[47]

The government was pressed by the trial court to justify its dismissal without following the provisions of the Tunney Act. In addition, Baxter's work as a legal consultant for IBM in 1975-76 raised the question whether a conflict of interest nullified the dismissal. The government petitioned the United States Court of Appeals for the Second Circuit in New York City to order the trial court to discontinue hearings into the propriety of the dismissal without adhering to the procedures set out in the Tunney Act. Meanwhile, Baxter was vindicated of any allegations of conflict of interest by the Office of the Solicitor General.[48] According to the Solicitor General, the dismissal was made by the "appropriate person . . . the dismissal was effective, and . . . the Department of Justice does not intend to proceed further with the case."[49] Former Department of Justice official Sanford Litvack dubbed the dismissal "a failure of the system," but, according to Baxter, it "was the most pro-competitive of all possible outcomes."[50]

While the stipulated dismissal liberated IBM from its 13-year suit with the government, it did not end the company's antitrust litigation. The European Economic Community's Commission filed a complaint against IBM charging that it had injured competitors through its "dominant position" by bundling the main memory of its 360 and 370 computers with CPUs, and by delaying disclosure of changes in interfaces for plug-compatible parts.[51] According to one observer, IBM is facing "substantially the same arguments all over again, this time before an administrative agency that is rooted in dated antitrust

---

[46] Pub L No 93-528, 88 Stat 1706.

[47] Trade Reg Rep (CCH) No 525, at 8 (Jan 18, 1982).

[48] Trade Reg Rep (CCH) No 549, at 6 (July 6, 1982).

[49] *Id.* The United States Court of Appeals for the Second Circuit ruled that the Tunney Act, Pub L No 93-528, 88 Stat 1706, also known as the Antitrust Procedures and Penalties Act, applied only to antitrust consent decrees and not to stipulations of dismissal under Fed R Civ P 41(a)(1). The district court, concerned that dismissal might be subject to the Tunney Act's procedural requirements, had declined to dismiss the case. The appellate court rejected the suggestion that Congress provided sub silentio for the Tunney Act to apply to dismissals, in view of the fact that Rule 41 existed in its present form for almost 30 years prior to the Tunney Act. The Tunney Act ". . . was enacted in response to the growing number of settlements by consent decree in antitrust suits filed by the Justice Department. . . ."

Congress determined that judicial approval of such consent decrees should be based upon specific criteria to ensure that the settlement terms would serve the public interest. Accordingly, the Act requires advance publication of the proposed decree and a *competitive impact settlement*, as well as a 60-day public comment period. 51 USLW 1029 (Aug 24, 1982).

[50] *Id.*

[51] *IBM's Antitrust Troubles Are Not Finished Yet*, Bus Week, Jan 25, 1982, at 24.

theories."[52]

IBM also faces the possibility of further antitrust litigation as it expands from its traditional base in the market for general purpose business computers into the markets for small computers and communications equipment. IBM, with its entrance into the satellite communications business in 1974, has bridged the technologies of computers and communications. These technological shifts are already "reshaping the $130 billion information processing industry."[53]

§4.04 —Private Suits Filed against IBM

The government has not been the only plaintiff in computer antitrust suits against IBM. The first private antitrust case involving IBM was filed in 1968 by Control Data Corporation (CDC).[54] Subsequent to the CDC complaint, Data Processing Financial and General Corporation (DPF&G); Applied Data Research, Inc. (ADR); and Programmatics, Inc. (PI) filed suits against IBM in the Southern District of New York. By order of the Judicial Panel on Multidistrict Litigation, these suits consolidated with the CDC action in the United States District Court for the District of Minnesota.[55] Both ADR & PI charged IBM with violations of §§1 and 2 of the Sherman Act. Specifically, they complained that IBM bundled its software with its hardware.

Neither ADR nor PI sold, manufactured, or dealt in hardware. ADR sold software in competition with IBM and other manufacturers, and PI sold special purpose software. ADR alleged that IBM sold its central processing units (CPUs) at an artificially high price, and furnished the systems software and other software at no additional cost. ADR also alleged that IBM had engaged in a campaign to further its monopoly and its attempt to monopolize the software market by wrongfully and deceptively "fostering and maintaining a viewpoint among computer users . . . that computer software is an intangible without market or property value."[56] PI complained of the same tactics as did ADR, and also alleged that shortly after PI had developed and marketed an improved sort program, IBM announced a similar program which it distributed free to its hardware purchasers.

CDC, the only plaintiff in direct competition with IBM, alleged 37 instances of monopolistic practices. Included within these allegations were references to the introduction of phantom fighting machines, bundling of software, and monopolistic control of the data service business. The DPF&G complaint

---

[52] *Id.*

[53] *The Odds in a Bell-IBM Bout,* Bus Week, Jan 25, 1982, at 22.

[54] Control Data Corp v IBM Corp, 421 F2d 323 (8th Cir 1970).

[55] *Id.* See also *Report on Unbundling in The Supersonic Seventies,* 17 Bus Automation 44, 64 (Jan 1970).

[56] Control Data Corp v IBM Corp, 421 F2d 323 (8th Cir 1970).

alleged that IBM's practices had damaged its mainframe leasing activities and its software and peripherals business.

These actions were all settled out of court, and thus failed to produce any substantive antitrust law. IBM was eager to reach settlement in order to curtail discovery proceedings at a time when the government was putting together its case against IBM on substantially the same claims.[57] These suits, however, illustrate potential hardware/software anticompetitive practices which can and do arise in the computer industry.

In another action, Memorex sued IBM claiming that IBM's Madrid disc drive created an illegal tying arrangement in violation of §1 of the Sherman Act and §3 of the Clayton Act.[58] Memorex charged that IBM's practice of selling the Madrid drive unit and the Madrid head/disk assembly for a single price actually constituted the sale of two products. The trial court directed a verdict on this claim for IBM on a finding that the Madrid aggregation was a single product and was recognized in the industry as such. This case differed from the CDC case because IBM was able to show that there was only one hardware product. The industry's recognition that a disk drive unit which included the read/write heads constituted a single product was a crucial factor in the court's decision to grant IBM's motion for a directed verdict.

IBM was also successful in countering allegations of illegal bundling in *Telex Corporation v IBM*.[59] Telex claimed that IBM's actions in reducing the price of its integrated file adapter for the 3330 disk drive constituted a tying arrangement between the file adapter and the 370/135 CPU. One claim focused on the fact that the integrated file adaptor or controller could be purchased at a lower price than buying the adapter separately. IBM defended this policy on the grounds that the integration represented a valid technological innovation at a decreased cost, and that there was no predatory intent. Both the trial and appeals courts agreed with IBM.[60] The courts took the position that IBM's integration of memory and CPUs in the 370/158 and 370/168 was an adaptation whose primary purpose was to achieve cost and performance improvements.[61]

To date, therefore, no private litigant has successfully proved that IBM unlawfully bundled its products. IBM settled the CDC, ADR, DPF&G, and PI cases before trial. The Memorex suit failed when IBM successfully proved that

---

[57] United States v IBM Corp, No 69 Civ 200 (SDNY Jan 17, 1969). See also Antitrust and Trade Reg Rep (BNA) No 792, at A-2 (Dec 12, 1976), for a discussion of the IBM settlement strategy by James T. Halverson, former chief of the FTC Bureau of competition.

[58] ILC Peripherals Leasing Corp v IBM Corp, 458 F Supp 423 (ND Cal 1978), *affd per curiam sub nom* Memorex Corp v IBM, Corp, 636 F2d 1188 (9th Cir 1980), *cert denied*, 452 US 972 (1981).

[59] Telex Corp v IBM Corp, 510 F2d 894 (10th Cir 1975).

[60] *Id*, 906.

[61] *Id*.

there was only one product, and the Telex suit failed due to IBM's assertions of technological innovation resulting in cost savings.

§4.05   —Unbundling: *Greyhound Computer Corp, Inc v IBM*

IBM was not as fortunate in escaping liability when it announced in June 1969 that it was unbundling.[62] IBM was subsequently sued by Greyhound Computer Corporation Inc. for breach of contract because it unbundled its software.[63] Greyhound alleged, but was unsuccessful in proving, that IBM had breached a contractual obligation created by its bundling practice of providing services to first users of IBM machines. Greyhound's major claim, however, was that IBM had violated §2 of the Sherman Act.

Greyhound leased computers, most of which were IBM mainframes, and competed with IBM in placing computers in the market. The strategy behind this leasing practice was explained by the Ninth Circuit Court of Appeals:

> Leasing companies operate on the premise that the useful life of a computer system will exceed the manufacturer's expectations as reflected in the manufacturer's rental rates. Because leasing companies calculate that the equipment will have a longer economic life, they charge less, assume the risk of technological obsolescence, and rely on their ability to lease the equipment long enough to make a profit.[64]

Greyhound's antitrust claim was that IBM had monopolized or attempted to monopolize the market for leasing general purpose digital computers for commercial applications, and a sub-market for leasing IBM-manufactured computers. IBM's market share was asserted as proof of the possession of monopoly power under §2 of the Sherman Act.[65] The second requirement for a §2 claim of attempting to monopolize, the willful acquisition or maintenance of monopoly power, was alleged to consist of IBM's adoption of four marketing practices instituted in 1969. Those practices were: inaugurating the fixed term plan (FTP); eliminating the technological discount; increasing the "multiplier;" and unbundling.[66] The trial court granted IBM's motion for a directed

---

[62] See Schmedel, *IBM Discloses Plan for Separating Its Computers and Services Prices,* Wall St J, June 24, 1969, at 38. See also Drattel, *Unbundling: The User Will Pay For the Works,* 16 Bus Automation 36 (Aug 1969).

[63] Greyhound Computer Corp Inc v IBM Corp, 559 F2d 488 (9th Cir 1977), *cert denied,* 434 US 1040 (1978).

[64] 559 F2d at 492 n 1. See also ABA Standing Committee on Law and Technology, Computers and the Law 125-26 (2d ed 1969).

[65] 559 F2d at 496. The court found sufficient evidence in the record to determine that IBM's share of the revenues from leasing of general purpose computers was 82.5% in 1964, 75.1% in 1967, and 64.68% in 1970.

[66] 559 F2d at 498. The fixed term plan (FTP) enabled IBM to lease its peripherals, which were being effectively competed against by computers, for longer than IBM's

verdict on the attempt to monopolize claims, but was reversed on appeal.[67]

Greyhound claimed that the manner in which IBM unbundled furthered its willful acquisition and maintenance of monopoly power. When IBM unbundled, it announced that it would no longer provide such services as education of user personnel, software support, and technological guidance and advice to its rental customers or to first users of purchased equipment, except upon payment of a separate charge. Prior to 1969, IBM had provided these services at no cost. The effect of these practices was to require lessors such as Greyhound to provide these services without charge to their lessees, even where the leases had been entered into prior to 1969. In reversing the directed verdict, the court of appeals noted that although the unbundling might actually have been a pro-competitive move, a jury could have concluded that it was anti-competitive from the way in which IBM unbundled.[68] The Supreme Court denied certiorari, and the case has been settled.[69]

§4.06 Predatory Pricing

IBM's fixed term plan (FTP) was a shift in policy away from short-term leases to long-term leasing. Prior to this, IBM had had a standard 30-day lease,

---

usual 30 day lease. The FTP, therefore, was able to *capture* or lock in many customers before competing plug compatible peripheral manufacturers could deliver their products to the market. In addition, the FTP had substantial penalties for early termination of the FTP lease. The technological discount had been a procedure whereby a leasee of IBM equipment could purchase the equipment at an ever decreasing price as the equipment became older and technologically inferior to newer equipment. The multiplier is the ratio between leasing computer equipment and purchasing the equipment. Maintenance must be fostered into the multiplier for the number to be valid. Multipliers in the IBM 360 series had been in the range of 40 to 48. Leasing companies, therefore, could expect a profit if they could lease the IBM equipment, after purchasing it from IBM or on IBM lease under the IBM technological discount plan, for 55 months or longer. The IBM 370 series, models 155 and 165, raised the multiplier to the 55 range, thereby effectively squeezing much of the profit out of the leasing services. Unbundling was the separation of hardware and system software and related services, by charging for both. See **§3.02** for more details. These four practices have been cited by every §2 claimant against IBM since Greyhound.

[67] Electronic News, Jan 18, 1982, at 4. *See also* Greyhound Computer Corp v IBM Corp, 1972 Trade Cas (CCH) ¶74205, *affd in part, revd in part,* 559 F2d 488 (9th Cir 1977).

[68] 559 F2d at 502.

[69] 434 US 1040 (1978). See Washington Post, Jan 27, 1981, at D-7, col 6. See also *IBM to Pay $17.7 Million in Legal Costs to Settle Greyhound Unit Antitrust Suit,* Wall St J, Jan 27, 1981, at 6, col 1.

> IBM said the payment was intended to cover a portion of Greyhound's legal costs, as indicated in a joint press release. But a Greyhound spokesman . . . said the company's legal costs were less than $17.7 million . . . Greyhound had sought more than $300 million in treble damages in the suit.

There was no showing that IBM had reduced its prices below its marginal or average costs.

cancelable after the first 90 days, for most of its hardware. In May of 1971, IBM announced its FTP which offered an 8 per cent price reduction on certain peripheral equipment under a one-year lease, and a 16 per cent reduction on two-year leases. The FTP also eliminated certain service charges, created substantial penalties for premature lease cancellation, lowered the purchase price, and gave purchasers a 12 per cent technological discount. Greyhound had claimed that the net effects of FTP was to *lock* users into an IBM rental base and to inhibit price competition. In upholding the trial court's directed verdict, the court of appeals stated, "Greyhound [has] failed to show that . . . [this] . . . was anything more than a reasonable response to competition."[70] There was no showing that IBM had reduced its prices below its marginal or average costs.

IBM also changed its policy with respect to the technological discount offered purchasers. A technological discount is given in recognition of the fact that rapid technological changes can render a particular model obsolete within a few years. The longer a model has been offered for sale, the greater the risk of technological obsolescence, and therefore, the greater the need for a reduction in the purchase price. Prior to 1963, IBM's discount had been 10 per cent per year up to a maximum of 75 per cent. Leasing companies made extensive use of the discount by purchasing equipment late in the product cycle at substantially reduced costs, and then offering equipment leases at reduced rates.[71] In 1963, IBM reduced the discount to 5 per cent per year, and limited the maximum to 35 per cent of the initial retail cost. When IBM announced the System 360 series, the technological discount was changed to a 12 per cent reduction after the first year of sale.

Greyhound alleged that IBM had manipulated the technological discount to restrict competition from leasing companies. Because of the new reduced technological discount policy, leasing companies incurred higher costs in acquiring equipment, and were forced to buy earlier in the produce cycle. The court of appeals held that there was sufficient evidence for a jury to infer that anti-competitive consequences were intended, and reversed the directed verdict in favor of IBM.[72]

Greyhound also alleged that IBM had increased the *multiplier,* which is the ratio between the sales price and the monthly rental fee charged to its leasees. As the multiplier increases, the number of months necessary to rent a computer system before it becomes less profitable than to have purchased rather than leased the computer system also increases. Greyhound contended that the increase in the multiplier was intended to limit competition from leasing companies. The court of appeals held that this issue should have been submitted

---

[70] 559 F2d at 498-99. See *Greyhound v IBM: Price Increases as a Form of Predatory Pricing,* 7 Rutgers J Computers, Tech & L 77 (1979).

[71] 559 F2d at 499.

[72] *Id.*

to a jury.[73]

Telex, in its suit against IBM, had also alleged that IBM engaged in predatory pricing.[74] Telex, a manufacturer of IBM plug-compatible peripheral devices, maintained that IBM had violated §§1 and 2 of the Sherman Act and §2 of the Clayton Act by monopolizing and attempting to monopolize the IBM plug-compatible peripherals market.[75] The trial court entered judgment in favor of Telex, awarding $259.5 million in damages. The court of appeals reversed, and the parties settled while the Telex petition for certiorari to the Supreme Court was still pending. One of the grounds for reversal was that the market definition should have been broadened to include all peripheral devices and not just IBM plug-compatible peripherals used on IBM equipment. The court of appeals also held that none of the acts complained of by Telex were predatory, but rather were reasonable responses to competitive market conditions.[76]

In support of its §2 claims, Telex had alleged that IBM engaged in five predatory acts. These included:

1. Announcement and institution of the 2319A disk storage facility product in September 1970

2. Announcement of the 2319B disk storage facility product in December 1970

3. Announcement of the fixed term plan (FTP) long term leasing program in May 1971

4. Announcement and implementation of extended term plan (ETP), another leasing plan, in March 1972

5. The pricing policy with regard to IBM memory products during 1970 and 1971

IBM's 2319A and 2319B disk storage facilities were essentially equivalent to IBM's prior 2314 offerings, except that they placed an integrated file adapter (the plug) in the central processing unit (CPU) rather than having an external disk control unit. This configuration allowed IBM to offer these products at significantly lower prices. It also made the 2319A and 2319B compatible only with the IBM 370 CPUs. Although IBM had effectively undercut Telex's price, the court of appeals held that since neither the 2319A nor the 2319B was priced below production costs (IBM's anticipated profit margin on the items was in excess of 20 per cent), there was no predatory pricing.[77] The characterization by the trial court of these product programs as predatory acts was based

---

[73] *Id* 501.

[74] Telex Corp v IBM, Corp, 510 F2d 894, 900 (10th Cir 1975).

[75] Sherman Act (Act of July 2, 1890) ch 647, 26 Stat 209, 15 USC §§1-7; Clayton Act (Act of Oct 15, 1914) ch 322, 38 Stat 730, 15 USC §§12-17 (§2 of the Clayton Act was amended by the Robinson-Patman Act, (Act of June 19, 1936) ch 592, 49 Stat 1526.

[76] 510 F2d 894, at 900.

[77] *Id,* 902.

not on the actual results which were achieved, but on IBM's predatory intentions at the time of the market development and during the marketing of these products.

Telex's allegations of predatory practices encompassing IBM's FTP and ETP were essentially identical to those asserted by Greyhound. Although the trial court found the practices to be predatory, the court of appeals held these practices to be a reasonable response to competitive in-roads and changing economic times. Telex and other lessors of peripheral equipment had always leased their equipment for longer periods of time than IBM and at lower prices. When the national economy took a down turn in 1970, many IBM rental customers returned their equipment to IBM, and began to lease equipment from IBM's plug-compatible competitors. Thus, IBM's actions in increasing lease durations and imposing substantial cancellation costs were found to be reasonable competitive responses.[78]

Telex also alleged that IBM's simultaneous price cuts for memory and price increases for CPUs effectively price balanced IBM's total system profitability by raising prices (and profits) for its CPUs, where it had no competition at the time, and lowering prices of products where IBM did face competition. This price balancing, according to Telex, was illegal predatory pricing. The trial court agreed that this memory/CPU price balancing was predatory pricing, but the court of appeals held that this was a legal competitive practice in the face of competitors' significant in-roads into IBM's shares of various submarkets.[79]

Following the trial court success of Telex, California Computer Products, Inc. (*CalComp*)[80] and Memorex[81] each sued IBM, alleging violations of §2 of the Sherman Act. Both made allegations essentially similar to those made by Telex, and both suffered directed verdicts against them.[82] In *CalComp*, the plaintiff had alleged that IBM monopolized the peripherals market. The appeals court held that a monopolist may be engaged in predatory pricing even when its prices are above average variable cost. The court stated, however, that even if IBM was a monopolist, it had the right to respond to the lower prices of its competitors. The court said that IBM had a right to redesign its products to offer equivalent or superior performance at a lower price, and was under no duty to help peripheral manufacturers survive or expand.[83]

Memorex made no attempt to show that IBM priced below its marginal costs,

---

[78] *Id,* 903-04.

[79] *Id,* 906-07.

[80] California Computer Prods, Inc v IBM Corp, 613 F2d 727, 731 (9th Cir 1979).

[81] ILC Peripherals Leasing Corp v IBM Corp, 458 F Supp 423 (ND Cal 1978), *affd per curiam sub nom* Memorex Corp v IBM Corp, 636 F2d 1188 (9th Cir 1980), *cert denied,* 452 US 972 (1981).

[82] *Id. See also* California Computer Prods Inc v IBM Corp, 613 F2d 727, 731 (9th Cir 1979)(CalComp).

[83] 613 F2d 727. See also Carley, *Laws Against 'Predatory Pricing' by Firms Are Being Relaxed in Many Court Rulings,* Wall St J, July 14, 1982, at 46, col 1. But cf *Computer Services and the 'Tie-in' Sale-A Case for Presuming Coercion,* 2 Rutgers J Computers & L 135 (1972).

but did fail in its attempt to prove that IBM's prices were below its short-run profit-maximums. The trial court in Memorex, using a liberal test for predatory pricing, held that prices are predatory if they are below either marginal or average variable cost. Under this standard, a price above marginal or average costs, even if below the short-run profit-maximizing price, is not predatory.[84] Memorex appealed the issue of whether pricing above marginal or average variable cost was presumptively nonpredatory, even when aimed at fledgling competitors, and whether such cost-based tests ignore the willful standard of monopolization under which all relevant factors are considered. The Court of Appeals for the Ninth Circuit upheld the trial court, based on its decision in *California* Computer Products.[85]

On review of the *Memorex* case, the Ninth Circuit, following its rationale in *CalComp,* held that IBM's price cuts, marketing practices, and product redesigns were reasonable responses to expanded competition from plug-compatible equipment manufacturers.[86]

In *Transamerica Computer Corp v IBM,* a California federal district court took a distinctly novel approach to pricing activities by monopolists.[87] Recognizing that IBM's reputation as a predator may act as a deterrent to potential rivals, the trial judge stated that "less egregious conduct may violate Section 2 if engaged in by a monopolist or by one attempting to monopolize if there is . . . specific intent [to exclude and proof of market power]."[88] The Areeda-Turner marginal cost standard was harshly criticized for ignoring the possibility that *deep pocket* firms could price above marginal or average variable cost, and still manage to drive out competitors.[89]

§4.07   Undue Frustration of Competition

Memorex had also alleged that IBM's change of design specifications was orchestrated solely for the purpose of frustrating plug-compatible competitors. Memorex challenged IBM's policy of not disclosing interface information on its central processing unit (CPU) compatible peripheral devices until the

---

[84] 458 F Supp at 442.

[85] 636 F2d 1188. See also Trade Reg Rep (CCH) No 494, at 2 (June 15, 1981).

[86] Trade Reg Rep (CCH) No 494, at 2 (June 15, 1981).

[87] Transamerica Computer Corp v IBM Corp, 481 F Supp 965 (ND Cal 1979), *affd,* 698 F2d 1377 (9th Cir 1983).

[88] 481 F Supp at 989.

[89] The court used a standard where pricing below average cost, if unreasonable, would constitute predatory conduct. 481 F Supp at 995-96. See generally *Predation Analysis,* 35 Vanderbilt L Rev 63 (1982) (for a discussion of the judicial treatment of predatory tactics by dominant businesses). See also Areeda & Turner, *Predatory Pricing and Related Practices Under Section 2 of the Sherman Act,* 88 Harv L Rev 697 (1975); Williamson, *Predatory Pricing: A Strategic and Welfare Analysis,* 87 Yale L J 284 (1977); Areeda & Turner, *Williamson on Predatory Pricing,* 87 Yale LJ 1337 (1978); Scherer, *Predatory Pricing and the Sherman Act: A Comment,* 89 Harv L Rev 868 (1976); and Areeda & Turner, *Scherer on Predatory Pricing: A Reply,* 89 Harv L Rev 891 (1976).

first customer shipment of the product.[90] Memorex claimed that this information was vital to plug-compatible manufacturers at the time of product announcement if they were to remain competitive. The trial court held that Memorex's profitability belied its need for such disclosure, and noted that such an order would deprive IBM of its lead time and incentive to innovate.

Memorex also argued that the New Attachment Strategy (NAS) for the 2319A and 2319B disk storage facilities was merely a technological manipulation designed to frustrate competition.[91] Memorex took the position that IBM had adopted this approach because it required the greatest number of interface changes. The court rejected this argument based on its findings that the NAS represented a product innovation superior to the alternate product Memorex posited as being equal. Memorex also challenged IBM's introduction of its Models 370/115 and 370/125 on the same grounds, and with the same results.[92]

One additional claim which Memorex advanced was that IBM had made inaccurate announcements concerning the availability of a Network Control Program for the 3705 teleprocessing central unit. Similar to the government's allegations in its suit with IBM, Memorex claimed the announcement was premature, and was intended to forestall sales of similar products by competitors. IBM had announced that the program would be available in March of 1973, but the actual delivery date to the first customers did not occur until October of that year. The court, however, found that there was no evidence that IBM had not honestly believed that the product would be available as announced.[93]

§4.08 Consent Decree

As discussed in §4.02, in 1956 IBM and the Department of Justice had entered into a consent decree. Several private litigants attempted, unsuccessfully, to use the consent decree against IBM. Control Data Corporation (CDC), Data Processing Financial and General Corporation (DPF&G), Applied Data Research, Inc. (ADR), and Programmatics, Inc. (PI) all made some reference to either the 1956 consent decree or the 1935 judgment in their complaints.[94] The CDC complaint did not seek enforcement of the provisions of the consent decree, nor did it attempt to base a separate cause of action upon it, but it did allege that one of the 37 instances of IBM's monopolistic practices grew out of IBM's failure to abide by what the decree required, a distinction the court found to be one without a difference. DPF&G's and ADR's complaints made some references to the 1956 decree, and both included a claim for single

---

[90] 458 F Supp 423.

[91] *Id* 440.

[92] *Id* 442.

[93] *Id.*

[94] CDC Corp v IBM Corp, 421 F2d 323 (8th Cir 1970). *See also* 306 F Supp 839.

damages on a third party beneficiary contract based on IBM's violation of the consent decrees. The complaints of ADR and PI alleged violations of the consent decrees.

IBM's pretrial motion in the *CDC* case to strike all references to the decree and to the 1935 judgment was granted.[95] The court stated that in actions for treble damages under the antitrust laws no reference could be made to *nolo contendere* pleas. The court questioned the use (and relevance) of acts committed 13 years earlier to prove current antitrust violations, and in any event, the statute of limitations barred claims based on these acts. The trial court rejected the litigant's attempts to enforce the decree directly by stating that:

> The law is rather clear that a third party, a stranger to the decree and not a party to the government action either directly or by intervention, cannot attempt to enforce it against the defendant.[96]

Whether or not the parties could intercede at that late date was not addressed by the court. The policy considerations cited by the court, however, made the intervention option seem doubtful.[97]

The court also rejected the third party beneficiary theory.[98] DPF&G had argued that the 1956 decree was unique in that it was intended to protect a specific, as yet *unborn*, class of plaintiffs, i.e., "users and prospective users" of IBM equipment. This construction of the DPF&G and IBM lease contracts, however, was barred by the court's reasoning that DPF&G could not do indirectly what it could not do directly through intervention, even though it was only seeking single damages under a contract theory. CDC argued that knowledge of the decree was necessary for the jury to evaluate IBM's practice of encouraging leasing. The failure of that argument, according to the court, was that if CDC could not prove its case without the decree, then there was no violation of the antitrust laws.[99] In sum, the prospects of private plaintiffs successfully using a consent decree entered in an antitrust suit brought by the government appear dim.

Minicomputers

§4.09   Bundling

Data General Corporation has a position in the minicomputer market analagous to IBM's position in the mainframe market. Data General provides a

---

[95] 421 F2d at 323.
[96] 306 F Supp at 845.
[97] *Id,* at 845-6.
[98] *Id,* at 846-8.
[99] *Id,* at 848.

complete line of hardware and software components, and has been sued numerous times for alleged antitrust violations. Private plaintiffs have contended that Data General violated §1 of the Sherman Act and §3 of the Clayton Act by illegal tying arrangements, and also monopolized and attempted to monopolize in violation of §2 of the Sherman Act.[100]

Several plaintiffs have alleged that Data General tied the licensing of its systems software to the sale of its central processing units (CPUs).[101] Ampex Corporation also alleged that Data General unlawfully tied the sale of its CPUs to the sale of its memory boards. All of the plaintiffs (except Data Compress Corporation) competed with Data General in the CPU market, but relied on Data General's systems software. All antitrust plaintiffs who sued Data General marketed a product dependent upon the separate availability of either the NOVA CPU or the NOVA systems software produced by Data General. Ampex also sold *add on* plug-compatible memory in competition with Data General.

The alleged tie-in between systems software and the CPUs revolved around two of Data General's marketing practices. Data General only licensed its software pursuant to an agreement which precluded the licensee from using the software on any hardware not manufactured by Data General. Systems software licensees were required to purchase a minimum hardware configuration of memory and peripheral devices. Ampex also complained of Data General's requirement that initial purchasers of the NOVA CPU buy a minimum of memory. Data General did not dispute the existence of any of these practices. Instead, it claimed that the systems software, CPU, and memory were only one product. In addition, Data General responded that it did not possess the requisite economic power in the tying product market, and that even if a tying arrangement were found, there was a justification for it.[102]

At trial, the jury concluded that but for a showing of economic power, Data

---

[100] *In re* Data Gen Corp Antitrust Litigation, 470 F Supp 855 (JPML 1979); *In re* Data Gen Corp Antitrust Litigation, 490 F Supp 1089 (ND Cal 1980), *revd,* 1982-1 Trade Cas (CCH) ¶64487 (ND Cal 1981). For a discussion of this case, *see* Stern, *supra* note 5. See also The Scott Report (Los Angeles, Calif) Oct 1981.

[101] 490 F Supp at 1089. *Fairchild Camera & Instrument Corp v Data General Corp,* No C 78 2418 (ND Cal, filed Oct 1978); *SCI Systems, Inc v Data General Corp,* No C 78-2417 (ND Cal, filed Oct 1978); *Digidyne Corp v Data General Corp,* No C 78-1261 (ND Cal, filed June 1978). In May, 1979, the Panel transferred three actions to this Court: *Bytronix Corp v Data General Corp,* No 78-3832-RF (CD Cal, filed Oct 1978); *Data General Corp v Ampex Corp,* No 79-1247 (DNJ, filed Aug 1978); *Data General Corp v Ampex Corp,* No 77-0636 (DNJ, filed Mar 1977). In June, 1979, the Panel conditionally transferred here *Data Compass Corp v Data General Corp,* No 79-1784-AA (CD Cal, filed Feb 1979). In November, 1979, the Panel conditionally transferred here three additional actions: *Data General Corp v Data National Corp,* No 78-2869-K (D Mass, filed Nov 1978); *Data General Corp v Ampex Corp,* No 79-1342-MRP (CD Cal, filed Apr 1979); *Data General Corp v Ampex Corp,* No 79-193-T (D Mass, filed Jan 1979).

[102] 490 F Supp at 1100. This was presented on plaintiff's Motion for Summary Judgment. For a per se violation it was necessary that Data General be shown to have sufficient economic power in the tying product market (systems software) to appreciably restrain competition in the tied product (CPUs).

General had imposed per se illegal tie-ins for which no valid business justifications existed.[103] This decision was overturned by the federal district court in San Francisco, which held that Data General did not impose a per se unlawful tying arrangement on its customers. The trial court found that competing manufacturers had failed to show that their alleged inability to compete with the manufacturer's CPUs was attributable to the software licensing restrictions. The trial court reasoned that the competitors could have failed to compete due to their inability to match Data General's quality and service standards, their inability to offer single-seller accountability, or their poor marketing strategies. The trial court found that Data General was not unfettered by the competitive restraints of the market, despite the tie-in of some customers to Data General's CPUs. The *uniqueness* of the manufacturer's software did not work as a competitive advantage over competitors who were unencumbered by legal or economic barriers from producing compatible software.[104]

§4.10 Miscellaneous Antitrust Actions

Digidyne Corporation (Digidyne), Fairchild Camera and Instrument Corporation (Fairchild), SCI Systems, Inc. (SCI), Ampex, and Bytronix Corporation also accused Data General of violating §2 of the Sherman Act.[105] Their allegations parallel allegations directed against IBM. The claims against Data General, however, differ significantly from the IBM claims in that the plaintiffs in the Data General actions attacked the business tactics of Data General rather than its marketing practices. The allegations were that Data General used harassment and threatened lawsuits to monopolize the NOVA-compatible minicomputer market.

Data General v Ampex was unusual in that Data General sought a declaratory judgment that it had neither violated federal antitrust law nor caused any antitrust injury to Ampex. Data General also alleged trade secret violations by Ampex.

Digidyne, which brought suit in June of 1978 against Data General, originally charged business libel, alleging that Data General had maliciously and falsely stated to Ampex and to other Digidyne customers that Digidyne had unlawfully used Data General's trade secrets and other proprietory information in the construction of a Digidyne computer.[106] In its amended complaint, Digidyne alleged that Data General had abused copyright laws and licensing agreements, and had threatened potential purchasers of its NOVA-compatible

---

[103] Telex Corp v IBM Corp, 510 F 2d 894, 1125 (10th Cir 1975).

[104] *In re:* Data Gen Corp Antitrust Litig, 1982-1 Trade Cas (CCH) at 72702-704 (ND Cal 1981).

[105] California Computer Prods, Inc v IBM Corp, 613 F2d 727, 731 (9th Cir 1979). Act of July 2, 1890, 617, 26 Stat 209, 15 USC §2.

[106] The discussion of Digidyne's and the other plaintiff's claims is derived from the court's discussion of those claims in *In re* Data Gen Corp Antitrust Litig, 470 F Supp 855 (JPMDL 1979).

products with lawsuits in an attempt to monopolize the market for manufacturing NOVA-compatible computer systems.

SCI also alleged that Data General restrained competition, and monopolized or attempted to monopolize the NOVA-compatible computer market. SCI claimed that Data General had engaged in a systematic program of harassing manufacturers of NOVA-compatible computers by bringing groundless actions against those manufacturers, including SCI. The allegedly groundless actions brought by Data General were for misappropriation of trade secrets and for interference with Data General licenses. SCI also claimed that the acquisition by Data General of another manufacturer was in furtherance of an attempt to monopolize the relevant market.[107]

Fairchild also filed suit against Data General, alleging that Data General had attempted to eliminate competition by Fairchild and others. In support of its §2 claim, Fairchild asserted that Data General had abused its copyright protection and licensing agreements, and had used litigation and threats of litigation against other manufacturers and their potential customers in order to eliminate competition.

Bytronix alleged that Data General had restrained competition in the market for minicomputer CPUs by asserting that manufacturers of NOVA-compatible CPUs were violating Data General's trade secrets. Bytronix also alleged that Data General had engaged in price-balancing between software and hardware, and had provided less than adequate service to users of Data General's equipment sold by its competitors.

Microcomputers

§4.11 Present Antitrust Involvement

Microcomputer manufacturers have remained unscathed by lawsuits raising antitrust claims. No group of microcomputer competitors has attacked a dominant manufactuer, as has occurred in the mainframe and minicomputer segments of the computer industry. It may be only a matter of time, however, before microcomputer manufacturers become involved in antitrust litigation, especially given the tremendous growth predicted for this segment of the industry. Gross sales of microcomputers are predicted to jump from $1 billion in 1981 to $9 billion in 1985. This tremedous growth potential is attractive to competition, and barriers to entry are low.

In a growth industry such as microcomputers, market structure will continue to develop, and with change will come the potential for antitrust litigation. In order to appreciate this potential, it is necessary to understand the current structure, growth rate, and marketing practices of the microcomputer industry.

---

[107] *Id.*

The present dearth of antitrust litigation involving microcomputer manufacturers may be explained in part by the lack of a clear natural leader. Tandy Corporation (Tandy), was close to being a dominant market power and with two other manufacturers, Apple Computer, Inc., and Commodore International, shared 75 per cent of the market, as of 1981, for small-computers.[108] A host of larger computer companies, including Hewlett-Packard (H-P), Texas Instrument (TI), and IBM have introduced microcomputers, but to date with the major exception of IBM's PC (personal computer), have not made significant in-roads into the market shares of Tandy, Apple, and Commodore.[109] As of spring 1983, IBM's PC has captured 25 per cent of the microcomputer market, and IBM's market share appears to be increasing even as the microcomputer market also increases. The big Japanese firms (Hitachi, Toshiba, Mitsubishi, and Nippon Electric) are also beginning to enter the microcomputer market.[110]

With one major exception, the marketing practices of microcomputer manufacturers mimic those used by mainframe and minicomputer manufacturers. Unlike mainframes and minicomputers, which are sold by direct sales force, microcomputers are typically sold in retail stores just like other consumer goods. Tandy's TRS-80 series is sold throughout its outlets, although Tandy may decide to employ a direct sales force to market its sophisticated business computers. Apple is also contemplating the use of a direct sales force to expand the distribution of its higher priced, more sophisticated computers.[111]

Tandy and Apple are full-line companies that manufacture microprocessors and peripheral equipment, and develop and market systems and application software.[112] Although neither Tandy nor Apple state that their hardware and operating software is bundled, it is clear from their advertising and public statements that they bundle their microprocessors and systems software.[113] At the present time there does not appear to be any significant competition in systems software, but it is safe to assume that such competition will develop.

As with mainframe and minicomputer systems, the major cost of a microcomputer system is attributable to its peripheral hardware. The significance of peripheral equipment cost is illustrated by the TRS-80 Model III's suggested retail price of $900.00. Compatible Radio Shack line printers range in price from $999.00 to $1,960.00.[114] It is readily understandable, therefore, why

---

[108] Taylor, *Small Computer Shootout,* Time, March 2, 1981.

[109] *Id.*

[110] *Id.* See also Uttal, *Japan's Big Push in Computers: Urged on by the Government,* Fortune, Sept 25, 1978, at 64; and Fortune, Oct 9, 1978, at 138.

[111] Apple Computer, Inc Prospectus, 4,600,000 Share Common Stock at 14 (Dec 12, 1980) [hereinafter cited as Apple Prospectus].

[112] *See* Radio Shack 1981 Catalog No 328, at 189; and Apple Prospectus, *supra* note 109, at 11-18.

[113] It is interesting that Apple has defined systems software as "a set of programs *supplied by Apple* that enable the user to supervise the computers' resources." Apple Prospectus *supra* note 111, at 12. (emphasis added)

[114] Radio Shack 1981 Catalog No 328, at 170-73.

significant competition exists in the peripheral equipment market for microcomputers. In addition to manufacturing peripheral equipment, both Tandy and Apple provide pre-built systems that bundle microprocessors and peripheral equipment. Both Tandy's TRS-80 Model II and Apple's Apple III are marketed with built-in disc drives and expandable memories.[115] Thus, the marketing premise of both Tandy and Apple appears to embody a package concept where a complete system is sold to the user.

Both Tandy and Apple provide full service for their microcomputers, and Apple, at least, has stated that its expanding business market may require it to institute a field service program.[116] Neither Tandy nor Apple has instituted leasing programs as they both prefer to sell their products directly to users via independent retail outlets. Although Apple disavows any contemplated leasing program, it has entered into an agreement with United States Leasing Corporation (USLC) to provide inventory financing for third-party leasing arrangements for commercial end-user customers. The USLC leasing plan offers these customers three and four-year leases with fixed purchase options, and permits users to add additional equipment to their leases.[117]

The microcomputer industry was once considered to cater to those who enjoyed computers as a hobby. Although the industry has a significant market for personal computers, recent product developments point towards a more sophisticated business market for microcomputers. Tandy's and Apple's top models are each priced over $3,000, and with a business use configuration of application software and peripheral devices, their price range is between $4,300 and $7,800.[118] Thus, the business market for microcomputers is expanding and will complement the minicomputer and mainframe markets. Despite the trend toward sophisticated business use, Apple has moved to enter the educational market.[119]

IBM has recently entered the microcomputer market, and has been very successful with its personal computer (PC). Contrary to its normal business practices in the mainframe market, in the microcomputer market IBM has extensively used third party vendor equipment in assembling its PC, has actively encouraged third party software firms to design application software for the PC, and has entered into retailing arrangements with third parties, including Sears, Roebuck. Many firms have begun to offer software and peripheral hardware which is compatable with the PC, and several firms are beginning to offer

---

[115] *Id.* Apple Prospectus, *supra* note 111, at 10.

[116] Apple Prospectus, *supra* note 111, at 16.

[117] Apple Prospectus, *supra* note 111, at 15.

[118] The price range is for the Apple III, Apple Prospectus, *supra* note 111, at 12; Tandy's TRS-80 Model II is similarly priced. Microcomputers are so inexpensive that extensive leasing seems rather unlikely. There may, however, be purchase money financing which is in effect leasing.

[119] "[I]n fiscal 1979, Apple introduced its products to the education market, which contributed to the increased awareness of the personal computer." Apple Prospectus *supra* note 111, at 9.

look-a-like microcomputers which are functionally equivalent to the PC. To date no antitrust litigation against IBM in the microcomputer market has occurred.

§4.12   Potential Antitrust Involvement

Because the dominant group of microcomputer manufacturers have followed the marketing practices of mainframe computer and minicomputer manufacturers, it is likely that these manufacturers, particularly Tandy and Apple with their packaged system marketing concept, face the same antitrust exposure experienced by IBM and Data General. Data General was unsuccessful in asserting that a minicomputer "CPU, main memory and operating system software consitute a single product which is commonly referred to as a computer."[120] It may be that as microcomputer systems become less and less expensive, the single product argument becomes more difficult to refute. Microcomputer manufacturers should, therefore, consider their antitrust exposure to: (1) illegal tie-in claims under §3 of the Clayton Act;[121] (2) monopolization and attempt to monopolize claims under §2 of the Sherman Act;[122] and (3) restraint of trade claims under §1 of the Sherman Act, which could also occur as *fair trading* claims due to the chain of distribution unique to microcomputers.[123]

§4.13   —Claims of Illegal Tie-Ins

Both Tandy and Apple employ a variety of bundling arrangements, principally between systems software and microprocessors, microprocessors and memory devices, and microprocesors and peripheral devices. All three of these arrangements in the mainframe and minicomputer markets have been attacked as illegal tie-ins. Mainframe and minicomputer manufacturers' practice of bundling central processing units (CPUs) and systems software have also been successfully attacked. The consolidated *Control Data* cases, which had implicated IBM's practice of bundling software and CPUs, encouraged IBM to unbundle in June 1969, just before the Department of Justice filed its civil antitrust suit against IBM.

Data General had also been accused of bundling software and hardware.[124] Data General's practice of bundling minicomputer CPUs and memory devices, and its software license requiring its licensees to purchase a minimum equipment configuration were attacked as illegal tying arrangements. Data General was unsuccessful in defending these arrangements on the basis that they were

---

[120] *In re* Data General Corp Antitrust Lit, 470 F Supp 855, at 856.
[121] Clayton Act (Act of Oct 15, 1914), ch 322, 38 Stat 730, 15 USC §14.
[122] Sherman Act (Act of July 2, 1890), ch 617, 26 Stat 209, 15 USC §2.
[123] 15 USC §1.
[124] 490 F Supp 1089, at 1124-25 (ND Cal 1980).

single products, or that as a business practice their bundling was justified.[125] One of Data General's asserted justifications was market demand—that its customers preferred such bundling. Tandy and Apple may well advance such an argument in support of their packaged system marketing practice, although this argument is weakened by the fact that both Tandy and Apple sell their microcomputers without disk drives if the user so desires, and likewise both companies also sell their microcomputers without video monitors. The courts have considered this a weak justification at best, especially when an unbundled option is not available.[126] While home-use consumers may desire such arrangements, sophisticated consumers and retailers who assemble different components into complete systems do not. Whether a particular business would benefit from an unbundled option would seem to depend on the computational needs of that particular business.

Tying arrangements have been treated harshly under the antitrust laws. The computer industry, given its unique technological aspects, has continually tested the general rule that tying arrangements are per se illegal.[127] The general prohibition of tying arrangements has consistently been applied to the mainframe and minicomputer markets, and its application to the microcomputer market is a strong possibility.

§4.14 —Claims of Monopolization and Attempts to Monopolize

It is generally accepted that there will be increasingly aggressive competition in the microcomputer industry. Intimations made by Apple which point towards a concentration on the educational market may subject Apple to a Sherman Act §2 claim for its activities in this market.[128] A likely submarket is the market for peripheral devices, and particularly, peripheral devices that are plug-compatible with either Tandy or Apple microcomputers.[129] As IBM's share of the microcomputer market grows, it may also become involved in §2 litigation.

The experiences of IBM and Data General reveal the vast potential for §2 claims in the peripheral devices market. As was noted in *Telex*, the originator of a product or series of products has several advantages.[130] When a new

---

[125] *Id.*

[126] 490 F Supp at 1122-23.

[127] *See* International Salt Co v United States, 332 US 392 (1947).

[128] See Chase, *Test of Time: As Competition Grows, Apple Computer Inc Faces a Critical Period,* Wall St J, Nov 11, 1981, at 1; *How Apple Will Keep Growth Going,* Bus Week, March 22, 1982, at 63. *See also* Apple Prospectus, at 9. See §§8.16-8.18 for a discussion of the antitrust implications of electronic fund transfer systems.

[129] With IBM's entry into the microcomputer market, the same plug compatible antitrust issues may arise as were seen in the mainframe market.

[130] *See* Telex Corp v IBM Corp, 510 F2d 894 (10th Cir 1975); California Computer Products, Inc v IBM Corp, 613 F2d 727 (9th Cir 1979); and ILC Peripherals Leasing

peripheral device is introduced the designer naturally has a 100 per cent share of the market for that device which gives the designer a competitive advantage until others can reverse-engineer the product or independently develop a competing device. A second advantage occurs where peripheral devices are dependent on the design specifications of a particular central processing unit (CPU). Thus, manufacturers of CPUs and peripheral devices can affect the peripherals market by changing either the CPU, the peripheral device, or the interface between the CPU and the peripherals. These advantages have aided companies which are full system manufacturers to become dominant firms.[131]

IBM and Data General, because of their natural advantages in their respective peripheral submarkets, and their attempts to maintain those advantages, have been attacked under §2.[132] Tandy and Apple, and possibly IBM, are in a similar position. Their development of microcomputers has created a market for peripheral devices in which they and other plug-compatible peripheral manufacturers compete. IBM, Apple, and Tandy, however, do sell technical information to competing makers of pheripheral devices at very low cost and also offer free engineering help. This seems the opposite of the *Telex* type case. Indeed most market analysts credit Apple's success to its very active encouragement of the outisde software and plug-compatible industries. Even so, as developers of CPUs and operating systems software, the conduct of Tandy, Apple, and IBM in changing interfaces, designing new configurations, developing product innovations, and any other conduct which affects the ability of plug-compatible peripheral devices manufacturers to compete with them, must be considered as potential bases for §2 claims. Tandy's and Apple's bundling of microprocessors and software, as well as other bundling schemes, may make it possible to allege price balancing since separate prices for these products are not established uniformly.

The market structure of the microcomputer industry—a few dominant full-line manufacturers, and many single or group product competitors—is strikingly similar to the structure of the mainframe and minicomputer markets. The potential for §2 claims in the microcomputer peripheral device market, therefore, appears great, although it is going to be hard to establish a pricing claim in the vigorously competitive microcomputer market. With several microcomputer models now selling at less than $100 retail, and with heavy competition

---

Corp v IBM Corp, 458 F Supp 423 (ND Cal 1978), *affd per curiam sub nom* Memorex Corp v IBM Corp, 636 F2d 1188 (9th Cir 1980), *cert denied,* 452 US 972 (1981).

[131] Actually in the microcomputer market, new peripherals are usually introduced by outside companies. Only after a proven market is shown for the device does the original manufacturer make it. For instance, IBM, as of early 1983, had not yet introduced a hard disk for its personal computer nor had it introduced complex multifunction memory/I/O/clock cards even though numerous small companies were selling these.

[132] Telex Corp v IBM Corp, 510 F2d 894 (10th Cir 1975); California Computer Products, Inc v IBM Corp, 613 F2d 727 (9th Cir 1979); and ILC Peripherals Leasing Corp v IBM Corp, 458 F Supp 423 (ND Cal 1978), *affd per curiam sub nom* Memorex Corp v IBM Corp, 636 F2d 1188 (9th Cir 1980), *cert denied,* 452 US 972 (1981).

at all levels, it would seem that market forces would give manufacturers little discretion in pricing.

Antitrust and Patents

§4.15   Patents in General

Evidencing a policy counter to the policy of the antitrust laws in encouraging competition, patent laws grant an innovator/inventor a monopoly for the patented product in return for disclosure of the invention. A patent is limited to 17 years. The United States Constitution provides that the: "Congress shall have the power . . . to promote the Progress of Science and Useful Arts, by securing for limited times to authors and inventors the exclusive right to respective writings and discoveries."[133] Pursuant to the constitutional grant of authority, Congress enacted the Patent Act which allows one who discovers any new and useful process, machine, etc., to obtain a patent.[134] The grant of a patent gives the holder the right to exclude others from making use of the fruits of the invention.[135] The patent holder may assign the patent outright or license the use of the patent to another, either exclusively or nonexclusively.[136] Antitrust considerations arise when a potential holder fraudulently seeks to acquire (or enforce) a patent, or when patent owners attempt to extend their monopolies through tying arrangements.[137]

§4.16   Fraudulent Procurement and Enforcement

In *Honeywell Inc v Sperry Rand Corp*, the court detailed the elements that, in addition to the elements necessary to prove a §2 Sherman Act violation, must be proven in order to recover antitrust damages based on an alleged fraud in obtaining a patent: willful and intentional fraud; and injury to business or property caused by the fraudulently procured patent.[138] Rather interestingly, good faith or an honest mistake was held to be a complete defense to an

---

[133] US Const art 1, §8, cl 8.

[134] 35 USC §101.

[135] *Id* §154.

[136] *Id* §261.

[137] For a discussion of antitrust implications in patent licenses, see Stedman, *The Patent-Antitrust Interface,* 58 J Pat Off Socy 316 (1976); Wood, *An Appraisal of Recent Cases Respecting Patents and Antitrust Laws,* 21 Bus Law 999 (1966); Gibbons, *Price Fixing in Patent Licenses and the Antitrust Laws,* 51 Va L Rev 273 (1965). See §§**2.02-2.05** for discussion of using patents for software protection.

[138] Honeywell, Inc v Sperry Rand Corp, 1974-1 Trade Cas (CCH) ¶74874 (D Minn Oct 19, 1973).

antitrust action based on a claim of fraud on the Patent Office.[139] Proof of fraud must be by clear and convincing evidence that the patent was obtained by fraudulent material misrepresentations involving affirmative dishonesty indicative of a deliberately planned and carefully executed scheme to defraud. Thus, the burden for recovering antitrust damages in a fraudulent patent procurement case is extremely high. Honeywell filed suit against Sperry Rand Corporation (SR) and Illinois Scientific Developments (ISD) alleging, among other claims, that SR and ISD had used an illegal patent portfolio to induce IBM and Bell Telephone Laboratories (BTL) to give up meritorious attacks on the validity of the ENIAC and other of defendant's electronic data processing patents. The central thrust of this claim was that SR, in connection with Dr. John W. Machly and J. Prespor Eckert, Jr., had fraudulently obtained a patent for the first computer (ENIAC). Honeywell was able to show that Machly and Eckert had concealed information as to possible co-inventors, and other information as to publication and prior public use, and that SR had concealed information as to co-inventors, publication, prior public use, and sale of the ENIAC computer. Although the patent was invalidated on grounds of prior use, the court, however, held that Honeywell had failed to show willful fraud in obtaining the patent by clear and convincing evidence.[140]

§4.17   Cross-Licensing

Generally, patent holders may enter into cross-licensing of patents (pooling) so long as it is not done to exclude third parties,[141] or to restrain competition by refusing to license competitors.[142] Honeywell alleged in its suit against the Sperry Rand Corporation (SR) that SR and IBM had entered into an illegal patent pooling agreement.[143] In 1956, SR and IBM had entered into a cross-licensing agreement whereby both parties would cross-license and exchange all their technological know-how relating to electronic data processing (EDP). In effect, SR and IBM created a technological merger of the two companies. At the time of the agreement, SR and IBM possessed 95 per cent of the market for electronic data processing (EDP) equipment.[144]

Honeywell claimed that SR had conspired with IBM: (1) to mislead the public, and its competitors as to the true extent of the transfer of information; (2) to prevent Honeywell and others from obtaining access to IBM's or SR's EDP patents; and (3) to maintain their positions of dominance by not actively attempting to include third parties in their information and patent exchange.

---

[139] *Id.*

[140] *Id* ¶95895.

[141] Hartford-Empire Co v United States, 323 US 386 (1945).

[142] Zenith Radio Corp v Hazel Time Research Inc, 395 US 100 (1969).

[143] 510 F2d 894. Honeywell, Inc v Sperry Rand Corp, 1974-1 Trade Cas (CCH) ¶74874 (D Minn Oct 19, 1973).

[144] *Id.*

Honeywell prevailed on its allegations on antitrust violations, but the court held that the action was barred by the statute of limitations.[145] Honeywell also complained of SR's discriminatory licensing of the ENIAC patent, claiming violations of §2 of the Sherman Act because SR had treated two of its competitors differently. IBM had paid only $11,100,000 for the license to use the ENIAC patent, but SR was demanding a royalty from Honeywell in excess of $250 million. In order to sustain its claim of a §2 violation Honeywell had the burden of proving: (1) that plaintiff took a license; (2) that the royalty rate charged plaintiff and that charged a competitor were unequal; (3) that in all relevant areas plaintiff and its licensed competitors were similar; and (4) that the discriminatory rate caused substantial impairment of competition in the relevant market. The trial court rejected this claim by Honeywell, holding that Honeywell had failed to prove injury because the ENIAC patent was invalid, and Honeywell could have litigated that claim earlier.[146]

§4.18   Tie-Ins and Tie-Outs

In 1936, the Supreme Court declared tying arrangements an antitrust violation.[147] The judgment entered against IBM for tying the lease of its tabulating machines to its punched card held that even if IBM's defense of patent protection had been accepted as a justification, §3 of the Clayton Act specifically prohibited tying. A valid business justification is the only defense to a tie-in.[148] In the computer industry, neither IBM nor Data General was able to justify a tying arrangement once two products were found to exist. In addition to the prohibition against tying products together, a patented article may not be licensed or sold on the condition that the licensee or buyer refrain from buying or dealing in another product. This is what is known as a tie-out and is also per se illegal.[149]

---

[145] *Id.*

[146] *Id*

[147] United States v IBM, 298 US 131 (1936). *See also* Curly, *Patent Acquisition and Restricted Licenses Under Antitrust Law,* B Seaton Hall L Rev 645 (1977).

[148] *See* United States v Jerrold Elecs, 187 F Supp 545 (ED Pa), *affd per curiam,* 365 US 567 (1960); Dehydration Process v AD Smith Co, 292 F2d 653 (1st Cir 1961). In both cases the courts found that there was a valid reason for the tying arrangements which could not be met by other, less restrictive means.

[149] *See* McCullough v Krammerer Corp, 166 F2d 759 (9th Cir 1948).

Antitrust and Copyright

§4.19 Copyright in General

The interface between copyright and antitrust laws was established by the United States Supreme Court in 1913 when the Court held that copyright holders were subject to antitrust regulation.[150] A copyright protects intellectual property by granting the owner a limited monopoly right similar to a patent, although the duration of the limited monopoly afforded copyright holders is the life of the author plus 50 years.[151] Copyright protection grants an author the exclusive right to prevent unauthorized use or copying of writings. The scope of writings is very broad and encompasses literature, photographs, works of art, and their reproduction. Ideas are not protectable by copyright, but protection is afforded the expression of those ideas. This is of critical importance in the area of computer software.

The Copyright Act of 1976 left the status of computer software unresolved. Many commentators believe that software would be more appropriately protected by copyright rather than patent law. In December 1980, the Computer Software Copyright Act of 1980 was enacted which amended §101 of the Copyright Act by adding a definition of a computer.[152] The 1980 Copyright Act also amended §117, stating that:

> not withstanding the provisions of section 106, it is not an infringement for the owner of a copy of a computer program to make or authorize the making of another copy or adaptation of that computer program provided: (1) that such a new copy or adaptation is created as an essential step in the utilization of the computer program in conjunction with a machine and that it is used in no other manner; or (2) that such new copy or adaptation is for archival purposes only and that all archival copies are destroyed in the event that continued possession of the computer program should cease to be rightful.

This amendment authorizes an author to distribute copies of a computer program *for use* of its intended function without affecting the protection afford-

---

[150] Straus & Straus v American Publishing Assn, 231 US 222 (1913). *But cf* Midway Mfg Co, 1981-2 Trade Cas (CCH) ¶64170 (ND Ill 1982), in which an antitrust violation by a copyright owner of electronic games was raised by the alleged copyright infringer as a defense to the copyright infringement.

The alleged copyright infringer had defended its activities on the basis of a purported agreement between the copyright owner and a competitor to split the world market for the electronic games. The defense failed, as the court held that there was no showing of how the copyright owner had used its monopoly over copyrighted material to exert anticompetitive power over noncopyrighted materials.

[151] 17 USC §302.

[152] Pub L No 96-517, 94 Stat 3015. See §§2.06-2.10 for a discussion of copyrighting computer software.

ed the copyright owner as claims of publication, abandoning, and not policing the copyright will not be recognized.

§4.20 Refusal to Grant License

The refusal on the part of a copyright owner to grant a license is permissible as long as the decision not to grant a license is made independently by the copyright holder. The right of the copyright owner to select persons with whom to deal may be challenged only when refusal by the copyright owner results from an agreement between the owner and third parties. Copyright licensing arrangements can be held to violate §1 of the Sherman Act if injury can be shown.[153]

In *United States v Singer,* the United States sued to enjoin Singer and two of its competitors from restraining interstate and foreign commerce in the importation, sale, and distribution of zigzag sewing machines in the United States.[154] The evidence showed a course of dealings between the defendant manufacturers which included cross-licensing on a nonexclusive and royalty-free basis for the purpose of supressing Japanese competition. The Court held that these actions constituted a conspiracy to exclude Japanese competitors in violation of §1 of the Sherman Act. To date no refusals to grant licenses for copyrighted software and a resulting §1 allegation have been reported.

§4.21 Amount Charged for License

The licensing of copyrights is often a lucrative proposition for the copyright holder because of royalty provisions, which presently are the only form of compensation allowed for copyrighted software. A court is bound to accept the terms of the license agreement,[155] and the licensor is free to exact the highest possible price, while the licensee can bargain a royalty rate as low as possible.[156] In *United States v General Electric,* the Supreme Court held that a bargained-for royalty in licensing agreements does not have to be reasonable to be valid.[157] If the proprietor of the copyright authorizes discriminatory royalty rates among licensees in competition with each other, thereby causing harm to one or more competitors, this discriminatory licensing agreement is an antitrust violation similar to the one alleged by Honeywell against Sperry Rand.[158] As with refusals to grant copyright licenses, thus far no software

---

[153] *See* Honeywell, Inc v Sperry Rand Corp, 1974-1 Trade Cas (CCH) ¶74874 (D Minn Oct 19, 1973).

[154] United States v Singer Mfg Co, 374 US 174 (1963).

[155] Brulotte v Thys Co, 379 US 29 (1964).

[156] Shapiro v General Motors Corp, 472 F Supp 636 (D Md 1979).

[157] United States v General Electric Co, 272 US 476 (1926).

[158] Honeywell, Inc v Sperry Rand Corp, 1974-1 Trade Cas (CCH) ¶74874 (D Minn Oct 19, 1973).

disputes have been reported involving discriminatory copyrighted software license royalty rates.

In conclusion, the computer industry has been a fertile source of antitrust litigation, producing a plethora of antitrust claims of monoplization and unlawful tying arrangements. In the arena of mainframes, IBM can certainly expect further antitrust litigation in the 1980s. Data General's various infringement suits and counterclaims of monopolization should yield guidelines in substantive antitrust law applicable to the minicomputer market. The microcomputer industry will not be immune from antitrust allegations and resulting litigation in the related areas of patents and copyrights. Antitrust law will also need to develop quite rapidly as technological developments such as systems software contained in firmware on a single chip becomes realities.

The Communications
Regulatory Environment

5

§5.19   Emerging Communications Technologies

Appendix 5-1   Comparison of Proposals for Restructuring AT&T

§5.01   Generally

Four major political and legal forces have affected the communications regulatory environment: the Federal Communications Commission (FCC), Congress, the Department of Justice (DOJ), and the courts. The FCC, *Computer Inquiry II,* ordered all enhanced services and most interstate customer premises equipment (CPE) detariffed. Also, dominant carriers are permitted to offer enhanced services and CPE only through a totally separate unregulated subsidiary.[1] Congress considered but did not enact the Communications Act Amendments of 1980 which would have required dominant concerns to offer enhanced services and CPE through a separate subsidiary, as well as effecting several other changes in the communications regulatory environment.[2] The third, and most important, factor influencing the telecommunications industry relates to the *United States v American Telephone & Telegraph Co (AT&T)* antitrust settlement. The parties have agreed on and the courts have accepted a divestiture plan in which the 22 Bell operating companies (BOCs) will be divested into 7 separate companies, with AT&T retaining Bell Laboratories, Long Lines, Bell Headquarters, and Western Electric.[3] The communications regulatory environment in the 1980s will remain in a state of flux while the structure and role of the parent AT&T and the BOCs are refined within these four legal arenas.

This chapter presents a brief discussion of the history of the 1934 Communications Act, followed by analyses of the FCC's *Computer Inquiry I* and *Computer Inquiry II.* The congressional response to the changing communications technology will then be examined. Finally, the interrelationship between the FCC decisions and the *United States v AT&T* settlement will be analyzed, followed by a general discussion of future trends in the communications industry based on the emerging legal environment.

---

[1] Amendment of §64.702 of the Commission's Rules and Regulations, 77 FCC2d 384 (1980), *modified on reconsideration,* 84 FCC2d 50 (1980), *further reconsideration,* 88 FCC2d 512 (1981), *appeal pending sub nom* Computer & Communications Industry Assn v Federal Communications Commn, No 80-1471 (DC Cir 1980). See generally Trebing, *Common Carrier Regulation—The Silent Crisis,* 34 JL and Contemp Prob 299 (1969) (contains an excellent concise legal history of telecommunications in the United States); G. Brock, The Telecommunications Industry (1981).

[2] For example S 2827, 96th Cong, 2d Sess (1980).

[3] [1980 Transfer Binder] Trade Reg Rep (CCH) ¶8699.

Federal Communications Commission Considerations

§5.02   The 1934 Communications Act and Interpretations

The Federal Communications Act of 1934 established the Federal Communications Commission (FCC), and empowered this regulatory agency with both rulemaking and adjudicatory authority.[4] The FCC was granted broad authority in the communications field.[5] Under the 1934 Act, Congress outlined the basic rules for regulating interstate and foreign wire and radio communications.[6] Interstate telephone service was established as a nationally regulated monopoly (but intrastate telephone operations remained subject to regulation by state public utilities commissions), and telephone companies were declared to be communications common carriers, i.e., firms which were regulated and which provided communications services to the public pursuant to a tariff.[7]

---

[4] 47 USC §151 *et seq* (1976). §151 explains that the FCC was created for the purpose of "regulating interstate and foreign commerce in communications by wire and radio so as to make available, so far as possible, to all the people of the United States a rapid, efficient, nationwide and worldwide and radio communications service with adequate facilities and reasonable charges . . ." See generally Berman, *Computer or Communications? Allocation of Functions and the Role of the Federal Communications Commission,* 27 Fed Com BJ 161 (1974); Davison, Babcock & Lesley, *Computers and Federal Regulation,* 21 Ad L Rev 287 (1969).

[5] The expansive nature of the FCC authority can be seen in United States v Southwestern Cable Co, 392 US 157 (1969), in which the FCC had requested legislation to regulate the Community Antenna Television System (CATV). However, no legislation was enacted. The legislators responded to the FCC's request by saying that the determination of jurisdiction was left to the courts. The FCC gradually exercised jurisdiction, and subsequently issued revised rules for regulating CATV.

The Court in Southwestern Cable held that "the FCC's authority recognized here is restricted to that which is reasonably ancillary to the effective performance of its responsibilities for the regulation of television in broadcasting . . ." The FCC has the authority to issue "such orders . . . as may be necessary in the execution of its function. . . ."

[6] 47 USC §153. Under §153(a) "wire communication" or "communication by wire" means the "transmission of writing, signs, signals, pictures, and sounds of all kinds of aid of wire, cable, or other like connection between the points of origin and reception of such transmission, including all instrumentalities, facilities, apparatus, and services (among other things, the receipt, forwarding, and delivery of communications) incidental to such transmission."

§153(b) similarly defines radio communications as "transmission by radio of writing, signs, signals, pictures, and sounds of all kinds, including all instrumentalities, facilities, apparatus, and services (among other things the receipt, forwarding, and delivery of communication) incidental to such transmission."

[7] See 74 Am Jur2d *Telecommunications* §§4-6 (1974); and 86 CJS *Telegraphs, Telephones, Radio, and Television* §§5-7 (1954). Tariffs, or rates, are established through a procedure in which a regulated common carrier requests approval of its tariff proposals. The appropriate regulatory authority approves a tariff which affords the common carrier an

The 1956 Western Electric Consent Decree

Before examining the cases leading up to *Computer Inquiry I* and *Computer Inquiry II,* an overriding salient fact should be noted. Under the 1956 *Western Electric* consent decree, AT&T was prohibited from offering, even through a separate subsidiary, any device that possessed the capability to perform a data processing function.[8] AT&T was also foreclosed from any direct or indirect activity in a unregulated market.[9] Thus, the FCC, in attempting to establish the legal distinction between data processing and communications, was in effect defining the limits of the 1956 *Western Electric* consent decree, and thereby, delineating the boundaries of the communications industry within which AT&T could operate. If the FCC were to classify a data processing service or product as a communications service or product, then AT&T was able to offer the service or product under tariff, and thus the objective of the 1956 *Western Electric* consent decree, to prohibit AT&T from entering the data processing industry, was thwarted.[10]

Early Cases

Whereas in 1956 the distinction between communications and data processing was relatively well-defined, advances in communications and computer technologies occurring after 1956 blurred the distinction between communications and data processing.[11]

Before these technological advances, AT&T offered end-to-end communications service. These technological developments involving the interaction of

---

opportunity to achieve a fair rate of return on its invested capital. This process provides a substitute for market forces which, in theory, regulate a competitive industry composed of many firms offering and buying the same or similar goods or services.

8 1956 Trade Cas (CCH) ¶68246. The defendants were each:

> enjoined and restrained from commencing, and after three years from the data of this Final Judgment from continuing, directly or indirectly, to manufacture for sale or lease any equipment which is of a type not sold or leased or intended to be sold or leased to Companies of the Bell System, for use in furnishing common carrier communication services, except equipment used in the manufacture or installation or equipment which is of a type so sold or leased or intended to be sold or leased.

9 *Id.* Under the 1956 Consent Decree, AT&T was "enjoined and restrained from engaging, either directly, or indirectly through its subsidiaries other than Western and Western's subsidiaries, in any business other than furnishings of common carrier communications services . . . "

10 See generally *AT&T's Access to New Markets Backed by Court,* Wall St J, Sept 8, 1981, at 1; *Judge Widens AT&T Business Scope,* Wash Post, Sept 5, 1981, at C-7. Judge Vincent P. Biunno of the US District Court for the District of New Jersey ruled September 4, 1981, that the FCC's 1980 Ruling on Competition and the 1956 Consent Decree did not conflict. Judge Biunno, ruling in March, 1980 at the request of AT&T that he interpret the 1956 Consent Decree, held that enhanced services could be offered by AT&T because it is a communications service.

11 See generally *The Computer Society, A Special Section,* Time, Feb 20, 1978; Bylinsky, *The Second Computer Revolution,* Fortune, Feb 11, 1980, at 230-32.

communications and computers gave rise to numerous cases in which the Bell System end-to-end service was challenged.

The *Hush-a-Phone* and *Carterphone* Decisions

Hush-a-Phone Corp v United States tested the legality of the tariff prohibiting all foreign attachments to AT&T's phone system.[12] Hush-a-Phone manufactured and sold a device that, when attached over the speaker of a telephone muffled the voice of the person speaking into the phone so that third parties near the speaker could not overhear the conversation. Several telephone companies threatened to suspend or terminate service to subscribers who continued to use Hush-a-Phone. On basis of the FCC tariff prohibiting foreign attachments. The FCC had concluded that the use of devices such as Hush-a-Phone was "deleterious to the telephone system" and would result in a general degradation of the quality of service.[13] On appeal, the decision was reversed and remanded to the commission. The Court of Appeals for the District of Columbia stated that the tariff was "an unwarranted interference with the telephone subscriber's right reasonably to use his telephone in ways which are privately beneficial without being publicly detrimental."[14] On remand, the commission invalidated the tariff prohibiting foreign attachments, but only as to Hush-a-Phones.

Another early case involved the Carterphone Corporation's production and sale of a radio transmitter that automatically switched on when the user was speaking, and then returned the radio to receiving status when the speaker was finished. By connecting the device to the phone system, a user was able to call any point on the phone system from a remote radio.[15] When the common carriers announced that the use of Carterphones on the telephone network was prohibited under the tariff prohibiting foreign attachments, Carterphone Corporation filed a private antitrust suit against the telephone companies to invalidate the tariff on antitrust grounds.[16] The court ruled that the FCC had primary jurisdiction, and referred the case to the commission. A hearing examiner approved the Carterphone radio transmitter for use on the telephone network, and ordered the carriers to change their tariffs to allow the use of the Carterphone device.[17] On appeal, the commission, without a hearing, affirmed the hearing examiner, and broadened the hearing examiner's decision to in-

---

[12] Hush-a-Phone Corp v United States, 238 F2d 266 (DC Cir 1956).

[13] Hush-a-Phone Corp v AT&T, 20 FCC 391, 420 (1955).

[14] 238 F2d at 269. See Smith, *Storming the FCC Fortress: Can the FCC Deregulate Competitive Common Carrier Services*, 32 Fed Com LJ 205, 221 (1980).

[15] There was no electrical connection between the AT&T equipment and the Carterphone.

[16] Carter v AT&T, 250 F Supp 188 (ND Tex 1966), *affd*, 365 F2d 486 (5th Cir 1966), *cert denied*, 385 US 1008 (1962).

[17] Use of the Carterphone Device (Initial Decision of Hearing Examiner), 13 FCC2d 430 (1967).

clude all harmless attachments provided by customers.[18] The FCC's decision was appealed, but the appeal was later withdrawn when the parties settled out of court.[19]

After World War II, microwave communications were developing slowly, and the FCC generally assigned frequencies only to common carriers and to government agencies. By the 1950s, however, numerous corporations were applying for licenses to operate their own microwave systems.[20] In 1967, the commission consolidated all the applications, and over the objection of common carriers changed its no-entry policy to allow private firms entry into the microwave field.[21] Although each applicant was assigned a portion of the radio spectrum above 890 millicycles, the private applicants were not allowed to share construction or use of a microwave system among themselves. If applicants had been permitted to share facilities or use of a microwave sytem, they could have combined together to provide themselves a total microwave system which would have been in effect a major unregulated carrier in competition with the existing regulated common carriers. Even without the ability to combine and share a microwave communications system, each individual applicant posed an economic threat to the existing carriers. The regulated common carriers, consequently, reacted defensively to protect their shares of the communications revenues by applying for new service offerings with drastically reduced long distance rates.[22]

Microwave Communications, Inc.

In 1964, Microwave Communications, Inc. (MCI) applied to the FCC for permission to provide low-cost voice and data communications links between urban centers. Substantial price reductions, as compared to the common carriers' rates, were proposed. Consumers would also have been granted complete flexibility in using the terminal equipment on an unqualified sharing of lines. Thus, a consumer needing only a portion of the MCI offering could purchase the service and resell what was not needed. In many instances, this sharing of lines would afford each customer substantial savings over AT&T's costs for similar lines on a nonshared basis. A hearing examiner approved a limited MCI

---

[18] Use of the Carterphone Device in Message Toll Telephone Service, 13 FCC2d 420 (1968), *reconsideration denied*, 14 FCC2d 571 (1968).

[19] See generally Walker, Mathison & Jones, *Data Transmission and the Foreign Attachment Rule*, 16 Datamation 60 (1969).

[20] See generally G. Brock, The Telecommunications Industry 180-87, 198-210 (1981).

[21] Allocation of Frequencies In the Bands Above 890 Mc, 27 FCC 359 (1969), *reconsideration denied*, 29 FCC 825 (1969).

[22] See AT&T, 38 FCC 270 (1964), 37 FCC 1111 (1964), *affd sub nom* American Trucking Assn v Federal Communications Commn, 377 F2d 121 (1966), *cert denied*, 386 US 943 (1967). See generally Note, *Regulation of Computer Communications*, 7 Harv J on Legis 208 (1970).

application connecting Chicago and St. Louis.[23] In affirming the hearing examiner, the commission stated that the proposed service by MCI would meet a significant unfilled communications need.[24]

After the initial MCI application was granted, other applicants petitioned the commission for construction of commercial microwave systems. After realizing that it was faced with a general licensing question, the commission in the late 1960s grouped together several of the applications.[25] Over the objections of the regulated common carriers, in 1970 the commission established a policy of approving individual applications.[26] Subsequently, the FCC approved the applications of numerous companies wanting to offer commercial microwave services.[27]

Bunker-Ramo Corporation

While the MCI dispute was in progress, a dispute arose between Bunker-Ramo Corporation and AT&T. Bunker-Ramo had previously provided a national stock quotation service on lines leased from AT&T, but in 1965 included a buy-sell provision in its service offering such that brokers using the stock quotation service could also transact business. AT&T contending that the additional service proposed by Bunker-Ramo was within its traditional communications monopoly, denied Bunker-Ramo access to the necessary communications lines. Bunker-Ramo finally withdrew its message offering petition. Western Union (substantially under FCC regulation) filed a tariff in 1967 for authority to provide the same service that Bunker-Ramo had applied for.[28]

Thus, the FCC, in allowing Hush-a-Phone to enter the limited mechanical phone attachments market, Carterphone to connect (although nonelectrically) with the phone system, and MCI to establish voice and digital communications service between major cities had breached the wall of AT&T's end-to-end service monopoly. Even though the Commission had not permitted Bunker-Ramo to establish a message-switching service in addition to its stock-quota-

---

[23] Microwave Communication Inc, 18 FCC2d 953 (1969), *reconsideration denied,* 21 FCC2d 190 (1970).

[24] Microwave Communications, Inc, 18 FCC2d 953, 966 (1969).

[25] Establishment of Policies and Procedures for Consideration of Applications to Provide Specialized Common Carrier Services in the Domestic Public Point-to-Point Microwave Radio Service and Proposed Amendments to Parts 21,43 and 61 of the Commission's Rules, 24 FCC2d 318 (1970).

[26] 29 FCC2d 870 (1971), *affd sub nom* Washington Util & Transp Commn v Federal Communications Commn, 513 F2d 1142 (9th Cir), *cert denied,* 423 US 836 (1975). See generally Smith, *Storming the FCC Fortress: Can the FCC Deregulate Competitive Common Carrier Services,* 32 Fed Com LJ 205, 222 (1980).

[27] See Comment, *Federal Communications Commission Regulation of Domestic Computer Communications: A Competitive Reformation,* 22 Buffalo L Rev 947 (1973).

[28] Western Union Tel Co, 11 FCC2d 1 (1967). The Western Union tariff was approved over the objection of Bunker-Ramo.

tion service, a major shift in FCC regulatory philosophy had occurred.[29] Based on the FCC's new policy of *free entry*, both regulated communications common carriers and some nonregulated communications carriers were permitted to compete for parts of the communications traffic which had previously been the exclusive domain of AT&T in its end-to-end communications service offerings.

§5.03 *Computer Inquiry I*

Against the backdrop of rulings described in **§5.02,** the Federal Communications Commission (FCC) determined that a full examination of the computer and communications interface was needed. In 1966 the commission initiated an *Inquiry* designed to answer the following two questions:

1. Under what circumstances should data processing, computer information, and message switching, or any particular combination thereof, be deemed subject to regulation pursuant to the provisions of the Communications Act?

2. Whether the policies and objectives of the Communications Act would be served better by such regulations or by such services evolving in a free, competitive market, and if the latter, whether changes in existing provisions of the law or regulations were needed.[30]

The commission received over 3,000 pages of correspondence, and submitted these responses to the Stanford Research Institute (SRI) for analysis.[31] In its final decision, the commission made three major rulings: (1) the FCC would retain its jurisdiction over those aspects of the computer industry in any way related to communications; (2) common carriers could not favor their own affiliates if they chose to enter the data processing industry; and (3) the principle of maximum separation was established in which the data processing affiliates were to be totally separated from their parent common carriers.[32]

---

[29] See generally Comment, *Computer Services in the Federal Regulation of Communications,* 116 U Pa L Rev 328 (1967), Smith, *Interdependence of Computer and Communications Services and Facilities: A Question of Federal Regulation,* 117 U Pa L Rev 829 (1969).

[30] Regulatory and Policy Problems Presented by the Interdependence of Computer and Communications Services and Facilities, 7 FCC2d 11, 17 (1966) (Notice of Inquiry). An additional issue relating to privacy was originally raised, but was later dismissed as being beyond the jurisdiction of the Commission.

[31] Dunn, *Policy Issues Presented by the Interdependence of Computer and Communications Services,* 34 Law & Contemp Probs 309 (1969); Dunn, *The FCC Computer Inquiry,* 15 Datamation 71 (1969).

[32] Regulatory and Policy Problems Presented by the Interdependence of Computer and Communication Services and Facilities, 28 FCC2d 291 (1970) (Tentative Decision); 28 FCC2d 267 (1971) (Final Decision), *reconsideration denied,* 34 FCC2d 557 (1972). See generally B. Gilchrist & M. Wessel, Governemnt Regulation of the Computer Industry 70 (1972); Note, *The FCC Computer Inquiry: Interface of Competitive and Regulated Markets,* 71 Mich L Rev 172 (1972).

In deciding to regulate the communications aspects of the data processing industry, and thereby limit AT&T to communications offerings only, the Commission was forced to define the difference between data processing and message switching. *Data processing* was defined as:

> the use of a computer for the processing of information as distinguished from circuit or mesage-switching. "Processing" involves the use of the computer for operations which include, *inter alia,* the functions of storing, retrieving, sorting, merging, and calculating data, according to programmed instructions.[33]

Message switching was defined as:

> the computer-controlled transmission of messages, between two or more points, via communications facilities, wherein the content of the message remains unaltered.[34]

The commission further refined the difference between message switching and data processing by defining *hybrid data processing* and *hybrid communications.* These two categories were defined as follows:

> (i)   *Hybrid data processing service* is a hybrid service offering wherein the message-switching capability is incidental to the data processing function or purpose.
> (ii)   *Hybrid communications service* is a hybrid service offering wherein the data processing capability is incidental to the message-switching function or purpose.[35]

The overall effect of the data processing definition was that firms whose primary thrust was data processing would not be regulated. The FCC was assuming that communications common carriers would police the line between hybrid data processing and hybrid communications.[36]

§5.04   —*GTE Service v FCC*

After exhausting administrative procedures, the communications common carriers appealed the Federal Communications Commission's (FCC's) *Computer Inquiry I* decision. *GTE Service Corp v FCC* affirmed the authority of the FCC to regulate communications common carriers who entered the data processing

---

[33] Computer Use of Communications Facilities, 28 FCC2d 267, 287 (1971); *see also* 47 CFR §64.702(a)(1).

[34] 47 CFR §64.702(a)(2).

[35] 47 CFR §64.702(a)(5).

[36] Computer Use of Communications Facilities, 28 FCC2d 274 (1971). See Berman, *Computer or Communications? Allocation of Functions and the Rule of the Federal Communications Commission,* 27 Fed Comm BJ 161 (1974).

field, but held that the FCC could not regulate data processors who merely used communications networks.[37] More importantly, the court upheld the FCC's requirement that communications common carriers wanting to enter the data processing industry establish a totally separate date processing subsidiary. However, the attempt by the FCC to prohibit the separate subsidiary from using the parent company's name was invalidated. Consequently, the separate subsidiary could obtain the goodwill benefits of its parent's name. Also, carriers were permitted to purchase data processing services from their separate subsidiaries.[38]

§5.05 —Post-*Computer Inquiry I* Developments

In the 1960s and 1970s, communications and computer technologies advanced ever more rapidly, with the data communications equipment sector at the forefront of this technological advancement.[39] Data communications technology has attained a high degree of specialization with front-end computers dedicated solely to communications functions acting as buffers between powerful mainframes and intelligent communications networks. These front-end computers provide many sophisticated functions including line control, character and message switching and handling, conversion of data and protocols, error control, message editing, and message queuing.[40] Computer mainframes, relieved of these communications functions, can be specifically designed to perform various data processing functions. Given these technological developments, the legal distinction between data processing and message switching which the Federal Communications Commission established in *Computer Inquiry I* became "technologically outdated."[41]

§5.06 *Computer Inquiry II*

Based on technological developments and the realization that the demarcation between data processing, hybrid categories, and communications defined in *Computer Inquiry I* were no longer technically valid, the Federal Communications Commission (FCC) initiated *Computer Inquiry II*.[42] In *Computer Inquiry II*, the FCC asked the industry for comments and new definitions dealing with

---

[37] GTE Service Corp v Federal Communications Commn, 474 F2d 724 (2d Cir 1973), *decision on remand,* 40 FCC2d 293 (1973).

[38] The FCC's requirement of separate subsidiaries was intended to reduce the possibility of cross-subsidization. *See* Note, *Federal Communications Commission - Review of Regulations Relating to Provisions of Data Processing Services by Communications Common Carriers,* 15 BC Ind & Com L Rev 162 (1973).

[39] See generally Frank, *Alive and Well,* 26 Datamation 112 (1980).

[40] *Id* 112, 114.

[41] Wiley, *Competition in Telecommunications,* 47 Antitrust LJ 1282, 1285 (1979).

[42] Amendment of §64.702 of the Commission's Rules and Regulations, 61 FCC2d 103 (1976) (Notice of Inquiry and Proposed Rulemaking).

data processing functions.[43]

Data-Speed 40/4 Controversy

Simultaneously with the initiation of *Computer Inquiry II,* AT&T announced that it would introduce the Data-Speed 40/4 communications terminal. AT&T proposed to offer the Data-Speed 40/4 as a tariffed communications item. Many terminal manufacturers, however, believed that the Data-Speed 40/4 was a *smart* data processing terminal, which pursuant to the Western Electric *1956* Consent Decree, could not be offered even through a separate subsidiary.[44] Thus, the opponents of AT&T were really arguing that the Data-Speed 40/4 represented an attempt by AT&T to enter the data processing industry. The Chief of the FCC Common Carrier Bureau agreed with the competitors of AT&T. The Commission, however, ultimately disagreed, and determined that the Data-Speed 40/4 could be offered by AT&T as a tariffed item.[45] The Second Circuit Court of Appeals upheld the decision of the commission.[46] As a result of the Data-Speed 40/4 dispute, an additional notice to the *Computer Inquiry II* was issued to deal specifically with the problem of terminals possessing communications and data processing capabilities.[47] Comments were also sought as to whether customer premises equipment (CPE) which performed any information processing function besides conversion should also be regulated.

Enhanced Services and Customer Premises Equipment

In the final decision of *Computer Inquiry II,* the Commission abandoned the procedures it had established under *Computer Inquiry I* for distinguishing be-

---

[43] *Id.* The Commission acknowledged the "technological advances, in hardware and software, which are tending to cause a blurring of the distinctions between data processing and communications. . . . In particular, the dramatic advances made in large scale integrated circuit technology, . . . minicomputers, microcomputers, and other special purpose devices. . . ."

[44] *See* United States v Western Electric Co, 1956 Trade Cas (CCH) ¶68246, at 71134 The Consent Decree prohibited AT&T from offering data processing equipment or services. *Id* at 71138.

[45] AT&T, 62 FCC2d 21 (1977). The initial vote by the Commission was tied, but the Commission finally voted that the Data-Speed 40/4 was properly classed as a tariffed communication item.

[46] IBM v Federal Communications Commn, 570 F2d 452 (2d Cir 1978). In interpreting §203(a) of the 1934 Act, the court held that the FCC's classification of a complex of small machines with communicative capacity to send and receive messages from a central computer as "communications" as opposed to "data processing" was not improper.

[47] Amendment of §64.702 of the Commission's Rules and Regulations, 64 FCC2d 771, 773 (1977). The FCC stated that "new technology has clearly made it possible for terminals to automatically perform many processing operations which they previously performed poorly or not at all—by employing techniques previously limited to central computers."

tween communications and data processing.[48] Instead, all network services were classified as either *basic* or *enhanced.* Basic service was limited to communications common carriers:

> offering transmission capacity for the movement of information, whereas enhanced service combines basic service with computer processing applications that act on the format, content, code, protocol or similar aspects of the subscriber's transmitted information, or provide the subscriber additional, different, or restructured information, or involve subscriber interaction with stored information.[49]

The commission, in December, 1980, further refined the distinction between basic and enhanced services by comparing basic service to a "transmission pipeline," in contrast to enhanced services which are dependent upon basic service, but are different in kind from the pipeline service.[50]

Regarding CPE, the Commission had noted in its May, 1980 Final Decision that, "in general, no regulatory distinction should be made between various types of carrier-provided CPE."[51] In the December, 1980 supplement, however, the Commission did create two subcategories for use during the transition

---

[48] Amendment of §64.702 of the Commission's Rules and Regulations, 77 FCC2d 384 (1980) (Final Decision).

[49] *Id* 387. In the Tentative Decision, the Commission had distinguished three categories of service—voice, basic non-voice (BNV), and enhanced non-voice (ENV). Carriers owning transmission facilities would have been required to provide ENV through a separate corporate entity. In addition, the Commission proposed new definitions for distinguishing between communications and data communications of ENV. Resale carriers would have been allowed to offer both ENV communications and ENV data processing services through common computer facilities. The Commission, however, opted for the basic/enhanced dichotomy as a more simplified terminology. *See* Amendment of §64.702 of the Commission's Rules and Regulations, 72 FCC2d 358 (1979) (Tentative Decision and Further Notice of Rulemaking).

[50] Amendment of §64.702 of the Commission's Rules and Regulations, 84 FCC2d 50, 54 (1980) (Memorandum Opinion and Order).

[51] 77 FCC2d at 388 (1980). In the Tentative Decision the Commission had proposed to define CPE based on whether the CPE performed more than a basic media conversion (BMC) function. After public comments, the Commission concluded that:

> [T]he public interest would not be served by classifying CPE based on whether or not more than a basic media conversion function is performed. We conclude that, in light of increasing sophistication of all types of CPE and the varied uses to which CPE can be put while under the user's control, it is likely that any given classification scheme would impose an artificial, uneconomic constraint on the design and use of CPE. In general, no regulatory distinction should be made between various types of carrier-provided CPE.

Full analysis of the problem of CPE is made impossible by the leaps in technological advancement that have taken place in the computer communications industry in the past five years. See generally *The Computer Society, A Special Section,* Time, Feb 20, 1978; Bylinsky, *The Second Computer Revolution,* Fortune, Feb 11, 1980, at 230-32.

period for detariffing CPE.[52] Equipment placed in service after January 1, 1983, and federally tariffed CPE would be detariffed as of January 1, 1983.[53] CPE which was tariffed at the state level and subject to the separations process was classified as *embedded CPE*.[54] Embedded CPE would not be subject to the January 1, 1983, detariffing deadline imposed on new CPE and interstate CPE, and a separate implementation proceeding would be instituted by the FCC.

By March 1, 1982, all carrier-provided CPE had to be "unbundled" from other service offerings, and carrier-provided CPE was also to be detariffed.[55] To prevent the rate base from being improperly inflated, the investment of "unbundled" CPE was required to be removed at the then-current book value from the jurisdictional rate base of each of the respective carriers. It is important to note that the FCC only detariffed, but did not deregulate, enhanced services and CPE.

Corporate Separations Requirements

Given the "significant potential to cross-subsidize or to engage in other anti-competitive conduct," the commission initially required both AT&T and General Telephone (GTE) to establish separate corporate entities to provide enhanced services or CPE.[56] Subsequently, the separate subsidiary requirement was applied to AT&T alone because of the risk that the largely captive monopoly ratepayers might be burdened by anticompetitive conduct by

---

[52] 84 FCC2d at 66-67. The Commission acknowledged that under the bifurcated approach, some customers during the transition period may pay different rates for equivalent CPE.

[53] Amendment of Part 67 of the Commission's Rules and Establishment of a Joint Board, 88 FCC2d 512 (1981) (Memorandum Opinion and Order on Further Reconsideration). In 1981 AT&T proposed to detariff all CPE at one time. This one step process was called the "flash cut" approach. The FCC, however, rejected this approach and reiterated its determination to follow its bifurcated approach in detariffing CPE.

[54] The Jurisdictional Separations process divides exchange and interexchange investment into local and interstate categories, and then further apportions the interstate component between the message and private line service categories on the basis of techniques described in a manual which is incorporated by reference in Pt 67 of the Commission's Rules. See 77 FCC2d at 447-50. In June, 1980 the Commission established a Federal-State Joint Board. See Amendment of Part 67 of the Commission's Rules and Establishment of a Joint Board, 78 FCC2d 837 (1980) (Notice of Proposed Rulemaking and Order Establishing a Joint Board). See also MTS and WATS Market Structure, 77 FCC2d 224 (1980) (Second Supplemental Notice); Amendment of Part 67 of the Commission Rules and Regulations, 89 FCC2d 1 (1982) (Second Further Notice of Proposed Rulemaking); and 90 FCC2d 52 (1982) (Decision and Order).

[55] 77 FCC2d at 447-50. See also 84 FCC2d at 65-67.

[56] 77 FCC2d at 388-89. The Commission stated that in weighing:

> [T]he public interest benefits of our objectives and the economic tradeoffs inherent in a separate subsidiary requirement, we have determined that limited imposition of the requirement will best serve the communications ratepayer and the public interest more generally.

AT&T.[57] The AT&T subsidiary would not have been permitted to own or to construct its own transmission facilities; thus, all transmission capacity would have had to be obtained from an underlying carrier pursuant to tariff. However, if no common carrier offered a specific basic service which the Bell subsidiary needed as part of an enhanced offering, the Bell subsidiary could request from the Commission a waiver of the prohibition of the Bell subsidiary's owning or controlling any transmission facilities.[58]

The December, 1980 supplement to *Computer Inquiry II* further curtailed the possibility of anticompetitive behavior by modifying the FCC's earlier position on research and development of hardware, firmware, and generic software. The final decision had required that all research and development by a parent for a subsidiary be performed on a compensatory basis. The subsidiary, however, had to perform its own design and development of nongeneric software.[59] In the December, 1980 supplement the commission, following the precedent laid down in the GTE/Telenet merger authorization, required the separate subsidiary: (1) either to perform internally or to have performed by an outside non-Bell affililated contractor, all software and firmware development; and (2) either to perform internally or to have performed by any outside firm (including a Bell System affiliated firm), research and development of equipment into which the software could be inserted.[60] The separate subsidiary could purchase any equipment from its parent as long as any software or firmware contained in the equipment was not customized, but was the same as that sold "off the shelf" to any interested party.

Information flow between parent and subsidiary concerning

---

[57] Amendment of §64.702 of the Comm Rules and Regulations (Second Computer Inquiry), 84 FCC2d 50, 72-75 (1980). The Commission explained its rationale for applying the separate subsidiary requirement only to AT&T by stating that the following factors were considered:

> (a) a carrier's ability to engage in anti-competitive activity through control over "bottleneck" facilities, i.e., local exchange and toll transmission facilities, on a broad national geographic basis; (b) a carrier's ability to engage in cross-subsidization to the detriment of the communications ratepayer; (c) the integrated nature of the carrier and affiliated entities, with special emphasis upon research and development and manufacturing capabilities that are used in conjunction with, or are supported by, communications derived revenues; and (d) the carrier's possession of sufficient resources to enter the competitive market through a separate subsidiary.

[58] 84 FCC2d at 78-79. The test for granting a waiver to the prohibition of the AT&T subsidiary owning transmission facilities was whether "any negative effects on ratepayers which may arise from grant of a waiver are outweighed by the possibility of imposition of unreasonable costs upon consumers, or unavailability of an enhanced service if waiver is not granted."

[59] 77 FCC2d at 479-81. Nongeneric software is often called application software in the data processing industry.

[60] 84 FCC2d at 79-81.

1. The basic network had to be released to everyone on the same basis and at the same time

2. Research and development had to be paid for on a fully compensatory basis

3. Proprietary information (e.g., customer lists) of the parent AT&T had to be disclosed to all interested parties at the same time and under the same terms and conditions[61]

A record of each transaction between the parent AT&T and its unregulated subsidiary had to be filed with the FCC. No restrictions were placed on transactions between unregulated Bell subsidiaries. The December, 1980 supplement also revised the restriction prohibiting affiliated Bell entities from purchasing equipment from the separate subsidiary, by prohibiting affiliated Bell entities from purchasing equipment from the separate subsidiary only if the equipment was not manufactured by the separate subsidiary. Finally, AT&T was ordered to account for all of its costs in establishing any separate unregulated subsidiaries.[62]

Over all, *Computer Inquiry II* favored AT&T by permitting AT&T to enter the rapidly growing enhanced services and CPE communications sectors. The restrictions separating the parent Bell affiliates and the separate Bell subsidiary (necessary to prevent cross-subsidization) can be modified to fit the divestiture of the Bell operating companies (BOCs) from the parent AT&T. These same separations requirements can be expected to form the basis of the future rules the FCC will implement to continue its regulation of the Long Lines division as the parent AT&T begins to compete in the unregulated sectors of the telecommunications industry.[63]

The divestiture whereby the assets of the Bell System will be divided between the parent AT&T (Bell Headquarters, Western Electric, Long Lines, and Bell Laboratories), and the BOCs is reviewable by the United States District Court for the District of Columbia and by the Department of Justice. Congress and the FCC can also be expected to review the division of the Bell System's assets, and to monitor the effects of the divestiture of the Bell System pursuant to the settlement of the *United States v AT&T* case.

---

[61] *Id* at 81-83. *See also In re* General Tel & Elecs Corp, 72 FCC2d 111, *modified,* 72 FCC2d 516 (1979).

[62] 84 FCC2d at 84.

[63] *See generally* 77 FCC2d at 475-86. In the May, 1980 Final Decision, the FCC, consistent with its enunciated policy of maximum separation, ruled that this degree of separation required: (1) separate maintenance of records and books of account; (2) no joint or common personnel; (3) separate offices; (4) that administrative services (such as legal services) be provided by the parent on a cost reimbursement basis; (5) no sharing of computer services; (6) no joint use of the same physical space; (7) that any technical information disclosed to the separate subsidiary be released to competitors of the subsidiary at the same time and on the same terms and conditions; (8) that no software or firmware be designed by the parent for the subsidiary except if the software or firmware was embedded in or integral to some of the CPE obtained from the parent.

§5.07 —Federal Communications Commission Actions Parallel to *Computer Inquiry II*

AT&T Price Studies

In 1974 the Federal Communications Commission (FCC) sponsored a study by Touche Ross & Company to analyze Western Electric.[64] The Touche Ross report concluded that Western Electric was able to avoid "certain costs incurred by outside manufacturers [in its] expense build up."[65]

To ensure that the prices Western Electric charged to the Bell operating companies (BOCs) were competitive with those of Bell nonaffiliated product sources, in 1977 the FCC approached the problem of cross-subsidization by analyzing the price studies prepared by AT&T.[66] The FCC concluded that these costs studies were not valid, but the Commission did not make any specific order regarding how AT&T should perform these studies in the future.[67] Instead, the Commission required AT&T to submit a proposal for achieving maximum separation of its equipment procurement and manufacturing functions, short of divestment of Western Electric.[68] Given the poor quality of the AT&T price studies, in July, 1981 the FCC approved an inquiry notice to examine the purchasing practices of the BOCs. In approving this inquiry notice, the commission relied heavily on the previous proceeding in which the commission had concluded that the BOC purchasing system created a bias in favor of Western Electric products, and that Western Electric had an input into virtually every step of the make/buy decision-making process.[69]

Although not specifically related to *Computer Inquiry II*, these proceedings indicate the philosophical approach the FCC has taken to formulate conduct changes in the Bell system which will prevent the unregulated AT&T from unfairly using price studies or make/buy decisions to favor itself at the expense of ratepayers using Long Lines.[70]

Uniform System of Accounts

In 1978 the FCC began to examine and revise the Uniform System of Accounts (USOA), which had remained virtually unchanged since its adoption in

---

[64] Touche Ross & Co, Final Report on the Comprehensive Review of the Western Electric Company (Jan 3, 1974) (FCC Contract RC-10195).

[65] *Id* 68.

[66] AT&T, The Assoc Bell Sys Cos, 64 FCC2d 1 (1977) (Final Decision and Order).

[67] *Id* 61-101.

[68] *Id* 43-45.

[69] *See generally* 64 FCC2d 1.

[70] See Wetherington, *Communications—The FCC, As an Alternative to Divestment of Western Electric, Ordered Greater Autonomy for the Bell Operating Companies in Purchasing Divisions,* 27 Cath UL Rev 1521 (1977).

1935.[71] The commission noted that the USOA was based on a company-wide breakdown of costs.[72] Given the multiservice telecommunications environment, the commission determined that the introduction of competition in the specialized services and terminal equipment areas necessitated more specific service-related cost and revenue information, with interstate and intrastate (as opposed to the company-wide data as provided by the USOA) breakdowns of cost for each service.[73] The ultimate goal of the revised USOA is a single data base for state and federal regulators, and the elimination of the cost studies AT&T has been required to perform in order to justify its requests for rate increases.[74] In addition to the goals of a single data base and the elimination of AT&T's cost studies, in light of *Computer Inquiry II,* the USOA will be revised in order to prevent cross-subsidization between the regulated Long Lines division and the unregulated divisions of AT&T. The FCC's study of the USOA is continuing through various proceedings.[75]

---

[71] Revision of the Uniform System of Accounts and Financial Reporting Requirement for Telephone Companies (Pts 31,33, 42 and 43 of the FCC's Rules), 70 FCC2d 719 (1978) (Notice of Proposed Rulemaking) (includes an examination of the early history of the USOA).

[72] *Id* 721. Historically, the primary rate-making criteria were overall investment and expense levels, property valuations, and depreciation rates. In recent years, rate cases have dealt increasingly with rate levels and rate structures of specific services. The starting point in setting appropriate rate levels and rate structures for specific services is the relative cost of providing the services.

[73] *Id* 724-25.

[74] The FCC stated that to remedy:

the inadequacies of the current USOA, we are proposing a comprehensive modification of the existing accounting system as a whole. . . . It is our intention that the revised accounting system which will result from this proceeding will constitute a single data base serving the following functions: (1) It will form the basis for financial reports, including both balance sheet and income statement reporting. (2) It will serve as a data base and a foundation for managerial decision-making and internal management reports by the carriers. (3) It will provide sufficiently detailed disaggregated cost and revenue information for derivation of costs and revenues of individual services and rate elements, for pricing decisions and other managerial decision-making by the carriers. (4) It similarly will provide detailed disaggregated cost and revenue information for derivation of costs and revenues of individual services and rate elements, for rate review and continuing surveillance purposes of this Commission (and other regulatory bodies which adopt the revisions) and provide a basis for rate prescription, where appropriate. (5) It will facilitate the breakdown of costs between interstate and intrastate jurisdictions ("Jurisdictional Separations"). (6) It will permit analysis of facility and plant utilization, including studies of the causes for each category of expenditure and review of service quality and service efficiency. And (7) it will be structured so as to allow for regulatory and independent auditing and tracing of questioned entries.

[75] Another aspect of the USOA, depreciation, has also recently been examined. See Amendment of Part 31 (Uniform System of Accounts), 83 FCC2d 267 (1980).

Manual and Procedures for the Allocation of Costs

In a related matter, the FCC in 1979 initiated a proceeding to develop procedures for AT&T to use in allocating costs among its various services.[76] The cost allocation procedures AT&T was to follow were within the general guidelines established by the FCC in Docket Number 18128.[77]

In 1980, the FCC had issued a notice of proposed rulemaking.[78] The commission stated that the cost allocation manual which it had proposed, although not a "perfect solution," was necessary to allow the commission to fulfill its statutory obligations.[79] This proposed manual was to be an interim manual, and more suggestions and comments were sought on long-term approaches to the potential problem of cross-subsidization. The commission was most concerned with cross-subsidization of private line services by message services, specifically that AT&T's dominant position in the provision of message service would allow it to overcharge message customers to cross-subsidize private line service, and thereby weaken or prevent competition in this area.[80] In an attempt to prevent cross-subsidization, private lines were to be aggregated into a single category for reporting purposes. To simplify, but still have the data verifiable, the FCC proposed to increase reliance on separations for allocation purposes. The interim manual did not lessen the burden on AT&T to demonstrate the validity of its tariff filings in that where the manual is silent, AT&T must "fully justify each tariff filing."[81]

---

[76] AT&T, 73 FCC2d 629, 630 (1979) (Notice of Inquiry). In its Notice of Inquiry, the FCC noted that:

> competitive methods for diverse telecommunications services remain in their infancy. Dominant carriers still possess sufficient market power to cross-subsidize among services and users. Such cross-subsidization might nullify or otherwise restrain the emergence of fully-developed competitive telecommunications markets. Consequently, the implementation of Commission-approved costing principles for dominant carriers generally, and AT&T in particular, is crucial to the promotion and further development of sustainable, competitive telecommunication markets of the future.

[77] *See* AT&T, Long Lines Department, 61 FCC2d 587 (1976), *reconsideration,* 64 FCC2d 971 (1977), *further reconsideration,* 67 FCC2d 1441 (1978), *aff'd sub nom* Aeronautical Radio, Inc v FCC, 642 F2d 1221 (DC Cir 1980), *cert denied* 451 US 920 (1981). The FCC had attempted in Docket 18128 to establish basic principles and standards of general applicability for determining cost of service and corresponding rate levels by service category.

[78] AT&T, 78 FCC2d 1296 (1980) (Notice of Proposed Rulemaking).

[79] 78 FCC2d at 1297.

[80] 78 FCC2d at 1298.

[81] *Id* 1298-99. The FCC also noted that the simplification of reporting requirements and added flexibility did not constitute a "carte blanche" to AT&T to engage in unjust, unreasonable or unlawfully discriminatory pricing practices. The Commission's: "interest in eliminating unnecessary complexity is related to our intent that the allocation of costs be verifiable and not unduly subject to management discretion . . . while existing separation procedures . . . may be amended in the near future, they nevertheless constitute an existing, externally mandated system of allocation which is readily subject to audit."

Three major types of allocation procedures were suggested by the commenting parties,[82] but the FCC concluded that each accounting method suffered fatal shortcomings.[83] The FCC did require AT&T to implement an interim plan, under which AT&T's interstate revenues, investment, and expenses had to be allocated to four service categories: MTS, WATS, Private Line, and ENFIA.[84] This FCC proceeding, concerning the establishment of a revised Manual and Procedures for the Allocation of Costs, continues.

Execunet Controversy

The *Execunet* controversy showed the further development of the FCC's free entry policy while *Computer Inquiry II* was being decided.[85] In *MCI Telecommunications Corp v FCC* (*Execunet*), the District of Columbia Circuit Court of Appeals

---

[82] *Id* 1307-12. AT&T proposed to modify the existing system, but the FCC viewed AT&T's proposed modified system as still impossible to understand and monitor. The second method, proposed by Walter Associations, Inc., was extremely complex, and in some areas went beyond an allocation technique and involved restriction on AT&T. The third method was the Western Union top-down approach. Although a simplified method, this top-down approach required identification of factors that would lead to the division of the interstate costs to various services (these factors were not identified in the report).

[83] *Id* 1329. In its Summary, the FCC concluded that a:

system of cost allocation must be understandable, verifiable, and, insofar as it assigns costs based upon forecasts or other inputs which are strongly subject to management discretion, capable of being checked for accuracy. . . . AT&T's cost allocation methods have prevented us from prescribing new rates in situations where filed tariffs have been found unlawful. . . . We believe that a cost allocation mechanism must be sufficiently understandable to permit us to take appropriate remedial action if we find that improper rates have been filed.

[84] *Id* 1311-12. MTS and WATS are acronyms for two of AT&T's service offerings. MTS stands for message telecommunications service, and WATS stands for wide area telecommunications service. Exchange Network Facilities for Interstate Access (ENFIA) was developed as a temporary category pending completion of the Commission's access charge investigation. See AT&T, Manual and Procedures for Allocation of Costs, 84 FCC2d 384, at 406 (1980) (Report and Order), 86 FCC2d 107 (1981) (Order), *reconsideration in pt,* 86 FCC2d 667 (1981) (Order on Reconsideration). In 1979 the Commission had approved an agreement (ENFIA agreement) which established the methods to be used to compute charges of AT&T and GTE subsidiaries for the origination or termination of certain interstate telecommunications services provided by carriers other than telephone companies (OCCs).

The ENFIA agreement is designed to provide an interim formula for the computation of such OCC access charges until this Commission or the Congress establishes a more comprehensive access compensation system. Paragraph 6 of the ENFIA agreement provides that the interim charges will be superseded by charges filed pursuant to an order of this Commission in the *MTS-WATS Market Structure Inquiry* (CC Docket No. 78-72) or charges established pursuant to new legislation relating to that subject. American Telephone and Telegraph Company and the Bell System Operating Companies Tariff FCC No 8 (BSOC 8) Exchange Network Facilities for Interstate Access (ENFIA), 90 FCC2d 202, 204 (1982)(Memorandum Opinion and Order).

[85] See G. Brock, The Telecommunications Industry 224-30 (1981).

ruled that the FCC could not deny specialized carriers the right to expand intercity telephone services in the absence of a finding by the FCC that such expansion was not in the public interest.[86] Later, the FCC ruled that AT&T was under no obligation to provide the local physical interconnections necessary for Microwave Communications Inc's (MCI's) *Execunet* service.[87] AT&T, complying with the FCC's declaratory ruling, refused to supply MCI with the requisite local physical interconnections for the Execunet service. MCI then challenged this declaratory ruling. The court specifically invalidated the FCC's ruling that AT&T was under no obligation to provide local distribution facilities for MCI's Execunet service.[88] Consequently, while *Computer Inquiry II* was progressing within the FCC, the effect of the court's decision was to allow MCI to offer specialized services such as Execunet.[89]

MTS and WATS Market Structure

In response to the *Execunet* controversy, in 1978 the FCC instituted a proceeding to determine "whether the public interest would be better served by conferring single source status upon MTS and WATS, in whole or in part, or by authorizing some other kind of industry structure."[90] Subsequently, in 1979 the FCC issued a supplemental notice requesting comments by interested parties on the optimal industry structure, and entry policy, for the MTS/WATS market.[91] The FCC concluded that, except for the Alaskan interstate market, the MTS/WATS market was open to entry, effectively permitting individual

---

[86] MCI Telecommunications Corp, 60 FCC2d 25 (1976), *revd sub nom* MCI Telecommunications Corp v Federal Communications Commn, 561 F2d 365 (DC Cir 1977), *cert denied,* 434 US 1040 (1978). A push button telephone subscriber to *Execunet* is able to reach any telephone in a distant city served by MCI by dialing a local MCI number followed by an access code and the phone number in the distant city.

[87] Petition of AT&T for a Declaratory Ruling and Expedited Relief, 67 FCC2d 1455 (1978) (Memorandum Opinion and Order).

[88] MCI Telecommunications Corp v Federal Communications Commn, 580 F2d 590 (DC Cir 1978), *rehearing denied,* (May 8, 1978).

[89] See generally Warren, *Intercity Telecommunications Competition After Execunet,* 31 Fed Com LJ 117 (1978).

[90] MTS and WATS Market Structure, 67 FCC2d 757, 758 (1978) (Notice of Inquiry and Proposed Rulemaking) (MTS stands for Message Telecommunications Service and WATS stands for Wide Area Telecommunications Service).

[91] 73 FCC2d 222 (1979). (Supplemental Notice of Inquiry and Proposed Rulemaking). The FCC encouraged the parties to describe regulatory policies the Commission should adopt with respect to the following:

(1) Entry Policy for the MTS, WATS Market.
(2) Accounting Practices.
(3) Allocations of Investments and Expenses Among Jurisdictions.
(4) Contractual Arrangements Among Carriers for the Distribution of Interstate Revenues.
(5) Charges to Carriers for the Use of Facilities of other Carriers.
(6) Other Forms of Tariff Regulation.

and corporate consumers to enter the MTS/WATS market.[92]

§5.08 —Communications Satellite Corporation and Satellite Business Systems

Computer system vendors and communications common carriers are interested in satellite communications technology because satellites provide an attractive opportunity for major cost reductions.[93] Significant reductions in the costs of communications are particularly attractive to computer system vendors as they expand their computer design options.

The Communications Satellite Act of 1962 established the Communications Satellite Corporation (COMSAT), which is owned half by the general public and half by overseas carriers.[94] COMSAT continues in operation, having launched several satellites, and establishing a communications network.[95]

In the late 1960s, the Federal Communications Commission (FCC) conducted a four-year study of the role of satellites in domestic communications, and in 1970 concluded that satellites could play a major role in domestic communications.[96] The FCC then invited potential satellite applicants to submit definite system proposals. In its 1972 *Domsat II* decision, the FCC, recognizing that each potential applicant presented possible antitrust problems, rejected the suggestion that entry be limited to one or a small number of entrants. The FCC did, however, indicate its willingness to approve applications involving joint ventures, given the advantages of risk sharing and pooling of technical and financial resources.[97] The FCC reserved the right to impose appropriate re-

---

[92] *See* 77 FCC2d 224 (1980) (Second Supplemental Notice of Inquiry and Proposed Rulemaking); 81 FCC2d 177, 202-03, 214 (1980) (Report and Third Supplemental Notice of Inquiry and Proposed Rulemaking); and 90 FCC2d 135 (1982) (Fourth Supplemental Notice of Inquiry and Proposed Rulemaking).

[93] See generally Kelley, *Satellites Save Money*, 26 Infosystems 42 (1979); *The Gold Mine in Satellite Services*, Bus Week, Apr 6, 1981, at 89-90.

[94] Communications Satellite Act of 1962, 47 USC §701 *et seq.*

[95] See generally Socol, *Comsat's First Decade*, 7 Ga J Intl & Comp L 678 (1977).

[96] Establishment of Domestic Communication - Satellite Facilities by Non-governmental Entities, 22 FCC2d 86 (1970) (Report and Order) (Domsat I). See generally Orr, *Satellite Communications Takes a Big Leap Forward*, 73 ABA Banking J 76 (1981). Evans, *Satellite Communications—The Legal Gap*, 11 Jurimetrics J 92 (1970).

[97] Establishment of Domestic Communications - Satellite Facilities by Non-governmental Entities, 35 FCC2d 844, 847 (1972) (Second Report and Order) (Domsat II). The Commission stated that the:

> presence of *competitive* sources of supply of specialized services, both among satellite system licensees and between satellite and terrestrial systems, should encourage service and technical innovation and provide an impetus for efforts to minimize costs and charges to the public. (emphasis added)

After the Domsat II decision, the FCC approved the applications of AT&T, RCA, Hughes Aircraft Co, GTE, and Am Satellite. *See* Satellite Bus Sys, 62 FCC2d 997, 1063-73 (1977); AT&T, 42 FCC2d 654 (1973); RCA Global Communications, & RCA Alaska Communications, 42 FCC2d 774 (1973); Hughes Aircraft Co (National Satellite

strictions on single and joint entrants to prevent any anticompetitive practices.[98]

AT&T and COMSAT proposed a domestic satellite system wherein AT&T would lease communications satellites and associated services from COMSAT.[99] To prevent antitrust abuses in the AT&T and COMSAT joint venture, the FCC required that: (1) COMSAT be a minority participant in the joint venture; (2) no AT&T officer or director serve as a director of COMSAT; and (3) COMSAT establish a separate corporate entity to operate the domestic satellite system.[100]

COMSAT had previously entered into a joint venture (called CML Satellite Corporation) with Lockheed Aircraft Corporation (Lockheed) and Microwave Communications, Inc. (MCI) to operate a domestic satellite communications system. In 1974, COMSAT and IBM filed a joint petition for FCC approval of changes in the corporate structure of CML.[101] It was proposed that after the withdrawal of Lockheed and MCI from the CML venture, COMSAT and IBM would operate a joint venture for a domestic satellite system. In 1975, the FCC rejected the COMSAT/IBM proposal, but delineated the conditions under which COMSAT and IBM could participate in a joint venture for a domestic satellite system. These conditions included requiring: (1) the joint venture to provide for interconnection of its customers' data processing and communications systems on reasonable terms and without discrimination; (2) the details of the interconnection to be submitted in advance to the FCC; (3) IBM to create a separate subsidiary to operate the satellite system; and (4) COMSAT and IBM to conform to one of three permissible forms of business organization.

Following the *balanced CML option* (one of the three permissible forms), in December, 1975, COMSAT, IBM, and Aetna Casualty and Surety Company (through its subsidiary, Aetna Satellite Communications, Inc.), applied to the FCC for a license to operate a domestic satellite system as a joint effort under the name Satellite Business Systems (SBS).[102] Opponents objected to the SBS proposal on numerous grounds, including antitrust considerations.[103] After extensive filings, in February, 1977, the commission denied the request by

---

Services), & GTE Satellite Corp, 43 FCC2d 430 (1973); and Am Satellite Corp, 43 FCC2d 348 (1973). The lack of an FCC evidentiary hearing was upheld by the Court of Appeals for the District of Columbia. See Network Project v Federal Communications Commn, 511 F2d 786 (DC Cir 1975).

[98] 35 FCC2d at 851; *See also* 62 FCC2d at 1037.

[99] The application of AT&T and Comsat was filed in response to Domsat I, 22 FCC2d 86 (1970) (Report and Order). *See generally* 35 FCC2d at 851-53.

[100] 38 FCC2d 655, 676-88 (1972). (Memorandum Order and Opinion). *See also* AT&T, 42 FCC2d 654 (1973).

[101] Petition for Approval of Changes in Corporate Structure of CML Satellite Corp, 51 FCC2d 14 (1975). CML stood for the three initial partners in the COMSAT joint venture; COMSAT, MCI, and Lockheed.

[102] Satellite Bus Sys, 62 FCC2d 997, 998 (1977).

[103] 62 FCC2d at 1014-15.

opponents for a formal evidentiary hearing, and granted SBS a license.[104]

American Satellite, Western Union, AT&T, and the Department of Justice appealed the FCC *SBS* decision on the grounds that the FCC had not properly reviewed the antitrust potential of the SBS joint venture in an evidentiary hearing. The District of Columbia Circuit Court of Appeals, *en banc,* upheld the FCC decision to permit SBS to operate a domestic satellite communications system.[105]

The various FCC proceedings which have involved applications for satellite communications systems offer further evidence of the FCC's open entry policy. The requirements for entry into this market are limited to a basic fitness requirement. A structural requirement that each entrant be a separate corporation will not be imposed by the FCC, although close antitrust scrutiny by the FCC of all satellite entrants can be expected. The FCC will likely continue to evaluate each entrant, and to adopt appropriate conduct constraints, such as the requirement imposed on SBS to treat all prospective customers equally.

The Congressional Scene

§5.09 Congressional Efforts to Revise the 1934 Communications Act

After the Department of Justice filed the *United States v AT&T* antitrust case in 1974, Congress began to study the telecommunications industry, and several bills nearly passed either the House or the Senate.[106] An early attempt to revise the 1934 Communications Act occurred in 1976 in the AT&T-supported Consumer Communications Reform Act.[107] Opponents charged that the bill should have been called the Monopoly Protection Act of 1976 in that it would have removed most of the Federal Communications Commission's (FCC's) authority over the national communications network, and given this authority to the states' public utilities commissions. Specifically, the bill would have: (1) transferred jurisdiction over station equipment and terminal equipment from the FCC to the states; (2) given the states authority to set intercommunications rules, define station equipment, and dictate the terms under which the equipment could be marketed; and (3) permitted states to control the interconnec-

---

[104] 62 FCC2d at 1029-32, 1061-99.

[105] United States v Federal Communications Commn, 652 F2d 72 (DC Cir 1980).

[106] *E.g.,* S 3192, 94th Cong, 2d Sess, 122 Cong Rec 3982-83 (1976); and HR 12323, 94th Cong 2d Sess, 122 Cong Rec 1676-77 (1976). Similar measures were reintroduced in 1977. *See* HR 8, 95th Cong, 1st Sess, 123 Cong Rec 78 (1977); and S 530, 95th Cong, 1st Sess, 123 Cong Rec 1757 (1977). See generally Loeb, *The Communications Act Policy Toward Competition: A Failure to Communicate,* 1978 Duke LJ 1 (contains an excellent review of the historical origins and passage of, and developments affecting, the Communications Act of 1934 through the mid-1970s).

[107] S 3192, 94th Cong, 2d Sess, 122 Cong Rec 3982-83 (1976).

tion of interstate specialized common carriers to the AT&T local distribution networks.[108] Opponents of the legislation sponsored a Pro-Competition Resolution, and after hearings in committees on communications in both houses, the bill died.[109]

A 1978 House bill would have required AT&T to divest Western Electric, and a 1979 House bill would have required AT&T to deal at arm's length with all of its subsidiaries.[110] Both bills were hotly opposed by AT&T as allegedly being seriously detrimental to the ability of AT&T to operate the national core communications network.[111] In December 1979, HR 6121 was introduced, and successfully moved through subcommittee, but was adversely reported by the Committee of the Judiciary due to antitrust concerns.[112] Although several bills were introduced in the Senate in 1977 and 1978, and numerous hearings held, these bills suffered a fate similar to that of the House bills.[113]

The two ill-fated 1980 bills, HR 6121 and S 2827, agreed on the concept of a separate subsidiary, but disagreed in the degree of separation that would have been required. Each would have modified the 1956 *Western Electric* consent decree. Both houses agreed on the concept of supporting the local urban networks through access charges, although the first six years of developing access charges were to be administered differently. Both the House and the Senate agreed that to maintain reasonable rural telephone rates a subsidy for rural networks would be necessary.[114]

§5.10   —1981 Packwood Bill (S898)

In 1981, Senator Packwood introduced S 898 titled Telecommunications Competition and Deregulation Act of 1981.[115] Senator Packwood announced at the bill's introduction that "it has been our view that Congress, not the courts or the Federal Communications Commission, should establish national

---

[108] See generally Biddle, *Computer Industry Association Position Statement* [Consumer Communications Reform Act of 1976], Telecommunications, Nov 1976, at 18; and Ellinghaus, *What the Public Should Know About the Consumer Communications Reform Act,* Telephony, Oct 4, 1976, at 84.

[109] HRJ Res 285, 95th Cong, 1st Sess (1977) (introduced by Wirth (D Colo)); SJ Res 30, 95th Cong, 1st Sess (1977) (introduced by Hart (D Colo)).

[110] *See* HR 13015, 95th Cong, 2d Sess (1978), and HR 3333, 96th Cong, 1st Sess (1979).

[111] See Sarasohn, *Telecommunications Rewrite Tries to Unfetter Industry,* Cong Q, Feb 16, 1980, at 389.

[112] *See* HR Rep No 1252 pt 2, 96th Cong, 2d Sess 3 (1980).

[113] See generally O'Riordan, *An Examination of the Application of Common Carrier Regulation to Entities Providing New Telecommunications Services,* 29 Case W Res L Rev 577 (1979).

[114] S 2827, 96th Cong, 2d Sess (1980); HR 6121, 96th Cong, 2d Sess (1980). See generally Sarasohn, *AT&T Restructured: New Objections Show Dare of Communications Rewrite,* Cong Q, July 12, 1980, at 1943.

[115] S 898, 97th Cong, 1st Sess (1981).

communications policy."[116] In effect, S 898 was an attempt to deregulate the telecommunications industry, and to offer parameters for future regulation of the telecommunications field.[117] Under S 898 the Federal Communications Commission (FCC) would have been encouraged to foster competition in the market for interexchange telecommunications. Regulation would have been required only as necessary, (e.g., in the case of a market where no alternative carriers were available to provide telecommunications services), but regulation was not a foregone conclusion where more than one service was available.[118] Carriers would have been regulated according to certain classifications set forth in the bill.[119] The FCC would have retained the power to regulate all markets to ensure the availability of telecommunications services at reasonable rates,[120] and the power to regulate dominant carriers (the term was defined within the bill).[121] AT&T was specifically designated as a dominant carrier, and thereby kept within the regulatory authority of the FCC by specific intention.[122]

S 898 proposed several amendatory additions to the Communications Act of 1934, each specifically directed towards AT&T.[123] For example, S 898 would have required AT&T to establish a separate subsidiary to compete in deregulated markets,[124] and would have provided procedures for AT&T to follow in conducting its research and development and its manufacturing activities during the interim period until full separation from the affiliates was achieved.[125] Requirements for a *fully separated affiliate* were clearly defined,[126] with a timetable provided for AT&T to follow in the process of cutting loose its operating companies.[127] Nothing in the language of S 896 required the total divestiture of the subsidiary companies, though strict requirements were established for the relationship of the *affiliates* to the parent company, including the subsidiary that would offer enhanced services. The fully separated affiliate and the parent: (1) could have only one common director;[128] (2) could not have any

---

[116] 127 Cong Rec S3544 (Apr 7, 1981).

[117] See generally Trienens, *Deregulation In the Telecommunications Industry: A Status Report,* 50 Antitrust LJ 409 (1982).

[118] S 898, 97th Cong, 1st Sess 102, §201 (1981).

[119] *Id* §§201, 205.

[120] *Id* §203.

[121] *Id* §204.

[122] *Id* §§205, 229.

[123] *Id* §§223, 227-29.

[124] *Id* §§223, 227-28.

[125] *Id.*

[126] *Id* §§223, 227.

[127] *Id* §§223, 228. §228(a) states that until such "time as the American Telephone and Telegraph Company and its affiliates (hereinafter referred to in this section as AT&T) establish fully separated affiliates pursuant to this section and §227, the provisions of this section shall apply in any case. . . ."

[128] *Id* §§223, 227(a)(1).

joint officers or employees;[129] (3) would each have to maintain separate books and records, and these records would have to be fully auditable;[130] (4) could not have any joint or common property with an exception for international telecommunications facilities or properties;[131] and (5) could engage in joint institutional advertising only on a compensatory basis.[132] Overall, the dominant regulated carriers were prohibited from conducting business with their fully separated affiliates on a preferential basis, and were prohibited from cross-subsidizing the unregulated separate subsidiary.[133] The FCC role in the reorganization of AT&T under S 898 would have been that of watchdog. Before offering unregulated services, AT&T would have had to have received FCC approval of a plan for complying with the transition to fully separate affiliates.[134] The FCC would have been permitted to waive the proposed statutory transition schedule if intervening forces rendered AT&T incapable of compliance.[135]

The 1956 *Western Union* consent decree would have been construed to permit AT&T to enter the data processing field through an unregulated subsidiary.[136] Consequently, AT&T and its affiliates would have been permitted to provide telecommunications services or equipment,[137] and information services as long as these services and products were offered by fully separated affiliates.[138] S 898 passed the Senate in October 1981; however, due to later events in the courts, no further action was taken on the Packwood bill.

§5.11 —1981 Wirth Bill (HR 5158)

In December, 1981, Representative Tim Wirth introduced HR 5158, a bill to reform Title II of the Communications Act of 1934.[139] In January, 1982, the Department of Justice and AT&T announced a proposed settlement of the seven-year *United States v AT&T* antitrust suit. The settlement agreement would have required AT&T to divest its 22 local operating companies (constituting two-thirds of AT&T's assets), and the Justice Department to lift the restrictions imposed on AT&T in the 1956 *Western Electric* consent decree. Those restrictions had kept AT&T from entering the telecommunications field or any other

---

129 *Id* §§223, 227(a)(2).

130 *Id* §§223, 227(a)(3).

131 *Id* §§223, 227(d)(1).

132 *Id* §§223, 227(d)(2).

133 *Id* §§223, 227(e)(1).

134 *Id* §§223, 228(a).

135 *Id* §§223, 228(c)(6)(A), 228(c)(6)(B). Examples of intervening forces were labor strikes, war, severe economic depression, or acts of God.

136 S 898, 97th Cong, 1st Sess §§223, 229.

137 *Id* §§223, 229(d)(2)(B).

138 *Id* §§227-229.

139 47 USC §101 *et seq;* HR 5158, 97th Cong, 1st Sess (1981).

unregulated activity.[140]

The subcommittee hearing which followed became a focal point of debate over the adequacy of the proposed settlement. In March, 1982, the subcommittee unveiled a substitute bill which dealt with the perceived deficiencies of the *United States v AT&T* proposed settlement.[141] The subcommittee had undertaken a comprehensive review of competition in the telecommunications industry, and the results were printed in a lengthy staff report.[142] The substitute HR 5158 bill was designed: (1) to protect the viability of the local operating companies after divestiture; (2) to prevent local rates from increasing dramatically due to the loss of subsidization from long distance revenues; and (3) to guard against AT&T taking anticompetitive actions, especially in the unregulated sectors of the communications industry.[143]

HR 5158, approved unanimously in March, 1982, went substantially beyond both the proposed *United States v AT&T* settlement and S 898.[144] The purpose of HR 5158 was to guarantee the public a reliable, efficient, and diverse telecommunications service at reasonable and affordable rates.[145] To achieve this goal, the forces of open and competitive markets were to be relied upon rather than regulation.[146] Under HR 5158, the Federal Communications Commission (FCC) was directed to deregulate competitive markets, and to promote competition in those markets lacking competition.[147]

The FCC's authority over exchange, interexchange, and international transmissions would have been limited.[148] State public utilities commissions and the FCC were: (1) forbidden from considering the revenues or profits derived from the offering of any unregulated products or services (except for "Yellow Pages") by any affiliate or separate subsidiary of a regulated carrier in determining the revenue requirements of any regulated service of such carrier; and (2) prohibited from regulating new terminal equipment, new inside wiring, and resale or shared use of any transmission service or enhanced service.[149] The FCC would have been required to classify carriers that owned interexchange transmission facilitites as either dominant carriers, regulated carriers, or deregulated carriers (AT&T would have been the only dominant carrier under

---

[140] See *House Panel Approvel Bill Adding New Limits to AT&T,* Cong Q, March 27, 1982, at 688.

[141] *Id.*

[142] *House Comm on Energy and Commerce, Subcomm on Telecommunications, Consumer Protection and Finance, Telecommunications in Transition: The Status of Competition in the Telecommunications Industry,* 97th Cong, 1st Sess (Comm Print 1981).

[143] HR 5158, 97th Cong, 1st Sess §§201, 205 (1981).

[144] House Panel Approves Bill Adding New Limits to AT&T, Cong Q, Mar 27, 1982, at 688.

[145] HR 5158, 97th Cong, 1st Sess §201(a) (1981).

[146] *Id.*

[147] *Id* §201(b)-(c).

[148] *Id* §211.

[149] *Id.*

the bill).[150] Telephone companies that were presently providing joint long distance and local exchange services would be classified as regulated carriers.[151]

Interexchange Transmission

After an initial transition period of five years, the FCC would have exercised sole authority over all interexchange (toll) transmission, whether intrastate or interstate, except for intrastate toll transmissions of exchange carriers serving not more than 500,000 customer access lines. Deregulation of any given carrier would have depended upon a determination by the FCC that there were adequate alternatives to the service/facility.[152] Alternatives would have been considered adequate if they were substitutable in quality and comparable in both economic cost and geographic range to the relevant service or facility.[153] Regulated carriers would have been compelled to furnish, upon reasonable request, *regulated services* or services for which there were inadequate facilities available.

The tariffs established for these services were required to be just, reasonable, and nondiscriminatory.[154] No tariff for a given regulated service was permitted to include any costs associated with the provision of any other service or product, and the burden of showing a tariff to be just and reasonable was placed on the carrier.[155] Carriers offering enhanced services would have been compelled to do so on an unbundled basis. To prevent cross-subsidization, facilities constructed for the purpose of enhancing service, as opposed to transmission, would not have been included in the regulated rate base.[156]

Exchange Transmission

To prevent the use of local exchange facilities to create a bottleneck to restrict interexchange, enhanced services, or terminal equipment competition, HR 5158 would have required exchange carriers after 1986 to offer all interexchange carriers access on an equal basis including equal access in type, quality, and range of supporting functions. Exchange carriers would have also been required to interconnect any terminal equipment, inside wiring, or transmission services or facilities that met federal technical standards.[157]

In order to protect exchange carriers, all interexchange transmission offered by a dominant carrier would have been required to originate and terminate through the facilities of an exchange carrier until 1988. This would prevent a

---

[150] *Id* §212.

[151] *Id.*

[152] *Id.*

[153] *Id* §213.

[154] *Id* §§212-213, 221-223, 226.

[155] *Id* §§223, 226.

[156] *Id* §§222, 226, 228.

[157] *Id* §§232, 233.

dominant carrier from *bypassing* a local exchange for the sole benefit of large users of long distance service. To subsidize the costs of exchange service in rural or remote areas, all interexchange carriers would have been compelled to contribute to a National Telecommunications Fund.[158] The payments from this fund were also intended to ease the transition from the current jurisidictional separation rules to a system which allocated costs between exchange and interexchange services. Exchange access charges would have been frozen relative to the Consumer Price Index (CPI) until such time as the access charges took effect.[159]

Telecommunications Equipment

The FCC would have retained authority to establish technical standards for transmission facilities and services, and interconnection of terminal equipment.[160] After a transition period of two years, no regulated carrier nor any regulated exchange carrier would have been able to file a tariff which included any cost associated with or caused by the provision of terminal equipment or inside wiring.[161] Terminal equipment would have had to have been offered on an unbundled basis. In order to foster competitive procurement and thereby promote the development of a domestic competitive industry for the manufacture of transmission facilities. The bill would also have required regulated carriers and regulated exchange carriers affiliated with facilities manufacturers and to provide specifications to all manufactures and to procure all products on a nondiscriminatory basis.[162]

Dominant Carriers

HR 5158 would have required AT&T to offer transmission facilities and services through a separate subsidiary.[163] Not more than 50 per cent of the subsidiary's board of directors could consist of employees, officers, or directors of AT&T.[164] All transactions between the parent and subsidiary were to be on an arm's length basis.[165] Joint ventures by AT&T and the subsidiary would have been prohibited.[166] The subsidiary would have been required to conduct its own marketing, sales, advertising, installation of equipment, hiring and training of personnel, maintenance, operations, manufacturing, and re-

---

[158] *Id* §234.
[159] *Id* §§232, 233.
[160] *Id* §§241, 242.
[161] *Id* §242.
[162] *Id* §243.
[163] *Id* §251.
[164] *Id* §252(b).
[165] *Id* §252(d).
[166] *Id* §252(g).

search and development.[167] Finally, the subsidiary would have had to maintain its own books, records, and accounts.[168] All of AT&T's transmission facilities and services would have been required to be offered through the subsidiary on a regulated basis, and AT&T would have been forbidden from constructing, owning, or operating duplicate, unregulated transmission facilities until effective, facilities-based competition came into being.[169]

Telecommunications Industry

Carriers would have been allowed to meet, plan, and agree, under the auspices of the FCC, on matters affecting the design, maintenance, management, development, and coordination of any network of telecommunications services or facilities, although meetings with the purpose or effect of violating federal or state antitrust laws were prohibited.[170] To promote the widest possible diversity of information sources, no dominant carrier or its separate subsidiary would have been allowed to offer any information services over its own transmission facilities, except for limited directories; time or weather information; printed directory advertising; electronic directory information; and audio information services.[171] Mergers between owners of transmission facilities would have been limited, and regulated exchange carriers would have been barred from providing cable television or broadcasting services in areas in which they were offering exchange services, with an exception for carriers serving rural areas.[172]

Protection of Ratepayers in Transition

To protect ratepayers in the transition to a competitive market for telecommunications, installed terminal equipment would have had to continue to be made available to the customer under regulation until it was fully depreciated. Alternatively, customers would have had the option of purchasing installed equipment for a price determined by a state public utilities commission. State public utilities commissions would also have had the authority to auction fully depreciated or returned installed equipment so as to aid in the orderly development of a competitive secondary market in terminal equipment, and to ensure that ratepayers were fully compensated for the transfer of equipment to carriers' unregulated activities.[173]

The bill would also have established a transitional joint board, composed of three FCC commissioners and two state commissioners: (1) to review exchange area boundary disputes; (2) to establish the formulas for funding and the

---

[167] *Id* §252(h).

[168] *Id* §252(c).

[169] *Id* §253.

[170] *Id* §261.

[171] *Id* §263.

[172] *Id* §264.

[173] *Id* §§271, 272.

procedures for distributing funds from the National Telecommunications Fund; (3) to modify the jurisdictional separation and settlements procedures as necessary for the orderly transition to the system of exchange access charges; (4) to determine joint and common costs for long distance services; and (5) to advise the FCC on equal exchange access.[174] The legislation would have given ratepayers the fruits of the research they had funded at Bell Laboratories by requiring AT&T to grant nonexclusive licenses for all patents currently existing or developed within two years of passage of the bill for products manufactured in the United States.

Viability of Operating Companies

Prior to asset valuation, AT&T would have been required to distribute to its shareholders securities which represented interests in the assets (or businesses) of the newly-created (spun-off) operating companies. Because divestiture was to occur before valuation of the assets, officials of the operating companies would be under a legal duty to promote and protect the independent corporate interests of the operating companies. No particular form of reorganization was imposed; the bill simply required that divestiture occur and that, after reorganization, no operating company's securities could include any interest in another operating company or in AT&T.[175] A key component in asset valuation would have been the allocation of debt, some of which AT&T would have had to assume in return for its acquisition of billions of dollars of the operating companies' assets. The bill provided that AT&T take an equitable distribution of the operating companies' debt with respect to the interest rate and dates of maturity of the debt instruments.

Litigation Considerations

§5.12 Private Plaintiff Antitrust Litigation against AT&T

For the last several years, AT&T has been continuously involved as a defendant in anywhere from 20 to 60 active antitrust suits.[176] Given this large number of antitrust suits, and the obvious drain on the AT&T management in supporting this level of litigation, there appeared to be a trend in the late 1970s and early 1980s for AT&T to settle, when and where appropriate, as many cases as possible.[177] Increasing the pressure to continue this settlement

---

[174] *Id* §273.

[175] *Id* §252(j)-(k), 253(e)-(f).

[176] *E.g.* Current Case Table, Trade Reg Rep (CCH) (Sept 13, 1982) (29 cases listed in the Current Case Table and many more in the main Case Table).

[177] E.g. Telecommunications Rep, Mar 3, 1980, at 5 (Discusses the settlement of the 1977 *ITT v AT&T* case in which AT&T agreed to purchase two billion dollars of

trend, AT&T, in June 1980, suffered an antitrust trial loss in *MCI Communications, Inc v AT&T*, which, after trebling, amounted to 1.8 billion dollars.[178]

§5.13   *United States v AT&T*

In November, 1974, the Department of Justice filed an antitrust suit against AT&T in the United States District Court for the District of Columbia. The Department of Justice alleged that AT&T used its position of dominance in the telecommunications industry to suppress new competition, and maintained and enhanced its monopoly in violation of §2 of the Sherman Act.[179] The Department of Justice sought divestiture of Western Electric, Bell Labs, the Long Lines division, and some or all of the Bell operating companies (BOCs).[180] After divestiture, AT&T would no longer be a vertically integrated firm, nor would AT&T be able to offer end-to-end telecommunications services.

After one appeal to the Supreme Court, in 1978 the parties finally began exchanging documents. After three years of discovery and almost a year of stipulation negotiations, there appeared to be an eleventh-hour settlement in January, 1981.[181] The parties, however, were not able to reach a settlement, and in March 1981, trial began. In June, 1981, the Department of Justice ended its case-in-chief, and in August 1981, after AT&T's motion for summary judgment was denied, AT&T began the presentation of its case.

Reopening of the *1956 Western Electric Consent Decree*

In January, 1956, the Department of Justice and AT&T had entered into a consent decree in which AT&T agreed not to engage in "any business other

---

telecommunications products and services offered by ITT, if competitively priced, over a 10 year period. A deposit of two hundred million dollars was required of AT&T which is returned to AT&T at the rate of 10% of any AT&T purchases. The remaining balance would be returned in either 1990 or 1995 pursuant to the detailed terms of the agreement. The two billion dollars of purchases by AT&T from ITT over 10 years represent less than 2% of Western Electric's annual sales to the Bell System over the 10 year period.

[178] Antitrust & Trade Reg Rep (BNA), No 969, A-3 (June 19, 1980). On appeal, the Seventh Circuit remanded on the issue of damages. Antitrust & Trade Reg Rep (BNA), No 1098, 112 (Jan 20, 1983).

[179] 15 USC §2. See generally Department of Justice, Plaintiff's First Statement of Contentions and Proof v AT&T, Western Electric Corp, and Bell Laboratories 3 (1978).

[180] Department of Justice, *supra* note 179 at 527. Specifically, the Department of Justice sought:

the separation of AT&T's ownership of intercity facilities from its ownership of local facilities and the separation of the current providers of telecommunications services from the manufacturer of telecommunications equipment and its allied research and development facilities.

[181] Antitrust & Trade Reg Rep (BNA), No 998, A-15 (Jan 22, 1981).

than the furnishing of common carrier communications services."[182] In March, 1981, AT&T filed a motion with the United States District Court for the District of New Jersey, Judge Victor Biunno presiding, seeking a construction of the 1956 *Western Electric* consent decree which would not bar AT&T from furnishing or manufacturing equipment and facilities in connection with providing "customer premises equipment' and 'enhanced services' " as defined by the Federal Communications Commission (FCC) in its *Computer Inquiry II*.[183] The FCC believed its detariffing rather than deregulating enhanced services and customer premises equipment (CPE) would permit AT&T under the terms of the 1956 *Western Electric* consent decree to offer these services and products through a separate subsidiary.[184] Judge Biunno ruled that the FCC's decision in *Computer Inquiry II* and the 1956, *Western Electric* consent decree were not in conflict with each other, and the Department of Justice filed an appeal.[185]

In January 1982, Assistant Attorney General William Baxter submitted to Judge Biunno a proposal for the modification of the 1956 *Western Electric* consent decree. Judge Biunno accepted Baxter's proposal, and transferred supervision of the consent decree to the federal district court in Washington, D.C. for consolidation with the AT&T antitrust case already underway in that court, Judge Harold Greene presiding.[186] Baxter's proposed modifications were placed before the Washington, D.C. district court in the form of a stipulation for voluntary dismissal between the parties.

The proposed modifications to the consent decree would have eliminated all provisions of the 1956 *Western Electric* consent decree, and replaced them by provisions that would have required AT&T to divest itself of its 22 Bell operating companies (BOCs) "by means of a spin-off of stock of the separated BOCs to shareholders of AT&T, or by other disposition."[187] The divested

---

[182] United States v Western Elec Co, 1956 Trade Cas (CCH) ¶68246 Pt V. See also II A. Kahn, The Economics of Regulation: Principles and Institutions 295 (1971).

[183] United States W Elec, Inc, Notice of Motion and Motion for Construction of Judgment of Jan 24, 1956, 1981-1 Trade Cas (CCH) ¶63,975.

[184] 84 FCC2d 106. The National Telecommunications Information Administration (NTIA), part of the Department of Commerce, is the principal advisor on telecommunications policy to the President, and is charged with the responsibility of insuring that the views of the Executive Branch are effectively presented to the FCC. The NTIA responded to the Petition for Reconsideration of the Second Computer Inquiry, by supporting the FCC in its construction of the 1956 Western Electric Consent Decree. *See* Exec Order No 12046, 2-401, 43 Fed Reg 24348 (June 5, 1978) (The National Telecommunications and Information Administration Petition for Reconsideration of the Second Computer Inquiry) (June 12, 1980) (Pt V-The Effect of the Consent Decree on AT&T's Participation in Deregulated Markets).

[185] United States v Western Electric Co, 1981-2 Trade Cas (CCH) ¶64275, at 74206 (DNJ filed Sept 3, 1981). See AT&T's Access to New Markers Backed by Court, Wall St J, Sept 8, 1981.

[186] 42 Antitrust & Trade Reg Rep (BNA) No 1047, at 82, text of opinion at 110 (Jan 14, 1982).

[187] 47 Fed Reg 4166 (Jan 26, 1982). Department of Justice, Antitrust Division— United States v Western Electric et al, Proposed Modification of Final Judgment; United

BOCs would assume control of the intrastate localized exchange systems, with AT&T retaining ownership of its Long Lines division, Western Electric, and Bell Laboratories. AT&T would also have been permitted to provide customer premises equipment (CPE).

AT&T was given 18 months after the entry of the final decree[188] for internal reorganization and divestiture of the local operating.

Within six months after the entry of the final decree, AT&T's plan for divestiture of the BOCs was to be submitted to the Justice Department for approval. The BOCs had to be provided with whatever facilities, personnel, systems, and rights to technical information were necessary to allow the BOCs to function as adequate local exchange systems.[189]

The divested BOCs would have been allowed to provide only exchange and exchange access (and other natural monopoly services), subject to state regulation.[190] Thus the proposed decree would have precluded the BOCs from offering any form of interchange services, information services, or CPE.[191] These markets would have been left to AT&T to pursue. The BOCs would have been permitted to provide directory services (within the definition of *exchange access*),[192] but this provision was generally interpreted as *White Pages* services rather than the lucrative *Yellow Pages* services, which were left in the control of AT&T.[193]

The proposed decree would have required the divested companies to provide access to all intercity carriers on an equal basis with that afforded AT&T.[194] The operating companies were also required not to discriminate against AT&T's competitors when procuring or interconnecting equipment or services;[195] establishing or disclosing technical specifications;[196] or planning new facilities or services.[197]

The BOCs could not discriminate between AT&T and other interexchange carriers when offering or procuring products or services. The BOCs would have been required to provide equal services at equal tariffs to all interexchange carriers.[198] All exchange access rates were to be cost based,[199] although the BOCs could seek court relief from this requirement when equal access was

---

States v AT&T, *et al;* Stipulation for Voluntary Dismisal, §I(4) [hereinafter cited as Decree].

[188] Decree, *supra* note 187, at §I(A).

[189] *Id* §I(A)(1).

[190] *Id* §II(D).

[191] *Id* §II(D)(1)(2).

[192] *Id* §IV(F).

[193] L. Glasser, AT&T Settlement: Terms, Effects, Prospects 346-47 (1982).

[194] Decree. *supra* note 187, at §I(B).

[195] *Id* §II(B)(1).

[196] *Id* §II(B)(2).

[197] *Id* §II(B)(3).

[198] *Id* §II(A).

[199] *Id* app B(B)(2).

not possible (this relief from the requirement for equal charges is found in Appendix B to the proposed decree).[200] Where access by an interexchange carrier was not equal, the BOCs could offer a lower charge to a carrier requiring less exchange access.[201]

Under the proposed decree, all supply and license contracts between the BOCs and AT&T's remaining subsidiaries would have been terminated.[202] The BOCs would have retained priority status in all dealings with AT&T, Western Electric, and Bell Laboratories until September 1, 1987. This priority status was to enable the BOCs to fulfill the requirements of the proposed decree in continuing, at the BOC level, research, development, manufacturing, and other support services.[203]

Once separated from AT&T, there would have been no restrictions on the consolidation of the 22 BOCs into one national or several regional companies.[204] Thus, although AT&T and the various BOCs could not share ownership, personnel, facilities, or accounting records, joint ownership of multifunction facilities as among the BOCs could occur via lease or other arrangements, as long as each BOC maintained control over its own exchange telecommunications and exchange access functions.[205]

The BOCs, whatever their final configuration, could share costs to support a centralized organization for engineering, administration, and other services to insure a viable national communications network.[206] After divestiture the BOCs would be required to provide, through a centralized organization, a single point of contact for coordination of all operating companies to meet the requirements of national security and emergency preparedness.[207]

The proposed decree did not specify whether regulation of these requirements was to be left in the hands of the FCC, or was to be left to the state public utilities commissions. Assistant Attorney General Baxter claimed that it was his understanding that BOC tariffs are within the jurisdiction of the FCC under the Communications Act.[208]

After divestiture of the BOCs, AT&T will no longer be precluded, as it was in the 1956 *Western Electric* consent decree, from entering any type of business it might choose.[209] Antitrust prohibitions against AT&T's ownership of cable television, broadcast, electronic news, or other mass media would have been

---

[200] *Id* app B(A)(1).

[201] *Id* app B(B)(4).

[202] *Id* §I(A)(3).

[203] *Id* §I(C).

[204] *Id* §I(A)(4). Later developments indicate that there will be seven regional holding companies.

[205] *Id* §I(A)(2).

[206] *Id* §I(B).

[207] *Id.*

[208] L. Glasser, *supra* note 193, at 350. Communications Act of 1934, as amended, 47 USC §1 *et seq.*

[209] L. Glasser, *supra* note 193, at 347.

reduced to typical antitrust concerns, rather than the increased restrictions imposed by the 1956 *Western Electric Consent Decree.*

§5.14 —Problems with Proposed Consent Decree

Language Ambiguities

The proposed consent decree introduced new terminology without providing specific definitions of all terms. For example, Bell operating companies (BOCs) were permitted to provide *exchange telecommunications* and *exchange access;* and AT&T was permitted to offer *interexchange communications* and *customer premises equipment (CPE).* There was, however, no clear delineation between the realms of *exchange* and *interexchange* telecommunications. It is also unclear whether premises wiring is CPE (within the realm of AT&T) or part of the amorphous *exchange telecommunications* reserved for the BOCs.

The Divestiture Plan

AT&T was permitted six months after the settlement was final to formulate a divestiture plan. Critics of this arrangement feared that if AT&T was permitted unilaterally to decide what path the divestiture would take, AT&T would intentionally structure the divestiture so as to ensure the continued weakness of the BOCs as independent companies.[210] Competitors of AT&T requested that Judge Greene withhold final approval of the settlement until after the divestiture plan was finalized. AT&T argued that the Justice Department would have final approval of the divestiture, and that AT&T's obligation to its shareholders ensured a fair division of assets inasmuch as the shareholders of AT&T would also be shareholders in the new companies.[211]

The Long-Term Viability of the BOCs

AT&T and Assistant Attorney General Baxter initially proposed the removal of *Yellow Pages* advertising, terminal equipment rentals, and intrastate toll services from the BOCs, which would have effectively denied the BOCs access to traditional sources of revenue.[212] Confining the BOCs to local telephone services without the opportunity to expand or augment services may present the BOCs with severe financial difficulties within a few years since technological advancements may make their present services unnecessary.[213] One technique to ensure the viability of the BOCs would be to increase the access charge interexchange carriers must pay to interconnect with the local exchanges.[214]

---

[210] The Scott Report, Apr, 1982, at 11-12 (No 7).

[211] *Id.*

[212] *Id* at 12-13.

[213] See generally *The Proposed AT&T Consent Decree: A Preliminary Analysis,* 9 Media L Notes 2 (1982).

Future technological advances may even preclude the need for these carriers to connect with the BOCs. In fact, AT&T has warned that if access changes into local exchange areas become unreasonable, AT&T will use technology presently available to bypass the local exchange areas, and instead connect its Long Lines directly to its customers.[215]

Potential for Higher Local Telephone Rates

The loss of the terminal equipment rental market and the loss of long distance subsidies may force the BOCs to increase local telephone rates as much as 46 per cent to maintain current revenue levels.[216] AT&T may also be permitted to bypass local exchanges and thereby deal directly with portions of the local services market, which would siphon off a very profitable portion of the BOCs' market revenues.

The Nationwide Telecommunications Network

There may be a need for legislation to ensure cooperation and reduction of interconnection problems between interexchange carriers and the BOCs. Under the proposed settlement, the BOCs, left with the local exchanges, would be under state as well as federal regulation.[217] Inconsistencies in regulation may develop between the local exchange carriers and the Long Lines facilities.[218]

Regulation of BOCs and Independent Telephone Companies

Given the new economic and regulatory environment, the question arises as to whether continued regulation of the independent phone companies and the BOCs will hinder or promote the expansion of the telecommunications industry. Some industry observers feel that to permit competition between the independents and the various BOCs would promote expansion of the industry [219], whereas other observers feel that to allow the BOCs to expand into any communications market would place too much power in the BOCs.[220]

---

[214] See generally *Some Policy-oriented Reflections on the AT&T Antitrust Settlement,* 29 Fed B News & J 372, 373-74 (Nov 1982).

[215] See also *AT&T Trust Accord Could Stir Problems For Local Units, FCC Staff Report Warns,* Wall St J, Jan 29, 1982, at 2.

[216] The Scott Report, Apr, 1982, at 13-14. AT&T Settlement: Terms, Effects, Prospects 19 (1982). See generally L. Glasser, *supra* note 193. See also *The Proposed AT&T Consent Decree: A Preliminary Analysis,* 9 Media L Notes 2, 5 (Apr 1982). See generally *Wide Changes are Expected Following Two Settlements,* NY Times, Jan 9, 1982, at 36.

[217] See generally L. Glasser, *supra* note 216, at 351.

[218] The Scott Report, *supra* note 216, at 14-15.

[219] L. Glasser, *supra* note 216 at 27.

[220] The Scott Report, *supra* note 216, at 16.

Patent Licensing and Competitive Problems

The 1956 *Western Electric* consent decree required that all components manufactured by Western Electric covered by patents be made available to competing equipment manufacturers. The proposed settlement contained no similar requirement.[221] AT&T, consequently, would have been able to use the revenues obtained from the licensing of its patent to support research and development work leading to additional patents, and thereby ensure its competitive advantages. AT&T currently holds the patents for basic semiconductor and laser technologies, which will permit AT&T to extract large license fees if it chooses to grant licenses) for these patents.[222] If AT&T chooses not to license its patents to competitors, these competitors may be precluded from producing equipment capable of connecting with the AT&T network.

Cross-Subsidization by AT&T of New Operations

If AT&T were permitted to move into unregulated markets, the temptation to fund its new operations with revenues from the Long Lines division would be strong. Competitors in these unregulated markets asserted that given this tremendous financial base, AT&T's new operations would have an unfair advantage. Competitors, therefore, strongly urged the separation of Western Electric and Bell Laboratories from AT&T.[223]

Access to Technical Information by Competitors

The proposed consent decree required the BOCs to share information regarding future equipment needs with all manufacturers, but did not place the same requirement on AT&T and Long Lines. In as much as two or more years lead time is frequently necessary for new equipment to be placed in service, giving Western Electric advance notice of equipment specifications would provide Western Electric with an unfair advantage over other manufacturers in the production and sale of such equipment.[224]

AT&T's Possible Expansion into Electronic Publishing and Cable Television

AT&T may, depending on the interpretation of the consent decree, be permitted to enter the electronic publishing and cable television markets. Technically, the language of the proposed decree would have permitted AT&T to expand its operations into these markets. The newspaper organizations as well as numerous legislators opposed permitting AT&T access to the publish-

---

[221] *AT&T Accord Seen Ending Licensing Rule,* Wall St J, Jan 29, 1982, at 2.

[222] The Scott Report, *supra* note 216, at 16.

[223] *Id* 16-17.

[224] *Id* 17.

ing market.[225] Some believed that there might be First Amendment ramifications. Representative Tim Wirth stated that:

> The settlement fails to adequately safeguard against the threat to information diversity from AT&T being permitted to engage in information publishing over its remaining monopoly transmission facilities . . .—its long distance lines.[226]

AT&T downplayed its ability to monopolize these markets, claiming that divestiture would eliminate this possibility.[227] The 1956 *Western Electric* consent decree prohibited AT&T from owning cable television facilities in areas it serviced. Since AT&T will no longer own local telephone services, this prohibition is no longer applicable.

§5.15 —Federal Communications Commission Perspective on Proposed Consent Decree

The Federal Communications Commission (FCC) reviewed the proposed consent decree, and concluded that there were three major areas of concern.[228] Under the proposed decree, the Bell operating companies' (BOCs') exchange areas would each be limited to individual states unless Judge Greene permitted an exchange area to cross over into an adjoining state.[229] In theory then, one could argue that each of the seven BOCs is merely a holding company for a group of state-oriented local exchange areas with state public utilities commissions exercising exclusive authority over each exchange area. If each exchange area were under the regulation of an individual state's public utilities commission, then the FCC would have no jurisdiction over either the individual exchange areas or the BOCs. The position of the FCC was that the FCC had authority over the BOCs based on the FCC's continued "superintendency of the national phone network.[230] The FCC also voiced its concern over the structure and pricing levels for access charges into the local exchange areas.[231]

Although Judge Greene, the FCC, and state public utilities commissions could all, in theory, attempt to enforce their individual views on proper access tariffs, the FCC stated that it alone had authority to regulate access tariffs. As

---

[225] *Id* 17-18.

[226] *Id* 18.

[227] Id.

[228] *FCC Analysis of AT&T Antitrust Consent Decree, reprinted in* L. Glasser, AT&T Settlement: Terms, Effects, Prospects 344-462 (1982) [hereinafter cited as FCC Analysis].

[229] 47 Fed Reg 4166 (Jan 26, 1982). United States v Western Elec Co, Proposed Modification of Final Judgment; United States v AT&T; Stipulation for Voluntary Dismissal, at (IV)(6)(4).

[230] FCC Analysis *supra* note 228, at 351.

[231] *Id.*

the BOCs file tariffs, the role of the FCC in setting access tariffs will continue to evolve.

Given the new structure of the communications industry under the proposed consent decree, the FCC will also need to modify its "separation, accounting, and depreciation policies."[232]

Timing issues between various dates set in *Computer Inquiry II* and dates discussed in the proposed *United States v AT&T* settlement will require a great deal of attention to prevent different dates for similar changes being enforced by the FCC and by Judge Greene.[233] The FCC stated that it would be helpful if Judge Greene would include a *Terminal Railroad* clause in the final decree to ensure that interpretations by AT&T and the BOCs of the decree are subject to lawful agency orders issued by the FCC.[234] In addition to *Computer Inquiry II,* the FCC has stated that as many as 12 of its ongoing proceedings are "substantially affected" by the proposed settlement.[235]

---

[232] *Id.*

[233] *Id* 352.

[234] *Id* 373. The Terminal Railroad clause concept is taken from Terminal RR v United States, 266 US 17, 25 (1924). Paragraph 6 of the decree stated that:

> Nothing in this decree shall be taken to affect in any wise or at any time the power of the Interstate Commerce Commission over the rates to be charged by the Terminal Railroad Association, on the mode of billing traffic passing over its lines, or the establishment of joint through rates or routes over its lines, or any other power conferred by law upon such commission.

[235] FCC Analysis *supra* note 228, at 356. A complete checklist of the Consent Decree impact on major FCC matters follows:

CC Doc No 78-72 (Access Charges)	S P
ENFIA III	S P
BSOC Tariffs Nos 9 & 10	S P
CC Doc No 80-286 (Joint Board)	P
Doc No 20828 (Computer II)	S P
CC Doc No 81-893 (Computer II Implementation Proceeding)	S P
CBI-SNET Reconsideration	S P
Doc No 20188 (Depreciation/ELG)	P
CC Doc No 78-196 (USOA)	P
CC Doc No 79-105 (Station Connections)	P
CC Doc No 79-318 (Cellular)	P
CC Doc No 80-742 (License Contracts)	S P
CC Doc No 80-53 (Procurement)	S P
WPC-3071 (Fiber Optics Filing)	U
Rate of Return Regulation	U
CC Doc No 79-187 (1978 Earnings)	U
CC Doc No 79-245 (Cost Manual)	U
Interstate Service Tariffs	U
CC Doc No 79-252 (Competitive Carrier)	U
CC Doc No 78-72 (Alaskan Entry)	S
CC Doc No 81-2126 (Registration)	S
NTIA Joint Planning/Ownership Petition	S
CC Doc No 80-634 (Comsat)	S

§5.16 —Proposed *United States v AT&T* Consent Decree and HR 5158

The most recent form of HR 5158 represented an attempt by the House Telecommunications Subcommittee to deal with the alleged deficiencies of the modifications to the 1956 consent decree contained in the proposed *United States v AT&T* settlement.

HR 5158 would have provided that "Yellow Pages" advertising, which produce an annual national revenue of approximately $2 billion, remain with the Bell operating companies (BOCs) because such listings are a natural function of the local companies, and this revenue would help to keep local phone rates low.[236] Pay telephone operations and maintenance would also have remained with the local operating companies. The provision for "Yellow Pages," would have given the local companies more revenue and ameliorated their need to charge higher local rates. All installed terminal equipment would have remained with the BOCs, and would have continued to be provided under tariff until fully depreciated. After five years, the operating companies would have been permitted to sell, but not manufacture, new terminal equipment, including computers, through separate subsidiaries. The bill would have provided protection for employees' rights and benefits during the transition period to deregulation (labor protection provisions would have been extended to all carriers which were permitted to establish a separate entity). AT&T would have been prohibited from setting up its own information services and offering these services over company phone lines. This provision, lacking in the proposed settlement, had been sought by newspaper publishers and others who viewed AT&T's ability to provide such services as anticompetitive.

Reaction to HR 5158

The Wirth bill, which attempted to deal with what were viewed as deficiencies in the proposed settlement, was met by strong opposition from AT&T. According to AT&T, the bill would have disrupted the nation's phone system by placing undue burdens on long distance lines. Representative Wirth contended that committee members sympathetic to AT&T resorted to procedural delays such as forcing the reading of the 130-page bill line by line, and demanding extensive debate on each amendment.[237]

As a result of these efforts by the opponents of HR 5158, Representative

---

CC Doc No 80-176 (International Resale)	S
CC Doc No 80-632 (TAT-4)	
Cable TV Cross Ownership	S

S–Substantively Affected (i.e., new policies may be necessary)

P–Procedurally Affected (e.g., new mechanisms may be needed to achieve established policy goals)

U–Generally unaffected

[236] *House Panel Approves Bill Adding New Limits to AT&T,* Cong Q, Mar 27, 1982, at 688.
[237] *Supporters of AT&T Bill Block Major Change,* Cong Q, July 17, 1982, at 1696.

Wirth, in a surprise move, withdrew his bill from consideration, claiming that AT&T had waged a campaign of "fear and distortion," and that "[t]he only way to pass legislation [in the time remaining] would be to accept an agreement dictated by AT&T."[238]

§5.17 —Modifications of Proposed Consent Decree by Judge Greene

Judge Greene insisted in his August, 1982 opinion that the proposed settlement plan be modified in several critical areas.[239] Representative Wirth praised Judge Greene's opinion, stating that it was a positive first step, yet he cautioned that congressional action was still needed to establish a comprehensive telecommunications policy.[240]

Although Judge Greene recognized that he had no power to order changes to the consent decree, he was able to insist on modifications to the settlement agreement by threatening the parties with a resumption of the trial if they did not agree to his modifications (Judge Greene gave the parties 15 days to consider whether they would accept his modifications).[241] Because Judge Greene's opinion contained several statements indicating that there was sufficient evidence to support the government's position, AT&T, faced with Judge Greene's ultimatum, and recognizing the very real possibility that it could lose the case on the merits if the trial resumed, agreed to his modifications.[242]

Judge Greene had enunciated ten modifications, four of which constituted major changes to the proposed consent decree:[243]

1. AT&T was to be barred for seven years from "electronic publishing" activities using its own transmission lines (this prohibition would not include the offering of directory or time/weather services). Judge Greene noted the potential for AT&T to discriminate against competitors and to deter potential competitors, although he also noted that AT&T, at the present time, had no plans to enter this field[244]

2. Divestiture, the keystone of the settlement, was found by Judge Greene to be an appropriate remedy, noting that the charges that AT&T may have monopolized the intercity communications and telecommunications

---

[238] *AT&T Bill Dropped, Killing Rewrite Efforts*, Cong Q, July 24, 1982, at 1773.

[239] Antitrust & Trade Reg Rep (BNA) No 1077, at 317 (Aug 12, 1982).

[240] *Courts AT&T Ruling Refocuses Attention on New Legislation*, Cong Q, Aug 14, 1982, at 1986.

[241] *Judge's Power in Settlements Outlined in AT&T Decisions*, Natl LJ, Aug 23, 1982, at 3.

[242] *Id.*

[243] Antitrust & Trade Reg Rep (BNA) No 1077, at 317 (Aug 12, 1982).

[244] *Id* 318.

product market "may be well taken."[245] As part of this divestiture, the Bell operating companies (BOCs) would be given the following powers: (a) to provide, but not manufacture, customer premises equipment (CPE); (b) to publish the "Yellow Pages" (AT&T must provide all facilities, personnel, systems, and rights to the information necessary to produce the advertising directories); and (c) to request the court to remove the restrictions on the local companies from providing long distance service and maintenance[246]

3. The local companies to have debt ratios of approximately 45 per cent, and the quality of the debt to be equal to that of AT&T

4. The local companies' billing services had to indicate to customers that they could choose an independent carrier for long distance service. These carriers had to be given the same access as AT&T received, or, in the alternative, price discounts

Finally, the order reserved the court's jurisdiction to ensure that the purposes of the decree were carried out, and prohibited the implementation of a reorganization plan without the court's approval.[247]

Judge Greene supported the removal of the restrictions imposed on AT&T by the 1956 *Western Electric* consent decree, finding that AT&T's monopoly power had its root in AT&T's control of the local operating companies, and "with the divestiture of these local exchange monopolies, continued restrictions are not required unless justified by some other rationale."[248]

In late August 1982, the Justice Department sent Judge Greene a proposed order incorporating all of his conditions.[249] The Justice Depatment had feared that the local companies would monopolize the selling of complex exchange equipment used by businesses, but Judge Greene rejected this idea calling the possibility "remote," and noted that this possibility was balanced by "the certainty that [the local companies] would provide healthy competition for AT&T."[250]

In October, 1982, AT&T filed a four-volume plan which laid out the seven regions in which the local companies would operate, and also outlined *local access and transport areas (LATAs)* within which the local companies would provide services.[251] Other carriers were allowed to provide long distance service linking the LATAs. The filing of this plan by AT&T was the first major step

---

[245] *Id.*

[246] *Id* 317.

[247] *Id.*

[248] *Id* 318. United States v Western Electric Co, 1956 Trade Cas (CCH) ¶68246 (DNJ 1956).

[249] Antitrust & Trade Reg Rep (BNA) No 1079, at 381 (Aug 26, 1982).

[250] *Id.*

[251] NY Times, Oct 5, 1982, at B1.

in the divestiture which is to be concluded by February 24, 1984.[252] For a comparison of the major provisions of *Computer Inquiry II*, the *United States v AT&T* consent decree, the Wirth bill (HR 5158), and the Packwood Bill (S898) concerning the restructuring of AT&T, see **app 5-1**.

Future Trends in the Telecommunications Industry

§5.18   Emerging Legal Structure

In his historical analysis of AT&T's development and growth, Gerald Brock reviewed the numerous strategic decisions AT&T's management has made throughout AT&T's existence.[253] One such decision was AT&T's acceptance of the 1913 "Kingsberry Commitment" in which AT&T agreed not to continue in its attempt to take over the telecommunications industry. As a result, the competition between AT&T and the independent telephone companies was greatly reduced.[254]

Given a history of strategic decisions by AT&T's management, it is not surprising that during deliberations within Congress and the Federal Communications Commission (FCC) over the future structure of AT&T, AT&T not only was willing to acccept a separate subsidiary as part of its revised structure, but proposed procedures to establish the subsidiary and actually began to create the subsidiary.[255] AT&T agreed with Assistant Attorney General Baxter to spin off the Bell Operating Companies (BOCs), retaining Western Electric, Bell Laboratories, Long Lines, and Bell headquarters, rather than risk an unfavorable result in the *United States v AT&T* antitrust litigation.

Initially, the AT&T separate subsidiary, under *Computer Inquiry II* and both the Packwood and Wirth bills, would have been the deregulated portion of AT&T, while AT&T would have remained subject to FCC and state public utility commission regulation. Pursuant to the *United States v AT&T* consent decree, however, the AT&T parent (Bell headquarters, Western Electric, Bell Laboratories, and the portion of Long Lines offering enhanced services pursuant to *Computer Inquiry II*) will be deregulated, while the portion of Long Lines offering basic services (and enhanced services until the procedures established under *Computer Inquiry II* have been fully implemented) will be regulated. The future legal structure of AT&T, therefore, will reflect AT&T's status as a substantially unregulated corporation, with a decreasing portion of itself con-

---

[252] *Id.*

[253] G. Brock, The Telecommunications Industry (1981).

[254] *Id* 155-58. In more detail, under the 1913 "Kingsberry Commitment" AT&T unilaterally agreed to dispose of its Western Union stock, to allow interconnection with competing independents, and to refrain from further purchases of competitors in return for the US Attorney General's decision not to pursue antitrust litigation against AT&T and the Bell System.

[255] Copethorne, *Key Word at AT&T Is "Bus"*, 26 Datamation 64 (May 1980).

tained in a separate regulated subsidiary (as the FCC continues its deregulation of the telecommunications industry under *Computer Inquiry II*.

The two-part legal structure imposed upon AT&T must be extremely flexible to encourage advancement in telecommunications technologies, but rigid enough to prevent cross-subsidization from regulated to nonregulated affiliates. Cross-subsidization would penalize monopoly ratepayers and unfairly enhance the competitive position of the unregulated portion of American Bell.

In addition to the FCC's regulation of basic services and deregulation of enhanced services pursuant to *Computer Inquiry II*, the FCC will remain active in the regulatory arena through its proceeding to revise the Uniform System of Accounts (USOA), its proceeding involving the Manual and Procedures for the Allocation of Costs, and its administration of access charges for the local exchange areas. The FCC will continue to exercise overall supervision of the national telecommunications network, as well as numerous other related communications areas. Given this pervasive enforcement of the nation's communications policy, the FCC will undoubtedly continue to play a major role in regulating the seven regional companies despite the fact that practically all local exchange areas will be within individual states. Customer premises equipment (CPE) will be deregulated, and AT&T will be allowed to offer CPE. The BOCs will be able to offer CPE under tariff only where unregulated CPE providers are unwilling to provide CPE (e.g., in isolated or other unprofitable areas).[256]

§5.19 Emerging Communications Technologies

The 1980s will witness an enormous growth in the information industry which is based on advancing computer and communications technologies, e.g., satellites, fiber optics, cellular, Digital Electronic Message Service (DEMS), teletext (over-the-air one-way transmission of material such as airline schedules and stock market news), and videotexts (involving two-way communication such as the Community Antenna Television System).[257] These technologies, which possess the potential for continually increasing the capability of carrying larger amounts of data at greater speeds, and with lower unit costs, will require a flexible legal structure if they are to develop to their fullest potential.[258] As these technologies develop further they will have a dramatic

---

[256] For example, in remote rural areas where there is limited demand for CPE, it may not be profitable to offer CPE, and thus the BOCs may need to offer CPE on a tariff basis.

[257] See generally *Micro-Electronics: A Survey*, The Economist, Mar 11, 1980, at 3; Noyce, Microelectronics, Scientific American, Sept 1977, at 68. See Hardman, *A Primer on Cellular Mobile Telephone Systems*, 29 Fed B News J 385 (1982); Sinter, *Private, Intra City Data Communications Networks*, 29 Fed B News J 414 (1982); Pare, *The New Video Technologies*, NY Times, Apr 14, 1982, at 29.

[258] See generally Hinden, *Large Scale Integration Latches on to the Phone System*, Electron-

impact on the legal and regulatory structure and environment of the telecommunications industry. The Bell operating company (BOC) legal structure, for example, is premised on the continued technological and economic viability of the local exchange areas.

Given the emerging legal structure of deregulated interlocal exchange (i.e., between cities) communication and customer premises equipment, and regulated intralocal exchange (i.e., intracity) communication, an ever-increasing variety of communications technologies can be expected to appear in the communications marketplace. Although AT&T and the BOCs will dominate in their respective areas, numerous competitors offering new products and services can be expected to enter, or even to create, new markets for these goals and services.[259] A shakeout of these new competitors is inevitable.[260] In addition, the effects of the asset division between AT&T and the BOCs can be expected to continue well into the late 1980s, as will the effects of *Computer Inquiry II.*

Overall, the pace of change in the market for communications technology can be expected to increase rapidly in the 1980s. The intermix of Federal Communications Commission and state public utility regulation, therefore, will need to remain flexible to adopt to changing communications technologies, and changes in the economics of the communications marketplace.

---

ics, June 5, 1980 at 114; and Branscomb, *Computer Technology and the Evolution of World Communications,* 47 Telecommunications J 208 (1980).

[259] See *Telecommunications: Everybody's Favorite Growth Business—The Battle For a Piece of The Action,* Bus Week, Oct 11, 1982, at 60. See generally Uttal, *What's Ahead for AT&T's Competitors,* Fortune, Dec 28, 1981, at 79.

[260] Oren & Smith, *Critical Mass and Tariff Structure In Electronics Communications Markets,* 12 Bell J Econ 467 (1981) (theoretical analysis of minimum size to offer successfully communications services).

Appendix 5-1

Comparison of Proposals for Restructuring AT&T

Critical Question	Proposal			
	Computer Inquiry II	1982 Consent	Wirth Bill	Packwood Bill
1. What will be the role of market competition?	CPE* & enhanced services	AT&T deregulated	AT&T partially deregulated	AT&T deregulated
2. Who will own Bell Labs?	AT&T	AT&T	Initially separate company	AT&T
3. Who will own the Bell Operating Companies?	AT&T	Separate companies	Initially separate companies	AT&T
4. Who will own Western Electric?	AT&T	AT&T	Initially separate company	AT&T
5. Who will own Long Lines?	AT&T	AT&T— Partially a separate subsidiary	AT&T	AT&T
6. Who will own Yellow Pages?	AT&T	BOCs	AT&T	AT&T

* Customer premises equipment

Critical Question	Proposal			
	Computer Inquiry II	1982 Consent	Wirth Bill	Packwood Bill
7. Who will control the pay telephones?	AT&T	BOCs	AT&T	AT&T
8. What will be the role of the FCC?	Continued active	Many questionable areas	Active regulator	Active regulator
9. What will be the role of the states?	Lesser role as CPE is deregulated	Active in exchange areas in access charges	Active regulator	Active regulator
10. How will the employees be protected?	AT&T left intact	Neutral	Statutory protections	Neutral
11. How will the stockholders be protected?	AT&T still dominant	AT&T must set up BOCs as financially viable	Neutral	Neutral
12. How will equipment be transferred upon divestiture?	FCC will need to interface *Computer Inquiry II*	Not resolved	Not addressed	Not addressed

Critical Question	Proposal			
	Computer Inquiry II	*1982 Consent*	*Wirth Bill*	*Packwood Bill*
13. Who will be able to sell customer equipment?	AT&T separate subsidiary	AT&T not BOCs	AT&T separate subsidiary	AT&T separate subsidiary
14. Where will research and development take place?	Bell Labs	Bell Labs & BOCs	Bell Labs	Bell Labs
15. What will happen to existing Bell Lab patents?	AT&T keeps	AT&T keeps	Open to public license	AT&T keeps
16. What will be the BOCs' responsibilities?	Not addressed	Manage local exchange areas	Not addressed	Not addressed
17. What will happen to the AT&T/BOC license agreements?	Remains	Leases	Revised	Revised

Critical Question	Proposal			
	Computer Inquiry II	1982 Consent	Wirth Bill	Packwood Bill
18. Will telecommunications carriers be required to interconnect?	Yes	Yes	Yes	Yes
19. Will AT&T be allowed to go into data processing?	In a separate subsidiary	Yes	In a separate subsidiary	In a separate subsidiary
20. Will any safeguards against price discrimination be established?	FCC monitors	Court & FCC monitors	FCC monitors	FCC monitors
21. How will the public be protected?	FCC	FCC & court	FCC	FCC
22. Will telecommunications carriers be allowed pricing flexibility?	Some	Yes	Yes	Yes

A Legal and Technical Assessment of the Effect of Computers on Individual Privacy

6

Development of Computerized Databanks

§6.01 Introduction, Purpose, and Definition

Alexander Solzhenitsyn once observed that "as every man goes through life he fills in a number of forms . . ., each containing a number of questions. . . . There are thus hundreds of little threads radiating from every man."[1] Modern computer technology permits each of these threads to be collected, combined, and analyzed in an efficient and timely fashion.[2] Consequently, there is a growing mass of data on individuals being legally collected by government and private industry.[3] This information includes census and tax information, medical and credit reports, arrest and criminal records, résumés, and even magazine subscription data. When aggregated, this information has the potential to be used as an instrument of control. At a minimum, the information accumulated in centralized data files may be used to trace and regulate an individual's movements and activities.[4] In extreme circumstances, this information could be used to blackmail, or coerce individuals to act as pawns in a totalitarian society. Many observers have expressed concerns that the computer, with its limitless capacity for storing information, and its ability to retrieve almost anything that has been stored in it, may engender a surveillance system that will turn society into a transparent world in which individuals' homes, their finances, and their associations will be bared to a wide range of observers.[5]

---

[1] Linowes, *Must Personal Privacy Die in the Computer Age?*, 65 ABAJ 1180 (Aug 1979).

[2] A fundamental issue of privacy is the amount of freedom each individual possesses. *Freedom* is of course directly related to the numbers of people in a defined space. Herbert wrote that beyond a

> critical point within a finite space, freedom diminishes as numbers increase. This is as true of humans in the finite space of a planetary ecosystem as it is of gas molecules in a sealed flask. The human question is not how many can possibly survive within the system, but what kind of existence is possible for those who do survive.

F. Herbert, Dune 493 (1965).

[3] See generally A. Miller, The Assault on Privacy (1971); A. Westin, Privacy and Freedom 158-68 (1967); Bazelon, *Probing Privacy*, 12 Gonzaga L Rev 587, 588-619 (Summer 1977).

[4] See A. Miller, *supra* note 3, at 38-46. This rather widespread fear led to considerable opposition to the federal government's proposed National Data Center in 1967 as well as the 1981 proposal by President Reagan to create a centralized data file in the Department of Health and Human Services in order to track welfare recipients.

[5] V. Ferkiss, Technological Man 227 (1969); Miller, *The National Data Center and Personal Privacy,* The Atlantic 53 (Nov 1967). *See also* Osborn v United States, 385 US

Despite this negative potential, the use of collected data is indispensable in modern society. To an ever increasing extent, information on individuals is needed in order to formulate policies for solving social, economic, and political problems inherent in modern society. Prior to the development of the computer, vast data collection and interpretation was either impossible or impracticable.[6] A number of contemporary prophets have predicted that the advent of these new information transfer technologies will prove to be as significant as the invention of movable type.[7]

An inherent problem in the development of computers, including data storage and data manipulation, is its effect on individuals' privacy. This chapter will examine the effect of computers on privacy from historical, contemporary, and futuristic perspectives, including an evaluation of statutory responses to the protection of individual privacy both in the United States and abroad.

Before considering privacy, the term must be defined. Certainly the simplest and perhaps most valid definition was penned by Justice Brandeis in his famous dissent in *Olmstead v United States,* in which he said that privacy "is the right to be let alone."[8] Other writers have defined privacy in more comprehensive terms, for example Professor Alan Westin, who defines privacy as:

> The claim of individuals, groups, or institutions to determine for themselves when, how, and to what extent information about them is communicated to others. . . . Each individual is continually engaged in a personal adjustment process in which he balances the desire for privacy with the desire for disclosure and communication. The individual does

---

323, 353 (1966) (Justice William O. Douglas dissenting); Lopez v United States 373 US 427, 450 (1963) (Justice William Brennan dissenting).

[6] Ruggles, Pemberton, & Miller, *Computers, Data Banks, and Individual Privacy,* 53 Minn L Rev 211, 213 (1968).

[7] A. Clarke, Profiles of the Future 265-79 (1962); See also M. McLuhan, The Gutenberg Galaxy 11-79 (1962); H. Kahn & A. Weiner, The Year 2000, 88-98, 348 (1967); A. Westin, *supra* note 3, at 165.

An example of the scientific community's views of the impact of the computer on our society is the following excerpt from a speech by Dr. Glenn Seaborg, Chairman of the Atomic Energy Commission, reprinted in *Hearings on Computer Privacy Before the Subcomm on Administrative Practice and Procedure, Senate Comm on the Judiciary,* 90th Cong, 1st Sess 248 (1967):

> Springing from our Scientific Revolution of recent decades is what is being called our "Cybernetic Revolution." This revolution which, comparatively speaking, is only in its infancy today amplifies (and will to a large extent replace) man's nervous system. Actually, this is an understatement because computers amplify the collective intelligence of men—the intelligence of society—and while the effect of the sum of man's physical energies may be calculated, a totally different and compounded effect results from combining facts and ideas. . . . Add this energy source to the productive capacity of the machine driven by an almost limitless energy source like the atom and the resulting system can perform feats almost staggering to the imagination. That is why I refer to cybernation as a quantum jump in our growth.

[8] 277 US 438, 478 (1928).

so in the face of the processes of surveillance that every society sets in order to enforce its social norms.[9]

Professor Thomas Emerson described privacy in these broad terms:

> Generally speaking, the concept of a right to privacy attempts to draw a line between the individual and the collective, between self and society. It seeks to assure the individual a zone in which to be an individual, not a member of the community. In that zone he can think his own thoughts, have his own secrets, live his own life, reveal only what he wants to the outside world. The right of privacy, in short, establishes an area excluded from the collective life, not governed by the rules of collective living.[10]

In this chapter, privacy is defined as the unitary concept of separation of self from society.[11]

§6.02 The Development of Computer Technology in Relation to Privacy

After World War II, the United States witnessed a tremendous increase in commercial and governmental activities, with a concomitant increase in the volume of transactions requiring record-keeping. Compared with the prewar years, numbers of bank checks written, college students, and pieces of mail all doubled; and the number of income tax returns quadrupled, as did the number of social security and other transfer payments.[12] Automated data processing developed into an industry in itself, largely to serve the demands of business and industry for fast, accurate, and efficient data handling.[13]

During the late 1960s, business and social planners began to use the concept of systems analysis—the mathematical simulation of a complex activity or task—which had originally been developed for engineering applications. In particular, systems analysis was applied to health care delivery, income transfer payments, air pollution, urban transportation, and higher education. The introduction of the disciplined methods of computer-assisted management gave business and social planners new tools for evaluating the performance of programs and institutions dealing with social problems. This auditing process included:

---

[9] A. Westin, *supra* note 3, at 7.

[10] T. Emerson, The System of Freedom of Expression 545 (1970).

[11] *Id.*

[12] Department of Health, Education and Welfare, Records, Computers, and the Rights of Citizens 7-10 (1973).

[13] See generally B. Gilchrist & R. Weber, The State of the Computer Industry in the United States 54 (1973); M. Holoien, Computers and Their Societal Impact 43-44 (1977); D. Tomeski & W. Lazarus, People-Oriented Computer Systems: The Computer in Crisis 130-32 (1975).

1. Tracking transactions between organizations and their clients
2. Measuring performance against goals
3. Providing information for planning
4. Assessing workload and productivity

Each of these functions necessarily involved the collection and storage of data on individuals. For example:

1. Administrative data were needed for management of individual transactions
2. Statistical data were needed for planning and assessing program performance
3. Intelligence data were needed for judging individuals' character and qualifications for employment, credit, welfare assistance, and other aid
4. Health data were needed to provide adequate health care and medical assistance

Consequently, the demand generated by all these uses of personal data, and the corresponding record-keeping systems to store and process these data, challenged conventional legal and social controls to protect individual privacy.

§6.03 Present Status and Future Trends

Computer technology can be expected to continue to increase the capacity, speed, and complexity of machines for storing and analyzing data concerning individuals. The federal government continues to sponsors development of advanced computer systems for its various military and domestic programs. Strong economic pressures exist worldwide for automating various operations in the public and private sectors. Additionally, public opinion is becoming progressively more receptive to the provision of better data and faster information processing. There is a tremendous infusion of venture capital into computer development. Computational development has even been described as the "last frontier of entrepreneural capitalism."[14]

Given this pattern of rapid innovation and technological development, policymakers have legitimate concerns that computational technology can infringe on individual privacy. As early as 1972, Professor Westin wrote that computer technology then existing could maintain a computerized, on-line file containing the equivalent of 20 single-spaced pages of typed information about the personal history and selected activities of every man, woman, and child in the United States. Further, it was possible to retrieve information on

---

[14] As Michael Shields, a catalog marketer for Apple Computers, stated: "Living here in the Silicon Valley of northern California is like riding in the nose cone of the Space Shuttle. We are riding into the future." *Striking it Rich: A New Breed of Risk Takers is Betting on the High Technology Future*, Time, Feb 15, 1982, at 36-41.

any given individual within 30 seconds.[15] While Americans may enjoy the convenience and speed of information processing, a Louis Harris poll once found that nearly two-thirds of the people interviewed were concerned about threats to their privacy. Nearly one-third said the United States was, or soon would be, much like the fictional Oceania in George Orwell's post-World War II novel *1984,* a nation that kept every activity of its citizens under constant surveillance.[16]

The major areas of computer technology which will affect personal privacy are as follows:

1. *Input.* The direct-entry input devices and optical scanning methods represent techniques by which data, either numeric or alphabetic, can be entered directly into machine readable form. Some forecasters even believe voice input devices will become widespread by the late 1980s[17]

2. *Storage.* Larger memory storage capacities are being developed so that great volumes of personal data can be entered into direct-access storage for on-line access. One new storage technique is laser beam technology, which allows data to be stored at the molecular level

3. *Configuration Arrangements.* More flexible options are becoming available for arranging the configuration of computer systems. Minicomputers and microcomputers can be used for self-contained record-keeping and data processing applications. There are also improved capacities for linking terminals into on-line systems, thereby giving greater flexibility to organizations and governments. Some organizations have become more decentralized in their record-keeping activities, while others have elected to use large, multiterminal centralized systems

4. *Database Management Software.* Considerable improvement is expected in database management software. The movement toward management information systems (MIS), which allow separate data files to be unified and processed, will continue. Some experts believe that continued upgrading of MIS will depend in large degree on the development of better understanding of business, social, and political processes and relationships, as well as major administrative reforms within these organizations

5. *Availability of Computers.* The development of low-cost microcomputers and relatively inexpensive terminal links into commercial time-sharing

---

[15] A. Westin, Databanks in a Free Society 321-30 (1972). While there may not exist a single giant databank to hold all this information, it is possible to link separate computer systems within a separate organization or between organizations. Given the linkage technology already available, and if problems of common personal identifiers, compatible record formats, and appropriate software instructions for the desired use could be worked out, there would never be a need for a mammoth central processing unit to operate this data system.

[16] *Report on Privacy: Who is Watching You?,* US News & World Rep, July 12, 1982, at 34-37.

[17] *To Each His Own Computer,* Newsweek, Feb 22, 1982, at 56.

services has greatly increased the availability of computers to small organizations and individuals. In 1981, over $2.2 billion was spent on personal computers worldwide. Assuming an average cost of $500-$1,500 per microcomputer, means that over a million were sold in 1981 alone.[18] It was estimated that over three million personal computers would be sold in 1982, and predictions for 1985 run to over 50 million personal computers in use worldwide.[19] As computers are made more readily available to individuals, more personal data is captured and available in machine readable form

6.   *Communications Systems.* Cheaper and more specialized communications systems for data transmission have been developed since 1975, including microwave systems, satellites, cable television channels, and laser communications[20]

7.   *Output Devices.* More flexible and less expensive computer output technology has been developed, including computers used as "support" for microfilm and microfiche systems. Consequently, the sorting and preparing of hard-copy media through computer-output-to-microfilm devices will continue to increase in use.[21] Hardware costs will continue to decline, but the increasingly complex software systems that users are demanding will rise in cost over time[22]

Given these continuing technological advances, the computer will remain the logical tool for coping with the so-called information explosion. It has been estimated that by 1987, while six to seven times the present volume of new information will be produced, the ability of computers to process this information will increase a hundred times over that of today's computers. Thus, the capacity of computers to process information may equal or exceed the amount of information to be processed.[23]

The present state of computer development and the projected future use of computer technology raise a number of implications for life in a highly computerized society. Four major issues have repeatedly been identified concerning the impact of computers on society: automation, power, individuality, and

---

[18] *The Seeds of Success—Apple Computers,* Time, Feb 15, 1982, at 41.

[19] *To Each His Own Computer, supra* note 17, at 50.

[20] It is expected that the breakup of AT&T will lead to the continued development of telecommunications systems capable of providing efficient and effective methods for data transmission. See **ch 5.**

[21] National Academy of Sciences, Libraries and Information Technology: A National System Challenge 75 (1971).

[22] As Ben Rosen wrote in his widely read *Electronics Letter,* "Software [is] the tail that wags the personal computer dog." *The Tail that Wags the Dog,* Newsweek, Feb 22, 1982, 55.

[23] See Douglas, *Beyond the Industrial Revolution,* Science News, Oct 4, 1975, at 220; Etzioni, *Effects of Small Computers on Scientists,* Science, July 11, 1975, at 93.

privacy.[24]

Automation

The Industrial Revolution initially supplemented and eventually replaced, the muscles of men and animals with the technology of machines. Computational technology has now begun to replace, or at least supplement, some aspects of human thought processes with electronic machines. These changes have had, and will continue to have, considerable significance to society. Not only are people relieved of burdensome, tedious, repetitive, and boring positions, but productivity and production costs are also optimized.[25] Some observers believe that computers create more jobs than they displace, while other experts theorize that computers in the future will take away more jobs than they create.[26]

Power

There is a saying that information is power. Computers create the potential for a few individuals to accumulate massive amounts of data that can be readily accessed. The very existence of sophisticated computers necessarily creates a power gap between those technically trained persons who can interpret and use these data for socially beneficial purposes, and those who do not have computational skills. In quite a different scenario, failures of computer systems can create chaos and catastrophe. Recent system failures like the 1970s power blackouts in New York City, the nuclear power plant shutdown at Three Mile Island, and air traffic control problems in Southern California have led to chaotic situations.

Individuality

Historically in the United States, the right of the individual to pursue happiness has been a value of considerable importance. Computers have altered this individuality to a great degree as a person's very essence can be reduced to numbers on a terminal screen. Computers have proven to be particularly useful for handling aggregations of data such as fiscal and credit transactions, medical records, consumer habits, and communications. With access to so much accumulated data, however, social planners might easily begin creating a society that can be dealt with in terms of masses, rather than in terms of

---

[24] S. Rothman & C. Mosmann, Computers and Society (1972); W. Mathews, Master or Messiah? The Computer's Impact on Society 32-36 (1980).

[25] Note the growing use of robots to perform repetitive processes in the manufacture of automobiles, steelwork, electronic circuits, and other assembly line products. Japan has already developed robots to build other robots. See *Japan's High-Tech Challenge,* Newsweek, Aug 9, 1982, at 48.

[26] *Machines Smarter than Men? An Interview with Robert Weiner,* US News & World Rep, Feb 24, 1964, at 84-86.

individuals.[27]

Privacy

Issues of individual privacy and the confidentiality of communications and personal data are raised by the increasing use of computers for data collection and information processing. Some observers have strenuously argued against the trend to link databanks containing information on individuals because such trends could well serve as the beginning of so-called "individual data images."[28] Professor Westin has argued that a computational technology which is capable of integrating several databanks into networks holds potentially grave implications regarding personal privacy.[29] With these networks, personal data provided by an individual for one purpose could potentially be used later for quite another purpose. The likelihood that an individual will know that such uses are being made of these data is slim.

Further, there appears to be no discernable legal or social impetus at this point in time to increase controls protecting privacy. As Professor Westin has observed, privacy is a quality-of-life issue that usually takes second place to economic and foreign policy concerns. According to his assessment:

> Many consider the in-roads in the U.S. slight compared with the ruthless obliteration of privacy in totalitarian nations. They pooh-pooh any suggestion that, with the U.S. system of constitutional rights, Orwell's *1984* nightmare could ever happen here.
>
> What's more, privacy advocates find it difficult to prove that abuses are widespread. Proponents of the Carter bill [in 1979, President Carter sent to Congress a package of proposals to safeguard personnel and medical records, but none of the bills passed] to protect medical records cited two major cases of abuse, one in Canada and one in Denver. Congressional opponents said the lack of other evidence showed that the bill was "a solution in search of a problem."
>
> Some experts think a major scandal is needed to break reform proposals loose. Comments sociologist James Rule of the State University of New York: "The trend now seems to be to get government off people's backs. It may take a disaster in the privacy area, such as Three Mile Island in nuclear power, to get action that would protect privacy."
>
> By then, warn privacy advocates, record-keeping technology may be so advanced it will be impossible for Americans to hold any personal information secret for long. Says Professor Trubow of John Marshall Law School: "If we have such a disaster, it will be too late then to do anything

---

[27] Michael, *Decisions and Public Opinion,* in A. Van Tassel, The Complete Computer 153 (1976).

[28] Koehn, *Privacy, Our Problem for Tomorrow,* Sys Mgmt 8-10 (July 1973).

[29] A. Westin, Privacy and Freedom 158-68 (1967).

about it. All personal information will be in the public domain.''[30]

Threat to Individual Privacy

§6.04   Key Forces Threatening Privacy

The dawning of the computer age has brought privacy concerns to the forefront of the public consciousness. These concerns have stirred increasing alarm in the writings of numerous individuals. Marshal McLuhan, for example, characterized computerization as a major threat to all people, particularly the poor and the middle class.[31] The recent developments of computer technology have given rise to incredible capacities of computers to collect, store, and analyze information. The threats posed to the individual from these capacities arise in a myriad of situations. Barron described some of the major threats presented by databanks as:

1. Illicit access to personal information with a malicious intent
2. Unexpected consequences of making information freely available by mechanical means
3. Use of information for purposes other than that for which it was collected
4. Actions based on inaccurate or outdated information
5. Placement of the individual at a disadvantage as against large organizations with ready access to large amounts of computerized information
6. Sanctity of information merely because it is stored in a computer[32]

Other threats involve the *secrecy* of personal information; unauthorized or illicit collection methods and omissions; the invisibility of the data collection and analysis processes; and the regulation of computers.[33]

Professor William Beaney believes that the major effect of the computer on privacy is that computers separate the individual from the decision whether personal information will be released. This loss of control can take two forms: loss of access control, and loss of accuracy control.[34] When an individual is the sole source of information, the individual has at least a marginal degree of control over what others know about him or her. The advent of the computer databank gives a new source of personal information to society, over which the individual, whose personal information is stored, has no access control. Distri-

---

[30] *Report on Privacy, supra* note 16.

[31] A. Westin, Privacy and Freedom 95 (1967).

[32] Barron, *People, Not Computers,* in J. Young, Privacy 320 (1978).

[33] Organization for Economic Cooperation and Development, Policy Issues in Data Protection and Privacy 148 (1974).

[34] Beaney, *The Right to Privacy and American Law,* 31 Law & Contemp Prob 253 (1966).

bution of personal information from such a source also vitiates that individual's control over the accuracy and reliability of the personal information that is released. Judge Bazelon argued that the role of law is to mediate between an individual's right to privacy and society's right to know. There are, however, four forces in contemporary America that make the need for some mechanisms to protect privacy even more compelling.[35] These four forces are eavesdropping, sophisticated databases, the growing need for information, and increased regulation.

Eavesdropping

There are increasingly more sophisticated devices becoming available for eavesdropping. Professor Westin documented both governmental and private sector actions geared to penetrate private places, and to intercept private conversations, all without the knowledge of the parties involved.[36] The assumption that persons can carry on a conversation in a home or room, presumably out of the earshot of others, therefore, is no longer justified.

Sophisticated Databases

The growth of efficient systems for storing, manipulating, and sharing data has increased the potential for the invasion of individual privacy.[37] When records were kept on paper and requests for information had to be manually processed in writing, central files which combined credit information, employment histories, and arrest records were unknown. One could often keep someone from having certain information simply by not telling that person where to look for it. Unless the person was willing to do a great deal of searching, the past as well as the present could often be hidden and forgotten. In the 1980s, governments and businesses maintain extensive records in computer databanks. Management information systems (MIS) which allow computers to be linked together can give a comprehensive picture of a person's finances, employment, education, and reputation—not just present data, but historical data as well. These MIS are not immune from being tapped and having information stolen by outsiders, nor is there anything to prevent those with legal access from checking the records of selected individuals.

Growing Need for Information

The third force is the growing need of business, government, and even academia for information. As the ability to handle larger volumes of data expands, so does the perception of the need for additional data. Professor Miller attributes this explosion of information and record-keeping not only to computer technology, but also to the entry by the federal government into the

---

[35] Bazelon, *Probing Privacy*, 12 Gonzaga L Rev 587, 597-600 (Summer 1977).

[36] A. Westin, Privacy and Freedom 158-68 (1967).

[37] A. Miller, The Assault on Privacy 21 (1971).

taxation and social welfare fields. Many governmental agencies are beginning to ask complex, probing, and sensitive questions on a multitude of forms, covering one's associations, medical history, and attitudes toward various institutions and people.[38] Similar trends are apparent in social science and market analysis research carried out by universities and private research organizations. Lie detector tests and personality examinations which touch on sexual preferences, religious beliefs, and other personal habits are not uncommon in private industry.[39]

Increased Regulation

The fourth force comes from the inevitable pressure to regulate individual lives more tightly in a complex economy. As population grows and resources diminish, individual economic freedom will most probably give way to increased governmental intervention. While people may in principle condemn this larger role for government, their demands for economic security, education, adequate health care, and better criminal justice systems all support an increasing governmental role in society. The danger is that government will exert unnecessary social controls in the process of providing these alleged benefits. As more people come to depend on government to fulfill more and more needs, they may find themselves with less autonomy and control over their private lives.[40]

Bazelon argues that the law must increasingly intervene to guard against this erosion of privacy. Insofar as the Constitution protects privacy, government should be subject to these same limitations. However, to prevent invasions by those in the private sector, there must also be administrative regulations and statutes.[41] Whenever law affecting privacy is made, whether by the courts, the legislature, or the executive branch, policymakers should analyze and mediate among the inevitable competing interests.[42] This action, according to Bazelon, is probably the only way to protect individual privacy in the 1980s and beyond.

§6.05   Types of Personal Information

The use of computers to store personal information might be best illustrated by the use of *hypothetical*, composite cases in which individuals applied for, but were refused, a loan, a life insurance policy, and a credit card. These individuals sought legal advice and were given specific options as to how they might

---

[38] *Id.*

[39] A. Westin, *supra* note 36, at 133-70 and 216-78. See also *Report on Privacy: Who is Watching You?*, US News & World Rep, July 12, 1982, at 34, 35-36.

[40] Some social commentators criticize Westin's notions of privacy and individualism as antagonistic to the general welfare. See Benn, *Privacy, Freedom, and Respect for Persons,* XIII Privacy Nomos 18-23 (1971).

[41] Bazelon, *supra* note 35, at 600.

[42] A. Westin, *supra* note 36, at 370-77.

remedy their situations. While the cases are hypothetical, they typify the extent to which information on an individual can be used, even abused, once it is stored in a computer databank.

Mr. Smith

John Smith, a 36 year-old engineer and honorably discharged veteran, was denied a Veterans' Administration (VA) guarantee on a home mortgage. He first requested to review his file at the savings and loan association where he applied for the loan. The accepted banking practice in the United States generally is to allow the customer to review the file, but not his credit report or the appraisal on the house for which the loan application is made.[43] A review of Mr. Smith's file revealed information that he had once been convicted of a felony, and the bank official told him that the credit report contained other adverse information. The bank told him the name of the credit reporting agency that supplied this information.

Mr. Smith and his attorney then called the credit reporting agency. Under the Fair Credit Reporting Act, 15 USC §1681 *et seq* (1976), Mr. Smith had the right to review his entire file, except for medical information (see **§6.07**). As a general practice, credit reporting agencies base credit reports on contacts with their own customers who have requested reports on individuals over the past years. They also contact references supplied by the credit applicant—generally merchants and banks who have a record of that applicant's buying and paying habits. Information supplied by these sources, as well as court records of such items as divorce decrees, garnishments, or bankruptcies, are then supplied to the requesting merchant; in this case the savings and loan association.[44]

To the surprise of Mr. Smith, his file contained a notation that he had been identified as a person known "to have had attacked or ridiculed a major doctrine of the Christian faith or the American way of life."[45] As required, the

---

[43] Banks generally consider credit reports and appraisals to be the banks' own information. It should be noted that when a potential customer completes a credit application, he or she gives consent to the bank to consult practically anyone or any institution about the person's credit, character, and general reputation.

[44] One Denver, Colorado credit reporting agency had over 2.5 million names in its computer as of February, 1980, and served over 2,000 members in Colorado alone. This is what is considered in the industry to be just a "local" firm. See **ch 8,** specifically **§8.20.**

[45] Linowes, *Are New Privacy Laws Needed?*, 44 Vit Speeches Day 436 (1978). The United States Commission on Privacy was told by one of the nation's three largest credit reporting agencies that it uses the services of organizations which purport to identify people with anti-American values. Lists of individuals classified in various categories are sold to business entities, and the establishment of such lists is greatly facilitated by computers. For example, many state motor vehicle departments sell lists of automobile owners, and the Federal Aviation Administration sells lists of FAA-certified pilots. Such lists are of great interest to oil companies and automobile insurance companies. The Internal Revenue Service sold aggregate statistics on income of United States taxpayers broken down by Zip Code to national magazines such as *Time, Look,* and *Newsweek;* it

credit reporting agency reinvestigated the notation after he protested, and finally concluded that the notation, based solely on the fact that his father had been investigated in the 1950s by the House Subcommittee on Un-American Activities, was not applicable to him. The agency, therefore, deleted the notation from his file, and notified the savings and loan association.

The alleged felony conviction was, in fact, a conviction for civil disobedience when he was involved in a sit-in as a civil rights worker in the South in 1965. The bank had obtained this information from his veteran's files, which also contained·the name and address of his exwife. With this information and the credit reporting agency's file,[46] it conducted its own investigation, including contacting the FBI,[47] whose files also showed the conviction.

Mr. Smith has two possible remedies: (1) he may seek expungement of his criminal record, or (2) he may sue the VA under the Privacy Act of 1974, 5 USC §552a. Expungement (i.e., sealing parts of a record) is generally available only when there is either an acquittal or a dismissal of the charges as well as a showing of "significant abuse of authority" by the law enforcement officials.[48] Expungements have been ordered, however, in cases where the sole purpose of an arrest was to harass civil rights workers.[49] On the other hand, a suit to obtain expungement is both uncertain and time-consuming. A better option is to seek a remedy under the Privacy Act. If the VA refuses to amend his military record, he may ask a court to compel the VA to amend.[50] The VA can argue it is exempt from the requirements of the Privacy Act because its disclo-

---

has also sold such lists to mailorder firms such as Sears Roebuck & Co. Such statistics are useful in identifying high-income areas for advertising targets. A. Miller, The Assault on Privacy 82 (1971). "Welcome Wagon," the friendly person who shows up at your door when you move into a new city, offers gifts to new residents in exchange for information on religious affiliation, occupation, and service needs. This information is then sold. A. Westin, Privacy and Freedom 160 (1967). The company that classified Mr. Smith obtained its information from lists of authors, speakers, signed group advertisements in newspapers, and investigations by the long-defunct House Subcommittee on Un-American Activities. Linowes, *Must Personal Privacy Die in the Computer Age?*, 65 ABA J 1183 (Aug 1979).

[46] If the bank already had this information, it could have notified the VA, whose activities are excluded from the provisions of the Right of Financial Privacy Act under the circumstances described here. 12 USC §3401 *et seq.*

[47] FBI activities are also excluded from the provisions of the Right to Financial Privacy Act. 12 USC §3401 *et seq.*

[48] As early as 1974, the FBI maintained over 200 million fingerprint cards, including over 19 million relating to criminal activity. The FBI exchanges such information with other federal, state, and local law enforcement agencies, insurance companies, national banks, the Federal Deposit Insurance Corporation, and the savings and loan industry. *See* Menard v Saxbe, 498 F2d 1017, 1021 (DC Cir 1974). (Weinstein, *Confidentiality of Criminal Records: Privacy v the Public Interests*, 22 Vill L Rev 11205-11 (1977), points out that data collection, not just computerization, is at least part of the problem. The criminal justice system has a genuine need, however, for data to prevent crime, move caseloads, and analyze statistics).

[49] United States v McLeod, 385 F2d 734 (5th Cir 1967).

[50] Under 5 USC §552a(g)(2)(A), the FBI is protected in its disclosures to the VA.

sure to the bank was a "routine use" of such records.[51] Moreover, Mr. Smith, as part of his application for the mortgage, undoubtedly signed a waiver permitting the bank and the VA to investigate and use any information they received concerning him. Mr. Smith can argue that any information disclosed under the Privacy Act must be "timely,"[52] and it is certainly arguable whether a 17 year-old conviction is timely.

The remedies available to Mr. Smith, either to seek expungement or to sue under the Privacy Act, are both uncertain as to outcome and extremely time-consuming. The house he was seeking to purchase will most likely have been sold to another bidder. His best nonlegal remedy may be to seek a conventional loan from another bank which does not use the same credit reporting agency.

Ms. Brown

Mary Brown, a 32 year-old television reporter in perfect health and with an excellent financial reputation, was informed that she would not be issued an insurance policy because, as the company informed her, it had received adverse information about her.[53] At the office of the insurance company, she was shown her file with the exception of her medical and credit reports, and she was given the names of the credit reporting agency and the doctors the company had contacted for this information.[54] The insurance company informed Ms. Brown that it had received an adverse report from the Medical Information Bureau (MIB), and that this report had been used to supplement the credit and medical reports.[55]

The MIB, which is subject to the requirements of the Fair Credit Reporting Act, was required to show Ms. Brown her file, again excluding medical infor-

---

[51] *See* 5 USC §552 a(b)(3).

[52] Under 5 USC §552 a(e)(6), the Fair Credit Reporting Act does not permit disclosures of convictions over seven years old.

[53] This tends to be an accepted industry practice.

[54] Again, although this is an accepted industry practice, routine medical information such as a blood pressure reading may be disclosed to the individual.

[55] The MIB is an association of 700 life insurance companies whose members underwrite 90% of the life insurance policies in the United States and Canada. Members may obtain information on the records of over 11 million people contained in the MIB computer files. Whenever an applicant is denied life insurance, the life insurance company reports this information to MIB. This list is not checked for accuracy and the person is placed on a list of "persons with impairments." The traits constituting an "impairment" have included nervousness, sexual deviation, and unhealthy appearance. The purpose of MIB is to prevent an applicant who is a poor risk and who is refused insurance by one company from applying to subsequent companies and withholding certain information. While the MIB will not divulge such medical information directly to an applicant, it will provide this information to the applicant's personal physician, who then may tell the applicant about it. Under MIB rules, such medical information is to be used only to supplement the life insurance company investigation. See Stern, *Medical Information Bureau: The Life Insurer's Databank,* 4 Rutgers J Computers & L 1-19 (1974).

mation. The file contained a report from a neighbor who stated that Ms. Brown entertained people of questionable character at all hours of the day and night and, further, that Ms. Brown was a drug user.[56] The insurance company reinvestigated this report after Ms. Brown disputed it. The company found that the neighbor, nearly senile, disliked Ms. Brown because her dog strayed into the neighbor's yard on occasion. With this information, the insurance company deleted the report.

While the file of the credit reporting agency contained no adverse comments, the report of the doctor did. The doctor had indicated that Ms. Brown disclosed to her college physician that her mother had been treated by a psychiatrist.[57] The college should not have released this information without Ms. Brown's consent.[58] The Family Educational Rights and Privacy Act, however, does not provide a private remedy; it merely permits the Secretary of Education to terminate federal funds to the institution.[59] Ms. Brown does have a remedy against the credit reporting agency for continuing to carry the doctor's report. Because the adverse information is over seven years old, the agency is precluded from disclosing it, even if it is true.[60] If the agency refuses to delete the information and inform the insurance company, the agency may be liable for both actual and punitive damages.[61]

Mr. White

Richard White, a 44 year-old small businessman who owns his own hardware store, was denied a credit card. The credit card company showed Mr. White his file, with the exception of his credit report, but did tell him the name of the credit reporting agency. The file at the credit reporting agency showed that shortly after Mr. White graduated from college some 22 years earlier, he was adjudicated as bankrupt and received welfare for a year. Under the terms of the Fair Credit Reporting Act, bankruptcies which occurred over 10 years prior to a report may not be disclosed.[62] Thus, the agency is required to delete such

---

[56] Linowes, *Must Personal Privacy Die in the Computer Age? supra* note 45, at 1182. This was an actual case reported to the Privacy Commission in 1978.

[57] This is another actual case reported to the Privacy Commission in 1978. In that case, the person was a young woman who was refused employment as a public school teacher because she had reportedly told her school doctor that her mother had once seen a psychiatrist. See Diamond, *How to Protect Your Privacy,* McCall's 51 (Feb 1980).

[58] 20 USC §1232g(b)(1).

[59] Girardier v Webster College, 563 F2d 1267, 1276 (8th Cir 1977) (a former student could not use the Family Educational Rights and Privacy Act to force a college to release his or her transcript after the student had defaulted on a National Defense Student Loan and was discharged in bankruptcy).

[60] 15 USC §1681c(a)(6).

[61] *Id* §1681n.

[62] *Id* §1681c(a)(1), but, where the credit report is used in connection with a transaction or life insurance policy involving an amount in excess of $49,999, or employment at a salary of $20,000 or more, there are no time restrictions placed on reporting bankruptcies.

information and inform the credit card company, or be subjected to actual and punitive damages. Other types of adverse information are subjected to a seven-year limitation on disclosure. The agency may not, therefore, legally report that Mr. White received public assistance,[63] The more interesting question is how the credit reporting agency obtained the information that Mr. White had received public assistance, since these records are subject to strict requirements of confidentiality under the law.[64] It is possible that this information was obtained as a result of the requirement that Mr. White supply his social security number when he obtained public assistance,[65] and when he applied for the credit card. A computer search for information based on social security number might very well have revealed such data. In any case, the agency has the duty to delete this information from its files and notify the credit card company. The credit card company then has the discretion to issue a credit card based upon this changed information.[66]

As these three hypothetical cases illustrate, computer storage and retrieval of personal information in all areas of an individual's life has become increas-

---

[63] *Id* §1681c(a)(6).

[64] 42 USC §602(a)(9). In Colorado, information on individuals applying for public assistance since 1972 is now in computer files. Printouts of these files contain a note that the recipient is responsible for the confidentiality of the files. *See* Colo Rev Stat §26-1-112(3) (1973) and IV Colorado Department of Social Services Manual §§4711-14.3.

[65] Chambers v Klein, 419 F Supp 569 (DNJ 1976), *affd*, 564 F2d 89 (3d Cir 1977). Requiring disclosure of a social security number in order to secure Aid to Families With Dependent Children benefits is a violation of neither the Privacy Act nor the Constitution. Of course, the use of social security numbers makes access to different computer files containing personal information easier. Davis, *A Technologist's View of Privacy and Security in Automated Information Systems,* 4 Rutgers J Computers & L 264, 273 (1975).

[66] Credit card companies are in and of themselves a major source of personal information on millions of individuals. In order to obtain a credit card, an applicant must provide a significant amount of financial, credit, and personal information. When the user subsequently uses the card, information concerning the items purchased, travel movements, and financial status are posted to the user's account. By 1973 over 50% of all American families had at least one major credit card. Credit card companies such as American Express, VISA, and MasterCard include specific instructions on their applications that the information requested, and later transactions, will be used and exchanged by other companies. In turn, this information is sold in order to generate further profits for the credit card companies. One startling example of how supposedly confidential information can be used was the sale of a list containing pregnancy information from a laboratory conducting such tests to a diaper service. In turn, the diaper service mailed advertisements to the names on the list. One flyer reached a house in which the husband was the first to arrive home one evening. He learned of his wife's pregnancy from the cheerful greeting and "congratulations" on the cover of the flyer. See Comment, *The Privacy Side of the Credit Card,* 23 Am UL Rev 183, 187 (1973). In Denver, Colorado, banks seem to be quite concerned about protecting the confidentiality of their customers' files. Most banks keep only a customer's balance, available credit line, and past few months' transactions on computer files. The rest of the customer's information is stored by month, not by name, on microfiche, which is stored under tight security in the bank's vault.

ingly pervasive. The burden of correcting inaccurate information or deleting dated material lies most often with the individual rather than the agency. This is so because in many computerized databanks the cost to delete data (whether dated, accurate, or inaccurate) is significantly higher than the cost to perpetually store it. The real threat to privacy, therefore, may not be the fact that computers can collect and store so much information about an individual, but that information that is inaccurate or dated can be repeatedly used to judge the character, reputation, employability, or creditworthiness of the individual without that person even knowing what information was used to make the decision or where the information originated.

Domestic Legal Protection of Individual Privacy

§6.06   Judicial Response—Constitutional and Common Law Cases

The origin of the "right" to privacy is an early *Harvard Law Review* article by Warren and Brandeis.[67] Privacy was finally defined by the Supreme Court some 38 years later by then Justice Brandeis. His oft-quoted dissent, as discussed in §6.01, stated that privacy is simply, "the right to be let alone."[68] He argued further that it "is not the breaking of [a person's] doors, and the rummaging of his drawers, that constitute [the invasion of privacy], . . . but it is the invasion of his indefeasible right of personal security, personal liberty, and private property. . . ."[69]

In the mid 1900s, the Supreme Court found a right to privacy in various amendments to the United States Constitution, even though the specific word *privacy* does not appear in the text of either the Constitution or any amendment. In 1958, some 30 years after the Brandeis dissent in *Olmstead v United States*, the Court, in *NAACP v Alabama*, found a "vital relationship between freedom to associate and privacy in one's associations,"[70] in ruling that the NAACP was protected by the First and Fourteenth Amendments in the "right of the members to pursue their lawful private interests privately. . . ."[71]

The Court decision that specifically held that a constitutional right of privacy exists was *Griswold v Connecticut*, in which a state statute making it a crime to prescribe or use contraceptive devices was struck down.[72] In *Griswold*, Justice Douglas found a right of privacy emanating from the "penumbras" of the First,

---

[67] Warren & Brandeis, *The Right to Privacy*, 4 Harv L Rev 193 (1890).

[68] Olmstead v United States, 277 US 438, 478 (1928) (Brandeis, J, dissenting).

[69] *Id* 474-75.

[70] NAACP v Alabama, 357 US 449, 462 (1958).

[71] *Id* 466.

[72] 381 US 479 (1965).

Third, Fourth, Fifth, and Ninth Amendments.[73]

Although quite willing to find a constitutional right to privacy in more personal areas, the Court has been rather reluctant to hold that such a right exists for individuals in commercial settings (i.e., areas involving banking and credit card institutions). In 1976, in *United States v Miller* the Court held that a bank depositor has no "legitimate expectation of privacy" as to copies of checks, financial statements, and other documents which the bank depositor had supplied to the bank.[74] The Court reasoned that because such records were merely business records, rather than the depositor's private papers, and because the depositor voluntarily revealed personal affairs to the bank by surrendering these records, the depositor also took the risk that this information might be conveyed to others.[75]

In 1972, the Court in *Laird v Tatum*, in a 5 to 4 decision, ducked the question of whether the existence of a broad system of domestic surveillance by the United States Army "chilled" the First Amendment rights of those being watched.[76] Information about the activities of the plaintiffs had been stored in a computer at Fort Holabird, Maryland. These data were freely dispensed to numerous military and civilian intelligence officials throughout the country. The holding was limited to a finding that the mere existence, without more, of broad governmental investigative and data-gathering activities was insufficient to constitute a justiciable claim.[77] Chief Justice Burger added, however, that the ruling intimated "no view with respect to the propriety or desirability, from a policy standpoint, of the challenged activities."[78] The dissenting opinion observed the dangers that exist as long as computer files were, are, and continue to be kept on the membership, ideology, and policies of every political activist group in the United States.[79]

In 1977, the Court again dealt directly with the question of privacy. In *Whalen v Roe*, the Court held that sensitive information may be stored and retrieved without an invasion of a person's right of privacy as long as the security of the computer is adequate and the information stored therein is passed on only to

---

[73] *Id* 484. *See also* Roe v Wade, 410 US 113 (1973) (right of privacy includes the right to have an abortion); Katz v United States, 389 US 347 (1967) (overruled *Olmstead*, wiretaps without a warrant or the permission of at least one of the communicating parties ruled an illegal search, i.e., illegal wiretap is an invasion on a reasonable expectation of privacy).

[74] United States v Miller, 425 US 435, 442 (1976) (Supreme Court upheld the constitutionality of the Bank Secrecy Act of 1970, 12 USC §1829b(d), which requires banks to retain copies of such transactions and records). *See also* California Bankers Assn v Shultz, 416 US 21 (1974).

[75] United States v Miller, 425 US 435, 443 (1976).

[76] 408 US 1 (1972).

[77] *Id* 10.

[78] *Id* 15.

[79] *Id* 24-25 (Douglas, J dissenting).

the appropriate officials.[80] Justice Stevens, writing for the majority, stated that the Court was "not unaware" of the threat to privacy from computerized databanks, but the right to collect personal information "is typically accompanied" by a duty to avoid disclosure, and that the proper concern and duty were shown in this case.[81] Justice Brennan, concurring, noted that databanks increase the opportunity for abuse, and that future developments in computer technology may very well necessitate a judicial curb on this technology.[82]

Although there have been a number of privacy and computer-related cases since the 1977 *Whalen* decision, none have gone beyond the appellate level.[83] Consequently, even though computer technology has continued to advance, the Court has yet to address the issues that Justice Brennan noted.

§6.07   Legislative Response—Federal Statutory Developments

Due in part to growing public concern about perceived violations resulting from computerized databanks, and due in part to the Supreme Court's reluctance to find constitutional violations of privacy in certain areas, as personal credit information, Congress has enacted various statutes dealing with privacy violations.

Fair Credit Reporting Act of 1970

The first major legislation in the area of credit data was the Fair Credit Reporting Act.[84] There are two main goals of the act: to protect individuals from inaccurate reports; and to prevent invasions of privacy. The applicability of the act is limited to reports for purposes of credit, employment, insurance, or related benefits.[85] In order to guard against inaccuracies, the act gives the individual the right to have access to and the right to challenge data which a

---

[80] 429 US 589 (1977).

[81] *Id* 605. (The information in the databank included the names and addresses of all the people in the state of New York who had acquired drugs such as opium and cocaine with a doctor's prescription. The security system of the computer included a locked wire fence, an alarm system, and "off-line" reading of the data files and tapes, i.e., no computer terminal outside the computer could read or record the information. Plaintiffs argued that the mere availability of their names and addresses in the databank created a concern that people in need of such drugs would refuse to seek medical assistance for fear of being discovered and being stigmatized as being drug addicts. This argument was rejected.)

[82] *Id* 607 (Brennan, J, concurring).

[83] *See, e.g.,* United States v Westinghouse Elec Corp, 638 F2d 570 (3d Cir 1980); Ash v United States, 608 F2d 178 (5th Cir 1979); Doe v Webster, 606 F2d 1226 (DC Cir 1979); United States v Choate, 576 F2d 165 (9th Cir 1978); and United States v Benlizar, 459 F Supp 614 (DDC 1978).

[84] 15 USC §1681 *et seq.*

[85] Organization for Economic Cooperation and Development, Policy Issues in Data Protection and Privacy 170 (1974).

credit reporting agency may have in its data files. The Act also mandates procedural requirements, placing civil penalties on credit reporting agencies if they do not correct inaccurate information.[86] The Act allows the individual to have access to both the data and their source. If credit is denied, either wholly or partially, to an individual based on the credit report, the Act requires that the creditor provide the individual the reason for its rejection and the name and address of the credit reporting agency.[87]

Under the Act, whenever a creditor requests a credit report from a credit reporting agency, the individual must be notified within six months that there has been a credit request, the scope and nature of the request, and the name of the creditor who requested the information.[88] Probably the most important provision in the Fair Credit Reporting Act is the individual's right to challenge the accuracy of the information contained in the credit reporting databank files.[89] As long as the challenge is not frivolous or irrelevant, the agency must reinvestigate and delete the information if it is found to be unverifiable. If the dispute is not resolved, the individual may file an account of the supposed inaccuracy with the credit reporting agency. This account must then be included in all subsequent reports that the agency passes on to requesting creditors.

In addition to access to a credit agency's reporting files, the act requires reasonable procedures to be followed by agencies in assuring the accuracy and proper use of credit information.[90] If an agency is negligent in these areas, an individual who is harmed may recover actual damages, costs, and attorney's fees.[91] If the action of the agency is willful, punitive damages may also be awarded.[92] Criminal penalties, including fines up to $5,000, imprisonment up to one year, or both, may be rendered for the willful misappropriation or unauthorized disclosure of credit information.[93] Federal courts are given jurisdiction over violations, without regard to the amount in controversy.[94] To protect against intrusions on the privacy of an individual, the Act constrains the purposes for which credit reporting agencies may provide information for use. Proper uses include determining eligibility for additional credit or disclosure pursuant to a court order.[95] Time limitations are also imposed on the length of time certain derogatory information may be retained by the credit reporting agency. For example, bankruptcy information can be retained for only 10 years, and records of arrests, indictments, or convictions can be re-

---

[86] 15 USC §1681(n).
[87] *Id* §1681(m).
[88] *Id.*
[89] *Id* §1681(i).
[90] *Id* §1681(e).
[91] *Id* §1681(o).
[92] *Id* §1681(n).
[93] *Id* §1681(q), (r).
[94] *Id* §1681(p).
[95] *Id* §1681(b).

tained for only seven years.[96]

There are, however, certain weaknesses in the Fair Credit Reporting Act. The Act lacks a formal procedure for assuring that an individual has due process, and it uses a rather haphazard approach in dealing with disputes about the accuracy of credit information contained in an individual's file.[97] For example, objections and accounts by an individual in unresolved disputes concerning the accuracy of credit information are not reported retroactively to prior recipient-creditors of the individual's file. Further, the Act only mandates that a credit reporting agency provide the individual with an oral report of the contents of the credit files. The agency need not provide the individual with direct access to or a written copy of the file.[98] Finally, civil action remedies are difficult to recover for the aggrieved individual because the burden of proof is on the plaintiff-individual, and it is often difficult to show actual monetary damages.[99]

Privacy Act of 1974

The Privacy Act of 1974 (5 USC §552a), which supplemented the Freedom of Information Act (5 USC §552), was the second major piece of legislation that dealt with privacy. The Act prohibits federal government offices from disclosing personal information about an individual without the individual's written consent, unless it falls within one of eleven exceptions (e.g., court order, criminal or civil law proceeding, disclosure to Congress).[100] Restrictions on disclosures include not only hard copy, but display and telephone transmissions as well.[101] The Act also requires that federal agencies: reveal their data collection activities relating to individuals; make public their justifications for the collection and use of such data; and give individuals a right of access to the collected information.[102]

The right of access permits the individual to make an inspection of the data in the presence of a companion. The individual may request any corrections and, if these are denied, may file a statement of disagreement.[103] The agency holding the information then has 10 days to respond to the statement of disagreement. If the agency refuses to amend the information, the individual has 30 days to request a review of the agency refusal. If the review supports

---

[96] *Id* §1681(c)(a)(1).

[97] See Task Force, Canadian Department of Justice and Communications, Privacy and Computers 164 (1972).

[98] Organization for Economic Cooperation and Development, *supra* note 85, at 174.

[99] *Id* 177.

[100] Other exceptions where release is allowed are: for agency internal record keeping, as required by §552, for routine use, for census use, when recipient gives written assurances the record will not be divulged, for National Archives use, where there are compelling circumstances, for use of Comptroller General. 5 USC §552a(b)(1-11).

[101] 5 USC §552a(b).

[102] Organization for Economic Cooperation and Development, *supra* note 85, at 101.

[103] 5 Computer L Serv (Callaghan) §5-2, art 5, at 2.

the agency, the individual has a right to judicial review.[104] If the agency agrees to amend the individual's file, it must notify those agencies or individuals to whom the record has been previously disclosed.[105] It should be emphasized, however, that an agency is not mandated to, and thus many times does not, maintain records of those to whom disclosures have been made.

In regard to the release of information, the federal agency is required to inform the individual of the name of each agency or authority requesting the information, to determine whether the request is voluntary or mandatory, and then to determine intended uses to which the information will be put.[106] In addition, the agency must publish an annual notice of each record system it maintains, including:

1. The name of the system
2. Its location
3. The categories of data files maintained
4. Routine uses and users
5. Its storage policies
6. The retrieval method or methods
7. Access control
8. Retention and disposal of data policies
9. Procedures to notify individuals as to the existence of, and requests for, their files
10. Inspection and challenge procedures[107]

Individuals who believe their rights have been violated, and who have been denied relief by the offending agency, may sue in federal court for injunctive relief and civil damages.[108] Damages for willful violations of the act cannot exceed $1000 plus attorney's fees. Criminal misdemeanor charges and fines of up to $5000 can be imposed on employees for wrongful disclosure.[109] Miscellaneous provisions of the Privacy Act prohibit the use of social security numbers in databank files. The Act also established a Privacy Protection Study Commission that spent two years studying state and local privacy protection.[110]

---

[104] *Id* 14.

[105] *Id* 5.

[106] Organization for Economic Cooperation and Development, *supra* note 85, at 101.

[107] *Id.*

[108] *Id.*

[109] *Id* 13.

[110] *Id.*

Family Educational Rights and Privacy Act

The Buckley-Pell Amendment to the Privacy Act of 1974, called the Family Educational Rights and Privacy Act, provides that federal funds may be terminated as to any institution of higher education that denies the right of parents to inspect the educational records of their children.[111] The Act does not apply to confidential letters of recommendation, financial statements of the parents of college students, or in the case of the student who has waived his or her rights in these matters.[112] The Act also provides that no funds will be provided to the institution if it releases such records to persons other than school officials "with a need to know," state and federal education officials, research organizations, and persons with a lawful subpoena.[113] No private remedy is provided for the student or parents. The only remedy is the federal denial of funds to the offending institution.[114]

Freedom of Information Act

The Freedom of Information Act (5 USC §552) was passed in order to force federal agencies to reveal their records, procedures, and statements of policy to requesting members of the public. The Act provides that each agency must publish a description of the place and method by which the public may obtain such information. The required publication is in the *Federal Register.* Exceptions are allowed in cases where the information request would:

1. Constitute a "clearly unwarranted invasion of personal privacy"
2. Jeopardize national defense matters
3. Impinge upon internal personnel rules
4. Release confidential financial information or trade secrets, personnel and medical files, geological information, and inter- or intra-office agency memoranda
5. Reveal investigatory records which can be obtained only by a valid subpoena[115]

Persons who are refused the right to inspect legitimate federal records may sue to enjoin the agency from withholding the information, and recover costs and attorney's fees.[116]

---

[111] 20 USC §1232g.

[112] *Id* §1232g(a). (Waivers may not be required as a condition of admission or receipt of financial aid.)

[113] *Id* §1232g(b).

[114] *See* Girardier v Webster College, 563 F2d 1267, 1276-77 (8th Cir 1977).

[115] 5 USC §552. *See id* §552(a) and Rose v Department of the Air Force, 425 US 352 (1976).

[116] 5 USC §552(a). *See also* Mervin v Bonfanti, 410 F Supp 1205 (DDC 1976); House Committee of Governmental Operations, Subcommittee on Governmental Information and Individual Rights, A Citizen's Guide on How to Use the Freedom of Information

Tax Reform Act of 1976

The Internal Revenue Service is exempted from statutes denying access to an individual's personal records that are held by third parties such as banks (*see United States v Miller*). In the Tax Reform Act of 1976, however, Congress established a requirement that the taxpayer be given notice in cases where records of the taxpayer's transactions are subpoened from a bank, credit reporting agency, or other party.[117]

Right to Financial Privacy Act of 1978

The basic purpose of the Right to Financial Privacy Act (12 USC §340 *et seq*) was to restrict federal government access to financial records. In apparent response to *United States v Miller* (see §6.06), Congress acted to impose a duty of confidentiality on financial institutions.[118] Financial institutions often serve as creditors, and, therefore, their records are likely to contain credit reporting agency reports. Financial institutions are also likely to provide such information to other banks and credit reporting agencies, as well as to the federal government.

The methods by which the federal government may obtain access to such financial records are specified. These methods include obtaining: (1) the written consent of the individual; (2) a subpoena; (3) a court order; or (4) a search warrant.[119] Whenever the federal government seeks access to financial records, the individual must be notified.[120] The individual may challenge the right of governmental access in all but search warrant cases. A civil remedy against the government of the financial institution is available to the individual.[121] Damages include a fine of $100 per violation, actual damages, punitive damages if the violation is willful, court costs, and attorney's fees.[122] The effective date of the act was March 10, 1979.

Fair Credit Billing Act

The Fair Credit Billing Act strengthens the protection an individual has from inaccuracies in credit data.[123] The detailed provisions of the Act for correcting billing errors establish a procedure whereby the obligor must identify his or her account, and register the alleged error and his or her reasons for believing that there is an error. The creditor then has 30 days to respond. Upon receipt

---

Act and the Privacy Act, in Requesting Government Documents, HR Rep No 793, 95th Cong, 1st Sess (1977).

[117] 26 USC §7609(a).

[118] 12 USC §3401 *et seq;* United States v Miller, 425 US 435 (1976).

[119] *Id* §§3402-3408.

[120] *Id* §§3404(c), 3405(2), 3406(c), 3407(2), 3408(4), 3412(b).

[121] *Id* §3417.

[122] *Id.*

[123] 15 USC §1666(a).

of the obligor's notice that there may be an error, the creditor may not issue an adverse report as to the obligor's credit.

Federal Reports Act

The Federal Reports Act has a provision which is of particular importance to the protection of data privacy.[124] Section 3508 imposes restrictions on the exchange of information between federal agencies, and establishes penalties for any unauthorized disclosures.[125] This provision limits the utilization by the agency of the defense of justification when it seeks to acquire confidential information on an individual.[126]

§6.08   State Legislation

As stated earlier, Supreme Court policy has generally been to provide more stringent protection in those areas of individual privacy rights which are more personal in nature (e.g., abortion, contraception, and wiretaps), but less protection in other, more public-oriented areas (e.g., credit reports and bank records). In addition, the overall Court policy continues to be one of allowing individual states to define privacy rights. In *Katz v United States,* the Court held that the "protection of a person's general right to privacy—his right to be let alone by other people—is, like the protection of his property and of his very life, left largely to the law of the individual States."[127]

While the notion of privacy is a relatively new area for the Supreme Court, it is even newer for the states. At the state level, the legal protection afforded privacy remains limited, inconsistent, and fragmented. While some privacy interests are protected, these protections are narrow in scope. Certain specific areas are protected, yet only 10 states have provisions in their constitutions which expressly protect privacy.[128] With two exceptions (Arizona and Washington), the right to privacy has been included in state constitutions only since 1968. Alaska and Montana have adopted what might be called a *free-standing* declaration of the right of privacy i.e., a separate section of the state constitution which deals only with the right of privacy. Similarly, California has de-

---

[124] 44 USCA §3501.

[125] *Id* §3508(b).

[126] *See* United States v Davey, 426 F2d 842 (2nd Cir 1970).

[127] 389 US 347, 350-351 (1967).

[128] Alaska Const art I, §22; Ariz Const art II, §8; Cal Const art I, §1; Fla Const art I, §12; Hawaii Const art I, §5; Ill Const art I, §§6, 12; Louisiana Const art I, §5; Mont Const art II, §10; SC Const art I, §10; Wash Const art I, §7. See Cope, *Toward a Right of Privacy*, 5 Fla St UL Rev 630-745 (1977) (includes an excellent discussion of state legislation in the privacy area as well as a full text of each state's statute; the Florida Constitution protects "private communications"; the Arizona and Washington Constitutions protect "private affairs"; the remaining constitutions protect "privacy").

clared privacy an "inalienable right."[129] Seven other states confer more limited recognition on the privacy right by tying it closely to another constitutional provision—the prohibition against unreasonable searches and seizures. Florida, for example, extends protection "against the unreasonable interception of private communications by any means."[130] The Illinois, Hawaii, Louisiana, and South Carolina privacy provisions are somewhat broader, protecting against "invasions of privacy." Washington and Arizona have privacy sections which are narrower, serving as the functional equivalent of the prohibition against illegal searches and seizures.[131]

States have also responded by protecting privacy through judicial interpretation. Some state courts have imported a constitutional right of privacy into general provisions of their respective state constitutions.[132] The resulting privacy rights which have been judicially created, however, have often been very limited. Some states which originally extended recognition to a state right of privacy through judicial action later inserted an express privacy provision into the appropriate section of the state constitution by legislative means.[133] The experiences of the states to date reveal that the notion of a state constitutional privacy provision greatly aids individuals by adding a degree of protection from outside intrusion into devices like computer databanks.

An examination of the varied state solutions suggests that the most efficacious approach to the protection of privacy is for a state to add a "package" of privacy measures to their respective state constitution. There are three essential elements to such a privacy package. The first is the inclusion of a provision relating to the interception of communication. This provision is normally within the section on searches and seizures. Second is a free-standing right of privacy, following the Alaska, California, or Montana models. This free-standing right of privacy protects against governmental intrusions. Finally, appropriate constitutional language should be added, where necessary to ensure that the courts and legislature have a mandate to fashion remedies against intrusions by the private sector.[134] If a state were to adopt such a package, the result would go far toward protecting the right of privacy of an individual across the spectrum of possible invasions, including those involving computer databanks. Most states, unfortunately, have lagged behind in the privacy area. For example, in Colorado, other than various restrictions on the dissemination of information concerning people who apply for welfare assist-

---

[129] Cope, *supra* note 128, at 636-37.

[130] Fla Const art I, §12. *See also* Cope, *supra* note 128, at 637.

[131] Cope, *supra* note 128, at 637.

[132] *See* Breese v Smith, 501 P2d 159 (Alaska 1972) (right to be let alone as to preferred hair length); Melvin v Reid, 297 P 91 (Cal Dist Ct App 1931) (invasion of privacy tort); Cason v Baskin, 20 So 2d 243 (Fla 1945) (invasion of privacy tort).

[133] The states of Alaska, California, and Florida all adopted privacy provisions subsequent to the dates of the court decisions cited *supra* note 132.

[134] See Cope, *supra* note 128, at 730-43, for a discussion of these considerations.

ance, little state privacy law exists.[135]

Transnational Aspects of Individual Privacy

§6.09 Transborder Data Flows

The development of complex computer systems with greatly enhanced data processing capabilities enabling vast quantities of data to be transmitted within seconds across national frontiers, has made it necessary to consider international privacy protection of personal data. Privacy protection laws have been introduced, or will shortly be introduced, in approximately half of the Organization for Economic Cooperation and Development (OECD) member countries to prevent what are considered to be violations of certain fundamental human rights.[136] The privacy rights which have considerable bearing on international law and their interpretation within the United States include those involving unlawful storage of personal data, the storage of inaccurate data, and the abuse or unauthorized disclosure of such data.[137]

While certain countries have enacted legislation aimed at protecting individual privacy, there is a danger that disparities in national legislation might hamper the free flow of appropriate and necessary personal data across national borders. Transborder data flows have significantly increased in recent years, and can be expected to continue to increase with more widespread use of computers and telecommunications technologies. Overly restrictive legal constraints, or disparities in such constraints, could lead to potentially serious disruptions in important sectors of the international economy as banking and insurance.[138]

A recent report by the United States House of Representatives Committee on Governmental Operations outlines the issues in the international regula-

---

[135] *See* Colo Rev Stat §26-1-112 (1973 & Supp 1977) (later repealed).

[136] The OECD has 24 members: Australia, Austria, Belgium, Canada, Denmark, Finland, France, West Germany, Greece, Iceland, Ireland, Italy, Japan, Luxembourg, the Netherlands, New Zealand, Norway, Portugal, Spain, Sweden, Switzerland, Turkey, the United Kingdom, and the United States. *See* World Almanac and Book of Facts (1980). The members who have introduced, or will introduce, privacy protection laws are: Austria, Canada, Denmark, France, West Germany, Luxembourg, Norway, Sweden, the United States (all these countries have introduced legislation), Belgium, Iceland, the Netherlands, Spain, Switzerland, and the United Kingdom (these countries have prepared draft bills). OECD, Guidelines on the Protection of Privacy and Transborder Flows of Personal Data (1981).

[137] *Id* 5.

[138] For a detailed article on transnational data flow regulation, see Patrick, *Privacy Restrictions on Transnational Data Flows: A Comparison of the Council of Europe Draft Convention and OECD Guidelines,* 21 Jurimetrics J 405 (1981). See **ch 9.**

tion of transborder data flows.[139] The difficulty of the problems involved can be observed from the conclusions of that report, which included:

1. A diversified consumer products company rented a house which straddled the border of two European countries to maintain the option of having computer tapes in the venue most expedient to management purposes[140]

2. A German multinational had established a central personnel information system in Sweden for administration and planning, containing information on the family, nationality, skills, and so on of its employees. Company officials were denied the right to export this information from Sweden[141]

3. A United States company complained about a specific problem it had with the Federal Republic of Germany: its wholly-owned subsidiary is regulated under bank law . . . requiring total processing [of all data] within the country, . . . thereby excluding the possibility [and economies] of on-line processing [as it can do in the case of its other subsidiaries] from its Chicago data center[142]

These problems are due, in part, to individual nations passage of differing privacy protection laws to control what many argue is an inherently international commodity—information.[143]

According to Professor Ved Nanda:

[International] law has been rather slow in responding to the "information revolution"—the development and application of technology in electronics, information processing and distribution, and telecommunications, resulting in sophisticated computers, cable and two-way television, direct broadcast satellites, and the like.[144]

Professor Nanda also argues that there must not be a rush to pass laws limiting transborder data flows in order that there develop a "balance between the needs and interests of society for free flow of information and of the individual for adequate safeguards of personal data and protection of privacy."[145] The focus of legislation by member countries of OECD has been on the protection

---

[139] House Comm on Governmental Operations, Subcomm on Government Information & Individual Rights, International Information Flows: Forging a New Framework, HR Rep No 1535, 96th Cong, 2d Sess (1980).

[140] *Id* 24.

[141] *Id* 18.

[142] *Id* 17.

[143] See Patrick, *supra* note 138, at 406.

[144] Nanda, *The Communication Revolution and the Free Flow of Information in a Transnational Setting*, 30 Am J Comp L 411 (Supplement 1982).

[145] *Id.*

of personal privacy without careful consideration given to balancing the need of society for information.

Present legal norms primarily apply to issues which can be fixed to a definable geographic locus where responsibility can be attached and jurisdiction can be established. Data transmission and storage do not follow formal geographic boundaries, thus traditional legal approaches have proven unsatisfactory to governments attempting to ensure that personal computer data-banks are safe and reliable. A related issue is with whom does responsibility lie with respect to internal data networks and commercial time-sharing services which operate across national borders. There are four possible parties to whom responsibility may attach in a simple data communication transaction: the originator of the data message; the telecommunications carrier; the data processor; and the recipient of the data.

§6.10 —Legal, Political and Economic Issues

Two major issues surround transnational data flows: what legal instruments governments must develop in order to track what computerized data exist, and, assuming that information is the lifeblood of economic or political organizations, what legal framework can be developed to ensure that agreements among various public and private parties can be enforced to make possible a continuous, uninterrupted flow of data vital to economic prosperity and national security. Data flowing across borders are necessarily affected by multiple jurisdictions. As the internal laws of countries differ, the legal assessment of the data and their uses may also differ. The thrust of legislative efforts has been on the regulation of personal information. While some law also exists for telecommunications and the regulation of economic information, the regulation of transborder data flows is almost nonexistent.

In some instances, the purpose of processing data in a specific country may be to obtain special protection for personal information. Personal data files could easily be placed outside the jurisdiction of the country in which the persons are located. Consequently, national authorities would need multiparty governmental agreements to be able to obtain disclosure of a particular personal data file. An example of a *data vault* is found on a localized level in Canada, where several provinces have passed legislation prohibiting the disclosure of data files in the province to individuals or governments outside the province (see §6.11). Another reason for locating a file abroad and placing the file under the jurisdiction of a foreign country that has stricter privacy legislation is to encourge persons to allow the storage of certain privileged personal information. Consequently, the high standards of the country will be seen as correlating with the high standards of the company.

The most obvious reasons for moving personal data files and processing to a foreign country is that more lenient privacy legislation may exist in that country. This lenient country is thus a *data haven.* Countries as the Bahamas are creating data havens and are probably the crux of the problem represented by transborder data flows. It is feared that national privacy legislation will be ineffective due to transborder *datadrains*. This fear is well-placed, primarily because of the practical difficulties in attempting to control foreign datadrains. For instance, it is difficult to decide the legality of the use of merged data in files maintained in a foreign country whose privacy laws allow such mergers, but where the use takes place in a country whose laws do not allow for such mergers. Consequently, this type of problem is a major threat to the establishment of effective international privacy legislation.

Data throughflow is the transportation of information across a country without the data being used in that country. For example, in transmitting data from Germany to the United States, data might be transmitted telephonically to London, and then by satellite or undersea cable to the United States. England is a passive way station in the data flow between Germany and the United States. Some data processing, however, may take place in London. One example is the creation of a temporary file for faster or compatible transmission. The data are not used in England, and typically do not include information on English subjects. Consequently, rarely will there be any English privacy problems associated with this data throughflow. There may, in fact, be little reason to restrict such throughflow with national legislation. In contrast, if Sweden were the throughflow country, even though the file is temporary and established to facilitate more economic and faster throughflow, existing Swedish law places restrictions on even the creation of a machine readable file (see **§6.11**). The file, therefore, cannot be established without the prior issuance of a license by the Swedish government.

Another consideration is the use of foreign service bureaus so that the processing of data for use in one country takes place outside that country. The privacy issue is not the nature of the data processed, but rather the effect of the relevant national privacy legislation which governs where the data are processed. One other important consideration is the nature and extent to which data collected in one country can be marketed in another country. Examples range from subscriptions to foreign periodicals (name and address information) to foreign credit reporting for credit cards and other forms of credit (specific information on individual assets and creditworthiness). Although name and address information may seem trivial, as economies among countries become more interrelated, the sharing of personal information by credit reporting agencies takes on increasingly greater economic and legal significance. In many countries, particularly those in Scandinavia, the use of data among credit reporting agencies in foreign countries has been severely restricted.

A final consideration is the growth of multinational corporations. When companies expand across national borders, there naturally arises a need for flows of personal data across these boundaries. Companies engaged in international trade must transmit commercial and personnel information between countries. Employees naturally tend to be more concerned over privacy issues than suppliers or clients because of the nature of data stored in personnel files. Two approaches have been taken to restrict access to personnel data. Sweden requires a license to create and export personnel information, whereas Norway has incorporated data agreements and restrictions on access to personnel data into contracts between employees and management for local and multinational corporations.

Outside of the personal data context, transnational data regulations, which tend to limit and constrain the extent and movement of data across national frontiers are in basic conflict with the administrative and technological programs of most multinational organizations. One traditional tenet of national sovereignty has been the ability of a country to control and manage significant domestic, economic, and social activities. Telecommunications and computer technologies reduce the ability of a country to control and manage internal activities as well as the in- and out-flows of data. In an interdependent, high-technology world, the concept of political and economic interdependence, in which economics and social activities of one country are decided and carried out among groups of nations, is not warmly accepted by individual sovereign states. An example is the Canadian government's position on information communications and data sharing between Canada and the United States. The Canadian government is very concerned over the southward drain of computerized data to the United States, and its own inability to control this drain. According to the Canadian Minister of Science and Technology:

> Transnational data flow has created the potential of growing dependence, rather than interdependence, and with it the dangers of loss of legitimate access to vital information and the danger that industrial and social development will be governed by decisions of interest groups residing in another country.[146]

Similar concerns about dependency and loss of access to economically necessary data have also been voiced in France, where the economic data bases used to develop monthly and quarterly forecasts of European economic trends are designed in the United States and disseminated to Europe via networks owned by American firms.

Economic issues tend to be a product of legal and political issues. Currently, many nations are attempting to protect their domestic computer industries (and jobs) by passing privacy legislation aimed at gaining an economic advantage over other nations in the areas of computers and data processing. Information processing is a major growth field where thousands of jobs will be created, and possibly lost, to foreign nations. The added dimension of developing viable national information industries with the necessary technical infrastructure must be considered by any foreign nation in passing laws in this area.

Telecommunications falls within this area because the laws and policies passed by individual nations will affect the services telecommunications carriers may offer. The telecommunications rates and tariffs governments levy will also enhance or limit transborder data flows. Moreover, how telecommunica-

---

[146] Speech by J. Hugh Faulkner, Canadian Minister of Science and Technology, before the United Nations (Aug 1977).

tions carriers view their role in new fields such as electronic funds transfer, electronic mail, interactive home communications, and international data traffic monitoring will also have a major effect on transborder data flows.

§6.11 Selected Examples of Foreign Privacy Legislation

Numerous foreign countries, particularly European countries and Canada, have enacted privacy legislation. The following is a brief overview of selected examples of the legislation which has been passed.

Canada

At the national level, the protection of privacy in Canada has been incorporated into the Canadian Human Rights Act.[147] The act provides for annual publication of a catalog which identifies each federal information bank, the type of records each contains, and the derivative uses of such records.[148] There are many exceptions to this publication requirement, the majority of which deal with information on international relations, national security, federal-provincial relations, and law enforcement.[149] The Act also provides for an individual's right of access to records concerning that individual, including a right to correct any inaccurate information.[150] A member of the Canadian Human Rights Commission is designated as Privacy Commissioner in charge of receiving and investigating complaints under the act.

The province of British Columbia enacted a Privacy Act in 1968 which created a tort action for the willful invasion of privacy. Proof of damages is not required by the complaining party. Manitoba enacted a similar provision in its privacy legislation in 1970.[151] In the United States, the Privacy Act affords only a civil cause of action for damages.[152]

Quebec enacted a Consumer Protection Act in 1972.[153] In this Act, §§43 to 46 provide some relief for persons subject to credit reports. These four sections allow individuals the right to examine credit reports and to register their comments on the reports.[154] This legislation differs from that in the United States in that the United States legislation restricts the type of information that

---

[147] II Can Stat ch 33, §2(b) (1976-77).

[148] *Id* §51(1).

[149] *Id* §§53-55.

[150] *Id* §§2(b), 52.

[151] *See* 5 BC Rev Stat ch 336 (1979); Man Rev Stat ch 74 (1979); Task Force, Canadian Department of Justice and Communications, Privacy and Computers 137 (1972).

[152] Organization for Economic Cooperation and Development, Policy Issues in Data Protection and Privacy 13 (1974).

[153] Que Stats ch 74 (1971).

[154] Task Force, *supra* note 151, at 140.

may be collected and the uses to which it may be put.[155] The Quebec Act, however, has no provisions to ensure the accuracy of credit reports since it lacks specific requirements and procedures for correcting false information.

Saskatchewan has enacted the Credit Reporting Agencies Act, which is penal in nature and regulates credit reporting agencies through licensing.[156] These licensed agencies are governed by rules regulating: (1) release of information; (2) permissible contents of these reports; (3) disclosure to the individual; (4) registration of disagreements; and (5) a requirement that agencies inform the recipients of information that certain of the information is disputed by the individual.

Sweden

The major privacy legislation in Sweden is the Data Act of 1973. The Act is innovative in its recognition of computerization, and its adoption of the right of access by individuals in light of computerization.[157] The Act prohibits computer databanks from holding personal information without the permission and supervision of the Swedish Data Inspection Board, which has broad powers to control the operations of databanks.[158] The regulations of the board extend to the: (1) type of data that may be collected; (2) design and technical equipment of the data systems; (3) notice and access to the public; (4) disclosure of information; (5) storage of data; and (6) security of the systems.[159] Penal sanctions include fines and imprisonment of up to one year for negligent or willful violations of the Act.[160] A two-year sentence may be incurred for unauthorized access or alteration of data, which is referred to as a *data trespass*.[161] Section 23 of the Act creates civil liability for damages from inaccurate information, and the damages an individual must show need not be solely pecuniary.

West Germany

Under the West German Data Protection Law of 1970, data banks were placed under the supervision of a Data Protection Officer who has the authority to levy criminal sanctions for privacy violations.[162] In 1976, the Federal Data Protection Law (FDPL) was enacted with an effective date of 1978. The FDPL protects privacy by regulating the type of information that may be stored, processed, and transmitted. Under the FDPL, specific types of data are not

---

[155] Organization for Economic Cooperation and Development, *supra* note 152, at 170.

[156] Sask Stat ch 23 (1972).

[157] Organization for Economic Cooperation and Development, *supra* note 152, at 149.

[158] Data Act of May 11, 1973 (Sweden).

[159] *Id.*

[160] *Id* §20.

[161] *Id* §21.

[162] Enacted by the West German State of Hesse. Gesetz und Verordnungsblatt fur das Land Hessen, Teil 1, Nr 41 published in Wiesbaden, Oct 12,1970.

excluded, but rather the secret or confidential nature of data is the bar to the use of the data.[163] Section 3 of the FDPL protects the processing of data when the individual has given consent or there is some legal authorization concerning the use of the data. The FDPL also seeks to regulate the contents of the data files and the right to access.[164] Under the FDPL, after a data file is created, the general nature of its contents must be reported through official government channels to the Data Protection Officer.[165] The Data Protection Officer has the discretion to allow public access to these reports.[166]

As under the Federal Credit Reporting Act (15 USC §1681 *et seq*) in the United States, individual access is denied under the FDPL where it would prejudice the function of the data base.[167] Disputed data are deleted from a data base when there is no longer a need for the particular data base. Time limitations for the retention of data bases are based on need, not specified time limits as in the United States.[168] The one serious deficiency in the FDPL is its lack of a provision for notification of disputes between individuals and the data banks. Individuals, however, may report their disagreements to the Data Protection Officer.

France

The French Data Processing, Files, and Liberties Law of 1978 created a supervisory commission to enforce and regulate the implementation of the law. Methods of gathering information are subject to regulation under Article 25 of the law. An unusual provision of the law is that databanks must provide a processing list to the public which includes the authorization, purpose, access rights, categories of information, and recipient organizations.[169] The right of access by an individual is subject to a preliminary inquiry by the commission as to the relevance of and necessity for the disclosure. If the commission decides favorably on the request by the individual to inspect his or her file, the databank must provide a complete copy of the file to the individual. There is also a provision which entitles an individual to have the file corrected, updated, or deleted. There is no provision in the French Data Processing Law, however, for settling or resolving disputes between individuals and databanks.

Norway, Denmark, and Austria

Unique legislation exists in several other countries. The Norwegian Private Register Bill, §3-3, mandates the legal presumption of obsolescence of any

---

[163] Federal Data Protection Law of 1976 (BDSG)(W Ger).

[164] *Id* §3.

[165] *Id* 163.

[166] *Id.*

[167] *Id.*

[168] *Id* See also Bigelow, *Transborder Data Flow Barriers,* 20 Jurimetrics J 8 (1979).

[169] France: Law No 78-17 Art 22 (Jan 6, 1978) reproduced in 5 Computer L Serv (Callaghan) Appendix, ch 9 §5.2a, No 4 (1979).

personal credit information of an unfavorable nature which dates back more than five years.[170] In Austria, the Data Protection Bill, §11(1), requires that databank users correct or delete inaccurate or imcomplete information on individuals that the users discover after receiving the information from the databanks. Note that the burden of the accuracy of information lies with the user, not the individual or the databanks.[171] The Danish Private Registers Bill goes even further, in that when even a credit bureau discovers that its information on an individual is incorrect, the bureau must: make the necessary corrections; notify the individual; and send correct and updated reports to any organizations or individuals who have requested credit information within the previous six months.[172]

It appears that several foreign nations have begun to realize the importance of protecting confidential, personal information. At the same time, the line distinguishing responsible use of data, and the abuse or exploitation of it is extremely uncertain.[173] The various national privacy laws that have been passed, therefore, could be said to represent a consensus on basic principles that should be incorporated into national privacy legislation.

Potential Developments to Protect Individual Privacy

§6.12   Some Suggested Controls—Self-Discipline and the Ombudsman Approach

Several developments which are presently occurring and which may be useful in protecting individual privacy will now be examined, although these developments are intended merely as suggestions for possible controls.[174] Obviously, laws alone will not guarantee individuals a right of privacy. These technical controls aid in filling lacunae in the law.

Industry Self-Discipline.

Self-discipline by the credit industry can be viewed as an inexpensive mode of control. By developing standards or a professional code of ethics, some observers believe that industries like credit reporting agencies can police themselves. The Code of Ethics for the Association of Credit Bureaus of Canada serves as a tool for self-discipline in the Canadian credit reporting

---

[170] F. Hondius, Emerging Data Protection in Europe 113 (1975).

[171] *Id.*

[172] *Id.*

[173] Patrick, *Privacy Restrictions on Transnational Data Flows: A Comparison of the Council of Europe Draft Convention and OECD Guidelines,* 21 Jurimetrics J 405 (1980).

[174] *See* R. Smith, Privacy: How to Protect What's Left of It xi-xiii (1980).

industry.[175] The disadvantages of an industry self-discipline system are that there is no responsible person or entity who may be held accountable for breaches of the code. In addition, there are no specific penalties to ensure compliance, and there is no outside authority to enforce the code or standard of conduct. Thus, enforcement of the code is principally based on "moral suasion."[176]

Ombudsman

Another control system is through an inquiry and complaint mechanism, commonly known as an ombudsman. West Germany already has an ombudsman called the Data Commissioner.[177] The ombudsman does not have regulatory or legislative powers, but can recommend regulations and legislation.[178] While the ombudsman would likely lack formalized power to effect a course of conduct, the prestige of the incumbent, and periodic reports to Congress, could provide considerable clout when it came to enforcement.[179] Although essentially remedial in nature, the ability to publicize potentially adverse effects of data collection and invasions of privacy would carry a fair degree of weight.[180] Some of the suggested functions of the ombudsman include: (1) consideration of specific injuries from misuse of information; (2) advice and comment on potential databank development; (3) research on data classification; (4) adjudication of complaints; (5) establishment of professional standards; (6) examination of types of information stored and used; (7) licensing of databanks; (8) requirement of periodic reports on systems procedures by operators of databanks; and (9) prior approval for interchange or collation of information between different systems.[181]

The simplicity and low cost of the ombudsman approach makes it particularly attractive. The ombudsman approach also gives an immediate response to the individual concerning any privacy concerns. A problem with the ombudsman approach is that it tends not to review systemic problems, i.e., the ombudsman generally does not look at the system as a whole. Rather, it concentrates on individual databanks and individual complaints. Another drawback is that there can be no investigation until a complaint has been made. Difficulties may also arise in a situation in which the ombudsman lacks the necessary technical expertise to analyze a problem.[182] This type of an approach, moreover, has not enjoyed widespread usage in the United States due

---

[175] Task Force, Canadian Department of Justice and Communications, Privacy and Computers 164 (1972).

[176] *Id.*

[177] *Id.*

[178] I. Roger, Computers: Privacy and Freedom of Information 7 (1970).

[179] Task Force, supra note 175, at 162.

[180] R. Freed, Computers and Law: A Reference Work 42 (1976).

[181] Roger, *supra* note 178, at 7.

[182] Task Force, *supra* note 175, at 162.

to the lack of understanding or acceptance of the ombudsman concept. Implementing an ombudsman system in the United States, therefore, may be difficult.[183]

§6.13 —Single Identification Number and Centralized Databanks

Single Identification Number

The use of a single identification number (SIN) for all records and information on an individual could reduce the social harm caused by identification errors. A SIN system would also be faster and more cost-effective in compiling and retrieving information. The SIN would also promote the centralization of data which could facilitate implementation of other technical controls. West Germany already employs a SIN system.[184] Under the West German system, if a person changes residences, only one agency needs to be notified of the move, and all other governmental agencies will automatically be notified. Sweden, Norway, Finland, and Denmark also have SIN systems.[185] Sweden uses 10-digit number, which refers to an individual's birthdate, geographic location, and check number.[186] Although there have been proposals for this type of system in the United States and Canada, neither country has adopted a SIN system. The United States' proposal to utilize social security numbers as the basis of a SIN system was dropped in 1970.[187]

Opponents claim that a SIN system will inevitably lead to a loss of individual anonymity. A SIN system can also be abused.[188] Other risks associated with personal data, particularly computerized credit information, may not be eliminated by a SIN system (see §6.05 for examples of the risks involved). By decreasing the identification factors to a single number, the possibilities for mismatching information on an individual may be increased. If errors are made with respect to the assignment of the SIN, the information on an individual may be irretrievably lost or destroyed.

Centralized Data Banks

In many respects, centralized databanks (CDBs) serve a function similar to that of a SIN system. Centralization could standardize all records, including credit data, into one central intelligence system. Like the SIN, the idea of a

---

[183] R. Freed, *supra* note 180, at 42.

[184] Task Force, Canadian Department of Justice and Communications, Privacy and Computers 86 (1972).

[185] *Id.* 87.

[186] *Id.*

[187] *Id.*

[188] *Id* 85.

CDB is attacked on the basis that such centralization provides the potential for too much power and control—the *1984*-Orwellian fear.

The Dunn Report issued in 1965 supported the establishment of a federal data center in the United States with a broad base of access.[189] The report focused its attention on the problems associated with maximizing volume, capacity, and usage. A subsequent investigation in 1966 by the House Special Subcommittee on Invasion of Privacy also examined issues relating to privacy.[190] In later reports and hearings, the concern over misuse and control of disclosure became paramount. The public discussions showed that there was a perceived need for a system of safeguards which would include coding procedures, codes of conduct, and data verifications.[191] CDBs might perpetuate facts from the past of an individual without methods or provisions for updating old information.[192] Miller refers to this as the "inability of a computer to forget."[193] Another privacy consideration is the high probability of error when data are collected from several sources.[194] As one observer has noted, errors in identity are "especially likely when a large number of similar names are assembled in one [computer databank]."[195]

Miller, an advocate of the right of privacy, engaged in several attacks on the proposed national data center during 1966 and 1967.[196] A surveillance device controlled by the federal government was particularly objectionable to him. A national data center "would be augmented by numerous subsystems or satellites operated by the state and local governments or by private organizations." Given the rapid development of the computer industry, it would be particularly attractive for unauthorized intruders to gain access to one centralized file containing information on literally millions of individuals.[197] Miller also discussed several other risks already mentioned, including data inaccuracies, misuse, and interagency use.

§6.14 —Right to Know and Systems Controls

Habeas Data: The Right to Know

The right to know has several aspects: the right of an individual to be informed of the information that is collected as well as to know its location.

---

[189] Bigelow, *The Privacy Act of 1974*, 1 Computer L & Tax Rep 112, 117 (1975).

[190] *Invasion of Privacy: Hearings before the Special House Subcommittee on Invasion of Privacy of the House Committee on Governmental Operations*, 89th Cong, 2d Sess(1966).

[191] Bigelow, *supra* note 189 at 124.

[192] *Id* 122.

[193] A. Miller, The Assault on Privacy 53 (1971).

[194] Bigelow, *supra* note 189, at 134.

[195] *Id.*

[196] A. Miller, *supra* note 193, at 53.

[197] *Id.*

The right to inspect these data to ascertain their legitimacy, and the right to challenge the data and insert objections into the record.[198] The perceived need to know of the existence of data files arises out of what psychologists call a "fear of invisible records." It is important for the individual to know what others know about him or her so that he or she may act accordingly.[199] After inspection of these files, the individual must be given the opportunity to challenge the information if it is inaccurate, incomplete, dated, or improperly obtained.[200] This is especially important if the files contain opinions or assumptions such as political labels or attitudes.[201] The right to access has been referred to as *habeas data.*[202]

The second aspect of this right to know allows the individual the right to inspect the record. Open access provides a means of holding the databank and its personnel accountable.[203] In Canada, if the individual disagrees with the information, the individual may insert personal statements into the file.[204] There are, however, problems with this aspect of the right to know. Legal problems may arise when someone other than the individual inspects the record, as in the case of minors or incompetents.[205] If access is extended to include sources and uses of the information, there might be an undue burden placed on the custodian of the data, which might increase the difficulty in obtaining confidential information.[206]

Costs in providing access may present another problem. In 1972, the Younger Committee estimated that the cost of mailing a complete printout on every individual in the United States could reach approximately $2 million (approximately 10 cents per person) plus mailing costs.[207] If such a report included a full explanation of codes, as would be the case for credit reports, the costs could double.[208] In the United States, the Fair Credit Reporting Act of 1970 allows databanks to charge the individual who requests access.[209] There is an element of irony in the right to access. The mere act of requesting access and the subsequent visit to the databank allow the databank another opportunity

---

[198] Organization for Economic Cooperation and Development, Policy Issues in Data Protection and Privacy 147 (1974).

[199] *Id.*

[200] *Id.*

[201] *Id.*

[202] *Id.*

[203] *Id* 59.

[204] Task Force, Canadian Department of Justice and Communications, Privacy and Computers 155 (1972).

[205] Organization for Economic Cooperation and Development, *supra* note 198, at 150.

[206] *Id.*

[207] Task Force, *supra* note 204, at 155.

[208] *Id.*

[209] 15 USC §1681 *et seq.*

to gather information on the individual.[210]

Systems Controls

At the data collection and storage phase, additional qualifications and guidelines may also be imposed.[211] Limitations can be placed on what data may be collected. Any data which are entered must be checked for accuracy. Once the data are in the file, measures to protect the nature of their representation can be established. Guidelines on when data should be updated or deleted can also be implemented.[212] Given massive but inexpensive storage capacities, it may be more costly to delete or update data than to retain it. Regulations, therefore, are particularly important.

Questions on the accuracy of data may be more problematic. Factual mistakes should be corrected, but debates may arise in areas where accuracy is a question of context. For example, an accurate account of unpaid debts may present a biased view if there is no explanation of the justification for nonpayment by the individual. If a question of context arises, the individual should be allowed to enter a personal accounting into the record. This approach is in use in Canada.[213]

Data must be protected while they are in storage. The concern here is primarily one of confidentiality because there are dangers of unauthorized persons gaining access to the information, and either pirating it or altering it. One method to ensure confidentiality is to develop an integrity program providing guidelines for access by outside sources.[214] Another method is *threat monitoring*—printouts and logs of who has accessed the files.[215] Access controls such as passwords, authentication, and authorization are additional safeguards to prevent illegal intrusion into the data file.[216] Controls restricting access to the machinery itself may also be incorporated into the software program to prevent access to the files.[217] Physical processing restrictions which revoke certain features of the computer system are also available to protect stored data.[218]

Finally, data output or dissemination must be protected. There could be restrictions placed on exchanges of information between databanks or limitations on exchanges to those with a demonstrable "need to know" or who have a common connection with the primary purpose for which the data were

---

[210] Task Force, *supra* note 204, at 156.

[211] *Id* 150.

[212] *Id* 151.

[213] *Id.*

[214] I. Roger, Computers: Privacy and Freedom of Information (1970).

[215] *Id.*

[216] *Id.*

[217] *Id.*

[218] *Id.*

collected.[219] Other controls include requiring: individual approval for all data exchanges; approval when the data are being used for other than their intended purpose; or provision of a list of exchanges to the individual on a regular basis.[220]

§6.15   —Computer Security and Cryptology

Computer Security

Security is the technical means by which confidentiality is ensured.[221] The degree of protection depends upon various factors including: (1) circumstances of the databank use; (2) sensitivity of the stored information; (3) its economic value; and (4) its availability for use outside the databank.[222] Examples of computer security techniques include passwords; limited access; audit logs; physical security; limitations on data links; and automatic labeling of sensitive files.[223] The costs of protecting privacy within a computerized system are primarily in the area of computer security. The expenses include: (1) analysis; (2) design and implementation of the protective system; (3) tests and validations; (4) operation and maintenance; (5) salaries of security personnel; and (6) computer time and costs to maintain the system.[224] The costs of hardware security may include key-cards, closed circuit television, and shielded transmission cables.[225] The costs of developing password and audit procedures and the number of times these are used are added cost factors. If passwords are used only for sign-on and file-open stages, processing times and costs may be lower. Access controls, however, may easily increase processing times by 10 per cent and increase main memory storage requirements by 20 per cent, thereby dramatically increasing total computer cost.[226]

One commentator has suggested that these safeguards may cost more in "management attention and psychic energy than in dollars."[227] These costs should be regarded as insurance against privacy invasions. Several provisions have been adopted which permit the computer databank industry to pass on added security costs to the individuals who are the subjects of the data, rather than to the consumer of the information. The access mechanism expenses, for example, are the burden of the individual under the New York Fair Credit

---

[219] Task Force, *supra* note 204, at 153.

[220] *Id.*

[221] Task Force, Canadian Department of Justice and Communications, Privacy and Computers 153 (1972).

[222] Organization for Economic Cooperation and Development, Policy Issues in Data Protection and Privacy 246 (1974).

[223] *Id* 244; Task Force, *supra* note 221, at 103.

[224] Organization for Economic Cooperation and Development, *supra* note 222, at 248.

[225] *Id* 249.

[226] *Id* 250.

[227] R. Freed, Computers and Law: A Reference Work 45 (1976).

Reporting Act.[228] France has adopted a similar provision.[229]

Cryptology

Cryptology encompasses signal security and signal intelligence. Signal security includes all ways of keeping human messages secret, including telegrams and telephone conversations, and electronic messages between computers. Various techniques exist for putting messages into secret form by code or cipher. The elements of the message—letters, electronic pulses, or voice sounds—can be scrambled or replaced by other elements. The receiver, who must know the key or secret procedures used in encryption, then reverses the process to read the original message.

Signal intelligence comprises all methods of extracting information from transmissions. These methods can include intercepting messages which are in plain language, electronic impulses, radio, or radar transmissions. Cryptanalysis breaks the codes or ciphers. The use of cryptology has great utility in making it difficult for outsiders to intercept messages passing over lines or by radio signal between users and computer databanks. As with general databank security measures, cryptology has the potential to limit access and thereby allow legitimate access only to those who have the right to know otherwise confidential information. While costs may rise with the use of cryptology, these increased costs may well be considered further insurance against privacy intrusions.

Future Legal Trends to Protect Individual Privacy

§6.16   Legal Trends in the United States

There are additional legal steps which may be taken in order to protect individual privacy. Additional legal protection is particularly needed because of the increased tension between the need for efficient and rapid availability of confidential data, and the requirements for data compartmentalization to protect individual privacy rights.

Constitutional Amendment and/or Federal Statutes

Craig C. Halls has argued that a constitutional amendment and additional federal statutes are needed: (1) to balance the interests between the need for data and privacy protections; (2) to restrict access of outsiders to confidential information; and (3) to provide stricter sanctions and penalties for improper dissemination of personal data. To obtain effective privacy rights, Halls concluded, federal sanctions and protections must be implemented because only a nationwide system will adequately protect privacy. Reliance on state laws will not work in that a state privacy protection system "will be only as strong as the

---

[228] Gen Bus Law §380d(a)(2)(McKinney 1977).

[229] France: Law No 78-17, art 35 (Jan 6, 1978) reproduced in 5 Computer L Serv (Callaghan) Appendix, ch 9 §5.2a, No 4 (1979).

weakest state law."[230] In enacting legislation, the following values must be considered:

1. Limitations on the type of data maintained, segregating criminal from non-criminal data

2. Strict controls on the process of collection (for example, by editing invalid or nonapplicable questions from government forms), and controls over the persons and processes recording the data. Respondents should be informed whether the information must be given. Those who collect information must have a legitimate interest in it

3. Notice of the existence of the records and access to the records for the individual; notice informing the individual of who has seen his or her files and when; and procedures to contest the accuracy and currency of this information

4. Automatic expungement of out-of-date or obsolete data

5. Access to records only on a "need to know" basis. Information collected for one purpose should not be used for another purpose; agency records should not be subject to discovery for criminal prosecutions in other jurisdictions

6. Categorizations of files as personal or statistical. Wherever possible, identity should be stripped from the records

7. Possible relief from, but without entirely eliminating, the present obstacles to discovery and proof

8. Physical access limited to on-site retrieval

9. Restricted exchange of personal information between government agencies with the number of physical copies of files kept to a minimum[231]

Those who believe a general right of privacy could be established by constitutional amendment or federal statute are, in effect, proposing that the courts be the major mechanism to oversee and enforce privacy. A drawback to enacting additional laws is that the injured party must still bring an action as the courts can not initiate actions against databanks which allegedly violate the statutes. Finally, given today's political climate, it is unlikely that one could successfully enact a constitutional amendment to protect privacy.

Federal Control Agency

A federal agency could be established to supervise and control governmental acquisition, storage, and release of computerized information.[232] This

---

[230] Halls, *Raiding the Databanks: A Developing Problem for Technologists and Lawyers*, 5 J Contemp L 264-65 (1979).

[231] *Id.*

[232] Note, *Agency Access to Credit Bureau Files*, 12 BC Ind & Comm L Rev 110, 125 (1970).

agency would govern situations arising out of facts similar to those found in *United States v Davey* where the Internal Revenue Service required a consumer credit company to produce credit reports for several individuals including the defendant.[233] A data processing and management office could act as a watchdog over federal utilization of computerized data and impose sanctions for violations of the privacy standards. If a federal control agency were given the authority to register and license the data systems, conformance to privacy safeguards could then be a condition precedent to obtaining a license.[234]

State Control Agency

State agencies could oversee the computerized credit reporting industry. The advantage of a state system is that it could use licensing and registration as a means of enforcement as well as a means to monitor credit reporting agencies. Giving a state agency broad powers may, however, endanger privacy in that the particular state would then have access to these confidential data. Moreover, the state agency may be given the power to interfere in the event of a violation, but not the power to correct the situation.[235] The advantages of the flexibility of a state control agency may be outweighed by the drawback of its heavyhanded effect.[236] On a larger scale, many of the stated concerns about a state privacy protection system may also be applicable to a federally mandated privacy protection system.

Code of Fair Information Practices

State adoption of Codes of Fair Information Practices have also been proposed. A model code was developed in 1976 by the Ombudsmen Committee on Privacy of the Association for Computing Machinery.[237] The code contained the following recommendations:

1. There should be no information system containing personally identifiable data whose existence is unknown to the data subject
2. Personally identifiable data should not be collected unless the information system is safeguarded by a level of security commensurate with the sensitivity of the information
3. There must be a reasonable method for the individual to find out what information is stored on him or her and how that information is used
4. There should be no disclosure of any personal information to any organization or individual until the data subject has given permission for the

---

[233] 426 F2d 842 (2d Cir 1970).

[234] Note, *supra,* note 232, at 127.

[235] Organization for Economic Cooperation and Development, Policy Issues in Data Protection and Privacy 92 (1974).

[236] Task Force, Canadian Department of Justice and Communications, Privacy and Computers 160 (1970).

[237] Ombudsmen Committee on Privacy, Association for Computing Machinery, *Privacy, Security, and the Information Industry* 72-79 (1976).

disclosure in writing. Such permission may be revoked by the individual at any time, and if it is not revoked, the permission shall expire automatically at the end of one year

5. Personally identifiable information collected for one purpose shall not be used for any other purpose without the knowledge and consent of the data subject

6. In the event of a demand made by means of a compulsory legal proceeding, a reasonable attempt should be made to contact the data subject and to advise him or her of the demand prior to such information being given to the authorities

7. There must be a reasonable method for an individual to contest the accuracy and completeness, pertinence and necessity of the data; to have data corrected, amended, or expunged if they are inaccurate or dated; and to ensure that when there is a disagreement about a correction or expungement, the individual's claim is noted and included in subsequent disclosures

8. Any organization creating, maintaining, using, or disseminating confidential information must ensure its reliability for intended use and take precautions to prevent misuse of such confidential information

9. Before creating a databank containing confidential information, a study should be completed to demonstrate the necessity for the information system as well as the relevance of the collected data to their intended use. The concept of *useful life* should also be addressed

10. An individual should have the right to have the personal information removed from any file if the organization maintaining it cannot show any legal, useful, specific, and productive purpose for maintaining it[238]

It is noteworthy that this model code does not distinguish between the public and private sectors. These guidelines would apply equally even though it may be more difficult to control the private sector. A privacy protection code would be a sound foundation upon which states could develop a system for personal privacy which maximizes the utility of the computerization of information and minimizes the abuses that may occur. The major issue at this point is not whether the computerization of personal information will take place, but rather, how can restriction on this collection process be formulated to ensure an appropriate degree of personal privacy.

§6.17   Transnational Trends

Recognizing that information is a powerful resource with political, economic, social, and cultural dimensions, governments are motivated to consider regulatory or other control mechanisms to protect and promote national interests in the area of privacy. The public and private collectors, users, processors, and transmitters of this information, realizing that such mechanisms may result

---

[238] *Id.*

in constraints and costs attaching to transnational data flows, are seeking to participate in these governmental decisions.

According to Professor Nanda, two international organizations, the Organization for Economic Cooperation and Development (OECD) and the Council of Europe, have taken major initiatives toward the establishment of an international legal regime concerning transborder data flows.[239] The recommendations of both organizations recognize that there must be a balance between the need for individual privacy protection and the free flow of information. Professor Nanda feels that the most significant of the OECD principles is the Individual Participation Principle

> which has already been reflected in the privacy legislation of the OECD members. The Principle recognizes the right of an individual to obtain confirmation regarding the existence of data pertaining to the individual; to have such data communicated to him or her within a reasonable time in a reasonable manner and intelligible form at a charge, if any, which is not excessive; to be given reasons for the denial of such request and the opportunity to challenge such denial; and to challenge data relating to the individual and have it erased, rectified, completed or amended if the challenge is successful.[240]

In 1980, the Council of Europe adopted the Convention for the Protection of Individuals with Regard to Automatic Processing of Personal Data, which was opened for signature at Strasbourg, Germany on January 28, 1981.[241]

> Its Preamble recognizes the twin objectives of protecting individual privacy and allowing for the free flow of data across frontiers. Unlike the OECD . . . the Convention is limited to automated (computerized) personal data—both files and automatic processing of personal data in the public and private sectors—and, unlike the nonbinding recommendatory nature of [the OECD] Guidelines, the Convention is a binding international instrument conferring rights of data subjects which are legally enforceable in states which become parties to the Convention. However, there are striking parallels between the Guidelines and the Convention which provides for accession even by non-member states.[242]

Third World countries continue to be extremely sensitive about the introduction of high technology within their borders because most of these nations have only recently attained political independence and are striving for economic independence as well. These developing nations fear that the immediate

---

[239] Nanda, *The Communication Revolution and the Free Flow of Information via Transnational Setting,* 30 Am J Comp L 411, 423-25 (Supplement 1982).

[240] *Id* 423-24.

[241] *Id* 424.

[242] *Id.*

introduction of outside technology and economic assistance may make them dependent on nations in Europe or on the United States.

Until recently, all equipment, related support materials, and many of the operating personnel for computer and telecommunications companies have had to be imported because these developing nations lack local expertise. Local users have generally been required to modify their local practices and traditional methods instead of the vendors adapting their equipment and programs to meet local needs. Now, however, developing nations are attempting to develop their own expertise and industries. As national policies become more fully developed, developing countries will turn to transnational data flow issues. The focus on transnational data flows could include requests to multinational corporations for assistance and access to databanks containing information on economic forecasting, marketing, and statistical research. These developing countries will begin to take a more active role in the preparation of technical standards, allocation of radio frequencies, and other decisions affecting international communications policies and data flows.

While the principles contained in the development of national information policies include elements of individual privacy protection, they also include elements generally associated with the protection of local self-interest. If national information capabilities are to be considered inherent to the sovereign rights of all countries, it follows that national policies designed to develop endogenous industries will ensure the ability of these countries to acquire the expertise necessary to guarantee this sovereignty. These national information policies must, however, also be considered in relation to the traditional principles of the international arena which includes: (1) the free flow of information among nations; (2) the promotion of free and fair trade; and (3) the recognition that there is an increasing interdependence among all nations. The general conclusion that can be drawn from this review of foreign experience is that, like the United States, most of the industrialized and developing nations are working on the problems of definition and development of protections for individual liberties balanced by the understanding that there must also be a free flow of information.[243]

The next step is to pass an international convention ensuring that privacy protections are maintained. Given the increasing interdependence among all nations in areas of international trade, business, banking, communications, and travel, there is an urgent need to develop and approve binding statutes and agreements that will govern information flows while ensuring the protection of individuals' personal privacy needs. Without such protection, continued development of high computer and telecommunications technology and the sharing of this knowledge among all nations may not take place at a pace that will benefit all parties involved. Furthermore, without such international protections, abuses in areas of illegal data storage, inaccurate data transmissions, and unauthorized data disclosures are likely to continue.

---

[243] *Id* 425-26.

Computer Crime

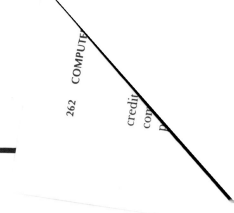

§7.01   Introduction

The ever-increasing use of computers has created a number of economic, social, and political problems. Computers are being used in a wide variety of business and governmental settings, including securities trading, banking, transactions, payrolls, inventories, and tax-related activities.[1] Just as computers facilitate information gathering and processing, so too do they provide new, less hazardous avenues for the commission of nearly all sorts of crimes.[2] Absent adequate safeguards, most computer systems are vulnerable to unauthorized or criminal activity.[3] The vulnerability of computer systems makes the successful commission of computer-related crimes appear possible without much risk of detection. There is often little if any evidence that a crime has been committed. As a tool of the would-be computer criminal, computers provide a quick, efficient, and relatively easy means of committing crimes such as fraud, deceit, embezzlement, or the outright theft of money, services, or information. Computers can be the target as well as the tool of crime, e.g., destroying another's computer program, shutting down another's computer system, or simply creating delays and confusion in another's computer network.[4]

The increasing availability of computers to the general public; the number, complexity, and significance of their applications; their ability to store and manipulate data; the amount of data concentrated in individual computer facilities (and the economic value of that information); and the complexity of computer technology have produced an "awesome opportunity for crime."[5] John C. Keeney, a former Deputy Assistant Attorney General in the Criminal Division of the United States Department of Justice, stated that:

> Our political, economic and social institutions have grown increasingly dependent upon computers to the point that their illicit manipulation or malicious destruction can potentially wreak havoc on society. . . . Computers have become a part of everyone's life and are being integrated into virtually every facet of human activity at an ever increasing rate. The very existence at the present time of a broad base of computer usage and computer knowledge, and its projected increase in the years to come, suggests that we will experience an increase in the opportunities for computer-related abuses in the years ahead.[6]

---

[1] Tunick, *Computer Law: An Overview,* 13 Loy LAL Rev 315, 326 (1980).

[2] *Id.* See also Whiteside, *Annals of Crime: Dead Souls in the Computer,* New Yorker, Aug 22, 1977, at 35, 50.

[3] See Rapoport, *Programs for Plunder,* Omni, Mar 1981, at 79, and Swanson & Territo, *Computer Crime: Dimensions, Types, Causes & Investigations,* 8 J Police Sci & Ad 304, 306 (1980).

[4] A. Bequai, Computer Crime 4 (1978). See also Sokolik, *Computer Crime—The Need for Deterrent Legislation,* 2 Computer LJ 353, 363 (1980).

[5] Rothman, *Computer Crime, The Menace Grows,* D&B Rep, July-Aug 1981, at 7. See also Bequai, *Computer Crime: A Growing and Serious Problem,* 6 Police LQ 22 (1976). See generally Norman, *Computer Fraud—The Villian's View of the Opportunity,* 24 Elec & Power 824 (1978); and Lancaster, *Rise of Minicomputers, Ease of Running Them Facilitates New Frauds,* Wall St J, Oct 5, 1977, at 1.

[6] *Federal Computer Systems Protection Act: Hearings on S 1766 Before the Subcomm on Criminal Laws & Procedures of the Senate Comm of the Judiciary,* 95th Cong, 2d Sess 27 (1978) [hereinafter cited as Hearings].

While opportunities for crime involving computers (as either the tool or the object of the crime) are increasing, experts disagree on such basic matters as: what constitutes *computer crime;*[7] what is the best course of preventive action; and whether a need exists for legislative and prosecutorial activities specifically directed towards the computer-related aspects of crime.[8]

Although there seems to be general agreement that the number and impact of computer-related crimes have increased and are likely to increase further in the future, accurate information on the incidence of computer crime is still not available. The incidence of computer crime is believed to be greater than reported because of a number of factors unique to these phenomena:

> (1) no consensus as to what should be classified as a computer crime; (2) the reluctance of victims to report such crimes; even though discovered, many computer crimes go unreported; and (3) the difficulty of detecting computer crimes. In the majority of cases, detection has been a matter of accident, rather than a result of security or auditing efforts.[9]

Each of these factors will be discussed in greater detail below. In addition to the problem of limited detection and reporting, the difficulties that relatively uninformed prosecutors, judges, and juries face in dealing with the complexities of computer technology under existing laws have obscured the full extent of the incidence of computer-related crime.

There are a number of serious problems confronting the effective prevention and prosecution of computer crime. The greatest single problem is that present laws do not adequately address the phenomenon of computer crime. Thus, successful prosecutions under traditional criminal statutes are rare. This is primarily due to a misunderstanding of what constitutes computer crime. Computer abuses should not have to be classified within traditional crimes in order to gain the protection of the law. One commentator has stated that:

---

[7] See Parker, *Computer Abuse Research Update,* 2 Computer LJ, 329, 341 (1980) (little agreemeent among district attorneys on what constitutes computer-related crime); SRI International, Computer Crime: Criminal Justice Resource Manual 5 (1979) (in effect, definition includes all intentionally caused losses associated in any way with computer use); Bureau of Justice Statistics, US Dept of Justice, Expert Witness Manual: Use of Outside Experts in Computer Related Crime Cases 1-1 to 1-3 (1980) (no universally accepted definition of computer-related crime; agreed that definition involves use of computer to commit act which law already defines as criminal); *Federal Computer Systems Protection Act: Hearings on S 240 Before the Subcomm on Criminal Justice of the Senate Comm on the Judiciary,* 96th Cong, 2d Sess 44 (1980) (statement of John K. Taber) ("I do not believe that computer crime can be meaningfully defined . . . I believe there are basic crimes, theft, so far and so on, but I think that 'computer crime' is a meaningless term.") [hereinafter cited as S 240 Hearings]

[8] *Compare* Hearings, *supra* note 6, at 71 (statement of Susan Nycum) (fact that presently no federal or state statute covers unauthorized transferrence of electronic impulses described as troublesome "loophole") *with* S 240 Hearings, *supra* note 7, at 47 (statement of John K. Taber) (computer crime insignificant; existing criminal law adequate).

[9] Sokolik, *supra* note 4, at 363.

The aspect of wrongful intrusion into a processing queue, which is most difficult to fit into traditional charging language, is therefore the one that most justifies statutory description. The intrusion engenders a ripple effect, which can disrupt or even destroy property. The property, though in the form of impulses invisible to the keenest microscope and beyond the grasp of the nervous system, nontheless can represent and effect personal endeavor and individual rights.[10]

The further evolution of computer technology will create new opportunities for crime, and in all likelihood these crimes will entail larger and larger sums. The costs of computer abuses to the public have been estimated at $10 billion annually, and there is the potential for greater losses in the future.[11] As computer technology continues to advance, "[s]ome existing avenues for crime will be precluded; [and] computer-related crimes will increasingly displace other kinds of white-collar crime."[12]

§7.02   Definition of Computer Crime

Computer crime is a general term covering a number of different kinds of occurrences in, around, and through a computer that can be classified, if not necessarily prosecuted, as illegal acts.[13] Most computer-related crimes can be placed in the amorphous category of white-collar crimes, although Don Parker of Stanford University claims that computers have played a role in nearly every sort of conventional crime, including fraud, theft, embezzlement, bribery, burglary, sabotage, espionage, conspiracy, extortion, and kidnapping.[14] However, John Taber, a computer systems programmer for IBM, contends that computer crime is a myth,[15] "a misnomer applied to several crimes that may or may not involve computers. . . ."[16] Taber's perspective is based on his feeling that the mystique surrounding computers and computer technology leads to an exaggeration of conventional crime when its occurrence is even

---

[10] Tunick, *supra* note 1, at 326.

[11] Volgyes, *The Investigation, Prosecution, and Prevention of Computer Crime: A State-of-the-Art Review*, 2 Computer LJ 385, 389 (1980). See generally *The Spreading Danger of Computer Crime*, Bus Wk, Apr 20, 1981, at 86.

[12] See generally L. Krauss & A. MacGahan, Computer Fraud and Countermeasures 3-24 (1979); D. Parker, Crime by Computer (1976); T. Whiteside, Computer Capers (1978); *Computer Crime Rising*, Sec Distr & Mkt, Sept 1978, at 82.

[13] Volgyes, *The Investigation, Prosecution, and Prevention of Computer Crime: A State-of-the-Art Review*, 2 Computer LJ 385, 387 (1980). See also A. Bequai, White-Collar Crime: A 20th Century Crisis 105-13 (1978).

[14] SRI International, Computer Crime: Criminal Justice Resource Manual 3 (1979).

[15] Taber, *On Computer Crime (Senate Bill S 240)*. 1 Computer LJ 517 (1979). But cf Comment, *Computer Crime - Sentate Bill S 240*, 10 Mem St UL Rev 660 (1980). See also A. Bequai, Computer Crime 1 (1978); Watkins, *Computer Crime: Separating the Myth From the Reality; It's the Crime Figures That are Suspect*, 14 CAM 44 (1981).

[16] Taber, *supra* note 15, at 534.

remotely linked to a computer.[17]

When crimes are committed that involve computers, many aspects of the crime may be beyond the understanding not only of the general public but even that of the prosecutor assigned to bring the culprits involved to justice.[18] In order to understand what is meant by *computer crime* in any given context, it may be helpful to look at some of the various definitions of the term.[19]

Although many definitions of computer crime have been offered, an easy understanding seems to have eluded prosecutors, judges, and legislators. Simply stated, computer crime is the use of the computer or its technology as a target of or a tool for illegal purposes. An illegal purpose can signify any number of traditional crimes including theft, fraud, or embezzlement of money, services, or information. This broad definition can be divided into two general categories:

1. Theft or vandalism of computer hardware, firmware, and software (computers as the *victims* of crime)

2. Theft, sabotage, espionage, fraud, or embezzlement committed through use of a computer (computers as the *facilitators* of crime)[20]

A more technical definition divides computer crime into three categories:

1. Computer abuse: any intentional act involving a computer where one or more perpetrators made or could have made gain, and one or more victims suffered or could have suffered loss

2. Computer crime: illegal computer abuse

3. Computer-related crime: *any illegal act for which knowledge of computer tech-*

---

[17] *Id* 518-28. See also T. Whiteside, Computer Capers 3 (1978):

> The intimidating effect of the computer is not confined to people who have only an ordinary citizen's knowledge of its functioning but often extends to managers and chief officers of big corporations who employ computers on a large scale. It seems that a sort of computer mystique has helped make possible a significant increase in illegal manipulation of the computer, in which it and its technology have been used as instruments of embezzlement, fraud, and theft.

[18] A. Bequai, Computer Crime 47-53 (1978). See generally Hemphil & Hemphil, *Prosecuting Computer Criminals,* Sec World, Aug 1978, at 62; Bequai, *Legal Problems in Prosecuting Computer Crime,* Sec Mgmt, July 1977, at 26.

[19] A. Bequai, Computer Crime 3 (1978).

> There is no widely accepted definition of computer crime. Some authorities define it as making use of the computer to steal large sums of money. Others include theft of services within this definition. . . . Some take an open approach . . . , viewing it as the use of a computer to perpetrate any scheme to defraud others of funds, services, and property.

An adequate definition of computer crime should encompass the use of a computer to perpetrate acts of deceit, concealment, and guile that have as their objective the detaining of property, money, services, and political and business advantages.

[20] A. Bequai, *supra* note 19, at 4.

nology is essential for successful prosecution[21]

The first definition, although broad, divides computer crime into two basic categories, the second of which, the use of a computer to commit crime, is the less familiar type of computer-related crime and is the category emphasized in this chapter. The second definition draws fine distinctions that will become more relevant in §7.09.[22] Suffice it to say, computers are not the creators of new crimes, but the targets of or the very efficient tools used to commit traditional crimes.[23]

A discussion of the stages of the computer process is helpful in understanding how computers can be both a tool and a target of the computer criminal. The five phases of computer operations are: (1) input; (2) programming; (3) processing in the central processing unit (CPU); (4) output; and (5) data communications. A computer system is vulnerable to different crimes at each of these phases. The following is a brief summary of each of the five stages of information processing and the vulnerabilty a system has at each phase.[24]

In the input stage, data is entered into the system in machine-readable form. Several input devices are in use including optical scanners, remote terminals, card readers, and magnetic tape units. During this phase the computer is vulnerable to the omission of documents, the creation of entirely false records, and the input of false data through the alteration of amounts, names, or other information.[25]

In the second stage of the computer process, the programming phase, the program gives the computer step-by-step instructions for the performance of specified tasks. Since it is the program that controls the operation of the computer (a computer can only perform functions as dictated by a program), a criminal can cause the computer to carry out the criminal's purpose by inserting the criminal's own program. Programs themselves are vulnerable to several types of criminal abuse, including alteration, theft, and destruction.

In the actual processing phase the CPU manipulates data according to the dictates of the program: storing, retrieving, and transmitting data as instructed. The CPU can be the object of criminal attack through the alteration or misuse of the computer input processor. The CPU can also be manipulated by improper instructions. One of the most common crimes occurring at this phase of the computer process is the unauthorized extraction (raiding) of data from another's computer system to obtain computer program data which another

---

[21] SRI, *supra* note 14, at 3 (emphasis in original).

[22] See §7.09.

[23] A. Bequai, *supra* note 19, at 4.

[24] Survey, *White Collar Crime: Computer Crime*, 18 Am Crim L Rev 370, 372 (1980). See also A. Bequai, Computer Crime 9 (1978); Nycum, *Computer Abuses Raise New Legal Problems*, 61 ABAJ 444 (1975).

[25] Tunick, *Computer Law: An Overview*, 13 Loy LAL Rev 315, 329 (1980). See also A. Bequai, *supra* note 13, at 107-08.

company may have developed.[26] The CPU is vulnerable to wiretapping,[27] electromagnetic pickup,[28] browsing,[29] and piggyback entry.[30]

The fourth stage encompasses the output function. In this phase, data received from the CPU is translated into readable form, e.g., printouts and terminal displays. The most common abuses directed at this stage of processing include thefts of customer and mailing lists, and other confidential marketing data. Even lists of registered voters have been stolen.[31]

The final stage of the computer process is data communication. Data communication involves the use of telephone circuits to transmit data between computers and remote terminals. A computer system is probably most vulnerable to penetration by unauthorized persons through the use of telephone circuits.[32]

§7.03   Targets of Computer Crime

Any computer can be a target for computer crime in the broadest sense of the term. Information of value stored in a computer, whether at home or at an office, can be the target of theft, or of tampering by a knowledgeable individual who gains access to that system without authorization. If this generalized assertion seems removed from the mainstream of everyday existence, consider that the majority of banks have computerized part, if not all, of the records they keep. Financial institutions are an obvious target for the computer criminal. Many financial institutions make use of computerized clearinghouses to conduct transfers of cash, negotiable instruments, and other valuable commodities. Where transactions can be conducted via telecommunications links,

---

[26] Tunick, *supra* note 25, at 329, See also A. Bequai, *supra* note 13 at 108.

[27] Survey, *supra* note 24, at 373, *Wiretapping* usually involves the connection of a *tap* directly to the telephone or teleprinter lines that transmit the data in order to intercept and record information. A. Bequai, *supra* note 19, at 12.

[28] *Electromagnetic pickup* usually involves a device designed to intercept the radiation generated by the CPU, telephone and teleprinter lines, or microwave communications. A. Bequai, *supra* note 15, at 13. See also Survey, *supra* note 24, at 373.

[29] *Browsing* means the utilization of an "unauthorized terminal in a system that does not expose terminal entry, thereby allowing the 'browser' to gain access to the computer." A. Bequai, Computer Crime 12-13 (1978).

[30] *Id* 13. *Piggyback entry* is the process by which messages from the computer to the user are selectively intercepted. Once interception is achieved infomation is either added or deleted as the case may be, and then a modified message is released to the user. See SRI, *supra* note 14, at 25-77.

[31] Tunick, *Computer Law: An Overview,* 13 Loy LAL Rev 315, 330 (1980). See also A. Bequai, *supra* note 13, at 108.

[32] Tunick, *supra* note 31, at 331. See also A. Bequai, *supra* note 13, at 108-09. In one case a major oil company used telephone lines between distant computers to evaluate what bid it should make on an important on-going project. A competitor tapped into the telephone line, discovered the bid that would be made by the company, and then entered a lower bid. L. Krauss & A. MacGahan, Computer Fraud and Countermeasures 12 (1979). See generally Robertson, *Oil Computer Leaks,* Elec News, July 28, 1975, at 10.

a criminal with the requisite equipment and knowledge can obtain access to the necessary records, and effect the transfer of cash and other valuables to an account controlled by the perpetrator. This is only one of many techniques that can be used to obtain funds from a financial institution. Moreover, this crude technique assumes that the perpetrators are not employees of the firm they are raiding. Thefts of funds via computer are more easily accomplished by those inside an organization.

Thefts are not the only crimes employees may commit against an employer or an employer's computer. Sabotage and espionage are available to the malcontent with the training and awareness of the company computer system often without much danger of the saboteur or spy being caught as there will be few traces left of the act. Employees have sabotaged employers by erasing valuable information from disks and tapes through the placement of a magnet in a storage area.[33] Employees with more extensive technological training have sabotaged operations in more subtle ways, e.g., by altering a program so that it produces consistently erroneous information. Sabotage has been accomplished in more spectacular fashion by causing a crash or shutdown of the entire computer system.[34] Espionage may involve the outright theft of programs or information regarding a competitor's trade secrets, or it may be limited to accessing a competitor's balance sheet.[35] This type of computer abuse may be accomplished with the aid of an employee of the violated firm, or via telephone lines from a safe distance away. Copies can be made of important documents, and unless elaborate safeguards are in place which are unknown to the computer abuser, no record of the copying will appear.

In the case of sensitive or secret materials, damage is often apparent only after it is too late. For example, once software has been pirated or trade secrets have been stolen, the damage is already done. The accelerated nature of software development gives the inventor of a new program perhaps six months or less of exclusive control over the invention before it can be independently duplicated. A stolen program will supply an able competitor with the edge he or she may need to surpass the original inventor's program. A protracted court battle may stop the original pirate's activities, but it will not prevent indpendent developers from generating essentially the same software program. A court action may, as a matter of principle, afford the victim some satisfaction in having a judgment entered against the defendant, but will ultimately be of little utility. Once a trade secret is revealed it is no longer afforded protection as intellectual property, and practically speaking, it may no longer be of value to the original owner. The original inventor may win the battle against the first unscrupulous programmer, but lose the war to legitimate developers who

---

[33] Rivlin, *A Multimillion Dollar Crime Has Just Been Committed in this Room*, 10 Student Law 15, 17 (1982).

[34] See generally Mandell, *Computer Security - Sabotage Fears Discounted*, 20 Computers & Automation 29 (1971).

[35] See generally *Espionage in the Computer Business*, Bus Wk, July 28, 1975, at 60; Hoyt, *The Computer as a Target for the Industrial Spy*, 1 Assets Protection 41 (1975).

come into the marketplace with essentially the same product and destroy the inventor's competitive edge.

The discovery that Hitachi attempted to purchase IBM trade secrets illustrates that computer-related crimes are an international as well as domestic problem.[36] Though this may seem an isolated course of events, it is important to note that this is an instance where the culprits were discovered. There is no estimate of how many similar attempts to obtain information have not only been successful, but have also remained undetected or unreported.

§7.04   Victim Unwillingness to Report Computer Crime

The number of actual computer crimes is uncertain. The amount of monetary loss resulting from these crimes has not yet been accurately determined. Much of this uncertainty is because most computer crimes go unreported.[37]

A number of factors affect the failure to report computer-related crimes. First, victims of computer crime, depending on the degree of loss involved, often view the pursuit of the criminal as fruitless. Second, victims often want to avoid the embarrassing acknowledgment of the penetration of their organization.[38] Particularly for a financial institution, a public admission of loss via

---

[36] Hitachi and another Japanese electronics firm, Mitsubishi Electric Corp, face charges of attempting to illegally obtain IBM proprietary information in two similar, but apparently unrelated incidents. Eighteen people have been charged with conspiracy to transport stolen property, and one person has been charged with receiving stolen documents.

The Justice Department said the conspiracy involved separate efforts by representatives of Hitachi and Mitsubishi to obtain confidential information from IBM to assist in the development of computers and computer-related products. Justice Department sources said the Japanese companies were seeking "state of the art technology," including machines, programming information, architectural plans, and manuals explaining how to use the equipment. Rocky Mountain News, June 23, 1982, at 3.

[37] Sokolik, *Computer Crime—The Need for Deterrent Legislation*, 2 Computer LJ 353, 359 (1980). This same author states that:

> Computer frauds lack visibility: a change in a computer program can be removed after the offense has taken place, or the change may affect only a miniscule portion of the processed data, or the fraudulent manipulation may be programmed to take place at a predetermined future time. Indeed, in the vast majority of cases, detection has been a matter of sheer accident, rather than as a result of an ongoing security or auditing effort.

See also Walker, *Theft by Computer—The Invisible Crime*, 42 J Ins 40 (1981).

[38] Volgyes, *The Investigation, Prosecution, and Prevention of Computer Crime: A State-of-the-Art Review*, 2 Computer LJ 385, 394 (1980); Bureau of Justice Statistics, US Dept of Justice, Expert Witness Manual: Use of Outside Experts in Computer-Related Crime Cases 1-7 (1980); see Law Enforcement Assistance Administration, US Dept of Justice, The Investigation of Computer Crime 5-6 (1980) (citing examples where companies refused to report such crimes) [herinafter cited as LEAA]; Interview with John P. Bellassai, Director of Criminal Justice Division, Koba Assoc, Washington DC (June 4,

computer crime could be threatening to the institution's image of security and stability within the business community. The seemingly innate distrust of the computer by the general public makes any acknowledgement of the computer's shortcomings, such as its vulnerability to thieves, particularly painful. Some institutions would rather write-off a loss that might encourage any public aggrandizement of the evils of the computer.[39] Third, management may simply be unaware of the vulnerability of their computer system to criminal attack. Once an attack has taken place and security measures against any intrusion taken, management feels reporting would prove futile.

It is also known that some crimes go unreported and unprosecuted because the perpetrators of the crimes are not turned over to law enforcement authorities. In fact, the perpetrators may be hired by the victim's organization as security officers in an attempt to prevent future break-ins or thefts, and to preclude the likelihood of unsavory publicity.[40]

Other reasons often mentioned for inadequate reporting include:

1. A real or imagined fear of loss of public confidence

2. The difficulty of proving that a crime has been committed, and the subsequent risk of a false-arrest charge

3. A concern about possible liability for the lack of prevention and recovery of losses

4. A belief by the computer user (and sometimes by the computer manufacturer) that public exposure would be tantamount to an admission that the computer is vulnerable to still further penetrations, as well as providing instruction on how to repeat penetrations[41]

§7.05 Forms of Computer Crime

The nature of the criminal act committed in a computer related crime generally falls into one of the following categories:

1. Misappropriation of computer time

2. Theft of software (computer programs, source codes, etc.)

3. Theft of computer data or information generated or stored in computer

4. Theft of services acquired by using the computer as a tool

---

1981) (large corporations maintain files of cases which are not released to outsiders). Statistics relied on by the FBI claim that only 15% of all computer crimes which are detected are brought to the attention of law enforcement officials. *But* Federal Computer Systems Protection Act: Hearings on S 240 Before the Subcomm on Criminal Justice of the Senate Comm on the Judiciary, 96th Cong, 2d Sess 80 (1980) (additional submission of John K. Taber) (no evidence to support this contention).

[39] Volgyes, *supra* note 38, at 394.

[40] *Id.* See also Tunick, *Computer Law: An Overview,* Loy LAL Rev 315, 326 n 48 (1980).

[41] Sokolik, *supra* note 37, at 359.

5. Destruction or vandalism of computer hardware

6. Destruction or interruption of computer processes causing confusion and delay

7. Theft of trade secrets (often concurrent with the theft of software or programs)

8. Theft of money, financial instruments (negotiable instruments), and property

The last catagory is probably the most common crime and usually involves computers used for payroll, accounts payable, receivables, and financial recordkeeping functions.[42]

These catagories may be regrouped or consolidated into four, broader categories:

1. Theft of services, e.g., an authorized person using computer time for unauthorized purposes

2. Utilization of information contained in a computer's memory for personal profit

3. Utilization of computers employed for various types of financial processing to obtain assets

4. Theft of property via computers[43]

Methods used to commit these crimes vary widely. Within the computer community certain modus operandi are given specific names that describe the method used. The following list of descriptions of common techniques is by no means exhaustive. However, it should give the reader an idea of the variety and complexity of some of the common methods.

Data diddling is the *rearrangement* or outright change of information while it

---

[42] See Survey *White Collar Crime: Computer Crime,* 18 Am Crim L Rev 370, 372 (1980).

[43] One study lists four main categories of computer crime:

(1) introduction of fraudulent records or data into a computer system; (2) unauthorized use of computer related facilities; (3) alteration or destruction of information or files; (4) theft, whether by electronic means of otherwise, of money, financial instruments, property services, or valuable data.

General Accounting Office, Computer Related Crimes in Federal Programs 1 (1976), cited in Volgyes, *The Investigation, Prosecution, and Prevention of Computer Crime: A State-of-the-Art Review,* 2 Computer LJ 385, 389 (1980). Another classification states that computer crimes include:

(1) sabotage and vandalism against a computer system itself;

(2) theft of computer services;

(3) property crimes (theft of property through the use of a computer); and

(4) data crimes (theft of information, whether output data or intercepted data).

A. Bequai, Computer Crime 13-14 (1978). See Swanson & Territo, *Computer Crime: Dimensions, Types, Causes & Investigations,* 8 J Police Sci & Ad 304, 306-07 (1980); see also Computer Crime: A Growing and Serious Problem, 6 Police LQ 22, 28 (1976).

is being prepared for input into the computer. Thus, technically speaking, this computer-related crime occurs prior to computerization of information.[44]

A *trojan horse* involves the covert placement of an instruction within a program so that the computer will perform an unauthorized function, but outwardly continue to allow the authorized program to perform its intended purpose.[45]

The *salami technique* is an automated form of theft that involves the creation of a program that takes small amounts of money from a large number of accounts, in effect taking small slices without noticeably reducing the whole. The best example of this would be the rounding down of accounts when interest is added. Detection is very difficult because no single account holder suspects any loss.[46]

Superzapping derives its name from a macro-utility program developed by IBM as an emergency systems diagnostic tool. The program permits a computer operator to override all system controls, and modify or disclose any of the contents in the computer system. A superzapping program can be dangerous or even disastrous in the wrong hands as it could be used to alter or obtain information at any point in the computing process.[47]

Trap doors are debugging tools used by programmers which act as markers for insertion of additional code, or for modification of existing code in a computer program. Normally these trap doors are eliminated in the final edit. Trap doors which remain in code, intentionally or unintentionally, mark the most likely positions for alteration of the computer program. The unscrupulous programmer can use trap doors to compromise the performance of a computer system.[48]

A *logic bomb* is a computer program executed at periodic times under specific conditions. In one incident, a programmer placed a logic bomb in a computer which caused the erasure of his name whenever it appeared on an employment termination list. Logic bombs can also be structured to perform less obvious tasks, such as crashing the system or downgrading performance of the system once or several times over a period of time.[49]

Data leakage is the covert removal of data or copies of data from a computer system by highly technical means.[50]

Wire tapping enables a thief, after purchasing about $200.00 worth of easily

---

[44] SRI International, Computer Crime: Criminal Justice Resource Manual 9-11 (1979).

[45] *Id.* 11-12.

[46] *Id.* 13-17. Interest due on an account, for example, might equal $.04232, but the automated round down would only credit $.04 to the account. The fractions of cents rounded off are then diverted into an account controlled by the thief. The resulting "round-downs" could equal thousands of dollars.

[47] *Id* 17-18.

[48] *Id* 19-20.

[49] *Id* 21.

[50] *Id* 24.

obtainable equipment, to tap a phone line. As more computer centers are linked to one another via telephone, and as more valuable information is transmitted between these centers, wire tapping may become a more frequent crime.[51]

Simulation and modeling techniques enable a would-be thief to use a computer to simulate and model a contemplated crime beforehand. Because computer modeling requires large amounts of computer time, modeling a crime before its commission occurs on a limited basis.[52]

Piggybacking can be done in physical or electronic fashion. In the physical form of piggybacking, an unauthorized individual will attempt to enter a secured or limited access area in conjunction with authorized personnel. The simplest form of this type of piggybacking is for the intruder to carry computer-related materials, and wait for an authorized person to come along and open the door into the secured area. Electronic piggybacking can be done via a terminal that has been activated by authorized personnel, and then left on and unattended. Improper sign-off after use is another avenue for the unauthorized use of computer equipment. Improper sign-off, which leaves the terminal in an active state, causes the computer to *think* that the terminal is still in use by an authorized user.

Impersonation occurs when an unauthorized person assumes the identity of authorized personnel in order to access a computer system. Despite the best security measures available, any individual with the proper combination of physical characteristics, or the requisite knowledge of passwords, codes, or procedures can impersonate another individual.[53]

Scavenging occurs when the thief literally picks through whatever discarded material may be found in or around a computer system. Pieced together, these computer leavings aid the thief in penetrating the security of the computer system. Simple forms of scavenging may entail going through the trash to find discarded printouts, scratched tapes, or carbon portions of multiple-part computer forms, whereas more technical forms involve using the computer to search for information that remains after pertinent processing has been completed.[54]

Undoubtedly, the greatest obstacle to the effective prosecution of computer-related crimes is the increasing complexity of computers, which has made detection and investigation of computer-related crimes an almost insurmountable task.[55]

---

[51] *Id* 27-28.

[52] *Id* 28-29.

[53] *Id* 25-27.

[54] *E.g.*, buffer registers (devices with memory capacity that link programs together) that have not been cleared after use can yield important information that could compromise a system. *Id* 23-24.

[55] Tunick, *Computer Law: An Overview*, Loy LAL Rev 315, 326 (1980). See also T. Schabeck, Computer Crime Investigation Manual 1 (1979). See generally *Computer Crooks Difficult to Detect*, Security Letter, Jan 24, 1978, at 4.

§7.06   Detection of Computer Crime

Detection, as opposed to investigation, of computer crimes usually implies *internal* measures designed to discover or uncover computer abuses. Detection hinges on the security measures a computer user takes with regard to the computer system during both operational and nonoperational periods. Detection of computer crime depends on proper in-house audit procedures to ensure that misuse of a computer is detected before the perpetrator has a chance either to commit the same crime again, or if the crime in question was a one-time occurrence, to abscond with the fruits of the crime. Depending on the frequency of auditing activities, the perpetrator could well be in another country before the crime is even discovered.

Although most instances of computer crime are discovered in the course of regular audit activities, some computer crimes are detected entirely by accident. In *Ward v Superior Court* the only clue that led to discovery of the crime was the coincidental dumping of punched cards that occurred concurrently with the telephone intrusion of the system.[56] ISD, a computer service company located in California, had developed a computer program which gave it a competitive edge over similar computer companies in the area. On January 19, 1971, an employee of UCC, another computer service company, used his company's data phone to gain access to the ISD computer, and instructed it to transmit the program over the telephone wires to the UCC office. The transaction took only six seconds to complete. Upon arrival at the UCC office, the electronic impulses were transformed into a computer printout. Fortunately for ISD, an unintended punched card dump of the program occurred contemporaneously with the intrusion. The cards showed that the system had been accessed, and the time of the access. A check with the telephone company indicated that the call into the ISD computer had come from the UCC office.[57]

Even though the prosecutor had the advantage of the punched card activity, it was difficult to find an appropriate charge under California's criminal statutes. The defendant was not charged with theft of computer time because the six seconds it took to steal the program was "deemed too short to represent a loss in duration—though not in effect."[58] The UCC employee was charged with grand theft in the amount of the market value of the program, and theft of a trade secret, a statutory offense in California.[59] Although the prosecutor

---

[56] Ward v Superior Ct, 3 Computer L Serv Rep 206 (Cal Super Ct 1972).

[57] The program which was tampered with did not have traps to detect intruders; the perpetrators just happened to call into the computer at that point in the program cycle where punched cards were automatically dumped. Because of this chance coincidence, the victim was able to pinpoint the time the intrusion occurred, and to determine what portion of the computer's storage had been accessed. *Id* 207-08.

[58] See Ingraham, *On Charging Computer Crime*, 2 Computer LJ 429, 432 (1980).

[59] Under §499C(b) of the Calif Penal Code a person is guilty of theft if, "with intent to deprive or withhold from another thereof the control of a trade secret . . . [he or she] steals, takes, or carries away any article representing a trade secret." Also under §487(1) grand theft is theft committed when money, labor, or real or personal property is unlawfully taken and the value exceeds two hundred dollars ($200).

had a product of definable commercial value, he was still forced to express the theft of the program in terms of asportation to come within the definition of theft under the California Penal Code. The court ruled that under California law, the asported program had to be tangible or in readable or visual form before it could gain the protection of the law. The court ruled that but for the print-out there would have been no asportation and thus no crime in this case, since magnetic symbols conveyed across telecommunications lines would not constitute an article representing a trade secret. The court stated:

> Based upon the record here, the defendant Ward did not carry any tangible thing representing ISD's Plot/Tran's Program from the ISD computer to the UCC computer unless the impulses which defendant allegedly caused to be transmitted over the telephone wire could be said to be tangible. It is the opinion of the Court that such impulses are not tangible and hence do not constitute an "article" within the definition contained in Section 499c (a)(1) [of the California Penal Code] as inclusive of "object, material, device, substance or copies thereof, including any writing, record, recording, drawing, sample, specimen, prototype, model, photograph, microorganism, blueprint or map."[60]

The *Ward* case shows the need for educating the courts in the basics of the computerized world. For example, according to traditional legal standards, six seconds is not significant, but six seconds is ample time to commit a crime when the perpetrator is working through a computer. One of the often overlooked lessons of *Ward* is that the criminal act was discovered entirely by chance. If the punched card dump had occurred even seconds after the commission of the six second crime, the victim might not have been able to learn the identity of the thief, or even discover that a robbery had occurred.

Computer crime detection assumes that the steps followed in committing the crime can be traced. If the perpetrator was an employee or some other person with authorized access to the facility, the computer crime is substantially easier to detect. Many times, however, this is not the case, and suspects must be sought in the outside world, making computer crime detection substantially more difficult.

§7.07 Investigation of Computer Crime

Depending on the nature of the computer crime and the security measures employed at a computer facility, it may be possible to narrow the list of suspects by considering which individuals had access to the information or equipment used to commit the crime, as well as the technical skills required to commit the criminal act. In *data diddling,* for example, the list of suspects would include those people who had access to the information collected for input into

---

[60] Ward v Superior Court, 3 Computer L Serv Rep 206, 208 (Cal Super Ct 1972). See also Ingraham, *supra* note 58, at 433.

the computer system. In the case of a *logic bomb* or a *trojan horse,* the list of suspects would be limited to those individuals who possessed the technical knowledge needed to implement such a complex computer crime.

Investigation, although it can be carried out in-house by those in charge of data processing, generally connotes law enforcement participation in the form of state and local police departments, the Fedeal Bureau of Investigation (FBI), and any number of state and federal administrative agencies, nonagencies, and commissions.[61]

The complexities of computer-related crime present law enforcement officials with unique and serious problems.[62] One of those problems is the potential for the complexities of the computer to overwhelm investigators.[63] External investigators, including law enforcement personnel, may be hampered in an investigation by their unfamiliarity with the technological world of computers. Without an accurate understanding of how the crime was committed, the prosecutor is faced with the sometimes difficult task of ascertaining whether state or federal law was violated. Mistakes in filing the proper charge or choosing the proper forum can result in dismissal or acquittal. As a result of the lack of technical expertise, the special problems encountered during the investigation of computer-related crimes, including the special precautions necessary to collect and protect evidence, and even the *language* of the computer community, may have to be taught to investigators before an effective investigation can begin.[64] Even in cases where investigators may already be familiar with computer-related criminal activities, an investigation may be hampered by a lack of funds and personnel, which are common at all levels of law enforcement, whether local, state, or federal.[65]

State and local police forces particularly suffer from a lack of trained personnel and inadequate budgets.[66] The personnel in most law enforcement departments are usually uninformed about the technical aspects of computer

---

[61] See A. Bequai, Computer Crime 59 (1978).

[62] Bureau of Justice Statistics, US Dept of Justice, Expert Witness Manual: Use of Outside Experts in Computer Related Crime Cases 1-7 to 1-11 (1980) (detailed list of unique features of computer-related crime and litigation); Swanson & Territo, *Computer Crime: Dimensions, Types, Causes & Investigations,* 8 J Police Sci & Ad 304, 311(1980) ("The investigation of computer crime requires special awareness and, as the complexity of schemes increases, definite technical capabilities.")

[63] See generally Shaw, *How Can You Fight What You Don't Understand,* L & Or, July 1977, at 5.

[64] See generally, Schabeck, *Investigators Tackle Computer Crime* Sec World, Feb 1977, at 31.

[65] A. Bequai, *supra* note 61, at 57.

[66] *Id.* Bequai states:

At the local level, more than 50 percent of these agencies employ fewer than 5 full-time employees. Almost 70 percent of these employ fewer than 10 full-time employees. One Presidential Commission has described local law enforcement as being made up of small, separate groups, each acting independently of the other and, many times, in ignorance of what an adjoining jurisdiction is doing.

technology. This may explain why local law enforcement bodies appear to be ignorant of the very existence of computer-related crimes.

The obstacles confronting effective investigation at the federal level can be characterized as problems of fragmentation and bureaucratic inertia. Fragmentation and inaction are caused by the restriction of each federal regulatory agency to a specialized area of the law.[67] As a result of their inadequate budgets, these agencies cannot keep pace with the speed and versatility of computer technology.[68] In addition, present investigations take too long. By the time some investigations have been completed, especially at the federal regulatory level, the computer felon is gone and the damage has been done. Political pressures can also take their toll as investigations may be stopped in mid-stream, or even before they have begun.[69] Greater public scrutiny of our federal investigatory system is needed to ensure that it functions competently and in the public interest.

§7.08 —Search and Seizure

New and sophisticated investigative techniques are needed to keep pace with the highly complex and varied practices used to commit computer crimes. The development of any new investigative technique, however, must be accomplished with the requirements of the fourth amendment kept in mind. To meet the constitutional requirements of the fourth amendment, a search must be reasonable. A search conducted pursuant to a valid search warrant is considered prima facie reasonable. The fourth amendment requires that a search warrant describe the object or purpose of the search, what is to be seized, and where the search and seizure will take place. Moreover, these matters must be described with specificity. Search and seizure of evidence of computer-related crime is relatively new phenomenon. Even assuming the investigatory phase is fruitful, law enforcement and investigatory personnel, poorly trained in computer technology, may find it difficult to describe accurately the nature and object of their search. As a result, there may be a need to consult with experts in order to describe to a judge or magistrate what was stolen or misused. Computer language and operations are often highly technical, and the computer vocabulary is rapidly changing as technology advances. In *Ward v Superior Court,* the judge was asked to sign a search warrant authorizing the seizure of "computer memory bank or other data storage devices, magnetically imprinted with Information Systems Design (ISD) remote plotting computer pro-

---

[67] For a more detailed discussion of the federal investigatory structure, see A. Bequai, *supra* note 61, at 59.

[68] See generally *The Push-Button Criminals of the '80s: Rapid Advances in Electronics are Providing Opportunities for Sophisticated Thieves and Saboteurs,* US News & World Rep, Sept 22, 1980, at 39.

[69] Some investigations believe that organized crime itself has made in-roads into the investigatory agencies decision processes. See A. Bequai, *supra* note 61, at 75.

grams."[70] Even if the judge happened to know what the search warrant was designed to find, there is still the question of whether the local police officers would know where or how to look for the object of the search.

If the official requesting the search warrant does not know the form of the evidence sought at the scene of the search, a computer expert should accompany the official to meet with a judge or magistrate for the search warrant.[71] This is only one problem. Even with the help of experts in specifically describing the evidence to be seized, it is uncertain whether the specific computer abuse committed is a crime in a particular jurisdiction.

Evidence seized pursuant to an invalid search warrant will be suppressed before or during trial. If the suppressed evidence is the only evidence which could have been used to convict the perpetrator, the culprit will go free. There is presently an open question as to what role the fourth amendment plays in a situation where a computerized corporation or institution has asked the FBI, local law enforcement authorities, or even a private detective firm to *oversee* its computer operations so as to prevent or deter unauthorized uses. Even if this type of surveillance is deemed a search within the meaning of the fourth amendment, the question of whether the search would be considered reasonable within the meaning of the fourth amendment is still open. This question is not easily answered because questions concerning consent and the scope of the consent granted by authorized users create curious constitutional issues. There is also a question of whether the government, ostensibly under the guise of this *private consent,* can constitutionally participate in a private undertaking without being guilty of violating the *silver-platter doctrine,* which would render the search unreasonable and therefore unconstitutional.[72]

§7.09   Problems of Prosecution—21st Century Crime and the 20th Century Courts

Well-trained investigators, including law enforcement officials and prosecutors, are a crucial link in the eventual conviction of computer criminals. But this aspect of enforcement is also an integral facet of another critical link: the applicable criminal statute. Where an apparent violation has occurred, the prosecutor must know how to classify it in terms of an offense recognized by the appropriate federal or state law.[73]

---

[70] Ward v Superior Court of the State of California, 3 Computer L Serv Rep (Cal Super Ct 1972). See Becker, *The Trial of a Computer Crime,* 2 Computer LJ 441, 443 (1980).

[71] *Id* 444.

[72] See McCormick's Handbook of the Law of Evidence 372 (E. Cleary ed, 2d ed 1972) for a discussion of the silver platter doctrine.

[73] Ingraham, *On Charging Computer Crime,* 2 Computer LJ 429, 437 (1980). Ingraham states:

> No investigation should be initiated without the clear guidelines afforded by the available statutes, and no case should be accepted for filing without explicit

Although the majority of computer-related crimes are basically "the same crimes that have been prosecuted since the apple was plucked," it is difficult to match a specific computer crime with the traditional criminal statute.[74] As a result, computer technology must be made to fit such statutes by implication.[75] In the majority of cases the perpetrators of computer abuses are charged with one or more of several common law crimes, including larceny, burglary, embezzlement, or false pretenses. Courts often find, however, that computer crimes do not meet with the rather technical statutory requirements of these traditional common law crimes, and as a result, many crimes go unpunished.[76] In many jurisdictions, especially those without adequate specialized computer abuse statutes, computer-related crimes may fall through the cracks of the criminal code. Even the most modern computer crime statutes embody certain elements of common law crimes, and the commission of a computer crime may not meet all the necessary requirements.[77]

Technically, a computer crime is committed every time a computer is used without the authorization of the proper parties. From a statutory perspective, however, this is not a workable definition for lawmakers and law enforcement personnel. For example, computer time may be used without permission, but also without the owner of the machine suffering a significant loss. Just as the theft of small office supplies in small quantities is generally not the subject of

---

satisfaction of the statutes. The enormity of the loss and the prestige of the victim set in motion influences which can trigger the crippling raglan reflex under which the attitude of "charge something now and amend it later" may swamp the circuits.

[74] *Id* 438. See generally, *Computer Crimes Not Amenable to Prosecution Under Current Law,* Sec Letter, Nov 2, 1977, at 2.

[75] See Tunick, *Computer Law: An Overview,* 13 Loy LAL Rev 315, 325 n 48 (1980) (charging the correct crime can be major problem). See generally Nycum, *The Criminal Law Aspects of Computer Abuse,* 5 Rutgers J Computers & L 271, 276-95 (1976) (discussion of the problems associated with matching computer-related technological crimes to traditional statutes); and Bureau of Justice Statistics, US Dept of Justice, Expert Witness Manual: Use of Outside Experts in Computer Related Crime Cases 1-9 (1980) (difficulties of charging under traditional criminal statutes).

[76] Volgyes, *The Investigation, Prosecution, and Prevention of Computer Crime: A State-of-the-Art Review,* 2 Computer LJ 385, 398-400 (1980). Few computer-related crime prosecutions are carried all the way through to trial because the respective governmental authorities are often willing to settle most cases by consent decree. Taken from an interview with John P. Bellassai, Director of Criminal Justice Division, Koba Associates, Inc, Washington, DC (June 4, 1981). See *White Collar Crime: A Survey of Law,* 18 Am Crim L Rev 165 n2928 (1980). See also *Accused Computer Bank Robber Cops a Pleas to Avoid Prosecution,* Sec Sys Dig, Feb 28, 1979, at 4. See generally Bequai, *Legal Problems in Prosecuting Computer Crime,* Sec Mgmt, July 1977, at 26.

[77] *E.g.,* asportation. In *Ward* the computer printout was the only evidence the court would accept to prove that asportation had occurred. If the perpetrator in *Ward* had not created a printout, but had instead left the information on a disk or tape, the court would have had to decide whether to admit into evidence magnetically-stored evidence. If the court had decided not to admit this evidence, there would not have been a conviction as not all the necessary elements of the crime would have been proved.

criminal prosecution, for the same reasons it is not practical to prosecute every theft of computer time. Many of the present federal and state statutes which are being used to address the multifaceted nature of computer crime are antiquated, inadequate, and confusing.[78] Due to the absence of well-defined computer criminal statutes, many prosecutors are forced to *shoehorn* a crime committed with the aid of a computer into a common law criminal statute in order to bring the case to trial. To shoehorn a computer abuse into traditional criminal statutory concepts is often time consuming and complicated, which consequently leads to low conviction rates. As one commentator has stated:

> Charging the correct crime can be a major problem. Because criminal codes rarely are written with computer crime in mind, the prosecutor often must attempt to fit a computer crime into a category when the fit might not be comfortable. For example, if software is misappropriated using a remote terminal, the prosecution, depending upon state law, may take any of several forms, e.g., misappropriation of trade secrets, larceny, telephone abuse, and forgery.[79]

§7.10   —Prosecution Under The Federal Criminal Code

Federal Bureau of Investigation Director William Webster stated at a meeting of the American Society of Industrial Security (ASIS) that "there is at present no existing effective legislation governing our [federal] jurisdiction to meet the threat of computer fraud."[80] Although computer-related crime may be prosecuted under any of 40 sections of the federal criminal code, there is none that specifically addresses computer crime.[81] Most of these statutes "were written to combat abuses other than computer crimes" and, as a result, prosecutors have had to fit computer technology into traditional criminal law molds.[82]

---

[78] See generally Comment, *Computer Crime - Senate Bill S 240,* 10 Mem St UL Rev 660 (1980); Computer Crime Law Inadequate, Crime Control Dig, Feb 21, 1977, at 9.

[79] Tunick, *supra* note 75, at 325, n 48.

[80] Dun's Rev, Jan 1980, at 106.

[81] *Federal Computer Systems Protection Act: Hearings on S 1766 Before the Subcomm on Criminal Laws & Procedures of the Senate Comm of the Judiciary,* 95th Cong, 2d Sess 3 (1978) (statement of Sen Paul Laxalt) [hereinafter cited as Hearings]. See also Nycum, *The Criminal Law Aspects of Computer Abuse Part II: Federal Criminal Code,* 5 Rutgers J Computers & L 297 (1976). See generally Volgyes, *The Investigation, Prosecution, and Prevention of Computer Crime: A State-of-the-Art Review,* 2 Computer LJ 385, 396-97 (1980) (lists of federal criminal code sections possibly applicable to computer-related abuses) and *White-Collar Crime: A Survey of Law,* 18 Am Crim L Rev 165, 379-80 (1980) (partial listing of applicable sections of federal criminal code). Computer crime may also be prosecuted under the Electronic Funds Transfer Act. 15 USC §1693 *et seq.*

[82] "All forty of the statutes were written to combat abuses other than computer crimes and, as such, Federal prosecutors have been handicapped because they have had to

Because interstate wires are frequently used in the movement of computer impulses, the federal wire fraud statute is available for the prosecution of computer crimes.[83] In one case the Third Circuit Court of Appeals upheld the conviction of two defendants on wire fraud charges stemming from the defendant's scheme to defraud Trans World Airlines of receipts from passengers who paid cash for one-way tickets.[84] The court had to read the wire fraud statute broadly in holding that the interstate wire impulses used to imprint the tickets were *essential* in order to execute the fraudulent scheme.[85]

In *United States v Computer Services Corp,* a different view was taken of the use of interstate wires.[86] A federal official allegedly bribed a contracting officer to obtain a federal contract, and then overbilled the government for computer software. The court dropped the wire fraud charge, holding that no wire fraud had been committed (even though interstate wires were used to provide Computer Science Corp.'s computer service) because there was no allegation that any false representations had been communicated over the interstate wires.[87]

The federal mail fraud statute has also been used to prosecute computer-related crimes.[88] In *United States v Kelly,* the defendants, who had used their

---

construct their cases on laws that did not envision the technical aspects of computer crime." Hearings, *supra* note 81, at 11 (statement of Sen Abraham Ribcoff). See also Roddy, *The Federal Computer Systems Protection Act,* 7 Rut J Computers, Tech & L 343, 352 (1980).

[83] 18 USC §1343. Under 18 USC §1343 any scheme to defraud or obtain money or property by fraudulent pretenses through the use of wire, radio, or television communications which cross state lines is a violation of this federal law. Thus, the use of remote computer terminals connected with CPUs via telephone lines would be within the meaning of this statute.

[84] United States v Giovengo, 637 F2d 941, 942 (3d Cir 1980).

[85] *Id* 945. The court concluded that:

Use of interstate wires was integral to [the defendant's] scheme. . . . Authorization for the printing of TWA airline tickets comes from Kansas City, and communications between the airport terminal . . . and the Kansas City computer which coordinates sales are carried over interstate wires. Without access to interstate transmissions, [the defendants] would have had no tickets to sell to TWA customers. . . . The use of interstate communications was thus "incident to an essential part of the scheme." Pereira v United States, 347 US at 8. We conclude that Paladino's use of interstate wires was "for the purpose of executing" the fraudulent scheme he devised with Giovengo.

[86] United States v Computer Ser Corp, 511 F Supp 1125 (ED Va 1981).

[87] *Id* 1135. The court stated that:

[T]he only involvement of the interstate wires in this case was the use of the wires to provide this service. There is no allegation that the service was in any way deficient or fraudulent. None of the false representations are alleged to have been communicated over the interstate wires. For this additional reason, therefore, Section 1343 is inapplicable.

[88] 18 USC §1341. Under 18 USC §1341 the essential elements of mail fraud are a scheme to defraud, use of the mails for the purpose of executing the schemes, and intent to defraud. See Volgyes, *supra* note 81, at 396. The mail fraud statute has been used to prosecute computer felons who copied programs, or acquired information or other assets controlled by a computer via the mails.

employer's computer facilities without authorization for the development of a private business venture, were found guilty of mail fraud for furthering their fraudulent scheme by mailing certain promotional materials.[89]

Computer Sciences Corp limited convictions for computer-related mail fraud. The defendants, in addition to wire fraud, had been charged with violating both the mail fraud statute and the false claims statute.[90] The defendant's submission of false claims to the government for computer services was accomplished by sending false invoices through the mail. The court, in a decision which may have serious ramifications for computer crime prosecutions, held that when an alleged offense violates more than one statute, a prosecutor *should* charge the defendant with the more specific statute.[91]

The use of §641 of the federal criminal code[92] in computer-related cases is dependent on how a judge or court interprets *things of value* and *property*.[93] Several federal courts have recently broadened their definitions of things of value, in order to facilitate convictions of computer-related crimes.[94] In *United*

---

[89] United States v Kelly, 507 F Supp 495, 499 (ED Pa 1981). The court held that the defendants, by their actions, had defrauded the employer of their "loyal and faithful services as employees."

[90] Computer Services Corp, 511 F Supp 1125 (ED Va 1981); 18 USC §287.

[91] *Id* 1135. The court stated that:

> Anytime a computer company is providing services to the government and that company is alleged to have submitted false claims regarding that service, wire fraud, under the theory the prosecutors have followed in this case, *could* be charged. Still, the false claims statute is *the more particularized* statute under which the claims *should* be brought. (emphasis added)

[92] 18 USC §641. 18 USC §641 prohibits the embezzlement, theft, unauthorized conversion, sale, or dispostion of federal property—whether it be from government agencies or corporations in which the federal government has a proprietary interest. The statute does not specifically indicate whether computer data is property within its purview.

The statute does state that any person who sells without authority any "records ... or thing of value" of the United States shall be guilty of a crime. Under this language, computer data could gain legal protection if the phrase *thing of value* were construed to include tangible as well as intangible property. There appears to be no clear-cut definition among the various circuits as to what is meant by thing of value. For a list of cases addressing this point see Survey, *White Collar Crime: Computer Crime*, Am Crim L Rev 370, 375 nn 1761-1768 (1980).

§641 also raises the question whether the unprivileged copying of computer data or a computer program constitutes a conversion for purposes of the statute. The issue has not been resolved by the courts. In United States v Hubbard, the theft of government information was held to violate §641 because tangible copies of such information are government property. But the court declined to reach the issue of whether the unprivileged copying of computer data constituted a conversion with the statute. The court also intimated that if §641 did encompass this type conversion, serious first amendment issues would be raised.

[93] See Roddy, *supra* note 82, at 356.

[94] *See, e.g.*, United States v Girard, 601 F2d 69 (2d Cir), *cert denied*, 444 US 871 (1979), where the Second Circuit found violations of §641 in the unauthorized sale of computerized Drug Enforcement Administration files. The court expressly defined *things of*

States v Sampson, a federal district court, in denying the defendants' motion to dismiss a §641 indictment, rejected the argument that computer time and storage capacity were "mere philosophical concepts as distinguished from interests capable of being construed as property."[95]

Other sections of the federal criminal code which are applicable to computer-related crimes include provisions for dealing with banking abuses,[96] statutes forbidding malicious destruction or damage to federal government property,[97] statutes forbidding disclosure of confidential information,[98] and statutes dealing with the interstate transportation of stolen goods and money.[99] Another potentially valuable prosecutorial tool is found in the recently-enacted legislation dealing with electronic funds transfer systems.[100]

---

value to include *intangibles* such as the contents of a computer program, and *records* to include computer printouts. 601 F2d at 71. See Note, *Selling DEA Computer-stored Data was Theft under 18 USC 641,* 22 Crim L Rep 2478 (1978). United States v Truong Dinh Hung, 629 F2d 908, 924 (4th Cir 1980) (thing of value in some §641 cases encompasses unauthorized disclosure of government information); and United States v May, 625 F2d 186, 191-92 (8th Cir 1980) (intangible flight time considered thing of value).

Many state statutes define "res of larceny" as a thing of value. For a comprehensive list see Gemignani, *Computer Crime: The Law in '80,* 13 Ind L Rev 681, 693 n52 (1980).

[95] United States v Sampson, 6 Computer L Serv Rep 879 (ND Cal 1978). The court stated that the utilization of computer time was inseparable from the physical identity of the computer itself. *Id* at 880. The proposed Federal Computer Systems Protection Act of 1979 stated that *property* means "anything of value, and includes tangible and intangible personal property, information in the form of electronically processed, produced or stored data." See Krieger, *Current and Proposed Computer Crime Legislation,* 2 Computer LJ 721, 726 (1980) (citing text of Act).

[96] *See* 18 USC §656 (theft, embezzlement or misapplication of funds by bank officer or employee). *See also* 18 USC §657 (misuse of funds by lending, credit and insurance institutions).

[97] *See* 18 USC §1361 (willfully injuring or committing any depredation against any property of the United States).

[98] *See* 18 USC §1905 (proscribes disclosure of confidential information by an officer or employee of the United State in course of employment or official duties).

[99] 18 USC §§2314, 2315 makes it a felony to transport stolen goods, securities, fraudulent state tax stamps, articles used in counterfeiting, or property or money worth $5000 across state lines. The issue created by these provisions is whether the transportation of stolen copies of computer programs across state lines or the interstate transmission of electronic signals will trigger this statute. In United States v Lester, 282 F2d 750 (3d Cir 1960) photostatic copies were deemed property within the meaning of §2314.

[100] EFT is the transfer of data relating to financial transactions over a series of communications networks. It starts with the input at the point of sale, and terminates in computerized bookkeeping at a bank miles away. EFT represents the movement of funds from the account of the buyer to that of the seller, or from that of an employer to that of an employee. *See Expert Witness Manual; Federal Computer Systems Protection Act: Hearings on S240, Senate Comm on the Judiciary, Subcomm on Criminal Justice,* 96th Cong, 2d Sess, 1-11 (1980).

Criminal Activity Within Electronic Funds Transfer Systems

Computers already allow for the withdrawal and deposit of money in savings or demand accounts, and technology exists for even greater computerization of these and other more intricate transactions.

The term *electronic fund transfer* is defined by the Federal Electronic Funds Transfer Act (EFT Act),[101] (a title under the Consumer Credit Protection Act 15 USC §1601 *et seq*) as "any transfer of funds, other than a transaction . . . which is initiated through an electronic terminal, telephonic instrument, or computer . . . [to] authorize a financial institution to debit or credit an account."[102] The EFT Act sets forth the rights and liabilities of all participants in EFTs, and provides consumer safeguards when funds are transferred.[103]

The House Committee on Banking, Housing and Urban Affairs reported that the cost savings and convenience of EFT systems to consumers and financial institutions are substantial.

> Direct deposit of payroll or government benefits gives the consumer quicker access to his money . . ., and eliminates the danger of theft or delay in the mails. . . . In short EFT's can provide greater convenience, lower cost, increased security, and more efficient services.[104]

EFT systems offer the potential for reducing the number of common-law crimes such as robbery, burglary, and larceny.[105] Traditionally vulnerable people such as the elderly and the disabled are less likely targets in a cashless EFT system. As the common-law felon realizes that people no longer will use the mails to transport money, keep money in their homes, or keep money on their persons, he or she is less likely to commit robbery, burglary and larceny.[106]

Cashless EFT systems will at the same time increase opportunities for computer-related crimes.[107] With the disappearance of paper audit trails, computer

---

[101] 15 USC §1693.

[102] 15 USC §9693(a)(6).

[103] 15 USC §1693(a)(6).

[104] S Rep No 915, 95th Cong, 2d Sess *reprinted in* US Code Cong & Ad News, 9403-04. Today it costs about 30 cents to process a check, whereas the EFTS would reduce the cost to about six cents. Obviously, the EFTS will also substantially reduce the amount of paper work required by all concerned.

[105] A. Bequai, Computer Crime 182 (1978).

[106] *Id* 182-83.

[107] *Id* 181. See Bequai, *The Spreading Danger of Computer Crime*, Bus Wk, Apr 20, 1981, at 89 ("The new risks are nowhere more evident or potentially devastating than in the banking industry's electronic fund transfer systems (EFTS).") Roddy, *The Federal Computer Systems Protection Act*, 7 Rutgers J Computers, Tech & L 343, 351 (1980) ("the technology which makes the system possible also makes it vulnerable to attack"); Sokolik, *Computer Crime—The Need for Deterrent Legislation*, 2 Computer LJ 353, 357 (1980) (EFT exposes more of general population to the impact of computer technology, and to the risk of computer crime). See generally *White Collar Crime Conference: Dealing with*

felons can make increasing use of the defense that the misdeed was caused by computer error and was not intentional. Present law enforcement and prosecutorial systems are ill-equipped to handle the expected increase in EFT crimes. Without legislation and sophisticated investigative techniques, convictions for EFT system abuses will be much less likely.

In response to the perceived vulnerability of EFT systems to computer fraud, Congress included a criminal provision in the EFT Act.[108] Section 1693(n) of the EFT Act imposes criminal penalties for deliberate violations, and for fraudulent use of a debit instrument (defined as the device which triggers a system's computerized mechanism, e.g., an EFT card)[109] to gain money, goods, services, or anything else of value. While computer abuses of an EFT system will likely fall within the proscription of §1693n(c) the statute does not address the evidentiary problems in trying EFT systems criminals. Because this new EFT criminal provision is relatively untested, its effectiveness in combating and in deterring computer crime remains to be seen.

§7.11 —Prosecution Under State Statutes

Only a handful of states have passed legislation which specifically addresses computer crime.[110] In the majority of states the prosecution of computer-related crimes has relied primarily on laws that deal with offenses involving

---

EFT's, Sec Mgmt, Feb 1978 at 32; *Federal Reserve Moves to Guard EFTS*, Sec Mgmt, Aug 1978, at 16.

[108] 15 USC §1653(n)(b) (1-3) proscribes the illegal use of any "counterfeit, fictitious, altered, forged, lost, stolen or fraudently obtained debit instrument." §1693n(b) is similar to 18 USC §641, in that it proscribes the knowing receipt, concealment, use, or transportation of money, goods, services, or "anything else of value" worth $1,000 or more.

[109] 15 USC §1693(n)(c) ("card, code, or other device, other than a check, draft, or similar paper instrument, by the use of which a person may initiate an electronic fund transfer"). See generally Northrup, *Bank Cards vs the Underworld*, Banking, May, 1975, at 66.

[110] Several states have passed legislation dealing directly with computers and computer crime. Colorado is one of the states which has enacted legislation specifically addressing computer crime. The Colorado Computer Crime Law defines *property* as "including but not limited to, financial instruments, information, including electronically produced data, and complete software and programs in either machine or human readable form, and any other tangible or intangible item of value." Colo Rev Stat §§18-5.5-101, -102. Other states which have enacted similar legislation as of late 1982 include Arizona, California, Florida, Illinois, Michigan, New Mexico, North Carolina, Rhode Island, Utah, and Virginia. Hawaii, Maryland, Massachusetts, Minnesota, Missouri, New Jersey, Pennsylvania, South Dakota, and Tennessee all have proposed computer crime legislation. Sokolik, *Computer Crime—The Need for Deterrent Legislation*, 2 Computer LJ 353, 375 (1980). See generally Kreiger, *Current and Proposed Computer Crime Legislation*, 2 Computer LJ 721, 745-72 (1980) (text of existing and proposed legislation).

property or habitation and occupancy,[111] *shoehorning* the criminal act into such statutory or common law crimes as larceny, burglary, embezzlement, false pretenses, extortion, malicious mischief, forgery, receipt of stolen property, and even arson.[112] Where no specific computer crime statute exists, prosecutors are forced to squeeze computer offenses into a less than logical criminal charge. By focusing on related criminal offenses, however, even if they do not exactly cover the act committed, the prosecutor has a greater chance of delivering a verdict of guilty. Even in those state jurisdictions which have addressed the problem of computer crime by enacting computer crime statutes, these new laws have often been saddled with the elements of common law crimes.[113]

Many of the recently-enacted computer crime statutes have expanded the traditional definitions of property to include the intangible items of value that comprise much of computer technology, e.g., computer programs.[114] Valuation of stolen computer programs and data, which determines whether the crime is a misdemeanor or a felony, may be more realistically approached under these new statutes. Even with these specialized statutes, however, there are still gaps through which the computer felon may escape prosecution.

It appears that the majority of states will continue to rely on traditional criminal laws to prosecute computer crimes. In those states which hesitate or refuse to adapt to the peculiar procedural and substantive problems associated with computer abuses, effective prosecution will remain elusive.

The inadequacy of both state and federal laws in dealing with computer crime is illustrated by the case of *United States v Seidlitz*.[115] The defendant illegally used a terminal in one state (Virginia) to gain access to a computer system in another state (Maryland) in order to acquire certain computer data. The defendant was charged with interstate transportation of stolen property. Maryland applied a common law test of tangibility to determine what constituted property. Because electronic impulses were deemed not to be property within the meaning of the Maryland statute, the defendant was acquitted of this charge. The defendant was, however, convicted of interstate wire fraud—a federal offense. If the defendant had gained access to the Maryland computer from a phone within the state of Maryland, he would have been acquitted of all charges.

---

[111] A. Bequai, Computer Crime 25 (1978); Sokolik, *supra* note 110, at 375.

[112] A Bequai, *supra* note 111, at 29-35.

[113] Sokolik, *supra* note 110, at 376.

[114] *Id.*

[115] In United States v Seidlitz, 589 F2d 152 (4th Cir. 1978), *cert denied*, 441 US 922 (1979) the Fourth Circuit let stand a ruling by the federal district court that transmission over telephone lines of electronic signals from a CPU to a remote terminal at the defendant's office did not violate §2314. One study has indicated that if this interpretation of §2314 prevails, the statute "may apply only to cases in which securities, money, or other tangible property obtained through the criminal use of a computer are physically transported between states." Survey, *White Collar Crime: Computer Crime*, 18 Am Crim L Rev 370, 377 (1980).

Defenses

Many computer-related prosecutions are based on statutes not restricted to computers and their use. Most defenses, in turn, focus on the statutory requisites defining the commission of an offense, with defendants arguing that their actions are outside the scope of a particular statute.[116]

§7.12 Trial and Evidence Difficulties in Prosecuting Computer Crime

If an investigation produces sufficient evidence of illegal computer conduct, criminal charges will be issued against the perpetrator by the prosecutor's office. But the prosecutor's problems do not end with the investigative and charging process. The trial of a defendant charged with a computer crime poses difficult substantive and procedural hurdles for the prosecution.

Educating Judges and Prosecutors

As in any complex litigation, the major problem in successfully prosecuting a computer crime is acquainting the necessary parties with the intricacies of the issues involved. The complexity of computer technology is coupled with the general public's unfamiliarity with criminal procedures and legal standards. Given the general public's ignorance about computers and how they work, in any computer-related criminal prosecution there is the problem of conveying to a lay jury the legal significance of the perpetrator's acts. Juries are more familiar with crimes against the person, and with property crimes involving more familiar articles of property.

The methods used by the computer criminal will generally require explanation, in simplified terms, as to what kind of crime was committed. Some computer crimes may be simple, such as embezzlement or software theft. The *methods* used by a computer criminal, however, may be beyond the understanding of the judge and jury, and even in some instances, the prosecutor. In other cases, explaining exactly *what* was stolen may prove a challenge for the prosecutor. The prosecutor, therefore, may have to not only teach the language of computers to the judge and jury, but also basic concepts about computers and their operation.

When a prosecutor is faced with educating a judge and a jury, it is best to present at trial only that technology necessary to prosecute the case at hand. Whenever possible, common points of reference should be used to communicate the issues, and the use of analogies to commonplace objects and experiences when speaking of computer technology will keep the judge and the jury

---

[116] See Roddy, *The Federal Computer Systems Protection Act,* 7 Rutgers J Computers, Tech & L 343, 356-57 (1980) ("when a statute is not specifically applicable, the decision to prosecute may be abrogated, when not abrogated, the court may feel constrained to find that the criminal activity is not within the reach of law.").

better attuned to the central issues of the case.[117] The prosecutor should not overwhelm the judge and the jury with computer jargon, although it is essential that the words used to explain the applicable computer technology are as accurate and technically correct as possible.[118] Because computers are not capable of committing crimes on their own, strict distinction should be made and maintained between computers as machines that perform tasks as programmed, and the humans who operate them. Computer errors are the product of human miscalculation or simple mistakes, and computers should not be presented to the trier of fact (either the judge or the jury) as suspect characters. Any attempt to do so (whether by the prosecutor or by defense counsel) should be understood as a lack of technical understanding on the part of the speaker.

Special Problems of Computer Evidence

The nature and use of computerized or computer-generated evidence presents a unique set of problems to the investigators and prosecutors of computer crimes.[119] In computer crimes, unlike traditional crimes, there is rarely a paper trail to lead the investigator to the perpetrator of the crime. In some cases the identity of the criminal must be discerned indirectly through the methods used to commit the crime. If computer crime investigators are not properly trained, they may not understand where to begin to look for clues. Even where the list of possible suspects has already been narrowed by the victim, it may still be necessary for the victim to assist the investigator in uncovering the culprit. When drafting a search warrant, it is difficult to determine beforehand where or in what form evidence of the crime might be found. In the case of crimes thought to have been committed from remote locations (linked telephonically to the main computer), it may be difficult for investigators to determine exactly what to look for to support the prosecution's case. The lack of paper trails in computer-related crimes makes it difficult to know what to list on a search warrant. Search and seizure laws, which require a specific description of the evidence sought, do not permit investigators to rifle through all the computer-related materials which may be present in the suspect's home or office. The law enforcement officers sent to collect computer-related evidence may be unfamiliar with computer technology, in which case the prosecutor may have to educate searchers as to exactly what they are looking for.

Prosecutors may not be able to compile the evidence needed for an indict-

---

[117] For a brief discussion of analogies between computers and computer-related equipment that can be used for technical presentations see SRI International, Computer Crime: Criminal Justice Resource Manual 124 (1979).

[118] *Id* 125-27.

[119] See generally Abelle, *Evidentiary Problems Relevant to Checks and Computers*, 5 Rutgers J Computers, Tech & L 323 (1976) (discussion of evidentiary problems); Comment, *A Reconsideration of the Admissibility of Computer-Generated Evidence*, 126 U Pa L Rev 425 (1977) (discussion of issues surrounding admissibility of computerized records).

ment.[120] For example, evidence may consist of components of an operational computer system, in which case it may not be possible to gather the needed evidence without shutting down a business' operations.[121] Prosecutors may not be able to identify precisely the component to be seized without an inordinate amount of description.[122]

Once the evidence is validly seized, law enforcement officials must take great care in order to preclude any problems that arise in establishing a chain of custody, and in preserving evidence which could be damaged by improper handling.[123] It is critical that the computer evidence be properly identified. Conventional methods of identifying evidence may be harmful to the information the evidence contains. For example, the pressure of a ballpoint pen on the label of a floppy disk may destroy the information it contains. A chain of custody must be carefully maintained in that one reel of magnetic tape may look exactly like any other reel of tape. Magnetic evidence must be stored at a temperature where it will not be harmed, and well away from substances or machinery that emit magnetic fields which can harm the stored information. Magnetic tape should never be touched, bent, or creased. Where the evidence consists of paper (e.g., paper tapes, punch cards, printouts, etc.), precautionary measures need to be taken to ensure that the evidence is neither bent nor torn, and that edges are not knicked. Paper clips and rubber bands should not be used, and punched cards should be stored in their proper sequence and kept in such a manner as to ensure that the cards do not become warped. Where continuous forms are used, they should not be separated because the information contained on the forms may be significant only in the order in which it appears. When it becomes necessary to seize electronic machinery it is best to consult the manufacturer as to its proper storage and care.[124]

A possible pitfall in computer crime investigation is that the investigation may be limited to the computer itself, and the environs of the computer may be neglected. Not all evidence of computer-related crime is in the form of computer hardware and paper inputs and outputs. In some cases, evidence may be found in log books that record usage of the computer equipment, or in the telephone bills of perpetrators who have made long distance telephone calls to commit their crimes.

---

[120] See Rothman, *Computer Crime, The Menace Grows,* D&B Rep, July-Aug 1981, at 7 (quoting computer security consultant R. Jacobson) (company that suffered 34 computer crimes in 1980 was able to proscute only three; others not prosecuted due to lack of evidence needed for indictment).

[121] See Law Enforcement Assistance Administration, US Dept of Justice, The Investigation of Computer Crime 19 (1980).

[122] *Id* at 21.

[123] See Bureau of Justice Statistics, US Dept of Justice, Expert Witness Manual: Use of Outside Experts in Computer Related Crime Case 1-10 (1980).

[124] For a more detailed list of special care needed for computer evidence see SRI International, *supra* note 117, at 111-12.

§7.13 —Admission of Computer-Related Evidence Under the Current Rules of Evidence

Once computer evidence is collected and properly cared for, the usual criminal standards for courtroom presentation—authenticity, accuracy, admissibility, and chain of custody—are applicable. The litigator who attempts to introduce computer-related evidence faces the same procedural and evidentiary obstacles as presented by other kinds of evidence. The general unfamiliarity of the trier of fact with computer technology may require that the evidence be presented with an explanation of relevant computer technology in the simplest and most quickly understandable terms to avoid confusion and mistake as to why and on what basis the evidence is being presented.

The major obstacles to the admission of computer-generated evidence are the hearsay rule,[125] the best evidence rule,[126] and the procedural problems associated with laying the proper foundation for authentication.[127]

Hearsay has been defined as an out of court statement (or conduct) offered in court to prove the truth of the matter asserted in that statement.[128] Since the commission of a computer crime rarely involves an eyewitness account, the prosecution often must rely on computer records or printouts to prove that a computer crime was even committed, and that the defendant committed the crime. When internal documentation of unauthorized or illegal transactions is offered at trial as proof of the crime, the hearsay rule may be invoked by the defendant(s). A computer printout is considered an out-of-court statement, and when it is offered in court for the truth of what it asserts, it is deemed to be hearsay. The admissibility of a computer printout or record, therefore, will depend on whether it fits under any of the exceptions to the hearsay rule.[129]

In the majority of states and at the federal level, the most commonly-used exception under which computer-generated evidence may be admitted at trial is the business records exception, which allows a prosecutor to enter into evidence "a data compilation, in any form."[130] A prosecutor must lay a proper

---

[125] McCormick's Handbook of the Law of Evidence §246 (E Cleary ed, 2d ed 1972) ("Hearsay evidence is testimony in court, or written evidence, of a statement made out of court, the statement being offered as an assertion to show the truth of matters asserted therein, and this testing for its value upon the credibility of the out-of-court asserter.").

[126] Id §229 ("The only actual rule that the 'best evidence' phrase denotes today is the rule requiring the production of the original writing.").

[127] Id §543 (authenticity, although difficult to define, means in the most limited sense proof of authorship or other connection with writings; foundation consists of proving such connection). See Interview with John P. Bellassai, Director of Criminal Justice Division, Koba Assoc, Washington DC 50 (June 4, 1981) at 50 (discussing the existence of and exceptions to these obstacles) [hereinafter cited as Koba Assocs].

[128] McCormick's Handbook, *supra* note 125, at §246. See also Fed R Evid 801.

[129] Fed R Evid 803 (1-24). For a complete analysis of all exceptions, see S. Saltzburg, Federal Rules of Evidence Manual (2d ed 1977).

[130] Fed R Evid 803(6). See Rosenberg v Collins, 624 F2d 659, 665 (5th Cir 1980) (computerized business records admissible under Rule 803(6) like any other record of

foundation for the authentication of computer records, which may require having a financial officer or a general manager testify as to their responsibility for maintaining company records and the procedure for that maintenance.[131] The prosecutor faces a more difficult problem in showing that the records are accurate and reliable.[132]

A majority of states have adopted the Uniform Business Records as Evidence Act, while some 20 states have retained the common-law business records exception to the hearsay rule entitled the *shop-book* rule.[133] The business records exception and the shop-book rule require:

1. That the records must have been made routinely during the regular course of business

2. That the entry must have been made contemporaneously or within a reasonable time of the transaction recorded

3. That the entry was made by a person who is unavailable as a witness

4. That the person who entered the record must have personal knowledge of the event

5. That the person had no motive to misrepresent or misstate the facts.[134]

The rationale of the business records exception is that the records are reliable and necessary for the conduct of business. The element of reliability is supplied by the systematic checking used in creating the record, by regularity and continuity in the recordkeeping (which produce habits of precision), and by the duty to make an accurate record as part of a continuing job or occupation.[135] In those 20 states which have retained the shop-book rule, the proponent of the admission of computer-generated evidence faces a difficult task because computerized evidence is often not made contemporaneously with, or within a reasonable time of, the recorded event.[136] Furthermore, "many computer entries are not made in the routine of one's regular course of business."[137]

---

regularly conducted activity). Fed R Evid 803(8) includes "Records, reports, statements, or data compilations, in any form, of public offices or agencies."

[131] See Koba Assoc, *supra* note 127, at 65 (officers must testify that it was company practice to make entries into computer within reasonable time of transaction).

[132] *See* United States v Russo, 480 F2d 1228, 1239-40 (6th Cir 1973) (evidence admissible where procedures for testing accuracy and reliability of information fed into computer detailed at length by witnesses).

[133] McCormick's Handbook, *supra* note 125, at §305.

[134] A Bequai, Computer Crime 119 (1978).

[135] McCormick's Handbook, *supra* note 125, at §§281, 286-287.

[136] See A. Bequai, *supra* note 134, at 119.

[137] A large business conglomerate with offices and subsidiaries in many states and countries may not computerize its data for long periods of time. The entries in the computer system are certainly not made in the regular course of (doing) business. In many instances, the leader sheets on which the entries are routinely made are usually destroyed once the data are fed into the computers. *Id.*

Some state laws have compounded evidentiary problems by requiring that the party who made the computer entry have personal knowledge of the recorded event. The personal knowledge requirement is often attacked as being impractical on the one hand, and unrealistic on the other. One critic of the personal knowledge requirement has stated that:

> Few, if any, of those who are employed in the computer center have knowledge of a personal nature of the events they record or enter into the computer banks. The theory of computer security provides for just the opposite situation. This doctrine requires that no middle- or low-echelon personnel have knowledge of the entire process. The doctrine further requires that only those on a need-to-know basis should have access to the data. . . . Too few [personnel] will have sufficient access to acquire the base minimum requisites to meet the criteria of personal knowledge.[138]

These computer security measures can prove to be a double-edged sword. If employees and other personnel of a computerized firm play no role in computer security procedures, only top management will have personal knowledge of all the corporate events recorded somewhere in the company's computer system. This could prove problematic since top management itself has the capability of intentionally falsifying or otherwise misusing computer data for their own purposes, and when top management personnel are suspected of having committed computer crimes, computer-generated evidence would probably be considered as unreliable.[139] At the federal level much of the problem of requiring personal knowledge before a business record can be admitted into evidence has been overcome. Under Rule 803(6) of the Federal Rules of Evidence, lack of personal knowledge by the maker of business entries may not be used to affect the *admissibility* of business records, but only the *weight or credibility* of the records.[140]

Other hearsay exceptions, all of which have been adopted by the federal courts through the Federal Rules of Evidence, but not necessarily by every state, include: medical records;[141] recorded recollections;[142] public records and reports;[143] records of vital statistics;[144] market reports and commercial

---

[138] *Id* 120.

[139] The question of the reliability of computer-generated evidence occurs more frequently in the case of larger firms than in smaller enterprises because the business records kept by smaller businesses, generally speaking, are not as detailed as those kept by the larger firms with their complex computer systems. *Id* 120-21.

[140] Fed R Evid 803(6).

[141] *Id* 803(4). See also 6 Wigmore, Evidence §1707.

[142] Fed R Evid 803(5).

[143] *Id* 803(8).

[144] *Id* 803(9).

publications;[145] learned treatises;[146] and declarations against interest.[147] An admission by a party is not considered hearsay under the federal rules, although in many states it is.[148]

Hospitals and medical clinics alike are increasingly using computers to aid in processing their paper work. The admissibility requirements for medical records are similar to the requirements for business records. The party making the entry must testify that the records were made in the regular course of business, i.e., hospital operations, and that it was the routine of the hospital to make those entries. Thus, until new laws are passed or new technology is developed, medical records face the same obstacles to their admission into evidence as do business records, i.e., the input of the computer record may not have been contemporaneous with the event, and the printout of the medical reports may not have been prepared in the normal course of business.[149] It would appear, though, that as long as a proper foundation was laid and the evidence was reliable, medically-related evidence in the form of computer printouts would be admissible under this exception. Note, however, that the patient-client privilege may act as a bar to disclosure, precluding the availability of certain information, even if nonhearsay, for presentation at trial.[150]

The admissibility of computer-generated evidence under the public records and records of vital statistics exceptions is as yet unreported. As state and federal governmental bodies become increasingly dependent on computers to run their operations, requests for admitting this type of evidence under these exceptions will undoubtedly arise.[151] Computerized evidence in the form of market publications, journals, books, and published treatises might be admissible under the learned treatises and market reports and commercial publications exceptions to the hearsay rule, depending on a particular jurisdiction's definition of treatise.[152] The declarations against interest exception would not appear directly applicable to computer-generated evidence. A declaration by one of the parties involved in the litigation that the party did in fact falsify the data, or otherwise misuse a computer, would be a declaration against interest and admissible against the declarant.[153]

---

[145] *Id* 803(17).

[146] *Id* 803(18).

[147] *Id* 804(b)(3).

[148] *Id* 801(d)(2).

[149] See A. Bequai, *supra* note 134, at 107-08.

[150] *Id.* See also 8 Wigmore, Evidence §§2380-2391.

[151] The basis of this rule is in the belief that "public officials, in the performance of their daily tasks, will note daily events in their work, and the likelihood that they will leave information out is remote; the assumption is that public officials will perform their duties properly." A. Bequai, *supra* note 134, at 106.

[152] *Id* 105-06. See also Saltzburg, *supra* note 129, at 552; R. Hunter, Federal Trial Handbook 596 (1974); 6 Wigmore, Evidence §1704.

[153] A. Bequai, *supra* note 134, at 112. The declaration would be against the declarant's pecuniary or proprietary interest, and thus, there is little reason to doubt the authenticity of the declaration. See, *e.g.*, Donnelly v United States, 228 US 243 (1913).

Overcoming the hearsay hurdle does not automatically make the evidence admissible. In many state jurisdictions the party seeking the admission of a computer printout must also establish that the printout is the best evidence available, i.e., the original document. At common law it was believed that the *best evidence rule* afforded substantial guarantees against inaccuracies and fraud by its insistence upon the production of original documents. Generally, the best evidence rule states that if the contents of a writing are in issue, an original writing must be produced unless a valid justification for its unavailability is presented to the court.[154] The rule applies only when secondary evidence is offered to prove the contents of an original writing.[155] If a computer printout were offered not to prove the contents of what it stated, or what some other original document stated, but to prove only that an event took place, then the best evidence rule is inapplicable and would not prevent the admission of the printout.

The Federal Rules of Evidence provide several exceptions to the best evidence rule. If the party offering the computer printout can show that the original document is unavailable, whether it be lost or destroyed, economically inaccessible, or judicially unobtainable, then a copy will be admitted in lieu of the original.[156] If the unavailability of the original was due to acts constituting bad faith by the offering party, the copy cannot be admitted. The contents of an official record can be proven through the admission of a certified copy of the record itself.[157] Summaries of voluminous documents can also be admitted into evidence if the documents individually would be admissible, and if the opposing party has had the opportunity to inspect them.[158]

Some states have attempted to deal with the best evidence rule and the problem of reproductions of original information stored on tape or disk, and printouts made from stored information, by adopting the Uniform Photographic Copies of Business and Public Records Act. Section 1 of this Act provides, in part, that:

> If any business, institution, member of a profession or calling, or any department or agency of government, in the regular course of business or activity has kept or recorded any memorandum, writing, entry, print, representation or combination thereof, of any act, transaction, occurrence or event, and in the regular course of business has caused any or all of the same to be recorded, copied, or reproduced by any photograph-

---

[154] Fed R Evid 1006.

[155] "For example, if X denies having entered into a written agrement with Y, the latter may introduce secondary evidence as to the context of the agreement without producing the original writing. The issue is not the contents itself but rather whether X and Y had entered into an agreement." A. Bequai, *supra* note 134, at 137.

[156] Fed R Evid 1004. See also A. Bequai, *supra* note 134, at 138.

[157] Fed R Evid 1005.

[158] *Id* 1006. This Rule of Evidence provides that where the original writings, recordings, or photographs are so voluminous that it would be impractical to produce them in court, a summary may be allowed.

ic, photostatic, microfilm, microcard, . . . or other process which accurately produces or forms a durable medium for so reproducing the original, the original may be destroyed in the regular course of business . . . unless its preservation is required by law. Such reproduction, when satisfactorily identified, is . . . admissible in evidence. . . .[159]

The Federal Rules of Evidence have taken the most liberal approach to the best evidence rule. Although Rule 1002 requires an original writing, Rule 1001 defines writing as "matters, words, or numbers, or their equivalent, set down by handwriting, typewriting, printing, photostating, photographing, magnetic impulse, mechanical or electronic recording, or other form of data compilation."[160] Under Rule 1003, duplicates are admissible as long as they are authentic, and would not impose an unfair burden upon the opposing party.[161] It does not appear, therefore, that the hearsay and best evidence rule pose any greater obstacles to the admission of computer evidence than noncomputerized evidence has traditionally faced.[162]

Once the proffering party has laid a proper foundation, the opposing party bears the burden of showing that the proffered computer evidence (e.g., printouts) are inaccurate or unreliable. The greatest obstacle facing prosecutors (and defense attorneys) who seek to admit computer-produced evidence is the task of establishing the reliability of the evidence. Logically this would also seem to require proof that the entire computer system is or was reliable. In the face of evidence that a computer system has repeatedly broken down or regularly makes errors, a judge is likely to rule that the computer-generated evidence is unreliable. This type of information is generally kept under lock and key by the owners and lessees of computers. Thus, should the reliability issue surface under these circumstances, the proponent for the admission of the computer evidence is likely to face an almost insurmountable obstacle in obtaining copies of the information through discovery, and in having the computer evidence admitted at trial. Relatively few computer crime cases that have gone through a trial process and these provide little insight into how the reliability question will be handled by the courts.

---

[159] *Reprinted in* A. Bequai, *supra* note 134, at 139. The federal counterpart governing photographic copies of records maintained in the regular course of business is codified at 28 USC §1732. This statue, the Federal Business Records Act, provides that "[R]eproduction[s], when satisfactorily identified, . . . [are] as admissible in evidence as the original itself . . . whether the original is in existence or not. . . ." *See* United States v Fendley, 522 F2d 181, 184 (5th Cir 1975) (quoting Louisville & Nashville RR v Know Homes Corp, 343 F2d 887, 896 (5th Cir 1965)) (theory underlying Act is that business records in form regularly kept by company have probability of trustworthiness).

[160] Fed R Evid 1001.

[161] *Id* 1003 provides that: "A duplicate is admissible to the same extent as an original unless (1) a genuine question is raised as to the authenticity of the original or (2) in the circumstances it would be unfair to admit the duplicate in lieu of the original."

[162] For a more in-depth discussion of the best evidence rule as it relates to computer-generated evidence, see A. Bequai, *supra* note 134, at 137-41.

§7.14   Computer Crime versus Computer Punishment

For years white-collar crimes have been misunderstood, and have gone relatively unnoticed. Whatever progress has been made in prosecuting traditional white-collar crimes has come as a result of the prodding and persistence of enforcement authorities against a reluctant judiciary. Punishment for white-collar crimes is only now beginning to fit the crime committed. Computer crimes are similarly obscure and misunderstood. Unfortunately, the increased penalties for white-collar crimes are not necessarily applied when a traditional crime such as embezzlement is committed via the computer. Penalties for computer abuse presently resemble the penalties for the typical white-collar crime of years past.

The last phase of the trial process is sentencing, where punishment is meted out to the guilty. If the imposing of sentences is to be fair to the criminal and to the public, a judge must be familiar with the technology used to commit the computer crime. The punishment meted out must be severe enough to serve as a deterrent to others who may be tempted to duplicate the computer crime elsewhere, yet not overly harsh as a result of a lack of computer familiarity on the judges part. Sentencing of white-collar felons as compared to sentencing of non white-collar felons is a stark example of unequal treatment under the law.[163] A deaf person, for example, was sentenced to one to ten years in prison by an Ohio court for stealing one bottle of beer. Several months before, a Maryland court sentenced a computer felon who stole over $100,000 to three years probation.[164] These and other examples of unequal sentencing illustrate a complete misunderstanding of computer crime, and of the enormity of the social costs of computer crime. This example is also indicative of more practical contradictions. Not only do many states lack even a modicum of consistency in their own criminal laws, but unequal sentencing of computer criminals points up inconsistent enforcement of white-collar crime laws among the states. It also shows that present legislation is not only seriously inadequate in dealing with computer crime, but can severely hinder the successful prosecution of a case involving computer crime. Clearly, there must be changes.

---

[163] One commentator has stated that the sentencing of a computer felon is often a delicate decision for a judge because in the majority of cases the defendant has not had "any serious prior contact with the law [and is] white, middle class, gainfully employed, and well regarded in the community." Becker, *The Trial of a Computer Crime,* 2 Computer LJ 441, 453 (1980). Bequai states that:

> the likelihood of going to prison for securities fraud in the federal system is 21.5 percent, and most sentences average only 20.5 months; it is only 19.5 percent for embezzlement, the average prison sentence being only 21.3 months; for postal embezzlement (mail fraud), the likelihood of going to prison is only 19 percent, the average sentence being 11.6 months. However, the likelihood of going to prison for crime classified as the "every-day type" by the government is 47.3 percent, the average prison sentence being 50.5 months.

A. Bequai, Computer Crime 6 (1978).

[164] A. Bequai, Computer Crime 196-97 (1978).

With the law as it is, it is unlikely that the would-be computer felon will be deterred.[165] As the public becomes more cognizant of the serious nature of computer-related crime, pressure will come to bear on the state legislatures, Congress, and the courts to increase the severity of the penalties and punishments for computer crime.

§7.15   Deterrence—Security

Deterrence of computer crime can be achieved by technological and organizational means (security), by increased public awareness of the problem, and by legal sanctions that lessen the attractiveness of computer abuse.

Computers create an environment in which assets exist in the rather unique form of magnetic patterns and electronic impulses, which, at any given time, may be passing through a complex network of computer hardware and telephonic equipment or may be stored in a computer on a disk.[166]

The correlation between the commission of computer crimes and the vulnerability of computer systems has been established.[167] Technological solutions to computer crime focus on prevention of the crime. Theoretically, one method of preventing or deterring computer abuses would be to design or program a computer in such a way that a criminal intrusion would trigger the production (and preservation) of evidence of the intruder's activities. One technological computer crime prevention strategy presently being used is encryption of data as it travels over communications lines.[168]

Some companies have addressed the vulnerability issue by instituting several levels of access into the computer facility, in effect restricting access to their computer system to a few trusted personnel. But even trusted personnel are human, and have been known to manipulate computer operations to their financial advantage. Other companies, e.g., IBM, have spent millions of dollars

---

[165] Sokolik, *Computer Crime—The Need for Deterrent Legislation*, 2 Computer LJ 353, 357 (1980).

[166] Volgyes, *The Investigation, Prosecution, and Prevention of Computer Crime: A State-of-the-Art Review*, 2 Computer LJ 385, 390 (1980).

[167] Sokolik, *Computer Crime—The Need for Deterrent Legislation*, 2 Computer LJ 353, 369 (1980).

[168] A. Bequai, Computer Crime 22 (1978). See generally, *Encryption Receives Much Attention*, Sys Tech & Sci L Enforcement & Sec, Jan 1978, at 1; *Encryption Standard to Strengthen Computer Security Developed by NBS*, Crime Control Dig, Nov 20, 1976, at 6; *Encryption Standard to Strengthen Computer Security*, Sec Sys Dig, Dec 22, 1976, at 9; *New Encryption Products Available to Protect Computer Information*, Sec Letter, Dec 15, 1977 (pt 1), at 4; Hattery, *Data Encryption Hardware Gets NBS Validation*, Sys Tech & Sci L Enforcement & Sec, Nov 1977, at 1; Yasaki, *Encryption Algorithm: Key Size is the Thing*, Datamation, Mar 1976, at 164; Shaw, *Encryption Units, The Answer to Computer Crimes?*, L & Ord, Aug 1978, at 8; *NBS Data Encryption Standard Offers Certain Level of Security but is no Panacea, Conferees Say*, Sec Sys Dig, Feb 23, 1977, at 1; *Data Security Equipment to be a Billion Dollar Market Over Next Five Years*, Sec Sys Dig, Sept 13, 1978; *IBM Announces New Products to Protect Computer Information*, Sec Sys Dig, Dec 14, 1977, at 11.

in an effort to secure the design and use of their own computers.[169] Some companies have foregone the installation of security devices, either because of high costs, or because they have failed to overcome the inertia of ignorance concerning computer crime, instead taking the "it can't happen to me" attitude.

The integration of computers into the daily operations of a business requires that management be educated in the technology of the computer, and that careful and comprehensive planning should precede the purchase or development of a new computer system.[170] To secure computer systems from potential criminal abuses, computers should be programmed to guard against that abuse, and security codes should be used to prevent unauthorized access to confidential data.[171] Trusted employees should conduct a periodic review of all computer records.[172] The American Society for Industrial Security (ASIS) has proposed a number of guidelines to upgrade computer security. ASIS suggests that all computer users incorporate the following elements into their data-processing operations:

1. Separation of knowledge through division of responsibilities, job rotations, physical isolation, controlled access, and logging of stoppages and interruptions

---

[169] IBM has suggested four areas where computer users can take preventive action:
(1) rigid physical security;
(2) new identification procedures for input operators;
(3) new internal auditing procedures based upon retaining a fuller record of each computer transaction; and
(4) new cryptographic symbols to scramble information.
These and other suggested security measures are presented in Sokolik, *supra* note 167, at 370.

[170] "Planning takes on ever-increasing importance these days as the computer becomes not merely an essential element of nearly every business's financial, word-processing and other record-keeping processes, but is also linked with other parts of office systems—telephone and photo copiers, for example—to create an efficient and powerful information network."
Makower, *Business Computers: A Planning Guide,* United Mainliner, May 1981, at 113. See also McKenney & McFarlan, *The Information Archipelago—Maps and Bridges,* Harv Bus Rev, Sept-Oct 1982, at 109.

[171] A. Bequai, *supra* note 168, at 22. See generally *Wanted: Computers That Will Not Compute for Criminals,* Nation's Bus, Nov 1978, at 38; Ross, *Computer Data Security:* Reprogram the Emphasis, Sec Mgmt, Dec 1978, at 10; Davis, *Computer Controls: A Different Emphasis Preventing Errors or Fraud by Implementing Passive Controls Which Include: Documentation, Organizational Independence and Audit Trials,* 22 Nat Pub Acct 10 (1977); *Password Techniques Provide Safeguards for Computer Data, NBS Magazine Reports,* Crime Control Dig, July 25, 1977, at 8; *The Growing Threat to Computer Security: New Codes and Other Solutions are Coming, But They are Controversial,* Bus Wk, Aug 1, 1977, at 44; *Electronic Access Control Systems Have Many Applications,* 78 Off 74 (1973); Coiner, *Controlled Access System Uses Mag Cards to Restrict Entry for Tight Security,* 33 Ad Mgmt 14 (1972).

[172] Makower, *supra* note 170, at 123.

2. Written program instructions with threat monitoring and audit trails built in

3. Careful accounting of all input documents

4. Periodic changes in access codes and passwords

5. Scramblers and cryptographic applications in data transmission[173]

Although these suggestions and recommendations would go a long way towards curtailing some types of computer crime, a fail-safe security system is an unrealistic expectation. There has never been a bank that could not be robbed, and it is doubtful that there will ever be a computer system which cannot be infiltrated. Consideration must consequently be given to other forms of prevention.

Most computer experts recommend state licensing, or even a national licensing or certification system for computer personnel.[174] At present, many computer firms require polygraph testing and fingerprinting of job applicants.[175] August Bequai maintains that in-depth screening of prospective employees should be implemented by employers to ensure that applicants have the "professional integrity necessary" for sensitive jobs.[176] According to Bequai, in the past, only technical qualifications have been considered when hiring new personnel.[177] Employers should conduct complete reviews of prospective employees' backgrounds, with follow-ups on past employment to determine whether an individual has previously been involved in suspicious activities.[178]

Computer security should be taught as a matter of routine, and emphasized in the daily operations at a computer center.[179] Employees should be made to realize that discussing sensitive matters with outsiders may compromise the security of the computer system,[180] and revealing confidential data stored in the computer may constitute a violation of state and federal laws.[181] Allocating responsibility for programming duties among many individuals increases the likelihood that illegitimate activity on the part of an individual might be discovered. Access to information concerning the operations of a computer system should be on a need-to-know basis only, and instructions to personnel should

---

[173] Sokolik, *supra* note 167, at 369. *See also* Davis, *Computer Controls: A Different Emphasis* 22 Nat Pub Acct 10 (1977) (preventing errors or fraud by implementing passive controls which include: documentation, organizational independence and audit trails).

[174] A. Bequai, *supra* note 168, at 19.

[175] *Id.* See also Lee, *Polygraph and Pre-Employment Screening*, 13 Hous L Rev 551 (1976).

[176] A. Bequai, *supra* note 168, at 19. See also Guynes & Vanecek, *Computer Security: The Human Element: Screening Candidates for Electronic Data Processing Positions* 71 Personnel Administraton 26 (1981).

[177] A. Bequai, *supra* note 168, at 19.

[178] *Id.*

[179] *Id.* See generally Stone, *Some Security and Integrity Controls in Small Computer Systems,* J Acct, Feb 1976, at 38.

[180] A. Bequai, Computer Crime (1978).

[181] *Id* 20.

be in writing whenever possible to control access to sensitive information.[182] The electronic data processing manager should select an appropriate and effective security system, and ensure that all employees follow whatever security procedures are established. Regular and frequent computer audits will aid the data processing manager in monitoring activities. For smaller data processing operations elaborate control procedures may be inappropriate, but some form of access and use procedures are essential for every computer center. While no computer security system is tamper-proof, even the simplest procedures, dutifully applied, can provide some deterrence for the less technical forms of computer crime. One of the simplest forms of deterrence of computer crime is the segregation of the computer center from the general office by means of walls, doors, and some sort of controlled access, e.g., a log-in/log-out procedure which tracks the personnel who enter the facility.

§7.16 —Public Education and Awareness

When the automobile first appeared, many well-educated and intelligent people cast aspersions on its future as a means of transportation. The concept of electronic data processing was also unenthusiastically received by the public when first introduced. The folklore of computers causing all sorts of human suffering is well-rooted in modern culture, and computers have received unflattering portrayals in print and film media. The theme of *man versus machine* is becoming increasingly popular as computers become a familiar part of daily life.

This negative public attitude towards computers is reflected in the public's perspective of the problem of computer crime. Computer criminals, especially the perpetrators of large-scale crimes involving money or other valuables, are often portrayed in the press as folk heroes, in a fashion akin to the notorious swashbuckling image given the gunfighters of the Old West. Perhaps one reason for this public attitude towards computer criminals is that these individuals are viewed as Robin Hoods, fighting back against unjust and tyrannical machines.[183]

The public remains largely unaware of the scope of computer use in business and government. The pressing need for stiffer penalties for computer abuse, consequently, is not apparent to the public. As computers are integrated into everyday life, the public's awareness of the magnitude of computer crime will increase, and the acts of computer criminals will be considered a more serious matter. Computer crime should then lose its romantic image in the eyes of the public. Once the public becomes familiar with the problem of computer crime, legislatures can be expected to correct inconsistencies in criminal laws and evidentiary rules which have impeded the effective investigation and prosecu-

---

[182] *Id.*

[183] Sokolik, *Computer Crime-The Need for Deterrent Legislation,* 2 Computer LJ 353, 367 (1980).

tion of computer crime, and to enact laws providing for punishment more realistically reflecting the gravity of the crime committed.

§7.17 —Proposed Federal Lesiglation

Few states have adequate laws specifically addressing computer crimes. Uniformity in state laws is also sadly lacking.[184] Because of the increased interstate nature of computer operations and networks, the need for adequate and consistent state laws is essential for effective deterrence and prosecution of computer-related crimes. History dictates that the 50 states are unlikely to adopt any uniform system on their own initiative—at least not without a model upon which they can rely. The model in this case will undoubtedly have to come, as it has in the past, in the form of federal legislation.[185]

In 1976 the Senate Governmental Affairs Committee conducted an inquiry into computer security and computer crime.[186] The committee concluded that:

1. The government was unable to adequately secure its 10,000 computers against fraud, compromise, or physical assault

2. Personnel procedures could not guarantee the integrity of computer personnel

3. Title 18 of the United States Code should be amended to enhance the government's capacity to prosecute computer crime[187]

In 1979, as a result of this inquiry, bills were proposed in the House (HR 6192), and in the Senate (S. 240).[188] Senate Bill S.240, entitled the Federal Computer Systems Protection Act of 1979 (FCSPA), would have amended

---

[184] See Sokolik, *supra* note 183, at 381; Nycum, *Computer Abuses Raise New Legal Problems*, 61 ABAJ 444 (April 1975).

[185] Both the Federal Rules of Evidence, and the Federal Rules of Civil Procedure have been followed by many state legislatures in enacting uniform rules of evidence and civil procedure. See Comment, *Computer Crime-Senate Bill S240*, 10 Mem St UL Rev 660, 662 (1980). See SRI International, Computer Crime: Criminal Justice Resource Manual 21 (1976).

[186] Senate Comm on Govt Operations, Problems Associated with Computer Technology in Federal Programs and Private Industry; Computer Abuses, 94th Cong, 2d Sess (Comm Print) (focuses on computer-related crimes and computer security). See Survey, *White Collar Crime: Computer Crime*, 18 Am Crim L Rev 370, 383 n 1831 (1980).

[187] Survey, *supra* note 186, at 383 n 1832. See also General Accounting Office, Automated Systems Security—Report to the Congress by the Comptroller General of the United States (Jan 23, 1979) (Rep B-115369) (federal agencies should strengthen safeguards over personal and other sensitive data).

[188] Federal Computer Systems Protection Act of 1979, S 240, 96th Cong, 1st Sess, 125 Cong Rec 710 (1979); HR 6192, 96th Cong, 1st Sess, 125 Cong Rec H 12, 352 (1979). The predecessor to Senate Bill S 240 was Senate Bill S 1766 which failed to make it out of the Senate Committee on the Judiciary. S 1766 received a great deal of criticism for being over-inclusive. See generally *House, Senate Subcommittees Begin Major Inquiry on White Color Crime*, 23 Crim L Rep 2288 (1978).

Title 18 of the United States Code to make the unauthorized use of federal computers, as well as the interstate misuse of other computers, a federal offense.[189] Essentially the FCSPA would have made it a federal offense:

> to use a computer to perpetrate a fraud or theft; or to illegally gain access to, or alter, any computer or any computer software, program, or data contained in a computer, if the computer operated in interstate commerce, or was owned by, under contract to, or in conjunction with, any financial institution, the United States Government or any branch, department, or agency thereof, or any entity operating in or affecting interstate commerce.[190]

Traditional property concepts would have been broadened to include computer software programs in either machine or human readable form, and any other tangible or intangible item of value.[191]

Senate Bill S.240 also provided for rather stiff penalties. For violations which amounted to fraud and theft, a fine of not more than two times the amount of the fraud or theft, or imprisonment of not more than five years, or both, could be imposed by the federal courts.[192] For other unauthorized uses, the penalty could be as much as $50,000, or imprisonment of not more than five years, or both.[193] The punishment sections of this proposed act were criticized for being too harsh or inappropriate, e.g., unauthorized uses would have included computer games for which the user could be subject to a $50,000 fine or five years imprisonment or both.[194] The American Bar Association's (ABA's) Section of Criminal Justice recommended, as an alternative, a *gradation guide* which would match the degree of punishment to the degree of misuse.[195]

The proposed bill would also have brought a significant number of computer crimes under federal jurisdiction, thus giving federal prosecutors the benefit of the more liberal Federal Rules of Evidence. With broader evidentiary rules and property concepts, the rate of successful prosecutions could be substantially increased. As convictions increased, so would the reporting efforts of victims. The awareness that perpetrators of computer crimes were likely to receive their just measure would likely have overcome the reluctance of victims to report these crimes.

Some commentators criticized the proposed law for preempting state laws. They argued that Senate Bill S.240 would have given the federal government the power to prosecute cases that traditionally were considered within a state's

---

[189] Comment, *supra* note 185, at 665.

[190] *Id.*

[191] *Id* 665-666. The broadened property definition was contained in §3(c) of S 240.

[192] *Id* 666.

[193] *Id.*

[194] *Id* 666-67.

[195] *Id* 667-68.

jurisdiction.[196] On its face the statute did not explicitly preempt any state laws, although by its comprehensive nature it might have amounted to a de facto preemption.[197] The preemption argument is not totally sound, and should not serve as grounds for foreclosing the passage of needed legislation. Computer crimes must be prevented, and the federal system must act not only for its own sake, but as an incentive to state legislatures to enact similar laws. The Department of Justice took the position that where state and local agencies had the investigatory and statutory means of handling computer crimes, and there was no compelling federal interest, the federal government would defer to the states.[198] Alternatively, concurrent jurisdiction would exist where state or local bodies had neither the means nor the experience to prosecute such crimes.

No bills were enacted, although the advantages of such a law could be manifold.[199] More effective deterrence would come from increased publicity in computer circles about the federal law, as well as through an awareness of the stiff penalties that such a law would likely impose. Even a comprehensive statutory scheme, however, would not be effective unless computer crimes could be detected and successfully prosecuted. Private industry will have to assume much of the responsibility for developing computer fraud detection systems that are capable of producing evidence that will be admissible at trial. The interplay between detection and prosecution will require closer communication between private industry and law enforcement authorities. The training centers for law enforcement officers may provide one forum for improving the channels of communication.[200] A reeducation in computer technology from a law enforcement perspective should enable the private and the public sectors to combat the problem of computer crime more effectively. The relevance of this approach is borne out by the recent formation in some business and government circles of *fraud teams* to deal with computer-related crime. Fraud teams may include:

> . . . criminal investigators, data processors, accountants and auditors. Whether a fraud team is available or whether investigators, auditors, accountants and data processors join in a less formal arrangement, a full

---

[196] *Id.* Federal Computer Systems Protection Act: Hearings on S1766 Before the Subcomm on Criminal Laws & Procedures of the Senate Comm of the Judiciary, 95th Cong, 2d Sess, 11 (1978).

[197] Id.

[198] *Federal Computer Systems Protection Act: Hearings on S1766 Before the Subcomm on Criminal Laws & Procedures of the Senate Comm of the Judiciary,* 95th Cong, 2d Sess 11 (1978). See also Comment, *supra* note 194, at 662 n 21; and Justice Department Comments on S 1766 Sec Mgt, Nov 1978, at 62.

[199] See generally *Statement of the American Society for Industrial Security Concerning the Federal Computer Systems Act of 1977 Presented to Subcommittee on Criminal Laws and Procedures of the Committee on the Judiciary, US Senate* Sec Mgt, Nov 1978, at 24.

[200] See generally Becker, *Computer Crime Fighters Go to Boot at FBI Academy,* Sec World, Sept 1978, at 30; *FBI Trains Agents in Computer Crime Investigation,* Sys, Tech & Science for Law Enforcement & Sec, Jan 1978, at 4.

investigation of suspected or detected computer abuse, if it is to result in prosecution, may require understanding of some or all of the following areas:

documented types of computer-related crimes, electronic data processing concepts and equipment,

nature of computer vulnerabilities,

investigative auditing, and

applicable federal, state and local laws.[201]

§7.18   Conclusion

This chapter has dealt primarily with the legal problems of computer-related crimes, but it should also serve as a beacon for change in a larger context, one where issues of economics, business management, science and technology, and law have become interrelated through the use of computers.

Present-day computer systems can handle a multitude of tasks. The would-be computer felon can use this computer capability to his or her advantage in several ways:

1. The criminal can cover or disguise the crime by creating a confusing mass of data

2. The criminal can destroy the evidence of the crime by the same method used to perpetrate the crime

3. The criminal can inflict substantial damages on victims by jamming, or simply jumbling, the computer data output

The criminal can accomplish this by instructing the computer to perform tasks which generate data that appear correct to the user, but that are in fact erroneous or misleading. Present procedures often make it difficult to ascertain whether these acts were committed by unintentional human (or machine) error, or by the intentional acts of an unauthorized computer user.

Computer-related crimes are increasing as more and more people receive technical training that allows them to utilize computer systems in other than specifically authorized ways. Much of the training that programmers and analysts receive involves a *problem-solving* approach. Each new computer system is viewed as a puzzle to be unravelled, a challenge to their skills and intellect. Much computer abuse is committed in a sporting spirit, i.e., as if it were more of a game than an act of wrongdoing. Accessing the computer system of another without authorization simply to see if it can be done; converting a software program from one hardware system to another for the challenge of making it work; and building a new program based on another's legally-protected program, are probably the most frequently committed illegal acts.

---

[201] Volgyes, *The Investigation, Prosecution, and Prevention of Computer Crime: A State of the Art Review,* 2 Computer LJ 385, 395 (1980).

Not all computer-related crimes, however, require a high degree of training. Anyone who knows how to access a computer, whether directly or indirectly, can use this knowledge to alter records or to purloin information. It is relatively easy for a properly authorized employee to print out a record stored on tape or disk, and spirit it away for sale to a competitor. Moreover, technological advancements that allow computer transactions to be conducted over telephone lines are making it safer to commit computer-related crimes, as the computer criminal can be in a different city, or even a different country, from the computer being tapped, with little chance of being detected, and even less chance of being prosecuted. Finally, computer crime is increasing because more profit can be obtained through computers, making the stakes higher and more tempting for those who would commit computer-related crime.

Everyone involved with computers has a responsibility to curb the potentially catastrophic problem of computer-related crimes. The responsibility for security, detection, and investigation falls primarily on the business community, law enforcement authorities, and the general populace. Effective laws are the responsibility of voters, legislators, prosecutors, and judges.

Present state and federal laws are inadequate to handle computer-related crimes. New legislation specifically addressing the peculiarities of computer abuse must be enacted at both the state and federal levels. Legislators must realize that computer technology is dynamic, and that laws need to be updated, e.g., the need to remove the barriers imposed by antiquated property concepts. These new laws, however, should not be so narrowly tailored as to preclude prosecutors from effectively confronting new or unforeseen aspects of the everchanging computer revolution.

Stanley Sokolik has written that:

> Strong legislation which specifically focuses upon computer-crime [could] be salutary to the entire range of possible preventive and punitive actions: [by instilling the incentive to obey the law, and by encouraging victims to report and cooperate in the prosecution of computer felons]. Successful prosecutions under a specific computer-crime bill will increasingly exert a force for preventive action. All users, particularly those using the computer to fulfill a fiduciary responsibility, can be expected to strive to prevent those acts enumerated in the law, report the acts that do occur, cooperate in the gathering of evidence, and support a request for the maximum possible sentence and fine.[202]

One specialist in the computer crime area has even suggested that, because of poor reporting by businesses, laws may be needed which make the failure to disclose these crimes a crime.[203] Effective legislation would also eliminate

---

[202] Sokolik, *Computer Crime—The Need for Deterrent Legislation*, 2 Computer LJ 353, 374 (1980).

[203] A. Bequai, *supra* note 180, at 197. Banks are presently required by law to report crimes committed against them to authorities.

much of the uncertainty concerning charges prosecutors should file against suspects accused of computer abuses. The courts would no longer have to try "to link unauthorized use of computer technology to general criminal legislation that never contemplated the existence of computers."[204] Legislation specifically drafted to overcome the shortcomings and technicalities of present laws would go a long way towards enhancing the effectiveness of prosecutors in their efforts to combat the problem of computer crime.

---

[204] Sokolik, *supra* note 202, at 375.

Banking—Electronic Funds Transfer Systems

8

§8.01 Generally

Instantaneous communication has been a way of life for Americans since the invention and development of the telegraph and telephone. Later, television brought faraway events into our living rooms as the events were occurring. The instantaneous analysis of information by computers has permitted us to build space vehicles that explore the edges of our solar system and to fly ships whose manuevers are too complicated for a human astronaut to handle. Each of these developments seems quite ordinary to us now, but at the time of their inception, they were met with suspicion and awe—awe at the technological accomplishment and suspicion that these accomplishments were effecting fundamental changes in our lifestyles which were not necessarily positive.

There is a new revolution in our midst which involves both the high technology of our society—computers—and the most basic cultural aspect of civilization—money, or the exchange of value. The methods by which human beings have exchanged goods and services has gone through its own evolutionary pattern—from bartering to the use of precious metals or stones, and more recently from coins and currency to checks. Today, with the technology of computers and communications systems, value can be exchanged between and among financial institutions and individuals by way of electronic impulses—an electronic fund transfer (EFT) system.

The development of EFT systems is being hindered by a maze of banking laws and regulations developed at a time when our payment system was paper-based and, largely, enacted as a result of the 1930's financial crisis. The Depression era bequeathed to the financial services industry a legal structure requiring the segmentation and specialization of services and markets. Similarly, the regulatory structure for these various financial "classes" mirrors this segmentation in the restricting of market entry, the limiting of product lines, and the controlling of the price of services. Our financial markets, however, have evolved beyond this compartmentalized structure. In addition, this "cubbyhole" approach to the organization of financial services has been tainted by federalism—the clash between the state and federal government bodies which has been with us since the writing of the Constitution.

These conditions have been brought glaringly to light by the inability of some of these institutions to effectively meet the needs of our rapidly changing financial markets. The problem is that we are being inundated by paper and crippled by the expense and inefficiency of handling that paper, despite the fact that the technology exists to transform our paper payment system to one consisting of electronic impulses, thus ushering in the "cashless society."[1] Complicating this situation is the fact that our financial institutions are entering a revolutionary period wherein our traditional notion of banking services could easily be swept aside.[2] To date, the courts, federal and state legislatures, and the banking institutions have been slow to respond and unwilling to tamper with the system in place.

Historical/Legal Perspective of the United States Banking System

§8.02   The Dual Banking System

Banking operations in the United States today are conducted under a dual system consisting of national banks, chartered by the federal government, and state banks, incorporated and operating under the authority of the states. To trace the fitful beginnings of this dual system is to plunge into the traditional debate over federalism and state's rights.

The Early Years

The First Bank of the United States was chartered in 1791 for a twenty year term. With its main office located in Philadelphia, the financial center of the new nation, the bank established eight branches that issued paper money redeemable in gold and silver and made loans to both private business and government in the form of deposits and circulating notes.[3] Although this bank is considered to have functioned satisfactorily, it failed to have its charter renewed in 1811. The winds of political change had swept out the Federalists who had created the bank and replaced them with Jeffersonian Republicans who had a decidedly more parochial view.

The interregnum between the demise of the First Bank and the chartering of the Second Bank of the United States in 1816 was a period of financial instability, caused in part by the War of 1812. The number of state banks blossomed.[4] The state banks were often loathe to accept notes issued by banks in other parts of the country, thus making the transfer of funds difficult. In

---

[1] A. Bequai, The Cashless Society: EFT at the Crossroads (1981). See generally Baxendale, *Commercial Banking and the Checkless Society,* 1970 Rutgers J Computers & L 88. See **ch 5** for a discussion of the regulatory environment for the communications industry.

[2] House Comm on Banking, Finance and Urban Affairs, Financial Institutions in a Revolutionary Era, 97th Cong, 1st Sess (1981). See also Clarke, *Automation - The Bank's Legal Problems of the Present and Future,* 87 Banking LJ 110 (1970).

[3] D. Richardson, Electric Money: Evolution of an Electronic Fund Transfer System 27 (1979).

[4] W. Lamb, Group Banking 13 (1961).

addition, many state banks made speculative loans resulting in depreciation of their currency.[5] The positive influence of the Second Bank of the United States was not felt until 1819.[6] From 1819 to 1836, the bank achieved success in providing quality notes and expediting fund transfer. The Second Bank followed the path of its predecessor in failing to be rechartered in the Jackson era. From 1836 to 1841, the bank conducted business under a charter from the Commonwealth of Pennsylvania.[7] The banking system during the period from 1836 to 1863 consisted exclusively of state banks. The depreciation of paper money and the general lack of confidence in its redeemability during the American Civil War led to the establishment of a national banking system.[8]

The National Banking Act of 1863

In 1863, the National Banking Act was passed for the purpose of helping to finance the Civil War by stimulating the sale of government bonds used to secure bank notes in circulation and to provide a sound currency to circulate at a uniform value.[9] This act created a system of national banks, regulated and controlled by Congress, and headed by a Comptroller of the Currency.[10]

Federal Reserve System

The failure of the National Banking Act to sufficiently deal with the recurring money crises of the late 19th and early 20th centuries, led to the creation of the Federal Reserve System in 1914.[11] Congress had created a National Monetary Commission that recommended that a single institution be created to act as a central banking office.[12] Instead, the Congress created a regional system

---

[5] *Id* 14.

[6] *Id* 15.

[7] D. Richardson, *supra* note 3, at 27.

[8] W. Lamb, *supra* note 4, at 17.

[9] National Bank Act of 1864, ch 106, 13 Stat 99, 12 USC §165; D. Richardson, *supra* note 3, at 29. For a succinct explanation of the history of American banking, see 1 Fed Banking L Rep (CCH) ¶1104 *et seq.*
See Levin, *In Search of the National Bank Act*, 97 Banking LJ 741, 743 (1980), for a discussion of the legislative history of the National Banking Act. The National Banking Act began as the revised version of a law enacted a year earlier and was encapsulated in the Revised Statutes, located at 12 USC §38, but 10 other provisions have been scattered throughout the Code titles. Levin notes that 12 USC §36, the national branching statute with which this chapter is most vitally interested, is actually part of the Act of Mar 5, 1865, 13 Stat 484. As Levin states, however, the National Banking Act is a generic reference to all of the statutory laws dealing with U.S. banking law, and is, at the very least, a "convenient shorthand for reference."

[10] 1 Fed Banking L Rep (CCH) ¶1308-09, 1115.

[11] Federal Reserve Act, Dec 23, 1913, ch 6, 38 Stat 251, 31 USC §409 (other sections are dispersed throughout Title 12).

[12] 1 Fed Banking L Rep (CCH) ¶1116.

of "reserve banks,"[13] headed by a Board of Governors and appointed by the President.[14]

Each reserve bank serves a region comprised of several states or sections of states and differs from regular banks in that it does not operate for profit.[15] Banks that become members of the reserve are called "member" banks. Member banks must maintain certain legal reserves on deposit with the federal reserve bank in its region, but may draw on these reserves to procure currency and pay checks drawn on them.[16] Also, and more importantly, member banks may borrow funds from their reserve bank. Member banks, of course, include all national banks, but may also include state banks which have applied for and met reserve requirements. It is here that the first interface of federal and state banking law appears.

Federal Deposit Insurance Corporation

The Federal Deposit Insurance Corporation (FDIC) was organized as an independent agency under the Federal Reserve Act in June 1933 to prevent future loss of depositor's funds as had occurred during the bank closings of the Great Depression.[17] The Comptroller of the Currency sits as one of the FDIC's directors. Banks belonging to the Federal Reserve System are obliged to have their deposits insured by the corporation while other banks may choose to be insured by other means. Because state banks may be insured by the FDIC without being members of the Federal Reserve, their insured status makes them subject to federal regulation by the FDIC. This system of national and state chartered banks creates four categories of commercial banks:

1. National banks regulated by the Federal Reserve, the FDIC, the Comptroller and *state law* in the absence of federal preemption (i.e., branching)

2. State banks/FDIC insured are regulated by the FDIC and the state in which they were chartered

3. State member banks are regulated by the Federal Reserve and the state in which they were chartered and

4. State chartered banks/uninsured are regulated solely by the state in which they were chartered[18]

This duality of federal and state control creates a curious pattern of federal

---

[13] 1 Fed Banking L Rep (CCH) ¶¶1302, 1116; 12 USC §282 deals with Federal Reserve membership.

[14] 1 Fed Banking L Rep (CCH) ¶1304.

[15] 1 Fed Banking L Rep (CCH) ¶¶1306-1307.

[16] *Id.*

[17] 1 Fed Banking L Rep (CCH) ¶1117; 12 USC §1814.

[18] Scott, *The Dual Banking System: A Model of Competition in Regulation,* 30 Stan L Rev 1, 4 (1977) (Scott's article is an excellent analysis of the dual banking system and the efforts to reform the system).

dominance or preemption in some areas, and an overlay of federal and state law in others.[19] The issue of branching, which has shown itself to be so important to the evolution of financial systems and electronic funds transfer (EFT) systems, is the only area of banking law that is state dominated. The difficulties state dominance of the banking issues creates will be explored fully in the remainder of the chapter.

Current United States Banking System

§8.03   United States Banking Today

The traditional financial institutions that exist today—commercial banks, savings associations, and credit unions—and the laws that regulate them, came about in the wake of the Great Depression of the 1930s. The result was a system of specialized institutions with specialized product lines and markets, wherein commercial banks offered demand deposits and agricultural/commercial loans; savings and loan associations and mutual savings banks offered savings deposits and home mortgage loans; and credit unions offered small loans to their members. This compartmentalized structure of services and markets, solidified by the regulatory structure, has continued to the present day, despite the fact that changes in the marketplace have occurred which have made the system anachronistic.

In this revolutionary financial services era, the following categories of institutions offering a wide range of financial services have emerged:

1. Depository Institutions—These constitute our "traditional" notion of what a "bank" is and consist of commercial banks, chartered by either the state or federal government, as previously described

2. Nonbank Depository Institutions—These are the so-called "thrift institutions:" mutual savings banks, savings and loan associations, and credit unions

3. Nondepository Institutions—These institutions that include finance companies, brokerage-investment firms, retailers, mortgage companies, life insurance companies, and the new conglomerates formed as the result of mergers between large retailers such as Sears, Roebuck and Company and brokerage houses such as Dean Witter, can offer bank-like deposit liabilities and make loans, often on an interstate basis

---

[19] *Id.* See generally *Electronic Funds Transfer in Iowa: Implications for the Regulation of Competition Among Federal and State Financial Institutions,* 61 Iowa L Rev 1355 (1976); *Analysis of Enacted EFTS State Legislation,* 9 Modern Data 27 (1976); Browne, *A Regulatory Perspective on EFTS: Electronic Banking: The Decisions Are Yours,* 51 Mag Banking Ad 34 (Jan 1976); Prives, *Electronic Fund Transfer Systems and State Laws,* 93 Banking LJ 527 (1976).

§8.04 —Depository Institutions

The commercial bank is the mainstay of the banking system, providing a wide variety of customer services such as savings deposits and short term commercial lending. The main characteristic of a commercial bank is the *demand deposit* or checking account which, until recently, was a product line that could be offered only by commercial banks.[20] Commercial banks may be state or federally chartered, members or nonmembers of the Federal Reserve System, and insured or uninsured by the Federal Deposit Insurance Corporation (FDIC). There are approximately 14,500 commercial banks in the United States of which 10,000 are state banks. About 10% of these state banks belong to the Federal Reserve, with almost all state banks being insured by the FDIC.[21]

The McFadden Act provides a general definition of what constitutes "banking services:" (1) receiving deposits, (2) paying checks, and (3) lending money.[22] These categories do not cover the increasing number of services they provide including electronic fund transfer (EFT) accounts. Competitive difficulties arise, however, because banking services, as defined by the McFadden Act, are geographically restricted, whereas *nonbank* institutions may offer these services without geographical restriction.[23]

Although commercial banks have been prevented from offering certain services interstate (if the service falls within the McFadden three element test), commercial banks have been able to offer nationwide services through other means such as multi-bank holding companies, loan production offices, (LPO) and Edge Act corporations.[24]

In addition to the McFadden Act, the extent to which banking organizations can expand their operations is determined by the Bank Holding Company Act

---

[20] The Depository Institutions Deregulation and Monetary Control Act of 1980, Pub L No 96-221, 94 Stat 132, gave to thrifts the power to offer NOW accounts and share drafts which function similarly to checking accounts.

[21] Department of the Treasury, Geographic Restrictions on Commercial Banking in the United States 176 (1981) [hereinafter cited as White House Report]. See generally Mortimer, *Current Legal Problems Facing Commercial Banks Participating in Electronic Funds Transfer Systems,* 95 Banking L J 116 (1978); Murphy & Barrett, *Legal Problems of Applying Electronic Funds Techniques to Retail Banking,* 17 Jurimetrics J 111 (1976). See also Hall, *Where EFT in Wholesale Banking Stands Today and Where It Is Going,* 70 Banking 45 (1978).

[22] McFadden Act, ch 191, §36, 44 Stat 1224 (as amended at 12 USC §36). Such expanded services include: certificates of deposit, cash management services, private bond placements, credit cards, mortgage banking and consumer finance. See White House Report, *supra* note 21, at 77. See generally Klein, *Analysis of the Issues in the Legal Attempts to Restrict Banks from Furnishing Automated Customer Services,* 86 Banking LJ 579 (1969).

[23] The problem of branch banking and the McFadden Act is discussed in §8.07 and its effect on EFT development in §8.15. This issue is also related to competition in intrastate banking facilities (§8.21), and interstate banking (§8.22).

[24] These aspects of interstate banking, including Edge Act Corporations, are discussed in §8.22.

and the Bank Merger Act.[25] Bank holding companies were originally created to achieve statewide banking in *unit banking* states.[26] Some holding companies acquired or chartered banks in other states—thereby effectively "branching" interstate. In 1956, the so-called "Douglas Amendment" precluded further interstate bank acquisitions unless the law of the state in which the acquired bank was situated so allowed, but "grandfathered" *existing* interstate organizations.[27] Despite the inability to offer "full service" banking facilities (deposits received, checks paid, money lent), bank holding companies have been able to enter related activities on the lending side (finance companies, mortgage banking, and factoring), and also to offer uninsured deposit-like capabilities.[28]

The Bank Merger Act, as amended, provides that banks seek the prior approval of the Federal Reserve, the FDIC and the Comptroller of the Currency before being permitted to merge. Each agency has to gather information on the competitive factors involved. Any merger, the effect of which "may be substantially to lessen competition," would not be approved unless the anticompetitive effects "are clearly outweighed in the public interest by the probable effect of the transaction in meeting the convenience and needs of the community served."[29]

The loan production office (LPO) solicits loan business for the parent at either the commercial or retail level. The LPO uses the fiction that the loan is not completed until the "paperwork" is approved and the funds advanced—both of which are performed by the main office, not the LPO. Based on this fiction, the loan is not advanced out of state and, hence, there is no illegal branching activity. Edge Act and Agreement corporations were created to

---

[25] Bank Holding Company Act of May 9, 1956, ch 240, 70 Stat 133, *as amended,* 12 USC §1841-1850; Bank Merger Act of 1966, Pub L No 89-356, 80 Stat 7 (codified at 12 USC §1828(c)). See generally Peck & McMahon, *Recent Federal Litigation Relating* to *Customer-Bank Communication Terminals (CBCTs) and the McFadden Act,* 32 Bus Law 1657 (1977).

[26] White House Report, *supra* note 21, at 4. Some of the acquisitions in the 1930s took place in order to rescue failing banks.

Group banking is a type of multiple office banking in which independently incorporated banks are directly or indirectly controlled by a "holding company." 1 Fed Banking L Rep (CCH) at ¶3104.

Chain banking is a type of multiple office banking in which each bank in the chain is a separate legal entity with the control being accomplished by stock ownership or common directors. 1 Fed Banking L Rep (CCH) at ¶3103.

Branch banking is a type of multiple office banking in which a bank, as a single legal entity, operates more than one office. 1 Fed Banking L Rep (CCH) at ¶3102.

[27] In 1977, these 12 grandfathered organizations: were headquartered in five states and three foreign countries; had subsidiary banks in 24 states which controlled 1808 banking offices; and held approximately $57 billion in bank assets. White House Report, *supra* note 21, at 4.

[28] For example, the issuing of floating rate notes not subject to Regulation Q interest rate ceilings. See White House Report, *supra* note 21, at 5. Banks are prohibited from entering into nonbanking activities, but may do so by organizing holding companies of which the bank will be a subsidiary.

[29] 12 USC §1828(c)(5).

engage in international banking, either directly or through foreign offices.[30] Banks utilize "Edges" to enter financial centers outside of their home state, although only international trading can be transacted.[31] In summary, the regulatory structure under which commercial banking functions is sufficiently restricted so as to create a competitive disadvantage which has ramifications for EFT development.

§8.05 —Nonbank Depository Institutions

For certain long-term, noncommercial activities, characterized as investment banking, "thrift institutions" developed: mutual savings banks, savings and loan associations, and credit unions.

Mutual Savings Banks

Mutual savings banks (MSBs) have no capital stock, but the earnings inure to the benefit of their depositors after the payment of obligations or advances by the organizers.[32] Services offered by MSBs include: regular and school savings accounts, special higher yielding savings accounts, savings bank life insurance, unsecured personal loans, mortgage loans, and demand deposit accounts.[33] MSBs originally were depository institutions organized to encourage individual savings that would then be invested in long term investments such as mortgages.[34] The creation of "negotiable orders of withdrawal" (NOW Accounts) that are essentially interest earning checking accounts, has taken away the dominance and control of commercial banks over demand deposit dollars.

At their inception, MSBs were state-chartered and controlled. Their state charters can be converted to federal charters and thus, MSBs may exempt themselves from state law limitations on branch offices.[35] The Federal Home Loan Bank Board, established in 1932 by the Federal Home Loan Bank Act, supervises federally chartered MSBs and approves the establishment of MSB

---

[30] 12 USC §§611-631.

[31] White House Report, *supra* note 21, at 6. Interestingly, "Edges" could not branch interstate even though they could be incorporated in several states. Also, foreign banks were free to establish interstate branches. This was changed by the International Banking Act of 1978, Pub L No 95-369, 92 Stat 607, that limited non-U.S. banks to a single home state.

[32] 1 Fed Banking L Rep (CCH) ¶1314.

[33] Department of the Treasury, Geographic Restrictions on Commercial Banking in the United States, at 9 (1981) [hereinafter cited as White House Report]. For a discussion of the power of savings banks to provide NOW accounts see Annot, 64 ALR3d 1314 (1975).

[34] *Id.* The Financial Institutions Regulatory and Interest Rate Control Act of 1978 (FIRA), Pub L No 95-630, 92 Stat 3641, amended the Home Owner's Loan Act of 1933, 12 USC §1461.

[35] FIRA, *supra* note 34, at §1202; White House Report, *supra* note 33, at 88.

branches within the savings bank's own Standard Metropolitan Statistical Area (SMSA), its own county or within 35 miles of its home office, as long as the branch is within the bank's home state.[36] Thus, the Financial Institutions Regulatory and Interest Rule Control Act of 1978 permits federally chartered MSBs to branch intrastate without regard to state law, although MSBs still may not branch across state lines.[37]

Savings and Loan Associations

Savings and loan associations (S&Ls) are chartered by states and the federal government as either nonprofit or mutual corporations. The Federal Home Loan Bank Board (FHLBB) has jurisdiction over federally chartered S&Ls by authority of § 5(a) of the Home Owner's Loan Act of 1933.[38] There are no federal statutes that regulate the branching of S&Ls, and the courts have held that the board has the power to permit branching.[39]

In 1974, a federal S&L in Lincoln, Nebraska installed, with FHLBB approval, computer terminals in two "Hinky Dinky" stores. These terminals functioned as "place of business funds transfer systems," and permitted customers to communicate with the S&L by making deposits and withdrawals. In a withdrawal transaction, the computer debited the customer's S&L account, and credited the store's S&L account, while in the deposit transaction, the store's account was debited and the customer's credited. Nebraska contended that the store was engaging in the banking business unlawfully. The court held that these arrangements constituted neither illegal banking nor the carrying on of business at an unauthorized branch, as the creditor/debtor relationship never existed between the store and the customer.[40]

Credit Unions

A credit union (CU) is a cooperative association organized on the basis of a common bond of employment or interest, for the purpose of promoting thrift and creating a source of credit at reasonable rates for its members. The National Credit Union Administration charters federal credit unions and insures both federal and state chartered credit unions. The Federal Credit Union Act[41] contains no branching restrictions but the nature of credit unions, limited as they are to members who share employment, location or interest, means that

---

36 White House Report, *supra* note 33, at 88.

37 *Id;* FIRA, *supra* note 34.

38 12 USC §1464(a).

39 Bloomfield Fed Savings & Loan Assn v American Community Stores Corp, 396 F Supp 384 (D Neb 1975). See generally Annot, 73 ALR3d 1282 (1976). The Garn-St Germain Depository Institutions Act of 1982, Pub L No 97-320, 96 Stat 1469 gave S&Ls the power to make commercial loans.

40 State *ex rel* Meyer v American Community Stores Corp, 193 Neb 634, 228 NW2d 299 (1975).

41 Pub L No 95-22, 91 Stat 49 (1977), amending the Federal Credit Union Act, 12 USC §§1751-1790, gave credit unions authority to make 30-year real estate loans.

the issue of branch offices is usually of little significance.[42] Credit unions have also been able to challenge commercial banks for their market share of demand deposits by the development of the share draft which operates as a checking account.[43] Also, "central liquidity facilities" give credit unions access to a liquidity fund analagous to the Federal Reserve discount window.[44]

It should be noted that, at present, credit unions make up only 4% of the nation's savings,[45] but there are more CUs (22,000) than commercial banks, S&Ls, and MSBs combined and there are 100 credit unions with assets of $600 million or more.[46] New federal laws, coupled with the advent of electronic funds transfer have "thrown CUs into the competitive arena with banks and savings and loan associations," consequently, "banks are now viewing CUs as a major threat."[47] One author suggests that if present trends continue, credit unions will replace finance companies as the second largest source of consumer credit.[48]

§8.06 —Nondepository Institutions

A new variable has been added to the financial services market equation— that variable is the advent of nondepository institutions capable of issuing bank-like liabilities unhindered by the regulatory framework under which banks and thrifts must operate. These institutions—such as retailers, brokerage houses, and life insurance companies—not only operate on an unregulated basis, but they also issue liabilities which do not carry the protection of insurance.[49]

Brokerage Firms

Investment houses can compete for the "demand deposit" market by paying interest on idle balances in a customer's account, known as a "cash managment

---

[42] White House Report, *supra* note 33, at 88-89. As long as the *affinity* requirement is met, credit unions may expand nationwide or even worldwide—the Navy Federal Credit Union operates on a worldwide basis.

[43] White House Report, *supra* note 33, at 10.

[44] The Depository Institutions and Deregulation and Monetary Control Act of 1980 (DIDA), Pub L No 96-221, 94 Stat 132 gave "any depository institution in which transaction accounts or nonpersonal time accounts are held" access to the Federal Reserve discount window; Title XVIII of FIRA created the central liquidity bank for Credit Unions.

[45] Denver Post, Feb 7, 1982, at 14D, col 1.

[46] Edmonds, *Credit Unions: Competition by Statute*, 97 Banking LJ 426, 427 (1980) (an excellent overview of the growth of credit unions and their impact on competition in the financial services industry).

[47] *Id* 426.

[48] *Id* 434.

[49] Department of the Treasury, Geographic Restrictions on Commercial Banking in the United States, at 11 (1981) [hereinafter cited as White House Report].

account" (CMA).[50] This type of account was introduced by Merrill Lynch in 1977, and subsequently by other firms such as Dean Witter, Shearson, and Bache.[51] The account is open to those who place $20,000 in cash or securities in an account that, if in the form of cash, enters a CMA Money Trust that earns market rates of interest. The securities can be used to take out margin loans.[52]

In addition to CMAs, money market mutual funds offer liquidity liability, the proceeds of which are used to purchase bank certificates of deposit or other high yield, short term instruments.[53] Since most funds offer checking services, the account becomes an interest bearing demand deposit. At times when market interest rates exceed the deposit interest rate ceilings, money market fund accounts can grow rapidly at the expense of banks and thrifts.[54]

Life Insurance Companies

Premiums paid for insurance can be accumulated as an "account" which gains interest. Because insurance policies can be "cashed in," an insurance policy can act as a savings mechanism.[55] Some companies also permit the insured to borrow against the amount of premiums paid in; the unpaid loan is then offset against the policy amount. Insurance regulations are principally the domain of the states, and consequently, these regulations prescribe the requirements for an out-of-state insurance company to operate within a certain state. there are no real geographical limitations on insurance company expansion.[56]

New Wrinkle: Conglomerate Mergers

In 1981, there began a series of "invasions" of the securities/brokerage business: Prudential Insurance Company acquired Bache, American Express got Shearson Loeb Rhodes, and Sears bought Dean Witter. These acquisitions and mergers add a whole new element to the issue of what constitutes banking services, who should offer them and how should they be regulated, if at all. These financial conglomerates are large enough to develop electronic funds

---

50 *Id.*

51 *The Fight for Financial Turf,* Fortune, Dec 28, 1981, at 54.

52 *Id.*

53 White House Report, *supra* note 49, at 11.

54 Although the deposit interest ceiling, Regulation Q, is set to go out of existence in 1986, many small banks still hold low cost deposits on which they do not wish to see interest ceilings raised. "The banks and thrifts [Regulation Q] supposedly protects are damned by the money market funds if they don't pay more for deposits and damned by economics if they do. The one thing these institutions know for sure is that they detest the money market funds." Fortune, *supra* note 51, at 56.

55 White House Report, *supra* note 49, at 12 and 89.

56 White House Report, *supra* note 49, at 89.
See also the McCarran Act, 15 USC 1011, which provides that no act of Congress can be construed to invalidate, impair, or supersede any state law regulating or taxing insurance unless the act specifically relates to the insurance business.

transfer (EFT) systems and, because of the lack of regulation, may leave traditional financial institutions, strapped by the McFadden Act, to flounder. This area is discussed extensively in **§8.22.**

Branch Banking

§8.07   McFadden Act

Justice Douglas stated in *First National Bank in Plant City v Dickinson* that "it will come as a shock, where common sense is the guide, to learn that an armored car picking up merchants' cash boxes and checks is a branch bank."[57] In *Plant City,* the Supreme Court held that, under the McFadden Act, a national bank could establish a "branch" within the meaning of the federal definition only under the same conditions as state law would permit a state bank to do so.[58] The issue of branch banking has appeared as an impediment to not only the development of electronic funds transfer (EFT) systems, but also to that of interstate banking. In actuality, this impediment to interstate banking has been avoided through other mechanisms such as the bank holding company. Yet, EFT deployment has been stifled by court decisions interpreting the McFadden Act. A major area of concern is the terminal located off the bank premises.[59]

The National Bank Act of 1864 made no mention of "branching," although branch banks did exist, and the Act permitted national banks to "exercise . . . all such incidental powers as may be necessary to carry on the business of banking."[60] Branch banks mushroomed at the beginning of the twentieth century compelling the Comptroller of the Currency, in 1923, to recommend congressional action regarding branch banking.[61] That same year, the United States Attorney General ruled that the "incidental powers provision of the National Bank Act included the power to establish off-premises 'teller-windows' for the purpose of receiving deposits and paying checks."[62] The Supreme Court took exception to an opinion of the Attorney General in *First National Bank v Missouri ex rel Barrett,* where the Court stated that "the mere

---

[57] First Natl Bank v Dickinson, 396 US 122, 138 (1969).

[58] *Id* 130-33. McFadden Act, ch 191, §36, 44 Stat 1224 (as amended at 12 USC §36).

[59] An automatic teller machine (ATM) may be on-line or off-line. An off-line machine records each transaction on a tape which a courier physically transports each day to the bank for processing. An on-line machine is directly linked to the bank's computer which permits instantaneous processing of transactions. See generally *Customer-Bank Communication Terminals and Branch Banking,* 7 St Mary's LJ 389 (1975); *Customer-Bank Communication Terminals Under the McFadden Act,* 47 U Colo L Rev 765 (1976).

[60] 12 USC §24.

[61] First Natl Bank v Walker Bank & Trust Co, 385 US 252, 257 (1966). This case gives a good overview and background of the National Banking Act and the McFadden Act.

[62] 34 Op Atty Gen 1, 5 (1923).

multiplication of places where the powers of a bank may be exercised is not, in our opinion, a necessary incident of a banking business. . . ."[63] According to the Court, Congress alone could remedy the situation of inequality between state and national banks.[64]

One month later, Representative McFadden introduced a bill to permit national banks to have branches within cities, if the state banks were also allowed to do so. The bill was finally enacted in 1927 with Representative McFadden commenting that, as a result of the passage of this act, the National Bank Act had been so amended that national banks were able "to meet the needs of modern industry and commerce and *competitive equality* has been established among all member banks of the Federal Reserve System."[65] It was the multiplicity of small bank failures during the depression of the 1930s that spurred Congress to again begin consideration of permitting national banks to branch without regard to state law. This move was defeated, but the Banking Act of 1933, also known as the Glass-Steagall Act, amended the McFadden Act so that national banks could establish branches anywhere in the state, if state banks were so authorized.[66]

The amended McFadden Act, therefore, reflects the historic and continuing struggle for control over banking between the states and the federal government. It is embodied in the principle of competitive equality coined by Rep. McFadden. This doctrine of competitive equality compelled the Court to conclude in *Plant City* that if national banks were permitted to offer off-premises services regardless of state law, the national banks would gain a competitive advantage over state banks which would be forbidden to do so by state law.[67]

The McFadden Act defined "branch" in the following terms:

---

[63] First Natl Bank v Missouri *ex rel* Barrett, 263 US 640, 659 (1923).

[64] The issue involved in this case was a Missouri statute which provided "that no bank shall maintain in this state a branch bank or receive deposits or pay checks except in its own banking house." A national bank opened a branch bank in St. Louis, several blocks away from its main banking house.

[65] 68 Cong Rec 5815 (1927) (emphasis added).

[66] 12 USC §36(c) states that:

A national banking association may, with the approval of the Comptroller of the Currency, establish and operate new branches: (1) Within the limits of the city, town or village in which said association is situated, if such establishment and operation are at the time expressly authorized to State banks by the law of the State in question, and (2) at any point within the State in which said association is situated, if such establishment and operation are at the time authorized to State banks by the statute law of the State in question by language specifically granting such authority affirmatively and not merely by implication or recognition, and subject to the restrictions as to location imposed by the law of the state on State banks.

[67] 396 US at 122. See generally Hill, *Electronic Funds Transfer and "Competitive Equality": A Doctrine That Does Not Compute*, 32 Ark L Rev 347 (1978); Esslinger, *Eighth Circuit Short Circuits Electronic Banking: The Broadening Reach of Competitive Equality*, 21 St Louis ULJ 535 (1977).

The term "branch" as used in this section shall be held to include any branch bank, branch office, branch agency, additional office, or any branch place of business located in any State or Territory of the United States or in the District of Columbia at which *deposits are received, or checks paid, or money lent.*[68]

The key transactions on which to focus are: deposits received, checks paid, and money lent.

In *First National Bank v Walker City,* the Court held that national banks in Utah must comply with the Utah statute which permitted branching within the municipality where they were located, but only by taking over an existing bank.[69] The Comptroller had issued a certificate permitting a national bank to establish a branch under circumstances directly opposed to the Utah statute, arguing that, under McFadden, state law controlled only whether or where branches could be established, not the method of establishing a branch.[70] The Court rejected this argument, stating that where a state allows branching only by taking over an existing bank "it expresses as much 'whether' and 'where' a branch may be located as does a prohibition or a limitation to the home office municipality." The Court, emphasizing the doctrine of competitive equality in McFadden, stated that it is a "strange argument that permits one to pick and choose which portion of the law binds him."[71]

In *Plant City,* the court had been faced with the question of whether state or federal law defined "branch." Florida law completely prohibited branch banking. The Comptroller had granted a national bank operating in Florida permission to operate two off-premises services: (1) a mobile drive-in which consisted of an armored car equipped with a teller window and service counter which delivered cash in exchange for checks and received cash and checks at the depositor's premises; and (2) a secured recepticle to which customers had keys and in which monies were left to be picked up by an armored car.[72] The Court again stressed the McFadden Act's attempt to deal with "competitive tensions inherent in a dual banking structure," and found that although state law is critical in determining how, when, and where branch banks may be operated, it is Congress which defined branch, for "to allow the states to define the content of the term 'branch' would make them the sole judges of their own powers."[73] The Court then analyzed the off-premises services offered against

---

[68] 12 USC §36(f) (emphasis added). See generally *Push Button Banking is Running into Trouble: Electronic Funds Transfer Systems,* US News & World Rep, July 7, 1975, at 76; *Sudden Setback for Electronic Banking: Court Decision on Electronic Terminals as Branch Offices,* Bus Wk, Aug 18, 1975, at 32; *Electronic Tremor Shakes Banks: Question of Legality of Electronic Banking Terminals as Branches,* Bus Wk, Mar 10, 1975, at 26.

[69] 385 US 252.

[70] *Id* 261.

[71] *Id.*

[72] *Id* 125-28.

[73] *Id* 131, 133.

the McFadden definition and concluded that the "offering of any one of the three services mentioned in that definition will provide the basis for finding that 'branch' banking is taking place."[74] This does not mean that national banks cannot establish and operate terminals in a state that prohibits branch banks as long as that state does not define EFT terminals as branches.[75] It is clear that the inevitable consequence of the McFadden Act and its interpretation will be a degree of inequality in those situations where the state's definition of branch and the national definition do not coincide.

§8.08 —1980 Changes: The Depository Institutions Deregulation and Monetary Control Act

In early 1980, the Depository Institutions Deregulation and Monetary Control Act (DIDA), described as the most significant banking legislation since the passage of the Federal Reserve Act, was passed. DIDA enacted almost ninety specific recommendations of the Nixon administration's Hunt Commission.[76] The Hunt Commission, like the numerous financial studies which preceded it, studied and recommended far-reaching changes in the structure of the financial industry. The basic effect of these changes would be to deregulate financial institutions, with the intent of making all of these institutions truly competitively equal to banks. The promulgation of this Act was the first positive response to correct the legislative and regulatory lag created by the revolutionary changes that had occurred in the financial services industry since the 1930s. DIDA's nine titles cover a myriad of banking issues which are summarized below.[77]

Title I—Monetary Control Act of 1980

These provisions permit the Federal Reserve to set new and lower reserve requirements for *all* commercial banks, savings banks, and savings and loan institutions.[78] "Depository Institutions" are defined by DIDA as banks, savings banks, mutual savings banks, savings and loan associations, and credit unions, and the distinction between member and nonmember institutions of the Fed-

---

[74] *Id* 135.

[75] Independent Bankers Assn v Smith, 534 F2d 921, 948 (DC Cir 1976).

[76] Pub L No 96-221, 94 Stat 161, tit V (1980). See **ch 5** for a discussion of the regulatory environment of the communications industry.

[77] A compilation of DIDA's titles, an explanation of the DIDA, and selected Committee Reports is found in 810 Fed Banking L Rep (CCH) (Apr 15, 1980) (hereinafter cited as CCH).

An overview of DIDA's provisions can be found in Weaver & O'Malley, *The Depository Institutions and Monetary Control Act of 1980: An Overview,* 98 Banking LJ 100 (1981).

[78] Weaver & O'Malley, *supra* note 77, at 102.

eral Reserve was dropped for the purposes of DIDA.[79] This provision ends the opportunity for nonmember banks "opting out" of the responsibility of maintaining reserve requirements by simply withdrawing from or declining to join the Federal Reserve System. The Federal Reserve will, consequently, increase its control of the money supply.[80] Further, DIDA recognizes that demand deposits are not the consumer's only source of "transaction accounts"—accounts by which the account holder may withdraw or transfer funds to a third party—and that negotiable orders of withdrawal accounts (NOW accounts), savings deposits subject to automatic transfer (pre-authorized transfer from savings to checking account), and share draft accounts (an interest bearing account—a credit union's equivalent of the NOW account) all constitute "checkable accounts" which form the basis of our medium of exchange and, therefore, should be subject to Federal Reserve control.[81]

Title II—Depository Institutions Deregulation Act of 1980

This section provides for the phased withdrawal of limitations on maximum rates of interest and dividends, as provided for in Regulation Q, and removes the advantage that savings and loan associations have on savings interest.[82] In so doing, Congress recognized the failure of Regulation Q, passed in 1966 as a temporary measure, to protect the flow of home mortgage funds from thrift institutions to commercial banks.[83] Regulation Q interest rate controls had been instituted to shield housing/mortgages during periods of tight money. Instead, alternatives such as money market funds (which are uninsured) offered the saver a higher interest rate at the expense of insured financial institutions. Congress noted that Regulation Q succeeded in discriminating against the small saver since banks and thrifts could offer money market certificates only with a large deposit of $10,000 or more. This gave more affluent savers a better return and discouraged saving by the small saver.

Title III—Consumer Checking Account Equity Act of 1980

The provisions of this title permit both member and insured nonmember institutions to offer the pre-authorized transfer of funds from a savings account to checking or other accounts (known as automatic transfer accounts (ATs).[84] NOW accounts, which are, in essence, checking accounts that draw interest,

---

[79] CCH, *supra* note 77, at ¶¶1003, 2003 amending §19(b) of Federal Reserve Act, 12 USC §461(b).

[80] CCH, *supra* note 77, at ¶2001.

[81] CCH, *supra* note 77, at ¶2003.

[82] Weaver, *supra* note 77, at 106.

[83] CCH, *supra* note 77, at ¶2021.

[84] Weaver & O'Malley, *supra* note 77, at 107 Regulation Q, 12 CFR §1204.

can now be authorized by *all* depository institutions.[85] These NOW accounts are permitted for funds in which the entire beneficial interest is held by: one or more individuals; or organizations operated primarily for religious, philanthropic, charitable, educational or similar nonprofit purposes.[86] Title III also amends the Federal Credit Union Act by permitting credit unions to issue share drafts and utilize Federal Home Loan Bank Board settlement and draft processing services.[87] Savings and loan associations are now permitted to use remote service units (RSUs) to allow customers to make savings deposits and withdrawals from off-premises remote electronic service units which in some cases are located in various retail stores.[88]

Title IV—Powers of Thrift Institutions

Title IV permits savings and loan associations to issue credit cards, lend money on the security of NOW accounts, and make commercial real estate and consumer loans with up to 20% of their assets.[89] These provisions recognize the fact that thrifts, which have historically functioned as depositories and home mortgage lenders, were unable to fulfill the needs of the consumer who also required a checking account, loan, or trust services. This provision allows the savings and loan associations to compete for the savings market while remaining "housing oriented."[90] Mutual savings banks are also authorized to hold up to 5% of their assets in commercial, corporate, or business loans, provided that such loans are made within the state in which the mutual savings bank is located or made within 75 miles of the mutual's home office.[91] Mutual savings banks may also accept demand deposits in connection with a commercial, corporate, or business loan relationship.[92]

Title V—State Usury Laws

Under certain conditions, state usury ceilings are preempted on first residential mortgage loans made by banks, savings and loan associations, credit unions, mutual savings banks, mortgage bankers, and Housing and Urban

---

[85] *Id.*

[86] CCH, *supra* note 77, at ¶1204; amended §2(a) of Pub L No 93-100, 12 USC §1832(a).

[87] Weaver & O'Malley, *supra* note 77, at 107.

[88] These units, which had been authorized in 1974 by the Federal Home Loan Bank Board, gave savings and loan associations an EFT capability denied to commercial banks which could be forbidden the use of ATM or POS terminals by state branching statutes.

[89] Weaver & O'Malley, *supra* note 77, at 108.

[90] CCH, *supra* note 77, at ¶¶1301, 2040; amended §5(c) of Home Owner's Loan Act of 1933, 12 USC §1464(c).

[91] CCH, *supra* note 77, at ¶1309 amended §5(a) of Home Owner's Loan Act of 1933, 12 USC §1464(a).

[92] CCH, *supra* note 77, at ¶149.

Development (HUD)-approved lenders.[93] Congress concluded that where state usury laws require mortgage rates below market interest levels, mortgage funds dry up in that area and flow to other states where market yields are available. National housing policies and programs are, consequently, frustrated.[94] This Title also exempts deposit accounts of depository institutions from usury ceilings, thus permitting small savers to receive a market rate of return on their deposit accounts.[95]

Title VI—Truth in Lending Simplification

Promulgated to deal with the more "onerous" aspects of the "overly technical" Truth in Lending Act,[96] this section provides consumers with clearer credit information, making creditor compliance easier, limiting creditor civil liability for statutory penalties to only significant violations, and strengthening the restitution enforcement mechanism.[97]

Title VII—Amendments to the National Banking and Interstate Trust Company Laws

The period of time allowed to a national bank to dispose of real estate taken in connection with defaulted loans is extended under this title. The 6% interest ceiling on National Bank preferred stock is removed. The Comptroller of the Currency is given the power to examine national banks as necessary, and the right to revoke the trust powers of a national bank. This section also permits a national bank to purchase, under limited conditions, a limited amount of stock of a bank providing bank services.[98]

Title VIII—Regulatory Simplification

Because of the myriad of federal regulatory agencies involved in promulgating rules for financial institutions, Congress provided that such agencies cooperate so that their regulations are not duplicative or inconsistent. These regulations are to be simply and clearly written, and the regulations should not be unduly burdensome or costly.[99]

---

[93] Weaver & O'Malley, *supra* note 77, at 110.

[94] CCH, *supra* note 77, at ¶2051.

[95] CCH, *supra* note 77, at ¶¶1401, 2052.

[96] Weaver & O'Malley, *supra* note 77, at 112. Regulation Z, 12 CFR §226, comprises the rules promulgated by the Federal Reserve Board to simplify creditor compliance with the disclosure requirements of the Truth in Lending Act, Pub L No 90-321, 82 Stat 146 (as codified at 15 USC §§1601-1677, as Part I of the Consumer Credit Protection Act).

[97] CCH, *supra* note 77, at ¶2081.

[98] Weaver & O'Malley, *supra* note 77, at 113-15.

[99] CCH, *supra* note 77, at ¶¶2121, 1703; see also Weaver & O'Malley, *supra* note 77, at 115.

Title IX—Foreign Control of United States Financial Institutions

This title provides for a moratorium on foreign acquisitions of United States depository institutions.[100]

Effect of DIDA

The overall effect of DIDA has been to "homogenize" financial institutions and, thereby, increase the number of banking offices and services available to the public. Some commentators believe this will result in a "ferociously competitive environment . . . with banks and thrifts slugging it out among themselves and against non-bank giants."[101] The competitive situation is compounded by the fact that thrift institutions may freely branch without regard to state law, and thus, have electronic funds transfer (EFT) authority to branch intrastate, while a commercial bank's EFT authority is limited by state law if the transactions consummated by the terminal fall within one of the McFadden Act's three element definition of branch. The only exception to this occurs where state law grants EFT authority to branch as an *exception* to its branching statutes. As a result of DIDA, the main benefit to commercial banks is the ability to attract customers by paying the same interest rates to depositors as thrift institutions are permitted to pay. Interstate banking via an EFT system remains unaffected by the passage of DIDA. DIDA is, however, a formal, legislative recognition of the market forces which are compelling the birth of nationwide, multi-service, financial institutions. This congressional recognition is also to be found in Congress' ordering of a study into the possibility of amending the McFadden Act. This White House Report, delivered during the Carter administration is the subject of §8.09.

§8.09 —White House Report

The original attempt to permit branches for national banks without reference to state law was defeated by the Congress in 1929. The courts have upheld the restrictions placed on national banks by state law, thus throttling any opportunity to develop an intrastate or interstate banking structure.[102] Finally, in early 1981, a White House report was issued by the Carter administration which recommended that the President propose the substantial easing of restrictions on interstate banking.[103] The study was ordered by Congress in

---

[100] CCH, *supra* note 77, at ¶¶2131, 1802; see also Weaver & O'Malley, *supra* note 77, at 115.

[101] *America's New Financial Structure,* Bus Wk, Nov 17, 1980, at 1.

[102] See §8.07.

[103] The Appendix of this report contains a "compendium of research on branch banking" written by various members of the Departments of the Treasury and Justice, the Federal Deposit Insurance Corporation, the Federal Reserve Board, and the Office of the Comptroller of the Currency. These papers contain excellent, general back-

the International Banking Act of 1978 and specifically referred to a possible amendment to the McFadden Act. The administration, however, broadened the study to include interstate chartering and acquisitions which come within §3(d) of the Bank Holding Company Act (Douglas Amendment).[104] Entitled "Geographic Restrictions on Commercial Banking in the United States," the report, which has extensive and detailed reports in its appendix, recognizes that, in effect, interstate banking *already exists* through multi-bank holding companies, loan production offices, Edge Act Corporations, and credit card operations, and that it is only small business and household customers who are denied the benefits of interstate banking.[105] Describing the current financial system as "Balkanized" and referring to the present "mystical" fixation with state boundaries, the report concludes that the needs of our financial markets have evolved without a concomitant evolution in the statutory framework provided for the regulation of those markets.[106] The conclusions of the report were based on a spectrum of policy considerations including: (1) competition among traditional banking institutions and "bank-like" operations; (2) competitive equality; (3) economic efficiency; (4) institutional safety and soundness; (5) the impact on small banks; (6) credit availability; (7) the needs of local communities; and (8) the preservation of the dual banking system.[107]

The study concluded that the increasingly complex and changing needs of our financial markets required a liberalization of the geographic restrictions on the provision of financial services.[108] The two options available to achieve this result are a modification of the McFadden Act or; a modification of the Douglas Amendment, that limits the interstate acquisitions of bank holding companies. Finding neither approach superior to the other, the study chose a phased relaxation of the Douglas Amendment as having a "less intrusive" impact on the existing regulatory structure.[109] The report emphasized, however, that it still considered the McFadden Act restraints as anti-competitive in its frustration of the expansion of retail deposit-taking, and in the inequity the McFadden Act imposed on banks as compared to nonbank competitors.

The study also recommended that electronic funds transfer (EFT) deployment should be subject to "less onerous" geographic restrictions than those imposed on brick and mortar branches, permitting terminal deployment on a

ground information and a discussion of policy options. Department of the Treasury, Geographic Restrictions on Commercial Banking in the United States (1981) [hereinafter cited as White House Report].

[104] The International Banking Act of 1978, Pub L No 95-369, 92 Stat 607 (codified as amended 12 USC §3106(a) and 12 USC §3104).
See also the Bank Holding Company Act, ch 240, 70 Stat 133 (1956), *as amended,* Pub L No 91-607, 84 Stat 1760 (codified at 12 USC §§1841-1850) (1976).
[105] White House Report, *supra* note 103, at 7-8.
[106] *Id* 1-2.
[107] *Id* 4-16.
[108] *Id* 16.
[109] *Id.*

statewide basis and within Standard Metropolitan Statistical Areas (SMSAs), to facilitate service within multi-state metropolitan areas.[110] In this way, a resident of Philadelphia who works across the Delaware River in Camden, New Jersey could take part in a payroll deposit program or conduct banking from across the river, rather than having to travel back to Pennsylvania to conduct banking business. In response to concerns about the impact of EFT on small banking institutions, the report stated that

> the great majority of EFT terminals at present, and probably in the immediate future, are off-line, self-contained units to which scale economies do not significantly apply. Also, sharing of EFT networks among depository institutions would mitigate any tendency of EFT development to foster a concentration of resources, and appropriate antitrust standards could be designed to minimize any such tendency.[111]

These recommendations have yet to be acted upon by the Reagan administration.[112]

Present Elements of Electronic Funds Transfer Systems

§8.10   Definition of an Electronic Funds Transfer

Electronic funds transfer (EFT) is the generic term for a whole spectrum of transactions involving an exchange of value between and among financial institutions and consumers by way of electronic impulses.[113] These transactions include: cash withdrawals, deposits, credit card authorization, check verification, billing operations, point of sale payments, clearing house services, balance inquiries, shifting of funds from one account to another, direct payroll deposits, and preauthorized periodic payments.[114] The simplest way to view

---

[110] *Id* 20.

[111] *Id.*

[112] See *House Votes Emergency Aid For Ailing Savings & Loans; Senate Weighs Broader Bill,* Cong Q, Oct 31, 1981, at 2106 (Senator Jake Garn introduced S 1720, which became law as the Garn-St. Germain Depository Institutions Act of 1982, Pub L No 97-899.

[113] Mortimer, *Electronic Fund Transfers,* 33 Bus L 947 (1978).

[114] *Id.* See generally M. Bender, EFTS: Electronic Funds Transfer Systems—Elements and Impact (1975); *Electronic Funds Transfer Systems: A Symposium,* 25 Cath UL Rev 687 (1976); Ernst, *EFT and the Future of Banking,* 67 Banking 54 (1975); Johnson & Arnold, *The Emerging Revolution in the Electronic Payments,* 22 Price Waterhouse Rev 26 (1977); Naar & Stein, *EFTS: The Computer Revolution in Electronic Banking,* 5 Rut J Computers & L 429 (1976); Nelson, *Electronic Funds Transfer: A Program,* 32 Bus L 201 (1976); *Primer on Electronic Funds Transfer Systems: A Symposium,* 37 U Pitt L Rev 613 (1976); Benton, *Electronic Funds Transfer: Pitfalls and Payoffs,* Harv Bus Rev, July-Aug 1977, at 16; White, *Consumer Bill Paying Services in the Evolving Electronic Funds Transfer Environment,* 52 Mag Bank Ad 38 (1977).

EFT is that electronic blips and bleeps are being substituted for paper in our current paper-based payments system.[115]

The exchange of financial information by means other than paper is not really new. At the time of the passage of the Federal Reserve Act, the transfer of financial data was accomplished by telegraph, using a Morse code system. By the late 1930s, the Federal Reserve converted to teletype machines and then, in the 1960s, computers were introduced into the Federal Reserve Communications System (FED Wire). It was not until October 28, 1974, that the National Commission on Electronic Fund Transfers was created.[116] The Commission, was formed for the purpose of conducting a thorough study and investigation, and recommending "appropriate administrative action and legislation necessary in connection with the possible development of public or private electronic fund transfer systems."[117] Public hearings and formal solicitations for public comment and papers occurred for 21 months. The Commission then issued a preliminary report in February 1922, and its final report in October 1977.[118]

The types of EFT services which are potentially available to both individual and business customers are classified by the Commission into two broad categories: (1) *information services* which involve the access to or transmission of data related to financial transactions, and (2) *funds transfer* which involve the actual movement of funds in or out of a deposit account.[119] Information services include credit authorization for credit card purchases, check verification (that permits a nondepository institution to verify the existence of funds), and check guarantee, whereby a consumer has a check payment guaranteed. Also included are "file look-up" functions which permit a consumer or financial institution to access account files for information. Funds transfer services are divided into four functions: deposit, debit, debit with overdraft privilege, and credit functions. Within the debit function, the Commission identified four areas: (1) debit for cash withdrawal; (2) debit for bill or loan payment; (3) debit for purchase; and (4) debit for interaccount transfer. Credit functions are classified into the areas of credit purchase and cash advance against an existing line of credit.

---

[115] Maki, *EFTS: Living in a Legal House of Cards,* Comm LJ 49 (1979).

[116] 12 USC §§2401-2408.

[117] 12 USC §2403(a). The Association of Data Processing Service Organizations issued a paper criticizing the makeup of the Commission for its failure to include anyone "with special experience and qualification in the computer industry". Computerworld, Nov 19, 1975, at 1. See also Baker, *Agenda for the National Commission on Electronic Fund* Transfer, 93 Banking LJ 389 (1976); Winkler, *The National Commission on Electronic Fund Transfers: Problems and Prospects,* 1977 Wash ULQ 507.

[118] Nat Comm on Electronic Fund Transfer, EFT in the United States, Policy Recommendations and the Public Interest; The Final Report of the National Commission on Electronic Fund Transfer (1977) [hereinafter cited NCEFT]. See generally *Update on EFTS,* 6 Rut J Computers & L 155 (1978); Dowe, *Where EFTS Stands Today,* 37 Ad Mgt 58 (1976); *US Has a Date with Electronic Banking,* 118 Forbes 69 (1976).

[119] NCEFT, *supra* note 118, at 36.

§8.11 Automated Teller Machines

The automated teller machine (ATM) is the most familiar aspect of the electronic funds transfer (EFT) system to the public, and is presently being utilized on an ever-increasing scale.[120] The ATM can perform a wide variety of transactions for a consumer at any time of the day or night: deposits; cash withdrawals; transfers between accounts; balance inquiries; and small, short term loans. Due to the marketing ingenuity of advertising companies, the ATMs have usually been given names such as "George" or "Mac." The terminals may be found both on and off bank premises. An ATM may be either *off-line* or *on-line*. An off-line terminal records each transaction on tape and a courier or bank employee transports the tapes to the bank for processing. Bank clerks review the tapes each day. Some machines are equipped with a memory which stores lists of delinquent accounts or stolen cards.[121] The on-line terminal is directly linked, via telephone lines, to the bank's computer which processes each transaction instantaneously, and can, therefore, protect against overdrafts.[122]

Consumers access the terminal by the use of a plastic card and by entering a personal identification number (PIN). Some terminals are located in secured areas whose entrance must be accessed by use of the plastic card. After the card is entered in a machine outside the door, the ATM reads the card and then unlocks the entrance to the terminal. When the card is placed in the terminal, it asks for the entry of the PIN. If the PIN is not entered, the transaction will not be consummated. Some terminals have the capacity to retain the card if the customer is not able to enter the correct PIN after several tries.[123]

The most outstanding benefit of the ATM (and the reason for its general acceptance by the public) is the availability of a wide range of simple, frequently performed bank services on a twenty-four hour basis. By performing (1) tasks which, performed by a human teller, would cost much more, (2) by permitting banks to close unprofitable branches without losing accounts; and, (3) by eliminating costly weekend and extended banking hours, banks are encouraged to make the original outlay of funds to install this expensive, but cost justfied equipment.[124] The success of the ATMs can also be attributed to the fact that they straddle both the paper and electronic payments systems, assisting the paper-based transactions while aiding in the development of the

---

[120] A. Bequai, The Cashless Society: EFT at the Crossroads (1981), at 33. See **§7.03** for a discussion of computer crime against ATMS. There are more than 10,000 ATMs in the United States. ATMs are referred to as "Customer-bank Communications terminals" or (CBCTs).

[121] *Id* 34. A majority of the ATM devices in use operate off-line.

[122] *Id.*

[123] N. Penney & D. Baker, The Law of Electronic Fund Transfer Systems 6-7 (1980).

[124] *Id* 6-13. A single on-line ATM can cost in the neighborhood of $35,000. See A. Bequai, *supra* note 120, at 34.

electronic.[125]

ATM services can be offered under various types of arrangements: a shared system, an interchange system, a piggybacking system, and a single institution system. A "shared" system involves a group of institutions which operate the system while an "interchange" is a system of seperate institutions with ATMs who permit each others' customers to use their machines.[126] In a "piggyback" system, an institution with ATMs allows the customers of other banks to use their machines and in a "single institution" system, only customers of that institution may utilize the EFT facilities.[127]

Security

Security poses a problem if the customer's access card and PIN are misappropriated. Because of the ease with which people forget the many numbers in their lives, PINs are often kept near the access card. If the consumer's wallet is stolen, the criminal can easily gain cash from the machine.[128] Other problems include counterfeit cards, listening devices, "spoofers,"[129] and "skimming."[130] The possibility of robbery at the ATM location can be minimized by enclosing the machine within "access control devices" which allow only cardholders to gain entry, as previously described.[131]

§8.12   The Point of Sale Terminal

The point of sale (POS) terminal provides many of the automated teller machine (ATM) services to the customer at the merchant's store or point of sale of the goods and services. Many people view this aspect of the electronic funds transfer (EFT) system as the single most important factor in the ultimate

---

[125] N. Penney & D. Baker, *supra* note 123, at 6-2.

[126] The Rocky Mountain Switch is a *shared* system. Colorado's mandatory sharing statute is found at Colo Rev Stat §11-6.5-104(1)(a) (1977). The Plus System, Inc, based in Denver, Colorado, is a nationwide shared ATM network of 26 banks, including such powers as the Bank of America and Chase Manhatten. When fully operational, the Plus System's services will be available to consumers in all 50 states on more than 9,000 ATMs.

[127] N. Penney, *supra* note 123, at 6-7.

[128] *Id* 6-8; See also A. Bequai, *supra* note 120, at 35.

[129] A *spoofer* is a device which can intercept the communications line between the ATM and the bank, and direct the ATM to empty itself of cash. Communication lines can be tapped and their data intercepted and altered. A. Bequai, *supra* note 120, at 36.

[130] *Skimming* is the transfer of the PIN from the original to a counterfeit card. This can be done only with an off-line system where the PIN is encoded on the magnetic stripe on the back of the card. In an on-line system, the PIN is encoded on the central computer's master file. Thus, on-line terminals are more secure than off-line. But on-line is still subject to spoofing.

[131] N. Penney, *supra* note 123, at 6-9; for a more detailed discussion of computer crime, in general, see **ch 7.**

success or failure of a universal EFT system.[132] POS brings a third party into the customer/financial institution communications link. POS devices, in many retail organizations, have replaced the cash register. The electronically transmitted data can simultaneously deposit into the merchant's account and charge the customer's account, even if the customer's bank is different from the merchant's. The terminal can perform an inventory control function for the merchant by recording sales, it minimizes errors on charge sales, and reduces need for staff for credit authorization.[133]

There are three types of POS systems:

1. *Simple model*—where both the merchant and the customer have accounts at the same bank. The "one-bank" model is very limited since it cannot handle regional or national EFT system transactions and is limited to stores and customers who share the offering bank.

2. *Transition model*—involves two or more banks, thereby eliminating the limitation of the simple model that both merchant and customer belong to the same bank.

3. *Network model*—distinguishable from the previous models by the introduction of "switches" or special subsystems. The *network switch* is a computer system that processes complex communications. This processing center will serve a variety of stores and banks in an area with multiple switches providing processing services for larger regional or national areas.[134]

The drawbacks of POS terminals are similar to those of the ATM: security breach, fraudulent manipulation of data and possible invasion of privacy of customer records.[135]

With respect to POS, the recommendations of the National Commission on Electronic Fund Transfers were tentative. While not precluding government involvement in POS operational switching and clearing facilities, the Commission saw the immediate role of the Federal Reserve to be "net settlement" among depository institutions.[136] Retailers, as one representative noted, have no interest in being in the banking business. They do not want to be susceptible to the authority of bank regulators because they have accepted payment through an EFT system. Retailers have no desire to be subject to reporting

---

[132] A. Bequai, The Cashless Society: EFT at the Crossroads (1981), at 30. See **ch 7** for a discussion of computer crime. This electronic accounting process, wherein the customer's account is instantaneously debited without the creation of a paper trail, is referred to as *data capture*. In a period of transition to data capture, the bank merely reserves the amount in the customer's account. Eventually, the paper trail reaches the bank, and the transaction is finalized.

[133] *Id* 32.

[134] *Id.*

[135] *Id* 33.

[136] National Commission on Electronic Fund Transfer, EFT in the United States, Policy Recommendations and the Public Interest, The Final Report of the National Commission on Electronic Fund Transfer (1977), at 78.

requirements designed for financial institutions.[137]

§8.13   The Automated Clearing House

The automated clearing house (ACH) is the unseen electronic funds transfer (EFT) component, though perhaps the most important. It functions as a regional check clearing facility, except that, instead of processing checks, an ACH serves as a central magnetic tape depository where information on payment transactions is processed.[138] The concept of an ACH originated in California in the late 1960s with the appointment of a Special Committee on Paperless Entries (SCOPE). Rules and regulations governing operations software and hardware were developed by 1972, and the California Automated Clearing House Association (CASHA) was established. Other clearing houses modeled on CASHA have been established in all twelve Federal Reserve districts.[139] These clearing houses, now numbering over thirty nationwide, are strongly supported by the Federal Reserve, with a major share of the volume being direct-deposit social security checks, military payrolls, and federal revenue sharing for states.[140] The Federal Reserve also provides operational services such as electronic data processing and transportation to and from banks that are members of the ACH.[141]

The ACH is the superstructure in the EFT system evolution. At present, ACHs are functioning by the use of "batch processing." To function as a true interbank clearing network, ACHs must be "on line."[142] Additionally, local networks connecting privately owned systems, such as retailers' point of sale devices, must become part of this larger structure which connects into a regional system.[143] In turn, the regional systems will eventually interconnect to form a national network.[144] The Federal Reserve Communications System (FED Wire) already functions on a national basis. National bank cards, such as

---

[137] Interview with Susan Ingram, Attorney, JC Penney Company, Inc, in New York City (Mar 1979).

[138] M. Bender, EFTS: Electronic Funds Transfer Systems—Elements and Impact (1975), at 41.

[139] Peat, Marwick & Mitchell, EFTS: A Strategy Perspective 7 (1977).

[140] *Id* 9.

[141] N. Penny & D. Baker, The Law of Electronic Fund Transfer Systems 3-7 (1980).

[142] *Batch processing* refers to data collected over a period of time, aggregated and processed as a group. An on-line or real time system is one where source data are collected through input devices which directly feed, and are controlled by, the computer itself.

[143] A. Little, The Consequences of Electronic Fund Transfer 71 (1975) (a report prepared by the National Science Foundation).

[144] An example of the transfer credit system is found where one bank transmits a transfer message to its Federal Reserve bank to debit its account. The Federal Reserve bank then credits the due-to account of another Federal Reserve bank, which in turn credits the account of the receiving bank. See generally M. Bender, *supra* note 138, at 13.

VISA and MasterCharge, already function with regional and national electronic communications.[145]

The National EFT Commission Report made recommendations for policy in the area of automated clearing houses. The Commission recommended continued participation by the Federal Reserve in providing ACH services. Continued Federal Reserve involvement will permit all depository institutions to utilize these services under rules promulgated by the Federal Reserve and the local ACH. At the same time, private development of ACH services would not be discouraged.[146]

§8.14   Economics of Electronic Funds Transfer

Revolutionary change does not occur in a vacuum. There must be some impetus forged by factors which will be benefitted by the change—a need for the change must be clearly perceived and acted upon. In the case of electronic funds transfer (EFT) development, the need for this change has been neither universally perceived, nor acted upon.

The View from Financial Institutions: Cost Reduction/Market Share

The interest of the financial service industry in EFT development stems mainly from: (1) increased operating costs; (2) increased customer usage of banking services; and (3) financial institutions taking part in price cutting for their services in this era of highly competitive financial services offerings.[147] Banks, therefore, see the *volume of services* they offer *increasing* while the *revenue* from servicing these transactions is *decreasing*.[148] This creates the vicious cycle of intensifying competition for the limited pool of deposits in a financial world wherein commercial banks no longer have an iron grip on demand deposit

---

[145] Bank card companies have nationwide on-line authorization systems. Each authorization center is connected by high speed data communication lines. These lines are also capable of paperless transmission of sales.

[146] National Commission on Electronic fund Transfer, EFT in the United States, Policy Recommendations and the Public Interest, The Final Report of the National Commission on Electronic Fund Transfer (1977), at 75. See generally, Berostran, Nationwide ACH Payments in 1978: The Future is Now, 54 Mag Bank Ad 32 (1978); Curren & Anderson, Quick Picture of Where ACH (Automated Clearing House) Stands and Where It's Going, 67 Banking 36 (1975); and Karr, Automated Clearing House: The Case for Barring Thrift Institutions, 95 Banking LJ 823 (1978).

[147] This increased competition is, in part, the result of the Depository Institutions Deregulation and Monetary Control Act of 1980, Pub L No 96-221, 94 Stat 132, which gave thrift institutions the power to offer quasi-demand deposit accounts in the form of NOW acounts and share drafts upon which interest can be earned. See §8.09.

[148] Hill, *Electronic Fund Transfer and "Competitive Equality": A Doctrine That Does Not Compute*, 32 Ark L Rev 347, 352 (1978).

dollars.[149] Some commentators actually foresee a reduced role for depository institutions as corporations develop "internal cash mobilization systems to manage funds on a corporate wide basis."[150] Banks, consequently, seek from EFT a *reduction in operating costs,* through the use of automated teller machines (ATMs), while *increasing the convenience of service* to the customer, as EFT acts to expand the hours and locations of bank accessability and services offered.[151] EFT may also improve bank productivity and customer recordkeeping.[152]

In this era when financial institutions and the services they offer are less compartmentalized, the market share is no longer protected. Therefore, these institutions must now actively compete for the depositor's dollar. Further, this competition has been intensified by the entry of nonfinancial institutions into the financial services industry. The EFT system has the potential of affecting the balance of power among financial institutions, both depository and non-depository in nature. After Sears, which has more credit card holders than MasterCharge, merged with Dean Witter, Sears now has the capacity to offer its own credit card holders bank-like liabilities.[153]

Cost/Benefit Analysis

One of the "Big-Eight" accounting firms attempted to give guidelines for a cost/benefit analysis of EFT.[154] In its report, it concluded that costs were difficult to discern accurately given that costs for equipment, personnel, and development are shared across a broad number of operating centers.[155] On the benefits side, it also stated that it was hard to quantify the intangible results of an EFT program such as new accounts or new deposits.[156] An American Management Association Publication estimated the cost to be 35 cents per customer transaction, while the American Bankers Association calculated 1.26 cents per transaction for other processing services.[157]

Financial Credit Industry View

This group, composed of small loan companies, sales finance companies, industrial banks, and industrial loan companies, have little contact with con-

---

[149] See §8.09.

[150] Quoted from Panel Discussion, *Electronic Funds Transfer,* 32 Bus L 201, 209 (1976); see also Hill, *supra* note 67, at 354.

[151] See generally Domm, *Electronic Banking—A Market View,* 92 Bankers Monthly 16 (1975); Long, *Banking Services in an EFT Society,* 37 U Pitt L Rev 640 (1976).

[152] Long, *supra* note 151. See also Rose, *More Bank for the Buck: The Magic of Electronic Banking,* Fortune, May 1977, at 202.

[153] Farley, *Dialing for Dollars - Electronic Funds Transfer Systems,* 37 U Pitt L Rev 613, 623 (1976).

[154] Peat, Markwick & Mitchell, EFTS: A Strategy Perspective (1977), at 35.

[155] *Id* at 37.

[156] *Id.*

[157] C. Martin, An Introduction to Electronic Funds Transfer Systems 10 (1978).

sumers, aside from the initial contact from a direct loan. Direct credit and debit functions, therefore, hold little interest for these institutions.[158] The EFT system could erode the market share of loans from this group to larger commercial banks. It has been argued that the nationwide organizational pattern of these companies could be condusive to electronic transfer.[159] A major retailer expressed a similar concern about a shift in sources of consumer finance services at a hearing before the U.S. Senate Subcommittee on Banking, Housing and Urban Affairs.[160]

Consumers' View

As one author noted, perhaps the dream of a cashless society wherein everyone benefits without harm, can be compared to the introduction of the seat belt buzzer and interlock system.[161]

> The vision that launched that technology, of course, was a vast reduction in the number of deaths and serious injuries from automobile accidents. The zeal of visionaries was fueled by the demonstrable ability of seat belts to prevent casualties and the very real social benefits that such prevention would produce. What they evidently failed to take into account, however, was that many drivers would not perceive the new technology as a benefit (despite mountains of data to the contrary) or would regard the benefit as outweighed by the cost, and would simply refuse to use seat belts.[162]

In the case of EFT, consumers appear to regard the present paper-based, check system as perfectly adequate to meet their needs.[163] Although consumers appreciate the convenience of ATM services, studies conducted in the 1970s indicate that consumers see no gain or benefit to be had in a total switch from paper to electronics.[164] In fact, one study indicated that consumers who favored direct payroll deposit did so because it also gave them free checking privileges.[165] One can see that EFT technology will change the way traditional services are delivered to the individual and business customer. Some authors

---

[158] These institutions at the end of 1974 held 39% of personal loans outstanding. (Speech by Dr. S. Lees Booth, NCFA senior vice president to Payments Systems Research Program Workshop, May 1975).

[159] *Id.*

[160] *Oversight on the Report of the National Commission to EFT: Hearings Before the Senate Subcomm on Banking, Housing and Urban Affairs*, 95th Cong, 1st Sess (1977) (statement by Paul R. Kaltinick).

[161] P. Schuck, Electronic Funds Transfer: A Technology in Search of a Market, The Economics of a National Electronic Fund Transfer System 151, 151-52 (a conference held Oct 1974, sponsored by the Federal Reserve Bank of Boston).

[162] *Id* 153.

[163] *Id.*

[164] *Id* 154. See also Lublin, *"Checkless" Banking is available, but Public Sees Few Advantages*, Wall St J, Nov 18, 1975, at 1.

[165] P. Schuck, *supra* note 161.

predict that it is only a matter of time before credit card companies, communication companies, and equipment vendors all attempt to offer financial services.[166] The profitability of network operation, in both local and regional clearing processing, is an important aspect of the economic picture.

Legal Issues Surrounding Electronic Funds Transfer

§8.15   Branch Banking and Electronic Funds Transfer

In late 1974, James E. Smith, Comptroller of the Currency, issued a ruling that Customer-Bank Communication Terminals (CBCT) were not branches.[167] The ruling stated that the use of "such devices at locations other than the main office or a branch office of the bank does not constitute branch banking."[168] The ruling also permitted banks to use CBCTs after giving written notice to the Comptroller's office 30 days before any device was put into operation.[169] The Comptroller attempted to distinguish the services offered at a brick and mortar branch as compared to those at a CBCT, noting that a CBCT customer cannot obtain a loan, purchase money orders, or open an account. Because subsequent verification of a transaction must be made before it is final, no check is actually cashed, nor deposit actually received. The CBCT, therefore, is "more closely analogous to a mailbox or a telephone through which the customer may communicate with his bank to accomplish certain routine trans-

---

[166] *Supra* note 154, at 27.

[167] After encountering pressure from several sources, a revised ruling was issued on May 9, 1975. The ruling clarified the original in three areas:

1. The use of CBCTS owned by third parties. The Comptroller's ruling was modified to make clear that national banks are permitted to participate in networks of CBCTS whether or not the bank itself owns or operates the terminals. *See* 40 Fed Reg 21700, 21701 (1975).

2. Geographic limitations. The Comptroller adopted a 50 mile radius as a measure of the natural market base of a banking office, stating that no national bank may establish for its exclusive use, a CBCT further than 50 miles away from the main office or its branch nearest to the CBCT. *See* 40 Fed Reg 21702.

3. Consumer protection. The Comptroller advised all national banks to disclose clearly and meaningfully to its customers all rights and liabilities in connection with both authorized and possibly unauthorized transactions involving a CBCT.

See Comment, *CBCTs: Stranded at the Altar*, 28 Baylor L Rev 356 (1976).

[168] Intepretive Ruling, 12 CFR §7.7491, *as amended*, 40 Fed Reg 21701 (1975).

[169] The Notice had to indicate the proposed location, general discription of the area and manner of installation; the manner of operation, the kinds of transactions, whether the device will be manned, whether the device will be shared, as well as information regarding the manufacturer, purchase or rental price, distance relative to other banks and devices, etc.

actions."[170] The Comptroller also noted the strong policy considerations:

> Defining such electronic communications devices as branches and applying to them the severe geographic and capital restrictions contained in the McFadden Act would stifle the development of modern banking and a newly evolving payments system.[171]

The most significant court challenge to the Comptroller's ruling came in *Independent Bankers Association of America v Smith.*[172] Based on the language of the McFadden·Act, the legislative history of the National Bank Act, and the Supreme Court decision in *Plant City,* the court stated that if the CBCT performed just *one* of the three basic transactions outlined in McFadden (deposits received, checks paid, or money lent), then the CBCT is a branch.[173]

As a result of this decision, the Comptroller suspended the ruling by stating that:

> National banks seeking to establish CBCTs must rely upon the advice of their own legal counsel. . . . However, national banks are cautioned that the Comptroller will not hesitate to use his supervisory powers to eliminate any unsafe, unsound or anti-competitive practices among national banks which might come to the Comptroller's attention.[174]

In *Colorado ex rel State Banking Board v First National Bank,* a national bank was enjoined from operating a CBCT in a shopping center located approximately 2.8 miles from the main building of the national bank.[175] The district court held that the CBCT was illegal because it met one of the McFadden Act's branching elements—deposits received—even though no checks were paid or money lent.[176] The court of appeals upheld the deposit function determination, but also found that the withdrawal of funds and transfer of funds between accounts also met the McFadden Act's requirements. The court of appeals

---

[170] 39 Fed Reg 44418 (1974). There is a crucial difference between customers instructing their banks by telephone, using an instrument not owned or operated by the bank, and using CBCTs which the bank established and operates. If it is not owned and operated by the bank, then it cannot possibly be a branch. *See* Comment, 6 Fordham Urban LJ at 585 (1978); see also Peck, 32 Bus Law 1657 (1977) (contains an extensive discussion of district and court of appeals holdings in this matter).

[171] 39 Fed Reg 44419 (1974).

[172] Independent Bankers Assn v Smith, 402 F Supp 207 (DDC 1975), *affd,* 534 F2d 921 (DC Cir), *cert denied,* 97 S Ct 166 (1976).
The IBAA is a 40 year old trade group consisting of about 50% of the commercial banks in the United States. It excludes banks or corporations controlled by multi-bank holding companies.

[173] 402 F Supp at 210.

[174] 40 Fed Reg 49077 (1975).

[175] State *ex rel* State Banking Bd v First Natl Bank, 394 F Supp 979 (D Colo 1975), *revd in part,* 540 F2d 497 (10th Cir 1976), *cert denied,* 429 US 1091 (1977).

[176] 540 F2d at 499.

stated that the district court had "unduly emphasize(d) form at the expense of substance."[177]

In *Missouri ex rel Kostman v First National Bank of St Louis,* Missouri law prohibited branch banking across county lines and the defendant operated two CBCTs in a county adjacent to the main office. In holding that the CBCTs did constitute branches, the court found that deposits were made, relying on congressional intent that national banks have the same right to branch as the banks of the state in which they operate.[178]

In *Illinois ex rel Lignoul v Continental Illinois National Bank & Trust Co,* the district court held that CBCTs received deposits but did not cash checks.[179] The court of appeals reversed the trial court, in part by holding that even cash withdrawals and installment loan payments constitute branch banking when done at a CBCT. The court focused on the fact that a payment order, whether accomplished by check, plastic card, or computer, is a routine banking function offered by a bank's main office and thus, when performed off-premises, comes within the scope of the McFadden Act.

In each of these cases, the defendant banks had argued, as had the comptroller, that deposits were "received" at the main office rather than at the CBCT location, since accounts were not credited or debited until after this information was communicated to the main office. The courts rejected this argument, based on the *Plant City* conclusion that the physical receipt of a deposit by the machine was a deposit within the meaning of McFadden. The judge in *Lignoul* noted that if the bank's argument were accepted, banks could circumvent McFadden by building brick and mortar offices, staffed by bank personnel who would accept deposits and then simply wire the information back to the main office.[180] The one court which held that CBCTs did not constitute branch banking was *Oklahoma ex rel State Banking Board v. Bank of Oklahoma,* wherein the court, motivated by policy considerations, accepted the bank's arguments, concluding that "the use of CBCTs by banks is necessary and essential for overall utilization by this country's payment system of electronic technology."[181]

§8.16   Antitrust Implications of Electronic Funds Transfer Systems

In this revolutionary period of change in the financial services industry, computer technology is playing an increasingly important role in determining

---

[177] *Id.*

[178] Missouri *ex rel* Kostman v First Natl Bank, 405 F Supp 733, 735 (1975).

[179] State *ex rel* Lignoul v Continental Ill Natl Bank & Trust Co, 409 F Supp 1167 (ND Ill 1975), *affd,* 536 F2d 176 (7th Cir), *cert denied,* 429 US 871 (1976).

[180] Peck, *supra* note 170, 1667-68.

[181] State *ex rel* State Banking Bd v Bank of Okla, 409 F Supp 71 (ND Okla 1975), *appeal dismissed by stipulation,* No 75-C-318 (ND Okla Mar 19, 1976).

the competitive advantage by which both traditional banking and new non-banking institutions will seek to increase their market share. The expense of creating banking computer systems creates pressure on these financial service industries to find ways to share costs with some institutions while denying access to others.

Antitrust Enforcement Statutes

The Sherman Antitust Act of 1890 was the first statute promulgated to halt the trend toward concentration of market power by large corporations. The original focus of the Act was Standard Oil and other trusts during the Gilded Era of the late 1800s. The two main provisions of the Sherman Act are: §1 which makes illegal "every contract, combination in the form of trust or otherwise, or conspiracy, in restraint of trade . . ." and; §2 which deems guilty of a felony "every person who shall monopolize, or attempt to monopolize, or combine or conspire with any other person or persons, to monopolize any part of the trade or commerce. . . ."[182] A §1 violation generally consists of restrictive agreements by two or more persons since a "contract" or "combination" cannot be entered into alone, while §2 violations may involve one or more persons given the emphasis on the development and possession of monopoly power.

The vagueness of the statute in defining the limits of legal or permissible conduct led to the passage of the Clayton Act of 1914[183] which concerned four specific acts which were restrictive or monopolistic and thus, could be illegal: (1) price discrimination or the sale of similar products to similarly situated buyers at different prices (§2); (2) "tying arrangements" or exclusive dealing contracts which condition sales on the cessation of dealings with the seller's competitors (§3); (3) mergers (§7) and; (4) interlocking directorates (§8).[184] The test of whether these acts were illegal was whether the effect of the acts "*may be* to substantially lessen competition" or tend to create a monopoly in any line of commerce.

The Federal Trade Commission Act of 1914 empowered the Federal Trade Commission to investigate unfair methods of competition, thus Sherman Act violations come within the umbrella of this Act.[185] Under this penumbra of statutes and regulatory agencies, those who wish to develop electronic funds

---

[182] 15 USC §§1-6. For a discussion of the antitrust aspects of computer technology see **ch 4.**

[183] 15 USC §§15-16.

[184] §2 of the Clayton Act was amended by the Robinson-Patman Act of 1936. 15 USC §13. Since Robinson-Patman requires a sale of "goods," there are differing opinions as to whether it could be applicable to EFT systems in the absence of a sale of goods.

[185] 15 USC §15. The Magnuson-Moss Warranty Federal Trade Commission Improvement Act, Pub L No 93-637, 88 Stat 2183 (1975), extended the Federal Trade Commission's jurisdiction to matters "affecting" commerce. Thus, EFT developers are exposed to antitrust suits from the Justice Department, the Federal Trade Commission, and private plaintiffs, who have the right to treble damages.

transfer (EFT) systems must face the spectre of antitrust exposure by taking part in any conduct which might "substantially lessen competition."

Joint Ventures: A Question of Sharing

The antitrust problems rooted in the development of EFT systems has been emphasized in recent years by the passage of state sharing statutes.[186] Further, the National Commission on Electronic Fund Transfers (NCEFT) recommended four possible sharing configurations: mandatory sharing, permissive/nondiscriminatory sharing, permissive sharing, and procompetitive sharing.[187]

These sharing arrangements fall within the definition of joint ventures—an association of two or more entities as owners of an enterprise formed for the purpose of carrying out a permanent corporate enterprise.[188] The shared activities may take the form of joint ownership of switching facilities or ownership and use of terminals, and must be limited to those activities necessary to

---

[186] The Justice Department objected to a proposed joint venture of commercial banks in Nebraska, stating that the mandatory sharing provisions of the Nebraska law tended to "undercut incentives to innovate and to create a 'free rider' problem with respect to those who join the system after it starts operating and thus avoid the initial risk taking." Letter of Donald I. Baker, as quoted in Katskee & Wright, *An Overview of Legal Issues Confronting the Establishment of EFT Services,* 2 Computer LJ 7, 18 (1980).

[187] The Final Report of the National Commission on Electronic Fund Transfers, EFT in the United States: Policy Recommendations and the Public Interest 94-97 (1977). Mandatory sharing would require that any institution providing EFT services share with any organization covered by the sharing structure. Permissive/nondiscriminatory sharing would permit a financial institution to refrain from sharing its system until another institution granted access. Permissive sharing would be a national policy of sharing designed to shield financial institutions from the antitrust laws in spite of the competitive effect. Procompetitive sharing, the policy endorsed by the NCEFT, allows that no sharing arrangement be precluded as long as it meets antitrust law standards. Retailers have spoken out against mandatory sharing of POS stating that this would reduce control over their point of sale and is not in the public interest. This is based on the theory that mandatory sharing will diminish competition among financial institutions providing EFT services. See Murray, *EFTS and Antitrust,* 37 U Pitt L Rev 678, 687 (1976). See also Morris, *Legal Background of a Shared EFT Network,* 34 Bus Law 527 (1979); Goldberg, *Shared Electronic Fund Transfer Systems: Some Legal Implications,* 98 Banking LJ 715, 722-23 (1981).

Mandatory sharing would seem to come within the state action antitrust exemption under the Parker doctrine. In Parker v Brown, 317 US 341 (1943), the Court upheld a California statute authorizing the establishment of agricultural marketing programs which had the effect of restricting competition and maintaining prices. In its recent decisions, the Court has looked for a clearly articulated, affirmatively expressed state policy, actively supervised by the state to find state action, and thus no antitrust violation.

[188] A joint venture may be formed by parents who are related horizontally or vertically, or who are potential competitors. See Pitofsky & Robert, *Joint Ventures Under the Antitrust Law: Some Reflections on the Significance of Penn-Olin,* 82 Harvard L Rev 1007 (1969), for a discussion of joint ventures.

accomplish the legitimate functions of the joint venture.[189] A joint venture is not a per se violation. Instead, the courts will generally look at the purpose of the venture and its economic benefit and determine whether there were less anticompetitive alternatives available to achieve the same results.[190] A key question in the joint development of EFT projects is whether the size of the joint venture itself diminishes the opportunity for competition. One argument raised by joint venture proponents is that the costs are so great that universal participation is essential from an economic viewpoint, while antitrust advocates point out that several discreet systems serving regional markets, which are technologically compatible, could be established.[191]

Entry

The most significant case dealing with the possible anticompetitive effects of a joint venture was *United States v Penn-Olin Chemical Co.*[192] In *Penn-Olin,* two chemical companies formed a joint subsidiary to produce sodium chlorate for the southeastern United States market. The Supreme Court held that a beneficial competitive effect could have been exerted on that market simply by having a strong, potential competitor "in the wings," and that this potential for competition had been eliminated by the formation of the joint venture.[193]

Financial institutions, therefore, which desire to create joint EFT ventures will argue that their costs and the risk of initiating the system are so great that horizontal sharing operations are the only feasible way to develop the system. The legality of the venture will depend on its scope in the context of the surrounding market. The creation of a permanent joint venture between competitors may be viewed as a merger between the parties.[194] The question of

---

[189] Katskee, *supra* note 186, at 17-18.

[190] The Antitrust Division of the Justice Department has listed the following factors for consideration in its Antitrust Guide:

> whether the creation of the joint venture itself unreasonably restrains competition; whether the joint venture has any unreasonable collateral restraints that must be struck down even if the joint venture is allowed; whether the joint venture is, in essence, a "bottleneck monopoly," which because of its importance to those in the business, must be open to all on reasonable and nondiscriminatory terms.

See US Justice Dept, Antitrust Division, Antitrust Guide for International Operations 20 (1977). See also N. Penney, *supra* note 141, at 18-3 to 18-29.

[191] Bernard, *Some Antitrust Issues Raised by Large Electronic Funds Transfer Systems,* 25 Cath UL Rev 749, 751 (1976). See generally Horodas, *Ownership and Control of Electronic Fund Transfer Systems in the United States,* 1 Computer LJ 501 (1979).

[192] United States v Penn-Olin Chem Co, 378 US 158 (1964).

[193] *Id* 173-74. "The existence of an aggressive, well-equipped and well-financed corporation engaged in the same or related lines of commerce waiting anxiously to enter an oligopolistic market would be a substantial incentive to competition which cannot be underestimated."

[194] As noted above, although there is a difference between a joint venture and a merger, the legal analysis of the potential competition is the same since the result of the joint venture is a "triumvirate of associated corporations." *Id* 169. The Federal

whether the merger will be allowed depends on whether the effect of the merger will be to "substantially lessen competition" or tend to create a monopoly in some *line of commerce* within a meaningful *geographic market.*

Antitrust liability is based on the extent of market shares within a defined *product* and *geographic* market. In bank mergers, it has been held that potential competition would be lost by the merger of a large, capable, potential entrant with the leading bank in a concentrated local market.[195] The proper defining of these markets, therefore, is critical.[196]

§8.17 —Geographic Market, Product Market, and Vertical Integration

Geographic Market

The Supreme Court in *United States v Philadelphia National Bank,* sought to define a bank's *geographic market,* stating that the issue was "not where the parties to the merger do business or even where they compete, but where, within the area of competitive overlap, the effect of the merger on competition will be direct and immediate."[197] The Court concluded that the geographic market was local, finding that "in banking, as in most service industries, convenience of location is essential to effective competition."[198] Similarly, for the retail-oriented electronic funds transfer (EFT) services such as the automated

---

Deposit Insurance Corporation (FDIC) has proposed that the authority to approve routine commercial bank mergers be delegated to regional FDIC administrators and the FDIC's Washington staff. The Department of Justice, which supports the proposal, suggested that market concentration standards be incorporated into the proposal, and that uniform standards for defining the relevant geographic market be established in order to ensure that all competitively harmful mergers would be identified. See Trade Reg Rep (CCH) No 572, at 9 (Dec 13, 1982).

[195] Baker, *Potential Competition in Banking: After Greely, What?* 90 Banking LJ 362, 367 (1973).

[196] Noble, *Antitrust Considerations Affecting Bank Growth: Greeley and Beyond,* 90 Baking LJ 381, 388 (1973).

> The legal objective is to draw the market in accord with economic realities— neither so narrow as to exclude competitors who have significant impact, nor so broadly as to dilute the market share of the merging firms which have no signficant impact on their competitive conduct. But antitrust litigation is, after all, an adversary proceeding. The closer the merging parties are geographically, the more likely the antitrust enforcer is to draw the market narrowly, so as to increase market shares; and the more likely the defendant is to draw the market broadly so as to acheive the opposite result. Put some distance between the merging banks and the roles are reversed: the defendant's interest is now served by drawing the markets narrowly, so that the banks are placed in different markets and treated as non-competitiors; whereas, if there is any reasonable basis for doing so, the enforcer is likely to draw the market broadly to include the two merging banks.

[197] United States v Philadelphia Natl Bank, 374 US 321 (1963).

[198] *Id* 358.

teller machine (ATM) and point of sale (POS) terminals, the relevant geographic market will remain local to a single community. Within that defined
area, the share occupied by the joint venture will be relevant, with the court
possibly inquiring into the market share of participants in demand deposits or
transaction services.[199]

Product Market: Line of Commerce

The Court in *Philadelphia National Bank* defined "commercial banking" as a
separate, relevant line of commerce to be used in evaluating bank mergers.[200]
The difficulty with the continued use of this definition is that it fails to take into
account the existence of both thrift institutions and nonfinancial institutions
which have been offering a full and varied panoply of financial services since
the 1963 *PNB* case. In the case of *U.S. v. Phillipsburg National Bank,* wherein two
of the largest commercial banks in Phillipsburg attempted to merge, the
Comptroller of the Currency approved the merger, pursuant to the Bank
Merger Act, by evaluating the competition from finance companies, savings
and loan associations, as well as other commercial banks.[201] The Court found
that the use of submarkets would be relevant "in analyzing the effects on
competition of a merger between a commercial bank and other type of financial
institution."[202] It is arguable that the Court, if faced with a joint venture or
merger case, in the recently deregulated financial markets, would redefine line
of commerce to include the more specialized submarkets such as "card
products" for those customers or merchants who use cards to the exclusion
of checks, or "ACH services" which may be distinct from traditional clearing
services.[203]

To date, the problems of entry have quickly disappeared once the Department of Justice expressed its objections to a sharing arrangement. In 1977, the
Department of Justice (DOJ) outlined its objections to the Nebraska Electronic
Transfer System (NETS). DOJ said that the venture would prevent individual
initiative by requiring that all services be designed collectively and emphasized
that, although all commercial banks would be allowed to join, thrift institutions
were precluded from participating.[204] The directors of NETS simply rewrote
their bylaws to comply with these objections. In 1977, DOJ also filed suit
against automated clearing house operations in California and Colorado which
denied use of their services to thrift institutions. Again, the bylaws were

---

[199] N. Penney & D. Baker, The Law of Electronic Fund Transfer Systems 18-11
(1980).

[200] 374 US at 356.

[201] United States v Phillipsburg Natl Bank & Trust Co, 399 US 350, 358-59 (1970).
See **ch 4** for a discussion of the antitrust issues of computer technology.

[202] *Id* 360.

[203] N. Penney, *supra* note 199, at 18-9. One author has suggested two lines of Commerce: business financial services and consumer financial services. R. Johnson, The
New Competition, 37 Bus Law 1363, 1371 (1982).

[204] Goldberg, *supra* note 187, at 727.

changed to permit this access and the cases were voluntarily dismissed.[205]

Vertical Integration Problems

The establishment of an EFT joint venture also constitutes a vertical integration into the newly created, computational financial communications industry. The hardware/software manufacturers who presently develop nonfinancial computerized systems would obviously be ready to supply equipment for financial communications systems.

James L. Pierce describes the combination of computer software and hardware and the communications network necessary to establish an EFT system as the "wholesale side" of EFT.[206] Pierce suggests that there exists an absence of conflict of interest among hardware/software firms and sufficient competition to make anti-competitive practice unlikely, but that depository institutions and merchants will have a conflict of interest between their wholesale and retail EFT activities. Merchants will want to be part of a system that has many depository institutions represented in it, while depository institutions will want many merchants while excluding other competing depository institutions.[207]

Another author suggests that the importance of antitrust enforcement in this area is clear when it is considered that these independent computer companies may be able to provide cheaper and more efficient EFT services than financial institutions by spreading their costs over a communications link which combines both financial and nonfinancial information.[208] This more efficient system could be foreclosed by an EFT joint venture which would deny its members the right to deal with those outside the venture—a clear §7 Clayton Act violation. This exclusion would give the joint venturers a competitive advantage over those financial institutions or merchants who could not gain access to the system, or could gain access only with the payment of fees. The question of access turns on whether or not the EFT system is so commercially necessary and desirable that competitors of EFT operators must make use of such systems as a matter of competitive survival.

---

[205] United States v Rocky Mountain ACH, Action #77-391 (D Colo 1977); United States v California ACH, Civ No 77-1643-LTL (D Cal 1977).

[206] Pierce, *The Competitive Implications of EFT*, 2 Computer LJ 133, 1345 (1980). See also Johnson, *The New Competition*, 37 Bus L 1363 (1982); Muething, *The Effect of the Use of Customer-Bank Communications Terminals on Competition Among Financial Institutions*, 45 U Cin L Rev 591 (1976).

[207] Pierce, *supra* note 206, at 144-46.

[208] Bernard, *supra* note 191, at 752.

§8.18 Access, Discrimination, Conglomeration, Standards, and Transaction Capabilities

Access

Under the antitrust laws, the finding that a joint venture is a *natural monopoly* could compel the cooperative arrangement to permit access to all competing entities. A natural monopoly is an enterprise whose economies of scale are so large in relation to potential demand that effective competition cannot exist as a matter of fact.[209] *United States v Terminal Railroad Association* stands for the proposition that access to this venture must be granted on a nondiscriminatory basis either through membership or the payment of reasonable fees for use when an *essential facility* is found to exist.[210] In *Terminal,* the association had acquired the only means of entry into St. Louis. The Court threatened the association with dissolution if it did not permit competing railroads to join in ownership or at least allow access at reasonable rates.

In *Associated Press v United States,* the Supreme Court extended the compulsory access rule to situations wherein no essential facility is found, but where a substantial amount of market power is derived from the sharing arrangement, or a substantial competitive advantage is created and those who have been denied access are without a reasonable way to create an alternative facility.[211] This compulsory access rule is based on the theory that those who obtain some competitive advantage by joint efforts may not inflict competitive harm on those to whom they have denied access.[212]

The automated clearing house (ACH) system could arguably be described as an essential facility since it seems logical that one clearing facility should be used on a regional basis, and that denial of access to certain institutions would result, not only in competitive disadvantage to those institutions, but possible inefficient handling of financial information. Similarly, the essential facility argument could be made for point of sale (POS) systems, although it has been suggested that because of the relatively low level of consumer acceptance for POS services, there are doubts that the essential facility argument could prevail.[213]

---

[209] The determination of a natural monopoly depends on an analysis of long run costs which may suggest that a facility is subject to pervasive and substantial economies of scale, thus requiring the finding of a natural monopoly. Absent a finding of natural monopoly, focus will be placed on the broadness of the venture in relation to the members' individual efforts. N. Penney, *supra* note 199, at 18-14. See **ch 4** for a discussion of the antitrust issues of the communications industry.

[210] United States v Terminal RR 224 US 383 (1912).

[211] Associated Press v United States, 326 US 1 (1945).

[212] This rule is also referred to as the "bottleneck theory" of antitrust, and is applied only where the large joint venture is justified as a benefit to society because of its economies of scale. See N. Penney, *supra* note 199, at 18-25.

[213] Goldberg, *supra* note 188, at 732.

Discriminatory Practices

As *Associated Press* indicates, even without the finding of an essential facility, restraint of trade can be caused by sheer market power. *Associated Press* could be used to attack electronic funds transfer (EFT) arrangements that restrict members from engaging in competing activities with the joint venture or preclude them from experimenting with alternate systems. These "collateral restraints" would clearly raise restraint of trade challenges, whereas collateral restraints that could be shown to be necessary, would survive challenge,[214] Price agreements, tying arrangements, and refusals to deal are all considered per se violations of §1 of the Sherman Act, and any one of these violations could be envisioned by an EFT system.[215] Any horizontal agreement among competitors or vertical agreement between suppliers and dealers would be considered a price fixing agreement. Price agreements could occur due to sharing information and technological data.[216] A tying agreement could occur in any number of ways: an employer whose payroll is part of a direct deposit arrangement could be compelled to take advantage of other services offered by the financial institution; or a POS merchant might be encouraged to maintain all of its accounts or fulfill its financial needs only with the services offered in the EFT bank which controls its terminals.[217] Refusals to deal could occur where the suppliers of EFT terminals to a certain system refuse to supply terminals to merchants or banks not a part of the system.[218] Further, precluding any institution, such as a savings and loan, from an EFT system, could be considered a "group boycott" which is a per se violation.[219] As has already been discussed, the joint venture or merger of banks to form an EFT system is subject to the restrictions of §7 of the Clayton Act. If the EFT system market were highly concentrated and a bank sought a merger rather than entering *de novo*, the potential competition from the entrant would be eliminated.[220]

Conglomerate Merger

Similar lessening of competition arguments could be made concerning the creation of financial services giants such as Sears and Dean Witter or American Express and Shearson.[221] Small banks fear the deregulation which has permit-

---

[214] N. Penney, *supra* note 199, at 18-24.

[215] Murray, *EFT and Antitrust - Some Reflections on the Possibilities*, 37 U Pitt L Rev 673 (1976) (contains a compilation of examples of potential antitrust problems). See also Ubell, *Electronic Funds Transfer and Antitrust Laws*, 93 Banking LJ 43 (1976).

[216] Murray, *supra* note 215, at 678.

[217] *Id* 681.

[218] *Id* 679.

[219] *Id* 680.

[220] *Id* 690. Murray suggests that an independent entry into the EFTS market would promote deconcentration in that market, *citing* United States v Marine Bancorporation, 418 US 602, 623-25 (1974).

[221] Conglomerate acquisition/mergers to date:

ted the merger of the large nonbank institutions entering a tight market. Of course, such nonbanking institutions offering a wide spectrum of financial services, presume that consumers desire this "one-stop shopping" convenience. One Prudential scenario suggests that a "family account" could be established whereby a customer would secure several different kinds of insurance but pay only a single premium. The "family account" would allow the customer to earn interest on credit balances in the account, or if the consumer could not pay, the consumer might be allowed to borrow against the cash value in an existing life insurance policy.[222]

The Independent Bankers Association of America, representing some 7,400 commercial banks, attempted to pressure the Reagan administration to stop the American Express/Shearson acquisition stating, "the size of the American Express empire when it is directly linked to the second largest brokerage house, means a concentration of economic power that is dangerous. . . . It creates a domestic and international bank outside of the regulatory scheme."[223] The efforts of the Independent Bankers Association, however, were unsuccessful. The Reagan administration is confident that these conglomerate mergers and acquisitions will provide consumers with better and cheaper financial services. Speaking before the House Monopolies Subcommittee, William F. Baxter, Assistant Attorney General of the Antitrust Division, and Lyle E. Gramley, of the Board of Governors of the Federal Reserve System both emphasized the need to deregulate banking and equalize competition among financial institutions.[224] Baxter stated that:

> the great changes in the financial services markets in recent years have resulted from vigorous competitive efforts to meet perceived consumer needs—needs that, largely because of legal constraints on regulated institutions, had gone long unmet.[225]

Further, Baxter noted that consumers will reap the benefits from consolidation, and that small institutions would continue to be profitable and to provide

---

Loeb Rhoades acquired Shearson - 1979
Blyth Eastman Dillon merged into Payne Webber - 1979
Salomon Brothers acquired Philbro - 1981
Shearson acquired by American Express - 1981
Bache acquired by Prudential - 1981
Dean Witter acquired by Sears Roebuck - 1981

Fortune, Dec 28, 1981.

[222] *Id* 64.

[223] Richard W. Peterson, legislative counsel to IBAA, quoted in Bus Wk, May 18, 1981, at 112.

[224] Antitrust & Trade Reg Rep (BNA) No 1022, at A-13 (July 9, 1981).

[225] *Id.*

needed services.[226] It is interesting to note that Baxter was unconvinced that there were economies of scale to be realized by these conglomerates, commenting:

> while there has been much talk about one-stop "financial supermarkets" that provide most or all of the services sought by their customers, it is far too early to make confident predictions whether consumers will prefer such arrangements to dealing with more specialized and accessible institutions.[227]

No matter what the antitrust implications of these mergers and acquisitions, these financial giants will be the institutions with the resources capable of developing EFT systems, and, therefore, will be subject to the doctrine of nondiscriminatory access previously discussed.

Electronic Funds Transfer Standards

The issue here is the development of one standard payment system. The problem breaks into two distinct areas: standardization of equipment (both hardware and software) and the types of transaction services which should be offered at terminal entry points.

Technical Standards

This area is of concern to both vendors (manufacturers) and purchasers. The major concern of the National Commission on Electronic Fund Transfer was the impact that standard setting would have on competition. The consensus of witnesses at the commission hearing was that well thought out, timely standards stimulate competition. The ability of dominant manufacturers in the data processing and communications fields to create standards outside the standard-making process, however, distorts competition.[228] The creator of this *de facto* standard can achieve a time advantage in the market place and competitors are unable to obtain timely information to develop compatible peripheral equipment.[229] This area was so fraught with controversy that the Commission declined to make any specific recommendations. The impact and importance of this aspect of EFT cannot be overlooked. If a national network is to function effectively there must be compatibility among systems.

---

[226] *Id* A-14. Gramley of the Federal Reserve commented that "consumers have clearly benefited from the interwoven effects of product innovation and institutional deregulation.

[227] Nat Comm on Electronic Fund Transfer, EFT and the Public Interest 102 (1977).

[228] *Id.*

[229] NCEFT, *supra* note 227, at 102.

Transaction Capabilities

The questions that have been raised in this area are: should there be any minimum capabilities at the terminal entry point and should terminal entry points be designed to accept the same types of activating devices, such as plastic cards, or touch-tone data entry? At present, there is diversity among the systems because of the proprietary nature and competitive factors of each system.[230] The American Bankers Association, however, has launched a pilot study to develop a prototype system to guide its members in developing electronic payments systems.[231]

Of note is the retailer perspective on mandated "bundling" of EFT services. In a recent presentation to a sectional meeting of the American Bar Association, an attorney for a major national retailer presented the retailers' point of view. Retailers are concerned about the payment vehicles which they must accept. For example, can a retailer have a debit function but not a credit function? The bundling of services will negate the retailer's ability to negotiate separately and competitively for different EFT functions.[232] There are presently no mandatory standards proposed either by private industry or government for EFT equipment. Minimum capability standards at terminal entry have also not been set. These two areas must be resolved, because of their important impact on EFT system competition.

§8.19   Consumer Concerns: The Uniform Commercial Code and the Electronic Funds Transfer Act

While electronic funds transfer (EFT) systems promise to provide more convenience and service, many consumers are concerned with protective safeguards. This concern received support in the report of the National Commission on Electronic Fund Transfers when it stated that:

> central to all the Commission's inquiries has been a recognition that the consumer's interest are primary in all regulatory, legislative, and policy decisions affecting EFT and the consumer's interest must be reflected in such decisions.[233]

Because our present payments system is paper-based, the source of consumer rights for paper payments is the Uniform Commercial Code (UCC). Consumer protection in the world of the computer came into existence as one of the titles of the Consumer Credit Protection Act of the Financial Institutions Regulatory

---

[230] M. Bender, EFTS: Electronic Funds Transfer Systems (1975), at 57.

[231] *Id.*

[232] Speech by Susan Ingram, Esq, to ABA in Dallas, Texas, Jan 1979.

[233] Nat Comm on Electronic Fund Transfer, EFT and the Public Interest xii (1977). See **§3.07** for the applications of the UCC to computer transactions.

and Interest Rate Control Act of 1978, also known as the Electronic Funds Transfer Act, and the rules implementing it are called Regulation E.[234]

The main source of law governing value exchanges, other than those executed for cash, is Articles 3 and 4 of the Uniform Commercial Code. The issue of the applicability of the UCC to electronic debit and credit transactions has been in controversy since these were first contemplated. Some authors argue that the UCC has no direct applicability because it pertains only to negotiable instruments and sets up requirements for negotiability that electronic impulses cannot meet.[235] Others contend that the UCC's "carefully integrated set of standards" have nationwide acceptance and should be amended or supplemented to apply to EFT systems.[236] Still others see the UCC as a "viable framework governing payment and transfer transactions during the transition from paper to paperless electronic operations."[237] Article 3 of the UCC is entitled *Commercial Paper* and deals with such instruments as checks, drafts, and promissory notes. Article 4 deals with the check collection process and is entitled *Bank Deposits and Collections.*[238] These articles establish the rights and responsibilities of both banks and their customers for items directing the transfer of funds. The UCC permits these rules to be varied by contractual agreement.[239] In contrast, consumer protections under the EFT Act, of necessity, deal with transactions which do not leave a paper trail, yet still must deal with the fundamental problems of standard of care, the allocation of risk,

---

[234] Financial Institutions Regulatory and Interest Rate Control Act of 1978, Pub L No 95-630, 92 Stat 3641. The Electronic Funds Transfer Act, Pub L No 95-930, 92 Stat 3728, tit XX (1978), 15 USC §§1693-1693r. For treatment of the EFT Act's major provisions, see generally Schellie, *The Electronic Fund Transfer Act,* 35 Bus L 1441 (1979); Einhorn, *A Banker's Guide to the Electronic Fund* Transfer Act, 96 Banking LJ 772 (1979); Jennings, *The Electronic Fund Transfer Act,* 25 Prac Law 11 (1979); Schellie, *Electronic Fund Transfer Act,* 35 Bus L 1275 (1980): Greguras, *How the New EFT Act Affects the* Financial Institution/Consumer Relationship, 11 UCCLJ 207 (1979); Brandel & Olliff, *The Electronic Fund Transfer Act: A Primer,* 40 Ohio St LJ 531 (1979). Regulation E, 12 CFR §226, comprises the rules promulgated by the Federal Reserve Board to implement the requirements of this act.

[235] Penney, *Questions Needing Answers - Effects of EFTS on the UCC,* 37 U Pitt L Rev 661 (1976).

The first fundamental issue raised was whether the term "item" applied to EFT. Item, as defined by UCC §4-104(1)(g) means "any instrument for the payment of money. . . ." The term instrument is generally construed to mean a writing in a "tangible form." Those that wish to bring the EFTS within the ambit of the UCC point out that a computer tape, or other computer record is a tangible form and constitute legal writings or instruments. Several states have added electronic transfers to the definition of item and instrument, and the Federal Reserve Board has modified its definition.

[236] Hill, *Electronic Fund Transfer and "Competitive Equality": A Doctrine That Does Not Compute,* 32 Ark L Rev 347, 355 (1978).

[237] Vergari, *Articles 3 and 4 of the Uniform Commercial Code in an Electronic Fund Transfer Environment,* 17 San Diego L Rev 287 (1980).

[238] *Id.*

[239] *Id* 290.

unauthorized issuances, material alterations, the stop payment function, and verification of transactions.

Scope of EFT Act

In the EFT Act, "electronic fund transfer" is defined as a transfer:

> initiated through an electronic terminal, telephonic instrument, or computer or magnetic tape, so as to order, instruct, or authorize a financial institution to debit or credit an account.[240]

The transactions this includes are: point of sale (POS) transfers, automated teller machine (ATM) transactions and telephone transfers. Specifically excluded from the Act's coverage are: original paper transactions with instruments such as checks, check guarantee or authorization services in which no crediting or debiting of an account takes place, security or commodity transfers, and trust accounts.[241] Thus, the Act does not conflict with the UCC, yet the UCC's flexibility makes it a good framework for reference in the transition period to a cashless society.[242] Incidental transfers authorized by phone to third parties are exempt if they are not made pursuant to a pre-arrangement with a financial institution.[243] Certain intrainstitutional transfers are also exempt in that there was no need to extend the Act's protection to these transactions which are automated only because of increased computerization.[244] The EFT Act defines "financial institution" broadly so as to bring within it all activity by both state and federal institutions as well as "any other person who directly or indirectly, holds an account belonging to a consumer."[245]

Allocation of Risk

There are several theories as to how to allocate liability: fault, a flat limitation on consumer liability, a combination of the two, and enterprise liability.[246] The UCC allocates loss on the basis of fault, although this may be altered by contract within the bounds of the UCC's good faith requirement.[247] This is to be contrasted to the EFT Act's minimum protections for consumers which

---

[240] Electronic Fund Transfer Act, §903(6), 15 USC §1693a(6); 12 CFR §205.2(g).

[241] *Electronic Fund Transfers: New Protections for Consumers, New Duties for Financial Institutions,* Fed Reserve Bull, Apr 1980, at 290. See generally Brandel, *Electronic Funds Transfer: Commercial and Consumer Law Aspects,* 82 Com LJ 78 (1977).

[242] Vergari, *supra* Note 237, at 294.

[243] *Id.*

[244] *Id* 291; Schellie, *supra* note 234, at 1277.

[245] Greguras, *supra* note 234, at 219; EFT Act §903(8), 15 USC §1693a(8); 12 CFR §205.2(i).

[246] Greguras, *The Allocation of Risk in Electronic Fund Transfer Systems for Losses Caused by Unauthorized Transactions,* 13 USFL Rev 405, 406 (1979).

[247] Vergari, *supra* note 237, at 295.

cannot be modified by agreement[248] and indicates a preference for the needs of the consumer.[249]

Unauthorized Transactions

The EFT Act gives consumers 60 days to identify unauthorized transfers and errors.[250] After this period, the consumer bears the loss, indicating a balance between the bank's duty to act reasonably and the consumer's duty to prevent losses. Further, if a customer's access card is used without authorization, the customer's liability is limited to the lesser of $50 or the value of the property or services obtained through the EFT terminal prior to the notification of the bank.[251] The customer's liability may not exceed $500 or the amount of unauthorized transfers which occur following the close of two business days after the customer learns of the loss, even if the customer fails to notify the bank.[252] The Act also places the burden of proof upon the financial institution to show that the fund transfer was authorized, or if unauthorized, to show that the conditions of liability have been met and the proper disclosures to the consumer have been made.[253]

In comparison, UCC § 3-406 allocates loss to anyone who "by his negligence substantially contributes to a material alteration . . . or the making of an unauthorized signature."[254] The reasons for this difference have been suggested as being: (1) an incentive to consumers to be careful in using access devices and reporting thefts; (2) an incentive to financial institutions to develop effective means of identifying authorized users, and (3) the greater ability of the financial institutions to prevent losses.[255]

---

[248] 15 USC §1693l. "Enterprise liability" limits coverage to the consumer and the financial institution and sets forth rigid procedures. Comment, *The Electronic Fund Transfer Act—A Departure from Articles Three and Four of the Uniform Commercial Code,* 1980 Wis L Rev 1008, 1013.

[249] Comment, *supra* note 248, at 1020.

[250] 15 USC §1693g.

[251] 15 USC §1693g(a).

[252] *Id.*

[253] 15 USC §1693g(b).

[254] If the consumer were to write his or her PIN on the transaction card which was then stolen, the thief would be able to access the account. This would be equivalent to signing a blank check. Under the UCC, the consumer would be liable for the amount of the check while the EFT consumer's liability would be limited to $50.00 if he or she followed proper notification procedures. Comment, *supra* note 248, at 1021-22.

[255] *Id* 1023-25. This article describes EFT's allocation as "redistributive allocation" in comparison with the UCC's method of permitting the trier of fact to determine the conduct of the parties as to its reasonableness. "Although the negligent consumer has an incentive up to $50/$500 to modify his conduct, if he does modify it, other users will absorb his losses to the extent the financial institution can pass the losses along in higher fees and lower interest rates paid on balances."

Error Resolution

Section 4-406 of the UCC imposes a duty of care upon the consumer to use reasonable care in examining the periodic statement and items to ascertain whether there have been any alterations or unauthorized signatures. If the customer fails to notify the payor bank and the bank has not been negligent, the customer may not assert the error against the bank. In contrast, the EFT Act gives the consumer 60 days after having been sent the periodic statement to notify the bank of error.[256] The bank then has 10 days to investigate the error, and one day to correct the error, if found.[257] If the bank provisionally recredits the consumer's account, it has 45 days to investigate, during which the consumer has full use of the account.[258]

Stop Payment

One of the important consumer protections in a check-based system is the ability to stop payment on a check. Section 4-403 of the UCC permits this, with the limitation that the stop order be received by the payor bank before the bank has made final payment.[259] Since EFT transactions are instantaneous, it is difficult to see how stop payment procedures could be applied to the EFT setting. One view is that if payment is to become final in a much shorter time, there should be some provision to permit customers to reverse charges to their accounts in a similar way to a stop payment.[260] The EFT Act provides for a stop payment function for preauthorized transfers, calling for three days' notice prior to the scheduled transfer.[261]

Disclosure/Documentation

Depository institutions must also provide a means for customers to verify a transaction. Under UCC §4-406 customers have an obligation to examine bank statements, exercising reasonable care and promptness to discover unauthorized signatures or alteration and notify the bank. Since the type of information that will be given under EFT is different, the duties of the customer may need some revision.

Under the EFT Act, at the time a consumer contracts for EFT services, a full and complete disclosure of the terms and conditions must be made.[262] Regulation E also provides that if the consumer contracts for EFT services with a third party, as an employer for automatic payroll deposit, wherein the institution learns of the agreement after it has been made, then the institution may make

---

256 15 USC §1693f(a).

257 15 USC §1693f(b).

258 15 USC §1693f(c).

259 UCC §4-403(1).

260 Penney, *supra* note 235, at 667.

261 15 USC §1693c.

262 Bulletin, *supra* note 241, at 293.

its initial disclosure before the first transfer is made.[263]

The terms which must be disclosed to the customer include: liability for unauthorized transfers, telephone number and address for reporting unauthorized transfers, the institution's working days, limitations and explanations of the types of transfers, charges, right to receive documentation of transfers, stop payment of preauthorized transactions, institutional liability for failure to stop or make certain transfers, disclosure of consumer's financial information to third parties, and error correcting procedures.[264] The Board has issued "model clauses" so as to facilitate institutional compliance with the Act.[265]

Regulation E requires that institutions provide consumers with notification of an unfavorable change in any of the original terms and conditions at least 21 days before its affect on the consumer's account would be felt.[266] Written documentation of all electronic transfers is also required by Regulation E.[267] This documentation consists of: automated teller machine (ATM) terminal receipts, documentation of preauthorized credits, and periodic statements. An ATM terminal receipt must show the amount, date and type of transfer, type of account, the identification or location of the terminal, account identification, and the identity of any third party involved. Extensive discussions are taking place concerning changes in UCC articles 3, 4 and 8, so as to be applicable to both an electronic and a paper payment system. The group, referred to as the "3-4-8" Committee, is preparing a New Payments Code for submission to the UCC Permanent Editorial Board.[268]

§8.20   Privacy Concerns and the Electronic Funds Transfer System

Due in part to the notoriety of George Orwell's "Big Brother" society in *1984* and Aldous Huxley's test-tube society in *Brave New World,* the future and the inevitablity of its technological achievement are met with a certain amount of resignation and feelings of impending doom. One of the common facts that science fiction writers seem to foresee is an assault on the citadel of privacy. A Louis Harris poll found that two-thirds of the people interviewed were concerned about threats to their privacy and one-third said that the United States would sooner or later be like Orwell's Oceania, a society which kept its citizens under constant surveillance.[269] Unfortunately, we are seeing in this

---

[263] *Id.*

[264] *Id.*

[265] *Id.*

[266] Schellie, *supra* note 234, at 1279; 12 CFR §205.8(a).

[267] Bulletin, *supra* note 241, at 293.

[268] N. Penney & D. Baker, The Law of Electronic Fund Transfer Systems (1982 Supplement), at S10-6.

[269] *Report on Privacy: Who is Watching You?,* US News & World Rep, July 12, 1982, at 34. See **ch 6** for a discussion of privacy problems and **ch 7** for computer crime.

new era of information collection, storage, and communication, the harbingers of this doom as tiny silicon chips are developed that can store huge amounts of information collected from vast numbers of sources.

Two national commissions—the Privacy Protection Study Commission (Privacy Commission)[270] and the National Commission on electronic Fund Transfers (EFT Commission)[271]—each studied the problem of confidentiality in the computer age and made recommendations as to its protection. The key to privacy in a world of computers is the access to the vast store of information which computers can store, sort, and retrieve about each of us—our occupation, home, financial worth, spending habits, affiliations, and associations. Further, the capacity of computers to give real-time information as to exactly *when* transactions took place, leaves us open to a type of electronic "alibi" system which we never would have imagined.[272]

The problem of privacy has its roots in the demand of businessmen and governments to know more and more about large numbers of people.[273] With a society of 230 million, highly mobile citizens, a great deal of information from driving violations to addresses for tax purposes is legitimately sought. At the same time, credit firms have compiled credit information on more than half of the United States' population. This credit information is bought and exchanged among financial institutions.[274]

It was in response to the Privacy Commission's report, and to provide relief from the effects of *United States v Miller,*[275] that Congress passed the Financial Institutions Regulatory and Interest Rate Control Act of 1978.[276] The Privacy Act seeks to protect consumers from unwarranted invasions of their financial privacy while permitting legitimate governmental investigation under certain specified procedures.[277] In contrast, the Electronic Funds Transfer Act deals with consumer protection such as documentation, distribution of cards, alloca-

---

[270] Privacy Protection Study Commission, Personal Privacy in an Information Society (1977) [hereinafter cited as the Privacy Report].

[271] National Commission on Electronic Fund Transfer, EFT in the United States, Policy Recommendations and the Public Interest, The Final Report of the National Commission on Electronic Fund Transfer (1977).

[272] Some of these "Big Brother" scenarios can be found in: Van Tassel, *Daily Surveillance, 1987, From a Nationwide Data Bank,* 24 Computers & People 31 (1975). See also Freed, *Legal Aspects of Computers and Confidentiality,* 18 Jurimetrics J 329 (1978); and Schick, *Privacy—The Next Big Issue in EFT,* 68 Banking J 70 (1976).

[273] Electronic Fund Transfers: New Protections for Consumers, New Duties for Financial Institutions, Fed Reserve Bull, Apr 1980, at 35.

[274] *Report on Privacy, supra* note 269.

[275] United States v Miller, 425 US 435 (1976); held that a bank customer had no standing to litigate government access to his financial records because there was no expectation of privacy by the customer in his bank's financial records.

[276] The Right to Financial Privacy Act of 1978, Pub L No 95-930, 1100, 92 Stat 3697, tit XI; Electronic Fund Transfer Act of 1978, 15 USC §1692.

[277] Kudlinski, Raiken & Hodgdon, *Confidentiality of EFT Information,* 13 USFL Rev 449, 454 (1979).

tion of risks or loss, disclosure, and error resolution.[278] There is, consequently, a significant gap in the legislation as the problem of financial information stored in computer data banks has not been specifically addressed by legislation.[279]

Privacy Concerns of EFT Systems

Imagine a consumer in a computer world where electronic funds transfer (EFT) systems exist on a national and international basis—the era of the truly "cashless society." In the cashless society, all purchases and bank transactions would be accomplished by means of a computer. Salaries could be deposited by way of preauthorized credits, while mortgage payments, life insurance, automobile insurance and hospitalization would be paid by preauthorized debits. POS terminals would instantaneously debit a retail purchaser's account and credit the merchant's account.[280] The time, place, date, identity of the parties, and goods are also transmitted. At the grocery store, a uniform product code scanner has replaced the cash register, thereby providing grocer and customer a complete list of the products purchased. Our privacy is threatened in at least five ways:[281]

1.   Each of these transactions has created an information trail which the use of cash would not have created

2.   Individual computer systems can store much more information per transaction than an ordinary paper system

---

[278] *Id.*

[279] There are four major pieces of legislation which deal with an individual's financial privacy:
1.   Fair Credit Reporting Act (FCRA), tit 6, 15 USC §§1681-1681t (1976)
2.   Fair Credit Billing Act (FCBA), tit 3, 15 USC §§1666-1666a (1976)
3.   The Equal Credit Opportunity Act (ECOA), USC §§1691-1691a (1976)
4.   The Privacy Act of 1974, tit 5, 5 USC §522a (1976)
The major drawback of the Privacy Act is that it applies only to data banks held by the federal government; once an individual's record leaves a federal agency it is no longer protected.

[280] This scenario is adapted from that found in N. Penney, *supra* note 123, at 15-23. See generally Bequoi, *Cashless Society: An Analysis of the Threat of Crime and the Invasion of Privacy,* 2 J Contemp L 47 (1976).

[281] N. Penney & D. Baker, The Law of Electronic Fund Transfer Systems (1980), at 15-23 to 15-27.
Penney suggested that the impact on privacy can be controlled by legislation affecting the following factors:
1.   Whether some or all transactions take place electronically
2.   The length of time the information remains in the system
3.   The accessability of the system
4.   Whether the system operates in real-time or batch mode
See generally *Electronic Fund Transfers, Branch Banks, and Potential Abuse of Privacy,* 6 Fordham Urb LJ 57, 571 (1978).

3. Every EFT system stores information in centralized, readable, easily re-
    trievable form. In contrast, manual paper systems are decentralized and
    access to them is difficult and costly

4. Since many EFT systems have "on-time" and "real-time" features, a
    customer's location at the time of the transaction can be pinpointed, thus
    permitting a type of surveillance upon which some very subjective judg-
    ments of the customer's activities could be made

5. Because many large scale EFT systems will require sharing arrangements
    to achieve economies of scale, financial records will be exposed to a
    greater number of financial institutions than the check-based system

Privacy Commission Findings

The Privacy Commission concluded that the information compiled by EFT
systems should be available only to the parties involved in the transaction and
their financial institutions. Further, the Privacy Commission recommended:

1. That individually identifiable account information generated in the provi-
    sion of EFT services be retained only in the account records of the
    financial institutions and other parties to a transaction, except that it may
    be retained by the EFT service provider to the extent, and for the limited
    period of time, that such information is essential to fulfill the operational
    requirements of the service provided

2. That procedures be established so that an individual can promptly cor-
    rect inaccuracies in transactions or account records generated by EFT
    services

3. That no governmental entity be allowed to own, operate, or otherwise
    manage, any part of an electronic payments mechanism that involves
    transactions among private parties[282]

By comparison, the EFT Commission adopted the Privacy Commission's first
two recommendations, but disagreed on whether the government should be
involved in the electronic payments system.[283] The EFT Commission focused
on the protection of confidentiality through procedures such as restricting
government agency's access to automated clearing house (ACH) transactions
to the extent that the private sector financial institutions would do so.[284]

Use of EFT Information

In a world where EFT systems operate on a national and international basis,
the number of institutions involved in financial transactions and, thus, the
number of institutions having access to an individual's financial record in-

---

[282] Privacy Report, *supra* note 269, at 121.

[283] *Id* 121-23.

[284] Kudlinski, *supra* note 276, at 453.

creases tremendously from a check-based system where the only parties involved are the consumer, the payor bank, the payee bank, and perhaps, a check clearing facility. This dispersal of information means that the consumer has less and less control over the use and accuracy of financial information. Further removed from the consumer's reach are computer support organizations, such as back-up storage, which will have access to the information contained on the hardware/software equipment they are servicing or storing.

Inaccurate Information

One of the major concerns of the Privacy Act of 1974 was the ability of the consumer to obtain financial records in order to check their accuracy, since inaccurate or outdated information could lead to a poor credit rating. This concern is especially applicable to EFT services and, even though the Privacy Act has been supplemented by the Right to Financial Privacy Act of 1978, the effectiveness of this legislation is not clear.[285] Robert Ellis Smith, publisher of the newsletter *Privacy Journal* was quoted as saying that the "nonchalant" attitude of many credit bureaus toward accuracy has caused unwarranted denials of credit.[286]

Conclusion

Alexander Solzhenitsyn described the tendency in modern life to reveal more and more personal information about ourselves as "hundreds of little threads radiating from every man, millions of threads . . . Each man, permanently aware of his own invisible threads, naturally develops a respect for the people who manipulate the threads."[287] As a result of the Privacy Commission's report, President Carter appointed a privacy study staff in the Commerce Department. This group, which has been adversely affected by the Reagan administration's budget cuts, is headed by Bernard Wunder, who argued against broad federal privacy laws and was quoted as saying, "I don't think we need to lose our sleep at night worrying that someone will gain access to our bank records."[288] Privacy and EFT development will continue to develop in an uneasy and fitful relationship. In the 1980s, many questions are being posed. The answers to these complex social and political questions have yet to be satisfactorily studied and implemented.

---

[285] *Id.* In 1978, the Federal Reserve announced a policy of retaining its individual transaction data records for sixty days after settlement and it has been a longstanding practice of the FED to grant access to individual transaction information only upon receipt of a subpoena.

See Note, *The Privacy Act of 1974: An Overview and Critique,* 1976 Wash ULQ 667. See generally Rule, Electronic Funds *Transfer and Federal Privacy Policy,* 18 Jurimetrics J 56 (1977).

[286] *Supra* note 269, at 35.

[287] A. Solzhenitsyn, Cancer Ward (1968).

[288] *Supra* note 269, at 37.

Future of Electronic Funds Transfers

§8.21   Open Competition Between Traditional Banking Sectors

In October of 1981, the House Committee on Banking, Finance and Urban Affairs issued an unofficial report entitled, "Financial Institutions in a Revolutionary Era."[289] The committee stated:

> In large measure it is the changing financial needs of individuals and corporations which have led to the increased homogenization of financial institutions. Banks, savings and loans, mutual savings banks, credit unions, mortgage banks, investment companies, and insurance companies are all offering, in many cases, similar and competing services to customers. The ability of all these institutions to speak to the needs of their customers, however, is limited by the differing regulatory frameworks under which they operate. Thus, the time has come to examine in more detail the supervisory and regulatory structure governing financial institutions.[290]

Although documents such as this and the Carter administration's task force report indicate that the leadership in this country recognizes the wide reaching change that has occurred in our financial industry, these reports share a common assumption which borders on misconception—that the financial institutions of the past and present will exist in the future. As stated by one commentator, the present institutions will continue to exist only if these institutions learn to adapt—a financial variation of Darwin's theory of survival of the fittest.[291] The emergence of financial conglomerates—Sears, Prudential, and Merrill Lynch among others—is the result of such innovations which manage to circumvent the present regulatory structure, thereby displacing the traditional banking institutions. Change in the structure and functioning of the financial services industry may occur as the result of legislation, or the inevitable acceptance of technological advance, or legal innovation which circumvents the legislative/regulatory scheme.

Inevitability of Change

An American Bankers' Association study has suggested that whereas, in the past, financial competition has focused on individual products and services, in

---

[289] House Comm on Banking, Finance and Urban Affairs, Financial Institutions in a Revolutionary Era, 97th Cong, 1st Sess (1981). See **ch 4** for a discussion of antitrust problems and **ch 6** for the regulatory environment.

[290] *Id* 6-7.

[291] Phillips, *Financial Institutions in a Revolutionary Era,* Trust & Estates, Feb 1982, at 14.

the future, the accent will be on broad financial relationships. The competitive objective in an electronic funds transfer (EFT) world will be to capture this financial relationship, and then sell the individual pieces of the product line.[292] The study outlined four levels of financial products and services which could be sold and administered, each on a different basis:[293]

Level I—Commodity products and services that can be understood and evaluated on an unaided basis by most consumers

Level II—Products and services that require a low level of judgment or that can be delivered on an impersonal, packaged basis

Level III—Products and services that require detailed technical knowledge or access to superior judgmental advice

Level IV—Products and services that require detailed knowledge of the customer's situation, sound judgment and good technical knowledge

Operating under this scheme, computerization can efficiently handle the lower level services which are, in essence, clerical in nature and leave to individual financial advisors, the Level III and IV services which require the human element. The Bankers Association study foresees:

a generation of customers who are convenience-oriented and who are comfortable with technology (and) already prefer electronic delivery of many of their financial services and will move to in-home shopping for financial services later in the decade.[294]

One author suggests that the success of the technological communications revolution in forcing a change in the financial services industry is inevitable because it has enhanced our ability to exchange assets at low cost and with great speed:

There is much more to the new technologies than simply shifting funds by wire among financial accounts. What has been evolving and will continue to evolve is an increased ability of households and businesses directly and indirectly to exchange, either through sale or through some form of hypothecation, an ever increasing array of assets (or, from the opposite vantage, liabilities) in day-to-day, hour-to-hour, or minute-to-minute transactions.[295]

Because of high transaction costs in the past, consumers kept positive balances

---

[292] *American Bankers Assn Study Looks at Future Services and Changes for the Banking Industry,* Trust & Estates, Feb 1982, at 28.

[293] *Id.*

[294] *Id.*

[295] Phillips, *supra* note 290, at 15.

in their checking accounts to minimize these transaction costs. Now, with the transaction costs lowered through technology,

> the extent to which anyone will hold these balances is bound to diminish.
> . . . We—households and businesses—will be willing to hold only those assets for which there are no preferred alternatives. . . . It is difficult to see the old type of deposit financial institutions liabilties—that is, non-interest bearing demand deposits, and various below-market yielding savings instruments—among this preferred group of assets.[296]

There has been a growing recognition of the need for an updating of banking law to meet the changing needs of the financial markets. A number of laws have been proposed, some of which have been narrowly written to deal with the immediate liquidity difficulty of thrift institutions, while others offer emergency provisions in a much broader reform of banking regulation.[297]

One of the problem areas addressed by these bills is the effect that money market funds have had on depository institutions. Money market funds are not subject to reserve requirements or interest ceilings, are not restricted geographically, and are ineligible for federal deposit insurance.[298] The Garn-St. Germain Depository Institutions Act of 1982 has, to some extent, equalized competition by allowing depository institutions to establish money market funds.[299]

The other areas for legislation include: (1) a modification of the Glass-Steagall amendment so that banks may compete with nondepository institutions in the financing of municipal revenue bonds;[300] (2) a modification or repeal of the McFadden Act and/or the Bank Holding Company Act, so as to permit interstate branching or Standard Metropolitan Statistical Area branching and EFT terminals on a statewide or regional basis;[301] and (3) interest rate deregulation.[302]

---

[296] *Id* (emphasis added). Phillips offers the example of wanting to purchase a dining room set. In order to pay for it, a loan might have to be taken out or funds withdrawn from other accounts so that, eventually, with time delays and high transaction costs, a positive balance would appear in the checking account and thus permit a check to be drawn in payment for the set. Now, a plastic card can be presented which simultaneously transfers to the merchant credits which he or she can use to increase his or her own assets or diminish his or her own liabilities.

[297] LaFalce, *Banking in the Eighties*, 37 Bus L 839, 840 (1982). In this article, LaFalce, who is a member of the House of Representatives, 36th District of New York, details the bills which have been proposed.

[298] *Id.* 844.

[299] Garn-St. Germain Depository Institutions Act of 1982, Pub L No 97-899.

[300] *Id.* 846-48.

[301] *Id* 848-51.

[302] *Id* 851-52.

Innovation

One author suggested that reactionary forces are too powerful to permit such revolutionary change through legislation.[303] Instead, it is foreseen that the growth of money market funds, new uses for credit and debit cards, electronic funds transfer, and other such innovations "often with great ingenuity . . . circumvent present regulations."[304]

Summary

A rational statutory and regulatory banking structure for our financial institutions is needed so that the financial services the people and the firms of this country need are provided fairly and efficiently in evolving financial marketplace. Market forces are shaping the services that are offered now and statutory restrictions keep many depository institutions from providing the services the market demands. Congress must examine the role of government as it affects all customers of financial institutions. The nation's economy and the public interest require a system of financial intermediaries which assures all segments of the population needed services while moving capital efficiently.[305] It is evident from statements such as this from congressional and government officials that the difficulties of the financial services industry have been recognized. Constructive change is now required.

§8.22   Amalgamation of Interstate Banking Activities

The issues of both interstate banking expansion and interstate electronic funds transfer (EFT) expansion must, of necessity, focus on the three element definition of the McFadden Act: receiving deposits, paying checks, and lending money. As noted previously, banks are forbidden to perform these functions interstate. Yet, banks have managed to circumvent the McFadden definition and, thereby, offer certain services interstate through the use of: loan production offices (LOPs) and multi-bank holding companies which are active in mortgage lending, commercial lending insurance, consumer lending, and credit cards.

In addition, other exceptions to interstate banking are found in money market funds and the merger of brokerage houses with other institutions which offer their customers what are essentially banking services. Nonbanking giants such as Sears, American Express, and Merrill Lynch have transformed themselves into financial service conglomerates by merging with securities/broker-

---

[303] Elliott, *Interstate Banking: A Personal View,* in Bank Expansions in the 80's: Mergers, Acquisitions and Interstate Banking 681-62.

[304] Phillips, *supra* note 291, at 14.

[305] House Commn on Banking, Finance and Urban Affairs, Financial Institutions in a Revolutionary Era, 97th Cong, 1st Sess (1981), at 7.

age houses. The banking industry has been turned into a "financial services" industry with the commercial banks operating at a competitive disadvantage since these "quasi-banks" are not restricted by the McFadden definition as commercial banks are, despite the fact that many of the services the conglomerates offer, as money market funds, come close to being checking accounts.

The exercise in creative legal reasoning which has permitted banks to circumvent McFadden focuses on the technicalities of the definition involved. The example of the loan production office (LPO) is illustrative: the LPO solicits business in a state where it is not chartered.[306] Using the legal fiction that the loan is not completed until the paperwork is done and the loan advanced, the LPO argues that the paperwork and actual disbursement of funds takes place at the home office in the state where the bank is chartered. Thus, the loan has been advanced *within* the chartering state and no illegal interstate activity has occurred. Similarly, if EFT activity is analyzed against the McFadden definition, it can be seen that it is the *deposit function* that renders the EFT transaction illegal as an interstate activity.

Element One: Paying Checks

A check, a paper, negotiable instrument, is payable at the office of the drawee, thus confining payment to the state where the bank is chartered. Since the system is paper-based, it has no impact on, nor use in EFT.

Element Two: Lending Money

The lending of money is currently being consummated by the loan production office which makes use of the fiction that the loan is not completed until the "paperwork" is approved and the funds advanced at the bank's main office. Based on this fiction, the loan is not advanced out of state, and there is no branching activity.

Element Three: Receiving Deposits

If performed interstate by the use of the mail, the transaction is legal. If accomplished by means of electronic impulses, the transfer is said to be consummated at the place where the customer initiated the transaction, not at the bank's location. This banking function is the focus of legal concerns and the focus of the consumer's effective use of EFT. Because of the absence of the paper document, an EFT transaction results not only in an electronic withdrawal of funds by the "drawer of the check," but also results in a deposit by the "payee." Because such transactions by definition involve a deposit, any interstate EFT transaction conflicts with the ban on interstate banking due to the deposit function.

If EFT development is going to occur in the absence of legislative action to

---

[306] *See generally* Note, *National Banks, Bank Holding Companies and Data Processing Services,* 14 Ga L Rev 576 (1980); 3 Fed Banking L Rep (CCH) ¶38641; 5 Fed Banking L Rep (CCH) ¶60918.

amend McFadden, similar legal ingenuity will have to be utilized to circumvent its strictures. This approach was suggested by one author who stated,

> what will happen is that a creative banker will design a system to deliver a full range of financial services to the consumer at places when and where the consumer dictates and not violate McFadden's archaic definitions of banking services. . . . Creative lawyering combined with developing technology will simply overrun McFadden and Douglas, rendering them moot.[307]

These technological advances involve the possibility of home banking by telephone or television. Some suggest that most Americans will be conducting their banking in this manner by the year 1990.[308] The advent of cable television, which distributes television signals by coaxial cable rather than through the air, as is the case with regular broadcasting, is part of the reason this future world exists in the here and now. Two way interactive service whereby subscribers are able to transmit signals as well as receive programming will permit the performance of a wide variety of functions from the home, including banking and shopping.[309] There already exists in Tennessee an in-home banking service whereby customers utilize their personal computers to pay bills and apply for loans.[310]

Another innovation is the computerized personal insurance planning service.[311] A New York savings and loan set up an insurance company as a subsidiary and offers advice as to how to utilize insurance as a savings tool. The customer enters the subsidiary office to explain the customer's needs and then watches the computer terminal as it devises a plan to meet those needs. In France, there is developing work being done on a *smart card* which has its own memory and intelligence in the form of a silicon chip sealed in plastic. It is believed that this card could become an all-purpose transaction device which would be more secure than credit/debit cards.[312]

If technology does not compel the expansion of the EFT and interstate banking, what legal techniques might be available to accomplish the purpose?

1. Bank service corporations (BSCs) can be utilized to operate an EFT network[313]

---

[307] Elliott, *supra* note 303, at 660, 663.

[308] American Banker, Nov 19, 1980, at 3, 22.

[309] In Columbus and Cincinnati, Ohio, where Warner Amex's QUBE system permits subscribers to answer questions by pollsters and order merchansdise through their television sets. See Noam, *Towards an Integrated Communications Market: Overcoming the Local Monopoly of Cable Television*, 34 Fed Comm LJ 209 (1982).

[310] Shockley, *EFTS Credit Cards and Interstate Banking*, *supra* note 302, at 689, 699.

[311] *Id* at 700.

[312] American Banker, Oct 13, 1980, at 1, 50, 52.

[313] The Bank Service Corporation Act, 12 USC §1981 *et seq*, allows two or more banks to invest more than 10% of their surplus and capital into a corporation the functions

2. Customer-Bank Communication Terminals (CBCTs) might be established by national banks if the state does not define CBCTs as branches or permits them as an exception to an antibranching statute

3. CBCTs may be permitted on an interstate basis if they are utilized on some basis other than ownership or rental[314]

4. Credit cards, such as VISA, already function on an interstate basis, and offer both credit and debit functions

The development of EFT, according to one observer, will not occur through legislation because "the forces of reaction are too powerful."[315] Instead, once new financial services are created and introduced, such as money market funds, it becomes difficult to legislate against these new services "because those who perceive it as beneficial are already entrenched."[316] As technology makes it less necessary to make a trip to the bank in order to make deposits and withdrawals, the "consumer market share will become less and less a function of brick and mortar locations."[317] It has been forecast by some authors that

> we will likely see national and regional consumer-oriented banking supermarkets accessed by personal computers. Smaller banks will then specialize in those banking services that still require hands-on treatment such as loans to local businesses. . . . Small banks may abandon consumer business and concentrate on their natural strength of service to local and

---

of which are defined as "check and deposit sorting and posting, computation and posting of interest and other credits and charges, preparation and mailing of checks, statements and notices and similar items, or any other clerical, bookkeeping, accounting, statitstical or similar functions performed for a bank." 12 USC §1861(b). According to Comptroller Staff Interpretive Letter No 160, by Richard V. Fitzgerald, national banks may establish a BSC to operate a EFT network since the ATM and interbank "switch" functions "seem to be precisely the kind of repetitive, clerical functions which are susceptible to automation and thus, presumably, the kind of functions that the BSC Act includes in its definition of banking services." The staff letter also concluded that "EFT services provided by a bank service corporation do not constitute branch banking by the participating national bank. . . . Consequently, a bank service corporation or its participants need not apply for CBCT branch certificate for terminals established by the corporation."

[314] IBAA v Smith, 534 F2d 921 (DC Cir) *cert denied*, 429 US 862, 951 (1976) indicated that

> any facility which performs the traditional bank functions of receiving or disbursing funds is a 'branch' within the meaning of §36(f) if (1) the facility is *established* (ie, owned or rented by the bank), and (2) it offers the bank's customers a convenience that gives the bank a competitive advantage over other banks. (Emphasis added)

Thus, if the CBCT were used on a transactional fee basis, its use would not constitute branch banking. See CCH ¶85234; Interpretive Letter No 153, John E. Shockley, Chief Counsel, July 7, 1980.

[315] Elliott, *supra* note 303, at 661.

[316] *Id* 662.

[317] *Id.*

regional businesses. As this develops, independent bankers' fear of large institutions may recede and their desire to combine with other small banks may lead to pressure from them for repeal of McFadden and Douglas.[318]

In 1983, the Senate Banking Committee began receiving testimony on the financial regulatory structure, especially in regard to possible mergers of banks and savings and loans with financial companies.[319] In testimony before the Committee, Treasury Secretary Donald Regan stated that federal regulators and state legislators should not allow banks and non-banks to blend until Congress has acted to reorganize the present financial structure.[320] Mr. Regan proposed lifting current restrictions on interstate banking and stated that he would not object if states acted unilaterally to remove such restrictions. Short of lifting all restrictions, Regan suggested that Congress should allow banks in contiguous states or in metropolitan areas that cross state lines to conduct business.[321]

Given the interaction of computational and communicational technology, and the drive by the banking industry to enter and compete in all areas of the financial industry, Electronic Funds Transfer (EFT) systems will continue to be introduced into the financial market place. The 1980's and 1990's will witness a continual state of flux as EFT systems encourage the push toward an eventual amalgamation of interstate banking activities.

---

[318] *Id* 662-63.

[319] The Wall Street Journal, Apr 7, 1983, at 3, col 2.

[320] *Id.*

[321] *Id.* See **ch 9** for a discussion of the international implications of information flow.

Import/Export Considerations Involving Computational Goods and Services   9

§9.01   Introduction

In international trade, and particularly where high technology goods and services are involved, there is a constant trade-off between the desire to promote free and competitive trade (with all the resulting benefits of greater product choice) and the conflicting government policy to protect national security. Exporting high technology goods and services, which results in the transfer of high technology, represents the epitome of this policy clash.[1] The mere export of high technology goods and services, however, is not the focus of this policy clash. Rather, it is the technology contained in these high technology goods and services which is the focus of the policy dispute. Technology represents the *thinking* behind the resulting product, good, or service, and is often equated with ingenuity.[2]

Technology transfer is generally accomplished by means of sales, licensing (involving patents, trade secrets, and know-how licensing), and joint ventures. In the past, the United States has been the international leader in the field of high technology research and development. In particular, the United States has led in the computerized high technology area. Other countries, most notably Japan, however, have been catching up, and in some instances pulling ahead of the United States in high technology.[3] This has led to a greater concern in the United States over importing Japanese high technology goods. In the past, computer technology imports into the United States presented little threat to the United States domestic computational market. The rapid advancement of the computers and electronics industries in countries like Japan has resulted in the United States domestic markets being an attractive target for foreign computational firms.

§9.02   United States Import/Export of High Technology Goods

International commercial transactions affecting United States commerce must comply with relevant United States antitrust legislation, including the Sherman, Clayton, Robinson-Patman, Webb-Pomerene, and Wilson Tariff Acts.[4] International transactions, however, by definition involve foreign gov-

---

[1] So-called high technology refers to those *systems of knowledge* that are the most advanced—that embody the greatest reaches, so far, of the human intellect. Technology transfer is the act of conveying know-how from one country to another. Research Monograph #47. The transfer of United States Technology to Other Countries. An Analysis of Export Control Policy & Some Recommendations by Theodore J Eckart. June, 1981 (Woodrow Wilson School). Center of Intl Studies, Princeton Univ 4 quoting Donald J Stickel, *Technology Arms Control,* Natl Security Affairs Monograph Series 78-5 (Washington D.C.: Research Directorate, National Defense University), 3-4.

[2] Technology, generally defined as know-how—ways of designing, manufacturing, or utilizing things, is the application of science to the manufacture of products and services. Technology is the know-how that transforms knowledge into products and services. It is the specific know-how needed to define a product that satisfies a defined need, to design the product, and to manufacture it, but it is not technology. It is an end-item. such as an automobile engine, a missile guidance system, an electronic circuit, a nuclear warhead, or a computer software program. Technology is not a piece of hardware, a science, or a specific product; rather, it is the system of knowledge that converts theory into practice. *Id.*

[3] Ramsey, *Japan's High-Tech Challenge,* Newsweek, Aug 9, 1982, at 48.

[4] Sherman Antitrust Act, ch 647 26 Stat 209, 15 USC §§1-7; Clayton Act, ch 323, 38 Stat 730, 15 USC §§12-27; Robinson-Patman Act, ch 592, 49 Stat 1526; Hart-Scott-

ernments, and foreign private entities. Additional political and economic considerations must, therefore, be taken into account because these considerations are translated into legal concerns when they are used as defenses in international antitrust actions. The most common of these defenses are the *act of state doctrine*, extraterritoriality, foreign government compulsion, and sovereign immunity.

§9.03   —United States Antitrust Laws

Criminal and civil sanctions exist for violation of United States antitrust laws. The principal prohibitions against monopolistic activities are found in the Sherman Antitrust Act (Sherman Act) which states that every "contract, combination . . . or conspiracy, in restraint of trade or commerce among the several states, or with foreign nations, is declared to be illegal."[5] Section 2 of the Sherman Act states that "every person who shall monopolize, or attempt to monopolize, or combine or conspire . . . to monopolize any part of the trade or commerce among the several States, *or with foreign nations,* shall be deemed guilty of a felony."[6] Thus, the criminal portion of the Sherman Act makes monopolistic activity a felony.[7] On the civil side, treble damages are awarded to victims of antitrust violations. By the clear language of the statute, therefore, the Sherman Act extends beyond the borders of the United States. The extent of this reach into international business transactions is a continuing area of conflict with the United States domestic courts, the Department of State, and foreign governments.

The Sherman Act has been violated if conduct resulting in a restraint of trade has a *direct and substantial* effect on United States commerce.[8] Although at first blush, United States commerce might appear to be affected only within the United States borders, a foreign firm (or a foreign-operated enterprise) can restrain competition in a United States market by flooding that market with imported goods that are priced below the minimum market price. This act of flooding the domestic market may be an antitrust violation.

Rodino Antitrust Improvements Act of 1976, Pub L No 94-435, 15 USC §18a; Webb-Pomerene Act of 1918, 15 USC §§61-65; Wilson Tariff Act, 15 USC §8. There is some question regarding the applicability of the Robinson-Patman Act to international high technology transactions, especially those involving services. For additional references on the subject of relevant United States antitrust law, see Davidow, *United States Antitrust Laws on International Transfer of Technology—A Government View*, 43 Fordham L Rev 733 (1975); Payne & Stroup, *US Antitrust Aspects of the International Transfer of Technology*, 15 NCJ Intl L & Com Reg 91 (1980); Dempsey, *Foreign Trade and Economic Injury—A Survey of U.S. Relief Mechanisms*, from The Laws of Transnational Business Transactions (V Nanda ed 1981).

[5] 15 USC §1 (emphasis added).

[6] 15 USC §2 (emphasis added). See also Areeda & Turner, *Predatory Pricing and Related Practices Under §2 of the Sherman Act*, 88 Harv L Rev 697 (1975).

[7] 15 USC §2.

[8] United States v Aluminum Co of Am, 148 F2d 416 (2d Cir 1945).

United States businesses injured by this type of conduct and other monopolistic activities are not the only persons capable of suing under the Sherman Act. The Department of Justice has stated that:

> the purposes of the Sherman Act enforcement are first, to preserve competition in domestic markets for the benefit of American consumers by prohibiting conduct which adversely affects competition in the United States and, second, to preserve American export opportunities by protecting American businesses against efforts to injure or limit those opportunities by anticompetitive conduct.[9]

Thus, even foreign governments allegedly injured by illegal antitrust activity have standing to sue for (treble) damages.[10] While the threshold consideration for an alleged international Sherman Act violation is a direct and substantial effect on United States commerce.

There is obviously a great potential for conflict between the United States and foreign countries where an international Sherman Act violation is alleged to have occurred. While trying to correct the negative impact of monopolistic activity in United States commerce, the Department of Justice as enforcer of the Sherman Act must respect principles of comity and not unduly interfere with the internal policies and practices of foreign countries involved. In an effort to determine whether or not to apply the Sherman Act to anticompetitive conduct which has occurred outside United States borders, United States courts have attempted to outline some standards for consideration. The two key cases in this context are *Timberlane Lumber Co v Bank of America*[11] and *Mannington Mills, Inc v Congoleum Corp.*[12]

In *Timberlane,*[13] the first of the two cases to attempt to develop standards for applicability of the Sherman Act to international antitrust violations, the court enunciated three threshold questions to be answered in determining whether or not a suit under the Sherman Act could be maintained. After discussing various defenses and procedural issues, the Ninth Circuit Court of Appeals stated that:

> A tripartite analysis seems to be indicated. As acknowledged above, the antitrust laws require in the first instance that there be *some* effect—actual

---

[9] Favretto, *Application of the Sherman Act to Joint Ventures & Operations of Multinational Corporations,* 50 Antitrust L J 408 (1982).

[10] Pfizer, Inc v Government of India, 434 US 308 (1978).

[11] Timberline Lumber Co v Bank of Am, 549 F2d 597 (9th Cir 1977).

[12] Mannington Mills, Inc v Congoleum Corp, 595 F2d 1287 (3d Cir 1979).

[13] Timberlane sued the Bank of America both in the United States and in Honduras, alleging that it "conspired to prevent Timberlane, through its Honduras subsidiaries, from milling lumber in Honduras and exporting it to the United States, thus maintaining control of the Honduras lumber export business in the hands of a few select individuals financed and controlled by the Bank." Timberlane Lumber Co v Bank of Am, 549 F2d 597, 601 (1976).

or intended—on American foreign commerce before the federal courts may legitimately exercise subject matter jurisdiction under those statutes. Second, a greater showing of burden or restraint may be necessary to demonstrate that the effect is sufficiently large to present a cognizable injury to the plaintiffs and, therefore, a civil *violation* of the antitrust laws. *Occidental Petroleum,* 331 F. Supp. at 102-103; Beausang, The Extraterritorial Jurisdiction of the Sherman Act, 70 Dick. L. Rev. 187, 191 (1966). Third, there is the additional question which is unique to the international setting of whether the interests of, and links to, the United States— including the magnitude of the effect on American foreign commerce— are sufficiently strong, vis-a-vis those of other nations, to justify an assertion of extraterritorial authority.[14]

Three years later, in *Mannington Mills, Inc v Congoleum Corp,* the Third Circuit Court of Appeals listed 10 factors for consideration in determining jurisdiction.[15]

In *Timberlane Lumber Co v Bank of America,* the Court of Appeals for the Ninth Circuit adopted a balancing process in determining whether extraterritorial jurisdiction should be exercised, an approach with which we find ourselves in substantial agreement. The factors we believe should be considered include:

1. Degree of conflict with foreign law or policy;
2. Nationality of the parties;
3. Relative importance of the alleged violation of conduct here compared to that abroad;
4. Availability of a remedy abroad and the pendency of litigation there;
5. Existence of intent to harm or affect American commerce and its foreseeability;
6. Possible effect upon foreign relations if the court exercises jurisdiction and grants relief;
7. If relief is granted, whether a party will be placed in the position of being forced to perform an act illegal in either country or be under conflicting requirements by both countries;

---

[14] *Id* 613.

[15] Both parties to the suit were in the flooring business. Congoleum had flooring patents in the United States and abroad. Mannington Mills was licensed to use Congoleum patents. Mannington Mills sued Congoleum because "Congoleum enforced the foreign patents by bringing and threatening the institution of infringement suits in foreign countries. This activity allegedly restrained the export trade of the United States by restricting the foreign business of Mannington and other American competitors in addition to demonstrating an intent to monopolize." Mannington Mills, Inc v Congoleum Corp, 595 F2d 1287, 1297-98 (1979).

8. Whether the court can make its order effective;
9. Whether an order for relief would be acceptable in this country if made by the foreign nation under similar circumstances;
10. Whether a treaty with the affected nations has addressed the issue.[16]

The Clayton Act is a statutory antitrust device designed to prevent monopolistic activity from occurring through mergers and acquisitions.[17] The key sections of the Clayton Act in the international context are §§1, 7, and 7a. Section 1 is important insofar as it brings international commerce within its reach. "Commerce . . . means trade or commerce among the several States and with foreign nations. . . ."[18] The key prohibitions are those found in §7. Section 7 states that:

> No person engaged in commerce or in any activity affecting commerce shall acquire, directly or indirectly, the whole or any part of the stock or other share capital and no person subject to the jurisdiction of the Federal Trade Commission shall acquire the whole or any part of the assets of another person engaged also in commerce or in any activity affecting commerce, where in any line of commerce or in any activity affecting commerce in any section of the country, the effect of such acquisition may be substantially to lessen competition, or to tend to create a monopoly.[19]

In 1976, §7a was added to the Clayton Act by the Hart-Scott-Rodino Amendment.[20] This amendment added a reporting, notification, and waiting requirement which mandates that firms of a specified size notify the Justice Department and the Federal Trade Commission of their intent to merge. These firms must then await approval before going ahead with their merger plans.[21]

The Clayton Act applies to both horizontal and vertical mergers. Simply put, a horizontal merger occurs between competitors. This applies to both real and potential competitors. A vertical merger occurs when one firm acquires a firm from which it gets supplies or vice-versa. The classic Clayton Act case dealing with international horizontal mergers is *United States v Jos Schlitz Brewing Co.*[22] In this case, Schlitz acquired Labatt's, the Canadian brewing company. Labatt's already owned another American brewery—General Brewing. Since Schlitz

---

[16] *Id* 1297-98.

[17] Clayton Act, ch 323, 38 Stat 730.

[18] 15 USC §12.

[19] 15 USC §18, *amended by* Pub L No 96-349, §6(a), 94 Stat 1157.

[20] 15 USC §18a, *added by* Pub L No 94-435, tit II, §201, 90 Stat 1390.

[21] Since the threshold size of the company for reporting purposes may change, it is advisable to check with the Federal Trade Commission and the Justice Department in order to determine what action is required. This is especially true when international concerns are involved.

[22] 253 FSupp 129 (ND Cal), *affd per curiam*, 385 US 37 (1966).

and General Brewing were competitors, the Schlitz-Labatt's merger was held to violate the Clayton Act.

U.S. v. Marine Bankcorporation is an example of a horizontal merger used to extinguish potential competition.[23] In the international setting, potential competition contemplates entry by an exporter into a foreign market. If the exporter is prevented from doing so by those who already occupy the market, §7 has been violated. An international vertical merger takes place when a United States firm acquires, or is acquired by, a foreign firm which either receives supplies from the United States firm or sells supplies to it, i.e., the two firms are in privity insofar as they are both links in the chain of production/distribution. In regard to this type of merger:

> The current administration takes the position that such a merger is almost always efficiency-producing and therefore procompetitive. Even a merger producing a significant percentage disclosure is not likely to be challenged by the government unless it produces a horizontal effect; that is, by closing off a source of supply or market outlet critical to viability of competitors at one, high-barrier, concentrated level of competition, it reduces competitors to the point of creating conditions for interdependence.[24]

A vertical merger, however, can restrict competition if the foreign firm is prevented, as a result of the acquisition, from entering the United States market on its own.

§9.04 —Defenses to Antitrust Violations

In addition to the United States statutes previously mentioned, the attorney dealing in the international high technology market must take into account other factors that may be potential roadblocks in the prosecution of an alleged antitrust violation. These include the *act of state* doctrine, foreign compulsion, sovereign immunity, extraterritoriality, and subject matter jurisdiction. Most of these are defenses that may be asserted by the opposing party. Although they may appear to be essentially the same, it is important to bear in mind the distinctions, however minor, that exist.

The act of state doctrine is a frequently raised defense that refers to an act of *sovereignty* exercised by a foreign government. The party asserting the act of state doctrine as a defense will claim that its acts are protected because they have been permitted by the foreign government, and that, therefore, the alleged acts cannot be prosecuted by United States courts. The act of state doctrine is an argument based on the separation of powers; i.e., the judicial branch of one government can not or should not interfere in the acts of a

---

[23] United States v Marine Bankcorporation, 418 US 602 (1974).

[24] Fox, *Application of the Clayton Act to International Mergers, Acquisitions and Joint Ventures*, 50 Antitrust LJ 477 (1982).

different branch of a foreign government. Each government should "respect the independence of every other sovereign state, and the courts of one country will not sit in judgment on the acts of the government of another done within its own territory."[25] When asserting the act of state doctrine as a defense, the party asserting it is really asking the United States court to *respect* the acts of the foreign government involved. Redress of grievances between governments should be resolved directly by those governments.

There has been some question as to whether such acts by the firms involved must be compelled by the foreign government. As the definition would seem to imply, however, this does not necessarily have to be the case (if it were, a defense of foreign compulsion might be more appropriate).

Generally, the act of state doctrine will be asserted by private firms or government firms; it will not be used by the foreign government itself (which would assert a claim of sovereign immunity). The possibility of overcoming this doctrine when it has been used as a defense will depend on the particular case. As has been pointed out, there are diplomatic considerations involved. The degree of respect to be accorded the acts of a foreign government will depend on the actual acts and their effect on United States trade in a particular market. This comes ultimately to a balancing test. In order for the act of state doctrine to be asserted at all, the alleged acts must occur within the jurisdictional boundaries of the foreign nation.

A foreign compulsion defense can be asserted when alleged antitrust acts of the offending firm have been forced or compelled by the foreign government involved. If this is truly the case, then there will be no antitrust liability; i.e., the offending firm cannot be found guilty of violating antitrust laws. *Compelled,* however, is the key word in an analysis based on foreign compulsion. The foreign government cannot merely have requested that the offending firm commit some act in violation of United States antitrust laws. Even slight pressure from the foreign government will not be strong enough to withstand an antitrust attack. The foreign government must have *forced* the offending firm to do those things which resulted in restraints of trade, for example, imposing laws that require or prohibit certain actions—such as sales to another country.

Although a firm need not be compelled by the *law* of the foreign government where a foreign compulsion defense is concerned, it is possible to be compelled without the benefit of laws.[26] Such was the case in *Interamerican Refining Corp v Texaco Maracaibo, Inc,* where the court simply concluded that "when a nation compels a trade practice, firms there have no choice but to obey. Acts of business effectively become acts of the sovereign."[27] The foreign compul-

---

[25] Underhill v Hernandez, 168 US 250, 252 (1897). When asserting the act of state doctrine as a defense, the party asserting it is really asking the United States court to *respect* the acts of the foreign government involved. Redress of grievances between governments should be resolved directly by those governments.

[26] Hawk, *Special Defenses and Issues Including Subject Matter Jurisdiction, Act of State Doctrine, Foreign Government Compulsion and Sovereign Immunity,* 50 Antitrust LJ 559, 571 (1982).

[27] Interamerican Ref Corp v Texaco Maracaibo, Inc, 307 F Supp 1291, 1298 (D Del 1970).

sion defense can be asserted by private foreign and domestic firms. The foreign compulsion inquiry, like that for act of state, is fact-oriented; it focuses on the truth of the claimed *compulsion*. Obviously, the defense will not hold up if the compulsion has been invited by the offending firm.

When a foreign government is a defendant in an antitrust suit, it will assert its sovereign immunity as a defense. The extent of the sovereign immunity defense is outlined in the Foreign Sovereign Immunities Act, enacted in 1976.[28] The two key elements of this defense concern the person committing the alleged antitrust act and the nature of that act. The person must be a foreign government: a sovereign entity. The act must be a public, as opposed to a commercial act. Therefore, an act which can only be undertaken by a government is protected by a defense of sovereign immunity. If the act is commercial, that is, it could be committed by either a foreign government or a private concern, the act will not fall within the protection of the defense.[29]

Because only a foreign government can use the sovereign immunity defense, this defense is not available to public or private domestic or foreign businesses. Like the act of state doctrine, diplomatic considerations come into play when sovereign immunity is asserted as a defense, and as in cases involving this doctrine, the considerations must include the doctrine of separation of powers. These sorts of issues are always present in any case involving a foreign government and possible interference with it.

Finally, there are two potential problems with prosecuting an international business transaction that violates United States antitrust laws: the concepts of extraterritoriality and subject matter jurisdiction. Extraterritoriality refers to the strength or reach of United States antitrust laws beyond United States borders. Basically, the inquiry is whether the statute violated allows for the assumption of jurisdiction outside of United States borders by United States courts for the purposes of enforcing these statutes at any time the United States or its businesses are involved. This is the case even though the Sherman and Clayton Acts specifically contemplate international, as well as domestic, restraints of trade affecting the United States.[30] It is evident that the same diplomatic considerations and conflict of law concepts are reflected in extraterritoriality inquiries. The United States cannot enforce its laws with respect to acts allegedly in restraint of trade when those acts take place in a different country that may allow such conduct, or when the restrictive acts have a relatively minimal effect on United States markets.

The Antitrust Division of the Department of Justice has stated that the *effects*

---

[28] Foreign Sovereign Immunities Act; 28 USC §1603(e).

[29] *See* International Assn of Machinists & Aerospace Workers v OPEC, 649 F2d 1354 (9th Cir 1981), *cert denied*, 50 USLW 3450 (US Jan 11, 1982). Foreign governments are not persons who can be defendants for the purposes of United States antitrust laws—this would seem to preclude any suit against a foreign government in the first place. This is ironic when one considers the fact that foreign governments are capable of suing under United States antitrust laws.

[30] Sherman Act, 26 Stat 209, 15 USC §17; Clayton Act, 38 Stat 750, 15 USC §§12-27.

doctrine, a test formulated in *United States v Alcoa,* will be used in antitrust cases against foreign firms whose acts have anticompetitive effects in the United States market.[31] In applying the effects test, a court determines if the conduct by the defendant foreign firm has "substantial and foreseeable effects" on a United States market. As with any test, however, the application is not always as intended. The comity rule can be (and many times is) arbitrarily applied.[32] Caught in the classic struggle between the desires for a hard and fast rule providing certainty, and a more flexible rule that can be adapted to particular factual situations appropriately, the Antitrust Division of the Justice Department proposed a test that would balance the interests of the United States and of the country where the offending firm was incorporated. Thus, this proposed test has two parts: (1) the court must determine what laws, if any, of the foreign country conflict with applicable United States law, and (2) the court must engage in a balancing act between the interests of the two countries.[33]

§9.05 Dumping

The issue of greatest concern to a country importing goods of another country is dumping by the foreign country. Dumping occurs when a country sells its exports in a targeted foreign market for substantially less than the prices charged for the same products in the manufacturer's home market. If successful, dumping can effectively force domestic manufacturers out of the domestic market for the particular product being dumped. On the other hand, antidumping measures can hurt trade by becoming protectionist in nature, thereby preventing healthy competition within the market. Antidumping measures which become overly protective naturally have substantial negative impact on international relations.[34]

Antidumping regulations and countervailing duties, often viewed as two solutions to the problem are imposed to remedy the effects of unfair competition on a particular market.[35] The ability of a manufacturer to dump its

---

[31] The effects test was formulated by Judge Learned Hand in his opinion in United States v Aluminum Co of Am, 148 F2d 416, 443 (2d Cir 1945). "It is settled law . . . that any state may impose liabilities, even upon persons not within its allegiance, for conduct outside its borders that has consequences within its borders which the state reprehends."

[32] Trade Reg Rep (CCH) No 510, at 5 (Oct 5, 1981)

[33] *Id.*

[34] See generally Barcello, *Antidumping Laws as Barriers to Trade- The U.S. and International Dumping Code,* 57 Cornell L Rev 491 (1972); Victor, *United States Antidumping Rules,* 10 St Mary LJ 217 (1978); Wilczynski, *Dumping and Central Planning,* 74 J Pol Econ 250 (1966); Coudert, *The Application of U.S. Antidumping Law in Light of a Liberal Trade Policy,* 65 Colum L Rev 189 (1965); Fisher, *The Antidumping Law of the U.S. - A Legal and Economic Analysis,* 5 Law & Poly Intl Bus 85 (1973); Ynetma, *The Influence of Dumping on Monopoly Price,* 36 J Pol Econ 686 (1928).

[35] For a discussion of both, see Ehrenhaft, *Protection Against International Price Discriminations: U.S. Countervailing and Antidumping Duties,* 58 Colum L Rev 44 (1958).

products on a foreign market at a cost to the consumer lower than the cost of similar products sold within the consumer's country can result from a number of factors: gentle down-sloping economies of scale, more efficient production, low-cost labor, low-cost materials, etc. Only the selling of goods at prices different between domestic and foreign markets will raise the issue of dumping. Countervailing duties are imposed on a product in response to subsidization by the government of the country in which the products were produced. Subsidization by a foreign government can come in the form of not imposing export taxes or lowering domestic taxes on goods destined for export which enable the manufacturer to offer its product in an importing country at a lower cost to the consumer. In order to offset the foreign country's unfair subsidization of its exporting firms, the importing country levies a countervailing duty upon the products of the foreign manufacturer. Essentially, the importing country imposes a burden on the imported product to counteract the unfair advantage given to the exporting manufacturer by the government of the exporting country.

The analysis focuses on the degree of interference with normal market activity caused by the exporting country's government subsidization. The distinction between reasonable and unreasonable government assistance becomes blurred, however, in the case of state-controlled-economy (SCE) countries.

Relevant Statutes

Two statutes regulate dumping on the United States market: (1) the Revenue Act of 1916 (1916 Act); and (2) the Trade Agreements Act of 1979 (1979 Act).[36] The 1916 Act allows individuals injured by dumping to sue the offending manufacturer in a private suit, and provides for recovery of treble damages by a successful plaintiff.[37] The 1916 Act also makes it unlawful for a manufacturer "commonly and systematically to import, sell, or cause to be sold" products in the United States at a price substantially below actual market price (wholesale) in the country of origin, with the intent to destroy or injure industry; to prevent an industry from being established; "or to restrain or monopolize trade or commerce in the United States."[38] The 1916 Act has not been extensively used. Perhaps one reason is the low success rate of suits brought under the 1916 Act. In *Outboard Marine Corp v Prezetel*, plaintiffs charged a Polish manufacturer of golf carts with importing their product into the United States for substantially less than the actual market value or wholesale price of similar products in principal markets of countries to which they were commonly ex-

---

[36] Revenue Act of 1916, 15 USC §72. Trade Agreements Act of 1979, Pub L No 96-39, 93 Stat 144, 19 USC §2501. Related articles: Prosterman, *Withholding of Appraisement Under the United States Antidumping Act-Protectionism or Unfair Competition Law*, 41 Wash L Rev 315 (1966); Comment, *The Antidumping Act- Tariff or Antitrust Law?* 74 Yale LJ 707 (1965).

[37] Revenue Act of 1916, 15 USC §72.

[38] *Id.*

ported.[39] The court held that the plaintiff had failed to state a cause of action under the 1916 Act because the Polish golf carts were manufactured for virtually exclusive importation into the United States, i.e., the golf carts were not manufactured for sale in Poland. As a result, the court decided that the 1916 Act provided no right to challenge dumping activity where the product was sold only in one market of one country.

Zenith Radio Corp. v. Matsushita was the first construction of the 1916 Act in 64 years.[40] Zenith alleged that Japanese manufacturers were dumping televisions, radios, phonographs, and tape and cassette recorders. The court found that a plaintiff, in an action under the 1916 Act, could attempt to establish a defendant's predatory intent by inference, and was not required to show that the predatory intent was accompanied by a dangerous probability of success. Previously Zenith had won a judgment in an administrative action for dumping against the same defendant.[41] The court in *Zenith*, finding that it had little discretion under the 1916 Act to determine what degree of similarity is required for goods to constitute *comparable goods*,[42] held that the Japanese electronic goods bound for the United States and those sold in Japan were not comparable under the 1916 Act.[43]

The Trade Agreements Act of 1979 (1979 Act) has been used more frequently than the 1916 Act.[44] The 1979 Act became law pursuant to the Tokyo Round of Multilateral Trade Negotiations (MTN) in early 1979. The 1979 Act repealed the Antidumping Act of 1921 (1921 Act),[45] although many of the substantive provisions of the 1921 Act can be found in the 1979 Act;[46] and the Tariff Act of 1930.[47]

The 1979 Act provides for imposition of an antidumping duty on dumped imports if the Department of Commerce, through the International Trade Administration (ITA), determines that an imported product has been, or is likely to be, sold in the United States at less than fair value (LTFV). Selling at LTFV essentially means that an imported product is being dumped on a

---

[39] Outboard Marine Corp v Pezetel, 461 F Supp 384 (D Del 1978).

[40] Zenith Radio Corp v Matsushita, 494 F Supp 1161 (ED Pa 1980); 494 F Supp 1190 (ED Pa 1980). See Schwartz, *Zenith Radio Corp. v. U.S.*: Countervailing Duties and the Regulation of International Trade, 1978 Sup Ct Rev 297 (1978).

[41] Zenith Radio Corp v United States, 437 US 443, 446 (1978).

[42] Zenith, *supra* note 41, at 1240. See Note, *Bounty or Grant: A Call for Redefinition in Light of the Zenith Decision*, 9 Law & Poly Intl Bus 1229 (1977); Arkin, *The Countervailing Duty Law After Zenith–Unanimity Can Be Beguiling*, 18 Va J Intl L 245 (1978).

[43] Zenith, *supra* note 41, at 450.

[44] Trade Agreements Act of 1979, Pub L No 96-39, 93 Stat 144, 19 USC §2501 *et seq*. See generally Weaver, *Subsidies and Duties Under the Trade Act of 1979*, 5 NCJ Intl & Com Reg 533 (1980); Peterson, *The Trade Agreements Act of 1979: The Agreement on Government Procurement*, 14 J Intl L Econ 321 (1980).

[45] Antidumping Act, ch 14, 42 Stat 9, 19 USC §§160-71.

[46] *Id, repealed by* Title I of Trade Agreements Act of 1979, Pub L No 96-39, *and replaced by* 19 USC §1673 *et seq*.

[47] Tariff Act of 1930, §13 (codified at 19 USC §1303 (amending 19 USC §1303)).

domestic United States market. The result of dumping is material injury (or the threat of it) to the domestic industry or the material retardation of the establishment of a domestic industry.[48] Three elements must be proven before an antidumping duty can be imposed: (1) that dumping has taken place; (2) that the domestic industry has been, or is threatened with, *material injury* or that the establishment of a domestic industry has been materially retarded; and (3) that dumping is the cause of the injury alleged.

Evidence of dumping is developed through preliminary investigations conducted concurrently by the Department of Commerce (ITA) and the International Trade Commission (ITC). The proceedings must end within 160 days of the commencement of the proceedings.[49] Final determination of LTFV sales and material injury follow within 75 days.[50] The dumping duty order must be published seven days thereafter.[51] An investigation may be suspended without determination under §734 if agreements are entered into between the United States and the foreign governments or exporters responsible for at least 85 per cent of the imports concerned.[52]

Less than Fair Value

One of the difficulties in a dumping investigation is to determine the fair value of the dumped product.[53] There are two tests used by the ITA to calculate fair value. Which test is used, and how it is used, depends upon the particular circumstances involved in the individual case. The test favored by the ITA to determine fair value is the foreign market value; i.e., the price at which the product is sold in the manufacturer's home market.[54] If the manufacturer's home market value is unavailable or cannot be determined, then the price in a third country's market may be substituted. There are many shortcomings in using the exporting country's market value or the market value of a third country as a yardstick for arriving at a fair value determination. For example, the costs of distribution, financing, and sales service may substantially differ in each country.

The second test is constructed value. The costs of various factors of production (labor, materials, etc.) are assigned to the good in question, and then a *fair value* of the product is computed. Under the constructed value test, the amount of the duty imposed is the difference between the constructed

---

[48] 19 USC §1673 *et seq.* The amount of the antidumping duty imposed is the difference between the foreign market value and the price at which the dumped product is sold for in the United States.

[49] 19 USC §1673 *et seq.*

[50] 19 USC §1673 *et seq.*

[51] 19 USC §1673 *et seq.*

[52] 19 USC §734.

[53] See Wharton, *Treasury Runs the Maze- LTFV Determination Under the Antidumping Act of 1921,* 8 Ga J Intl & Comp L 919 (1978).

[54] 19 CFR §§353.0-.23.

value and the price at which the product is actually being sold in the United States market.

State-Controlled Economy Countries

Products imported by a manufacturer in a state-controlled economy (SCE) country present a special problem in dumping controversies. In a SCE country, the government largely directs the course of economic activity, including export activity. For the most part, SCE countries are communist.[55]

Due to an SCE government controlling the flow of goods and services throughout the economy, it is unlikely that the price of products produced within an SCE country reflects either the actual or true cost of the product either to the manufacturer, or the price to the ultimate consumer in the importing country. This price distortion makes the determination of fair value even more complicated in dumping cases involving SCE countries since the source of that distortion is the government of the manufacturer state. Application of the foreign market value test, therefore, is probably useless since the foreign country's price is a controlled price within the SCE country. In these situations, the government of the manufacturer can provide the manufacturer a better, or unfair, opportunity to compete in a foreign market by unfairly pricing the exported product, or by unfairly lifting export taxes or subsidizing exports. Under these circumstances, the importing country can offset this subsidization by imposing countervailing duties. In effect, the SCE government is tampering with the free market system in which a manufacturer (in theory) competes in the acquisition of labor, capital, and raw materials necessary for manufacturing its products. Even in a non-SCE country, however, unions, government purchase of products, and government-sponsored research and development can distort a *free market* economy.

In the SCE government situation, the third country market test can be used to determine fair value or, alternatively, a constructed value for the product must be computed.[56] The use of a third country market as the measure has several significant shortcomings: (1) comparing a third country market to the market of the SCE country; (2) the cost differences, if any, of similar raw materials; and (3) the volumes of exports, if they too are different. Determination of a constructed value is also extremely difficult due to the many value-based assumptions which must be injected into the computation.

Dumping and High Technology Imports

Dumping also occurs in markets for high technology goods, and the same problems involved in a normal dumping case are present in high technology

---

[55] For earlier views on the subject, see Feller, *The Antidumping Act and the Future of East-West Trade*, 66 Mich L Rev 115 (1967); Anthony, *The American Response to Dumping from Capitalist and Socialist Economics- Substantive Premises and Restructured Procedures After the 1967 GATT Code*, 54 Cornell L Rev 159 (1969).

[56] 19 CFR §353.8.

dumping situations. These problems are intensified, however, in the high technology field. Computational technology is developing at an increasing rate, and thus the fair value of a computer product can be diminished during the three to nine month period it takes for a fair value analysis of the product to be completed by the ITA. The application of the antidumping laws, therefore, presents an extremely complicated task where high technology is concerned.

§9.06   Tariff Act of 1930

The pivotal clause of the Tariff Act of 1930[57] is §337, which prohibits "unfair methods of competition and unfair acts in the importation of articles into the United States."[58] This language parallels the language of §5 of the Federal Trade Commission Act,[59] which applies to unfair competition in domestic trade. Section 337 includes: (1) §§1 and 2 of the Sherman Act[60] (restraint of trade and monopolization); (2) §3 of the Clayton Act[61] (exclusive dealing and tying arrangements); (3) the Robinson-Patman Act[62] (price discrimination and predatory pricing); and (4) the Revenue Act of 1916 (dumping and predatory pricing).[63] Due to the expansive coverage of §337, the International Trade Administration (ITA) and the International Trade Commission (ITC) cannot possibly enforce all §337 violations.

The Unfair Imports Investigation Division, the prosecuting arm of the ITC, exercises its authority only in three instances: (1) where the resources of the complainant to prosecute a complaint are limited; (2) where the size of import trade involved indicates that the alleged violations are serious or continuous; and (3) where the jurisdiction of the agency is being established in new areas for the purpose of establishing import regulations.[64]

Section 337 gives the ITC the authority to undertake investigations of sus-

---

[57] 19 USC §1337.

[58] *Id.* This language parallels the language of §5 of the FTC Act, which applies to unfair competition in domestic trade. See LaRue, *Section 337 of the 1930 Tariff Act and Its Section 5 FTC Counterpart,* 43 Antitrust LJ 608 (1975); Musrey, *Tariff Act's Section 337: Vehicle for the Protection and Extension of Monopolies* , 5 Law & Pol Int Bus 56 (1973); Rosenthal & Sheldon, *Section 337: A View from Two Within the Department of Justice,* 8 Ga J Intl & Comp L 47 (1978); Glick, *Settling Unfair Trade Practices Cases Under Section 337 of the Tariff Act of 1930,* 21 Harv Intl LJ 129 (1980); Kaye & Plaia, *The Relationship of Countervailing Duty and Antidumping Law to Section 337 of the U.S. International Trade Commission,* 2 Intl Trade LJ 3 (1977); Easton & Laing, *A Comment-Kaye and Plaia on Section 337-Pricing Jurisdiction,* 3 Intl Trade LJ 359 (1978).

[59] Federal Trade Commission Act, ch 311, §5, 38 Stat 719 (codified at 15 USC §45).

[60] 15 USC §§1, 2.

[61] *Id* §14.

[62] *Id* §13.

[63] 15 USC §72.

[64] Easton & Neely, *Unfair Competition in U.S. Import Trade Developments Since the Trade Act of 1974,* 5 Intl Trade LJ 203, 219 n 45 (1980).

pected unfair methods of competition, and under the Trade Agreements Act of 1979, the ITC can begin an investigation upon request of an *interested party* who petitions the ITC.[65] An investigation may, however, be undertaken by the ITC on its own initiative. If the ITC decides to make an investigation, it must be completed within one year, unless the ITC determines that the case is *more complicated,* in which case the investigation must be completed within 18 months. The matter is then referred to the Unfair Imports Investigation Division, which becomes a party for the purpose of representing the public interest.[66] The case is referred to a presiding officer, in most cases an administrative law judge (ALJ), who must decide whether the evidence supports a finding of a statutory violation.[67] The rules of practice and procedure promulgated by the ITC provide for termination of investigations at any time by motion of any party.[68] In April of 1980, the ITC proposed rules for settlements by consent orders, but these rules have not yet been adopted.[69]

If the ITC finds the importer has violated the unfair methods of competition statute, there are a variety of sanctions which the ITC may impose on the offending importer. The strongest sanction available is complete exclusion of the product from the United States. The ITC can also issue a *cease and desist* order which is applicable to products already in this country, or can require that the manufacturer post an import bond to offset the effects of the unfair methods of competition. The exclusion order is an *in rem* action, whereas the cease and desist order is an *in personam* proceeding.

A §337 proceeding must comply with the Administrative Procedure Act (APA).[70] During the investigation, there is a hearing in which the involved parties are given notice and an opportunity to present evidence. Once a §337 investigation is undertaken and completed within a particular industry, one year must elapse before another investigation can be initiated in the same industry.[71] If good cause can be shown, however, the ITC can begin another investigation before the normal one-year period is over.[72] The good cause determination by the ITC is discretionary in as much as §337 does not set forth standards for good cause.[73] In *Sneaker Circus, Inc v Carter,* a good cause finding

---

[65] Trade Agreements Act of 1979, Pub L No 96-39, 93 Stat 144, 19 USC §2551.

[66] 19 CFR §2104(b).

[67] 19 CFR §210.53(a). The termination of an investigation is handled as a recommended determination.

[68] 19 CFR §210.51(a).

[69] 45 Fed Reg 24192 (1980). Proposed 19 CFR §210.51(d) provides that an order of termination based upon a consent order agreement would not constitute determination of whether there is a violation of §337, 5 USC §§551-559.

[70] Adminstrative Procedure Act, Pub L No 89-554, 80 Stat 378, 5 USC §§551 *et seq,* 701 *et seq.*

[71] 19 USC §1337(b)(1).

[72] 19 USC §1337(c).

[73] Sneaker Circus Inc v Carter, 457 F Supp 771 (1978), at 783.

by the ITC was challenged by the shoe industry plaintiffs.[74] Among other things, the plaintiffs claimed that in determining whether good cause existed in order to make a second investigation within a year, the involved parties were entitled to notice and an opportunity to present evidence. The court disagreed since no property rights were affected by a mere good cause determination, and no due process rights were operative. The involved parties were, however, afforded an opportunity to present evidence during the substantive hearing.

§9.07   The General Agreement on Tariffs and Trade

The General Agreement on Tariffs and Trade (GATT)[75] has served as a basis for world trade negotiations since 1947. The general principles agreed upon by members of GATT include a commitment (1) to reduce barriers to international trade through negotiation, and (2) to produce an environment in which trade is conducted on a nondiscriminatory basis. The agreement was entered into by the signatory countries in an attempt to develop a uniform approach to international commerce and equal treatment for all parties engaged in international trade. The agreements formulated by GATT are not binding. Rather, GATT merely establishes policies to be followed by its members. The agreements under GATT apply only as between governments, not between a government and a private enterprise located in another member country. The GATT trade agreements are not self-executing, and thus do not have independent effect under United States law. The Protocol of Provisional Application of GATT provides that an agreement be applied to the fullest extent not inconsistent with existing legislation.[76] Rather than possessing the status of binding domestic law, GATT has served as a forum for international trade policy negotiation. Congress has noted that even though the United States is a party to GATT, the United States membership need not completely determine United States trade policies because GATT is often: (1) inappropriate in a complex economy; and (2) observed only in the breach.[77] GATT has not been ratified by Congress.

The Trade Agreements Act of 1979 (1979 Act) implements many of the

---

[74] *Id* 796. See Peevy, *Notice and Opportunity to be Heard in a "Good Cause" Determination Proceeding Under Section 201(e) of the Trade Act of 1974 Are Not Required by the Provisions of the Act Itself or by Constitutional Due Process,* 9 Ga J Intl & Comp L 654 (1979).

[75] General Agreement on Tariff & Trade, Oct 30, 1947, 61 Stat pt 5, TIAS #1700, 55 UNTS 194, as amended by IV General Agreements on Tariffs & Trade, Basic Instruments & Selected Documents (1958).

[76] Protocol of Provisional Application, Art 1(b), 61 Stat A2051, TIAS No 1700, 55 UNTS 308 (1947).

[77] S Rep No 1298, 93d Cong, 2d Sess, reprinted in (1974) US Code Cong & Ad News 7186, at 7304.

principles and purposes of the General agreement.[78] Prior to the 1979 Act, United States law gave distinct preference to domestic government suppliers in bidding for procurement contracts, most notably under the Buy-American Act.[79] The 1979 Act gives the President authority to waive those portions of United States law which discriminate against foreign suppliers of designated goods.[80] Developing countries may be designated as equal bidders, although all other countries must be parties to GATT, or provide reciprocal benefits to United States corporations bidding for foreign government contracts, in order to be designated equal to domestic bidders.[81]

GATT applies to:

1. The sale of products (service contracts per se are excluded)

2. Services incidental to the supply of products are covered if the value of those services does not exceed that of the products; prospects valued above $150,000; and Special Drawing Rights (which protect small business from foreign competition)[82] and

3. Those agencies which each signatory nation has listed in an annex to the GATT[83]

The official policy of GATT is to oppose monopolies, and the primary aim of GATT is to achieve optimal resource allocation with minimal government interference.[84] It is unrealistic to expect, however, that GATT can accomplish its aims with no government intervention. In short, GATT embraces a laissez-faire view towards international commerce.

GATT also has mechanisms for dispute resolution. The first step in eliminating disagreements between parties is an initial consultation between the parties to the dispute.[85] Under the GATT procedures, it is hoped that the parties can

---

[78] Trade Agreements Act of 1979, Pub L No 96-39, July 26, 1979, 93 Stat 144; Pub L No 96-467, §14(a), Oct 17, 1980, 94 Stat 2225; Pub L No 96-609, Title II, §203(a), Dec 28, 1980, 94 Stat 3561.

[79] 41 USC §10(a)-16(a). Under the Buy-American Act, domestic bidders on contracts have a 6% price preference over foreign bidders, raised to 12% in the case of small business or given labor-surplus areas, and 50% for Dept of Defense Procurement.

[80] Trade Agreements Act of 1979, Pub L 96-39, 93 Stat 144.

[81] S Rep No 96-249, 96th Cong, 1st Sess at 22-3 (1979), *reprinted in* 1979 US Cong Code & Ad News 381. 408-09

[82] Pub L 96-39, 93 Stat 144.

[83] The United States has included the Defense Department as an entity, but excluded the Corps of Engineers of the DOD, as well as the Department of Energy, Department of Transportation, and others. (Senate Finance Comm Trade Agreements Act of 1979, S Rep No 249, 96th Cong, 1st Sess (1979), *reprinted in* 1979 US Code Cong & Ad News 1, 130. GATT does not apply to procurements by state and local governments, even those financed through federal funds.

[84] Protocol of Provisional Application, art I(b), 61 Stat A2051, TIAS No 1700, 55 UNTS 308 (1947).

[85] General Agreements on Tariff and Trade, opened for signature Oct 30, 1947, 61 Stat (5) and (6), 55 UNTS 187, TIAS No 1700.

reach an acceptable settlement. If the initial consultation between the parties proves unsuccessful, the dispute is referred to a panel composed of representatives of the signatory countries to decide.

§9.08   The Tokyo Round

In Spring 1979, The Tokyo Round of the MTN took place. This was the seventh of such negotiation meetings since GATT's inception in 1948. The Tokyo Round dealt with nontariff barriers to trade, notably dumping, subsidization, and domestic governmental protectionist procurement. Five separate agreements were reached. The first and most important of these is the Agreement on Government Procurement. Under its terms, the signatory countries agreed to allow foreign suppliers to compete for government supply contracts, which were traditionally open only to domestic companies. The United States looked favorably upon this agreement because of increased foreign markets for United States manufacturers.[86]

Recent studies estimate that this Agreement should open additional foreign markets which are valued at $20 billion to United States suppliers.[87] Defense concerns, on the other hand, could potentially be a reason for cutting off competition from foreign bidders in a government procurement situation.

The second agreement involved product standards. Under the Tokyo Round, the member countries agreed that no obstacles to trade could be created by standards codes for imported products that unreasonably restricted competition from foreign competitors. The codes intended to be affected by the agreement are those that are performance-oriented.[88] The third agreement defines restrictions on subsidies and countervailing duties. Under this agreement, signatory countries cannot subsidize their exports. Put another way, a government cannot underwrite the international undertaking of a particular industry so that the industry involved can effectively corner most of the international market for its product.[89] In fact, some subsidies are per se illegal. On the other hand, countervailing duties for an alleged GATT violation by foreign subsidization may not be imposed by a country unless it can be shown that there is both foreign interference in, and resulting substantial injury to, the domestic market.[90] Fourth, the Tokyo Round created a licensing code. This established procedural ground rules for the signatory countries to follow in issuing import licenses. Finally, the MTN agreements resulted in a uniform

---

[86] Davis, *Multilateral Trade Negotiations: The Tokyo Round,* 29 Fed B News & J 23, 24 (1982). Exceptions to the Government Procurement Agreement are health, safety, and welfare concerns of a particular nation. In these cases, a member country can limit the contract bidders to domestic suppliers.

[87] Senate Report, *supra* note 81, at 141.

[88] Davis, *supra* note 86, at 24.

[89] *Id* 24. See Staple, *Implementing "Tokyo Round" Commitments, The New Injury Standard in Antidumping and Countervailing Duty Laws,* 32 Stanford L Rev 1183 (1980).

[90] *Id* 24.

system for valuation of imports. The standard established was the actual transaction value. As with determining *less than fair value* (LTFV) for the purposes of dumping cases, arriving at an actual transaction value for imports can be difficult, if not impossible. If the actual transaction value cannot be ascertained, alternative methods of valuation were established at the Tokyo Round. Like LTFV alternatives, some of these include utilizing the transaction value of comparable goods in a third country-market that is similar.[91]

The general effect on United States trade as a result of the Tokyo Round appears to be beneficial. The Agreement on Government Procurement and the other four agreements reached will, if nothing else, establish uniform standards in all the signatory countries so that United States exporters will better understand the potential barriers they may expect to encounter. More importantly, it is expected that the MTN results will further open up international markets to United States exports.

§9.09 High Technology Import/Export Considerations

The role of high technology in the international market is vital, due to the role high technology plays in the economic and military development of a country. Ultimately, high technology imports and exports have a major impact on foreign policy and diplomatic relations between countries. Because of the far-reaching political as well as economic effects of high technology exports, many political factors are involved. In the United States, four governmental entities are involved in export policy: (1) the Department of Commerce through the International Trade Administration (ITA) and the Office of Export Administration; (2) the Department of Defense; (3) the State Department; and (4) the International Coordinating Committee on Strategies Trade with Communist Countries more commonly referred to as COCOM.[92]

Foreign countries have also adopted laws and created regulatory agencies to control technology transfers. These laws are often based on controlling technology transfer, nationalism, or revenue collection considerations rather than on antitrust principles. In addition to requirements imposed by foreign laws, import/export controls and financial regulations may also apply to international technology transfers. As a result, United States restrictions on technology transfer, and exports in particular, have been confused.[93]

Technology transfer can take place by any of three basic means: (1) sales; (2) licensing; or (3) joint ventures. An outright sale of high technology is fairly

---

[91] Davis, *supra* note 86, at 25.

[92] See Bingham & Johnson, *A Rational Approach to Export Controls,* 57 Foreign Aff 894 (1979); Berman & Garson, *United States Export Controls- Past, Present, and Future,* 67 Colum L Rev 791 (1967); Rubin, *United States Export Controls: An Immodest Proposal,* 36 Geo Wash L Rev 633 (1968).

[93] Comment, *Interagency Conflict: A Model for Analysis,* 9 Ga J Intl & Comp L 241 (1979).

straightforward. Licensing and joint ventures as methods of technology transfer present slightly more complicated elements.

Before engaging in a business venture involving technology transfer, one might also want to investigate patent and licensing laws in the acquiring country, antitrust restrictions, tax effects of the transfer,[94] and the possible triggering of the Foreign Corrupt Practices Act by the transaction.[95]

Foreign as well as domestic commerce falls within the reach of the Sherman Act[96] since an effect upon "trade or commerce among the several states, or with foreign nations" is sufficient to invoke subject-matter jurisdiction.[97] International licensing agreements are subject to United States antitrust surveillance.[98] Even an agreement between two or more foreign firms may be reached by United States antitrust law if the agreement produces a substantial effect on United States commerce. Dealings not directly in United States foreign commerce must have a substantial effect[99] on United States commerce before they are subject to United States antitrust jurisdiction. The sale, transfer, accumulation, or cross-licensing of technology is not necessarily violative of United States antitrust laws, under the Department of Justice Antitrust Guide for International Operations. The ancillary restrictions included in a licensing package, though, may create antitrust problems.[100]

The first step in analyzing a transaction is to determine whether the arrangement is actually a cartel device to divide or control markets, or if the agreement is a valid method for a licensor to protect its technology. Responsible attempts to protect a firm's technology are analyzed with the *Timken* test. After the initial *Timken* test is passed, the next step is a three-pronged ancillary restraints test.[101] Terms of a licensing agreement may restrict some competition, as long

---

[94] Comment, *Tax Incentives to Exportation: Alternatives to DISC*, 9 Ga J Intl & Comp L 441 (1979); Cabanellas & Bertone, *Host Country Taxation of Transfers of Technology Transactions*, 11 Ga J Intl & Comp L 495 (1981); Ruppert & Pansius, *Transfer of Know-How Under Section 351*, 55 Den LJ 223 (1978).

[95] Foreign Corrupt Practices Act of 1977, Pub L No 95-213, Title I, Dec 19, 1977, 91 Stat 1494-1498 (Title 15, §§78a note, 78m, 78dd-1, 78dd-2, 78ff).

[96] Sherman Act of 1890, 15 USC §§1-7.

[97] United States Aluminum Co, 148 F2d 416 (2d Cir 1945).

[98] See generally US Justice Department, Antitrust & International Operations, Trade Reg Rep (CCH) No 266, Feb 1, 1977.

[99] United States v Watchmakers of Switzerland (1963), Trade Cas ¶70,600 (SDNY 1962), *order modified*, (1965) Trade Cas ¶70,352 (SDNY 1965).

[100] See generally Blake, *Technology Licenses, Economic Development Antitrust Law*, 26 Am J Comp L 265 (1978).

[101] Timken Roller Bearing Co v United States 341 US 593 (1951), involved trademark license and accompanying ancillary agreements among three related companies. The Court emphasized that it was condemning "the aggregation of trade restraints" pursuant to which the companies had allocated markets (at 598). The Justice Department has emphasized this "aggregation of restraints" approach in two recent cases involving international technology licensing: United States v Addison Wesley Publishing Co, 2 Trade Cas ¶61,225 (SDNY 1976) (consent judgment), *approving* 41 Fed Reg 32615 (1976) (proposed consent judgments and competitive impact statement), and United States v Westinghouse Elec Corp No C-70-852-SAW (ND Cal Apr 22, 1970).

as the restrictions are: (1) clearly ancillary to some legitimate purpose; (2) appropriately limited in scope; and (3) do not significantly harm the public interest.[102] Areas of dispute under the Sherman Act include governmental rules which require: (1) package licensing;[103] (2) tying agreements;[104] (3) grant-backs;[105] and (4) unreasonable royalty payments.[106]

Methods of Technology Transfer

There are three ways, basically, that technology transfers are effected: through a direct sale of the technology, joint ventures, or by way of licenses. Of these three, high technology transfer from the United States to another country is best done through licensing. This is so because of the advanced nature of high technology. By licensing exports, they are thus regulated and the government is better able to track the fate of what represents our greatest advancements. Many governmental entities are involved in trying to monitor high technology transfers to foreign countries. The owner or inventor of high technology is generally protected by patents, trademarks, or trade secret or know-how agreements.

The direct sale of a technology is one method of exporting technology. The advantage of a sale method of technology transfer is that in its simplest form it is relatively direct. There is one major disadvantage, however, in using sales to export high technology. Although a product may be protected by a patent or trademark, one loses control over that product when it is exported. Later developments based on the exported item may be beyond the protective reach of the patent or trademark. Because of this disadvantage connected with an outright sale of technology, transfer by sale is probably the lease acceptable method of high technology transfer.

Licensing is the most common method of technology transfer. A license agreement is executed between a licensor and a licensee whereby the licensor agrees to give the licensee the right to make use of the high technology involved. This requires a transfer, to some degree, of the right to the use of the know-how or patented process involved. Therefore, when a technology transfer results from a license agreement, the original owner or inventor (licensor) is able to retain some power over the high technology that forms the basis for the agreement. Licensing, therefore, permits the use of high technology by someone other than the owner or inventor, while still protecting the interests of that owner or inventor in that product (high technology). Licensing by its

---

[102] See generally Webster & Herold, Antitrust Guide for Association Executives (1979).

[103] American Security Co v Shatterproof Glass Corp, 268 F2d (3d Cir), *cert denied*, 361 US 902 (1959).

[104] International Salt Co v United States, 332 US 392 (1947).

[105] United States v Associated Patents, Inc, 134 F Supp 74 (Mar 1955), *affd per curiam sub nom.* Mac Inv Co v United States, 350 US 960 (1956).

[106] Unreasonable in length of duration: Zenith Radio Corp v Hazeltine Research, Inc, 395 US 100 (1969); Bruhtte v Thys Co, 379 US 29, 32 (1964).

very nature, however, can conflict head-on with antitrust laws. In order to maintain greater control, the licensor will sometimes impose restrictive provisions within the licensing agreement. These include mandatory packaging, tie-ins, price-fixing, grant-backs, and field-of-use and territorial restrictions. These provisions tend to result in a restraint of trade, and are, therefore, violative of antitrust laws.

A mandatory package license involves a requirement by the licensor (within the licensing contract) that the licensee obtain a complete package of (in our case) high technology goods and services. The reason that such a provision may be problematic is that the licensee may well not need the entire package, and is therefore forced to pay for much more than is necessary or affordable. The package license is unlikely to result in a restraint of trade and consequent prosecution for antitrust violations unless it is particularly restrictive. The leading case on the subject is *American Security Co v Shatterproof Glass Corp*,[107] in which the court concluded: "Because licensor's package licensing requirement is imposed upon a foreign customer, the Department would be unlikely to seek to invoke United States antitrust enforcement jurisdiction absent a belief that it had some significant effect on overseas licensing opportunities for other United States firms or some impact on sales in the United States."[108]

A tie-in provision is one in which the licensor requires the licensee to use the licensor's own products and/or services in making use of the high technology upon which the licensing agreement is based. As a result of the agreement, the licensee may be foreclosed from using cheaper component parts or services provided by a competitor of the licensor. As with all the restrictive clauses discussed here, a factual inquiry would be necessary to determine the effect of these agreements on United States trade. Depending on the extent of the effect, antitrust law violations would be prosecuted. Obviously, if the effect on the relevant market in the United States is negligible, the Department of Justice would probably forego the time and expense of prosecution. As a result, it does not seem that these restrictive agreements can be considered per se violations of antitrust laws. Price-fixing is another common technique used in licensing high technology. The licensor requires a licensee to sell the product produced under license at a high minimum price, thereby preventing the licensee from competing in the licensor's market.

Grant-backs are potentially restrictive clauses found in licensing agreements. A grant-back clause requires the licensee to *grant back* any rights to new technology related to, or arising as a result of, the technology patents covered by the original licensing agreements between the licensor and licensee. This way, the licensee is prevented from using the patent license to forge technologically ahead of the licensor. The scope and duration of the grant-back clause

---

[107] American Sec Co v Shatterproof Glass Corp, 268 F2d 769 (3d Cir), *cert denied*, 361 US 902 (1959).

[108] *Id* 770.

would determine the likelihood of an antitrust proceeding.[109] Finally, field-of-use restrictions and territorial restrictions may be encountered in a licensing agreement. A field-of-use clause restricts "the end-use of the licensed product or process, or the end product which the licensee may produce with the licensed product or process, and may have the same effect as a variety of other restrictions."[110] A territorial restriction does not limit the use of the licensed product, but rather, limits the areas wherein the licensee can market the licensed product (or process) or end-product produced as a result of the licensing agreement. Through this device, the licensor can prevent the licensee from competing in the markets where the licensor is already present.[111]

Defense & Military Export Controls

The United States has demonstrated its intention to control exports of products which are or are related to military goods.[112] The Trading with the Enemy Act of 1917 was an early legislative attempt to deal with the export of military related products and technology.[113] Originally, the 1917 Act allowed the President to limit exports to enemy countries during war or periods of national emergency as unilaterally declared by the President. Because this automatically allowed the President to institute essentially wartime controls without congressional approval or declaration of war the power to impose control in a national emergency was removed in 1977, leaving the wartime control powers intact.[114] These controls extend to all exports to foreign coun-

---

[109] Griffin, *Problems Raised by Various Types of Restrictive Clauses,* 50 Antitrust LJ 499 (1982).

[110] Rosenthal, *Judicial Attitudes Towards the Tensions Between Antitrust, Federal Patent, and State Trade Secret Laws in International Technology Transfers,* 50 Antitrust LJ 525 (1982), citing Antitrust Section, American Bar Association, Monograph No 6, U.S. Antitrust Law in International Patent and Know-How Licensing, 15 n59, 18-19 n88 (1981).

[111] For example, the Andean Pact countries—Bolivia, Colombia, Ecuador, Peru, and Venezuela—as well as Brazil and Argentina, have made technology transfer payments a crucial part of their system of regulation of foreign capital. All technology transfer arrangements and payments in those countries must be registered and approved, and many ancillary restrictions common in the United States are prohibited. See Reeves, *Antitrust and International Licensing: A Primer,* 11 Cornell Intl LJ 263, 265-66 (1978). (Reeves suggests that uncertainty in foreign antitrust considerations can be mitigated by using rules of presumptive legality and presumptive illegality in many categories of international licensing restrictions. Another area of consideration is human rights. See generally Murphey & Downey, *National Security, Foreign Policy, and Individual Rights: The Quandary of United States Export Controls,* 30 Intl & Comp LQ 791 (1981); Comment, *United States Human Rights Policy: Effect on Exports,* 9 Ga J Intl & Comp L 329 (1979).

[112] See generally Bracken, *Public International Trade Law, Regulation of Imports and Exports,* 4 Intl Trade LJ 219 (1978); Finnegan, *A Code of Conduct Regulating International Technology Transfer: Panacea or Pitfall?,* 60 J Pat Off Socy 71 (1978); Comment, *Selected Materials on Technology Transfer,* 33 Rec AB City NY 346 (1978); Novotny, *Transborder Data Flow Regulation: Technical Issues of Legal Concern,* III Computer LJ 105 (1982).

[113] 50 USC §§2401-2402.

[114] National Emergencies Act of 1977, Pub L No 95-223, §101(a), 91 Stat 1625 (codified at 50 USC §5(b)).

tries designated as enemies.

Control of arms and munitions export was the target of the Neutrality Act of 1939.[115] It was replaced by the Mutual Security Act of 1954 which continued the authorization of the Department of State to control exports of munitions and related technology.[116] The Mutual Security Act was replaced by the Arms Export Control Act of 1976.[117] The State Department is responsible for controlling exports of munitions and related technology through the United States Munitions List. This list is developed and export controls are administered in coordination with the Director of the United States Arms Control and Disarmament Agency. Military goods and technologies contained in the list may only be exported through the licensing facilities of the State Department. The munitions list is referenced in the Export Administration Act (EAA) of 1979,[118] and limits the export of other goods or technologies controlled by the EAA that are used to design or produce goods on the list. This limitation has left open the possibility that other goods or technologies not limited by the EAA might be used to produce munitions list items without sanction.

§9.10   The Export Administration Act of 1979

The primary restriction on United States exports of technology is the Export Administration Act of 1979 (EAA),[119] which replaced and extended the Export Administration Act of 1969.[120] The purpose of the EAA is: (1) to control the export of technology and commodities from the United States; (2) to protect national security; and (3) to prevent depletion of scarce commodities. EAA formally adopted the *critical technologies* approach to the control of technology export. This approach was originally recommended in a 1976 report to the Department of Defense (DOD) entitled, "An Analysis of Export Control of U.S. Technology—A DOD Perspective" *(Bucy Report).*[121] The *Bucy Report* emphasized control of information transfer rather than end products, as transfer of the technology itself allows the transferee to adapt it to any system, includ-

---

[115] Ch 2, §12, 54 Stat 4 (1939) (repealed 1954).

[116] Mutual Security Act of 1954, 22 USC §1934 (1970).

[117] 22 USC §2571 *et seq* (as amended by the International Security Assistance Act of 1979, Pub L No 96-92, 93 Stat 701).

[118] Export Administration Act of 1979, §5(1), 50 USC §2404(1). See also Dvorin, *The Export Administration Act of 1979: An Examination of Foreign Availability of Controlled Goods and Technologies,* 2 NWJ Intl L & Bus 179 (1980); Flowe, *An Overview of Export Controls on Transfer of Technology to the U.S.S.R. in Light of Soviet Intervention in Afghanistan,* 5 NCJ Intl L & Com Reg 555 (1980); Evrard, *The Export Administration Act of 1979: Analysis of Its Major Provisions and Potential Impact on United States Exporters,* 12 Cal W Intl LJ 1 (1982).

[119] Export Administration Act of 1979, 50 USC §§2401-2402.

[120] Export Administration Act of 1969, Pub L No 91-184, 83 Stat 841.

[121] Reprinted in *Transfer of Technology and the Dresser Industries Export Licensing Actions: Hearings Before the Permanent Subcommittee on Investigations of the Senate Commission on Government Affairs,* 95th Cong, 2d Sess 33-89 (1978).

ing military systems. End products, on the other hand, may reveal little about the technology used to produce them. Accordingly, the *Bucy Report* recommended that detailed information about design and manufacturing processes, equipment essential or *key* in those systems, and products that necessarily carry the technology with them be strictly controlled.

As a result of the *Bucy Report* and its adoption by the DOD, the EAA required the DOD to publish the Initial Militarily Critical Technologies List by October 1, 1980.[122] The list contains 17 different types of critical technologies with sub-listings of more specific technologies.[123] The list was submitted for inclusion in the Commodity Control List (CCL) by the Secretary of Commerce and Secretary of Defense.[124] Technologies remain on the list only until replacement technology is available.[125] This enables the United States to maintain a technological advantage in each area while at the same time allows United States businesses and members of the International Coordinating Committee on Strategic Trade with Communist Countries (COCOM) to market the technology at the earliest possible time. As in the Export Administration Act of 1969, controls must be lifted if the goods and technologies become readily available outside the United States.

The critical technologies approach in the EAA is not without its problems. Since the approach restricts the flow of information itself rather than the end product, some basic constitutional issues are raised. In *United States v Edler Industries*,[126] an aerospace firm appealed their conviction for exporting, without a license, technical data about missiles on the United States munitions list. While the Ninth Circuit Court of Appeals reversed and remanded for a new trial, it held that the government had the power to restrict information that would directly aid foreign governments to produce arms on the munitions list. In so holding, the court was careful to note that the power to restrict would only exist if the technical data related in a significant fashion to that armament.[127] Otherwise, the court noted, without deciding, that Edler had advanced a colorable claim of First Amendment protection.[128] Since many of the technologies on the Initial Militarily Critical Technologies List may find more nonmilitary applications than military ones, a challenge to this approach may be successful.[129]

In many technology areas, the United States has a comparative advantage

---

[122] 45 Fed Reg 65014 (1980).

[123] *Id* 65015-65016.

[124] Export Administration Act of 1979, §5(c)(2), 50 USC §2404(c)(2).

[125] 45 Fed Reg 65014, 65015 (1980).

[126] 579 F2d 516 (9th Cir 1978).

[127] *Id* 521.

[128] *Id* 520.

[129] For further discussion of this area see Note, *The Export Administration Act's Technical Data Regulations: Do They Violate the First Amendment?*, 11 Ga J Intl & Comp L 563 (1981).

over communist nations.[130] Rather than totally prohibiting the transfer of technology to these communist countries, the EAA attempts to slow high exports to communist countries and thus enable DOD to maintain the necessary lead time to permit replacement or replenishment of critical technology.[131] If it were believed, for example, that the Soviet Union was five to eight years behind the United States in computer technology, and that it would take the United States three years to achieve the next computational technological advance, the United States export of existing computational technology should be withheld from export to the Soviets for at least three years. Consequently, the Soviets would continually remain five to eight years behind the United States.[132] Theoretical control of United States computational technology, however, must deal with the reality of international political policy without unnecessarily curbing international trade. Obviously, American export controls cannot inhibit Soviet acquisition of new computational technology without the cooperation of other nations.[133]

The Department of Commerce published the Commodity Control List (CCL) in January, 1965.[134] This list is still the primary source of information on export restrictions. Currently, commodities on the CCL, which is administered by the Office of Export Administration of the Department of Commerce, are divided into 10 categories.[135] Foreign countries are grouped into *embargo destinations.* The matrix on the list indicates the maximum value of a commodity that may be shipped to an embargo destination without a validated license. The list is followed by interpretations of the specific types of items to be included in a commodity category. If an exporter is uncertain of the proper CCL category, it is advised to consult the Office of Export Administration for guidance.

---

[130] Export Administration Act of 1969, Pub L No 91-184, 83 Stat 841.

[131] See E. Philbin, Soviet Technology States, Trends & Strategies, 128 (1978) (Air War College Report No 445).

[132] Davis, *Multilateral Trade Negotiations: The Tokyo Round,* 29 Fed B News & J 12 (1982) (statement of Dr. Ruth Davis, Deputy Director for Research & Advanced Technology for DOD).

[133] Among the problems with foreign policy export controls are the unilateral nature of the restrictions (affecting US goods only) and the frequently tactical nature of the objectives (discouraging USSR action against specific human rights protestors, for example). Such restrictions force US companies to competitive handicap in relation to suppliers from other countries, in that US political actions can cut off the export of US goods and services without warning, while goods from elsewhere are still available to the offending nations.

Enterprise Institute, Proposals for Reform of Export Controls for Advanced Technology 3 (1979).

[134] 15 CFR §399.1, *as amended by* 45 Fed Reg 43010 (1980). See also Comment, *National Security Protection: The Critical Technologies Approach to U.S. Export Control of High-Level Technology,* 15 J Intl L & Econ 575 (1981); Comment, *Export Controls: Restrictions on the Export of Critical Technologies-Initial Critical Technologies List 15 CFR 399.1 (1974), as amended by 45 Fed Reg 43010 (1980),* 22 Harv Intl LJ 411 (1981).

[135] For a list of goods *not* controlled by the Office of Export Administration, *see* 15 USC §370.10.

§9.11   —Export Trading Companies

High technology production is, of course, very expensive. The additional expenditures required to export high technology products often preclude smaller companies from participating in international markets. As a result, the Senate proposed the creation of Export Trading Companies (ETCs) to remedy this situation, which was enacted in 1982 as the Export Trading Company Act. Export Trading Companies (ETCs) perform all export functions for smaller businesses that would like to expand into the foreign market through exports, but are unable to because of their small size. ETCs act as intermediaries and perform all services necessary to become involved in international export trading. These services include financial services, analysis of foreign markets, transportation, and sales services.[136] In effect, under the 1979 Export Trading Act,[137] these ETCs are service organizations which encourage small and medium-sized businesses to enter the international markets. These ETCs are designed to aid exports and help in improving the negative balance of trade which has plagued the United States in recent years.[138]

An ETC is defined as a company organized under the laws of the United States or any state with the purpose of: (1) exporting United States produced goods or services; and (2) "facilitating the exportation of goods or services produced in the United States" by unaffiliated persons who provide one or more export trade services.[139] A unique feature of ETCs is that they are owned by banking institutions, although, these banking organizations are limited in the amount in which they can invest in an export trading company. If the investment exceeds the specified limit, the banking entity must have prior approval of its primary regulatory agencies: the Federal Reserve Board, Comptroller of the Currency, Federal Deposit Insurance Corporation, or Federal Home Loan Bank Board.[140] Title I of the Export Trading Company Act requires the establishment of guarantee programs to support exporting programs in case of inadequate financing. Title II is composed of amendments to the Webb-Pomerene Act.[141] The Department of Commerce is responsible for granting antitrust immunity to the export trading association prior to opera-

---

[136] Schwartzmann, *Export Trading Company Legislation: Birds, Commons & Peashooters,* 29 Fed Bar News & J 16 (1982).

[137] Export Trading Company Act of 1981, Pub L No 97-290, 96 Stat 1240-1245 (codified at 15 USC §§4011-4021).

[138] See generally, S734, 97th Cong, 1st Sess (1981).

[139] *Id* 18. See also Reinsch, *The Export Trading Company Act of 1981,* 14 L & Poly Intl Bus 47 (1982).

[140] Pub L No 97-290, 96 Stat 1240-45 (codified at 15 USC §§4011-4021).

[141] Under this title, the Department of Commerce is placed in charge of export trading associations and export trading companies. For all practical purposes, export trading companies and export trading associations may be treated as the same. For proposed rules regarding export trade certificates of review, see 47 Fed Reg 56,972 (1982), 48 Fed Reg 31 (1983), and 48 Fed Reg 10,596 (1983).

tion,[142] although the Department of Commerce can limit the extent of antitrust exemption as it deems appropriate.

As amended, Webb-Pomerene associations and ETCs must meet two new criteria in addition to those already required of existing Webb-Pomerene associations. An ETC "must not engage in trade or commerce" in the "licensing of patents, technology, trademarks, or know-how" (except when these transfers are incidental to a sale of goods or services), and export activities must serve to promote or preserve export trade.[143] The other requirements embody traditional antitrust and unfair competition considerations.[144]

In the future, smaller and middle-sized businesses will become more involved in export trade. This increased involvement by smaller and medium-sized firms in export is an advantage for the United States as well as for the individual firms. Most countries have traditionally linked the financial/banking functions with the business side of exporting. Opponents, however, to ETCs fear that banking organizations involvement in ETC's will blur the traditional distinction between commerce and banking. There is also a fear that lines drawn between legitimate cooperative activity and prohibited antitrust activities will become blurred, resulting in antitrust exposure to the participants. Other opponents argue that the Department of Commerce is not qualified to assume the responsibilities placed upon it.[145] The Foreign Trade Antitrust Improvements Act of 1981 has been proposed in Congress to resolve antitrust concerns in export matters.[146]

§9.12 United Nations Conference on Trade and Development Code of Conduct on Transfer of Technology

The draft of the United Nations Conference on Trade and Development (UNCTAD) Code of Conduct on Transfer of Technology (UNCTAD Code)[147] may place further limitations on the transfer of technology if adopted as a treaty by the participating nations. The UNCTAD Code was first drafted in

---

[142] See Schwartzmann, *supra* note 136, at 19. This would be an amendment to the Webb-Pomerene Act.

[143] §204(2)(a)(1), §204(2)(a)(6).

[144] §204(2)(a)(2-5).

[145] Schollenberger, *Export Trading Companies and S734*, 11 DJ Intl L & Policy 119 (1982).

[146] HR 5235 97th Cong, 1st Sess (1981); S795, 97th Cong. The bill is at this writing in the House Judiciary Committee as H2244. See Garvey, *The Foreign Trade Antitrust Improvements Act*, 14 L & Poly Intl Bus 1 (1982). For one author's predictions of how Congress will treat international trade legislation in the near future, see Kassinger, *The Trade Agenda of the 98th Congress*, Fed Bar & News Journal, Vol 30, No 4 (April 1983), at 219.

[147] The draft outline was prepared by a Group of Experts convened by the Secretary-General of UNCTAD. See Joelson, *United States Law and the Proposed Code of Conduct on the Transfer of Technology*, 23 Antitrust Bull 835 (1978).

response to the complaints of developing countries that restrictive clauses in their contracts for import of technology were oppressive and restricted the growth of technological industry. These clauses included limitations on technology export by the acquiring company, and grant back provisions which would give rights to any improvements gained by the acquiring company back to the seller, often at no cost. These complaints, and the interest of the United Nations (UN) General Assembly in promoting international trade as a medium of understanding, prompted the UN to assign drafting of the agreement to UNCTAD in 1974.[148]

The basic aim of the UNCTAD Code is to prevent restrictive trade practices in the transfer of technology. While a list of many practices was outlined in the draft UNCTAD Code, few were agreed upon. Two that were agreed upon were definitions of *exclusion dealing* and *exclusive sales or representation agreements.*[149] Another chapter deals with disputed mandatory contractual terms. The UNCTAD Code, if enacted as a treaty, would place another level of burden on the transfer of technology. Some benefits, however, may result from UNCTAD. With a mandatory UNCTAD Code, negotiations of agreements would be speeded up and a framework for dispute resolution would be created. Additionally, a UNCTAD Code would limit more restrictive legislation or retaliatory legislation passed as a result of an isolated incident. These benefits should enhance international trade in technology, which would benefit importer and exporter alike.

§9.13 The European Economic Community

In an effort to promote free trade and restrict unfair competition, the European states in 1948 formed a commercial alliance: the European Economic Community, generally known as the Common Market. Historically, the economic focus of most European states had been on cartels. In many European countries, cartels controlled numerous markets within their individual countries. The strength of the cartel was even greater due to the restrictive laws in

---

[148] GA Res 32/188, UN GAOR, Supp (No 45) 117, UN Doc A/32/45 (1977), adopted without a vote.

[149] This is part of the developing countries' elaborate attempt to weaken protection of patents, copyrights & trademarks. This attempt also includes weakening the major relevant international treaties. If it succeeds, it will discourage licensing, but encourage copying, as with the pirate Apples made in Taiwan.
Zuijdwijk, *The UNCTAD Code of Conduct on the Transfer of Technology*, 24 McGill LJ 562, 570 n 33 (1978). For other articles on the UNCTAD Code, see Jeffries, *Regulation of Transfer of Technology: An Evaluation of the UNCTAD Code of Conduct*, 18 Harv Intl LJ 309 (1977); Comment, *An International Code of Conduct on Transfers of Technology* 26 Intl & Comp LQ 210 (1977); Feinrider, *UNCTAD Transfer of Technology Code Negotiations: West and East Against the Third World*, 30 Buffalo L Rev 753 (1981); Dessemontet, *Transfer of Technology Under UNCTAD and EEC Draft Codifications: A European View on Choice of Law Licensing*, 12 J Intl L & Econ 1 (1977); Farabow, Jr & Bagarazzi, *Developments at the United Nations Conference on Science and Technology*, 70 Trademark Rep 134 (1980).

each country that hampered the flow of trade across national borders. The Common Market has shifted this cartel focus toward a free market economy among the member states.

The two most important sections of the European Economic Community treaty[150] dealing with cartel activity are Articles 85 and 86. These two Articles are designed to prevent unreasonable restrictive trade agreements in the Common Market. The rules of the Common Market supersede the national laws of the participating countries. Ultimately, the main objective of the Common Market is the freedom of movement of both goods and people. In Article 85, §§1 and 3 are the starting points of a Common Market antitrust violation analysis.[151] Section 85(1) prohibits "all agreements between undertakings, decisions by associations of undertakings and concerned practices which may affect trade between Member States and which have as their object or effect the prevention, restriction or distortion of competition within the common market."[152] It should be noted that (as with United States antitrust law) §85(1) is applicable only when trade between member states is prevented, restricted, or distorted. If an agreement between a firm of a nonmember state and a firm of a member state has only a negligible effect (or no effect at all) on trade in the Common Market, then the agreement will not fall within the prohibitive ambit of §85(1). Article 85 applies to both horizontal and vertical agreements. Horizontal agreements are those agreements made between competitors. Vertical agreements are those agreements made within a single company, but at different levels.

Section 85(3) allows for exemptions from the prohibitions of §85(1). Both private (individual) and block exemptions are available. Private exemptions will be granted upon application for a single agreement. Block exemptions are granted for multiple agreements of the same kind. In determining whether to grant exemptions, the deciding body (the composition of the body depends on the type of exemption requested) will balance the proposed advantages of such an agreement against potential adverse effects on market trade and competition resulting from it:

> To qualify for exemption from Article 85(1) the agreement must show appreciable objective advantages of such a character as to outweigh the disadvantages which it causes on the field of competition. The fact that the agreement is beneficial to the firm concerned will not suffice; it has to merit positive assessment from the point of view of the economy as a whole.[153]

---

[150] Reg 17/62, JO p 204/1962, OJ (Special ed. 1959-1962) 87, Reg 27/1962, JO p 1118/1962, OJ (Special ed. 1959-1962)(32; Reg 99/163, JO p 2263/1962, OJ (Special ed. 1963-1964) 47.

[151] §85(1) lists prohibited antitrust activities or associations; §85(3) lists exceptions to the prohibitions of §85(1). Treaty of Rome, March 25, 1957, Art 86, 298 UNTS 3.

[152] Treaty of Rome, *supra* note 151, at §85(1).

[153] Schlieder, *European Competition Policy,* 50 Antritrust LJ 661 (1982).

Article 86 is designed to maintain healthy competition. Like §85(1), Article 86 is prohibitive; it is forbidden for "one or more firms to abuse a dominant position in the Common Market."[154] Therefore, once a member state firm has achieved a dominant position in its market (through the competitive process), it is under a duty not to *affect trade* by abuse of its powerful place.[155] A firm (or *undertaking,* as it is referred to by the Common Market) holds a dominant position in the market when it can operate freely in the Common Market without having to take account of its competitors.

> The dominant position . . . relates to a position of economic strength enjoyed by an undertaking which enables it to prevent effective competition being maintained on the relevant market by giving it the power to behave to an appreciable extent independently of its competitors, customers, and ultimately of its consumers.[156]

Healthy competition is preserved to the extent that small businesses are protected from large competitors while they develop. More importantly, the Common Market protects the consumer as well: the free flow of trade resulting from this healthy competition allows consumers more freedom of choice, and greater opportunity to move items in commerce without encountering restrictive national barriers.

§9.14 —The Court of Justice of the European Communities

The judicial enforcement mechanism of the European Economic Community (Common Market) is the Court of Justice of the European Communities which enforces the European Economic Community treaty.[157] The Court also has jurisdiction over disputes involving the European Coal and Steel Community (ECSC) and the European Atomic Energy Commission (EAEC) treaties.[158]

The Court of Justice consists of nine judges, one judge from each member country of the Common Market. The judges, however, are independent and do not act as advocates for their countries. One of the nine judges acts as the president. There are also four Advocates-General: one each from the United Kingdom, France, Germany, and Italy. The role of the Advocates-General is

---

[154] Art 86, Reg No 59/62/EEC, 1 Common Mkt Rep (CCH) §2441 (July 10, 1962).

[155] United States v Aluminum Co of Am, 148 F2d 416 (2d Cir 1945).

[156] Ce 27/76 United States v Commission, (1978) & CR 207 sy 9165.

[157] Reg 17/62, JO p 204/1962, OJ (Special ed. 1959-1962) 87; Reg 27/1962, JO p 1118/1962, OJ (Special ed. 1959-1962) 132; Reg 99/163, JO p 2263/1962, OJ (Special ed. 1963-1964) 47.

[158] The court has an advantage over the Coordinating Committee on Export Controls because the Common Market has some power to carry out its aims. COCOM, which will be the focus of later discussions, has no such tool to enforce its agreements.

similar to that of an amicus curiae in the United States' court system. Although the Advocate General has no vested interest in the outcome of the case, the Advocate General acts as a friend of the court. The Advocates-General are individually assigned to cases before the Court of Justice. The Court's Registrar is the Common Market equivalent of the United States' clerk of the court. The registrar supervises all administrative aspects of the Court including financial matters.

Three types of cases can be tried before the Court: (1) direct actions; (2) staff cases; and (3) references for preliminary rulings. Direct actions generally take nine months from the filing of a complaint to the opinion stage, and are tried in open court. Staff cases are tried in chambers.[159] References for preliminary rulings last approximately six months. If the reference is a simple case for which there is a large body of law on the subject, and the issue is a technical one, the case can be handled in chambers. Otherwise, the reference is processed the same way as direct actions.

A direct action begins with filing a complaint with the Registrar of the Court. The complaint, like those filed in United States courts, sets forth the allegations and the relief sought. In addition, evidence is presented in the complaint. All issues that are to be litigated must be raised in the initial complaint. Within one month of service, the defendant must file an answer. The answer by the defendant contains all defenses, any counterclaims, and any new issues the defendant chooses to raise. Answers to answers can also be filed. No new issues or claims can be raised in the answers to answers, unless newly discovered evidence has come to light since the filing of the original complaint.

At this point in the process, interested parties may intervene. Following the filing of all necessary documents and the intervention of all interested or necessary parties, oral arguments are heard in open court. After these oral arguments by both sides, there is a second set of oral arguments, which consist of the Advocate-General's opinions of the case. After a period of deliberation, the Court reaches a decision, and an opinion is read in open court. The full text of the opinion is later published. The International Court of Justice of the

---

[159] Direct actions are those "brought by the Commission against a Member State which it considers to have failed to fulfill an obligation under the Treaties or under legislation issued in implementation thereof; actions instituted by a Member State against another Member State which it considers to have failed to fulfill such an obligation; actions for the annulment of an act of the Council or Commission having binding force (in certain circumstances a natural or legal person may institute such proceedings); actions against the Council or Commission for having failed to act (again available to natural or legal persons in certain circumstances); actions for damages consequent upon noncontractual liability where the Community is liable to make good damage caused by its institutions or its servants" while staff actions are employee-oriented, that is, they are, "brought by employees of the Communities against the institutions for which they work by virtue of the staff regulations governing their conditions of service." A. McKay, *The Court of Justice of the European Communities: Composition, Organization & Procedure,* in Enterprise Law of the 80's: European & American Perspectives on Competition & Industrial Organization 6 (Rowe, Jacobs & Joelson eds 1980).

European Communities has a heavy caseload.[160] In 1978, 268 cases were filed. Of these, 97 full opinions were delivered.[161]

§9.15   Japan

In recent years, Japan has played an increasingly important role in the international high technology scene. The involvement of Japan in international trade in all areas has increased dramatically since World War II. Before World War II, Japan was a predominantly agricultural country. The focus of businesses at that time was toward cartels. Like European countries before the formation of the European Economic Community, most Japanese businesses operated in the form of monopolies. Since the end of World War II, Japanese trade with the West has opened up greatly, and Western business influence has made its mark in Japan. Japanese business law, under the McArthur occupation,[162] has partially absorbed the Western antimonopoly philosophy.[163] This influx of antimonopoly philosophy has created a conflict in the Japanese approach to business: the Eastern pre-war cartel orientation must be balanced against concepts of free trade and competition.

There are two major governmental entities involved in Japanese international trade. The Japanese Fair Trade Commission (JFTC) controls antimonopoly policy in Japan. The JFTC was created by the Japanese Antimonopoly Act of 1947 (1947 Act).[164] American antitrust concepts are closely paralleled in the 1947 Act, and the JFTC is modeled after the United States Fair Trade Commission. The other major government agency is the Ministry of International Trade (MITI) which controls industrial policy in Japan. MITI was established in 1952 and appears to be more sympathetic to older Japanese cartel practices. The conflicting philosophies of the cartel and antimonopoly camps are often reflected in the friction between the goals of JFTC and those of MITI.

Any international business contract involving a Japanese firm must be filed with the JFTC within 30 days of its execution. In this way, the JFTC is able to monitor international business transactions in which Japanese businesses are involved and, oversee possible antitrust problems that might arise in the

---

[160] McKay, *The Court of Justice of the European Communities: Composition, Organization & Procedure,* in Enterprise Law of 80's: European & American Perspectives on Competition & Industrial Organization 3 (Rowe, Jacobs & Joelson eds 1980).

[161] *Id* 9.

[162] Kobayashi, *Technology Transfer in Japan: An Introduction to the Current State of Japanese Industry,* in Technology Transfer in Industrialized Countries 27 (Gec ed 1979).

[163] *Id* 28.

[164] Japanese Antimonopoly Act of 1947: Shiteki dokusen no kinshi oyobi kosei torihiki no kakuho ni kansuru horitso (Law Relating to Prohibition of Private Monopoly & Methods of Preserving Fair Trade)(Law No 54, 1947) in 2 CHS No 2270, enacted April 14, 1947; MITI Establishment Law, Law No 275 (1952).

course of trade.[165] The JFTC has also an enforcement arm (like the United States Department of Justice) to handle Japanese antitrust cases. For the most part, the JFTC prosecutes antitrust and unfair business practice cases. If the JFTC concludes that an antitrust violation of the 1947 Act has occurred, there are two sanctions which can be imposed upon the offending party: (1) a surcharge (based on damages caused by its monopolistic acts) can be imposed; or (2) the JFTC can issue a cease and desist order against the offender.

The business climate in Japan has been ripe for a rapid shift from agriculture to high technology. Research and development in Japanese high technology is primarily funded by private industry. The most significant high technology products presently exported by Japan are consumer electronics (which are obvious when walking through a local video arcade). Research and development is focused on private, nonmilitary uses of high technology.[166]

Finally, the Japanese high technology industry is characterized by the zero defect theory of management (ZD). As with almost all other aspects of Japanese life, the Japanese strive for perfection in the high technology business. The emphasis in this field is on efficiency. The ZD theory is Japan's way of bringing this emphasis to the forefront.[167]

§9.16   Middle East & South America

The Middle East has been a growing concern for the United States in the past decade.[168] Because of political, diplomatic and military considerations, transfer of high technology to the countries in the Middle East will be an important concern. Information in this area, however, is limited.[169]

§9.17   Communist Nations

A major concern with high technology export is exports to communist nations. High technology development in countries dominated by the Soviet Union lags behind Western computational technological developments. Given

---

[165] There is a strict separation between banking and commercial institutions in Japan.

[166] Kobayashi, *supra,* note 162, at 30-31.

[167] Kobayashi, *supra,* note 162, at 32.

[168] For articles discussing technology transfer to developing countries, see generally Silverstein, *Sharing United States Energy Technology with Less-Developed Countries: A Model for International Technology Transfer,* 12 J Intl L & Econ 363 (1978); Goekjian, *Legal Problems of Transferring Technology to the Third World,* 25 Am J Comp L 565 (1977); Matsui, *The Transfer of Technology to Developing Countries: Some Proposals to Solve Current Problems,* 59 J Pat Off Socy 612 (1977).

[169] On Mexico and South America, see generally Brill, Jr, *Transfers of Technology in Mexico,* 4 Den J Intl L & Poly 51 (1974); Kantor, *Restrictions on Technology Transfer in Latin America,* 68 Trademark Rep 552 (1978); Ebb, *Transfers of Foreign Technology in Latin America: The Birth of Antitrust Law?,* 43 Fordham L Rev 719 (1975); Nattier, *Limitations on Marketing Foreign Technology in Brazil,* 11 Intl L 437 (1977).

the radically different sociopolitical philosophies involved, the United States has a strong interest in restricting high technology transfer to communist nations.[170] High technology export restrictions have, however, been loosened in recent years along with a general improvement of relations between the United States and the Soviet Union. As diplomatic relations between the two nations have improved since the 1950s Cold War, the flow of high technology from the United States to the Soviet Union has dramatically increased. The effect the present administration will have on this flow of technology has yet to be defined.[171]

The Export Administration office is the chief entity in charge of high technology export to Communist nations. Computers and high technology in general fall within the *regulated commodity* category previously discussed.[172] As such, high technology requires a special validated license to be exported to the Soviet Union. Due to the delicate nature of high technology transfer to unfriendly countries, Congress imposes strict penalties on those who illegally export high technology without the requisite license to Communist countries. Criminal sanctions are available for offenders. In *United States v Brumage*, criminal sanctions against an offending exporter were upheld.[173] Defendant Brumage had been charged with willfully exporting technical and electronic equipment without a proper validated license with the knowledge that such exports were ultimately destined for Hungary and East Germany. Defendant made a motion to dismiss the criminal charges on the grounds that the Export Administration Act was: (1) void for vagueness and as applied; (2) did not properly notify the exporter of the possible criminal aspect of his conduct; and (3) that the term "communist-dominated" found in the statute was open to different interpretations. The District Court for the Eastern District of New York rejected this argument and denied the motion to dismiss.

The United States has attempted to provide a check on the export of computer technology to the Soviet Union by membership in the International Coordinating Committee on Strategic Trade with Communist Countries (COCOM). United States export control policy was initially premised upon unilateral controls to restrict both the export of goods and technologies from foreign sources and the transshipment of American goods. The United States, however, quickly recognized that effective inhibition of Soviet military and techno-

---

[170] See generally Osofsky, *U.S.-Soviet Trade: Problems and Prospects*, 27 Mercer L Rev 717 (1976); Pederrsen, *Joint Ventures in the Soviet Union*, 16 Harv Intl LJ 390 (1975); Berman, *Joint Ventures Between United States Firms and Soviet Economic Organizations*, 1 Intl Trade LJ 135 (1975); Loeber, *Capital Investment in Soviet Enterprises? Possibilities and Limits of East-West Trade*, 6 Adel L Rev 337 (1978).

[171] See generally Comment, *U.S. Technology Transfers to the Soviet Union and the Protection of National Security*, 1 L & Poly Intl. Bus 1037 (1979); Comment, *An Overview of Export Controls on Transfer of Technology to the U.S.S.R. in Light of Soviet Intervention in Afghanistan*, 5 NCJ & Com Reg 555 (1980); Nau, Technology Transfer and U.S. Foreign Policy (1980).

[172] 45 Fed Reg 65015, 65016 (1980).

[173] United States v Brumage, 377 F Supp 144 (EDNY).

logical development through export controls required other major industrial countries to adopt similar export controls. In November, 1949, the United States and six major allies formed a multinational Consultative Group on Export Controls to curtail Soviet development. COCOM, established in 1950, eventually assumed full responsibility for coordinating multilateral export controls. At present, 15 countries are members of COCOM. These include Japan and all the NATO countries except Iceland.

COCOM regularly composes confidential lists of items for which export should be monitored, restricted, or denied.[174] These goods and related technologies can be categorized as follows:

1. Those principally used for the development, production, or use of arms

2. Those from which technology of military significance can be extracted

3. Those of military significance in which the intended (Communist) destinations have deficient supply

The purpose of the COCOM embargo is to restrict the export of goods and technologies which increase the military capabilities of the Communist countries, thereby threatening the security of the Western nations.

The real problem with COCOM is that it has no enforcement powers. Congress has criticized COCOM as being ineffective for a number of reasons: (1) the organization operates without formal rules of procedure or enforcement powers; (2) there have been allegations that participating governments do not uniformly interpret and enforce COCOM controls; (3) nonmembers such as Sweden and Switzerland are at a relative competitive advantage in the international marketplace (and through them the Communist countries may eventually obtain the technology suppressed by COCOM); and (4) the COCOM control list does not accurately reflect advances in technology. Rapid advances that characterize the field of high technology may make current list-keeping extremely difficult. In addition, the fact that the lists are kept secret, at times impedes the smooth operation of COCOM.[175]

In an effort to coordinate various multilateral export agreements, the Export Administration Act of 1979 (EAA)[176] specifically mandates that the President enter into negotiations with COCOM members to achvieve greater concensus, given that COCOM decisions are not binding on member countries. The EAA has taken significant steps towards controlling and reducing foreign availability of goods and technology through negotiations with foreign nations, particularly within the COCOM forum.

---

[174] The original Consultative Group established secret lists of controls, in 1954 and 1958. Major reductions were made in the lists, and by 1958, sublists were maintained of items under surveillance and items embargoed. The current COCOM embargo list contains 105 item categories. The US unilaterally controls exports of an additional 38 industrial item categories.

[175] S Rep No 95-104, *reprinted in* 1977 US Code Cong & Ad News 362, 381.

[176] Export Administration Act of 1979, 50 USC §§2401-2420.

§9.18 Office of Export Administration

As part of the Export Administration Act of 1979 (EAA), Congress created the Office of Export Administration (OEA).[177] The OEA is a part of the Department of Commerce and is a centralized authority that oversees and enforces domestic statutes concerning exports of United States products (high technology in particular) overseas. OFA was designed to clarify and instill uniformity into the United States export legal system. The President was granted plenary power by EAA to participate in COCOM.[178] Participation in this organization of noncommunist countries can also be seen as an attempt to establish a uniform approach to export activities in regard to Communist countries.

With as much concern as there is regarding high technology exports and the fear that potentially destructive technology will fall into *enemy hands,* the United States government (and presumably those of other noncommunist nations) must look beyond mere export and consider re-export possibilities. It is entirely possible that technology transferred from the United States to, for instance, Sweden will be subsequently transferred from Sweden to the Soviet Union. Although the United States could not effectively curb this (unless of course, it chose not to allow high technology transfer outside of the United States), the United States can attempt to maintain some form of control on these exports by means of restricting the ability to re-export them. As a result, licenses must be obtained to avoid potential re-export penalties. Re-exports would not be allowed unless they are approved by the Office of Export Administration. This approval takes the form of a license.

International trade law is an extremely complicated subject. Issues and considerations that will be of particular concern to those involved in the export and import of high technology include the applicability of relevant United States antitrust statutes as applied to dumping and other related antitrust activities. Possible defenses that the offending importer may raise have also been reviewed. In the export area, the relevant laws of the importing country and the various ways that transborder technology transfer takes place are critical. Most importantly, the lawyer involved in the export of high technology should look to the Office of Export Administration for the necessary required licenses.

---

[177] Export Administration Act of 1979, §5(f)(5).

[178] *Id* §5(i). "The President shall enter into negotiations with the governments participating in the group known as the Coordinating Committee . . . ". Note that this section mandates presidential participation.

Epilogue

10

§10.01   Introduction

Although computer technology is still in its infancy, the dramatic effects it will have on modern society will be permanent and widespread. The broad structural change in the industrial world, magnified by increased energy prices, is actually the result of a conversion to high-technology from the traditional heavy industries that carried the United States economy for nearly a century. The impetus behind this computational structure is that a "given standard of living no longer requires the same amount of iron and steel, energy, rubber or glass it once did."[1] The devastating effect this technological change is having on industry has already begun to affect the world economy.

§10.02   Technological Revolution

The advent of electronics has changed the automobile industry so rapidly that steel and other labor-intensive industries must redefine their roles in terms of capacity and efficiency. The average car today contains at least 30 per

---

[1] Cook, *The Molting of America*, Forbes, Nov 22, 1982, at 161.

cent less steel and 28 per cent less rubber than it did just five years ago, meaning that even a major recovery in the auto industry would have only a mildly positive effect on today's steel mills. Detroit is no longer the bellweather of American industry, and it is inconceivable that it will ever regain that position.

There are two mutually exclusive methods of dealing with industrial change. The first method, reindustrialization, encompasses the use of domestic subsidies and import protection from foreign predators to preserve struggling industries which have gradually lost their competitiveness. The second method recognizes a new industrial revolution, i.e., the shift from a production and resource-oriented industry to computers, fiber optics, and other high-technology industries of the future. To attempt to preserve traditional industries would not only allow foreign competition to infringe on the commanding lead enjoyed by the United States in areas where the high-technology future is most promising, but would also delay the inevitable coming of the computational revolution. The potential dangers of such a delay are significant, including the elimination of domestic firms (and the people they employ) as primary benefactors of new industry. One observer has stated that it is:

> precisely through the shrinking of old industries—learning to make more with less—that new industries become possible and with them a broadening of the horizons of life for most people. The decline of old industries is sad. But is not a tragedy.[2]

Detroit is no longer America's employer. New jobs will come from the development and maturation of industries which already exist in an infant state. Led by electronics, these computational industries will assume a central role as the heart of the economy. For example, by 1990, there may be a need for 1.5 million programmers, more than three times as many as are working today.[3]

The basis of these new industries is the microprocessor—a "computer on a chip." The microprocessor has the unique capability of combining memory and logic on a microscopic chip, harboring enormous potential for small applications. The microprocessor will have an even greater impact on the new industrial revolution because it is a "base industry. . . . It's not really a product; it's process oriented, like oil, and other products and industries will live off it for decades."[4] Even engineers refer to the chip as the crude oil of electronics on which the entire computational industry depends.

The effect of this electronic solution for industry is already being felt in some unique and ironic areas. The price of many goods is continually being reduced, resulting in the opening of new market applications that were previously unaffordable. Gordon Moore of INTEL notes that microprocessor prices continue

---

[2] Cook, *The Molting of America*, Forbes, Nov 22, 1982, at 161, 163.

[3] Boraiko, *The Chip: Electronic Mini-marvel*, Natl Geographic, Oct 1982, at 421, 436.

[4] Cook, *The Molting of America*, Forbes, Nov 22, 1982, at 161, 165 (statement made by Regis McKenna of Palo Alto in an interview for this article).

to drop dramatically, and predicts ". . . wherever electronics is appropriate, the electronic solution is going to be the one that eventually dominates."[5]

§10.03 Computational Investment Frontier

Because of the economic role that the electronics industry will play in the future, the computer and its associated technology have the potential to become the newest investment frontier.[6] An investment frontier is a major development in a new or existing capital-intensive industry requiring massive annual expenditures, and lasting for many years. As a new investment frontier evolves capital expenditures are spread geographically throughout various business sectors, infiltrating the entire economy and providing significant increases in employment and consumer income. Previous investment frontiers include railroads, the telephone, and the automobile.

The driving force behind all investment frontiers is the allocation of scarce resources so as to maximize the production of those goods and services that consumers desire most and for which they are most willing to pay. The recent significant development of large capacity computers has led American businesses to increase their expenditures on computer hardware. As these firms become computerized, the decline in the rate of investment in computer hardware and related equipment will have to be offset by additional expenditures on software products. Each new and different problem, and every additional application for computers, requires that relevant software be produced or developed. This is the precise feature that qualifies the computer industry as an investment frontier. Thus, even if the necessary hardware is in place, expenditures for software development and implementation will ensure the computer industry's vital role in the economy.

§10.04 Foreign Technological Concerns

It is not surprising that the major source of foreign competition in the most vital areas of the computer industry comes from Japan. Just as in the auto industry, the Japanese have examined and refined technology that was born in the United States, and have then developed superior production techniques. The implications of Japan's expertise are dangerous and varied. Officials at the Department of Defense express concern that Japan will come to dominate the industry as weaponry and communications become totally reliant on chips produced overseas. The head of Japan's largest computer company claims that his company faces ". . . far keener competition in Japan than in the U.S."[7]

---

[5] *Id.*

[6] Hansen, Fiscal Policy and Business Cycles (1941).

[7] Boraiko, *The Chip: Electronic Mini-marvel,* Natl Geographic, Oct 1982, at 421, 440 (statement made by Dr Matami Yasufuku, Fujitsu Limited, in an interview for this article).

While conceding that Japan presents worthy competition, American producers remain confident. IBM's Dr. Lewis M. Branscomb is ". . . much surer of our ability to match them in production and productivity than of their ability to match us in innovation."[8] Dr. James S. Albus of the United States National Bureau of Standards sees a unique opportunity in Japan's technological advantage: "Japan has given us another Sputnik."[9]

§10.05 Consumer Technological Developments

Nowhere will the effects of the electronic revolution be felt at a greater level than in the home. As technology lowers prices, it creates new opportunities and applications for computers, and makes computers available to a larger, more diverse group of users. When connected to a telephone line (or to the even larger capacity cable television system), a computer can be used as a telecommunications terminal, and is capable of everything from delivering the daily newspaper to the processing of banking transactions. The possibilities are limitless, as are the problems related to new computational technologies.

At first glance, the thought of never having to stand in line at the bank, or of never receiving a late or soggy newspaper, or struggling with a shopping cart in a crowded supermarket aisle is extremely appealing. The idea of people working in their homes and communicating with the office via electronic mail is not limited to clerical and office employees. Sales people, technicians, and managers could eliminate or sharply reduce the need for long distance travel and their daily commute. The restrictions on employment which limit the handicapped, parents with small children, and other homebound, but potentially valuable employees, would disappear. These newfound freedoms will dramatically increase employment opportunities.

§10.06 Geometrically Increasing Legal Technological Interactions

As the technology evolving from the electronic revolution makes its impact on modern society, the corresponding legal implications will multiply in direct correlation to the availability of new applications. New applications will lead to new users with less education and experience, and a greater propensity for error as computers and related technologies infringe on the traditionally *people-oriented* aspects of society. Each of the previous chapters has dealt individually with computer technology in particular legal areas. These legal areas are all changing as computational technology impacts them. Moreover, the rate of change in each area is further increased from an arithmetic to a geometric rate because the legal areas are impacting each other as each is itself changing.

This geometric increase in technological interaction poses a threat to in-

---

[8] *Id* 421, 441.

[9] *Id* 421, 451.

dividual privacy because of the low cost of accumulating and storing large amounts of personal data. Americans, free-spirited and on the move, still value privacy, or at least the right to privacy. In order for computers to develop into the communications center of the home, immense amounts of information about personal lives and intimate data will have to be stored. Consider home shopping. Computers can be used to order everything from groceries to theater tickets, and the costs will be deducted from a bank account, or charged to a credit card. Necessary to these functions is a data base, beyond personal control, that will contain information about where one shops, what one eats and drinks, the movies one watches, and an endless list of the personal habits of the computer user. The temptation to retain this information for market research data (and the tremendous potential for abuse) is virtually uncontrollable. Legal protection of individual privacy by federal statutes, or state legislation is complicated by the ease of access to personal data and the ability of modern communications to transmit and disperse data.

The retention of personal information is not only an ideological concern from a privacy standpoint, but also offers the potential for computer theft. The development of the automatic banking machine as a popular tool for the electronic transfer and withdrawal of personal funds has provided additional opportunities for computer crime. For example, if the security codes to individual bank accounts or credit card numbers are discovered by an unauthorized computer user, bogus transfers and withdrawals can be made. In addition to stealing from bank accounts, computer thieves can charge merchandise against credit cards or charge accounts by altering files stored in the computers of businesses or financial organizations. The most dangerous aspect of computer theft (and the most appealing to the thief) is that computer crime is often undetectable. Without physical evidence, the victim may have no knowledge of the crime for some time, and even immediate detection may not be helpful because of the difficulty of tracing the action back to the location of the thief. False information of an accidental origin is also a significant aspect of the proliferation of computer use. In order for computer data to be accurate and therefore valuable, data files must be *purged* periodically. Information that is inaccurate because of clerical error, obsolesence, or changes of any nature must be removed or updated with current figures. An insurance company, for example, in addition to recording claims and payments, must make countless daily adjustments because of changes in the status of policyholders due to marriage, birth, or death in the family. Consider also an employee data file containing payroll information and the potential inaccuracies that can result when exemptions or deductions change, or a new tax law comes into effect. The cost of purging files and providing updated information is enormously expensive, so much so that some companies actually send out inaccurate statements to customers (and overpay or overcharge) instead of purging inaccurate data on a timely basis. This practice may continue since purging files is a labor-oriented process increasing in cost while the hardware costs of increased computer storage continue to decline.

The electronic revolution and its offspring, the home computer, have created interesting legal relationships, especially in the areas of responsibility and liability. Particularly where privacy is a concern, the technical aspects of computer development have historically outpaced government's response with appropriate protective legislation. The result is that where statutory protection exists, it is often ineffective. Attempting to follow precedent is precarious in an area where changing technology makes court decisions obsolete almost as fast as they can be published. The issue of liability for breaches of privacy resulting in individual consumer's suffering damages of a financial and personal nature has not yet been resolved.

The invasion of privacy caused by the storage and use of inacccurate data is evidenced by the effect it has on individual employment. Inquiries are routinely made into an individual's medical history or credit record for varied purposes: when applying for a job, seeking admission to a school or other organization, or when making a purchase with a check or on credit. The liability for incorrect information in this type of situation may be hard to assign, but the effect on the person being subjected to the inquiry is immediate and disastrous. A job applicant unknowingly subjected to a personal history check which erroneously reveals a series of past psychiatric treatments or a false criminal record may fail to secure employment. More importantly, this individual has no idea why employment was refused, and is given no opportunity to correct the erroneous information. Assessing liability in this example would be a challenge to the best legal experts. Perhaps the party injured by the inquiry mistakenly provided inaccurate information when completing an application form that became a *source document* (a standard form filled out by hand from which data is keyed into a computer) for the data file. Or, perhaps, the organization operating the computer information service was negligent during data entry, or failed to purge and update the records in a timely manner. It is possible that even if the damaging information was accurate, the organization operating the computer data bank violated existing privacy law by illegally dispensing confidential information. Any legislative solution requiring disclosure of information must, therefore, be sensitive to balancing the rights of the employer against those of the prospective employee.

The problem is compounded in instances of computer theft where the guilty party is not apprehended. The result is a conflict between banking institutions, computer service companies, and individual consumers as to who is responsible for the financial loss. Computer theft is not limited to misappropriating funds belonging to banks or individual consumers. The computer programs or *software* necessary to provide the detailed instructions required to carry out various transactions are extremely valuable and subject to piracy. Because these programs are complex and intricate in design, software development is expensive and time consuming. An effective programmer is not only highly trained and experienced from the standpoint of technical expertise, but also possesses an intimate understanding of the particular business applications being developed. Experienced programmers are mobile due to the demand for their services, and thus have ample opportunities to take programs with them as they move from job to job. While most programmer employment contracts stipulate that all work product developed on the employer's equipment during the term of employment remain the property of the employer, it is quite simple for a programmer to make and keep electronic copies of programs. Once copied, a program may require only slight modification to allow it to perform essentially the same functions, and yet render its identification and place of origin undetectable.

§10.07   Contracting and Software Protection

Legal implications of software protection are immediately apparent in two specific areas—ownership of developed programs, and the agreement of the programmer not to compete. The sources of potential danger in these areas are interrelated. A business that employs a programmer to develop and implement computer applications must necessarily open up the entire operation of the company to the programmer. Thus the programmer has access to detailed information concerning sales, new product development, financial records, and other strategic information that could literally destroy the business if made available to competitors.

Completed programs are a detailed reflection, on a step-by-step basis, of the daily operations of the business, making it imperative that title to the programs be retained by the user. Not only is title to the finished product important, but the timing of the title transfer at various stages of development is crucial. If termination of the programmer's employment occurs, for whatever reason, the user must have title to programs completed up to that time (along with sufficient documentation), or risk exposure of many vital business secrets.

Equally important is restricting the programmer from working for any competing organization for at certain time period after completing the program's development. From a competitive standpoint, a business organization installs a computer to become faster, more efficient, and therefore more profitable, and this competitive edge can be lost if crucial information is made available through the expertise of a former computer programmer.

The Electronic Funds Transfer System (EFTS) is an appropriate subject for conclusion of the discussion of the effects of the computational revolution. The implementation of EFTS has provided a valid test of problems inherent in any electronic solution. EFTS is perhaps the most obvious and familiar example of modern technology—nearly every bank customer owns or has access to a *cash card* or a credit card equipped for use in automatic teller machines. When combined with an easy to remember personal code, this card can magically produce cash from the stoic machines found on nearly every street corner and bank lobby. These machines can also frustrate the consumer to tears without ever changing its expression or tone of voice. An examination of EFTS demonstrates potential problems that must be confronted as society moves into the automated world of consumer transactions.

Problem areas can be categorized into three major groups: authentication, operator error, and system error. While problems of authentication are generally a result of either operator or system error, it is the major aspect of not only

EFTS, but any form of computer use by the individual consumer. The inter-related purposes of authentication define its inherent limitations: to be effective any EFTS authentication method must allow the valid user access to the system while refusing access to all unauthorized users. The difficulties of authentication become obvious when one considers that it depends entirely on the possession of a plastic card and the knowledge of a short (usually five digit) personal identification code.

Allocation of risk for damages caused by improper authentication has been approached by both state and federal legislation. Liability can be incurred for an improper authentication which results in theft or improper allocation of funds, and for improper refusal of a valid user which causes one to miss an installment payment or *bounce* a check because a transfer was not made on time. Although statutes provide guidelines for the assignment of liability, case law is still relatively new in this area.

Operator error has been significantly reduced through the improvement in the design of these machines, and through the development of more sophisticated software. As the number of users and the number of transactions per user increases, so do the number of improper transfers and withdrawals. The system improvements that have been implemented to correct problems in operator error have led to more reliable systems, reducing the potential for system error. In most states, the banking institution is held strictly liable for damages caused by machine error, either due to improper identification and authorization, or misappropriation of funds.

§10.08   Conclusion

An exciting time lies ahead in the legal arena as both legislative and case law respond to the technological changes in society. The future is bright for legal organizations and individuals who are willing to specialize in the computational industry or in other new industries that may evolve out of the computational revolution. Education and expertise will be crucial to understanding not only specialized legal areas such as software contracts or the intricacies of the Electronic Funds Transfer systems, but will also be imperative to comprehending the overall legal implications of computational technology. Computational technology will not only affect each major legal area at an arithmetic rate, but as each major legal area adapts to computational technology, the interaction among each legal area will cause the entire body of law to change at a geometric rate. Because of the geometric rate at which legal areas are affected, expertise in a specific, limited legal area will be insufficient to practice law in a computational-dominated environment. Opportunities exist, and more will be created, for persons with diverse backgrounds and technical abilities to enter the field of computer law.

Glossary

A

ADDRESS: Identification, label, or name which specifies the location of a particular storage location or I/O device.

APL: Symbolic programming language particularly suited for interactive programming and mathematical applications, noted for power and brevity.

ALGOL (ALGOrithmic Language): Programming language similar to FOR-TRAN, used widely in Europe.

ALGORITHM: A complete statement of specific actions comprising the procedure for solving a problem.

ANALOG: *Cf* **Digital.** An analog device operates on data in the form of continuous variable physical quantities such as an electrical signal or wave-form.

B

BACKGROUND PROCESSING: The execution of less-important jobs during periods of low demand for high priority job time.

BAUD: A unit of speed used in describing signaling capabilities of computer hardware, equal to the number of distinct elements, or states, per second.

BASIC (Beginners' All-Purpose Symbolic Instruction Code): Easy-to-learn symbolic programming language of general application, suited for use by people who are not professional programmers.

BINARY: Number system having a base of 2. Most digital computer components are essentially binary in character, having two states; on (1) and off (0). Any decimal or alphanumeric character can be represented in binary notation.

For example, the numeral 9 is represented as 1001, or $(1 \times 2^3) + (0 \times 2^2) + (0 \times 2^1) + (1 \times 2^0)$.

BIT (Binary Digit): Either of the two numbers—"0" or "1"—used to encode computer data. The bit is the smallest unit of binary notation. A bit is expressed by either a high or a low electrical voltage.

BRANCH: Transfer of program control to a program element other than the next instruction in sequential order.

BUFFER: Area of memory used as a storage location during input and output, primarily used to compensate for time or rate difference between devices.

BYTE: A group of eight bits operated upon as a unit, and used to encode a single letter, number, or symbol.

C

CPU (Central Processing Unit): The component of a computer system which controls the interpretation and execution of instructions. Main storage is generally considered part of the CPU.

CALL: Software instruction which invokes a function or subroutine.

CHIP: A small piece of silicon that is a complete semiconductor device, or integrated circuit.

COBOL (COmmon Business Oriented Language): Symbolic programming language designed for business data processing.

COMPILER: A system program or utility capable of preparing and executing a program in machine language from a source language program, by replacing each source language instruction with an object code instruction or subroutine.

CONDITIONAL TRANSFER: An instruction that will cause a transfer of program control from the next sequential instruction to some other instruction if a given condition is met.

D

DEBUG: The process of detecting, locating, and correcting errors or malfunctions in a program or piece of equipment.

DIGITAL: *Cf* **Analog.** A digital device accepts data in the form of discontinuous discrete elements, usually expressed symbolically, as by alphanumeric characters, and performs arithmetic and logical operations on the data.

E

EMULATOR: A system program or utility which allows a computer to mimic the characteristics of another computer of different design by allowing the emulating machine to accept programs or data intended for use on the different computer.

EPROM (Erasable Programmable Read-Only Memory): A type of memory in which stored information can be erased by ultraviolet light beamed in a window of the chip package. EPROMs can be reprogrammed repeatedly.

EXECUTIVE ROUTINE (aka "Monitor," or "Operating System"): Master program which controls the operation of a particular computer system and the execution of other programs implemented on that system.

F

FIELD: A group of characters treated as, and having meaning as, a unit; i.e., an item in a record is recorded in a given *field* within that record. E.g., a person's name is usually stored in a field of their payroll record.

FILE: An organized group of records, treated as a unit.

FLOWCHART-(PROGRAM FLOW CHART): A diagram representing the logical structure of a program using symbols to depict the types and sequence of specific operations.

FORTRAN (FORmula TRANslator): A symbolic programming language designed to be particularly well-suited to mathematical applications.

G

GATE: This term has two distinct meanings in semi-conductor technology: the controlling element of certain transistors, or a logic circuit that has two or more inputs that control one output.

H

HARDWARE: *Cf* **Software.** Physical components of a computer system.

I

INTEGRATED CIRCUIT: A semiconductor circuit combining many electronic components in a single substrate, usually silicon.

INTERPRETER: A computer system program or utility which translates a source code instruction into the necessary object code, and then executes that block of code before moving on to the next source code instructions.

K

K: Unit of measurement. Usually, an abbreviation for Kilo (1000), but in computer applications 1K has a value of 1,024 because it is a binary device based on powers of 2. Generally used in reference to size of addressable storage or memory. Thus, a 64K of memory can store $64 \times 1,024$ or 65,536 bytes of information.

L

LOGIC: The fundamental principles and the connection of circuit elements for computation in computers.

LOOP: A program element consisting of a set of instructions executed repetitively.

LSI (Large-Scale Integration):   This term is generally applied to integrated circuits containing from 500 to perhaps 20,000 logic gates, consisting of transistors, or 1,000 to 64,000 bits of memory.

M

MACHINE LANGUAGE: Form of instructions which can be used directly by a computer.

MASK: A glass photographic plate that contains the circuit pattern used in the silicon chip fabrication process.

MEMORY CHIP: A semiconductor device that stores information in the form of electrical charges.

MICROPROCESSOR: An integrated circuit that provides, in one chip, functions equivalent to those contained in the central processing unit of a computer. A microprocessor interprets and executes instructions, and usually incorporates arithmetic capabilities and some memory.

O

OBJECT CODE: The result of the "translation" process whereby a compiler or interpreter transforms source programs into a form which can be executed by a computer.

P

PL/1 (Programming Language 1):   A symbolic programming language well suited for file manipulation, and other business and scientific applications.

PROGRAM: A set of instructions set in a particular sequence in order to cause a computer to execute the operations necessary to perform a given task.

R

RAM (Random Access Memory):   *Cf* **ROM.** A memory in which any piece of information can be independently stored or retrieved. Its contents are only held temporarily.

RECORD: A group of related data items stored and manipulated as a unit.

ROM (Read Only Memory):   *Cf* **RAM.** A memory chip in which information is permanently stored during the manufacturing process.

S

SEMICONDUCTOR: An element whose electrical conductivity is less than that of a conductor, such as copper, and greater than that of an insulator, such as glass.

SERIAL-ACCESS: File type in which individual elements or records can only be located by reading through all the records which precede the record of interest.

SOFTWARE: *Cf* **Hardware.** Collectively, the programs, subroutines, and utilities, together with corresponding documentation and operations procedures, which are implemented upon computer equipment.

SOURCE CODE: A program written in a programming "language" such as BASIC, FORTRAN, or COBOL, which is readily understood by humans. Source code must be translated by an interpreter or compiler to be "understood" by a computer.

STATEMENT (aka "Instruction"):   An expression or command in a source language.

SUBROUTINE: A set of instructions which stand on their own to perform a particular service or operation, and which may be "called" from several different locations within a program or group of programs.

T

TRANSISTOR: A semiconductor device that acts primarily either as an amplifier or as a current switch.

U

UNCONDITIONAL TRANSFER: *Cf* **Conditional Transfer.** An instruction which invariably causes a branch in program execution.

UTILITY (UTILITY ROUTINE):   Software used to perform some common or generally useful service in computer operations. Often takes the form of a subroutine represented by a single instruction. E.g., sorting, merge, and file management.

V

VIRTUAL STORAGE: Addressable memory space, provided by use of secondary storage devices and associated software, used to increase the apparent effective size of internal storage to enhance the information-handling capacity of a given computer.

VLSI (Very Large-Scale Integration):   Integrated circuits containing on the order of 20,000 logic gates, or more than 64,000 bits of memory.

W

WAFER: A thin disk of semiconductor material on which many chips are fabricated at one time. The chips are subsequently separated and packaged individually.

WORD: A computer "word" is a group of information units (either bits or characters) of established length (number of characters) which is considered as an entity and is capable of being stored in a single memory location.

Cases

A

Abrams, *In re,* 188 F2d 165 (CCPA 1951) **§2.03**

Aeronautical Radio, Inc v FCC, 642 F2d 1221 (DC Cir 1980), *cert denied,* 451 US 920 (1981) **§5.07**

AH Emery Co v Marcan Prods Co, 268 F Supp SDNY (1967), *affd,* 389 F2d 11 (2d Cir), *cert denied,* 393 US 835 (1968) **§2.12**

Alfred Bell & Co v Catalda Fine Arts, Inc, 191 F2d 99 (2d Cir 1951) **§2.11**

Allocation of Frequencies in the Bands Above 890 Mc, 27 FCC 359, *reconsideration denied,* 29 FCC 825 (1969) **§5.02**

American Employers Ins Co v Goble Aircraft, 131 NYS2d 393 (1954) **§3.37**

American Security Co v Shatterproof Glass Corp, 268 F2d (3d Cir), *cert denied,* 361 US 902 (1959) **§9.08**

American Satellite Corp, 43 FCC2d 348 (1973) **§5.08**

Apple Computer, Inc v Franklin Computer Corp, 545 F Supp 812 (ED Pa 1982) **§2.09**

Aronson v Quick Point Pencil Co, 440 US 257 (1978) **§2.14**

Ash v United States, 608 F2d 178 (5th Cir 1979) **§6.06**

Associated Press v United States, 326 US 1 (1945) **§8.18**

AT&T, 38 FCC 270 (1964), 37 FCC 1111 (1964), *affd sub nom* American Trucking Assn v Federal Communications Comm, 377 F2d 121 (1966), *cert denied,* 386 US 943 (1967) **§5.02**

AT&T, 42 FCC2d 654 (1973) **§5.08**

AT&T, 62 FCC2d 21 (1977) **§5.05**

AT&T, 73 FCC2d 629 (1970) **§5.07**

AT&T, 78 FCC2d 1296 (1980) **§5.07**

AT&T, Long Lines Dept, 61 FCC2d 587 (1976), *reconsideration,* 64 FCC2d 971 (1977), *further reconsideration,* 67 FCC2d 1441 (1978), *affd sub nom* Aeronautical Radio, Inc v FCC, DC Cit No 77-1333 *decided* June 24, 1980, *revised* Nov 5, 1980 **§5.07**

G

GCA Corp v Chance, No C-82-1062 (ND Cal July 19, 1982) §2.09

General Aniline & Film Corp v Frantz, 50 Misc 2d 994, 274 NYS2d 634 136 (Sup Ct 1966) §2.11

General Tel & Elec Corp, *In re,* 72 FCC2d 111, *modified,* 72 FCC2d 516 (1979) §5.06

Girardier v Webster College, 563 F2d 1267 (8th Cir 1977) §§6.05, 6.07

Glovatorium v NCR, 684 F2d 658 (9th Cir 1982) §3.18

Goldstein v California, 412 US 546 (1972) §2.14

Gottschalk v Benson, 409 US 63 (1972) §§1.08, 2.02, 2.03

Graham v Sissor-Tail, Inc, 28 Cal 3d 807, 623 P2d 165 (1981) §3.25

Greyhound Computer Corp v IBM Corp, 438 F2d 423 (1978) §1.08

Greyhound Computer Corp Inc v IBM Corp, 559 F2d 488 (9th Cir 1977), *cert denied,* 434 US 1040 (1978) §4.05

Greyhound Computer Corp v IBM, 1972 Trade Cas (CCH) ¶74205, *affd in part, revd in part,* 559 F2d 488 (9th Cir 1977) §4.05

Grieb v Citizens Casualty Co, 313 Wis 2d 552; 148 NW2d 103, (1967) §3.36

Griswold v Connecticut, 381 US 479 (1965) §6.06

Gross v Seligman, 212 F 930 (2d Cir 1914) §2.09

GTE Service Corp v Federal Communications Commn, 474 F2d 724 (2d Cir), *decision on remand,* 40 FCC2d 293 (1973) §5.04

H

Hall Affiliates v Burroughs, No CV-79-001536 (Ala Cir Ct June 12, 1981) §3.18

Hamilton Natl Bank v Belt, 210 F2d 706 (DC Cir 1953) §2.11

Hancock v Texas, 402 SW2d 906 (Texas Crim App 1966) §2.13

Hartford-Empire Co v United States, 323 US 386 (1945) §4.17

Honeywell, Inc v County of Maricopa, 118 Ariz 171, 575 P2d 801 (1977) §3.29

Honeywell, Inc v Sperry Rand Corp, 1974-1 Trade Cas (CCH) ¶74874 (D Minn Oct 19, 1973) §§4.01, 4.16, 4.17, 4.20

Hughes Aircraft Co (National Satellite Services) & GTE Satellite Corp, 43 FCC2d 430 (1973) §5.08

Hush-a-Phone Corp v AT&T, 20 FCC 391 (1955) §5.02

Hush-a-Phone Corp v United States, 238 F2d 266 (DC Cir 1956) §5.02

I

IBAA v Smith, 534 F2d 921 (DC Cir), *cert denied,* 429 US 862 (1976) §8.22

IBM Corp v Catamore Enters, Inc, 548 F2d 1065 (1976) §§1.08, 3.09

IBM v Federal Communications Commn, 570 F2d 452 (2d Cir 1978) §5.06

W

Statutes

Regulations

Code of Federal Regulations

12 CFR §205.2(g) *§8.19*
12 CFR §205.2(i) *§8.19*
12 CFR §205.8(a) *§8.19*
12 CFR §226 *§§8.08, 8.19*
12 CFR §1204 *§8.04*
15 CFR §399.1 *§9.09*
16 CFR 700.7(b) *§3.13*
16 CFR 7001(a) *§3.13*
19 CFR §210.51(a) *§9.06*

19 CFR §210.51(d) *§9.06*
19 CFR §210.53(a) *§9.06*
19 CFR §§353.0-353.23 *§9.05*
19 CFR §358.8 *§9.05*
19 CFR §2104(b) *§9.06*
37 CFR §201.20(g) *§2.09*
37 CFR §202.10 *§2.11*
42 USC §1983 *§3.21*
47 CFR §64.702(a)(1) *§5.03*
47 CFR §64.702(a)(2) *§5.03*
47 CFR §64.702(a)(5) *§5.03*

Books and Articles

A

ABA Standing Committee on Law and Technology, Computers and the Law (2d ed 1969) **§4.05**

Abelle, *Evidentiary Problems Relevant to Checks and Computers,* 5 Rutgers J Computers & L 323 (1976) **§7.12**

Accused Computer Bank Robber Cops a Plea to Avoid Prosecution, Sec Sys Dig, Feb 28, 1979 **§7.09**

A Checklist for Computerizing Accounts Receivabale, 6 Pract Acct 45 (1973) **§1.07**

L. Albrecht, Organization and Management of Information Processing Systems (1973) **§1.07**

Allen & Rosa, *Integrating the Management of a Big City,* 25 Mgmt Focus 14 (May/June 1978) **§1.01**

R. Amara, Toward Understanding the Social Impact of Computers (1974) (Rept R-29) **§1.01**

American Arbitration Association, A Businessman's Guide to Commercial Arbitration 4 (1962) **§3.23**

American Bankers Assn Study Looks at Future Services and Changes for the Banking Industry, Trust & Estates, Feb 1982 **§8.21**

America's New Financial Structure, Bus Wk, Nov 17, 1980 **§8.08**

74 Am Jur 2d Telecommunications §§4-6 (1974) **§5.02**

Analysis of Enacted EFTS State Legislation, 9 Modern Data (1976) **§8.03**

Anderson, *Programmable Automation: The Bright Future of Computers in Manufacturing,* 18 Datamation 46 (Dec 1972) **§1.01**

Anochie, *Computers and Small Local Governments,* 10 Mgmt Info Serv Rep 1 (Feb 1978) **§1.01**

Anochie, *Using Minicomputers in Local Government,* 10 Mgmt Info Service Rep 1 (Aug 1978) **§1.01**

Anthony, *The American Response to Dumping from Capitalist and Socialist Economies-Substantive Premises and Restructured Procedures After the 1967 GATT Code,* 54 Cornell L Rev (1969) **§9.05**

Benn, *Privacy, Freedom, and Respect for Persons*, XIII Privacy Namos 18-23 (1971) **§6.04**

Benton, *Electronic Funds Transfer: Pittfalls and Payoffs*, Harv Bus Rev, July-Aug 1977 **§8.10**

Bequai, *Computer Crime: A Growing and Serious Problem*, 6 Police LQ 22 (1976) **§§7.01, 7.05**

Bequai, *Legal Problems in Prosecuting Computer Crime*, Sec Mgmt, July 1977 **§§7.02, 7.09**

Bequai, *The Spreading Danger of Computer Crime*, Bus Wk, Apr 20, 1981 **§7.10**

A. Bequai, Computer Crime (1978) **§§7.01, 7.02, 7.07, 7.08, 7.10, 7.11, 7.12, 7.13, 7.14, 7.15, 7.18**

A. Bequai, The Cashless Society: EFT at the Crossroads (1981) **§§8.01, 8.11, 8.12**

A. Bequai, White-Collar Crime: A 20th Century Crisis (1978) **§7.02**

Berman, *Computer or Communications? Allocation of Functions and the Role of the Federal Communications Commission*, 27 Fed Comm BJ 161 (1974) **§§5.02, 5.03**

Berman, *Joint Ventures Between United States Firms and Soviet Economic Organizations*, 1 Intl Trade LJ 135 (1975) **§9.16**

Berman & Garson, *United States Export Controls - Past, Present, and Future*, 67 Colum L Rev 791 (1967) **§9.08**

Bernacchi, *Selected Tax Problems*, in Brooks, Computer Law (1980) **§3.28**

Bernacchi, Davidson & Grogan, *Computer System Procurement*, 30 Emory LJ 395 (1981) **§3.08**

Bernacchi & Larsen, *Data Processing Contracts and the Law* 74, 79 (1974) **§§3.10, 3.27**

Bernard, *Some Antitrust Issues Raised by Large Electronic Funds Transfer Systems*, 25 Catholic UL Rev 749 (1976) **§§8.16, 8.17**

Bernstein, Private Dispute Settlements: Cases and Materials on Arbitration (1968) **§3.22**

J. Bernstein, The Analytical Engine: Computers, Past Present and Future (1964) **§1.01**

Berostran, *Nationwide ACG Payments in 1978: The Future is Now*, 54 Mag Bank Ad 32 (1978) **§8.13**

Biddle, Computer Industry Association Position Statement **§5.09**

Bigelow, *Footnotes to the Use of Computers in the Law*, 8 L & Computer Tech 99 (1975) **§1.08**

Bigelow, *Introduction - Symposium Computers in Law Society*, 1977 Wash ULQ 397 **§1.01**

Bigelow & Saltzberg, Computer L Newsletter, July 1980 **§3.20**

Bigelow, *The Computer and the Tax Collector*, 30 Emory LJ 357 (1981) **§3.28**

Bigelow, *The Privacy Act of 1974*, 1 Computer L & Tax Rep 112, 117 (1975) **§6.13**

Bigelow, *Transborder Data Flow Barriers*, 20 Jurimetrics J 8 (1979) **§6.11**

Biglow, *United States v IBM, 1969-1973*, 5 Computer L Serv §7-1, art 6 (1974) **§§4.02, 4.03**

Bingham & Johnson, *A Rational Approach to Export Controls*, 57 Foreign Aff 894 (1979) **§9.08**

Blasch, *Computer Models for Investment Analysis*, 20 Mgt Controls 272 (Dec 1973) **§1.07**

Blumental & Riter, *Statutory or Non-Statutory? Analysis of the Patentability of Computer Related Inventions,* 62 J Pat Off Socy 454 (1980) **§2.03**

Blumenthal, *Supreme Court Sets Guidelines for Patentability of Computer Related Inventions - Diamond v Diehr,* 63 J Pat Off Socy 117 (1981) **§2.04**

Blumenthal, *The Development of the Central Market System: Revolution-One Step at a Time,* 3 Rutgers J Computers & L 232 (1974) **§1.07**

Bonge, *Purchasing Managers and the Introduction of Computers,* 8 J Purchasing 25 (May 1972) **§1.07**

Boorstyn & Fliesler, *Copyrights, Computers and Confusion,* 56 Cal St BJ 148 (1981) **§2.09**

Boraiko, *The Chip: Electronic Mini-marvel,* Natl Geographic, Oct 1982, at 421 **§§10.02, 10.04**

Boswick, *Computer Systems Impact on Railways,* 36 Chartered Inst Tran J 179 (Jan 1975) **§1.01**

Boulden, *Computerized Corporate Planning,* 3 Long Rang Plan 2 (June 1971) **§1.07**

Boulden & McLean, *An Executive's Guide to Computer-based Planning,* 17 Col Mgmt 58 (Fall 1974) **§1.07**

Bowlin, Dukes & Ford, *The Computer, Broker of the Future: A Speculative Forecast,* 20 Computers & Automation 8 (April 1971) **§1.07**

Boyd, *The Computer Revolution — And the Railroads,* 20 Computers & Automation 25-27 (Feb 1971) **§1.01**

G. Brabb, Computers and Information Systems in Business (1976) **§1.07**

Bracken, *Public International Trade Law, Regulation of Imports and Exports,* 4 Intl Trade LJ 219 (1978) **§9.08**

Brandan, Checklists in Practicing Law Institute, Computer Law: Purchasing, Leasing, Licensing Hardware, Software and Services 217-43 (Brooks Ed 1980) **§3.11**

Brandel, *Electronic Funds Transfer: Commercial and Consumer Law Aspects,* 82 Com LJ 78 (1977) **§8.19**

Brandel & Olliff, *The Electronic Fund Transfer Act: A Primer,* 40 Ohio St LJ 531 (1979) **§8.19**

Brandon & Segelstein, *Data Processing Contracts Structure, Contents, and Negotiations* 13-19 (1976) **§§3.06, 3.13, 3.14, 3.40**

Branscomb, *Computer Technology and the Evolution of World Communications,* 47 Telecommunications J 208 (1980) **§5.19**

Brewster, *Controlling Inventory: On-Line Computer Systems,* 45 The CPA 35 (Sept 1975) **§1.07**

Brill, Jr, *Transfers of Technology in Mexico,* 4 Den J Intl L & Poly 51 (1974) **§9.15**

Briody, *Employment Agreements Not to Compete in California,* 47 J Calif State Bar 318 (1972) **§2.12**

Brock, *A Study of Prices and Market Shares in the Computer Mainframe Industry,* 52 J Bus 119 (1979) **§4.01**

G. Brock, The Telecommunications Industry (1981) **§§5.01, 5.02, 5.07, 5.17**

Brooks, *Profession Must Nurture Growth of Computer Law,* Legal Times of Wash, May 25, 1981, 12 col 1 **§1.01**

Brooks & Brewer, *Special Problems in the Mass Distribution of Hardware, Software and Firmware,* 1982 USC Computer Inst, §II §§**3.12, 3.13**

Brown, *Some Practical Thoughts on Arbitration,* 6 Litigation 8, 10 (1980) **§3.25**

Brown & Black, *Gas Measuring Computer Eliminates Winter Overruns,* 202 Popelines & Gas J 20 (July 1975) **§1.01**

Browne, *A Regulatory Perspective on EFTS: Electronic Banking: The Decisions Are Yours,* 51 Mag Banking Ad 34 (Jan 1976) **§8.03**

Bumstead, *Opening up High Technology Careers to Women (as computer workers),* 25 Occupational Outlook Q 26-31 (Summer 1981) **§1.03**

Bureau of Labor Statis, Computer Manpower Outlook Critchlow, (1974) **§1.03**

Bureau of Justice Statistics, US Dept of Justice, Expert Witness Manual: Use of Outside Experts in Computer Related Crime Cases (1980) §§**7.01, 7.04, 7.07, 7.09, 7.10, 7.12**

Bylinsky, *The Second Computer Revolution,* Fortune, Feb 11, 1980, at 230 §§**5.02, 5.06**

Bylinsky, *The Computer Stores Have Arrived,* Fortune, Apr 24, 1978 at 52 **§3.12**

C

Cabanellas & Bertone, *Host Country Taxation of Transfers of Technology Transactions,* 11 Ga J Intl & Comp 495 (1981) **§9.08**

Campenella & Fearon, *An Integrated Computer Materials Management System,* 6 J Purchasing 45 (Nov 1970) **§1.07**

Carley, *Laws Against "Predatory Pricing" by Firms Are Being Relaxed in Many Court Rulings,* Wall St J, July 14, 1982, at 46, col 1 **§4.06**

Carroll & Watson, *The Computer's Impact upon Management,* 23 Managerial Plan 5 (May/June 1975) **§1.07**

Carter, *A Simulation Approach to Investment Decision,* 13 Cal Mgmt R 18 (Summer 1971) **§1.07**

Cash Drawers that 'Talk Computer', Bus Week, Aug 29, 1970, 66-7 **§1.01**

Cavitch, Business Organization §234.02 (1974) **§2.12**

Cerullo, *Maximizing Computer Utilization in Business,* 9 Baylor Bus Studies 23 (Feb/Apr 1978) **§1.07**

G. Chako, Computer-aided Decision Making 1972 **§1.07**

Chandler, *Computer Transactions: Potential Liability of Computer Users and Vendors,* 1977 Wash ULQ 405 §§**3.07, 3.09, 3.18, 3.21**

Chase, *How Apple Will Keep Growth Going,* Bus Week, Mar 22, 1982, at 63 **§4.14**

Chase, *Test of Time: As Competition Grows, Apple Computer Inc Faces A Critical Period,* Wall St J, Nov 11, 1981, at 1 **§4.14**

Checkless Payroll Saving Hospital Dollars & Time, 20 Computers & Automation 50 (Oct 1971) **§1.07**

Checkless Payrolls Are Here, Industry Week, July 14, 1975 at 55 **§1.07**

Cheek, *Personal Computer Systems: Solutions in Search of a Problem,* 14 Bus Horizons 69 (Aug 1971) **§1.07**

Cheetham, *Progress with Computers,* Munic & Pub Serv J May 21, 1971 717 **§1.01**

Cheney, *Selecting, Acquiring, and Coping with your First Computer,* 17 J Small Bus Mgmt 43 (1979) **§3.05**

Chief Executives, Local Government and Computers, 13 Nation's Cities 17 (Oct 1975) **§1.01**

86 CJS *Telegraphs, Telephones, Radio, and Television* §§5-7 (1954) **§5.02**

Clarke, *Automation - The Bank's Legal Problems of the Present and Future,* 87 Banking LJ 110 (1970) **§8.01**

A. Clarke, Profiles of the Future (1962) **§6.01.**

Coiner, *Controlled Access System Uses Mag Cards to Restrict Entry for Tight Security,* 33 Ad Mgmt (1972) **§7.15**

Cole, *Automotive Industry and the Computer Industry: Common Language, Common Future,* 22 Computers & Automation 8 (Oct 1973) **§1.01**

Colorado Department of Social Services Manual §§4711-4714.3 **§6.05**

Coming: Another Revolution in Use of Computers, US News & World Rep, July 19, 1976, at 54 **§1.03**

Comment, *An International Code of Conduct on Transfers of Technology,* 26 Intl & Comp LQ 210 (1977) **§9.12**

Comment, *A Reconsideration of the Admissibility of Computer-Generated Evidence,* 126 U Pa L Rev 425 (1977) **§7.12**

Comment, *CBCTs: Stranded at the Altar,* 28 Baylor L Rev (1976) **§8.15**

Comment, *Computer Crime - Senate Bill S 240,* 10 Mem St UL Rev 660 (1980) **§§7.02, 7.09, 7.17**

Comment, *Computer Services in the Federal Regulation of Communications,* 116 U Pa L Rev 328 (1967) **§5.02**

Comment, *Consumer Warranty Law in California Under the Uniform Commercial Code and Song-Beverly and Magnuson - Moss Warranty Acts,* 26 UCLA L Rev 583 (1979) **§§3.12, 3.13**

Comment, *Electronic Fund Transfers, Branch Banks and Potential Abuse of Privacy,* 6 Fordham Urban LJ (1978) **§§8.15, 8.20**

Comment, *Federal Communications Commission Regulation of Domestic Computer Communications: A Competitive Reformation,* 22 Buffalo L Rev 947 (1973) **§§5.02, 7.17**

Comment, *Export Controls: Restrictions on the Export of Critical Technologies - Initial Critical Technologies List,* 22 Harv Intl LJ (1981) **§9.09**

Comment, *Interagency Conflict: A Model for Analysis,* 9 Ga J Intl & Comp L (1979) **§9.08**

Comment, *Patentability of Computer Software: The Nonobvious Issue,* 62 Iowa L Rev 615 (1976) **§2.03**

Comment, *Patent Law-Computer Programs for Processing Data with a Digital Computer Cannot be Patented Under Present United States Laws,* 4 Loy U Chi LJ 560 (1973) **§2.03**

Comment, *Patent Law—Patentable Subject Matter—Computer Software,* 24 NYL Sch L Rev 975 (1979) **§2.03**

Comment, *Selected Materials on Technology Transfer,* 33 Rec AB City NY (1978) **§9.08**

Comment, *Tax Incentives to Exportation: Alternatives to DISC,* 9 Ga J Intl & Comp L (1979) **§9.08**

Comment, *The Antidumping Act - Tariff or Antitrust Law?,* 74 Yale LJ (1965) **§9.05**

Comment, *The Electronic Fund Transfer Act — A Departure from Articles Three and Four of the Uniform Commercial Code,* 1980 Wis L Rev **§8.19**

Comment, *The Privacy Side of the Credit Card,* 23 Am UL Rev 183 (1973) **§6.05**

Comment, *United States Human Rights Policy: Effect on Exports,* 9 Ga J Intl & Comp L (1979) **§9.08**

Comment, *U.S. Technology Transfers to the Soviet Union and the Protection of National Security, An Overview of Export Controls on Transfer of Technology in the U.S.S.E. in Light of Soviet Intervention in Afghanistan,* 5 NCJ & Com Reg (1980) **§9.16**

The Computer and American Society, Am Philosophical Soc Proc, Oct 17, 1977, at 339 **§1.08**

Computer and Synthetic Freight Rates, 28 ICC Prac J (Nov/Dec 1970) **§1.01**

The Computer Room, 59 Pub Mgmt 2 (Dec 1977) **§1.01**

Computer Crime Law Inadequate, Crime Control Dig, Feb 21, 1977 **§7.09**

Computer Crimes Not Amenable to Prosecution Under Current Law, Sec Letter, Nov 2, 1977 **§7.09**

Computer Crooks Difficult to Detect, Sec Letter, Jan 24, 1978 **§7.05**

Computer Error Closes Nuke Plants, Indianapolis Star, Mar 16, 1979 at 1 **§3.21**

The Computer in Our Lives, 27 Infosystems 40 (Jan 1980) **§1.03**

The Computer Law Journal **§1.07**

The Computer Society, A Special Section, Time, Feb 20, 1978 **§5.02**

Computer Prepared Returns, 11 Taxn for Acct 284 (Nov 1973) **§1.07**

Computer Revolution at Dun & Bradstreet, Bus Week, Aug 27, 1979, at 72-76 **§1.07**

Computer Service for Port and Waterway Management, 52 Dock & Harbour Authority (Feb 1972) **§1.01**

Computer Services and the 'Tie-in' Sale-A Case for Presuming Coercion, 2 Rutgers J Computers & L 135 (1972) **§4.06**

Computers in Instruction: Their Future for Higher Education (R. Levien ed 1971) **§1.01**

Computers in Local Government, 7 Governmental Fin 3 (Aug 1977) **§1.01**

Computers in Manufacturing, 24 Infosystems 35 (1977) **§1.01**

Computers Rush into Your Daily Life, US News & World Rep, Nov 5, 1973 45 **§1.03**

Computer Technology for Textiles (a compilation of twenty-six articles from the October 1969 and March 1970 issues of *Textile Industries*) **§1.01**

Contino, *The Leasing of Computer Equipment,* 1982 US Computer L Inst §VIII **§3.30**

Cook, *Computer-Managed Parts Manufacture,* 229 Scientific Am 22 (Feb 1975) **§1.01**

Cook, *Computer Systems in the Federal Government,* 11 Printing & Pub 7 (July 1970) **§1.01**

Cook, *The Molting of America,* Forbes Nov 22, 1982 **§§10.01, 10.02**

Cope, *Toward a Right of Privacy,* 5 Fla St UL Rev 630 (1977) **§6.08**

Copethorn, *Key Word at AT&T is 'Bus'*, 26 Datamation 64 (1980) **§5.18**

1 Couch on Insurance §§7:18 (2d 1959) **§3.35**

13A Couch on Insurance 48:166 (2d rev ed 1982) **§3.36**

16 Couch on Insurance 62:184 (2d rev ed 1983) **§3.36**

Coudert, *The Application of U.S. Antidumping Law in Light of a Liberal Trade Policy*, 65 Colum L Rev (1965) **§9.05**

CPU Fails, Two Jets Nearly Collide, Computerworld, Nov 12, 1979, at 1 **§3.21**

Courts AT&T Ruling Refocuses Attention on New Legislation, Cong Q, Aug 14, 1982 **§5.17**

Curly, *Patent Acquisition and Restricted Licenses Under Antitrust Law*, B Seaton Hall L Rev 645 (1977) **§4.18**

Curren & Anderson, *Quick Picture of Where ACH (Automated Clearing House) Stands and Where It's Going*, 67 Banking (1975) **§8.14**

Curtis, *Theft of Secrets Continue*, 48 Electronics 63 (1975) **§2.13**

Customer-Bank Communication Terminals and Branch Banking, 7 St Mary's LJ 389 (1975) **§8.07**

Customer-Bank Communication Terminals Under The McFadden Act, 47 U Colo L Rev 765 (1976) **§8.07**

D

Dann v Johnston: Program Patentability Postponed, 1976 Det CL Rev 663 **§§2.03, 2.04**

D'Anna, *Transportation Information System (Western Electric)* 21 Computers & Automation 14 (Sept 1972) **§1.01**

Data Communications System Keeps Short-Haul Trucking Firm Competitive, 22 Infosystems 43 (1975) **§1.01**

Data Security Equipment to be a Billion Dollar Market over Next Five Years, Sec Sys Dig, Sept 13, 1978 **§7.15**

David, *The Little Red School House and the Big Black Box*, 19 Computers & Automation 15 (Dec 1970) **§1.01**

Davidow, *United States Antitrust Laws on International Transfer of Technology - A Government View*, 43 Fordham L Rev (1975) **§9.02**

D. Davidson, Computer Software Protection at 66-67 (1982) **§2.11**

Davis, *A Fresh View of Mini and Microcomputers*, Computer Design, May 1974 **§4.01**

Davis, *A Technologist's View of Privacy and Security in Automated Information Systems*, 4 Rutgers J Computers & L 264 (1975) **§6.05**

Davis, *Computer Controls: A Different Emphasis Preventing Errors or Fraud by Implementing Passive Controls Which Include: Documentation, Organizational Independence and Audit Trails*, 22 Nat Pub Acct (1977) **§7.15**

Davis, *Computer Programs and Subject Matter Patentability*, 6 Rutgers J Computers & L 1 (1977) **§2.03**

Davis, *Illustrative Computer Programming for Libraries*, Contributions in Librarianship and Information Science (1974) **§1.01**

Davis, *Multilateral Trade Negotiations: The Tokyo Round*, Federal Bar News & J, Jan 1982 **§9.07**

G. Davis, Computer Data Processing (1969) **§4.01**

Davison, Babcock & Lesley, *Computers and Federal Regulation,* 21 Admin L Rev 287 (1969) **§5.02**

Dempsey, Foreign Trade and Economic Injury-A Survey of U.S. Relief, Mechanisms, from The Laws of Transnational Business Transnational Business Transactions (V Nanda ed 1981) **§9.02**

Department of Health Education and Welfare, Records, Computers, and the Rights of Citizens (1973) **§6.02**

Dessemontet, *Transfer of Technology Under UNCTAD and EEC Draft Codifications: A European View on Choice of Law Licensing,* 12 J Intl L & Econ 1 (1977) **§9.12**

Diamond, *How to Protect Your Privacy,* McCall's 51 (Feb 1980) **§6.05**

Discovering a Vast Potential Market, Bus Week, Dec 1, 1980, at 91 **§3.12**

Doan, *A New-and Bigger-Computer Explosion,* US News & World Rep, April 20, 1981, at 62-4 **§1.03**

Dobyns & Block, *Adequate Disclosure of Computers and Programs in Patent Specifications* 56 J Pat Off Socy 574 (1974) **§2.05**

Domm, *Electronic Banking—A Market View,* 92 Bankers Monthly (1975) **§8.14**

Douglas, *Beyond the Industrial Revolution,* Science News, Oct 4, 1975, at 220 **§6.03**

Douglas, *Some Ideas on the Computer and the Law,* 2 Tex SUL Rev 20, 43 (1971) **§3.01**

Dowe, *Where EFTS Stands Today,* 37 Ad Mgt (1976) **§8.10**

Drattel, *Unbundling: The User Will Pay For the Works,* 16 Bus Automation 36 (Aug 1969) **§4.05**

Duff & Henry, *Computer-aided Management,* 9 Mgmt Decision 204 (Winter 1971) **§1.07**

Dunn, *Policy Issues Presented by the Interdependence of Computer and Communications Services,* 34 L & Contemp Probs 309 (1969) **§5.03**

Dunn, *The FCC Computer Inquiry,* 15 Datamation 71 (1969) **§5.03**

Dutton & Kramer, *Technology and Urban Management: The Power Payoffs of Computing,* 9 Admin & Socy 305 (1977) **§1.01**

Dvorin, *The Export Administration Act of 1979: An Examination of Foreign Availability of Controlled Goods and Technologies,* 2 NWJ Intl L & Bux (198—) **§9.08**

E

Easton & Neely, *Unfair Competition in US Import Trade Developments Since the Trade Act of 1974,* 5 Intl Trade LJ (1980) **§9.06**

Eastway & High, *Lease or Buy?,* New LJ July 28, 1979, at 4 **§3.31**

Ebb, *Transfers of Foreign Technology in Latin America: The Birth of Antitrust Law?,* 43 Fordham L Rec (1975) **§9.15**

Edmonds, *Credit Unions: Competition by Status,* 97 Banking LJ (1980) **§8.05**

Edwards, *Security and the New Technologies,* Banker, Oct 1979, at 41 **§3.35**

Ehrenhaft, *Protection Against International Price Discrimination: U.S. Countervailing and Antidumping Duties*, 58 Colum L Rev 44 (1958) **§9.05**

Einhorn, *A Banker's Guide to the Electronic Fund Transfer Act*, 96 Banking LJ (1979) **§8.19**

Electronic Access Control Systems Have Many Applications, 78 Off 74 (1973) **§7.15**

Electronic Brains in Classrooms (pocket calculators and mini-computers), US News & World Rep, Jan 13, 1979, at 30 **§1.01**

Electronic Funds Transfer, 32 Bus L 201 (1975) **§8.14**

Electronic Fund Transfers: New Protections for Consumers, New Duties for Financial Institutions, Fed Reserve Bull, Apr 1980 **§§8.19, 8.20**

Electronic Funds Transfer in Iowa: Implications for the Regulation of Competition Among Federal and State Financial Institutions, 61 Iowa L Rev 1355 (1976) **§8.03**

Electronic Funds Transfer Systems: A Symposium, 25 Cath UL Rev 687 (1976) **§8.10**

Elkouri & Elkouri, How Arbitration Works (3d ed 1973) **§3.22**

Ellinghaus, *What the Public Should Know About the Consumer Communications Reform Act*, Telephony, Oct 4, 1976, at 84 **§5.09**

Elliott, Interstate Banking: A Personal View in Bank Expansions in the 80's: Mergers, Acquisitions and Interstate Banking **§§8.21, 8.22**

Ellis, Trade Secrets §12 (1953) **§§2.11, 2.12**

T. Emerson, The Systems of Freedom of Expression 545 (1970) **§6.02**

Encryption Receives Much Attention, Sys Tech & Sci L Enforcement & Sec, Jan 1978 **§7.15**

Encryption Standard to Strengthen Computer Security Developed by NBS, Crime Control Dig, Nov 20, 1976 **§7.15**

Enterprise Institute, Proposals for Reform of Export Controls for Advanced Technology (1979) **§9.09**

Epstein & Bessel, *Minicomputers are Made of This*, 2 Computer Decisions 10 (Aug 1970) **§4.01**

Epstein & Bessel, *Mini-Menagerie: A Survey of the Minicomputer Field*, 2 Computer Decisions 20 (Aug 1980) **§4.01**

Ernst, *EFT and the Future of Banking*, 67 Banking 54 (1975) **§8.10**

Ernst, *Management, The Computer, and Society*, 20 Computers & Automation 8 (Sept 1971) **§1.07**

Espionage in the Computer Business, Bus Wk, July 28, 1975 **§7.03**

Esslinger, *Eighth Circuit Short Circuits Electronic Banking: The Broadening Reach of Competitive Equality*, 21 St Louis ULJ (1977) **§8.07**

Etzioni, *Effects of Small Computers on Scientists*, Science, July 11, 1975, at 93 **§6.03**

Evans, *Computer Program Classification: A Limitation on Program Patentability as a Process*, 53 Or L Rev 501 (1974) **§2.03**

Evans, *Satellite Communications — The Legal Gap*, 11 Jurimetrics J 92 (1970) **§5.08**

Evrard, *The Export Administration Act of 1979: Analysis of Its Major Provisions and Potential Impact on United States Exporters*, 12 Cal W Intl LJ (1982) **§9.08**

Ford's Computer Changes Models on the Fly, Bus Week, July 28, 1973 30B **§1.01**

Forrester, *Simplified Financial Modelling Via Time Sharing*, 139 J Accountancy 39 (Mar 1975) **§1.07**

Foster & Gluck, *Impact of Antitrust and Regulatory Actions on the Progress of Technology*, 18 Research Mgmt 7 (July 1975) **§1.02**

Fox, *Application of the Clayton Act to International Mergers, Acquisitions and Joint Ventures*, 50 Antitrust LJ 477 (1982) **§9.03**

N. Foy, Computer Management: A Common Sense Approach (1972) **§1.07**

Frank, *Alive and Well*, 26 Datamation 112 (1980) **§5.05**

Frank, *The New Software Economics*, Computerworld, (1979), at 17 **§2.01**

Freed, *Legal Aspects of Computers and Confidentiality*, 18 Jurimetrics J (1978) **§8.20**

Freed, *Protection of Proprietary Programs in Light of Benson and Talbot*, 13 Jurimetrics J 139 (1973) **§2.02**

Freed, *Software Protection: Introductory Observations on the Study Sponsored by the National Commission on New Technological Uses of Copyrighted Works*, 18 Jurimetrics J 352 (1978) **§2.06**

R. Freed, Computers and Law: A Reference Work (1976) **§§6.12, 6.15**

Friedman, *Checklist for Commercial Arbitration*, 37 Arbitration J 10 (1982) **§3.24**

Friedman, *Correcting Arbitrator Error*, 33 Arbitration J 9 (1978) **§3.25**

Frost, *IBM Plug-to-Plug Peripheral Devices*, 16 Datamation 24 (1970) **§4.01**

Frost, *Tying Clauses and Package Licensing*, 28 U Pitt L Rev 207 (1966) **§4.02**

The Future of Computers in Business Organizations, 1 J Contemporary Bus 1 (Spring 1972) **§1.07**

G

Gagliardi, *Software: What is it*, 8 APLAQJ 233 (1980) **§2.01**

Galbi, *Proposal for New Legislations to Protect Computer Programming*, 17 Bull Copyright Socy 280 (1970) **§2.06**

J. Galbraith, The New Industrial State (1968) **§1.07**

Gampert, *Home Input: the Computer Moves from the Corporation to Your Living Room*, Wall St J, Feb 4, 1977, at 1 **§1.01**

Garvey, *The Foreign Trade Antitrust Improvements Act*, 14 L & Poly Intl Bus (1982) **§9.10**

Gemignani, *Computer Crime: The Law in '80*, 13 Ind L Rev 681 (1980) **§7.10**

Gemignani, *Legal Protection for Computer Software: The View From '79'*, 7 Rutgers J Computers, Tech & L 269 (1979) **§2.03**

Gemignani, *Product Liability and Software*, 8 Rutgers Computer & Tech LJ 173 (1981) **§3.20**

Gemignani, *Should Algorithms be Patentable*, 22 Jurimetrics J 326, 328 (1982) **§2.04**

George, Computers, Science and Society (1970) **§1.02**

George Washington University Computers in Law Institute, The Law of Software (1968 & 1969) §2.01

Gerrity, *Design of Man-machine Decision Systems: an Application to Portfolio Management,* 12 Sloan Mgmt Rev 59 (Winter 1971) §1.07

Gibbons, *Price Fixing in Patent Licenses and the Antitrust Laws,* 51 Va L Rev 273 (1965) §4.15

Gibson & Nolan, *Managing the Four Stages of EDP Growth,* 52 Harv Bus Rev 76-88 (1974) §3.01

Gilburn, *Source Code Escrows: Meaningful Solution or Inadequate Protection?* Computer Negotiations Rep at 4-8 §3.10

Gilburne, *Structuring and Negotiating Software Development Contracts,* 1981 USC Computer L Inst, §X §3.11

Gilburne & David, *Structuring Agreements for Vertical Distribution of Hardware and Software,* 1982 USC Computer L §IX §§3.11, 3.17, 3.19

B. Gilchrist & R Weber, The State of the Computer Industry in the United States (1973) §6.02

B. Gilchrist & M. Wessel, Government Regulation of the Computer Industry (1972) §5.03

L. Glasser, AT&T Settlement: Terms, Effects, Prospects (1982) §5.13

Glavitsch, *Computer Control of Electric-Power Systems,* 239 Scientific Am 34 (Nov 1974) §1.01

Glick, *Settling Unfair Trade Practices Cases Under Section 337 to the Tariff Act of 1930,* 21 Harv Intl LJ (1980) §9.06

Gluck, Heissenbuttel & Hillman, *Model Railroading Simulation May Make Computers Love the LIR,* 2 Computer Decisions 32 (Aug 1970) §1.01

Goekjian, *Legal Problems of Transferring Technology to the Third World,* 25 Am J Comp L (1977) §9.15

Gold, *Factors Stimulating Technological Progress in Japanese Industries: The Case of Computerization in Steel,* 17 QR Econ & Bus 7-21 (Winter 1978) §1.01

Goldberg, *Shared Electronic Fund Transfer Systems: Some Legal Implications,* 98 Banking LJ (1981) §§8.16, 8.17

Government: New Review Showed Victory Over IBM Unlikely, Economic News, Jan 11, 1982, at 6 §4.03

Gorenstein, *Dual Standard of Patentability: A New Look at the Computer Issue,* 62 J Pat Off Socy 96 (1980) §2.03

Gottschalk v Benson: A Bright Light with a Dim Future, 28 Baylor L Rev 187 (1976) §2.02

Greene, Risk and Insurance (3d ed 1973) §3.37

Greenlee, *New Criteria for Patentable Subject Matter,* 47 Brooklyn L Rev 43 (1980) §2.04

Greguras, *How the New Eft Act Affects the Financial Institution/Consumer Relationship,* 11 UCCLJ (1979) §8.19

Greguras, *The Allocation of Risk in Electronic Fund Transfer Systems for Losses Caused by Unauthorized Transactions,* 13 USFL Rev (1979) §8.19

Greyhound v IBM: Price Increases as a Form of Predatory Pricing, 7 Rutgers J Computers Tech & L 77 (1979) **§4.06**

Griffin, *Problems Raised by Various Types of Restrictive Clauses,* 50 Antitrust LJ 499 (1982) **§9.08**

The Growing Threat to Computer Security: New Codes and Other Solutions are Coming, But They are Controversial, Bus Wk, Aug 1, 1977 **§7.15**

Guynes & Vanecek, *Computer Security: The Human Element: Screening Candidates for Electronic Data Processing Positions,* 71 Personnel Ad (1981) **§7.15**

H

Hall, *Where EFT in Wholesale Banking Stands Today and Where It Is Going,* 70 Banking (1978) **§8.04**

Halls, *Raiding the Databanks: A Developing Problem for Technologists and Lawyers,* 5 J Contemp L 264 (1978) **§6.16**

Hamburg, *US Supreme Court Affirm CCPA in Two Cases According Patent Protection to Inventions Relating to Computers,* 79 Pat & Trademark Rev 211 (1981) **§2.04**

Hamburg, *Inventions Relating to Computers or Use Thereof Again Being Considered by US Supreme Court,* 78 Pat & Trademark Rev 518 (1980) **§2.03**

Hammer, *IBM-Tightens Reins on Trade Secrets: Pledges Fight on Lawsuits,* NY Times, April 30, 1974 at 57 **§2.13**

Hammond, *Do's and Don'ts of Computer Models for Planning,* 52 Harv Bus Rev 110 (Mar/Apr 1974) **§1.07**

Hansen, Fiscal Policy and Business Cycles (1941) **§10.03**

Hardman, *A Primer on Cellular Mobile Telephone Systems,* 29 Fed B News J (1982) **§5.19**

Hardowy, *Computerized Financial Reporting Systems-How & Why,* 101 Can Chartered Accountant 26 (July 1972) **§1.07**

Hardy, *Computer Investment Systems: What They Are, How They Work,* 64 Banking 50 (Oct 1971) **§1.07**

Harris, Complex Contract Issues in the Acquisition of Hardware and Software 3 (1982) **§3.06**

Hattery, *Data Encryption Hardware Gets NBS Validation,* Sys, Tech & Sci L Enforcement & Sec, Nov 1977 **§7.15**

Hawk, *Special Defenses and Issues Including Subject Matter Jurisdiction, Act of State Doctrine, Foreign Government Compulsion and Sovereign Immunity,* 50 Antitrust LJ 559 (1982) **§9.04**

Head & Linik, *Software Package Acquisition,* 14 Datamation 24 (1968) **§2.01**

Hemphil & Hemphil, *Prosecuting Computer Criminals,* Sec World, Aug 1978, **§7.02**

Herman, *Manpower Implications of Computer Control in Manufacturing,* 93 Mo Labor Rev 3 (Oct 1970) **§1.03**

Hess & Waters, *Inventory Control and Stores Management,* 6 Soc Research Ad J 37 (Winter 1975) **§1.07**

Hilde, *Can a Coputer be an "Author" or an "Inventor"* 51 J Pat Off Socy 318 (1969) **§2.07**

J

Jacobs, *Computer Technology (Hardware and Software): Some Legal Implications for Antitrust, Copyrights and Patents,* 1 Rutgers J Computers & L 50 (1970) **§§2.02, 4.01**

Jacobs, *Ever Wonder how Tax Accountants Do All those Returns? Simple, they Just turn them over to some expert-namely, to a computer,* Wall St J, April 5, 1979, at 1 **§1.07**

Japan's High-Tech Challenge, Newsweek, Aug 9, 1982, at 48 **§§6.03, 9.01**

Jessetes, Regulation of Transfer of Technology: An Evaluation of the UNCTAD Code of Conduct, 18 Harv Intl LJ 309 (1957) **§9.12**

Jewkes & Sawers & R. Stillerman, The Sources of Invention (1968) **§§1.07, 1.08**

Joelson, *United States Law and the Proposed Code of Conduct on the Transfer of Technology,* 23 Antitrust Bull (1978) **§9.11**

Johnson, *Liability Security Need Senn,* Computerworld, Dec 6, 1982 at 83 **§3.35**

R. Johnson, *The New Competition,* 37 Bus L 1363 (1982) **§8.17**

Johnson & Arnold, *The Emerging Revolution in the Electronic Payments,* 22 Price Waterhouse Rev 26 (1977) **§8.10**

Joines, *Computerized General Ledger and Budgetary Accounting System,* Gov Fin, May 1976 at 26 **§1.07**

Jones, *At Last: Real Computer Power for Decision Makers,* 48 Bus Rev 75 (Sept 1970) **§1.07**

Jones, *Using Computers Southern Style (Southern Railway System),* 26 Atlanta Econ R 6 (Nov/Dec 1976) **§1.01**

Joss, *Data Collection Speeds Retail-Store Inventory,* 2 Computer Decisions 29 (March 1970) **§1.07**

Judge Widens AT&T Business Scope, Wash Post, Sept 5, 1981, at C-7 **§5.02**

Judge's Power in Settlements Outlined in AT&T Decision, Natl LJ Aug 23, 1982 **§5.17**

Jutila & Sass, *Uses of Computers for Corporate Strategy Development,* 10 Data Mgmt 73 (Sept 1972) **§1.07**

Juvigny, *Data-handling and the Protection of Workers' Rights,* 115 Internat Labour R 247 (Nov/Dec 1976) **§1.07**

K

A. Kahn, The Economics of Regulation: Principles and Institutions (1971) **§5.13**

H. Kahn & A. Weiner, The Year 2000 (1967) **§6.01**

Kamrany, *Technology: Measuring the Socioeconomic Impact of Manufacturing Automation,* 8 Socio-Econ Plan Sciences 281 (Oct 1974) **§1.03**

Kantor, *Restrictions on Technology Transfer in Latin America,* 68 Trademark Rep (1978) **§9.15**

Karp, *Management in the Computer Age,* 8 Data Management 24 (Dec 1970) **§1.07**

Karr, *Automated Clearing House: The Case for Barring Thrift Institutions,* 95 Banking LJ (1978) **§8.14**

Kassinger, "The Trade Agenda of the 98th Congress", Fed Bar & News Journal, Vol 30 No 4 (April 1983) at 219 **§9.12**

Katskee & Wright, *An Overview of Legal Issues Confronting the Establishment of EFT Services,* 2 Computer LJ 7, (1980) **§8.16**

Kaufman, *On Understanding the Computer and the Problem of Executive Decision-making in its Alien Technological Environment,* 11 Conference Bd Rec 52 (Oct 1974) **§1.07**

Kaye, Plaia, *The Relationship of Countervailing Duty and Antidumping Law to Section 337 of the U.S. International Trade Commission,* 2 Intl Trade LJ (1977) **§6.09**

Kayton, *Update of Legal Protection of Computer Software Via Patents,* APLAQJ 1980 273,274 **§2.04**

Kelley, *Satellites Save Money,* 26 Infosystem 42 (1979) **§5.08**

Kelley, *The Gold Mine in Satellite Services,* Bus Week, Apr 6, 1981, at 89 **§5.08**

Kellor, American Arbitration (1948) **§3.22**

Kennedy, Benson & McMillan, *Managing Negotiations* 99-110 (1982) **§3.41**

Kern, *Washington Tackles the Software Problem,* BYTE 128, 136 (1981) **§2.04**

Keston, Information Systems in Urban Government 20 Computers & Automation 21 (Sept 1971) **§1.01**

Kick, *A Profit-planning and Control System (PPCS) for the Small Firm,* 14 J Small Bus Mgmt 8 (Oct 1976) **§1.07**

Kim, *Unconscionability of Presumptively Biased Arbitration Clauses Within Contracts of Adhesion,* 70 Cal L Rev 1014 (1982) **§3.25**

Kirkpatrick, *Antitrust Enforcement in the Seventies,* 30 Cath UL Rev 431 (1981) **§4.01**

Klein, *Analysis of the Issues in the Legal Attempts to Restrict Banks from Furnishing Automated Customer Services,* 86 Banking LJ 579 (1969) **§8.04**

Klein, Computerizing Accounts Receivables, 77 Fin Mgmt 30 (Aug 1975) **§1.07**

Klein, *The Technical Trade Secret Quadrangle: A Survey,* 55 NWUL Rel 437 (1960) **§2.12**

Kleinfield, *Help Wanted,* Wall St J May 12, 1977 40 **§1.03**

Kobayashi, Technology Transfer in Japan: An Introduction to the Current State of Japanese Industry, from Technology Transfer in Industrialized Countries (Gec ed 1979) **§9.14**

Koch, *Basic Facts About Using the Computers in Instruction,* 38 Educ Dig 28 (Mar 1973) **§1.01**

Koehn, *Privacy, Our Problem for Tomorrow,* Sys Mgmt, July 1973, at 8 **§6.03**

Koenig, *Software Copyright: The Conflict Within CONTU,* 27 Bull Copyright Socy of USA 340 (1980) **§2.06**

Koller & Moshman, *Patent Protection for Computer Software: Implications for the Industry,* 12 Idea 1106 (1968) **§2.03**

J. Kraemer & J. King, Computers, Power, and Urban Management: What Every Local Executive Should Know (1976) **§1.01**

Luecke, *Computer Models: 'Black Box' or Management-oriented,* 10 Mgmt Adviser 17 (Jan/Feb 1973) **§1.07**

M

Machines Smarter than Men? An Interview with Robert Weiner, US News and World Rep Feb 24, 1964, at 84 **§6.03**

Maggs, *Computer Programs as the Object of Intellectual Property in the United States of America,* 30 Am J **§2.01**

Maggs, *Some Problems of Legal Protections of Programs for Microcomputer Control Systems,* 1979 U Ill Forum 453, 468 **§2.06**

Makower, *Business Computers: A Planning Guide,* United Mainliner, May 1981 **§7.15**

Maki, *EFTS: Living in a Legal House of Cards,* Comm LJ 49 (1977) **§8.10**

Man and Computer for Higher Education, M. Marois ed (1972) **§1.01**

'Managing' ROI on Business Contracts through Simulation, 10 Mgmt Adviser 28 (Jan/Feb 1973) **§1.07**

Mandell, *Computer Security - Sabotage Fears Discounted,* 20 Computers and Automation 29 (1971) **§7.03**

Manufacturing Management System: New Challenges and Profit Opportunities (F.Gruenberger ed 1974) **§1.01**

C. Martin, An Introduction to Electronic Funds Transfer Systems (1978) **§8.14**

Marton, *Copyright in the 1980's: Fifth Anniversary of the Revised Law,* 30 Fed B News & J 39, 42 (1983) **§2.11**

Maschino & Emmer, *An Automated Information System for Local Government,* 19 Mgmt Controls 257 (Nov 1972) **§1.01**

Mason, *Collective Bargaining Agreements Without Arbitration Clauses,* 7 U Dayton L Rev 387 (1982) **§3.22**

W. Mathews, Master or Messiah? The Computer's Impact on Society (1980) **§6.03**

Matsui, *The Transfer of Technology to Developing Countries: Some Proposals to Solve Current Problems,* 59 J Pat Off Socy (1977) **§9.15**

Matsui & Nukui, *Railway Freight Information System,* 22 Computers & Automation 22 (Sept 1973) **§1.01**

Matt, *An Effective Tool for the Optimization of* Distribution Systems, 5 Long Range Plan 48 (Dec 1972) **§1.01**

May, *A Landmark Year for Computers in High Schools* 19 Computers & Automation 26 (July 1970) **§1.01**

McCormick's Handbook of the Law of Evidence (2d ed 1972) **§§7.08, 7.13**

McFarlane, *Legal Protection of Computer Programs,* 1970 J Bus L 204 (1970) **§2.01**

McGonagle & McClain, *Negotiating Computer Contracts,* 2 Popular Computing 126 (1983) **§3.13**

McKay, The Court of Justice of the European Communities: Composition, Organization & Procedure, Enterprise Law of 80's: European & American Perspectices on Competition & Industrial Organizations (1980) **§9.13**

McKenney & McFarlan, *The Information Archipelago - Maps and Bridges*, Harv Bus Rev, Sept-Oct 1982 **§7.15**

McKenzie, *Automation and Labor Law*, 4 USFL Rev 229 (April 1970) **§1.01**

M. McLuhan, The Gutenberg Galaxy (1962) **§6.01**

Menkhaus, *Terminals: Pipelines to Computer Power*, 17 Bus Automation 48 (1978) **§4.01**

Merian, System Vendors and Duty of Care: Mini-Micro Systems 166 (1981) **§3.01**

N. Metropolis, A History of Computing in the Twentieth Century (1980) **§1.01**

Meyers, *How to Computerize Corporate Tax Operations*, 30 Tax Exec 17 (Oct 1977) **§1.07**

Michael, *Decisions and Public Opinion*, in A. Van Tassel, The Complete Computer (1976) **§6.03**

Micro Electronics: A Survey, The Economist, Mar 11, 1980 **§5.19**

Milguin, *Protecting and Licensing Software*, 1982 USCL Center Computer L Inst §I **§3.10**

Miller, *The CONTU Software Protection Survey*, 18 Jurimetrics J 354 (1978) **§2.06**

Miller, *The National Data Center and Personal Privacy*, The Atlantic 53 (Nov 1967) **§6.01**

A. Miller, The Assault on Privacy (1971) **§§6.01, 6.12**

Minicomputers That Run the Factory, Bus Week, Dec 8, 1973 68-73 **§1.01**

Monczka, *Time-shared Information Systems for Purchasing and Materials Management*, 7 J Purchasing 15 (May 1971) **§1.07**

Moore & Fearon, *Computer-assisted Decision-making in Purchasing* 9 Purchasing 5 (Nov 1973) **§1.07**

Moore & Fearon, *Computer Operating and Management-reporting Systems in Purchasing* 9 J Purchasing 13 (Aug 1973) **§1.07**

More Aggressive IBM Expected by Competitors Electronic News, Jan 18, 1982 **§4.03**

Morris, *Legal Background of a Shared EFT Network*, 34 Bus Law (1979) **§8.16**

C. Morrison, *Computer Suits Spur Specialty*, Nat LJ, Mar 29, 1982, at 1 **§1.07**

P. Morrison & E. Morrison, Charles Babbage and His Calculating Engines (1961) **§1.01**

Mortimer, *Current Legal Problems Facing Commercial Banks Participating in Electronic Funds Transfer Systems*, 95 Banking LJ (1978) **§8.04**

Mortimer, *Electronic Fund Transfers*, 33 Bus L 947 (1978) **§8.10**

Morris, *Protecting Proprietary Rights of Computer Programs: The Need for New Legislative Protection*, 21 Cath Univ L Rev 181 (1970) **§§2.11, 2.13**

Moses, The Home Computer in Your Future, 75 Graduate Women 42 (July/Aug, 1981), *reprinted in* The Computer Age (M. Dertouzos & J Moses, ed) **§1.01**

Moskowitz, *The Patentability of Software Related Inventions After Diehr and Bradley*, 63 J Pat Off Socy 222 (1981) **§2.05**

Moyer & Seitz, *The Marketing Implications of Automated Store Checkouts Impact of Point-of Sale Systems on Consumers, on Mass Distributors, on Smaller Retailers, and Manufacturers, and on Marketing Researchers,* 40 Bus Q 68 (Spring 1975) **§1.01**

Muething, *The Effect of the Use of Customer-Bank Communications Terminals on Competition Among Financial Institutions,* 45 U Cin L Rev (1976) **§8.17**

Murphey & Downey, *National Security, Foreign Policy, and Individual Rights: The Quandry of United States Export Controls,* 30 Int & Comp LQ (1981) **§9.08**

Murphy, *A Computer Model Approach to Budgeting* 56 Mgmt Acct 34 (June 1975) **§1.07**

Murphy & Barrett, *Legal Problems of Applying Electronic Funds Techniques to Retail Banking,* 17 Jurimetrics J (1976) **§8.04**

Murray, *Claims for Damage and Submission to Arbitration Clauses as Traps for Lethargic Businessmen,* 87 Com L J 359 (1982) **§3.27**

Murray, *EFTS and Antitrust,* 37 U Pitt L Rev (1979) **§8.16**

Murray, *EFT and Antitrust - Some Reflections on the Possibilities,* 37 U Pitt L Rev (1976) **§8.17**

Musrey, *Tariff Act's Section 337: Vehicle for the Protection and Extension of Monopolies,* 5 Law & Pol Intl Bus (1973) **§9.06**

Mylton & Walker, *Computer Models in Planning Container-Terminals,* 58 Dock & Harbour Authority 431 (April 1978) **§1.01**

Myrick & Sprowl, *Patent Law for Programmed Computers and Programmed Life Forms,* 68 ABAJ 920 (1982) **§2.05**

N

Naar & Stein, *EFTS: The Computer Revolution in Electronic Banking,* 5 Rutgers J Computers & L (1976) **§8.10**

Nanda, *The Communication Revolution and the Free Flow of Information in a Transnational Setting,* 30 Am J Comp L 411 (Supplement 1982) **§§6.09, 6.16**

NASA Jumbles Skylab Flight Data, Computerworld, July 9 1979 at 1 **§3.21**

National Academy of Sciences, Libraries, and Information Technology: A National System Challenge (1971) **§§6.03, 6.04**

National Banks, *Bank Holding Companies and Data Processing Services,* 14 Ga L Rev (1980) **§8.22**

Nat Comm on Electronic Fund Transfer, EFT and the Public Interest (1977) **§§8.18, 8.19**

Nattier, *Limitations on Marketing Foreign Technology in Brazil,* 11 Intl L (1977) **§9.15**

Nau, Technology Transfer and U.S. Foreign Policy, (New York ——) **§9.16**

Naylor, *The Future of Corporate Planning Models,* 24 Managerial Plan 1 (Mar/Apr 1976) **§1.07**

Naylor & Mansfield, *The Design of Computer-based Planning and Modeling Systems,* 10 Long Range Plan 16 (Feb 1977) **§1.07**

NBS Data Encryption Standard Offers Certain Level of Security but is no Panacea, Conferees Say, Sec Sys Dig, Feb 23, 1977 **§7.15**

Nelson, *Electronic Funds Transfer: A Program*, 32 Bus L (1976) **§8.10**

Nelson, *The Impact of Computers on the Legal Profession*, 30 Baylor Law Rev 829 (Fall 1978) **§1.08**

New Encryption Products Available to Protect Computer Information Sec Letter, Dec 15, 1977 **§7.15**

New: 'UnManned' Supermarkets, US News & World Rep, Nov 3, 1975 90 **§1.01**

Niehaus, Unconscionability and the Fundamental Breach Doctrine in Computer Contracts, 57 Notre Dame Law 547 (1982) **§3.09**

Nielsen & LoCascio, *Computer-assisted Planning in the Public Sector*, 10 Mgmt Adviser 34 (May/June 1972) **§1.01**

Nimtz, *Diamond v Diehr: A Turning Point*, 8 Rutgers J Computers, Tech & L 267, 268 (1981) **§2.04**

Noam, *Towards an Integrated Communications Market: Overcoming the Local Monopoly of Cable Television*, 34 Fed Comm LJ (1982) **§8.22**

Nordling, *Analysis of Common Carrier Tariff Rates*, 17 Datamation 28 (May 1971) **§1.01**

Norad System Goofs, Calls Missile Alert, Computerworld, Nov 19 1979, at 1 **§3.21**

Northrup, *Bank Cards vs the Underworld*, Banking, May, 1975 **§7.10**

Norman, *Computer Fraud—The Villian's View of the Opportunity*, 24 Elec & Power (1978) **§7.01**

W. Norman, The Impact of Computer Technology on Road Transport Planning (1969) **§1.01**

Note, *Agency Access to Credit Bureau Files*, 12 BCI & CLR 110, 125 (1970) **§6.16**

Note, *Automated Supermarket.* 219 Nation 518 (1974) **§1.01**

Note, *Bounty or Grant: A Call for Redefinition in Light of the Zenith Decision*, 9 Law & Poly Intl Bus 1229 (1977) **§9.05**

Note, *Coming Soon: Computerized Checkout Counters*, Changing Times, Feb 1975 53 **§1.01**

Note, *Computer Monitoring Shaves Fuel Use*, Aviation W & Space Tech, Dec 9, 1974) **§1.01**

Note, *Computer Program Patentability—The CCPA Refuse to Follow the Lead of the Supreme Court in Parker v Flook*, 58 NCL Rev 319 (1980) **§2.04**

Note, *Computer Programs as Goods Under the UCC*, 77 Mich L Rev 1149 (1979) **§3.07**

Note, *Computer Programs: Does the Copyright Law Apply?*, 5 Artists' Rights & Labor Relations 66 (1980) **§2.09**

Note, *Grocery Checkout by Computer-What it Means to Shoppers*, US NEws & World Rep, Dec 30, 1974 56 **§1.01**

Note, *Invention is Algorithm and Not Patentable*, 5 Computer L Serv Rep 518 (1976) **§2.—**

Note, *New Kind of Stock Market*, US News World Rep Dec 23, 1974, at 65 **§1.07**

Note, *Patentability of Computer Programs*, 27 U Miami L Rev 494 (1973) **§2.02**

O'Riordan, *An Examination of the Application of Common Carrier Regulation to Entities Providing New Telecommunications Services,* 29 Case W Res L Rev 577 (1979) **§5.09**

Orr, *Satellite Communications Takes a Big Leap Forward,* 73 ABA Banking J 76 (1981) **§5.08**

Osofsky, *US - Soviet Trade: Problems and Prospects,* 27 Mercer L Rec (1976) **§9.16**

P

Pantages, *A Look at Unbundling,* 15 Datamation 85 (1969) **§4.02**

Pare, *The New Video Technologies,* NY Times, Apr 14, 1982 **§5.19**

Parker, *Computer Abuse Research Update,* 2 Computer LJ 329 (1980) **§7.01**

D. Parker, Crime by Computer (1976) **§7.01**

Password Techniques Provide Safeguards for Computer Data, NBS Magazine Reports, Crime Control Dig, July 25, 1977 **§7.15**

Patrick, *Privacy Restrictions on Transnational Data Flows: A Comparison of the Council of Europe Draft Convention and OECD Guidelines,* 21 Jurimetrics J 405 (1980) **§§6.09, 6.12**

Payne, Stroup, *U.S. Antitrust Aspects of the International Transfer of Technology,* 5 NCJ Intl L & Com Reg (1980) **§9.02**

Peat, Marwick & Mitchell, EFTS: A Strategy Perspective 7 (1977) **§§8.13, 8.14**

Peck & McMahon, *Recent Federal Litigation Relating to Customer - Bank Communication Terminals (CBTs) and the McFadden Act,* 32 Bus Law (1977) **§§8.04, 8.15**

Pederrsen, *Joint Ventures in the Soviet Union,* 16 Harv Intl LJ (1975) **§9.16**

Peevy, *Notice and Opportunity to be Heard in a "Good Cause" Determination Proceeding Under Section 201(e) of the Trade Act of 1974 Are Not Required by the Provisions of the Act itself or by Constitutional Due Process,* 9 Ga J Intl & Comp L (1979) **§9.06**

Penney, *Questions Needing Answers - Effects of EFTS on the UCC,* 37 Pitt L Rev (1976) **§8.19**

N. Penney & D. Baker, The Law of Electronic Fund Transfer Systems (1980) **§§8.11, 8.16, 8.17, 8.20**

Perle, *Copyright and New Technology,* 25 Bull Copyright Socy 250 (1978) **§2.06**

Perlman, *Computer System Facilities Comprehensive Planning by Washington DC Local Officials,* 35 J Housing 351 (July 1978) **§1.01**

Perlman, *Materials Handling: New Market for Computer Control,* 16 Datamation 133 (May 1970) **§1.07**

The Personal Computer Strives to Come of Age Economist (London), May 19, 1979, 101 **§1.01**

Peters, *Could Computers be Doing and Saving a Lot More for Your School District?* 161 Am School Bd J 41 (May 1974) **§1.01**

Peterson, *The Trade Agreements Act of 1979: The Agreement on Government Procurement,* 14 J Intl L Econ (1980) **§9.05**

R

Raghavan, *Chipping Away: Demand Continues to Increase as Cheaper Technology Brings the Computer Within Reach of More Businesses and Homes,* 4 Singapore Bus 17.(June 1980) **§1.01**

Ramey, *Patentability of Software and Firmware* 3 Pat & Trademark Rev 147 (1980) **§2.01**

Rands, *Using Computers in Small Company Cash Management,* 4 Acct & Bus Research 231 (Autumn 1974) **§1.07**

Rapoport, *Programs for Plunder,* Omni, Mar 1981 **§7.01**

Ratchford & Ford, *A Study of Prices and Market Shares in the Computer Mainframe Industry.* 49 J Bus 194 (1976) **§4.01**

Raysman, *Warranty Disclaimer in the Data Processing Contract,* 6 Rutgers Comp & Tech LJ 265 (1978) **§3.09**

Real Time System Keeps Employee Time Real, 22 Infosystems 62 (Sept 1975) **§1.07**

Reeves, *Antitrust and International Licensing A Primer,* II Cornell Intl LJ 263 (1978) **§9.08**

Regulation of Computer Communication, 7 Harv J Leg 208 (1970) **§5.02**

Reid-Green, *A Short History of Computing,* 3 Byte 84 (1978) **§1.01**

Reinsch, *The Export Trading Company Act of 1981,* 14 L & Poly Intl Bus (1982) **§9.10**

Report on Privacy: Who is Watching You?. US News & World Rep, July 12, 1982, 34 **§§6.03, 8.20**

Report on Unbundling in the Supersonic Seventies, 17 Bus Automation 44 (Jan 1970) **§4.04**

Reznick, *Synercom Technology, Inc v University Computing Co: Copyright Protection for Computer Formats and the Idea/Expression Dichotomy,* 8 Rutgers J Computers, Tech & L 65 (1980) **§2.09**

D. Richardson, Electric Money: Evolution of an Electronic Fund Transfer System (1979) **§7.02**

Richter, *The Subject Matter Analysis for Computer Related Processes: A Matter of Characterizations,* 27 Loy L Rev 1140 (1981) **§2.04**

Rinkerman, *Computer Program Patentability,* 1 Computer L Rev 20 (1982) **§2.03**

Rivlin, A Multimillion Dollar Crime Has Just Been Committed in this Room, 10 Student Law 15, 17 (1982) **§7.03**

Robertson, *Oil Computer Leaks,* Elec News, July 28, 1975 **§7.02**

Robots: *Progress Depends on Computer Technology,* Kredietbank W Bul, June 5, 1981 at 1-5 **§1.01**

Robots to Take Over in Factories, 14 Ind Res 31 (Nov 1972) **§1.01**

J. Rockart & M. Morton, Computers and the Learning Process in Higher Education (1975) **§1.01**

Roddy, *The Federal Computer Systems Protection Act,* 7 Rut J Computers Tech & L (1980) **§§7.01, 7.11**

I. Roger, Computers: Privacy and Freedom of Information 7 (1970) **§§6.12, 6.14**

Root, Protecting Computer Software in the 80's: Practical Guidelines for Evolving Needs, 8 Rutgers Computer & Tech LJ 205 (1981) **§2.01**

Rose, *More Bank for the Buck: The Magic of Electronic Banking,* Fortune, May 1977 **§8.14**

Ben Rosen, *The Tail that Wags the Dog,* Newsweek, Feb 22, 1982, at 22 **§6.03**

Rosenthal, *Judicial Attitudes Towards the Tensions between Antitrust, Federal Patent, and State Trade Secret Laws in International Technology Transfers,* 50 Antitrust LJ (1982) **§9.08**

Rosenthal & Sheldon, *Section 337: A View from Two Within the Department of Justice,* 8 Ga J Intl & Comp L (1978) **§9.06**

Ross, *Computer Data Security: Reprogram the Emphasis,* Sec Mgmt, Dec 1978 **§7.15**

Ross, *Computers: Their Uses and Misuses: Some Do's and Don'ts for Management,* 15 Bus Horizons 55 (April 1972) **§1.07**

Ross, *Patentability of Computer 'Firmware'* 59 J Pat Off Socy 731 (1977) **§2.01**

Ross, *To Insure Patent on Software, Make it Reusable Hardware,* Electronic News, Jan 18, 1970 at 48 **§2.01**

Roth, *Choosing an Arbitration Panel,* 6 Litigation 13 (1980) **§3.25**

Rothman, *Computer Crime, The Menace Grows,* D&B Rep, July-Aug 1981 **§§7.01, 7.12**

S. Rothman & C. Mosmann, Computers and Society (1972) **§6.03**

Rowan, *Information Systems Technology in State Government,* 44 State Govt 113 (Spring 1971) **§1.01**

Rubin, *United States Export Controls: An Immodest Proposal,* 36 Geo Wash L Rev (1968) **§9.08**

Ruckman, *Firmware Patents Can be Firm,* IEEE Spectrum 35-40 (Aug 1980) **§2.01**

Ruggles, Pemberton, & Miller, *Symposium: Computers, Data Banks, and Individual Privacy,* 53 Minn L Rev 211 **§6.01**

Rule, *Electronic Funds Transfer and Federal Privacy Policy,* 18 Jurimetrics J (1977) **§8.20**

Rupert, *The Relationship of Patent Law to Antitrust Law,* 49 Antitrust LJ 755 (1980) **§2.02**

Ruppert & Pansius, Transfer of Know-How Under Section 351, 55 Den LJ 223 (1978) **§9.08**

Rupil, *How to Improve Profits Through Simulation,* 55 Mgmt Accounting 16 (Nov 1973) **§1.07**

S

Sager & Wood, *Electric Utility Corporate Models,* Pub Util Fort, Aug 3, 1972 at 30 **§1.01**

Safran, *What Non-Patent Attorneys Should Know About Patents,* 28 Prac Law 60 (1982) **§2.02**

Sales and Use Tax of Computer Software - Is Software Tangible Personal Property? 27 Wayne L Rev 1503 (1981) **§§4.01, 4.03**

Salton, *Computers & Libraries,* Lib J, Oct 15 1971 3277 **§1.01**

S. Saltzburg, Federal Rules of Evidence Manual (2d ed 1977) **§7.13**

Samuels, *Copyright and the New Communications Technologies,* 25 NYL Sch L Rev 905 (1980) **§2.06**

Sandver, Blaine and Wagner, *Time and Cost Savings Through Expedited Arbitration Procedures,* 36 Arbitration J 11 (1981) **§3.26**

Sarasohn, *AT&T Restructured: New Objections Show Dare of Communications Rewrite,* Cong Q, July 12, 1980, at 1943 **§5.09**

Sarasohn, *Telecommunications Rewrite Tries to Unfetter Industry,* Cong Q, Feb 16, 1980, at 389 **§5.09**

Sawhney, *Time-sharing Systems in Financial Planning,* 3 Fin Plan Today 346 (Jan 1980) **§1.07**

Schabeck, *Investigators Tackle Computer Crime,* Sec World, Feb 1977 **§7.07**

T. Schabeck, Computer Crime Investigation Manual (1979) **§7.05**

Schellie, *The Electronic Fund Transfer Act,* 34 Bus L 1441 (1979) **§8.19**

Schellie, *The Electronic Fund Transfer Act,* 35 Bus L (1980) **§8.19**

Scherer on Predatory Pricing: A Reply, 89 Harv L Rev 891 (1976) **§4.06**

Schick, *Privacy — The Next Big Issue in EFT,* 68 Banking J (1976) **§8.20**

Schlieder, *European Competition Policy,* Antitrust LJ (1982) **§9.12**

Schmedel, *IBM Discloses Plan for Separating Its Computers and Services Prices,* Wall St J, June 24, 1969, at 38 **§4.05**

Schmidt, *Legal Proprietory Interests in Computer Programs: The American Experience* 21 Jurimetrics J 345, 357 (1981) **§§2.01, 2.03, 2.04**

Schollenberger, *Export Trading Companies,* 11 DJ Intl L & Policy (198?) **§9.10**

Schorr, *Automated Deals,* Wall St J Oct 3, 1978, at 1 **§1.07**

P. Schuck, Electronic Funds Transfer: A Technology in Search of a Market, The Economics of a National Fund Transfer System (1974) **§8.14**

Schussel & May, *Wall Street Automation: A Primer,* 16 Datamation 109 (April 1970) **§1.07**

Schwartzmann, *Export Trading Company Legislation: Birds, Commons & Peashooters,* 29 Fed Bar News & J (1982) **§9.10**

Scott, *Failure to Disclose Computer Program Invalidates Patent,* The Scott Report, Cot 1982 at 1 **§2.03**

Scott, *New Legislation to Strengthen Software Copyright Protection,* Scott Report Nov 1982 at 2 **§2.08**

Scott, *The Dual Banking System: A Model of Competition in Regulation,* 30 Stan L Rev (1977) **§8.02**

The Seeds of Success—Apple Computers, Time, Feb 15, 1982, at 41 **§6.03**

Selling DEA Computer-Stored Data was Theft under 18 USC 641, 22 Crim L Rep 2478 **§7.10**

Shaw, *Encryption Units, The Answer to Computer Crimes?* L & Ord, Aug 1978 **§7.15**

Shaw, *How Can you Fight What You Don't Understand,* L & Ord, July 1977 **§7.07**

Michael Shields, *Striking it Rich: A New Breed of Risk Takers is Betting on the High Technology Future,* Time, Feb 15, 1982, at 36 **§6.03**

Shockley, EFTS, Credit Cards and Interstate Banking **§8.22**

Silverman, *The New Copyright Act: An Overview of the New Law,* 1977 Pat L Ann 363 **§2.07**

Silverstein, *Sharing United States Energy Technology with Less-Developed Countries: A Model for International Technology Transfer,* 12 J Intl L & Econ (1978) **§9.15**

W. Skees, Before you Invest in a Small Computer (1982) **§3.01**

Simolin, *Information, Computers and Local Government: an Administrator's Guide,* 10 Mgmt Info Serv Rep 1 (Feb 1978) **§1.01**

Simone, *Production and Inventory Control,* 11 Data Systems News 20(Oct 1970) **§1.07**

Sinter, *Private, Intra City Data Communications Networks,* 29 Fed B News J (1982) **§5.19**

C. Sippl & C. Sippl, Computer Dictionary and Handbook (2d ed 1972) **§4.01**

Slutsker, The Peripherals Proliferation: Technological Advances and Productivity Gains Spur Funding of Computer Peripherals Startups Despite the Country's Recession, Venture (1980) **§4.01**

Smith, *Automation Collection,* Credit & Fin Mgmt, May 1975 at 10 **§1.07**

Smith, *Interdependence of Computer and Communications Services and Facilities: A Question of Federal Regulation,* 117 U Pa L Rev 829 (1969) **§5.02**

Smith, *Storming the FCC Fortress: Can the FCC Deregulate Competitive Common Carrier Services,* 32 Fed Comm LJ 205 (1980) **§5.02**

Smith, *The Magnuson-Moss Warranty Act: Turning the Tables on Caveat Emptor,* 13 Cal W Reserve L Rev 391 (1977) **§3.13.**

C. Smith, Coordination and Control of Computer Technology in State Government: Constraints and Strategies, DPA Thesis, University of Southern California (1970) **§1.01**

Socol, *Comsat's First Decade,* 7 GA J Intl & Comp L 678 (1977) **§5.08**

Soden, *Planning for the Computer Services Spin-out,* 50 Harv Bus Rev 69 (1972) **§1.01**

Software Industry Analysis, Computer Yearbook 98 (1972) **§4.01**

Softwarre, Statutes, and Stare Decisis, 13 How LJ 420 (1967) **§2.13**

Sokolik, *A Strategy for Planning,* 26 Mich State U Bus Topics 57 (Spring 1978) **§1.07**

Sokolik, *Computer Crime — The Need for Deterrent Legislation,* 2 Computer LJ (1980) **§§2.13, 7.01, 7.04, 7.10, 7.11, 7.14, 7.15, 7.17, 7.18**

Soltysinski, *Computer Programs and Patent Law: A Comparative Study,* 3 Rutgers J Computers & L 1 (1973) **§2.03**

A. Solzhenitsyn, Cancer Ward (1968) **§8.20**

Some Policy-oriented Reflections on the AT&T Antitrust Settlement, 29 Fed B News & J 372 (Nov 1982) **§5.14**

Soon: A Computer in Every Home? US News & World Rep, Nov 21, 1977, at 77 **§1.01**

Spence, *Using the Computer to Teach: A New and Simple Approach,* 19 Electronics & Power 284 (July 1973) **§1.01**

Spencer, Computers in Society: the Wheres, Whys, and Hows of Computer Use (1974) **§1.03**

The Spreading Danger of Computer Crime, Bus Week, Apr 20, 1981 **§7.01**

Sprigg, *Controlling Direct Labor Costs Through Performance Reporting,* Cost & mgmt 49 (March-April 1975) **§1.07**

Sprowl, *A Review of Niblett's Legal Protection of Computer Programs and Diamond v Diehr and Some Thoughts on Patenting Computer Programs,* 1981 Am B Found Research J 559 **§2.04**

SRI International, Computer Crime: Criminal Justice Resource Manual (1979) **§§7.01, 7.02, 7.05, 7.11, 7.12, 7.17**

Staple, *Implementing Tokyo Round Commitments The New Injury Standard in Antidumping and Countervailing Duty Laws,* 32 Stanford L Rev (1980) **§9.07**

Statewide Computing Systems: Coordinating Academic Computer Planning (C. Mosmann ed 1974) **§1.01**

Stedman, *The Patent-Antitrust Interface,* 58 J Pat Off Socy 316 (1976) **§4.15**

Stern, *Copying ROMS: Right or Wrong,* Computer Design, Feb 1982 at 131, 132 **§2.09**

Stern, *Medical Information Bureau: The Life Insurer's Databank,* 4 Rut J Computers & L 1 (1974) **§6.05**

Stern, *ROMS in Search of a Remedy: Can they Find it?,* 1 Computer L Rev 4 (1982) **§2.09**

Stern, *Restricting Customers' Use of Software to Particular Computers - Proprietor's Right or Competitive House?* 1 Computer L Rep 194 (1982) **§§4.01, 4.09**

Stern, *Software Piracy and the Copyright Laws,* Computer Design 209 (Nov 1981) **§2.08**

Stone, Computer Simulation in Financial Accounting, 48 Acct Rev 398 (Apr 1973) **§1.07**

Stone, *Some Security and Integrity Controls in Small Computer Systems,* J Acct, Feb 1976 **§7.15**

Suchecki, *Digital Computer in Process Control,* Textile Industries 87 (1973) **§1.01**

Sudden Setback for Electronic Banking: Court Decision on Electronic Terminals as Branch Offices, Bus Wk, Aug 18, 1975 **§8.07**

The Superregisters: Computer Terminals Replace Cash Registers, Wall St J, Nov 20, 1972 at 1 **§1.01**

Supporters of AT&T Bill Block Major Change, Cong Q, July 17, 1982 **§5.16**

Survey, White Collar Crime: Computer Crime, 18 Am Crim L Rev 370 (1980) **§§2.13, 7.02, 7.04, 7.10, 7.11, 7.17**

Swanson & Territo, *Computer Crime: Dimensions, Types, Causes & Investigations,* 8 J Police Sci & Ad (1980) **§§7.01, 7.05, 7.07**

S. Swihart & B. Hefley, Computer Systems in the Library: A Handbook for Managers and Designers (1973) **§1.01**

T

Taber, *On Computer Crime (Senate Bill S 240),* 1 Computer LJ 517 (1979) **§7.02**

Taft & Reisman, *On a Computer-aided Systems Approach to Personnel Administration,* 5 Socio-Econ Plan Sciences 547 (Dec 1971) **§1.07**

Task Force, Canadian Department of Justice and Communications, Privacy and Computers (1972) **§§6.07, 6.11, 6.12, 6.14, 6.15, 6.16**

Woodfin, *Time-shared Computer Usage in the Corporate Tax Department*, 23 Tax Exec 519 (April 1971) **§1.07**

I. Woods, *The Insurance Aspects of Computer Litigation* (1979) **§3.36**

World Almanac and Book of Facts (1980) **§6.09**

Wydick, *Trade Secrets: Federal Pre-emption in Light of Goldstein and Kewanee*, 55 J Pat Off Socy 736, 739 (1973) **§2.14**

Wylczynski, *Dumping and Central Planning*, 74 J Pol Econ (1966) **§9.05**

Y

Yasaki, *Encryption Algorithm: Key Size is the Thing*, Datamation, Mar 1976, at 164 **§7.15**

Ynetma, *The Influence of Dumping on Monopoly Price*, 36 J Pol Econ (1928) **§9.05**

Z

Zammit, *Contracting for Computer Products*, 22 Jurimetrics J 337 (1982) **§§3.07, 3.09, 3.17, 3.18, 3.20**

Zartman & Berman, *The Practical Negotiator* 69-80 (1982) **§3.40**

Ziskind & Boldin, *A Computer Simulation Model for Investment Portfolio Management*, 2 Fin Mgmt 23 (Autumn 1973) **§1.07**

Zuijdwijk, *The UNCTAD Code of Conduct on the Transfer of Technology*, 24 McGill LJ (1978) **§9.11**

Index

469

Computer Technology and the Law

**1986 Cumulative Supplement
Current through July 1986**

John T. Soma
Professor of Law
University of Denver
College of Law

*Insert in the pocket at the back
of the bound volume. Discard
supplement dated 1985.*

Shepard's/McGraw-Hill, Inc.
P.O. Box 1235
Colorado Springs, Colorado 80901

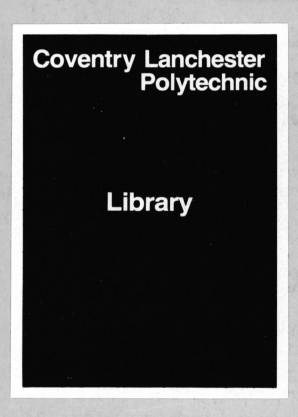
Bound Book ISBN 0-07-059642-5
Supplement ISBN 0-07-059644-1

New sections appearing in this supplement

Emergent Role of Computers in Society

1

---

§1.01 Introduction—The Computational Perspective

Page 1, note 1, at end of note add:

See also P. Ceruzzi, Reckoners: The Prehistory of the Digital Computer, from Relays to the Stored Program Concept, 1935-1945 (1983); J. Cortada, An Annotated Bibliography on the History of Data Processing (1983).

Pages 1-2, note 2, at end of note add:

See also Maloney, *Now it's the "stay-at-home society,"* US News & World Rep, June 28, 1982, at 64 (describing the rapidly expanding uses of home computers for entertainment, shopping, education, and health care); Simison, *R202 May Be A Wiz, But Robots For Home Use Still Can't Do Much,* Wall St J, Apr 25, 1985, at 39 (notes some of the current limitations on robots in the home and sketches the future in the field.).

Page 2, note 3, at end of note add:

See also *Symposium: Computer Law,* 30 Emory LJ 345 (1981).

Page 2, note 4, at end of note add:

See also Artandi, *Computers and the Postindustrial Society: Symbiosis or Information Tyranny?,* 33 Am Soc Info Sci J 302 (1982); Ruby, *Terminal Behavior,* PC Week, Nov 13, 1984, at 127-129 (discusses study of effect of computers on corporate communication and decision making); Longworth, *It's Fear and Loathing in the High Tech World,* Chi Tribune, Dec 3, 1984, at 1B (outlines remarks made at conference on computer and society; generally discusses dehumanizing by computer).

Page 2, note 5, at end of note add:

See also I. Reinecke, Micro Invaders: How the New World of Technology Works (1982) (discussing the effect of the microchip on offices, factories, supermarkets, and homes); Toong & Gupta, *The Computer Age Gets Personal*, 36 Tech Rev 26 (1983) (discussing the computing power of small computers now appearing on desks in homes and offices); Whalen & Mills, *Large Systems Thriving Despite PC Revolution*, Government Computer News, Dec 1984, at 49+ (discussing size, power, speed, and cost of new mainframes and supermainframes); Chabrow, *Tele-Commuting: Managing the Remote Workplace*, Information-WEEK, Apr 15, 1985, at 27ff (discussing trends and impact of remote and commuter workstations, includes list of organizations offering telecommuting information); Swartz, *Telecommuting's Expansion Poses Host of Legal Questions*, Information Week, Apr 15, 1985, at 38 (brief note of possible future situations with questions to be answered); Nulty, *How Personal Computers Change Managers' Lives*, Fortune, Sept 3, 1984, at 38-40+ (the effect of personal computers on management time, labor, communications.).

Page 2, note 6, at end of note add:

See also *Computers: Personal Models, Smaller and Smarter*, Bus Week, Mar 28, 1983, at 134.

Page 2, note 7, at end of note add:

See also Walsh, *Giving Demographics More Byte*, 5 Am Demographics 18 (1983) (a survey of companies providing census data via microcomputers for business and other uses); Kirkland, *Ma Blue: IBM's Move Into Communications*, Fortune, Oct 15, 1984, at 52-54+ (discussing IBM's communications directions, strategy, reasons, and results); Conference on Computer and Communications Law, hosted by the Arizona Law and Technology Institute and the Arizona State University College of Law (Jan 14-16, 1985).

Pages 2-3, note 8, at end of note add:

See also Dept of Education Office of Educational Research and Improvement, Computers in Education: Realizing the Potential (1983) (chairmen's report of a research conference held in Pittsburgh, Pennsylvania, November 20-24, 1982); House Comm on Educ and Labor, Subcomm on Elementary, Secondary, and Vocational Education; Hearing on National Centers for Personal Computers in Education: Hearing on HR 1134, 98th Cong, 1st Sess (1983); Sheingold, *Microcomputer Use in Schools: Developing a Research Agenda*, 53 Harv Educ Rev 412 (1983); Johnson, *Can Computers Close the Educational Equity Gap?*, 14 Perspectives 20 (1982) (use of computers to assist minority students); Loeb, *Class Machines: Computers May Widen Gap in School*

Equality Between Rich and Poor, Wall St J, May 26, 1983, at 201 (experiences of two Atlanta schools); Molnar & Babb, *The Electronic Age Challenges Education,* 16 Appalachia 1 (1982); Cong Office of Tech Assessment, Informational Technology and its Impact on American Education (1982) (report which examines the impact of advances in informational technology on education, and the use of computers in the classroom).

Page 3, note 9, at end of note add:

See also Snipes & Crook, *Introducing Computers into Local Government Administration,* 9 Current Mun Prob 66 (1982); Northrop, Dutton & Kraemer, *The Management of Computer Applications in Local Government,* 42 Pub Ad Rev 234 (1982); Garson, *Microcomputer Applications in Public Administration,* 43 Pub Ad Rev 453 (1983); *Minisymposium on Micro Computers in Local Government,* 44 Pub Ad Rev 57 (1984); Norris, *Computers and Small Local Governments: Uses and Users,* 44 Pub Ad Rev 70 (1984); Head, Federal Information Systems Management: Issues and New Directions (1982); *How Uncle Sam Misuses Computers,* Bus Week, June 28, 1982 at 88; King, *Local Government Use of Information Technology: The Next Decade,* 42 Pub Ad Rev 25 (1982); Norris & Webb, *Microcomputers,* 15 Baseline Data Rep 1 (1983) (based on a survey of microcomputer use in local governments); Whited, *Using Microcomputers in Urban Planning,* Planning Advisory Service Rep No 372 (Nov 1982). The General Services Administration, Office of Information Resources Management, publishes the following annual reports: Automatic Data Processing Activities Summary and Automatic Data Processing Equipment Inventory in the US Government. See also Wynter, *Federal Bid to Update Agencies' Computers Faces Many Obstacles: Once a High-Tech Pioneer, Government is Hindered By Bureaucratic Delays,* 62 Wall St J, Feb 13, 1985, at 31 (discussing need for government to update procedures and equipment prior to massive breakdown).

Page 3, note 10, at end of note add:

See also Marcin, *Computer Uses in Law Libraries,* 6 ALSA F 38 (1982); Badertscher, *An Examination of the Dynamics of Change in Information Technology as Viewed from Law Libraries and Information Centers,* 75 Law Libr J 198 (1982).

Pages 3-4, note 11, at end of note add:

Schindler, *See Computers, Communications Converging,* Information Sys News, Oct 15, 1984, at 42-43 (notes trend of manufacturers—IBM, AT&T—toward similar products).

Pages 4-5, note 14, at end of note add:

See also House Comm on Science and Technology, Subcomm on Investigations and Oversight, Robotics: Hearings June 2 & 23, 1982 (current state of robot technology; United States world market position; implications for labor); Org for Econ Coop and Development, Micro-electronics, Robotics and Jobs (1982); Miller, *Robotics: Future Factories, Future Workers,* 470 Annals Am Acad 9 (1983).

Socio-Economic Functions and Effects of Computers

§1.02   Technology and Economic Activity

Page 5, note 15, at end of note add:

See also Bazelon, *Coping with Technology Through the Legal Process,* 18 Jurimetrics J 241 (1978); Cohodas, *Special Report: Technology and the Law, New Technology Puts Strain on Old Laws,* Cong Q 135 (Jan 28, 1984); Foster, *The Effect of Technology on Institutions,* 15 J Econ Issues 907 (1981); Rahman, *The Interaction between Science, Technology and Society: Historical and Comparative Perspectives,* 33 Intl Soc Sci J 508 (1981); M. Vance, Social Aspects of Technology: A Bibliography (1982); B. Shearer & M. Huxford, Communications and Society: A Bibliography on Communications Technologies and Their Social Impact (1983); *The Power of Technological Innovation,* 48 Bus Q 83 (1983); N. Rosenberg, Inside the Black Box: Technology and Economics (1982) (relationship and speed of change in changing inter-industry relationships).

Page 5, note 16, at end of note add:

See also Nelson, Government and Technical Progress: A Cross-Industry Analysis (R. Nelson ed 1982); F. Mansfield, A. Romeo, M. Schwartz, D. Teece, S. Wagner & P. Brach, Technology Transfer, Productivity and Economic Policy (1982); Morone & Ivins, *Problems and Opportunities in Technology Transfer from the National Laboratories to Industry,* 25 Research Mgmt 35 (1982) (advocating that government, the national laboratories, and industry must change in order to effectively transfer technology from government labs to industry); Maguire & Kevich, *The Introduction and Diffusion of Technological Innovation in Industry: An Information Research Perspective,* 4 Progress Com Sci 163 (1984); Matley, *Sees The Need For a National Computer Policy,* Information Sys News, July 23, 1984, at 35 (editorial on need for a national computer plan similar to the Japanese and French models).

§1.03 —Computational Technology: Economic and Social Activity

Page 6, note 17, at end of note add:

See also Horowitz, *Printed Words, Computers, and Democratic Societies*, 59 Va Q Rev 620 (1983) (discussing the political and social impacts of computers and information technologies).

Page 6, note 18, at end of note add:

See also Dray & Menosky, *Computers and a New World Order: Is Adapting Computers to the Various Cultures of the World an Idea Whose Time Has Come or a Pipe Dream with Commercial Overtones?*, 86 Tech Rev 12 (1983).

Page 6, note 19, at end of note add:

See also *The Smart Machine Revolution: Providing Products with Brainpower*, Bus Week, July 5, 1976, at 38; Kallman & Krok, *Micros—Personal Computers with Power*, 32 Bus (Atlanta) 2 (1982) (discussing the rapid technological development of the microcomputer, or computer-on-a-chip, which is a small, inexpensive computing system with the capability of a minicomputer); Chace, *Mind Machines: Scientists are Laboring at Making Computers Think for Themselves*, Wall St J, Mar 29, 1983, at 1; Firnberg, *Future Trends in Computing*, 11 Long Range Plan 58 (1978); Madnick, *Recent Technical Advances in the Computer Industry and Their Future Impact*, 14 Sloan Mgmt Rev 67 (1973); Chace, *Silicon's Successor? Tomorrow's Computer May Reproduce Itself, Some Visionaries Think*, Wall St J, Jan 6, 1983, at 1 (organic computers, biochips, are computer circuits assembled from molecules); Bylinsky, *Here Comes the Second Computer Revolution*, 92 Fortune, Nov 12, 1975, at 134 (discussing the effects the development of the microcomputer has had and will have on business and consumers); Van, *Looking Beyond the Silicon Chip*, Chi Tribune, May 22, 1983, at 1; Beutel, *Government Regulation of Diagnostics Software: A Threat to Artificial Intelligence Software Developers*, 2 The Computer Law Feb 22 (1985)(discussing how government regulation will affect the artificial intelligence industry); Perrone & Associates, Jeffrey, Inc. Management Consultants Specializing in the creation of custom Expert Systems.

Technical Aspects of Computational Technology

§1.05   —Hardware Components of a Computer System

Page 8, note 20, at end of note add:

See also *New Memories Boost Minicomputer Capacity*, Bus Week, July 7, 1973, at 72; *A memory that costs one-quarter cent per bit: that will happen if Ampex (corporation)'s new process for making magnetic cores proves out*, Bus Week Feb 3, 1975 at 26; *Fairchild Bets on a Memory Chip; Memory Product Using Charge-Coupled Device (CCB)*, Bus Week, Jan 20, 1975, at 26; Bing, *How to Select Add-on Main Memory*, 14 Data Mgt 22 (1976); Kruschke, *An Overview of Add-on Memories*, 14 Data Mgt 12 (1976); *The bubble memory finally arrives: solid-state memories could replace disks in a big way—but not until the 1980s*, Bus Week, Mar 28, 1977, at 72; Shaffer, *Memory explosion: the pocket computer, other electronic gear may be available soon*, Wall St J, Mar 29, 1977, at 1; Uttal, *New technology scrambles the memory market: a couple of novel devices promise to become stars of the fast-growing computer-memory business, provided their costs come down far enough—and soon enough*, 97 Fortune, June 5, 1978, at 136; *The chip makers' glamorous new generation: the 64K has four times the capacity of the most popular chips (semiconductor devices) now in use*, Bus Week, Oct 6, 1980, at 117; *A groovy way of stretching computer memories*, 279 Economist 99 (1981); *No boom for bubble memory: the take-off never came; instead it stalled in marketing and production (chip that stores digital data in the form of minuscule "bubbles" of magnetism)*, Bus Week, May 4, 1981, at 152; Gardner, *Wang's Early Work in Core Memories*, Datamation 161 (1976); Bylinsky, *The Chip That Erases Repair Bills*, 106 Fortune, Oct 18, 1982, at 172 (discussing possible applications of EEPROMs (electrically erasable, programmable read-only memory)); Bylinsky, *The Next Battle in Memory Chips*, 107 Fortune, May 16, 1983, at 152; Robinson, *Gallium Arsenide Chips*, BYTE, Nov 1984, at 211+ (discussion of the newest technology in high speed integrated circuitry).

Page 8, text, last paragraph, after first sentence, add:

(Smith, *Five Voice Synthesizers*, BYTE, Sept 1984, at 337-46 (technical discussion of microchips used in voice synthesizer designs); Texas Instruments, Personal/Professional Computers: How Can They Help You?, (1983). (Outline of applications and introduction to TI Personal Computers. Good discussion of voice recognition/speech synthesis circuitry using TI technology.))

Page 8, text, at end of section add:

IBM Programming Announcement 284-92 (Local Area Networks)

IBM Programming Announcement 184-200 (Personal Computer Network Interconnects, notes indicate that 255 IBM PC's can be networked together using cable or CATV, 1,000 with adaptors on a campus)

IBM Programming Announcement 284-93 (Network Enhancement Software)

IBM Programming Announcement 284-94 (Network Emulation Program, a dial-up, noncable-connected system).

§1.06 —Software Components of a Computer System

Page 8, text, at end of section add:

Appelbe & Pournella, *Big Projects on Small Machines: Software Engineering on Microcomputers,* BYTE, Sept 1984, at 150-51+ (How to write a large program, system, or application on a microcomputer. Including costs, time, personnel, equipment.).

Computers and the Law

§1.07 The Origin of Computer Law

Page 9, note 21, at end of note add:

See also R. Freed, Materials and Cases on Computers and Law (1969); Gemignani, *The Case for Computer Law,* 88 Case & Com 3 (1983); Grossman & Solomon, *Computers and Legal Reasoning,* 69 ABA J 66 (1983); McGonagle, *The Electronic Law Library: The Expanding Role of Computerized Research,* 19 Trial 40 (1983); *The Case for Computers: LA Law Firms Tell Their Tales,* 5 LA Law 12 (1982); Butler, *The Computer Imperative,* 56 Ohio St BA Rep 760 (1983); Sprowl, *New Age of Computers in the Law Office,* 71 Ill BJ 478 (1983); Grillies, *How Lawyers Will Adapt to the Information Age,* 58 Fla BJ 73 (1984); Freed, *Will Lawyers Impede Computerization?,* 30 Emory LJ 345 (1981); Quade, *Computers: Don't Fear Them, Lawyers Told,* 68 ABA J 253 (1982); Quade, *Futureworld: Lawyers Become 'Computerniks,'* 68 ABA J 255 (1982); Heintz, *Of Bits and Bytes,* 5 LA Law 43 (1982); Leininger, *Creating a Role for Law and Computers at Stanford,* 15 Stan Rev 4 (1980); Arness, *Learning to Love Your Computer,* 11 Brief 32 (1982); Benoit, *The Drama and Intrigue of Innovation,* 5 LA

Law 38 (1982) (outlining the history of technological innovations and the computerization of the practice of law); Kidwell, *The Day the Machine Broke Down*, 69 ABA J 50 (1983); McLellan, *Microelectronics and the Law: More than Meets the Eye*, 87 Case & Com 3 (1982); Hambleton & Malone, *Computers and the Law*, 7 Ark Law 28 (1983); *Computers and Law*, New LJ, July 8, 1982, at 645; Bing, *New Technology and the Law: Likely Impact and Future Trends*, 1983 Computers & Law 2 (1983); Cameron & Rees-Potter, *Applications of Computer Technology to Law (1979-1982): A Selected Bibliography*, 16 Law Tech 1 (1983); Grunbaum, *Legal Connections*, PC Mag, Feb 19, 1985, at 273-75. (examines legal telecommunications versus local area networks).

Page 9, note 22, at end of note add:

An additional journal is Rutger's Computer & Technology Law Journal.

Page 9, note 23, at end of note add:

See also Carley, *On the Defense: Computer Companies Are Hauled into Court by Flurry of Lawsuits*, Wall St J, Nov 30, 1970, at 1.

Page 9, note 24, at end of note add:

See also M. Rothenberg, The History of Science and Technology in the United States: A Critical and Selective Bibliography (1982).

Page 9, note 25, at end of note add:

See generally *Information Management: Strategies for the Future*, 63 Nat F 2 (1983).

Page 10, note 30, at end of note add:

See also Brightman & Harris, *The Planning and Modeling Language Revolution: A Managerial Perspective*, 32 Business 15 (1982) (discussing potential impact of microcomputers and new planning languages on short-term planning); McGinnins & Ackelsberg, *Effective Innovation Management: Missing Link in Strategic Planning?*, 4 J Bus Strategy 59 (1983); Lewis, *The Modern Planning Office*, 48 Planning (APA) 12 (1982) (predicts that during the 1980's microcomputers will become a universal fixture in planning departments); Greenberg, *Executives Rate Their PC's*, PC World, Sept 1984, at 286-92. (Results of survey by Arthur Anderson & Co. Executives using more microcomputers than expected, and are happier.).

Pages 10-11, note 32, at end of note add:

See also Crooks, *Small Businesses and the Cash Management Culture*, 68 Econ Rev 48 (1983) (examining the spread of computerized cash management to small business and nonfinancial corporations);

O'Brien, *Cash Control System on the IBM Displaywriter*, 9 Legal Econ 28 (1983).

Page 11, note 34, at end of note add:

See also *Paperless Filing, Retrieval of Information Sought by SEC*, 155 J Acct 20 (1983).

Page 11, note 35, at end of note add:

Friedman, *Taking a Byte Out of Organized Crime*, Infosystems, Aug 1984, at 48-49 (use of computers in government crime investigation).

Page 11, note 36, at end of note add:

Neimark, *Psych-Out Software*, Datamation, Oct 15, 1984, at 32-34+ (discusses decision aid software and psychologically oriented software).

§1.08 The Computer-Legal Interface

Page 12, text, first paragraph, end of second sentence, add:

Computer Law Association, Legislative Update, May 13, 1985 (outline of Congressional action regarding computers in 1984 and 1985 by general topic, 7 bills attached).

Page 12, note 37, at end of note add:

See also Dombroff, *Demonstrative Evidence: Computer Reconstruction Techniques*, 18 Trial 52 (1982); *Discovery of Computerized Information*, 12 Cap UL Rev 71 (1982); *Guidelines for the Admissibility of Evidence Generated by Computer for Purposes of Litigation*, 15 UCDL Rev 951 (1982); McFarlane, *Criminal Trials and the Technological Revolution*, New LJ, Apr 8, 1983, at 327; Kelman, *Computer Evidence and the Police and Criminal Evidence Bill*, New LJ, Mar 9, 1984, at 237; Pengilley, *Machine Information: Is it Hearsay?*, 13 Melb UL Rev 617 (1982); Uelmen & Tunick, *Computer Searches and Seizures*, 10 Search & Seizure L Rep 165 (1983); Miller, *The Admissibility of Computer-Generated Evidence in Georgia*, 18 Ga St BJ 137 (1982); Quade, *Computing the Evidence: Technology Moves into the Courtroom*, 69 ABA J 882 (1983); Boccardo, Alexander & Kennedy, *How to Harness the Information Explosion*, 18 Trial 74 (1982); Kovach, *Application of Computer-assisted Analysis Techniques to Taxation*, 15 Akron L Rev 713 (1982); Onove, *Using Personal Computers in Tax Practice*, 70 ABA J 96 (1984); Shidler, *Computer Tax Research and Tax Research Sources*, 12 Colo Law 1960 (1983); Bigelow, *The Computer and the Tax Collector*, 30 Emory LJ 357 (1981); Moses, *Programs, Applications Make Microcomputers Increasingly Valuable Tools for Estate Planners*, 10 Est Plan 16 (1983); Robbins, *Selecting a Law Firm's Computerized Timekeeping and Billing Systems*, 72 Ill

BJ 256 (1984); Saxon, *Computer-aided Drafting of Legal Documents,* 1982 Am B Foun Res J 685 (1982); Gallet, *A Lawyer Looks at Law Office Automation,* 56 NY St BJ 19 (1984); Walshe, *Law Office Automation Gains Momentum,* 68 ABA J 292 (1982); Countryman, *Law Office Automation: What Does It Really Mean?,* 19 Trial 26 (1983); Shuey, *Legal Technology— 1982 Update,* 11 Colo Law 3015 (1982); Hoffman, *Computers for the Law Office: Some Guidelines for Coping with Rapid Marketplace Change,* 22 Law Off Econ & Mgt 260 (1981); Emerson, *Computers and the Law Firm: Three Ways to Automate Your Practice (pt II),* 18 Trial 20 (1982); Karasik, *The Computerization of an 11-Member Firm,* 69 ABA J 1236 (1983); Lockwood, *"Electronic Shock": The Impact of Computer Technology on the Practice of Law,* 7 Dalhousie LJ 743 (1983); Remer, *Goodbye Yellow Pads, Hello Computers,* 3 Cal Law 49 (1983); Brest, Brest & Horton, *Options in Office Computer Systems,* 3 Cal Law 34 (1983); Hoffman, *The Every Lawyer's Computer— Now and Tomorrow,* 55 NY St BJ 43 (1983); Pretty, *Harnessing a Personal Computer to Win Cases,* 69 ABA J 1438 (1983); Sprowl, *The New Age of Computers in the Law Office,* 24 Law Off Econ & Mgmt 223 (1983); Harper, *Computer Evidence is Coming,* 70 ABA J 80, (Nov 1984) (dsicussing the effect of computers on litigation and evidence in the courtroom); Cognition Corporation, Sales Brochure, 1984 (example of integrated software for the law office); Young, *Computer-Generated Evidence: When Is It Admissible at Trial?,* Trial, Jan 1985 at 15-18 (outlining the procedures generally necessary to admit computer evidence); Moran, *Computers For Small Cases: How Lawyers Can Set Up A Computerized System,* Trial, Jan 1985, at 20-26 (outlining a basic automated litigation support system); Lipson, *Computerizing Your Document System: For All Computer Models, Legal Specialties, and Software Packages,* Trial, Jan 1985, at 28-32 (recommending a simple system for document tracking and filing); Blau, *Software for the Law Office: Six Criteria To Evaluate It,* Trial, Jan 1985, at 34-38 (providing a checklist for document management.); Monti, *Automating Deposition Digests: How To Develop a System,* Trial, Jan 1985, at 40-42 (general how and why article); Piovia, A Common-Sense Guide to Law-Office Automation (1985) (how and what to automate, including checklists and sources).

Page 12, note 38, at end of note add:

See also Lambert, *Law in the Future: Tort Law: 2003 (pt I),* 19 Trial 90 (1983); Lambert, *Law in the Future: Tort Law: 2003 (pt II),* 19 Trial 62 (1983); Price, *IBM Rep. Denies VDT Harm From Radiation,* Govt Computer News 12 (Mar 29, 1985) (excerpts from speech to Computer and Business Equipment Manufacturers Association (CBEMA) by Peter Broadmore); Hoover, *Safety Information on Video Display Terminals,* Denver Post, Jan 20, 1985, at 3J (discussing the unmeasurable radiation danger from VDT's. Also notes three further sources for research).

Software Protection

2

§2.01 Definition of Software and Hardware

Pages 24-25, note 15, at end of note add:

See also Sprowl, *Bridging the Gap Between Technology and Legal Protection,* 5 Computer L Inst, Univ S Cal L Center I-1, *et seq* pt I (1984); and Sherman, *Special Problems in Dealing with Software Authors,* 191 Computer L Inst 337 (1984); Freed, *Legal Interests Related to Software Programs,* 25 Jurimetrics J 347 (1985); Bender, *Software Protection: The 1985 Perspective,* 7 W New England L Rev 405 (1985); Jensen, *Softright: A Legislation Solution to the Problem of Users' and Producers' Rights in Computer Software,* 44 La L Rev 1412 (1984); Ortner, *Current Trends in Software Protection: A Litigation Perspective,* 25 Jurimetrics J 319 (1985). See Baeza, *Acquisition and Exploitation of Mass-Market Software: Course Handbook Series Number 226,* Computer Software & Chips Protection and Marketing Program, 1986, Practicing L Inst #G4-3791, at 515-532 (mass market software marketing). See also Sandison, *Acquisition and Exploitation of Custom Software: Course Handbook Series Number 226,* Computer Software and Chips Protection and Marketing Program, 1986, Practicing L Inst #G4-3791, at 533-596 (custom software marketing strategies).

Patent Protection

§2.04 The *Diehr* and *Bradley* Decisions

Page 33, note 88, at end of note add:

Kreiss, *The Theory of Overclaiming and its Applicability to Diamond v. Diehr,* 5 Cardozo L Rev 97 (1983); Stout, *Protections of Programming in the Aftermath of Diamond v. Diehr,* 4 Computer LJ 207 (Fall 1983).

§2.04A   Patent Case Law Developments since *Diehr* and *Bradley* (New)

The Court of Customs and Patent Appeals (CCPA) has supplemented the *Diehr* and *Bradley* decisions to further refine the definitions of when a computer program is statutory subject matter. In *In re Abele*, 684 F2d 902 (CCPA 1982), the court ruled that if the claimed invention is an application of an algorithm, §101 will not bar the grant of a patent (*id* 907). In a companion case, *In re Pardo*, 684 F2d 912 (CCPA 1982), the CCPA restated the *Freeman-Walter* test, stating that first

> the claim is analyzed to determine whether a mathematical algorithm is directly or indirectly recited. Next, if a mathematical algorithm is found, the claim as a whole is further analyzed to determine whether the algorithm is applied in any manner to physical elements or process steps, and, if it is, it passes muster under Section 101.

684 F2d at 915.

In *In re Meyer*, 688 F2d 789 (CCPA 1982), the CCPA went even further in clarifying the *Freeman-Walter* test for computer software applications to scientific experiments by stating that in

> considering a claim for compliance with Section 101, it must be determined whether a scientific principle, law of nature, idea, or mental process, which may be represented by a mathematical algorithm, is included in the subject matter of the claim. If it is, it must then be determined whether such principle, law, idea, or mental process is applied in an invention of a type set forth in Section 101.

688 F2d at 795.

A recent decision concerning software patentability came from the District Court for the District of Delaware. This case involved a highly sophisticated computerized investment package, developed by Merrill Lynch, known as the Cash Management Account (CMA). A patent was issued for the CMA, known as the *442 patent*. Paine, Webber, Jackson & Curtis, Inc (Paine Webber) and Dean Witter had also been using a similar cash management system. Paine Webber sought a declaratory judgment of noninfringement, invalidity, and unenforceability of the 442 patent. *Paine, Webber, v Merrill Lynch, Pierce*, 564 F Supp 1358 (D Del 1983).

In analyzing the patentability of the CMA, the District Court first looked to the issue of the algorithm. The court noted that there was a distinction between a mathematical algorithm and a computer algorithm by stating that a "computer algorithm is a procedure consisting of operation to combine data, mathematical principles and equipment for the purpose of interpreting and/or acting upon a certain data input." *Id* 1367. The court went on to note that the CCPA has held that a computer algorithm, as opposed to a mathematical algorithm, is patentable subject matter (*see In re Pardo.*) *Id* 1368.

The court next turned to Paine Webber's contention that the 442 program was unpatentable because it defined nothing more than familiar business systems. Paine Webber urged the court to focus on the product of the CMA, whereas Merrill Lynch urged focus on the method of operation of the CMA. The court ruled that the focus of analysis should be on the operation of the program on the computer. The court then ruled that the 442 patent claimed statutory subject matter because the claims allegedly teach a method of operation on a computer to effectuate a business activity. *Id* 13. The case is currently on appeal to the new Court of Appeals for the Federal Circuit. In addition, Dean Witter has since paid Merrill Lynch $1 million in settlement. Wall St J, Dec 28, 1983, at 2, col 3. The only other activity in this case has been procedural. *See Paine, Webber, Jackson & Curtis v Merrill Lynch,* 587 F Supp 1112 (D Del 1984). See also Raysman & Brown, *Patent Protection for Software,* 190 NYLJ 1 (Nov 3, 1983).

A different approach to protecting an algorithm was tried in *United States Golf Association v St Andrews Systems DataMax, Inc,* 749 F2d 1028 (3d Cir 1984), in which the court ruled that a formula used to determine golf handicaps could not be protected under the Lanham Trade Marks Act.

§2.05   The Future of Patent Protection

Page 36, note 101, at end of note add:

See also White Consol Indus v Vega Servo-Control, Inc, 713 F2d 788 (CAFC 1983), where a patent held by White was ruled invalid for failure to satisfy the enablement requirement of 35 USC §112. In order to protect a trade secret, the court recognized that an applicant may refer to an element of a claimed invention held as a trade secret by name only and yet satisfy 35 USC §112 if equivalent elements are known (and known to be equivalents), and available to those skilled in the art. The court, however, ruled that the record was insufficient to show that other equivalent elements were known to those skilled in the art. *Id* 790. Consequently, a software developer who is seeking patent protection, and still attempting to maintain some trade secret protection, must be careful to satisfy the enablement requirement under 35 USC §112. Otherwise, the developer risks the possibility of a declaration of invalidity for an otherwise valid patent. *See also* Honeywell, Inc v Diamond, 499 F Supp 924 (DC 1980).

Page 36, note 104, at end of note add:

An additional hazard to patent protection is the threat of loss of protection to a junior claim. Cases exist wherein a senior claimant has been denied a patent either because the senior claimant had suppressed the invention or because the junior claimant had been first to reduce the invention to practice. *See* Piher, SA v CTS Corp, 664 F2d 122 (7th Cir 1981); Honeywell, Inc v Diamond, 499 F Supp 924 (DC 1980).

A software developer who wishes to seek patent protection must be careful to determine when a program has evolved from a conception to an invention reduced to practice. In *Piher, SA v CTS Corp*, the court stated that for an invention to be reduced to practice, all that is "required is a demonstration of practical efficacy and utility." In addition, the court stated that further "experiments in an attempt to refine the device is no evidence that it has not been reduced to practice. . . . [A] device is reduced to practice once it has been 'assembled, adjusted and used.' " 664 F2d at 127. The sequence of events to be concerned with is where a software developer first develops a new program, chooses trade secret protection, and then a second software developer creates a substantially similar program and receives a patent for the program. In this instance, the first developer may be totally foreclosed from using the program due to the second developer's patent.

See also Austin Powder Co v Atlas Powder Co, 568 F Supp 1294 (D Del 1983); GAF Corp v Amchem Prods, Inc, 514 F Supp 943 (ED Penn 1981); Shindelar v Holdeman, 628 F2d 1337 (CCPA 1980), *cert denied,* 451 US 984 (1981); Mobil Oil Corp v Dann, 421 F Supp 995 (DC 1976); and 3.5 D. Davidson, Advanced Strategies for Buying and Selling Computers and Software, Draft Manuscript Submitted to John Wiley & Sons, Inc (1985) for a discussion of self-help techniques; Syrowik, *Disclosing Computer Programs in an Application for a United States Patent—A Trap for the Unwary,* 26 Jurimetrics J 21 (1985); Hopkins, *The Status of Patent Law Concerning Computer Programs: The Proper Form for Legal Protection,* 33 Drake L Rev 155 (Winter 1983-1984); Weber, *Patenting Inventions that Embody Computer Programs Held as Trade Secrets,* 99 Wash L Rev 501 (July 1984); Gregures, *Software Packages: Trade Secret or Patent Protection?,* 15 Computer World 39 (Apr 27, 1981).

Copyright Protection

§2.06   Generally

Page 37, note 109, at end of note add:

See Petry, *Computer Software: Course Handbook Series Number 226,* Computer Software & Chips Protection & Marketing Program, 1986, Practicing L Inst # G4-3791, at 467-514(a general overview of computer software). See also Goldberg, *Copyright Protection for Computer Programs, Data Bases, and Related Works: Course Handbook Series Number 225,* Computer Software & Chips Protection & Marketing Program, 1986, Practicing L Inst # G4-3791, at 9-124 (copyright protection overview). For a look at the judicial and legislative response to copyright protection, see Levine, *Copyright and The Protection of Computer Software: Course Handbook Series Number 225,* Computer Software & Chips Protection & Marketing Program, 1986, Practicing L Inst #G4-3791, at 125-158.

Page 37, note 110, at end of note add:

See also Pecieroni, *The Ninth Circuit has Held that All Computer Programs are Copyrightable Regardless of Their Function,* 23 Dug L Rev 457 (Winter 1985).

Page 38, note 117, at end of note add:

Dunn, *Defining Scope of Copyright Protection for Computer Software,* 38 Stan L Rev 497 (Jan 1985); Kline, *Requiring an Election of Protection for Patentable-Copyrightable Computer Programs,* 67 J Pat & TM Off Socy 280 (June 1985).

§2.07   The Copyright Act of 1976

Page 43, note 143, at end of note add:

Surrel, *The Treatment of Computer Software Works Made for Hire under the Copyright Act of 1976,* 5 Computer LJ 579 (Spring 1985).

Page 44, note 151, at end of note add:

Fisher, *Copyright Act of 1976: Operating System Computer Programs Expressed in Object Code and Stored in ROM are Copyrightable,* 29 Vill L Rev 894; Samuelson, *CONTU Revisited: The Case Against Copyright Protection for Computer Programs in Machine Readable Form,* 1984 Duke LJ 663 (Sept 1984).

§2.08 The Copyright Act Amendments of 1980

Page 46, text, at end of section add:

Section 117 of the Copyright Act has been interpreted in regard to programmed read only memory. In *Atari, Inc v JS&A, Inc,* the United States District Court for the Northern District of Illinois ruled that a device marketed by JS&A (known as a "Prom Blaster"), which copied programmed read only memory cartridges used in home video games, contributed to the infringement of copyrights held by Atari.

JS&A sold the Prom Blaster, as well as nine of its own game cartridges (for which it gave its purchasers permission to copy) and blank cartridges. JS&A advertised the Prom Blaster as a means of making copies of home video game cartridges for archival purposes. Atari alleged that JS&A was contributing to the infringement of Atari's copyrights in several of its games by marketing the Prom Blaster as an inexpensive way to make and sell copies of Atari's protected games. Atari sought a preliminary injunction against future sales of the Prom Blaster, recovery of JS&A's profits on the sales of copies of games, and $1 million in punitive damages.

The district court determined that the critical issue was whether the primary use of the Prom Blaster was to make legal copies or to make infringing copies. The court ruled that with only nine JS&A games to copy with permission, it was clear that the primary use of the Prom Blaster was to duplicate other's video games. The court noted that while §117 of the Copyright Act permits archival copies, it does not allow the making of backup copies in all circumstances. The court read §117 very narrowly and found that copies could be made only to guard against destruction or damage by mechanical or electrical failure, and that JS&A had offered no evidence that the read only memory in this particular type of video game cartridge was subject to the danger of mechanical or electrical failure. *See Atari, Inc v JS&A, Inc,* No 83 C8333, (ND Ill Dec 6, 1983).

A source code listing of a computer program (generally of first and last 25 pages) must be deposited with the Copyright Office as a condition of registering a federal copyright. 37 CFR §202.20(c)(2)(vii). See generally Williams, *Copyright Registration for Secret Computer Programs: Robbery of the Phoenix's Nest,* 24 Jurimetrics J 357 (Summer 1984); Kelso & Rebey, *Problems of Interpretation Under the 1980 Computer Amendment,* 23 Santa Clara L Rev 1001 (Fall 1983); Stern, *Another Look at Copyright Protection of Software: Did the 1980 Act Do anything for Object Code?,* 3 Computer LJ 1 (Fall 1981); Mihm, *Software Piracy and the Personal Computer: Is the 1980 Copyright Act Effective?,* 4 Computer LJ 171 (Summer 1983); Stern, *Section 117 of Copyright Act: Charter of the Software Users' Rights or an Illusory Promise?,* 7 W New England L Rev 459 (Winter 1985).

§2.09 Copyright Case Law

Page 46, note 163, at end of note add:

Root, *Copyright Infringement of Computer Programs: A Modification for the Substantial Similarity Test,* 58 Minn L Rev 1284 (June 1984). See also Reysman & Brown, *Copyright Infringement by Nonidentical Software,* 93 NYLJ 1 (Apr 9 1985).

In Q-Co Indus v Hoffman, 625 F Supp 608, (SDNY 1985), IBM software did not infringe copyrighted Atari software because there was not substantial similarity between the two programs.

Page 46, note 164, at end of note add:

In M. Kramer Mfg Co v Andrews, 783 F2d 421 (4th Cir 1986), the court held that an electronic, coin-operated video poker game could not be copied by a competing firm because a copyright in an audiovisual game protects the actual software of the game's computer program.

Page 50, text, at end of section add:

Uniden Corporation recently lost a software copyright case, EF Johnson Co v Uniden Corp of Am, 623 F Supp 1485 (DC Minn 1985) because Uniden's software was an infringement of EF Johnson's copyrighted software (based on substantial similarity), *Computer Program Conversion As Possible Infringement,* 5 The Computer Law Monthly 199-200 (May 1986). For a detailed analysis of current problems and solutions to copyright protection of computer programs see Gesmer, *Developments In the Law of Computer Software Copyright Infringement,* 26 Jurimetrics J 224 (Spring 1986).

§2.09A Recent Developments in Copyright Case Law (New)

In 1983, the District Court ruling in *Apple Computer, Inc v Franklin Computer Corp,* 545 F Supp 812 (ED Pa 1982), was overturned by the Court of Appeals for the Third Circuit. *Apple Computer, Inc v Franklin Computer Corp,* 714 F2d 1240 (3d Cir 1983), *cert dismissed,* 104 S Ct 690 (1984). The circuit court addressed three basic issues: (1) the copyrightability of a computer program, whether in source code or object code; (2) the copyrightability of a computer program embedded in read only memory (ROM); and (3) the copyrightability of computer operating system programs.

As to the first issue, the district court had been uncertain as to whether a computer program in object code could be classified as a "literary work." The appeals court looked to the definition of *literary works* in 17 USC §101, which includes expression not only in words but also numbers, or other numerical symbols or indicia. The court ruled that a computer program, whether in object code or source code, is a literary work and is protected from unauthorized copying, whether from its object or source code version.

Concerning the second issue, the court returned to its analysis in *Williams Electronic, Inc v Artic International, Inc*, 685 F2d 870 (3d Cir 1982), as to computer programs made on a read only memory (ROM). The court reaffirmed its holding in *Williams* that the statutory requirement of fixation is satisfied through the embodiment of the expression in the ROM devices. A computer program, therefore, in object code embedded in a ROM chip is an appropriate subject of copyright protection.

The third issue addressed by the court concerned whether computer operating system programs, as distinguished from application programs, are proper subjects for copyright protection. Franklin argued that an operating system program is either a "process," "system," or "method of operation," and hence uncopyrightable. The court, however, noted that Apple was not seeking to copyright the method which instructs the computer to perform its operating functions, but only the instructions themselves. That court stated that since it is

> only the instructions which are protected, a "process" is no more involved because the instructions in an operating system program may be used to activate the operation of the computer than it would be if instructions were written in ordinary English in a manual which described the necessary steps to activate an intricate complicated machine. There is, therefore, no reason to afford any less copyright protection to the instructions in an application program.

714 F2d at 1251.

In addition, the court also raised the issue of the idea/expression dichotomy. The court, however, felt the record was not sufficiently clear for the issue to be decided at the appellate level. The court then granted Apple's motion for preliminary injunction. After the court's ruling, Apple and Franklin settled out of court.

See Harris, *Apple Computer, Inc. v. Franklin Computer Corp.—Does a ROM a Computer Program Make?*, 24 Jurimetrics 248 (1984); Goodrich, *Hard Law for Software*, 4 Cal Law 18 (1984); Warren, *Copyright: Computer Firmware: Is it Copyrightable?*, 36 Okla L Rev 119 (1983); Ashman, *Software Program Can be Copyrighted*, 69 ABA J 1750 (1983); Englander, *Copyrightability of Computer Operating Systems*, 41 Wash & Lee L Rev 1361 (Fall 1984); Touponse, *The Application of Copyright Law to Computer Operating System Programs*, 17 Conn L Rev 665 (Spring 1985); Weber, *Extension of Copyright Protection to Computer Operating Systems*, 7 W New England L Rev 829 (Winter 1985).

Apple Computer was involved in another infringement action which raised issues very similar to those addressed in *Apple Computer, Inc v Franklin Computer Corp. See Apple Computer, Inc v Formula International, Inc,* 725 F2d 521 (9th Cir 1984). In this later case, however, the court more fully addressed the issue of the idea/expression dichotomy.

In the *Formula* case, the court of appeals affirmed the lower court's granting of Apple's motion for preliminary injunction. The injunction prohibited Formula from copying computer programs having copyrights registered to Apple, from importing, selling, distributing, or advertising those copies, and from using the name "Pineapple" or any other mark or name confusingly similar to the trademarks used by Apple.

Formula asserted that the district court erred in granting the preliminary injunction by relying on a misapplication of 17 USC §101 *et seq.* Formula contended that the computer programs involved, because they control the internal operation of the computer, are only "ideas" or "processes," and therefore, unlike application programs, are not protected by copyright.

The court followed the ruling in *Franklin,* holding that the operating system programs were copyrightable because Apple was seeking to copyright only its particular set of instructions, not the underlying computer process. 725 F2d at 525. In addition, Formula raised the contention that the operating system programs were not copyrightable because they were not directly communicated to the computer user. The court, however, reasoned that

> Formula provides absolutely no authority for its contention that the "expression" required in order for a computer program to be eligible for copyright protection is expression that must be communicated to the computer user when the program is run on a computer. The Copyright Act extends protection to "original works of authorship fixed in any tangible medium of expression. . . ." The computer program when written embodies expression; never has the Copyright Act required that the expression be communicated to a particular audience.

Id.

Formula and Apple were recently back in court. Apple sued Formula for contempt of the preliminary injunction upheld in *Apple v Formula, supra.* Formula had changed the name of its computer and had removed all infringing computer programs. Formula continued to sell its computer, but began including a kit which included silicon chips the purchaser installed into the computer. One of the silicon chips contained an identical copy of a copyrighted Apple program. The court held that Formula was in contempt and ordered it to destroy or erase all infringing copies of Apple's programs and to pay Apple over $8,000.

Apple Computer, Inc v Formula International, Inc, 594 F Supp 617 (CD Cal 1984).

As a result of the *Franklin* and *Formula* cases, *supra*, it has now been uniformly accepted that all computer programs, whether used in RAM or in ROM, as an application or operational, can be copyrighted (provided they are original expressions). The cases have now, therefore, turned to other issues of copyright infringement.

One of the more interesting recent developments in the area of software copyright infringement stems from the fact that much of the software still being written is designed to be used on one or a few particular brands of computers. This has provided an incentive for others to develop identical programs that will run on other computers. There have been two recent federal District Court cases directly on this point.

The first case involved a computer program designed to control the operation of a dental laboratory. The *Dentalab* system, created by Whelan Associates, was originally designed for the IBM-Series I computer and was written in a language known as Event Drive Language (EDL). Rand Jaslow, a sales representative for Whelan Associates, attempted to prepare a computer program for dental labs written in BASIC language that could be run on the IBM PC. Although Jaslow claimed that his program was an original piece, the court, in finding that there had been a copyright infringement, noted that direct copying was sufficiently demonstrated by circumstantial evidence of access and substantial similarity (in this case, almost complete similarity).

Whelan Associates had also raised a trade name infringement claim. Whelan Associate's software was called *Dentalab* while Jaslow's was called *Dentcom.* The court ruled that there was a potential for confusion between the products due to the fact that the visual screens displayed by both programs were almost identical in format and the use of abbreviations and terminology. *Whelan Associates v Jaslow Dental Laboratory,* 609 F Supp 1325 (ED Pa 1985), 29 *Pat Trademarks & Copyright J (BNA)* 357.

The second case involved the attempt to convert a statistical computer package, designed to run on IBM computers, so that it would also run on Digital Equipment Corporation's VAX computer system. The defendant, S&H Computer Systems, Inc. acquired a copy of the *SAS* statistical software package through a license agreement with the plaintiff, SAS Institute, Inc. Unknown to the plaintiff, the defendant made unauthorized additional copies of the program and began a conversion of the program.

The court first ruled that SAS Institute held a valid copyright to the SAS program and that the additional copies of the program made by

S&H, in violation of the license agreement, constituted a copyright violation. As to the statistical program developed by S&H, the court ruled that it was a derivative work of the original SAS program. S&H argued that they had merely used ideas presented by the SAS program and that since the S&H program was written in a different computer language, the S&H program was its own original expression of ideas. The court rejected this argument with a single finding of fact that, to the extent that S&H copied from the SAS program source code and other copyrighted SAS materials, such copying was of expression, and not merely of ideas.

As to the issue of substantial similarity, the court made findings of 44 specific instances of copying. When S&H offered to remove the infringing lines of code, the court responded that it was not a computer programmer, and is simply not able to determine out of 186,000 lines of integrated product code, which of them reflect misappropriation. The court then cited *Tennessee Fabricating Co v Moultrie Manufacturing Co*, 421 F2d 279 (5th Cir), *cert denied*, 398 US 928(1970), for the proposition that it was enough that the starting point for S&H's redesign was SAS Institute's work. *SAS Institute, Inc v S&H Computer Systems, Inc*, Nos 82-3669 & 82-3670, 695 F Supp 816 (MD Tenn 1985).

Another area of software copyright infringement litigation activity has been in the so-called *typing service* cases. Many computer hobbyist magazines publish copyrighted computer program listings which the readers may enter into their computers and use. Entering many of these programs into a computer is a tedious and time consuming task. In one case, Amtype Co. established a *typing service* to input onto a disk, for a fee, all of the programs appearing in a particular issue of Nibble magazine. The court found that the defendant did not fall within the exceptions provided under §117 of the Copyright Act. Section 117(1) did not permit the purchaser of Nibble magazine to authorize the defendant to input the computer programs into a computer and §117(2) did not permit the purchaser to authorize the defendant to store the program on a disk for archival purposes—Nibble magazine had authorized the purchaser of the magazine to engage only in the input and storage activities. *Micro-SPARC, Inc v Amtype Corp*, 592 F Supp 33 (D Mass 1984). (For a related case, *see Rand McNally & Co v Fleet Management Systems*, 634 F Supp 604 (ND Ill 1984), in which the court ruled that the input of mileage data published in the plaintiff's distance guides into defendant's data base constituted copyright infringement.)

See generally Baumgarten, *Copyright Protection of Computer Programs*, 32 Fed Bar News & J 220 (1985); *Copyright Protection of Computer Programs Under Federal Copyright Laws*, 70 ALR Fed 176 (1985).

§2.10   The Future of Copyright Protection

Page 51, text, at end of section add:

The newest form of software protection is found in the Semiconductor Chip Protection Act of 1984, Pub L No 98-620, 98 Stat 3347, 17 USC §901. The act essentially gives the owner of a semiconductor chip 10 years of protection to exclusively reproduce, import, distribute and sell the chip. Intel Corporation became the first company to receive protection under the Act by registering its 27C256 semiconductor chip.

One important provision of the Semiconductor Chip Protection Act is the limitation of the above exclusive rights to reverse engineering. Section 906(a) permits the reverse engineering of a protected chip by allowing the analysis and evaluation of the concepts and techniques embodied in the protected chip and the incorporation of such analysis or evaluation into a new, original chip.

See generally Baumgarten, *Copyright and Computer Software (Including Data Bases & Chip Technology)*, 5 Computer L Inst, Univ S Cal L Center pt IV IV-1 *et seq* (1984); Baumgarten, *"Reverse Engineering" and other Exceptions Under the Semiconductor Chip Protection Act of 1984*, Presentation Made to the Computer Law Association "Update" Program—(May 13 & 14, 1985); Greguras & Williams, *Planning for the Operational Impact of the Semiconductor Chip Protection Act*, 2 Computer Law 12 (Mar 1985); Laurie & Everett, *The Copyrightability of Microcode: Is it Software or Hardware . . . or Both?*, 2 Computer Law 1 (Mar 1985); Stern, *Preemption and Relation of SCPA to Other United States Laws*, 2 Computer Law 9 (Jan 1985); and 3.3 D. Davidson, *Advanced Strategies for Buying and Selling Computers and Software*, Draft Manuscript submitted to John Wiley & Sons, Inc (1985). See also Baumgarten, *"Reverse Engineering" and Other Exceptions Under The Semiconductor Chip Protection Act of 1984: Course Handbook Series Number 225*, Computer Software & Chips Protection & Marketing Program, 1986, Practicing L Inst # G4-3791, at 159-179 (discussing exceptions to the Chip Protection Act); Baumgarten, *General Review of the Semiconductor Chip Protection Act (SCPA): Course Handbook Series Number 225*, Computer Software & Chips Protection & Marketing Program, 1986, Practicing L Inst #G4-3791, at 177-236 (general overview of SCPA); Wong, *The Semiconductor Chip Protection Act: New Law for New Technology*, 67 J Pat & TM Off Socy 530 (Oct 1985). Peters, *Registration of Computer Programs and Mask Works Fixed in Semiconductor Chip Products: Course Handbook Series Number 225*, Computer Software & Chips Protection & Marketing Program, 1986, Practicing L Inst # G43791, at 432-568 (how to register computer programs that are fixed in semiconductor chips).

See also Data Cash Systems, Inc v JS&A Group, Inc, 480 F Supp 1063 (ND Ill 1984), *Pat Trademark & Copyright J* (BNA) 612, where the court ruled that the defendant's dismantling of a device in the public domain and producing a similar device did not constitute unfair competition. See generally, Laurie & Everett, *Protection of Trade Secrets in Object Form Software: The Case for Reverse Engineering,* 1 Computer Law 1 (July 1984).

One of the areas that will see the most activity in the near future is the effort by businesses to stop internal copying of commercial software. Policies have been instituted to prevent employees from copying commercial software acquired by the corporation for in-house use by the employee. Most of this activity has been generated as a result of lawsuits filed by Lotus Development Corp., the maker of the popular Lotus 1-2-3 software.

Arguing that the language of the Copyright Act provides for statutory damages for each infringing copy made, Lotus has recently instituted two $1 million suits and one $10 million suit. To date, two of the suits (one, the $10 million) have been settled for undisclosed sums. Faced with the very real threat of a multimillion dollar lawsuit, businesses have suddenly become very serious about enforcing software license agreements among their employees. See Gilburne & Meyer, *Liability for Copyright Infringement Committed by Third Parties or Employees,* 2 Computer Law 1 (Apr 1985); and Gordon & Milligan, *Establishing Corporate Compliance Programs to Control Unauthorized Duplication of Microcomputer Software by Employees,* 2 Computer Law 11 (Apr 1985).

One of the most innovative and successful ways to eliminate the problem of corporate copyright abuse is through microcomputer software site licensing. Site licenses have been common practice for some time in the licensing of mainframe computer software for particular machines at particular sites. A site license for personal computer software permits the making of unlimited copies of a program, which otherwise violates the software's copyright.

The licensee pays a flat fee for the software which permits the unlimited copying of the software for business related needs and the right to upgrades and enhancements. The site license takes away the dilemma of a large corporation trying to oversee and prevent copyright abuse. Recent site licensing of microcomputer software has yielded up to 60 per cent savings in licensing costs for major corporations. See generally, Warner, *Exxon Sees Site Licensing Pact Slicing Software Costs,* 19 Computerworld 25 (June 10, 1985); Cooper & Sapronov, *Software Protection & Pricing in a LAN Environment,* 26 Jurimetrics J 162 (1986); Rubin, *Companies Benefit from Site-License Agreements,* 3 PC Week 60 (May 6, 1986).

One of the more interesting developments to monitor will be the treatment of software copyright infringements. It is now being argued that the full extent of the programmer's originality should be protected. Rather than comparing the programming code of computer programs, it has been asserted that the courts should also look to fundamental elements such as the product's design, arrangement, and presentations. See Russo and Derwin, *Copyright in the "Looks and Feel" of Computer Software,* 2 Computer Law 1 (Feb 1985).

Another issue which should also generate some activity in the near future is the copyrightability of computer databases. Databases are becoming more accessible to the general public. One who has compiled a database certainly wishes to protect it, and can do so through the Copyright Act. A database user has the right to access, copy and use portions of the database. The dilemma arises in the degree of copying and use that should or can be permitted and the type of use. The infringement of database copyrights promises to be one of the major centers of debate over the next few years. See generally, *Case Developments in Proprietary Rights* 1 Computer Law 24 (Aug 1984); Baker, *Of Copyrights and Databases,* Micro Communications 34 (Aug 1984); and Swartz, *On-Line Databases: The Legal Dilemma,* Business Computer Sys 28 (Jan 1985).

Finally, The Copyright Office has proposed changes to the deposit requirements for computer programs. The proposals are designed to clarify and expand the current regulations and would divide 37 CFR §202.20 (c)(2)(vii) into three classes: (1) computer programs and databases embodied in machine-readable form; (2) machine-readable copies of works other than computer programs and databases; and (3) works with visually-perceptible and machine-readable copies. See generally *Administrative Changes,* 2 Computer Law 27 (Apr 1985).

A secure test similar to the type used with deposited bar exams has been proposed for use with computer software by the Copyright Office. See Horwitz, *Proposed Changes In Regulations Governing Deposits of Computer Programs With the Copyright Office,* 26 Jurimetrics J 305 (Spring 1986), where the problems of software deposits are analyzed; Gesmer, *Developments in the Law of Computer Software Copyright Infringement,* 26 Jurimetrics J 224 (1986).

Trade Secret Protection

§2.11   Generally

Page 52, note 191, at end of third line add:

To date, nine states (California, Connecticut, Delaware, Indiana, Kansas, Louisiana, Minnesota, North Dakota, and Washington) have adopted the Uniform Trade Secrets Act. *See also* McCormack & Dodge Corp v ABC Management Sys, No 82-2-00204 (Wash Dec 22, 1983), which was decided, in part, under the Uniform Trade Secrets Act. The jury determined that trade secrets embodied in computer software had been misappropriated, and the court awarded attorney's fees of over $600,000 to the prevailing parties and exemplary damages of double

the Act, leading to an overall award of over $3 million. See generally Ruus, *The Impact of the Uniform Trade Secrets Act on California Trade Secret Law,* Trade Secret L Rep 4 (May 1985); and Dratler, *Trade Secret Law: An Impediment to Trade in Computer Software,* 1 Santa Clara Computer & High-Tech LJ 27 (1985).

§2.12 Employment Agreements

Page 55, note 207, at end of note add:

See also *Checklist—Employment Contracts re Intellectual Property Rights,* 1 Computer L Monitor 48 (1984).

Page 55, note 208, at end of note add:

See also Business Intelligence Servs, Inc v Hudson, 580 F Supp 1068 (SDNY 1984), wherein Business Intelligence Services (BIS) sought to enjoin Hudson, a former senior consultant, from working for a competitor (Management Technologies, Inc). Hudson had signed an employment agreement which contained a one-year noncompetition clause.

The district court noted that in the state of New York, a noncompetition clause is enforceable if the restriction is reasonable in scope and duration and necessary to protect against: (1) disclosure of trade secrets or other confidential information; (2) solicitation of customers; or (3) use of an employee's services which are unique or extraordinary. The court granted BIS's preliminary injunction, which prevented Hudson from working for any domestic or foreign competitor of BIS, on the grounds that BIS would suffer irreparable harm if Hudson went to work for Management Technologies, Inc, due to Hudson's extensive knowledge of BIS computer software and client information.

Also see Syntex Ophthalmics, Inc v Novicky, 701 F2d 677 (7th Cir 1983), in which a former employee was enjoined for a period of 20 years from using or disclosing any of the trade secret information contained in the plaintiff's laboratory notebooks unless such information had been publicly disclosed via patent or otherwise or was independently developed. The district court noted that 20 years represented the amount of employee time that it cost the plaintiff to develop the confidential data.

Page 55, note 209, at end of note add:

See also Haley, *Trade Secrets and the Skilled Employee in the Computer Industry,* 61 Wash ULQ 823 (1983).

Page 57, note 222, at end of note add:

See also Brown, *Protecting a Software Company Against a Spinoff Formed by Departing Employees*, 5 Computer Law Inst, Univ S Cal L Center pt II II-1 *et seq* (1984); and Heying, *Wrongful Termination: A New Common Law Remedy for Employees-At-Will?*, Ill BJ 584 (July 1985). *See also* SI Handling Sys, Inc v Heisley, 581 F Supp 1553 (ED Pa 1984), in which former employers were enjoined from using SI's *know-how*, which the court granted trade secret protection.

§2.14 Preemption of Trade Secret Protection

Page 63, note 259, at end of note add:

See also Bogglid v Kenner Prods, Div of General Mills, 576 F Supp 533 (SD Ohio 1983), wherein the district court held valid a license agreement which assigned a toy extruder device for 25 years or the life of any patent obtained, whichever was longer, regardless of whether any patents were issued. The court ruled that the enforcement of the agreement would not conflict with the patent laws. In ruling that the terms of the agreement were not preempted by federal patent laws, the court noted that the plaintiffs were not invoking the indeterminate protection of Ohio trade secret law. The court further stated that the plaintiffs

> are not seeking to prevent the public from manufacturing, selling or using this invention. Rather they seek to enforce the bargain they negotiated with defendant, i.e., the payment of royalties for a specified period in exchange for defendant's having the advantage of being first in the market place. We conclude, therefore, that plaintiffs did not use this agreement to extend their patent monopoly beyond the terms of the patents.

576 F Supp at 539.

Page 63, text, at end of section add:

Synercom Technology, Inc v University Computing Co, 462 F Supp 1003 (1978), upheld the concept that state trade secret protection and federal copyright protection can coexist so long as the plaintiff is not seeking to enforce the same or a substantially equivalent right under state law as would be provided under federal copyright protection. The district court noted that Synercom's argument in support of its unfair competition claim was based on the defendant's infringement of Synercom's copyright in its user manuals and not on the defendant's use of Synercom's input format. The court had already granted relief for the copyright infringement and ruled that "further relief for the same conduct under the theory of unfair competition would be unwarranted." 474 F Supp at 44.

One of the better reasoned cases concerning federal preemption of state trade secret protection came from the Court of Appeals of Wisconsin. *See M Bryce & Associates v Gladstone,* 107 Wis 2d 241, 319 NW2d 907 (1982), *cert denied,* 459 US 944 (1982). The plaintiff, M. Bryce & Associates (MBA), contended that the defendants, Arthur Young & Co and Harley-Davidson Motor Co, took and used for their own benefit MBA's trade secret software. This software contained a methodology for the design of management information systems. MBA had marked the trade secret documents with a copyright notice and date of publication, yet the court concluded that state trade secret protection was not preempted by federal copyright protection. The court noted that trade secret law protects content irrespective of form of expression, while copyright law protects form of expression but not the underlying ideas. 319 NW2d at 915. The court stated that if

> state trade secret protection was preempted by federal copyright law, MBA would have to turn to the federal copyright law for protection. Since copyright protection covers only the form of expression, its value to MBA in protecting MBA's interests would be limited. Only MBA's . . . manuals and forms would be protected but not MBA's methodology which is embodied also in [an] . . . oral presentation . . . . We conclude that such a preemption of trade secret law by federal copyright law incapable of providing equivalent protection would disrupt an area of property protection which has been found to be of great value.

Id 916.

See also Technicon Medical Information v Green Bay Packaging, 687 F2d 1032 (7th Cir 1982), *cert denied,* 103 S Ct 732 (1983), which was decided on unique procedural grounds where the copyright holder limited its publication under the Copyright Act; therefore, the preemption issue was not directly addressed. The court did, however, state in dictum that it did not perceive "an inherent conflict between the Federal Copyright Act and state trade secret law." 687 F Supp at 1038.

Not all courts, however, will provide as broad a scope of coverage. In *Videotronics, Inc v Bend Electronics,* the United States District Court for the District of Nevada ruled that federal copyright law did preempt state trade secret protection. Videotronics, which manufactures an electronic video poker game machine, sought a preliminary injunction to restrain Bend and others from manufacturing and selling a similar video poker game machine which used a read only memory (ROM) chip which Videotronics claimed was misappropriated by the defendants. The court ruled that protection for the ROM chip fell directly under the Copyright Act and, therefore, state unfair competition and misappropriation protection were preempted. Videotronics then sought a preliminary injunction against Bend Electronics to enjoin the infringement of the program. The injunction was denied on the basis of insufficient notice of a claim of copyright. It is important to note that the court was aware that the defendant was not an innocent infringer. The court ruled that although the defendant was *wholly aware* of the existence of the copyright, no protection would be afforded the plaintiff since there had been no substantial compliance with the copyright act. *Videotronics, Inc v Bend Electronics,* 586 F Supp 478, 484 (D Nev 1984).

See *contra, GCA Corp v Chance,* 217 USPQ 718 (ND Cal 1982) wherein the court held that trade secret and copyright protection both supported a grant of preliminary injunction against the copying of diagnostic and operating system programs. *Videotronics, Inc v Bend Electronics,* 564 F Supp 1471 (D Nev 1983).

§2.15   The Future of Trade Secret Protection

Page 64, note 262, at end of note add:

See generally 3.2 D. Davidson, Advanced Strategies for Buying and Selling Computers and Software, Draft Manuscript submitted to John Wiley & Sons, Inc (1985). See Brooks, *Reverse Engineering Computer Software: Is It Fair Use of Plagiarism: Course Handbook Series Number 226,* Computer Software & Chips Marketing Program, 1986, Practicing L Inst #G4-3791, at 7-122 (discussing reverse engineering, copyright protection and trade secret protection).

Suggested Legal Approach to Software Protection

§2.16   Generally

Page 65, text, at end of section add:

See *Checklist—Copyright, Patent, Trade Secret & Trademark: Some Basic Elements,* 1 Computer L Monitor 64 (1984); Mantle, *Trade Secret and Copyright Protection of Computer Software,* 4 Computer LJ 669 (1984); *The Current State of Computer Software Protection: A Survey and Bibliography of Copyright, Trade Secret and Patent Alternatives,* 8 Nova LJ 107 (1983); Visserman & Moran, *Legal Protection of Computer Software,* 81 Pat & TM Rev 457 (1983); Samuels & Samuels, *The Patentability of Computer-Related Inventions,* 6 Corp L Rev 144 (1983); Davidson, *Protecting Computer Software: A Comprehensive Analysis,* 23 Jurimetrics 337 (1983); Selinger, *Protecting Computer Software in the Business Environment: Copyright & Trade Secrets,* 3 JL & Comm 65 (1983); MacGrady, *Protection of Computer*

Software—An Update and Practical Synthesis, 20 Hous L Rev 1033 (1983); Harris, *A Market-Oriented Approach to the Use of Trade Secret or Copyright Protection (or Both?) for Software,* Jurimetrics J 147 (Winter 1985); and M. Scott, Computer Law (1984); Ortner, *Current Trends in Software Protection —A Litigation Perspective,* 25 Jurimetrics J 319 (1985); Conley & Bryen, *A Unifying Theory for the Litigation of Computer Software Copyright Cases,* 5 Computer LJ 55 (Summer 1985); Murphy & Zuck, *Trade Secrets and Noncompetition Agreements—Old Fashioned Remedies for Problems of High-Tech Industries,* LIX Fla BJ 37 (July 1985).

§2.16A   Software Protection Under Shrink-Wrap License Agreements (New)

The validity of shrink-wrap license agreements has been debated for some time. Legislatures are now beginning to supply the validity that many argued was lacking. The enforceability of shrink-wrap license agreements is discussed in **§3.12.** Since shrink-wrap licenses impact the ability of some computer software distributors to protect their software from unauthorized copies, the issue merits some discussion under Software Protection.

A shrink-wrap license is a license agreement which accompanies mass market, microcomputer software. The license is printed on, or attached to, the software package which is sealed by shrink-wrap. The license spells out the rights and obligations of each party (the licensee and licensor), particularly as to the licensee's right to copy and use the particular software. Removing the shrink-wrap automatically binds the licensee to the agreement.

There has been much criticism of this system. It is essentially adhesive. If the consumer wants the software, he or she has to comply with the licensor's preprinted form. There is no negotiation. Although there are implied warranties of merchantability, the consumer is essentially stuck with the product once the shrink-wrap has been removed. In effect, the opening of the package has gone beyond mere investigation to contractual obligation. In addition, there is no signed writing between the parties, possibly violating some states' Statute of Frauds provisions.

The shrink-wrap license agreement is, however, gaining validity. Louisiana has passed the Computer Software License Enforcement Act, 538, Act No 744 (1984), to be codified at LRS §§51-27-1951 to-1956. The act states that a software license will be enforceable if:

1. A notice or legend is clearly and conspicuously visible upon cursory examination of the package 2. The notice or legend is in capital letters and understandable 3. The notice or legend states that use of the software constitutes acceptance of the terms of the license or that opening the package will constitute acceptance of

the terms of the license 4. The notice or legend states that if a person does not agree with the terms of the license, they may, within a reasonable time, return the unused, *unopened* software. (Emphasis added.)

The Act also permits the inclusion of the following provisions in the license:

1. Retention of title to the software by the licensor 2. Prohibitions against copying 3. Prohibitions against modifying, adapting, decompiling, or reverse engineering the software 4. Prohibitions against further transferring the software 5. The right of automatic termination of the license in the event of breach of any of the terms by the licensee.

Illinois and California are both considering shrink-wrap legislation. (California Legislature, Regular Session 1985-86, Assembly Bill No 2296; State of Illinois, 84th General Assembly, 800.) See *Current Developments—Legislation,* 2 Computer Law 24 (Apr 1985) for a reprint and analysis of the bills. For related matters, see also Rice, *Trade Secret Clauses In Shrink-Wrap Licenses,* 2 Computer Law 17 (Feb 1985). See also Sahler, *Shrink-Wrapped Software Agreements,* 8 Licensing Law & Bus Rep 37 (Nov-Dec 1985); Einhorn, *The Enforceability of "Tear-me-open" Software License Agreement,* 7 Pat & TM Off Socy 509 (Oct 1985); Davidson, *"Box-Top" Software Licenses,* 41 Bench & B Minn 9 (Mar 1984).

§2.17 Foreign Perspectives

Page 66, note 269, at end of note add:

A political dispute has arisen in Japan over the type of protection which should be afforded to computer programs. A subcommittee of the Copyright Council has proposed a 50-year term of copyright protection for computer programs. The Ministry for International Trade and Industry (MITI), however, considers software to be an industrial product and has drafted a proposal that would offer the same 15-year term of protection to computer programs as is applied to Japanese patents. See *Japan Weighs Extending Copyright Protection to Computer Programs,* 27 PTCJ 309 (1984).

The MITI proposal also includes provisions for the equivalent of registration and deposit, effectively requiring a software author to disclose all of the program's source code. It has been suggested that a factor underlying MITI's position could be that, given the current situation in which Japan uses much more software produced in the United States and other foreign countries than it creates and exports, the net effect of the proposed law would be to advance Japan's use and

understanding of foreign software at relatively little cost to its own
software production efforts. See Klasson, *Japanese Copyright Proposal
Could Damage Software Trade,* 1 Computer L Strategist 3 (1984).

In addition, senior United States trade officials are very concerned
about the MITI proposal. The United States trade delegation has
indicated that should MITI's proposal be enacted into law, retaliation
by the United States government and American corporations is likely.
The delegation warned that the United States is prepared to remove
copyright protection for Japanese software. In addition, United States
software firms would be likely to file suit to restrict sales of Japanese
software on the grounds that Japan has unfairly or unduly harmed or
burdened their interests. See 27 PTCJ 424 (1984).

Page 67, text, at end of section add:

The amount of copyright protection afforded to a computer
program varies with each foreign jurisdiction. In *Apple Computer, Inc v
Computer Edge Pty, Ltd,* an Australian Court ruled that computer
programs are not "literary works" within the meaning of Australia's
copyright statute. The Federal Court of Australia (New South Wales
District), however, reversed ruling that the country's Copyright Act
encompasses protection for computer programs. A majority of the
court determined that computer programs, in source code form, are
"literary works" and that object code is protectable as an "adaptation"
of the source code. See *Computer Programs Are Subject to Copyright
Protection in Australia,* 28 PTCJ 256 (1984).

(See also Wilson, *Current Issues in Australian Computer Law,* 4 Scott R
No 7 at 1 (Apr 1985)).

In addition, the Canadian government is currently considering
revisions to that nation's copyright act. Included in the revisions is a
proposal that computer programs and data bases be subject to
copyright protection. The protection for computer programs would,
however, be limited. While programs in human-readable form would
continue to receive the same protection as traditional literary works,
programs in machine-readable form would be protected for a limited
period of five years from the date of creation (as opposed to 50 years
plus the life of the author for traditional works). After this five-year
time limit, any person with access to the program in human-readable
form could use it to make a machine-readable program, which would
not constitute an infringement of either the underlying human-
readable program or of any other machine-readable program based
upon that human-readable program. See 28 PTCJ 132 (1984).

Copyright protection for software has become the most widely
accepted form of protection with most of the developed nations
judicially accepting the concept. Aside from Japan and Australia, the
Federal Republics of Germany and France have both approved of
copyright protection for software, FRG *Visicorp* v Basic Software GmbH

September 21, 1982 Munich District, France. *Tribunal de Commerce de Paris,* 9 Mars 1982, RIDA 1983, no 116.

The largest barrier to universal copyright protection stems from the antiquated copyright statutes. The Canadian copyright law was passed in 1971 (Act Respecting Copyright ch 55 1971); Belgium's law is dated 1958, (Law on Copyrights 1958); France, Law on Literacy and Artistic Property (1957) law #57-298; Great Britain, the 1956 Copyright Act. The wording of these laws tends to create uncertainty regarding copyright protection. Phrases such as "protection is provided for written compilations or notations made by hand printing, typewriting, or other similar process" (see Britain's 1956 Copyright Act and Bishop, *Protection of Computer Programs in the UK,* 5 NWJ Intl L & B 346-55 (1982)) remain in many of the world's copyright laws and were written at a time when computers were to be found only at universities and the biggest corporations. Protection of software when these laws were written was provided by the differences in operating systems that made simply copying the code onto a disk or tape and running it on another machine impossible. See Tapper, *Copyright in Computer Programs: An International Perspective,* 1 Santa Clara Computer & High-Technology LJ 13 (Jan 1985); Hayden, *Copyright and the Right to Copy: Japan's Proposed New Legislation,* 58 Law Inst J 414 (Apr 1984); Stover, *Copyright Protection for Computer Programs in the United Kingdom, West Germany and Italy: A Comparative Overview,* 7 Loy LA Intl & Comp LJ 279 (Spring 1984); Karjala, *Lessons from the Computer Software Protection Debate in Japan,* 1984 Ariz St LJ 53 (Winter 1984); Argy, *Legal Protection of Computer Software in Australia,* 1 J L & Intl Sci 256 (1983); Gilbert, *International Copyright Law Applied to Computer Programs in the United States and France,* 14 Loy U Chi LJ 105 (Fall 1982).

These laws were not written to deal with computer software and technology, and until the old laws are amended trade secret protection will be as important in the international technology trade as copyrights. (See generally Keplinger, *Software Protection in Europe and Other Civil Law Jurisdictions,* Computer Law Inst 381 (1984); Baumgarten, *Copyright Protection of Computer Programs,* 35 Fed Bar & J 220, (1985).)

Interest in prodding foreign nations into action on copyrights has been expressed in the United States Senate with a bill introduced by Senator Frank R. Lautenberg (D-NJ) (S 339) that would provide for reciprocal protection to software. The scope of protection for foreign software would equal that protection given United States software in the particular foreign country. See Legislation note 29 Pat Trademark & Copyright J (BNA) 358 (1985).

A bill of this type has been introduced several times without much success. The principal problem with this sort of law is it would require not only judicial interpretation of foreign laws but also interpretation of foreign laws that in many cases have not been interpreted locally. The ability for the United States to force other nations to enact legislation seems dubious at best. It will probably be the marketplace pressures that force the updating of laws and expansion of software protection as such laws will become necessary to attract the foreign technology necessary to remain internationally competitive.

§2.18   A Two Step Matrix Approach to Protect Software

Page 67, note 374, at end of note add:

See Price, *Counterfeiting of Computer Goods, and Trademarks: Strategy and Tactics with Customs on Infringements: Course Handbook Series Number 226,* Computer Software & Chips, Protection & Marketing Program, 1986, Practicing L Inst #G4-3791, at 285-466 (discussing trademarks and customs in relation to prevention of counterfeiting). See also Einschlag & Michaelson, *Patent and Trade Secret Protection of Software: Patentability of Programs—Nature and Scope of Trade Secret Protection: Course Handbook Series Number 225,* Computer Software & Chips Protection & Marketing Program, 1986, Practicing L Inst 3G4-3791, at 403-430 (an overview of trade secret protection); Gregures, *Software Packages: Trade Secret or Patent Protection?,* 15 Computer World 39 (Apr 27 1981); Kemp, *Trade Secret and Copyright Protection for Mass-Marketed Computer Programs,* 90 Commercial LJ 525 (Dec 1985); Solomon, *The Copyrightability of Computer Software Containing Trade Secrets,* 63 Wash ULQ 131 (Spring 1985).

Computer Contracts

3

§3.01 Introduction

Page 72, note 1, at end of note add:

A multivolume set of checklists, contract provisions, forms, and agreements for use in computer contracting is published by Sunscape International Inc., Orlando, Fla. For a discussion of and sample acceptance, performance, and fulfillment provisions, see Course Handbook Series Number 191, at 277-336 (The Computer Law Inst 1984).

For an excellent review of various approaches to buying, selling, leasing, negotiation, warranty and tax considerations in computer hardware and software acquisitions see Davidson & Davidson, Advanced Strategies for Buying and Selling Computers and Software, submitted to John Wiley & Sons, Inc (Apr 15, 1985).

Page 73, note 2, at end of note add:

See also Joseph, *Computer Contract Challenges,* 5 Computer LJ (Winter 1985); Davidson & Davidson, Advanced Strategies for Buying and Selling Computers and Software, submitted to John Wiley & Sons, Inc (Apr 15, 1985).

Contract Issues

§3.02 The Hardware Market

Page 73, text, at end of section add:

One computer hardware manufacturer sought to contractually prohibit its dealers from engaging in telephone or mailorder sales practices. Because the court accepted the manufacturer's reasoning that dealer assessment of customer needs' for custom assembly of equipment configuration, hands-on instruction, and dealer availability for future problem solving are all essential aspects of customer service, the prohibition recently withstood a challenge that it was an unlawful restraint of trade in violation of §1 of the Sherman Antitrust Act. (*See OSC Corp v Apple Computer, Inc,* No CV 81-6132-PAR(Gx) (CD Cal Jan 11, 1985) in which the court found Apple's mail order prohibition to be a permissible nonvertical restraint on trade; see generally *infra* 4 Antitrust Considerations in the Computer Industry).

§3.03   The Software Market

Page 75, note 6, add:

For a further discussion of custom software contracting issues *see* Raysman & Brown, Computer Law (Law Journal Seminars Press 1984); and Wise, *Custom Software,* presented at American Patent Law Association 1984 Institute on Law and Computer Related Technology.

§3.04   The Software Life Cycle

Page 76, text, at end of section add:

For a discussion dealing with avoiding "distribution channel lock-in" and maintaining market flexibility during the product life cycle of software (and hardware), see Gilburne, *The Grant of Marketing Rights Early in the Product Life Cycle of Hardware and Software: The Problem of Distribution Channel Lock-in,* 1 Computer Law 28 (1984). See also Gilburne, *Software Publishing: Sourcing and Distributing Microcomputer Software,* 5 Computer L Inst, Univ S Cal L Center pt VIII VIII-1 *et seq,* (1984).

§3.05   Systems Approach to Contracting

Page 77, note 9, at end of note add:

See also Gordon & Starr, *Emerging Issues in Computer Procurements,* 5 Computer L Inst, Univ S Cal L Center pt XI XI-1, *et seq* (1984).

§3.06   Request for Proposal

Page 77, note 11, at end of note add:

See also 5 J Auer & CE Harris, Major Equipment Procurement 126-85 (1983).

§3.07   Application of the Uniform Commercial Code to Computer Transactions

Page 78, note 12, to beginning of note add:

For an overview of UCC law in the context of computers, see Davidson & Davidson, Advanced Strategies for Buying and Selling Computers and Software, submitted to John Wiley & Sons, Inc (Apr 15, 1985);

Page 78, note 12, at end of note add:

See also Scott, *Warranty of Title: The "Other" U.C.C. Warranty,* 8 The Scott Rep 7 (1985).

§3.08   Computer Contract Problems

Page 80, note 29, at end of note add:

See also *Checklist—Acquisition Contracts for Computer Systems,* 1 Computer Law Monitor 16 (1983).

§3.09   General Contract Provisions and Commercial Computer Contracts—Warranties

Page 80, note 30, change the UCC reference to:
UCC 2-312(1)(a).

Page 80, note 30, at end of note add:

For a thorough discussion, see Gross, *Computer Sales and Leases: Breach of Warranty, Misrepresentation, Failure of Consideration as Defense or Ground for Affirmative Relief,* 37 ALR 4 110 (1985); Scott, *Warranty of Title: The "Other" U.C.C. Warranty,* 8 The Scott Rep 7 (1985).

Page 81, note 33 at end of note add:

; for a thorough discussion of computer products warranties with reference to both federal and state law, see Rice, *Computer Products and the Federal Warranty Act,* 1 The Computer Law 8, (Sept 1984); for a discussion of the challenges involved in drafting an effective disclosure of warranty under the UCC and the issues in turn faced by the buyer under such a contractual disclaimer, see Joseph, *Computer Contract Challenges,* 6 Computer/Law Journal 379 (1985); for a discussion of possible trends in microcomputer hardware warranties, see Swartz, *Paving the Way for Buyer Protection,* Business Computer Sys 26 (Oct 1984).

Page 81, note 34, at end of note add:

For a discussion of the applicability of the warranty of merchantability to computer software contracts, which concludes that UCC 2-314 should not apply to such sales, see Durney, *The Warranty of Merchantability and Computer Software Contracts: A Square Peg in a Round Hole,* 59 Wash L Rev 511 (1984).

Page 81, note 39, at end of note add:

Any subsequent purchaser (buyer of used equipment) will generally be bound by the limited warranty disclaimers and damage exclusions contained in the original sales contracts even though he or she was not a party to those contracts. *See* Datamatic Inc v International Business Machs Corp, 613 F Supp 715 (1985).

Two state legislatures have struggled with bills to prohibit vendors and manufacturers from disclaiming, modifying, and limiting their warranties in an arbitrary manner. Bill 5091 in New York is virtually dead. However, in California Bill 1507 has passed the Assembly and is presently being considered by the Senate. *See California Computer Warranty Bill Awaiting Senate Vote; New York Computer Warranty Bill to Go Back to Committee,* 2 The Computer Law 31 (Aug 1985).

Page 82, note 41, at end of note add:

See also AMF, Inc v Computer Automation, Inc, 573 F Supp 924 (SD Ohio 1983), where the district court stated that the test utilized under UCC 2-316 is not dispositive, particularly in non-form contracts. The court noted that the trend was to determine if the bargaining strength and commercial sophistication of the parties made it reasonable to assume that the limiting language was brought to the attention of the parties. 573 F Supp at 929.

Page 82, note 42, at end of note add:

See also AMF, Inc v Computer Automation, Inc, 573 F Supp 924, 930 (SD Ohio 1983). The Ninth Circuit recently issued an opinion, RRX Indus, Inc v Lab-Con Inc, 772 F2d 543 (9th Cir 1985), where a breach of contract suit involving defects in software was upheld. The limitation of remedies provision failed of its essential purpose and thus an award of consequential damages was upheld. The Computer Law, May 1986, at 196.

Page 82, note 43, at end of note add:

See also Consolidated Data Terminals v Applied Digital Data Syss, 708 F2d 385 (9th Cir 1983), where baud rate specifications for a terminal screen were ruled to prevail over a general disclaimer of warranty liability. *Id* 391.

Page 83, note 47, at end of note add:

See also Barnhart v Dollar Rent A Car Syss, Inc, 595 F2d 914 (3d Cir 1979) (following *Carl Beasly Ford*); Binks Mfg Co v National Presto Indus, 709 F2d 1109 (7th Cir 1983) (following *IBM v Catamore*); and Mostels Corp v Chemetron Corp, 642 SW2d 20 (Tex 1982) (referring to *WR Weaver* in upholding the parties' agreement to limit a warranty).

§3.10 —Other Contract Clauses

Page 84, note 50, at end of note add:

The difficulty of this situation is created by the fact that the vendor wants to minimize the vendee's access to the source code, and retain exclusive possession of the source code to preserve trade secret protection. At the same time, the vendee prefers to have possession of the source code, or at least maximize its access to it. In order to provide both parties with the fullest possible protection, three distinct contracts are strongly suggested: (1) an object code license agreement; (2) a source code escrow agreement; (3) and a maintenance agreement.

Each of the three contracts must be supported by separate consideration. Separate consideration reduces the possibility of having the entire set of contracts voided in a bankruptcy proceeding of either the vendor or vendee because one of the contracts (or a part of one) may be executory in nature. A trustee appointed under a bankruptcy proceeding has the power to reject any executory contract of the debtor. The policy behind permitting the trustee in bankruptcy to reject a contract is to relieve the debtor's estate of ongoing burdens. In order to prevent the only copy of the source code from becoming part of the bankrupt estate of the vendor, the escrow agreement must relieve the vendor of as many of its rights in the source code as possible prior to its filing a bankruptcy petition. Transfers out of escrow of any assets which are conditioned on the insolvency or financial condition of the debtor will not be upheld. The escrow provision should be tied to some event distinguishable from bankruptcy, such as the vendor's failure to maintain the software.

See also Gilburne, *The Use of Escrows for Source Code and Technical Design Specifications in OEM Transactions,* 1 Computer Law 1 (1984); Lewis, *A Custody Agreement for a Computer Source Code (with Form),* 29 Prac Law 59 (1983).

Page 85, note 53, at end of note add:

See also Kane, *Response Time Warranties in Computer System Acquisition,* 1 Computer Law 40 (1984).

Page 85, note 54, at end of note add:

See also AMF, Inc v Computer Automation, Inc, 573 F Supp 924, 932 (SD Ohio 1983).

Page 85, text, at end of section add:

A forum selection clause should also be included in the computer contract whenever the parties are located in different states and foreign jurisdictions. In determining the reasonableness of the forum selection clause, most courts will consider the following factors: (1) the identity of the law which governs the construction of the contract; (2) the place of execution of the contract(s); (3) the place where the transactions have been or are to be performed; (4) the availability of remedies in the designated forum; (5) the public policy of the initial forum state; (6) the location of the parties, the convenience of prospective witnesses, and the accessibility of evidence; (7) the relative bargaining power of the parties and the circumstances surrounding their dealings; (8) the presence or absence of fraud, undue influence, or other extenuating circumstances; and (9) the conduct of the parties. *D'Antuono v CCH Computax Systems, Inc,* 570 F Supp 708, 712 (DRI 1983). *See also Horning v Sycom,* 556 F Supp 819 (ED Kan 1983).

Companies whose business activities bring them within the accounting and recordkeeping requirements of the Foreign Corrupt Practices Act of 1977, 15 USC §78m(b)(2), (d), dd-1, dd-2, and ff(c) (1982), (FCPA), should bear those requirements in mind when designing computing facilities and negotiating contracts for hardware and software. Considering the severity of the penalties provided for in FCPA, it would be worthwhile for the relevant acquisition group of such companies to involve personnel familiar with accounting accuracy requirements of the Act. For further discussion, see Scott, *Computers and the Foreign Corrupt Practices Act,* The Scott Rep (Jan 1985).

§3.11 Marketers/Developers Software Contracts

Page 87, note 58, at end of note add:

See also P. Hoffman, Software Contract Forms (1984); Hoffman, *Software Development and Services Agreements,* 24 Jurimetrics 58 (1983).

Page 88, note 60, at end of note add:

See also Hansen, Jr, *Software Distribution, Remarketing and Publishing Agreements,* 4 Computer LJ 625 (1984).

Page 88, text, at end of second full paragraph add:

See Davidson, *Constructing OEM Nondisclosure Agreements,* 24 Jurimetrics 127 (1984).

Page 89, text, at end of section add:

Due to the high demand and short supply of the highly specialized skills of computer programmers and systems analysts, the software marketer/developer must be careful in its employee agreements to maintain adequate program development confidentiality, and at the same time offer its employees an attractive employment agreement. See McCoy, *Attracting and Retaining Key Employees in the Computer Industry: An Analysis of Various Strategies—pt I,* 1 Computer Law 1 (1984); McCoy, *Attracting and Retaining Key Employees in the Computer Industry: An Analysis of Various Strategies—pt II,* 1 Computer Law 14 (1984).

Given the dramatic increase in the size of the software developer industry sector, an additional concern for the software developer is adequate financing. The financing of the software developer generally influences the types of contracts a software developer will be willing to enter. See Halloran, *Venture Capital and Public Offering Negotiation,* 5 Computer L Inst, Univ S Cal pt XIII XIII-1 *et seq* (1984).

§3.12   Contracts for Mass Marketing of Software

Page 91, note 66, at end of note add:

For an example of a legislative approach to the enforcement of shrink-wrapped license agreements, *see* La Rev Stat Ann §15:1961-66 (West 1984).

See also Computer Law Institute, Course Handbook Series Number 191, at 597 *et seq,* for a discussion of special problems involving software warranties and indemnities for mass distributed software.

Page 91, text, at end of section add:

Some computer clubs are now "renting" popular mass market software programs at 20-40 per cent of the purchase price. A disclaimer that copying the rented software is a copyright violation is typically noted in a conspicuous manner. An additional clause in the mass market software contract, beneficial to the developer/distributor, should be to the effect that the consumer/licensee agrees not to "rent" the software to anyone. This provision would at least be a deterrent to legitimate clubs who might otherwise be tempted to participate in this quasi-illegal activity.

Given the rapid development of local area networks (LANs) for microcomputers using mass-marketed software, an additional clause to include in the mass market software contract should be to limit the application software to one user at a time. See generally Hollman, *Emerging Issues in Software License Agreements,* 5 Computer L Inst, Univ S Cal L Center pt IX IX-1 *et seq* (1984).

§3.14   Custom Development of Software

Page 94, note 83, at end of note add:

See also Gordon & Starr, *Emerging Issues in Computer Procurements*, VI Computer/LJ 119-42 (Summer 1985) for a review of the advances made by vendors in contracting for the distribution of new technology.

Page 95, note 87, at end of note add:

See generally Lentz, *Contracting for Performance in the Procurement of Custom Computer Software*, 13 Golden Gate UL Rev 461 (1983); Kriendler, *Contracting for the Development of Customized Software*, 12 The Scott Rep 1 (1985).

§3.15   Time Sharing and Service Bureau Contracts

Page 96, note 88, at end of note add:

See Grogan, *Negotiating and Drafting Service Bureau Contracts*, 11 The Computer Law 11 (Dec 1984).

Page 96, note 89, at end of note add:

See also *Checklist—Service Bureau Contracts*, 1 Computer L Monitor 32 (1983).

Additional Legal Concerns

§3.16   Computer Tort Theory

Page 98, note 90, at end of note add:

See generally Walker, *Computer and High Technology Product Liability in the 1980's*, The Forum, Tort and Insurance Practice Section, ABA Vol 19 No 4, (Summer 1984). *See* Page Co Appliance Center, Inc v Honeywell, Inc, 347 NW2d 171 (Iowa 1984) remanding the code and reversing judgment for appliance store which sued computer manufacturer for damages arising out of alleged radiation from computer interfering with appliance store's television reception and thus sales.

A computer malfunction apparently triggered excessive radiation doses to two cancer patients after the operator of the machine entered an erroneous command and then corrected it. See *Fatal Dose Given*, Denver Post, June 21, 1986, at 8A, col 1.

§3.17 —Vendor-User Conflicts

Page 98, note 92, at end of note add:

; Gemignani, *Overview of the Legal Aspects of Computer Related Failures,* 8 Rutgers Computer & Tech LJ 173 (1981) (product liability and software); Hafif, *Breach of Contract, Tort, or Both?,* 21 Trial 39-42 (1985) (an overview of the various damages which have been awarded plaintiff in a computer contract dispute based on Micro/Vest Corp v Computer-Land Corp, 198 Cal Rptr 404 (1985)); RRX Indus v Lab-Con, 772 F2d 543 (9th Cir 1985) (on appeal the Ninth Circuit rendered its decision in this case and, in effect, created a type of strict liability for vendors with licenses permitted to recover all damages suffered as a result of defective software, regardless of the terms of the contract or the intent of the parties); Gesmer, Choate, Hall & Stewart, *Proving Damages in Computer Vendor User Litigation,* V The Computer Law 10-13 (Dec 1985); Scott, *Ninth Circuit Decision May Have a Major Impact On Software Contracts,* 12 The Scott Rep 12ff (Sept 1985): Scott, *EEC Adopts Strict Product Liability Law,* V The Scott Rep 11ff (Nov 1985); Brocklesby v USA, 753 F2d 794 (9th Cir 1985). (California's strict liability law).

§3.18 —Fraud and Misrepresentation

Page 98, note 93, delete text and substitute:

See Zammit, *Contracting For Computer Products,* 22 Jurimetrics J 337, 352 (1982); Schachter, *Tort Theories in Computer Litigation,* 38 The Record 431-32 (1983), an excellent overview of misrepresentation as a theory for recovery in computer contract disputes.

Page 100, text, at end of section add:

It has been suggested by some commentators that disgruntled computer purchasers who cannot prove misrepresentation, and, therefore, have to rely on breach of warranty claims (which often lead to discouraging results), might also be able to turn to the doctrine of unconscionability. *See contra,* Himelson, *Frankly, Incredible: Unconscionability in Computer Contracts,* 4 Computer LJ 695 (1984).

§3.19 Negligence

Page 101, note 105, at end of note add:

See also Ales-Peratis Foods Intl, Inc v American Can Co, 164 Cal App 3d 277, 209 Cal Rptr 917 (1985). The plaintiff was not in privity with the manufacturer and did not incur physical injury or property damage. The court of appeals held that commercial consumer can recover from the manufacturer for solely economic loss caused by negligently manufactured products.

§3.20   Computer Malpractice

Page 101, note 107, at end of note add:

See also Galler, *Contracting Problems in the Computer Industry: Should Computer Specialists be Subjected to Malpractice Liability?*, 50 Ins Counsel J 574 (1983).

§3.22   Arbitration in the Computer Contracting Context

Page 104, note 125, at end of note add:

See generally Friedman, Using Alternative Dispute Resolution to Settle Computer Disputes (American Arbitration Association 1984); ADAPSO, An Adapso program for the Computer Software and Services Industry (available from ADAPSO, 1300 N. 17th Street, Suite 300, Arlington, VA 2209).

§3.24   —The Burroughs Model Clause and the American Arbitration Association Clause

Page 105, note 127, delete text within parenthesis and insert:

as amended and adopted April 1, 1985

Page 105, text, after the STANDARD ARBITRATION CLAUSE, add:

The American Arbitration Association has initiated a Computer Dispute Advisory Committee with the guidance of computer industry members to develop its role in resolving computer related controversies. The Association of Data Processing Services Organizations (ADPSO) has recently published an Alternative Dispute Resolution (ADR) program to provide industry-specific information and procedures to improve ways in which debates are resolved in the computer software and services industry. ADPSO suggests the following ADR contractual provisions:

SEQUENTIAL SETTLEMENT

The parties shall seek to resolve any controversy between them, first, by negotiating with each other in good faith; next, if negotiation is unsuccessful, by mediating in good faith; next, if mediation is unsuccessful, by employing a mini-trial procedure in good faith; and finally, if the mini-trial procedure is unsuccessful, by arbitration provision of this agreement.

NOTE: The above should be modified to meet the needs of the situation. Any one or more of the steps may be omitted; rarely if ever would all be appropriate. Time limits may be stated for each phase. Preference may be made to specific outside persons or individuals to serve as mediator, arbitrator or mini-trial advisor. The agreement may be limited to specific kinds of controversy, or to a single, specific, preexisting controversy.

ARBITRATION

For the submission of future disputes to arbitration:

Any controversy or claim arising out of or relating to this contract, or the breach thereof, shall be settled by arbitration. (Specify location if desired.) Each party shall select one arbitrator, and the two thus selected shall select a third who shall serve as chair. The decision of the three arbitrators shall be by majority vote. Judgment upon their award may be entered in any court having jurisdiction thereof.

For the submission of existing disputes to arbitration:

We, the undersigned parties, hereby agree to submit to arbitration the controversy described in the attached memorandum. We further agree that each of us shall select one arbitrator, and the two so selected shall select a third who shall serve as chair. The decision of the three arbitrators shall be by majority vote. We further agree that we will faithfully observe this agreement and that we will abide by and perform any award rendered by the arbitrators and that a judgment of the court having jurisdiction may be entered upon the award.

Alternative Dispute Resolution, a publication of the ADPSO Committee on Alternative Dispute Resolution, at 8.

ADPSO further suggests the following special provisions to define the parameters of the arbitration agreement

In applying its rules, (insert name of administering organization) shall make reasonable efforts to:

a) include on its arbitration panel an arbitrator or arbitrators with appropriate specialized expertise; and

b) bring the proceedings to final conclusion as promptly as consistent with its proper outcome, irrespective even of delays to which counsel for the parties may consent; and

c) limit the costs, expenses and other burdens of the proceedings to the maximum reasonable extent.

Alternative Dispute Resolution, a publication of the ADPSO Committee on Alternative Dispute Resolution, at 9.

Page 105, note 131, at end of note add:

See also Bernacchi & Kruth, *Checklist Vital for Arbitration Clauses,* 1 Computer L Strategist 7 (1984).

§3.25 —Procedures and Practice

Page 106, note 132, at end of note add:

CAR §7 now requires that three copies of the demand be filed.

Page 106, note 135, first line, delete "clerk" and substitute:

administrator

Page 106, note 139, at end of note add:

In addition, CAR §29 (1973) (Order of Proceedings) provides guidelines for the arbitrator to follow during a hearing.

Page 107, note 142, at end of second sentence add:

Rule 10 of the CAR addresses the concerns of the absence of discovery in the arbitration process by allowing for a prehearing conference.

§3.27 —Arbitration versus Litigation

Page 108, note 152, add:

Friedman, *Sue or Settle: What to Do When Your Client's Computer Doesn't Work,* 1 The Computer Law 10 (Nov 1984).

Pages 108-109, note 153, at end of note add:

As of February, 1984, the American Arbitration Association provides new Expedited Rules, wherein an award is issued five days after the hearings are closed for disputes of $15,000 and under.

Page 109, note 155, at end of note add:

This disadvantage can, however, be overcome by screening prospective arbitrators with certain questions agreeable to both parties.

Taxation

§3.28   Introduction

Page 110, note 158, add:

See also McCoy, *Unitary Taxation: A Primer for the Expanding Technology Company,* 1 The Computer Law 10 (Nov 1984); Callison, *Tax Aspects of Computer Software Development,* 13 Colo Law No 6 (June 1984); Maloof, *Tax Treatment of Sale of Software,* 2 The Computer Law 3 (Mar 1983); *High Technology and the Tax Reform Act of 1984,* Computer L Inst, Course Handbook Series No 191, at 9 (1984); Osborne, *Going to Market: Tax Considerations for Inventors and Programmers in the Computer Industry,* 67 J Pat & Trademark Off Socy 149-59 (March 1985); for a discussion of the tax consequences of computer hardware and software purchases, see Malone, *Computer Hardware and Software Purchasing: Tax Implications,* 2 Akron Tax J 119-29 (1984).

Page 110, note 159, at end of note add:

Also see generally Adam, Gordon & Starr, *Contractual, Financial, and Tax Issues in Major Procurements,* 4 Computer LJ 465 (1984); Rabinovitz & Whalen, *Selected Problems in Taxation of Computer Software,* 4 Computer LJ 605 (1984); Markey III, *State and Federal Taxation of Computer Software: A Functional Approach,* 4 Computer LJ 737 (1984); DiBernardo, *The Taxation of High Technology,* 61 Taxes 813 (1983). See also Note, *IRS Private Letter Rules Software Company Subject to Personal Holding Company Tax Although Engaged in Business,* 2 The Computer Law 2 (Feb 1985).

§3.29   Federal Tax Considerations

Page 110, note 160, at end of note add:

Congress is at present struggling with President Reagan's "Treasury II" proposal submitted on May 29, 1985. If Treasury II is enacted into law without substantial change, the ITC would be eliminated. See Berwind, *The President's Tax Reform Proposals: Their Impact on High Technology Firms,* 2 The Computer Law 1-5 (July 1985) for insight into possible changes in taxation in this area.

Page 111, note 161, at end of note add:

McGee, *Computer Software and the Investment Tax Credit,* 5 Computer/LJ 3 (Winter 1985).

Page 112, note 172, at end of note add:

See also Rogers, *Wrap Leases,* 5 Computer L Inst, Univ S Cal L Center pt XX-1 *et seq* (1984); Ruidl, *Investment Credit and Related Party Leases: The Impact of the Peterson Case,* 61 Taxes 238 (1983).

Page 112, note 173, at end of note add:

For a general dicussion of the R&D tax credit, see McGee, *Computer Software and the Research Credit,* 5 Computer/LJ 3 (Winter 1985).

Page 113, note 177, at end of note add:

See also Beach, *Capital Gain Treatment of a Sale of Computer Software by a Research and Development Limited Partnership,* 68 Cornell L Rev 554 (1983); Wasserman, *Section 174 and Computer Software Development,* 61 Taxes 813 (1983).

§3.30 State and Local Taxation

Page 113, note 179, at end of note add:

See also Cowdrey, *Software and Sales Taxes: The Illusory Intangible,* 63 BUL Rev 181 (1983); Stohlgren, *The Nature and Taxability of Computer Software,* 22 Washburn LJ 103 (1982).

Page 113, note 180, at end of note add:

See also Comptroller of Treasury v Equitable Trust Co, 296 Md 459, 464 A2d 248 (Md 1983); Chittenden Trust Co v King, 465 A2d 1000 (Vt 1983), wherein computer programs on magnetic tape were deemed tangible personal property subject to Maryland sales tax and Vermont compensating use tax, respectively.

See generally Fitzgerald, Jr. *Imposition of Sales/Use Tax on Computer Software,* 39 J Mo B 291 (1983). See *How the States Tax Sales of Computer Software,* 45 C.C.H. State Tax Rev 44 (Oct 30, 1984); see also Computer Law Institute, *State Taxation of Computer Software and Services,* Course Handbook Series No 191, at 263 (1984).

§3.34 Introduction

Page 116, note 187, at end of note add:

For a discussion of the different approaches to valuation of databases, see Lipton, *How Much is Your Data Worth,* Business Computer Sys (Aug 1984); *see also* Friedman, *Customized Policies for Micro Protection,* Micro Manager 18 (July 1984).

Negotiating Strategies

§3.43   Other Negotiating Concerns

Page 128, note 218, at end of note add:

See also L Davis, D Allen, T Bowman & J Armstrong, A User's Guide to Computer Contracting: Forms, Techniques and Strategies (1984); R Raysman & P Brown, Computer Law: Drafting and Negotiating Forms and Agreements (1984); J Auer & C.E. Harris, Computer Contract Negotiations (1981).

Antitrust Considerations in the Computer Industry

4

§4.01 Generally

Page 130, note 1, at end of note add:

See, e.g., Trade Reg Rep (CCH), No 580 (Feb 7, 1983) (Computer Chip Testing Equipment Meter Challenged by FTC). See also Trade Reg Rep (CCH), No 614 (Sept 19, 1983) (Text of National Productivity and Innovation Act of 1983, HR 3878); Trade Reg Rep (CCH), No 617 (1983) (Remarks by William F. Baxter, Assistant Attorney General in charge of the Antitrust Division delivered before the Town Hall of California, October 1983, concerning the Reagan administration's legislative proposal to improve the legal climate for private sector research and development, by enacting the National Productivity & Innovation Act of 1983. Baxter commented that the bill deals with incentives for all types of R&D and seeks to improve the ability of the owners of technology to develop and fully disseminate their technology after it is created.)

Several computer companies have formed joint research and development (R&D) efforts. See McCracken, *Antitrust Issues in Structuring Joint R & D Ventures*, 5 Computer L Inst, Univ S Cal L Center pt VI VI-1 *et seq* (1984). Joint ventures among major competitors are becoming increasingly popular. A good example of a narrow joint venture is the General Motors-Toyota joint venture. Weinbaum, *Antitrust Problems In Conducting the Joint Venture's Business Activities*, 54 Antitrust L J 3, Nov 1985, at 999-1001. Joint ventures may be useful in the computer industry; however, antitrust issues will always be present. See also Davidow, *Special Antitrust Issues Raised By International Joint Ventures*, 54 Antitrust L J 3, Nov 1985, at 1031-1038. See generally Pitofsky, *A Framework For Antitrust Analysis of Joint Ventures*, 54 Antitrust L J 3, Nov 1985, at 893-914. See also Jacobson, *U.S. and Japan Cooperating in High Technology Research and Development*, 2 The Computer Law 7, July 1985, at 6. See also 5 Trade Reg Rep (CCH) ¶50447 (May 23, 1983) (remarks before the National Association of Manufacturers in Washington, DC on May 10, 1983, by William F. Baxter, Assistant Attorney General, Antitrust Division. Mr. Baxter discussed the effects of United States antitrust laws on competition in the world economy, particularly with regard to joint ventures for research and development, technology licensing, misuse of intellectual property, and enforcement differences between product and process patents); Trade Reg Rep (CCH), No 649 (May 16, 1984) (text of report by Senate Committee on the Judiciary on S 1841, The National Productivity and Innovation Act, Report 98-427); Reback, *Antitrust Issues in Pricing Computer Software*, 5 Computer L Inst, Univ S Cal L Center pt V V-1 *et seq* (1984). Kump, *Litigation Between Competitors: Antitrust and Tort Liability for Sham Litigation*, 1 The Computer Law 7, Aug 1984, at 9-16 (discussing especially the application of the Noerr-Pennington Doctrine); Whalley, *The National Cooperative Research Act of 1984*, 23 Antitrust L 3, Feb 1985, Illinois State Bar Association Center, at 1-2+ (basic discussion of applicability of new Act and its effects); CCH Trade Regulation Reports-Number 686, *Joint Research Venture Notices*, at 5 (outline of first three joint venture research notices under Act of 1984, one covering hardware research, another regarding software); Katsh, *Congress Reduces Antitrust Roadblocks for Basic and Applied R & D Joint Ventures*, 2 The Computer Law 1, Jan 1985, at 32-38 (discussing the uses and advantages of the Act of 1984); CCH Trade Regulation Reports-697, *Cooperative Research*, at 10. (outlining joint effort between Bell Communications and Honeywell on gallium arsenide integrated circuits-IC's).

For recent developments in the computer industry concerning antitrust issues, see Leback, *Antitrust Developments Affecting the Computer Industry: Course Handbook Series Number 209*, Computer L Inst, 1985, Practising Law Inst #G4-3775, at 769.

Page 130, note 2, at end of note add:

The Justice Department's new guidelines give a "green light" to exclusive dealing and tying arrangements. See Ryan & Schnitz, *The Justice Department's Guidelines on Vertical Restraints*, 74 Ill Bar J 2, 66-73 (Oct 1985). See also McCracken, Gibson, Dunn & Crutcher, *The Vertical Restraints Guidelines: Theoretical Purpose and Practical Effects*, 2 The Computer Law 8, 10-12 (Aug 1985) (an analysis of vertical restraints).

Page 132, note 11, at end of note; add:

See generally, Brooks, *Patents, Copyrights, Trademarks, and Literary Property: Course Handbook Series Number 191*, Computer L Inst, 1984, Practising L Inst #G4-3758, at 702-04 (discussing antitrust issues in computer cases).

Mainframes

§4.03 *United States v IBM*

Page 135, note 32, at end of note add:

For a discussion of the government's economic analysis by one of IBM's expert economic witnesses, Franklin M. Fisher, see F. Fisher, J. McGowan, & J. Greenwood, Folded, Spindled, and Mutilated: Economic Analysis and *US v IBM* (1983).

§4.04 Private Suits Filed Against IBM

Page 141, text, at end of section add:

Hollander, *Antitrust-Tying Sale of "Initial Loading" Program to Sale of "Dump-Restore" Program*, 2 The Computer L Monitor 2, Nov 1984, at 81-83 (discussing *Innovation Data Processing v. IBM*).

§4.06 Predatory Pricing

Page 146, note 89, at end of note add:

IBM recently joined the new United States Corporation for Open Systems. The Open Systems will oversee standardization of networking equipment. It remains to be seen if such standardization will lead to less competition and increased antitrust violations. Computergram International, London, No 369, Feb 10, 1986, at 1, col 1.

Page 146, text, at end of section add:

The issue before the Ninth Circuit Court of Appeals was whether the pricing policy of the dominant manufacturer in an industry is conclusively presumed to be nonpredatory and legal under the Sherman Act when products are priced above average total cost. The court held that where a dominant manufacturer prices its products above average total cost, such prices are not conclusively presumed nonpredatory. If the challenged prices exceed average total cost, however, the plaintiff must prove by clear and convincing evidence that the defendant's pricing policy was predatory. *Transamerica Computer Co, Inc v International Business Machines Corp*, 481 F Supp 965 (ND Cal 1979), *affd*, 698 F2d 1377 (9th Cir 1983), *cert denied*, 104 S Ct 370 (1983).

American computer manufacturers sued Japanese electronic manufacturers for conspiracy to maintain artificially high prices in Japan while maintaining low prices for products exported to the United States. The United States Supreme Court held that American manufacturers could not recover antitrust damages against the Japanese because the American stood to gain addtional profits from the low prices. The case was reversed and remanded. *Matsushita Electric Industrial Co, Ltd v Zenith Radio Corp*, 106 S Ct 1348 (1986).

§4.08 Consent Decree

Page 148, text, at end of section add:

IBM has recently requested that the United States Department of Justice, Antitrust Division, jointly petition with IBM to have its 1956 consent decree vacated. To date, no action has been taken by the Antitrust Division.

§4.09 Bundling

Page 149, note 100, at end of note add:

Digidyne Corp v Data Gen Corp, 734 F2d 1336 (9th Cir 1984), *cert denied*, 105 S Ct 3534 (July 1, 1985). See Kayne, *Date General v Digidyne Corp: Tying the Hands of the Computer Industry*, 4 Comp L Rep 1, July 1985, at 1 (a discussion of the *Data General* case and its implications). See also Helein, *Software Lock-in and Antitrust Tying Arrangements: The Lessons of Data General*, 5 Computer L J 329-45 (Winter 1985) (general analysis of the *Data General* tying arrangements).

Page 150, text, at end of section add:

Another antitrust case involving bundling is: *Advisory Information & Management Systems v Prime Computer*, 1984-2 Trade Cas (CCH) ¶ 66,237 (ND Tenn 1984). See Gilburne, *Manufacturer's Ban on "Hardware-Only" Sales Did Not Constitute Per Se Illegal Price Fixing*, 2 The Computer Law 1, Jan 1985, at 40-41 (discussing the *Prime Computer* case); and Harlow, *Trade Secret Policy vs. Antitrust Policy: Four Lessons from the Tension*, I Trade Secret L Rep 1, May 1985, at 18-23 (discussing the application and effect of the Data General litigation on trade secret versus antitrust decisions).

§4.10 Miscellaneous Antitrust Actions

Page 150, note 105, at end of note add:

See also Hollander, *Antitrust-Tying Sale of "Operating System" Program to Sale of Central Processing Unit (CPU)*, 2 The Computer L Monitor 2, Nov 1984, at 83-84 (discussing the *Data General* case after the Court of Appeals decision); Johnston, *Product Bundling Faces Increased Specter of*

Illegality Under the Antitrust Laws, 1 The Computer Law 8, Sept 1984, at 1-13 (discussing the *Data General* case after the appellate decision).

Page 151, note 107, at end of note add:

For a different approach to monopolization *see* Computer Identics Corp v Southern Pac Co, 756 F2d 200 (1st Cir 1985) (appeals court affirmed trial court decision, dismissing an action for conspiracy to restrain trade in the computerized railroad control industry).

Microcomputers

§4.11   Present Antitrust Involvement

Page 152, note 110, at end of note add:

For an in-depth analysis of foreign competition in the microcomputer industry see Gerla, *Competition On the Merits-A Sound Industrial Policy For Antitrust Law*, XXXVI U Fla L Rev 553 (1984).

§4.12   Potential Antitrust Involvement

Page 154, note 123, at end of note add:

See Lavey, *Antitrust Issues Critical to Structuring Vertical Channels of Distribution for Computer Businesses*, Computer L Inst, Legal Times/ Harcourt Brace Jovanovich 562 (1983). See also Flumenbaum & Pfeffer, *Advanced Antitrust Issues in Computer Distribution to the Mass and Other Markets*, Computer L Inst, Legal Times/Harcourt Brace Jovanovich, 687 (1983); Eisenstat, *Structuring Distributor And Dealer Agreements For Distribution of Computer Hardware*, 4 Computer L Inst, Univ S Cal L Center pt XII XII-1 *et seq* (1983); Lavey, *Pricing And Other Selected Antitrust Issues Critical To Structuring Vertical Channels Of Distribution*, 4 Computer L Inst, Univ S Cal L Center pt XV XV-1 *et seq* (1983).

Another critical antitrust concern is distributor terminations. A manufacturer may have legitimate business reasons for terminating a distributor, but a dealer termination may be a Sherman Act §1 violation if the termination results from concerted action of the manufacturer and other distributors. A manufacturer has a general right to deal, or refuse to deal, with whomever it pleases, but it must do so independently. In distributor terminations, the issue is whether the concerted action was designed to fix prices (judged per se illegal), or was designed as nonprice restrictions (judged under the rule of reason). The test for distinguishing concerted action on nonprice restrictions from price-fixing agreements was most recently articulated in Monsanto Co v Spray-Rite Serv Corp, 104 S Ct 1464 (1984). Monsanto refused

to renew respondent's distributorship term. Spray-Rite brought a
Sherman Act §1 action alleging that Monsanto and some of its
distributors conspired to fix the resale prices of Spray-Rite products
and that Monsanto had terminated Spray-Rite's distributorship in
furtherance of the conspiracy. At trial, the jury found that the
distributorship termination was pursuant to a price-fixing conspiracy
between Monsanto and one or more of its distributors. Monsanto's
conduct was therefore per se illegal.

The Seventh Circuit Court of Appeals affirmed the trial court at 684
F2d 1226 (1982). The court held that proof of termination following
competitor complaints was sufficient to support an inference of
concerted action. The Seventh Circuit also held that an antitrust
plaintiff can survive a directed verdict motion by showing that the
manufacturer terminated a price-cutting distributor in response to, or
following complaints by, other distributors. The Supreme Court,
however, rejected the appellate court's standard of proof required to
submit the case to a jury in distributor termination litigation, but
affirmed the judgment under a new test enunciated by the Court. The
Supreme Court standard is that there must be direct or circumstantial
evidence that reasonably tends to prove that the manufacturer and
others had a conscious commitment to a common scheme designed to
achieve an unlawful objective. *Monsanto*, 104 S Ct 1464 (1984). The
Court stated that there was sufficient evidence for the jury to conclude
that petitioner and some of its distributors conspired to maintain resale
prices and that Spray-Rite's termination was part of, or pursuant to,
the conspiracy. *Id* at 10-11. Monsanto was therefore guilty of violating
§1 of the Sherman Act.

Vertical dealer distribution agreements, therefore, may contain
nonprice vertical constraints, but may not contain vertical price
constraints. Typical vertical nonprice constraints can generally be
classified in the following categories: (1) marketing approach and
style; (2) personnel numbers and training; (3) required product inventory; (4) service capacity and spare parts inventory; and (5) customer
geography and type of restrictions. A consent decree has been signed
regarding unfair trading practices by one microcomputer manufacturer. See *In re* Commodore Business Mach Inc, File No 832-3191
(Aug 3, 1984); and Gilburne, *Trade Practices—Commodore Agrees Not to
Advertise Products of Products' Capabilities Unless They Exist at Time*, 1 The
Computer Law 7, Aug 1984, at 29-30 (discussing the Commodore
consent decree).

Page 154, text, at end of section add:

The Racketeer Influenced and Corrupt Organizations Act (RICO),
18 USC §§1961-1968, has been actively discussed as a supplement to
a civil antitrust claim, where the plaintiff can allege that the defendant
has violated at least two federal laws in the past 10 years. Although

there have been few successful civil RICO cases, if successful, a plaintiff under RICO will receive treble damages. See Schwab, *Misappropriation of Trade Secrets as a RICO Claim*, 5 Computer L Inst, Univ S Cal L Center pt III (1984).

Given the current administration's attitude of deregulation, one potential area of antitrust involvement may be state antitrust laws as typified by *Pima County v Digital Equipment Corp*, (C538594)(Maracopa Dist Ct 1985); and *Arizona v Digital Equipment Corp*, (C538593) (Maracopa Dist Ct 1985).

§4.13 —Claims of Illegal Tie-Ins

Page 155, note 127, at end of note add:

See Steinberg, *Antitrust Litigation with Competitors: Tying and Horizontal Restraints*, 17 Computer Litigation Resolving Computer Related Disputes and Protecting Proprietary Rights 725 (1983). Joseph, *Tie-Ins and Exclusive Dealing in the Distribution and Franchising Arenas: Emerging Issues and Principles After Hyde*, Panel discussion hosted by the 33rd Annual Antitrust Spring Meeting Section of Antitrust Law of the American Bar Association (Mar 21, 1985) (panel discussion regarding the impact of the *Jefferson Parish* decision on antitrust law and computer issues).

For a look at antitrust tying principles in the highly competitive area of computer software marketing and sales see Webb, *The Application of Antitrust Tying Principles to Computer Software Distribution*, The Scott Rep July 1985, at 1-6. For an example of a court not finding a tying arrngement, *see* AI Root Co v Computer Dynamics Inc, 615 F Supp 727 (ND Ohio 1985) (Court held no per se tying existed and no evidence of group boycott was found).

Page 155, text, at end of section add:

The Ninth Circuit decision in the *Data General* case, *Digidyne Corp v Data General Corp*, 734 F2d 1336 (9th Cir 1984), *cert denied*, (July 1, 1985) [*Data General III*] sent a clear message to computer manufacturers: software may not be licensed on the condition that customers also purchase hardware from the manufacturer. However, the decision gave precious little guidance to manufacturers as to the prices that could be charged for various system components sold or licensed individually, when considered in light of the Supreme Court's recent decision regarding tie-in practices, *Jefferson Parish Hospital District No 2 v Hyde*, 104 S Ct 1551 (1984). This has prompted further questions in the area including:

1. the question of when components comprise separate products;
2. the presumption of market power arising from copyright
3. the prices which may be charged for bundled sets

The law of tying is in complete disarray and will probably not come into clear focus until the Supreme Court next considers a tie-in case. In the interim, *Data General III* presents practitioners and marketing executives with serious problems, the most severe of which is proper pricing of unbundled products. In this area, the cases are so inconsistent that companies may engage in aggressive pricing activities only at extreme risk. See the article by Reback, *Further Reflections on Data General and the Law of Pricing Unbundled Products*, 1 The Computer Law 10, Nov 1984, at 1-7 (outlining issues present in *Data General* decision at the Court of Appeals level). And note the continuing saga of IBM in court, *Innovation Data Processing, Inc v IBM Corp*, 585 F Supp 1470 (D NJ 1984). See also Young, *Consumer Preferences, Efficiency and Data General: The Implications of Jefferson Parish for the Joint Provision Of Computer Programs and Hardware*, 2 The Computer Law 6, June 1986, at 11.

§4.14 —Claims of Monopolization and Attempts to Monopolize

Page 155, note 129, at end of note add:

See Johnston & Kump, *Attempted Monopolization Claims in Litigation With Competitors*, 18 Computer Litigation Resolving Computer Related Disputes and Protecting Proprietary Rights 757 (1983).

Antitrust and Patents

§4.15 Patents in General

Page 157, note 135, at end of note add:

The "exclusive right" mentioned in the Constitution and embodied in the Patent Act is actually a theory of a negative right. It is the right to exclude others from making, using, or selling the patented invention. Competitors, however, are never totally excluded. Many times they can devise ways to perform substantially the same function as the invention without infringing the patent. The patent holder therefore realizes a limited negative monopoly over its invention. See 2 Hamburg, C1 1983-84 Patent Law Handbook 125 (1983). See also Reilly, *Impact of the New Patent and Trademark Fee Bill: What Hath Been Wrought?*, 65 J Pat Off Socy 166 (1983); Sobel, *The Antitrust Interface with Patents and Innovation: Acquisition of Patents, Improvement Patents and Grant-backs, Non-Use, Fraud on the Patent Office, Development of New Products and Joint Research*, National Institute on Industrial and Intellectual Property, 53 Antitrust LJ 681-712 (1984); Turner, *Basic Principles in Formulating Antitrust Constraints on the Exploitation of Intellectual Property Rights*, National Institute on Industrial and Intellectual Property, 53 Antitrust

LJ 3, at 485-502 (1984). For an annotated guide to software copyrights see Pearson & Toedt III, *An Annotated Guide to Establishing and Registering U.S. Computer Software Copyrights,* 3 The Computer Law 2, Feb 1986, at 22.

Page 157, note 137, at end of note add:

Burton, *Patents in the Antitrust Context,* Antitrust and the Patent Laws: Current Issues in Distribution, Litigation and Software Licensing Presented by The Antitrust and Trade Regulation Committee of the Colorado Bar Association Section on Corporation, Banking and Business Law and the Patent, Trademark and Copyright Section (Sept 27, 1984); Jones, *Antitrust and Patent Licensing Problems: Are the Nine "No-Nos" The Nine "Maybes"?,* 53 Okla BJ 1568 (1982); Lipsky, *Current A.T. Division Views on Patent Licensing Practices,* 50 Antitrust LJ 515, 518-19 (1982).

§4.16   Fraudulent Procurement and Enforcement

Page 158, note 140, at end of note add:

A patent infringement suit must meet the requirement of clear and convincing evidence concerning bad faith for a court to allow antitrust liability. Loctite Corp v Ultraseal Ltd, 781 F2d 861 (Fed Cir 1985). See generally Laurie, *The First Year's Experience Under the Chip Protection Act or "Where Are the Pirates Now That We Need Them?",* 3 The Computer Law 2, Feb 1986, at 11 (an analysis of the effectiveness of the Chip Protection Act).

Antitrust and Copyright

§4.19   Copyright in General

Page 160, note 152, at end of note add:

See also Bendekgey, *Trademark Rights in Computer Product Configurations: If It Looks Like a DEC and Feels Like a DEC, Does It Infringe a DEC,* 3 The Computer Law 3, Mar 1986, at 15; Cohen & Scarborough, *The Copyrightability of Computer Programs as Literary Works: Return to a Statutory Approach,* 3 The Computer Law 3, Mar 1986, at 25 (articles covering proprietary rights of computer hardware and software).

For an overview of computer clones and counterfeiters see generally Davis III, *Computer Software—The Final Frontier: Clones, Compatibility and Copyright,* 2 The Computer Law 7, July 1985, at 11; Phillipes, *Cracking Down on Copycats, Fighting Counterfeiters of Trademarked Products Has Recently Become Fashionable,* 5 Cal Law 15 (1985). See generally Conley

& Bryan, *A Unifying Theory for the Litigation of Computer Software Copyright Cases,* 63 NCL Rev 563-616 (Apr 1985). For a view of copyright protection litigation see Weber, *Copyright Law—The Extension of Copyright Protection to Computer Operating Programs* (case note, *Apple Computer Inc v Franklin Computer Corp),* 7 W New England L Rev 829-45 (Winter 1985).

§4.20   Refusal to Grant License

Page 161, note 153, at end of note add:

See also Milgram, *Antitrust Issues In Licensing Computer Technology,* 4 Computer L Inst, Univ So Cal L Center pt III III-1 *et seq* (1983). A related issue here is exclusive territorial license. Territorial provisions are not directly addressed in the Copyright Act. Copyright law, however, does permit a geographically exclusive license unless the territorial limitation in the copyright license is intended to broadly divide the market between the parties. In United States v Chicago Tribune-New York News Syndicate, Inc, 309 F Supp 1301 (1970), the court held that agreement between a defendant corporation and its newspaper customers to supply them with copyrighted features restrained trade. Defendant corporation agreed to not sell these features to other newspapers within a specified territory. The territorial restriction was found arbitrary and unreasonably broad, and therefore in restraint of trade. Vendor site licensing has become increasingly popular; however, each vendor's definition of a site license varies. See Vale & Harding, *Practical and Legal Issues Relating to the Marketing Of Microcomputer Software by Means of Site Licenses,* 2 The Computer Law, Aug 1985, at 1.

§4.22   Antitrust and Trade Secret (New)

The Data General litigation has created a whole litany of answers to long-asked antitrust questions. Included among the competing policy questions addressed by the litigation are at least four practical lessons in the relation of trade secret and antitrust policies.

First, a trade secret program that affects or excludes competition will not be saved by an argument of *only protecting our confidential information.* A number of cases have made clear the anticompetitive nature of lessor-imposed prohibitions against the lessee dealing in competing products. For example, *Krampe v Ideal Industries, Inc,* [1973] Trade Cas (CCH) ¶74,439 (ND Ill 1972) and *Dubuit v Harwell Enterprise Inc,* 336 F Supp 1184 (WDNC 1971). The Data General case instead contained a prohibition against using their operating system with any other hardware, relying on the argument that the operating system could not be reproduced without utilizing trade secrets and infringing Data

General's copyright. *Digidyne Corp v Data General Corp,* 734 F2d 1336, 1341-44 (9th Cir 1984), *cert denied,* (July 1, 1985)[Data General III].

Second, if the trade secret program is part of a broader intellectual property protection scheme, the confidential information plan may be weakened simply because of the plan. This irony stems directly from jury instructions allowing the consideration of the effect on competition of the combined copyright/trade secret/*lock-in* of customers method of protection. That instruction was approved by both the trial and appellate courts. *In re Data General Corp. Antitrust Litigation,* 529 F Supp 801, 811-12 (ND Cal 1981)[Data General II]; *Data General III,* 734 F2d 1336, 1341-44. Although most businessmen will want to utilize whatever works, antitrust cases examine the effect of the challenged practices. A multiple claim approach may present a picture of greater effects.

Third, no matter what program is used internally and how it is enforced, any involvement of outside entities greatly enhances exposure to antitrust liability. Note that this practice existed in the *Kodak* case where the court found the trade secret appropriate but the combination formed by Kodak unacceptable. The Second Circuit stressed that what may be legal when done alone may become anticompetitive when done in concert with others. *Berkey Photo, Inc v Eastman Kodak Co,* 603 F2d 263, 301 (2d Cir 1979), *cert denied,* 444 US 1093 (1980). This makes clear the need to maintain trade secret protection programs individually. Under the National Cooperative Research Act of 1984, 15 USC §4301n, this liability may be somewhat limited but these joint ventures should be closely examined for antitrust risk, especially when the market is just beginning to develop.

Fourth, trade secret protection programs will be upheld only if they *delay* competitors' development of the product. If they prevent competitive development, another story is written. The trial court in Data General instructed that barriers to incoming trade were impermissible.

California does not recognize employee noncompetition agreements after termination from high technology companies. See Russo, Derwin & Hale, *The Impact of the Uniform Trade Secret Act on California Trade Secret Law,* 3 The computer Law 3, Mar 1986, at 1. See also Palenski, *Computer Personnel Under The Fair Labor Standards Act,* 3 The Computer Law 2, Feb 1986, at 27 (an overview of the problem involving employees of computer industries).

§4.23 Dynamic Distribution Procedures and Antitrust Concerns (New)

Given the relatively short life cycle of most software and hardware, the hardware and software developer must be able to use numerous channels of distribution during the modest life cycle. These channels may include direct selling, original equipment manufacturing (OEM), mail order, traditional wholesale and retail outlets, and franchising arrangements. See, for example, Cantor, *Franchising: A Distribution Technique and its Regulation,* 2 The Computer Law 4, Apr 1985, at 18-24 (discussing the issues involved in and the definitions of franchising).

As a firm shifts from one marketing procedure to another, Sherman Act §7 and Robinson-Patman Act Section 1 become concerns. See the article by Reback, *Of Bits, Bytes and Price Discriminations: The Robinson-Patman Act,* 1 The Computer Law 7, Aug 1984, at 1-8 (discussing application of the act to computer firms). *See Computronics, Inc v Apple Computer, Inc,* 600 F Supp 1274 (DC Wis 1985) (court precluded defendants' motion for summary judgment on the Robinson-Patman Act claim). The antitrust concern is particularly strong when an entire distribution channel is eliminated, as discussed in the articles by Gilburne, *Marketing Strategies Aimed at Alleviating "Free Riding" Fears do not Constitute Sherman Act Violations,* 2 The Computer Law 1, Jan 1985, at 39-40 (discussing the *Computer Place* litigation), and the case of *OSC Corp v Apple Computer, Inc,* 601 F Supp 1274 (DC Cal 1981) discussed in Andrews Publications, *Antitrust Issues: California Judge Explains Decision Allowing Apple to Terminate all Mail-Order Dealers,* Computer Industry Litigation Reporter, Jan 28, 1985, at 2,014+ (discussing reasoning behind decision in *OSC Corp v Apple* case); and Stern, *Commentary on O.S.C. v Apple,* Computer Law Rep, 1983, at 81. *See also Computer Connection v Apple Computer Corp,* 621 F Supp 569 (DC La 1985) (court allowed Apple to enforce standardized practices which resulted in termination of an authorized dealer). Computer manufacturers have developed a method of regulation that involves termination of dealer agreements to market and sell computer products. See Note, *Monopolies —Computer Manufacturers' Elimination of Mail Order Sales,* The Comp Law Monitor, Nov 1985, at 164, col 2.

The Fourth Circuit Court of Appeals held that a manufacturer of marine electronics did not violate §1 of the Sherman Act when it stopped selling its products to a mail order company. *National Marine Electronic Distributors, Inc v Raytheon Co,* 778 F2d 190 (4th Cir 1985). See also *Current Developments, Antitrust, Evidence of Dealer Complaints Insufficient to Establish Conspiracy to Terminate Mail Order Dealer,* 3 The Computer Law 2, Feb 1986, at 40, col 2 (discussion of the rationale behind the decision in *National Marine*).

§4.24   Mergers and Acquisitions (New)

Mergers and acquisitions have always been a fertile field for antitrust litigation. Despite the deregulation policy of the Reagan administration, this remains true today. Recently, such acquisitions have caused a closer scrutiny for the computer/high technology field. This has occurred in part because of the general belt-tightening experienced throughout the industry. However, other mergers have been motivated by the availability of undervalued or prospectively attractive investments for those firms having the available funds. Finally, the new National Cooperative Research Act of 1984, 15 USC §4301n has caused certain combinations not otherwise likely to have occurred.

One time the antitrust division of the Justice Department acted on an acquisition was the IBM purchase of the outstanding stock of ROLM. ROLM was the primary source for United States military specialized computers. IBM had announced a future entry to the field. The consent decree IBM eventually signed required the divestiture of the milspec portion of ROLM in an effort to preserve competition in the field, as discussed in CCH Trade Regulation Reports-Number 680, *Mil-spec Computers—Competitive Impact Statement,* at 5 (mentions required IBM filing resulting from ROLM acquisition), and CCH Trade Regulation Reports—Number 678, *Computer Industry Acquistion Challenged by U.S.; Restructuring Permitted,* at 1 (discussing IBM acquisition of ROLM).

The Communications Regulatory Environment 5

§5.01 Generally

Page 164, note 3, at end of note add:

Beginning January 1, 1984, American Telephone & Telegraph Company (AT&T) officially divested its 21 local operating companies. AT&T now consists of the regulated Interexchange Division (ATTIX), Western Electric Company, Bell Laboratories, and AT&T Information Systems (ATTIS). A brief description of each operating division follows.

Under ATTIX, Long Lines will offer domestic and international intercity communication services. AT&T and the independents account for about 96 per cent of the long distance market. This area falls under the jurisdiction of the FCC. In recent years, competition has become increasingly significant, as other common carriers such as MCI and Sprint (GTE) have underpriced AT&T. The specialized carriers have aimed aggressive marketing programs towards residential customers.

Western Electric manufactures a wide line of telecommunications products, including standard telephones, private business exchanges, digital and analog switches, processors, microwave equipment, fiber optics, software, and electronic components. Western Electric will no longer be restricted to the Bell System in its sales efforts. The operating companies will remain a major source of business, however, for Western Electric.

Western Electric has two principal subsidiaries, Teletype Corporation and Bell Telephone Laboratories. Teletype manufactures and sells teleprinters and associated equipment for the transmission of data communications. Bell Labs, jointly owned with AT&T, provides research, development, and engineering design services.

AT&T Information Systems (ATTIS) was formed in June 1982 and began selling enhanced services and new customer premises equipment on January 1, 1983. Enhanced services encompass information processing, while customer premises equipment (CPE) consists of basic telephone and private business exchange (PBX) equipment. ATTIS topl lease and sell new CPE. After January 1, 1983, ATTIS began marketing new CPE, but the operating companies will only be able to offer new equipment from inventory during 1983. On January 1, 1984, the existing CPE was transferred to ATTIS, and the operating companies may once again market new CPE.

Revenues will be derived from the leasing and/or sale of existing CPE, the sale of new CPE, and enhanced services. Leasing is expected to be an important aspect of ATTIS' operation, especially for equipment such as PBXs. Existing CPE will be phased out, perhaps over a 10-year period, through a combination of asset sales to customers and retirements.

AT&T International is engaged in the overseas market for Western Electric and other Bell System products and services. AT&T intends to mount a joint effort with N.V. Philips of the Netherlands to compete in the European market. The purpose of the new venture with Philips is jointly to develop, manufacture, and market digital switching equipment and other items. The international market is an area in which Western Electric should be able to provide more competitive equipment for International to distribute.

AT&T has a number of other subsidiaries, including Advanced Mobile Phone Service (AMPS) and Overseas and Cable Services and Operations. The AMPS subsidiary has applied for licenses to construct cellular radio systems in many major cities. These cellular radio systems were assigned to the Bell operating companies (BOCs) at divestiture. AT&T is working with other parties in some cities, such as Centel in Chicago and GTE in other cities. AT&T owns a number of underseas cables with other international carriers, including foreign agencies.

On January 1, 1984, the BOCs were spun off from AT&T with all assets necessary to provide regulated exchange service, exchange access, and printed directory service. The division of assets was based on book value, as proposed by AT&T and confirmed by the court, rather than on market value. The decree requires maintenance of BOC debt ratios of about 45 per cent. The BOCs are organized into seven regional operating companies.

Each regional operating company will need rate relief to offset revenues which will be transferred to the new AT&T. Regulation, service territory growth, and operating cost controls will determine the relative strength of the seven regional companies.

Before the divestiture, AT&T was the world's largest corporation. As compared to the new, smaller AT&T, its total assets have decreased by more than two-thirds. See *American Telephone & Telegraph: The*

Upcoming AT&T Divestiture and Its Implications for Investors, Sherson, American Express (1983); §§5.13-5.17; Verueer & McGrew, *Greene Defines Process for BOC Waiver Requests,* Legal Times, Feb 4, 1985, at 16 (analyzes Judge Greene's orders which define the process by which the BOC's can seek waivers of "line of business" restrictions. Judge Greene's general philosophy is that the "BOC's are in danger of ignoring . . . their central responsibility—namely, the provision of local telephone service."*Id*at 20.); Geller, *Communications Law A Half Century Later,* 37 Federal Comm LJ 73 (1985) (points to changes in the industry and the failure of the Communication Act to respond); Jones & Quillan, *Broadcasting Regulation: A Very Brief History,* 37 Federal Comm LJ, 107 (1985); Burch, *Common Carrier Communications by Wire and Radio: A Retrospective,* 37 Federal Comms LJ 85 (1985) (traces the evolution of common carrier regulation); Homet, *"Getting The Message": Statutory Approaches to Electronic Information Delivery and the Duty of Carriage,* 37 Federal Comms LJ 217 (1985) (advocates the development of legislation); Lloyd, *Federal, State, and Local Regulation of Video and Telecommunication Systems—The Actual and the Ideal,* 6 Computer LJ 283 (1985) (1985) (an overview of the 1934 Communications Act); M. Snow, Marketplace for Telecommunications ch 4 (1986) (deregulation, divestiture, and competition in United States telecommunications).

Federal Communications Commission Considerations

§5.02 The 1934 Communications Act and Interpretations

Page 165, note 5, at end of note add:

See *FCC and Cable Information Services: an Analysis of the Scope and Mandate of the Communications Act,* 54 U Colo L Rev 257 (1983); Note, *Teletext and the FCC: Turning The Content Regulatory Clock Backwards,* 64 BUL Rev 1057 (1984) (in exempting teletext from content regulation, the FCC has failed to regulate the telecommunications industry); Note, *To Defer Or Not to Defer: The Question for The D.C. Circuit in Reviewing FCC Decisions,* 36 Federal Comm LJ 293 (1984) (review of agency action); Fogarty & Spielholz, *FCC Cable Jurisdiction: From Zero To Plenary in Twenty-Five Years,* 37 Federal Comm LJ 113 (1985) (traces the Evolution of FCC cable jurisdiction under the Communications Act); Meyerson, *The Cable Communications Policy Act of 1984: A Balancing Act on the Coaxial Wires,* 19 Ga L Rev 543 (1985) (FCC power before and after the Cable Act); McKenna, *Preemption Under the Communications Act,* 37 Federal Comms LJ 1 (1985) (includes FCC preemption of CPE interconnection and opening common carrier service to competition).

Page 168, note 18, at end of note add:

See Fuhr, *Telegraphs and Telephones: Competition in the Terminal Equipment Market after Carterphone,* 28 Antitrust Bull 669 (1983).

§5.03 *Computer Inquiry I*

Page 171, note 36, at end of note add:

McKenna, *Preemption Under the Communications Act,* 37 Federal Comms LJ 1, 37 (1985) (*Computer Inquiry I & II:* preempting state regulation of CPE and enhanced services).

§5.05 —Post-*Computer Inquiry I* Developments

Page 172, note 39, at end of note add:

See also Williams, The Communications Revolution (1982); Rapport, *Launching Into the Telecommunication Age: The Dawn of the Electronic Era,* 56 Fla BJ 208 (1982).

§5.06 *Computer Inquiry II*

Page 176, note 60, at end of note add:

McKenna, *Preemption Under the Communications Act,* 37 Federal Comms LJ 1 (1985) (*Computer Inquiry I & II,* preempting state regulation of CPE and enhanced services).

§5.07 —Federal Communications Commission Actions Parallel to *Computer Inquiry II*

Page 178, note 70, at the end of note add:

The FCC has recommended that the Department of Justice adopt a proposal allowing AT&T to sell customer premises equipment (CPE) directly to the customers rather than through a separate subsidiary. The proposal would not apply to enhanced services. The Department of Justice agreed with the FCC evaluation and cited AT&T's loss of market power in the customer premises equipment field. See Department of Justice Furnishing of Customer Premises Equipment and Enhanced Services, CC Dk No 85-26 (Apr 9, 1985); also see for short discussion 699 Trade Reg Rep 5 (1985).

Page 180, note 80, at end of note add:

See Johnson, Competition and Cross-Subsidization in the Telephone Industry (1982).

Page 182, note 86, at end of note add:

Among the provisions of the Federal Communications Act of 1934, 47 USC §151 *et seq*, is its requirement, in 47 USC §201(a), that communications carriers establish physical connections, "interconnections," with other competing or noncompeting communications carriers. In pertinent part, the text of 47 USC §201 provides as follows:

> 201. *Service and charges.*—(a) It shall be the duty of every common carrier engaged in interstate or foreign communication by wire or radio to furnish such communication service upon reasonable request therefor; and, in accordance with the order of the Commission, in cases where the Commission, after opportunity for hearing, finds such action necessary or desirable in the public interest, to establish physical connections with other carriers, to establish through routes and charges applicable thereto and the divisions of such charges, and to establish and provide facilities and regulations for operating such through routes.

Page 183, note 92, at end of note add:

See also Hearing Before the Senate Comm on Commerce, Science and Transportation, Communications Problems in Alaska (1982), 97th Cong, 2d Sess (Serial no 97-135).

§5.07A   *Computer Inquiry III* (New)

Computer Inquiry III is designed to address some of the more controversial issues which arose under *Computer Inquiry II.* Several requests for waivers of the *Computer II Inquiry* had been made. For example, AT&T requested permission for its separate corporation to market transmission services on a resale basis; additionally AT&T requested permission for its customer premises equipment (CPE) and enhanced service company to obtain software developed by unseparated elements of AT&T without having to give the same rights to third parties. The FCC granted most of the relief sought, while imposing conditions to minimize the potential for anticompetitive abuse. See *AT&T Provisions of Basic Services via Resale by Separate Subsidiary*, 98 FCC 2d 478 (1984), *on reconsideration*, FCC 85-379 (released Aug 1, 1985) *appeal pending sub nom* MCI v FCC, No 84-1402 (DC Cir filed Aug 9, 1984); furnishing of CPE and enhanced services by AT&T, FCC 85-86 (releases Feb 22, 1985); *FCC Removes Separation Requirements Imposed on AT&T under Computer Inquiry II*, 2 Computer Law 29 (1985). However, concern developed that the waiver process was too slow, uncertain, and constraining.

In August, 1985, the *Computer Inquiry III* Notice of Proposed Rulemaking was released. The basic changes were in a long, detailed release. First, porposals for specific changes in the *Computer Inquiry II* rules. The second proposal would completely displace the existing rules. The third proposal concerned miscellaneous issues not addressed elsewhere. The notice points out that these proposals are not mutually exclusive. All these proposals would increase computer intelligence and could be displayed in the network.

Through *Computer Inquiry III* the FCC view appears to be changing to the idea that many efficiencies and economies can be achieved only if the computer intelligence that is needed to provide enhanced services is integrated into telephone company facilities. Additionally, *Computer Inquiry III* continues the debate over what measures are necessary to maintain fair competition and promote user choice. See generally Marks & Casserly, *On Introduction to the FCC's Third Computer Inquiry*, 2 Computer Law 1 (1985); Roth, *FCC Seeks Update of Telecom Policy*, Government Computer News, Aug 30, 1985, at 77.

§5.08 —Communications Satellite Corporation and Satellite Business Systems

Page 184, note 97, at end of note add:

For a discussion of the FCC pricing review guidelines, see *In re* Guidelines for Dominant Carriers' MTS Rates and Rate Structures, FCC CC Dkt No 84-1235 (1984).

Page 184, note 102, at end of note add:

See also R. Hall, The New Telecommunications Landscape 21 (1984); Burch, *Emerging Competitive Forces in International Communications: Satellites and Cables*, 54 Antitrust LJ 227 (1985).

The Congressional Scene

§5.09 Congressional Efforts to Revise the 1934 Communications Act

Page 185, note 106, at end of note add:

See also the hearings before the House Comm on Energy and Commerce, Subcom on Telecommunications, Consumer Protection, and Fin Record Carrier Competition Act of 1981 (1981), 97th Cong, 1st Sess (Serial no 97-83). The hearings concerned domestic and international telecommunication services that deal primarily in the transmission of information that originates or terminates in written or graphic form, with some emphasis on the position of Western Union and its competitors.

§5.10 —1981 Packwood Bill (S 898)

Page 187, note 116, at end of note add:

Current bills pending include the following: S 66 (Baker, R-Tenn & Goldwater, R-Ariz), which amends the Communications Act of 1934 to provide a national policy regarding cable television (and is a companion to HR 4103); S 999 (Baker, R-Tenn), which amends the Communications Act of 1934 to provide for improved international telecommunications (and is a companion to HR 4464); S 1660 (Packwood, R-Or), which preserves Universal Telephone Service (and is a companion to HR 4102); HR 4102 (Wirth, D-Colo), which preserves Universal Telephone Service (and is a companion to S 1660); HR 4103 (Wirth, D-Colo), which amends the Communications Act of 1934 to provide a national policy regarding cable television (and is a companion to S 66); and HR 4464 (Markey, D-Mass & Bryant, D-Tex), which amends the Communications Act of 1934 to provide for full and effective competition in international telecommunications markets (and is a companion to S 999).

§5.11 —1981 Wirth Bill (HR 5158)

Page 189, note 142, at end of note add:

See also the House telecommunications report released, 108 Pub Util Fort, Dec 3, 1981, at 56.

Page 193, note 175, at end of note add:

See Mayo, Hensler & Smith, *The AT&T Valuation Controversy,* 17 Merg & Acq 20 (1982); White, *Breaking up Bell: Plans to Split AT&T Confuse and Worry Stock, Bond Holders; A Maze of Fractional Shares Seem Likely to Develop,* Wall St J, Oct 12, 1982, at 1.

Litigation Considerations

§5.12   Private Plaintiff Antitrust Litigation against AT&T

Pages 193-194, note 177, at end of note add:

Peters, *Is The Third Time the Charm? A Comparison of the Government's Major antitrust Settlements with AT&T this Century*, 15 Seton Hall 252 (1985).

Page 194, note 178, at end of note add:

MCI Communications Corp (MCI) and American Telephone and Telegraph Co (AT&T) petitioned the United States Supreme Court to review a decision vacating a $1.8 billion antitrust award and remanding for a retrial of damages. The Court denied certiorari. The United States Court of Appeals had affirmed 7 of 17 findings of monopolization by AT&T, reversed findings of predatory pricing, vacated the award, and remanded the case for a new trial on damages only (1982-83 Trade Cas (CCH) ¶65,137). The Seventh Circuit Court had held, in reversing the predatory pricing findings, that under any cost methodology, MCI had failed to establish that AT&T priced its services below its average total cost. The Seventh Circuit previously had declined to reconsider the case and had made minor modifications of its opinion. MCI Communications Corp v AT&T, 462 F Supp 1072 (ND Ill 1978), *affd*, 594 F2d 594 (7th Cir 1979), *cert denied*, 440 US 971 (1980). See also Waller, *The "New" Law of Monopolization: An Examination of MCI Communications Corp. v AT&T*, 32 De Paul L Rev 595 (1983); Campbell, *MCI v AT&T—The Predatory Pricing Debate*, 64 Chi B Rec 272 (1983). MCI's attempt to seek damages at retrial that were not sought at trial received a setback when the United States Court of Appeals ruled that the question of new damages was not appropriate for an interlocutory appeal. 680 Trade Reg Rep 3 (1984); Bell, *The Decision to Divest: Incredible as Inevitable?*, IEEE Spectrum, Nov 1985, at 46 (divestiture was as much a clash between the participants philosophy as it was about antitrust laws).

§5.13   *United States v AT&T*

Page 194, note 179, at end of note add:

The government stated its case quite directly:

> AT&T through its Long Lines Department engaged in a pattern of conduct designed to maintain and expand its existing telecommunications service monopoly. In order to deter potential competitors and eliminate actual competitors AT&T has engaged

in predatory pricing, refusals to supply transmission service, preselling, and other marketing and operational practices available to it as the monopoly supplier of long distance service. These exclusions of competitors were often in violation of the Communications Act and Federal Communications Commission (FCC) policy, as well as the antitrust laws. In addition, AT&T has also used its control over the 23 Bell operating companies and the power of the monopoly of local telephone service to deter would-be competitors in telecommunications. The local monopolies—whose services are needed by all long distance carriers to reach their individual customers—refused to deal with these potential competitors of their affiliated Long Lines Department or did so only on highly discriminatory terms and conditions, effectively shielding Long Lines from their competition. The evidence proves that defendants employed their control of the Bell operating companies to develop and implement uniform, system-wide policies aimed at discouraging the development and expansion of any competition in telecommunications services to prevent any diminution of their overall telecommunications monopoly.

Brief for the United States, 1 Nov 1978, at 4.

AT&T, in its defense, contended that there were at least three reasons why the government's charges were not true:

(1) Because defendants do not possess monopoly power in any of the markets or submarkets which they are alleged to have monopolized; (2) because defendants' position in the telecommunications industry, even if it reflected market power—which it does not—is a product, not of monopolization, but of the technology of communications, governmental statutes, and policies regulating telecommunications carriers, and the efficiencies of the Bell System in providing telecommunications products and services; and (3) that the conduct challenged by the Government —whether considered discretely or as a continuing course of conduct—reflects, not an effort or scheme to monopolize, but a wholly proper discharge by defendants of their common carrier obligations.

Brief for AT&T, Jan 8, 1979, at 198-99.

Page 194, note 181, at end of note add:

See also *Hearings before the Senate Comm on the Judiciary, DOJ Oversight: US v AT&T*, pts 1-2, Aug 6, 1981-Mar 22, 1982, regarding the Department of Justice oversight. 97th Cong, 1st and 2d Sess (1982) (Serial no J-97-53.)

Page 196, note 198, at end of note add:

Refusal by one of the new telephone companies to grant its former parent access to lines for coinless public telephones violated the AT&T reorganization consent decree (1982-2 Trade Cas (CCH) ¶65,900), according to the Federal District Court in Washington, DC. The operating company, Pacific Bell, was ordered to provide the access. Pacific Bell had objected that the California Public Utilities Commission had jurisdiction over the matter, and therefore the federal court rule did not apply. Pacific Bell's reliance on the primary jurisdiction doctrine was misconceived. The access refusal was not a dispute involving possible federal antitrust jurisdiction, but a judgment already entered by a federal court, the court explained. According to the court, when a party is in violation of the terms of such a judgment, the court is not justified in deferring to a state regulatory body. A decree requirement that operating companies grant nondiscriminatory exchange access to all interexchange carriers was designed to prevent a "bottleneck" monopoly barring competitors from providing service. If an operating company had the authority to determine when it would provide access, it could become the arbiter of future services between defined local access and transport areas, and thereby shape the competition to suit its needs. In other words, a BOC "could act as the Bell System was alleged to have acted prior to divestiture." The refusal to provide the necessary connections potentially stifled competition, and for that reason it could not be in the public interest. Innovations presented by the coinless phones were in the public interest and were the type of advances that the decree was designed to foster. See Trade Reg Rep No 645, Apr 17, 1984.

See also English, New Telecommunications Landscape 87 (1984), Jan 18, 1982 at 1; *Stipulations Speeded Trial But Imposed Steep Costs,* Legal Times of Wash, Jan 18, 1982, at 1.

Page 197, note 208, at end of note add:

See Johnson, *Deregulation and Divestiture in a Changing Telecommunications Industry,* Pub Util Fort, Oct 14, 1982, at 17; Graham, *The State's Role in the New Age of Communications,* 56 Fla BJ 210 (1982).

§5.14 —Problems with Proposed Consent Decree

Page 198, note 213, at end of note add:

See also F. Starkey, The New Telecommunications Landscape 63 (1984).

Page 199, note 214, at end of note add:

See also Wilson, *Telephone Access Costs and Rates,* Pub Util Fort, Sept 15, 1983, at 18; A. Kahn, Some Thoughts on Telephone Access Pricing (1983).

Page 199, note 215, at end of note add:

Local telephone companies face a serious competitive threat from new technologies: microwave/satellite, cable television, and cellular radio. The technologies are beginning to capture local traffic from the local telephone companies. The local phone companies can counter these threats by upgrading their systems. Their ability to compete can be adversely affected by inappropriate access charges. See P. Netschert, The New Telecommunications Marketplace 69 (1983).

Page 199, note 216, at end of note add:

See the hearings before the Senate Comm on Commerce, Science, and Transportation, AT&T proposed settlement: pts 1-2, Jan 25-Mar 25, 1982, 97th Cong, 1st and 2d Sess (1982) (Serial no 97-92) (possible effect of the AT&T consent decree on telephone rates).

Page 199, note 217, at end of note add:

See *NARUC Committee on Communications Reviews Key Telecommunications Issues,* Pub Util Fort, Mar 31, 1983, at 49.

Page 199, note 219, at end of note add:

See N. Pilz, F. Weber & I. Gibbons, The New Telecommunications Marketplace 3 (1983); Langley, *Ma Bell's Orphans: Regional Phone Firms Vie for Investor Dollars,* Wall St J, Oct 19, 1983, at 1; *Trading Bell: New Telephone Stocks Stir Big Board Activity, Mostly By Professionals,* Wall St J, Nov 22, 1983, at 1.

Page 201, note 225, at end of note add:

See R. Neustadt, The Birth of Electronic Publishing: Legal and Economic Issues in Telephone, Cable, and Over-the-air Teletext and Videotext (1982) (print-type information distributed over television, radio, cable television, and telephone wires; communications policy implications).

§5.15 —Federal Communications Commission Perspective on Proposed Consent Decree

Page 201, note 230, at end of note add:

Johnson, *Deregulation and Divestiture in a Changing Telecommunications Industry*, Pub Util Fort, Oct 14, 1982, at 17; Graham, *The State's Role in the New Age of Communications*, 56 Fla BJ 210 (1982).

Page 201, note 231, at end of note add:

Robinson, *An assessment of state and federal jurisdiction to regulate access charges after the AT&T divestiture*, BYU L Rev 376 (1983).

Page 202, note 232, at end of note add:

Saddler, *The Rule Slashers: In Rush to Deregulate, FCC Outpaces Others, Pleasing the Industry; But Critics Say Some Steps, Such as Phone-rate Plan, Are at Public's Expense*, Wall St J, Dec 7, 1983, at 1.

Pages 202-203, note 235, at end of note add:

Many of these proceedings are continuing today. Since the finalization of the *United States v AT&T* settlement, the FCC has instituted a number of new proceedings to deal with the rapidly changing computer and communications technologies. The following is an update of the FCC's continuing dockets and a summary of the recently instituted FCC proceedings which deal with communications common carriers and the telecommunication services and products market:

1. CC 78-72, MTS and WATS Market Structure-Access Charge (establishes mechanism by which local telephone exchange companies are to recover the costs of providing access services to interexchange carriers)
2. CC-81-893, Detariffing Customer Premises Equipment (establishes criteria and procedures for the removal of embedded CPE from regulated service in accordance with the principles articulated in *Computer Inquiry II*)
3. CC 79-252, Competitive Carriers (deregulation of competitive common carrier services)
4. CC 83-1147, Deregulation of AT&T (inquiry into long-run regulation of AT&T-COM's basic domestic interstate service)
5. CC 83-1145, Investigation of Access and Divestiture Related Tariffs
6. CC 83-1375, AT&T-IS Resale (proposal to permit AT&T-IS to resell tariffed services offered by AT&T-COM and other carriers
7. Gen 80-756, Communication Code and Protocol Inquiry (establishes rules governing provision of code and protocol services by

carriers subject to structural separation of basic and enhanced offerings)

8. Gen 83-841 ISDN (inquiry into efforts to specify standards for Integrated Services Digital Networks)

1 Telematics 24 (1984).

§5.16 —Proposed *United States* v *AT&T* Consent Decree and HR 5158

Page 203, note 236, at end of note add:

See Wines, *The Big Guns Have Joined the Battle Over How to Break Up the Bell System: AT&T and Many of Its Telecommunications Rivals Have Lined Up on Opposite Sides Over a Bill That Could Determine Bell's Future,* Nat J, June 19, 1982, at 1085.

Page 204, note 238, at end of note add:

See the hearing before the House Comm on Energy and Commerce, Subcomm on Telecommunications, Consumer Protection, and Financial Prospects for Universal Telephone Service, Mar 22, 1983, 98th Cong, 1st Sess (Serial no 98-11) (possible impact of the AT&T reorganization and recent FCC actions on telephone rates); Langley, *Ma Bell's Shepherds: AT&T Sends a Horde of Lobbyists to Fight a Phone-bill Proposal,* Wall St J, Nov 1983, at 1.

§5.17 —Modifications of Proposed Consent Decree by Judge Greene

Page 205, note 245, at end of note add:

See Katz & Willig, *Toward Competition in Phone Service: The Case for Freeing AT&T,* 7 Reg 43 (1983).

Page 205, note 247, at end of note add:

After six months of deliberation, Judge Greene approved the basic principle of the settlement—divestiture of the local phone companies—and after another year he issued his final opinion, which sought to achieve three objectives:

(1) Promotion of true and fair competition in the telecommunications long distance and equipment markets, (2) preservation of AT&T as a dynamic force, capable of research, manufacturing, and marketing in technologically advanced fields, and (3) protec-

tion of the principle of universal telephone service, accessible to all segments of the population regardless of income.

Opinion of Judge Greene, July 8, 1983.

Page 205, note 248, at end of note add:
See Lavey & Carlton, *Economic Goals and Remedies of the AT&T Modified Final Judgment,* 71 Geo LJ 1497 (1983).

Page 205, note 250, at end of note add:
See Besen, *Regulation, Deregulation, and Antitrust in the Telecommunications Industry,* 28 Antitrust Bull 39 (1983); Knieps, *Regulating by Partial Deregulation: The Case of Telecommunications,* 35 Ad L Rev 391 (1983); *Resale, Shared Use Regulation: Can the "Invisible Hand" Hold on to Ma Bell?,* 35 Fed Com LJ 209 (1983); Baker & Baker, *Antitrust and Communications Deregulation,* 28 Antitrust Bull 1 (1983).

Page 206, text, at end of section add:
Seeking the modification of the consent decree became big business for the BOC's when Judge Harold H. Greene entered a series of orders that allowed six of the seven RHC to expand into new business areas that included equipment leasing, computer sales and service office products, real estate and several foreign business enterprises.

This decision provided and important indication on the court's approach to further modifications. The original decree provided for no expansion of the BOC's into areas outside the basic natural monopoly services regulated by tariff (see MFJ 11). Judge Green's concern over the health of the BOC's is believed to have led to this liberal interpretation of the consent decree.

The modification of the decree allowed business restrictions to be removed if the BOC could show that the BOC would be unable to use its monopoly power to impede competition in the new market.

Within seven months of his decision, the BOCs were before Judge Green again with new requests for waivers of the line of business restrictions. Greene, who was concerned about the diversion of resources to the new enterprises, declined to grant any new waivers and indicated that he would not consider granting any waivers to allow the BOCs to enter the interexchange telecommunications market, information services market, or the equipment manufacturing market.

Along with the three forbidden areas, Judge Greene also listed four restrictions that would apply to all activities conducted pursuant to line of business waivers:

1. The new business must be operated by a subsidiary

2. The new subsidiary cannot rely on the RHCs for financing and must obtain credit without permitting creditors to seek recourse against the RHCs upon default
3. The total estimated revenue of the subsidiary cannot exceed 10 per cent of the RHCs estimated revenue
4. The BOC must agree that MFJ visitorial privileges for the Department of Justice will apply to the subsidiary

The court stated its opinion regarding the rush of applications for the waiver of the line of business requirements when it said that the court "did not have the slightest belief or intention that within a very short period of time, the Regional Holding Companies would seek to transform themselves from custodians of the nation's local phone service into conglomerates for which such service was at best a pedestrian sideline." United States v AT&T, __ F Supp __ (DDC 1984) (July 24, 1984 slip op at 24).

It appears that Judge Greene and the RHCs are testing each other's limits but it seems likely that the RHCs will continue to expand into new lines of business. Judge Greene, however, will act as a brake on that growth. See Verveer & McGrew, *Greene Defines Process for BOC Waiver Request*, Legal Times, Feb 4, 1985, at 16.

Future Trends in the Telecommunications Industry

§5.18   Emerging Legal Structure

Page 206, note 253, at end of note add:

AT&T's acceptance of the government's proposed settlement of its antitrust suit against AT&T was another strategic management decision. AT&T's attorneys were willing to settle because they knew that the Reagan administration wanted to bring the long and costly case to an end. It was reported that AT&T believed that the trial was not going well for their side, and they were anxious to move into computers and related services from which the Bell System had been barred. K. Brimmer, Annual Review of Information Science and Technology 33 (1982). See also M. Irwin, Markets Without Boundaries (1985) and Negotiating Telecommunications Contracts: Business and Legal Aspects (1985).

Page 206, note 255, at end of note add:

See also Warner, *Pressing Case: Newspaper Publishers Lobby to Keep AT&T From Role They Covet*, Wall St J, July 9, 1982, at 1.

Page 207, note 256, at end of note add:

See also Howard, *Vertical Integration: Should the AT&T Doctrine be Extended?*, 52 Antitrust LJ 259 (1983). A federal district court has approved a consent decree permitting GTE to acquire certain telecommunications enterprises of Southern Pacific Company, which includes *Sprint* long distance service. Unlike AT&T, GTE will be permitted to engage in competitive and monopoly enterprises. See Trade Reg Rep 50833.

Page 207, text, at end of section add:

A new legal issue has arisen over the BOC's right to enter into the cable television business. The FCC on January 30, 1985 granted the Chesapeake & Potomac Telephone Company (C&P) the right to construct cable television transport facilities for the exclusive use of the District of Columbia's winning franchisee, District Cablevision.

The opponents of the decision claim that such action is in violation of the consent decree that divested BOCs from AT&T.

The FCC based its decision on C&P's lack of authority over the cable programming. A true test of the ruling's compliance with the consent decree has not been made but the opponents of the move have appealed to the Justice Department and have filed suit in district court. Nelson, *D.C. Cable Franchise Losers Challenge Phone Company Ties*, 7 Legal Times No 35, at 1 (Feb 4, 1985).

(For general articles on the deregulated telecommunications, see *Telematics*, a journal specializing in the communication industry.)

Several changes have been advocated in the legal structure. An argument for an amendment to the act requiring more public service announcements has been made, Note, *In the Public Interest; An argument calling for an Amendment to the Federal Communications Act Requiring More Public Service Announcements in the Broadcast Media*, 7 Computer LJ 223 (1985). Additionally, concern has been shown for the needs of the hearing-impaired. Comment, *Community Television of Southern California v. Gottfried: Defining the Role of the Television Industry in Serving the Needs of the Hearing Impaired*, 19 New England L Rev 899 (Fall 1984).

§5.19 Emerging Communications Technologies

Page 207, note 257, at end of note add:

See also J. Tydeman, H. Lipinsky, R. Adler, M. Nyhan, & L. Zwimpfer, Teletext and Videotex in the United States: Market Potential, Technology, Public Policy Issues (1982); Wines, *The FCC and Its Critics Are at Odds on How to Control the Video Explosion*, Nat J, Aug 14, 1982, at 1408; R. Wiley, Introduction to Communications Issues (1983); A. Pearce & P. Verveer, Some Policy-Oriented Reflections on the AT&T Antitrust

Settlement (1983); Oliver, *A Further Analysis of OFPP's Continuing Effort to Change the Competitive Forces in the Government Marketplace*, 29 Fed B News & J 317 (1982).

Pages 207-208, note 258, at end of note add:

See also Fagan, *Direct Broadcast Satellites and the FCC: A Case Study in the Regulation of New Technology*, 29 Fed B News & J 378 (1982); E. Noam, Telecommunication's Regulation Today and Tomorrow (1984).

Federal and state regulators and the telecommunications industry itself are entering a new era. As competition grows, it is inevitable that regulation and the roles of state and federal regulators must change. See R. Romano, The New Telecommunications Marketplace 99 (1983).

For a discussion of the growth of multiple computer networks that are linked by telecommunication channels, see Lavey, *Recent Telecommunications Developments Affecting Computer Networks*, 2 Comp Law 1 (1985).

Page 208, note 259, at end of note add:

See also O'Reilly, *More Than Cheap Talk Propels MCI*, 107 Fortune, Jan 24, 1983, at 68; *Telecommunications: The Global Battle*, Bus Week, Oct 24, 1983, at 126; *The New Technology in the Communications Industry: Legal Problems in a Brave New World*, 36 Vand L Rev 867 (1983); I. Stelzer, The Post-decree Telecommunications Industry (1982) (discussing changes in the telephone and telegraph equipment industries, some predating the AT&T agreement to divest itself of its operating subsidiaries); Schroeder, *Telecommunications in the Eighties*, Editorial Research Rep, Feb 4, 1983, at 91; J. Eidenberg, The New Telecommunications Landscape 4 (1984).

Page 208, note 260, at end of note add:

See also M. Loewenstein, The New Telecommunications Marketplace 127 (1983); Wines, *Transition to a New Era of Telephone Service Could be a Painful Passage*, Nat J, Jan 15, 1983, at 104; Alessio, *Managing the Transition to Telecommunications Deregulation*, Pub Util Fort, July 7, 1983, at 21; Inman, *Phone wars: AT&T Tells Everyone Its Long-distance Calls are Better Than MCI's*, Wall St J, Oct 27, 1983, at 1; Langdale, *Competition in the United States Long-distance Telecommunications Industry*, 17 Regional Studies 393 (1983); Katz, *Toward Competition in Phone Service: The Case for Freeing AT&T*, 7 Reg 43 (1983). Marks, *Regulations and Deregulation in the United States and other Countries*, 25 Jurimetrics 5 (1984).

Page 208, text, at end of section add:

The deregulation of the telecommunications industry has given rise to a more aggressive AT&T which has revamped the unregulated portions of its corporation.

AT&T has created ATTTEC (ATT Technologies) to handle the growth and development of the unregulated operating units which include AT&T Information Systems (formerly American Bell Inc.), AT&T Technologies Incorporated (formerly Western Electric), AT&T Bell Laboratories (formerly Bell Laboratories), and AT&T International. AT&T believes that the vertical integration of the operating units under ATTTEC will create a more efficient system for bringing new technology from Research and Development to the customer.

IBM has committed to becoming a force in the telecommunications field; it has increased its stake in Satellite Business Systems and is now seeking to trade its interest in SBS to MCI in exchange for a 16 per cent interest in MCI (Computerworld, July 1, 1985, at 1, col 4). IBM has purchased Rolm Corporation, a manufacturer of PBX-like communications systems. IBM has also allied itself with a government owned firm in an effort to win an exclusive contract from AT&T to provide public data communication services in Italy. IBM has also attempted to make inroads into other markets through joint development agreements but has been thwarted by government intervention.

The battle lines in the communications industry are being drawn between AT&T and IBM. AT&T has the advantage in technology and expertise, but AT&T's ATTTEC will have to live up to its expectations if AT&T is to keep the edge over IBM and its numerous acquisitions. IBM lacks AT&T's communication skills and is aggressively seeking to acquire already-developed skills from the outside. IBM has the capital resources to become competitive with AT&T but IBM's ability to properly manage and control the current influx of technology and the future R&D needed to remain a force in the market remains an unanswered question.

The confrontation between AT&T and IBM will be fascinating to observe and may also generate huge advancements in communication technology. Hannan, *Ring Out the Old: AT&T Streamlines Operations,* Gov't Computer News 4 (Jan 21, 1985), Schultz, *Ring in the New: IBM Grows, Reorganizes,* Gov't Computer News 4 (Jan 21, 1985).

Another growth field in the telecommunications field is database access. Telecommunications software that provides easy access to other computers has been made more powerful and simple enough for nonhackers to use (See Pallaro, *Communications Software: The Expanding Horizon,* PC Week, Sept 18, 1984, at 47). This software has created a market for various database access systems that include stockmarket and news reports. The ability to quickly access hugh databases on any number of topics may give the personal computer industry another boost as a new market of buyers is tapped.

A Legal and Technical Assessment of the Effect of Computers on Individual Privacy

6

Development of Computerized Databanks

§6.01   Introduction, Purpose, and Definition

Pages 214-215, note 5, at end of note add:

Concern for the impact of computers on privacy has even resulted in a variety of symposiums and regular publications. One publication is entitled *Public Journal: An Independent Monthly on Privacy in a Computer Age.* The *Privacy Journal* attempts to provide "consistent and timely coverage of new legislation, new court cases, new technology, and new public attitudes about privacy." In business since 1974, this publication has reported on topics ranging from computerized data banks to interactive televising systems and electronic banking. See generally *Privacy Journal.* See the *Washington EFT Letter* and the *Washington Credit Letter Privacy Report.* See also *Proceedings of the 1984 Symposium on Security and Privacy,* sponsored by the Technical Committee on Security and Privacy, IEEE Computer Society, in Oakland, California, April 29-May 2, 1984.

§6.02   The Development of Computer Technology in Relation to Privacy

Page 216, note 13, at end of note add:

See Yalonis & Padget, *Tapping Into On-Line Data Bases,* PC World, May 1985, at 120-26 (what is available and what the decision criteria are); Federal Data Base Finds, Information USA, 1984-85 (directory of free and fee-based databases and files available from the federal government); Krajewski, *Database Types,* BYTE, Oct 1984, at 137+ (brief look at different types of database structures and relationships); Hayden, *Database Growth: 23% Annually,* Mgmt Information Sys Week, Wed, Nov 7, 1984, at 48 (discusses growth of databases—2,500 at writing— and the strictly defined industries experiencing growth; mentions two reports on database industry by Cox, Lloyd Assoc Ltd); NEWSNET Sales Brochure, 1984 (publications databases divided into business specialities for online access); Hewes, *Gateways to On-Line Services,* PC World, May 1985, at 149-56 (discusses gateway systems to ease access to multiple online databases).

§6.03 Present Status and Future Trends

Page 218, note 16, at end of note add:

See also *Privacy Lost: Have Computers Already Collected More Data About Us Than Is Safe?,* Student Law, Dec 1983, at 15-20.

Page 219, note 20, at end of note add:

Some government agencies have begun to use fiber optic lines rather than coaxial cables or twisted pairs in order to avoid electronic surveillance. See Toadvine, *Fiber Optics Foil Electronic Spying,* 5 Govt Computer News 45 (Jan 17, 1986).

Page 219, note 23, at end of note add:

The growing use of microcomputers in corporations raises many concerns for today's management of information systems (MIS) directors. According to Newton-Evans Research Company, the most frequently cited concern by MIS directors is that of privacy and/or security violations. These issues are complicated further by the loss of control over information management resources due to the increased use of desktop microcomputers. See Egan, *Study: Micro Privacy A Worry,* Mgmt Information Sys Week 14 (1984).

An effective computer security system is a necessity to ensuring privacy protection. The importance of computer security cannot be overstated. Corporations, as well as federal, state, and local governments, have a duty to provide adequate security systems. A variety of security measures are today being discussed and utilized. Management policies and controls, however, may be better deterrents to computer crime and possible privacy invasions than laws or sophisticated technological techniques. See Buss & Solerno, *Common Sense and Computer Security,* 62 Harv Bus Rev 112 (Mar-Apr 1984).

Page 220, note 24, at end of note add:

Information security and privacy are top issues for information systems management for reasons of increased public awareness, the potential for large losses, and legal responsibilities of management in assuring adequate protection. See *Information Security and Privacy*, 24 EDP Analyzer 1 (Feb 1986).

Page 222, note 30, at end of note add:

Technological advances are impacting individual privacy in areas other than computer applications. Cordless telephones broadcast conversations by radio waves; this speech can be picked up as an ordinary radio signal. While the 1968 federal wiretapping law defines a wire communication as any conversation carried "in whole or in part" by wire and cordless telephones operate, at least partially by wire, it has been held that there is "no reasonable expectation of privacy," Kansas v Howard, 679 P2d 197 (Kan 1981), and that court authorization was not needed to listen in on the conversation, Rhode Island v Delaurier, No 84-76-CA. See Who's Listening?, 71 ABA J 20 (May 1985). Privacy considerations in cordless telephone conversations are evaluated in *Privacy Rights in Cordless Telephone Conversations*, 18 J Marshall L Rev 1015 (Summer 1985).

Threat to Individual Privacy

§6.04   Key Forces Threatening Privacy

Page 222, note 33, at end of note add:

Government computer centers are working to increase safeguards protecting sensitive or classified information from unauthorized users where computers currently have little or no security measures installed. See *Center Works to Increase Safeguards*, 4 Govt Computer News, Sept 24, 1985, at 24.

Page 223, note 37, at end of note add:

Concern over potential threats to individual privacy are now being addressed by data processing trade journals. *Datamation* examined the increasing use of various databases by law enforcement agencies in an article entitled *The Electronic Cops*, Datamation 115 (June 15, 1984). In addition to growing reliance being placed on the National Crime Information Center database, governmental agencies now access commercial databases to obtain additional information on individuals. While law enforcement has been made both easier and more efficient through the use of computers, there remains a great risk of misuse or abuse of data when inaccurate or obsolete data is not purged from the database.

Errors in online databases used by law enforcement agencies have been responsible for the misidentification and arrest of people with like names or other similarities to that contained in the warrant system. Suits have been brought both in Los Angeles and New Orleans by people who have spent time in jail because their name was the same as that of a listed suspect. According to an article entitled *A Bad Rap*, 71 ABA J 24 (Jan 1985), a 1982 Office of Technology Assessment survey of the FBI's computerized criminal history system revealed that approximately 56% of the dispositions were not reported and 20% of the information was simply inaccurate.

Also see *Privacy in the Computer Age*, 4 Phil & Pub Poly 1, n 3 (Fall 1984).

Design flaws in multi-user systems can leave the system vulnerable to clandestine programs that copy, corrupt or scan input data. See Boebert, Kain, & Young, *Trojan Horse Rolls Up to DP Gate*, 19 Computerworld, Dec 2, 1985, at 65-69. Likewise, disgruntled employees can compromise a system's security even though they may have authorized access to the system. See Atkins, *Jesse James at the Terminal*, 19 Computerworld, Nov 25, 1985, at 47-48.

Page 224, note 39, at end of note add:

University of Chicago Law Professor Frank Zimring suggests the group that will know the most about us and is therefore the more appropriate cause for concern is the private financial sector, rather than the government. See *Privacy in Peril: Technology and Government Erode Protections*, Law Scope, May 1983, at 565-69. See also Brownstein, *Computer Communications Vulnerable as Privacy Laws Lag Behind Technology*, 16 Natl J 52 (Jan 14, 1984).

§6.05 Types of Personal Information

Page 230, text at end of section add:

The impact of misused computer-supplied data was reported in the popular media after a flight attendant was detained and arrested on the basis of a warrant issued for a different, but similiar named woman. See Strossier & Siegel, *A Computer Sent Me to Jail*, Woman's Day, Nov 1985, at 124.

Domestic Legal Protection of Individual Privacy

§6.07   Legislative Response—Federal Statutory Developments

Page 234, note 100, at end of note add:

In Doyle v Wilson, 529 F Supp 1343 (D Del 1982), the United States district court stated that the constitutional privacy right generally covers only the intimate facets of an individual's personal life, such as marriage, procreation, contraception, family relationships, child rearing, and education. The court, therefore, followed the rulings of other courts which require that mandatory disclosure of one's social security number does not so threaten the sanctity of individual privacy as to require constitutional protection.

In Delaware, it is the state treasurer's practice to require a social security number before refunding a motor vehicle fine. The plaintiff Doyle, entitled to a motor vehicle fine refund, refused to reveal his social security number. The state treasurer's office in turn refused to pay the refund. The court noted that §7 of the Privacy Act of 1974 allows the "disclosure of a social security number to any Federal, State, or local agency maintaining a system of records . . . if such disclosure was required under statute or regulation . . . to verify the identity of an individual." If an agency requests such disclosure, however, it shall "inform that individual whether that disclosure is mandatory or voluntary, by what statutory or other authority such number is solicited, and what uses will be made of it." Privacy Act of 1974, 5 USC §522a note.

The court also stated that the 1976 Amendment to the Social Security Act allows a state to use social security numbers for identification in the administration of any tax, general public assistance, driver's license, or motor vehicle registration law. Social Security Act, 42 USC §405(c)(2)(C).

The court in *Doyle* held that refusing to reveal a social security number may be an individual's option under the Social Security Act or Privacy Act. It noted that §7 of the Privacy Act generally prohibits a state from penalizing an individual in any way because of failure to reveal the social security number upon request, except in narrowly defined circumstances. The court also stated that Congress indicated, in enacting §7 of the Privacy Act, its concern that widespread use of a common, standard identification number in collecting information could lead to the establishment of a national data base. A national data base could facilitate government surveillance of American citizens.

Page 234, note 102, at end of note add:

There is also legislation pending in Congress. Senate Bill 66 forbids any government body or private individual from intercepting broadband communication unless specifically authorized to do so by the program originator, system operator, or federal law. This legislation covers common carriers, electronic mail services, and also cable transmission. It defines cable transmission as wire communications. If passed, this privacy legislation will preempt similar state law and provide a unified substitute for the variety of different state and local regulations. S 261, 98th Cong, 1st Sess, §17 (1983). See also Neustadt & Swanson, *Privacy and Videotex Systems*, 8 BYTE 96 (1983).

Pages 236-237, note 116, at end of note add:

Harvard Law School Professor Arthur Miller argues that the Freedom of Information Act "probably does more to end privacy in the United States, ostensibly in pursuit of the public's right to know, than any other enactment in the last 50 or 60 years." See *Privacy in Peril, Technology and Government Erode Protections*, Law Scope, May 1983, at 565-69.

Page 238, note 126, at end of note add:

See M. Scott, Computer Law (1984) for an additional analysis of existing federal privacy statutes.

The Department of Housing and Urban Development has proposed to amend a section of its Privacy Act system of records to allow the agency and the IRS to match their files in order to track delinquent borrowers. If the amendment is passed, debtors and the IRS will receive Form 1099GS informing them of their additional tax liability. Govt Computer News 17 (June 21, 1985).

Bill HR 1721, authored by Rep. Glenn English, if passed, would establish a federal Data Protection Board. Not only would the board have oversight duties, but it would also prepare guidelines and model regulations, investigate Privacy Act compliance, and assist United States companies with foreign data protection laws.

§6.08 State Legislation

Page 239, note 129, at end of note add:

In 1983, the 25-member California Commission on Personal Privacy issued its report stating that many personal privacy protections can only be delivered by Congress. The commission recommended a variety of national programs to protect privacy. One recommendation was the establishment of a Federal Privacy Board to oversee Federal Privacy Act enforcement, study privacy issues, and recommend other regulations. See *Privacy in Peril, Technology and Government Erode Protections*, Law Scope, May 1983, at 565-69. States have continued to address privacy issues. California Assemblywoman Gwen Moore has proposed an amendment to the state constitution which will protect electronic information systems and databases against unreasonable searches and seizures. This amendment, if enacted, would require that if a warrant is issued, it must describe the electronic information system and database to be searched and the person and things to be seized. Govt Computer News 1 (May 24, 1985).

Also see Leech, *The Illinois Personnel Records Statute: New Rights for Employees, New Risks for Employers*, Ill BJ 386 (Mar 1985). This article reviews the legislation which grants employees the right to review and dispute information included in an employer's personnel files.

The New York assembly has introduced several bills impacting computer-related legal issues. One would establish a state security officer to provide security checks to protect the integrity of information stored in the state's computer system. The remaining two bills would amend the general business law to cover computer use and management, and would amend the state penal code to include computer programs and data, stored or in transit, in the definition of property.

Page 239, text, following carryover paragraph add:

There are four states with right to privacy statutes, each of which specifically recognizes an individual's right to privacy. Mass Gen Laws Ann ch 214, §1B (West 1984) states:

> A person shall have a right against unreasonable, substantial or serious interference with his privacy. The superior court shall have jurisdiction in equity to enforce such right and in connection therewith to award damages.

Virginia's Privacy Protection Act of 1976 relates more directly to the use of computers in collecting personal information. Virginia Code §2.1-377 (1976). Section 2.1-378 of the Act begins:

> A. The General Assembly finds:
> 1. An individual's privacy is directly affected by the extensive collection, maintenance, use and dissemination of personal information;
> 2. That the increasing use of computers and sophisticated information technology has greatly magnified the harm that can occur from these practices;
> 3. That an individual's opportunities to secure employment, insurance and his right to due process, and other legal protections are endangered by the misuse of certain of these personal information systems; and

4. That in order to preserve the rights guaranteed a citizen in a free society, legislation is necessary to establish procedures to govern information systems containing records on individuals.

The Virginia Privacy Protection Act does not render personal information confidential and does not generally prohibit information dissemination. Rather, the act requires that certain procedural steps be taken regarding the acquisition and dissemination of information. The act also provides for injunctive relief where a public official acquires information properly in his or her capacity as a public official, but disseminates it improperly in his or her capacity as a private person. *Hinderliter v Humphries*, 224 Va 439, 297 SE2d 684 (Va 1982).

In 1977, Wisconsin enacted its privacy law. The right of privacy is recognized and interpreted in accordance with the developing common law privacy right. The Wisconsin law allows actions for the unreasonable invasion of privacy. Wis Stat Ann §895.50 (West 1983).

Finally, in 1980, Rhode Island enacted its privacy statute, RI Gen Laws §9-1-28.1 (Supp 1983). It states:

It is the policy of this state that every person in this state shall have a right to privacy which shall be defined to include any of the following rights individually:
(1) the right to be secure from unreasonable intrusion upon one's physical solitude or seclusion; . . .
(2) the right to be secure from an appropriation of one's name or likeness; . . .
(3) the right to be secure from unreasonable publicity given to one's private life; . . .
(4) the right to be secure from publicity that reasonably places another in a false light before the public; . . .

The statute further allows any deprivation or violation of the privacy right to be actionable. *Id.*

Other states use a more general approach to privacy protection. Greater emphasis is placed on what constitutes a privacy invasion and what rights of action are allowed. The Alabama Code defines *Offenses Against Privacy* as:

(1) Eavesdrop. To overhear, record, amplify, or transmit any part of the private communication of others without the consent of at least one of the persons engaged in the communication, except as otherwise provided by law.
(2) Private Place. A place where one may reasonably expect to be safe from casual or hostile intrusion or surveillance, but such term does not include a place to which the public or a substantial group of the public has access.

(3) Surveillance. Secret observation of the activities of another person for the purpose of spying upon and invading the privacy of the person observed.

Ala Code §13A-11-30 (1975).

Arkansas Stat Ann §5-1108 (1947) states that no authority shall be given "to any person, agency, or corporation or other legal entity to invade the privacy of any citizen . . . ."

The privacy statute in New York states:

A person, firm or corporation that uses for advertising purposes, or for the purposes of trade, the name, portrait or picture of any living person without having first obtained the written consent of such person, or if a minor of his or her parent or guardian, is guilty of a misdemeanor.

NY Civ Rights Law 8 §50 (McKinney 1976).

In New Hampshire "[a] person is guilty of a misdemeanor if he [or she] unlawfully and without the consent of the person entitled to privacy therein, installs or uses

(a) in any private place, any device for observing, photographing, recording, amplifying or broadcasting sounds or events in such place; or
(b) outside a private place, any device for hearing, recording, amplifying or broadcasting sounds originating in such place which would not ordinarily be audible or comprehensible outside.

NH Rev Stat Ann §644:9 (1974).

In Delaware, one is guilty of a privacy violation when he or she:

1) Trespasses on property intending to subject anyone to eavesdropping or other surveillance in a private place; or
2) Installs in any private place, without consent of the person or persons entitled to privacy there, any device for observing, photographing, recording, amplifying or broadcasting sounds or events in that place or uses any such unauthorized installation; or
3) Installs or uses outside a private place any device for hearing, recording, amplifying or broadcasting sounds originating in that place which would not ordinarily be audible or comprehensible outside, without the consent of the person or persons entitled to privacy there; or
4) Intercepts without the consent of all parties thereto a message by telephone, letter or other means of communicating privately, including private conversation; or

5) Divulges without the consent of the sender and the receiver the existence or contents of any message by telephone, telegraph, letter or other means of communicating privately if the accused knows that the message was unlawfully intercepted or if he [or she] learned of the message in the course of employment with an agency engaged in transmitting it.

Del Code Ann tit 11, §1335 (1979).

Utah and Oregon have privacy statutes similar to Delaware's in that they declare an individual guilty of a privacy violation when he or she eavesdrops or trespasses upon another. Utah Code Ann §769401 (1953); Or Rev Stat §164.245 (1981). Oklahoma's statute also permits actions based on privacy invasions. Okla Stat Ann tit 21, §839.1 (West 1983). Vermont allows tort claims against the state for privacy invasions. Vt Stat Ann tit 12, §5602 (1973). Michigan and North Dakota have privacy statutes that emphasize eavesdropping.Mich Comp Laws Ann §750.539 (West 1968); ND Cent Code §14-02-10 (1981). New Mexico and South Dakota privacy statutes concern wiretapping procedures. NM Stat Ann §30:12:11 (1978); SD Codified Laws Ann §23A-35A (1979). Minnesota, Pennsylvania, and Washington have privacy statutes covering the privacy of communication. Minn Stat Ann §626A.01 (1984); Pa Stat Ann tit 72 §731 (Purdon 1949);Wash Rev Code Ann §9.58.070 (1977).

Page 239, note 132, at end of note add:

An analysis and compendium of state law has been published by the United States Department of Justice. See *Compendium of State Privacy and Security Legislation, 1984 Edition: Overview, Privacy and Security of Criminal History Information,* NCJ-98077 (Sept 1985).

Page 240, text, at end of section add:

In addition to state legislative action to protect the privacy of individuals, most cable television franchises issued in recent years include privacy requirements. The National Cable Television Association and the Videotex Industry Association have formed groups to help draft industry-wide privacy guidelines. Warner-Amex and Cox, two of the largest companies offering cable service, have issued codes of behavior concerning privacy. There is also increasing support for a uniform national standard to preempt state and local regulations. For the time being, though, it appears that industry attempts at self-regulation regarding the privacy issue will increase. See Neustadt & Swanson, *Privacy and Videotex Systems,* 8 BYTE 96 (1983).

Transnational Aspects of Individual Privacy

§6.09   Transborder Data Flows

Page 240, note 138, at end of note add:

See Beling, *Transborder Data Flows: International Privacy Protection and the Free Flow of Information,* 6 B C Intl & Comparative Law 591 (1983). The author focuses on the guidelines proposed by the Council of Europe and the Organization for Economic Cooperation and Development. See *Information Flow Vital to Global Economy,* 6 Transnatl Data Rep 239 (July-Aug 1983). See also Zimmerman, *Transborder Data Flow: Problems with the Council of Europe Convention, or Protecting States From Protectionism,* 4 Nw J Intl Law & Bus 601 (Autumn 1982). Transborder data flow continues to be a topic of concern, particularly in Europe. See Cooper, *Transborder Data Flow and the Protection of Privacy: The Harmonization of Data Protection Law,* 8 Fletcher J 335 (Summer 1984). See also Ortner, *The Privacy Protection Aspect of Transborder Data Flow,* 21 Intl Bus L 171 (Apr 1984) and Matthews, *Protection of Rights of Individuals in the EEC in Relation to Automatic Processing of Data,* Intl Bus L 410 (Oct 1984).

An examination of transborder data flow issues also raises the concern that without international cooperation adverse consequences of adopting new technology will be felt on a national level particularly as a loss of jobs. Additional fears that maintaining a database in a single nation will result in cultural bias were addressed in Minc, *The Informationization of Society* in Policy Implications of Data Network Development in the OECD Area, 154, 156 (1980). The development of such a cultural bias is strongest, but not limited to, in the developing nations.

Transborder data flow control may take the form of industrial protection, privacy protection, and censorship, but as information networks and communications expand, governments will have to address the issues of content regulation, historical precedents set by the evolution of printing and publishing, and self-regulation. See Kesler, *The Legal Realities of Transborder Data Flows,* The Scott Rep, Aug 1985, at 8.

Page 241, note 143, at end of note add:

Most of the national data protection laws in foreign countries provide for:

1. A centralized administrative body that licenses or registers all computerized data bases containing personal information maintained within the country
2. Authority within the data protection agency to inspect the record systems periodically to determine compliance with regulations

for maintaining data bases, and to impose penalties for noncompliance

3. Prohibitions on the collection of certain types of personal information (in Sweden, for example, certain lifestyle information is banned, while in France it is illegal to document religious or union affiliation)

4. Guarantees of the rights of individuals to have access to their records in order to verify or correct them

See Yurow, *Transborder Data Flow Data Protection*, Govt Computer News, Mar 1984.

§6.11 Selected Examples of Foreign Privacy Legislation

Canada

Page 245, note 147, at end of note add:

See also Adams, *Canada's Future TDF Policy: Reconciling Free Flow with National Sovereignty*, 6 Transnatl Data Rep 405 (Oct-Nov 1983).

Sweden

Page 246, note 157, at end of note add:

See also Freese, *The Right to be Alone in Sweden*, 6 Transnatl Data Rep 447 (Dec 1983).

West Germany

Page 247, note 163, at end of note add:

See Riccardi, *The German Federal Data Protection Act of 1977: Protecting the Right to Privacy?*, 6 Boston C Intl & Comp Law 243 (Winter 1983).

Page 248, text, at end of runover paragraph add:

United Kingdom

On July 12, 1984, the United Kingdom enacted the Data Protection Act of 1984 with the intended purpose to protect private individuals from the threat of recording and use of erroneous information about them on computers and, secondly, to enable their data processing industry to participate freely in the European market. The Act also provides for the registration of data users and compensation for damage by reason of data inaccuracy.

Brazil

Brazil has one of the most comprehensive schemes for regulation of computer imports and data flow yet implemented. It allows the establishment of domestic information industries, seeks to ease balance of payments troubles, and minimize reliance on foreign technology. Additionally, the Special Secretariat for Informatics (SEI) has established regulations concerning software registration and approval of all databases.

Page 248, note 173, at end of note add:

See 128 Solicitors J 584 (31 Aug 1984) and Chalton, *The U.K, Data Protection Act of 1984: A New Statutory Right to Privacy*, 4 The Scott Rep 1 n 5 (Feb 1985) for an analysis of this Act.

See Bortnick, *International Information Flow: The Developing World Perspective*, 14 Cornell Intl LJ 333 and Ripper & Wanderley, *The Brazilian Computer and Communications Regulatory Environment and Transborder Data Flow Policy*, Transborder Data Flow Policies (1980).

Potential Developments to Protect Individual Privacy

§6.12   Some Suggested Controls—Self-Discipline and the Ombudsman Approach

Page 250, text, at end of section add:

To satisfy national and international privacy regulations, multinational corporations should take procedural steps regarding the acquisition, use, and dissemination of information. The company should develop a corporate privacy code and privacy compliance program. This approach is recommended by Coombe, Jr. & Kirk, in *Privacy, Data Protection, and Transborder Data Flow: A Corporate Response to International Expectations*, 59 Bus Law 33, at 57-64 (Nov 1983). The code should cover all data protection and privacy elements. These elements include:

1. Public concern for personal data and the need for its protection
2. Recognition of the subject's privacy rights and remedies for their enforcement
3. Regulations governing collection, storage, and use of personal information
4. Denial of personal data disclosure to unauthorized third parties

5. Establishment of a corporate structure to address data protection, privacy, and transborder data flows

See Coombe, Jr. & Kirk, *supra* at 58.

An effective privacy compliance program must ensure that privacy is an organizational concern. The program should utilize corporate counsel, internal auditors, and top management. For each corporate geographical division, subsidiary, and affiliate, a data coordinator should be appointed to coordinate the privacy program. The data coordinator, who must be familiar with corporate practices, procedures, and the company's EDP systems should:

1. Ensure uniform application, consistent identification, description, proper registration, and reporting of company EDP systems

2. Report problems and suggest responses thereto

3. Assist in the training of company personnel concerning applicable data protection and privacy matters

See Coombe, Jr. & Kirk, *supra,* at 62.

Along with the data coordinator, a data controller should be appointed for every jurisdiction in which the company does business. It is the data controller's job to ensure an effective privacy compliance program. As such, the data controller ensures compliance with local law, oversees program implementation, and acts as a liaison between the area data coordinator and the local privacy protection authority. See Coombe, Jr. & Kirk, *supra,* at 62. See also Buss & Martin, *Managing International Information Systems,* 60 Harv Bus Rev 153 (Sept-Oct 1982).

§6.14 —Right to Know and Systems Controls

Page 253, note 210, at end of note add:

The Cable Communications Policy Act of 1984 set forth privacy protection for cable television subscribers. Subscribers must be notified of the scope of data collection, retention, and disclosure. Any disclosure of personally identifiable data must have the prior written or electronic consent of the concerned subscriber. Also, cable subscribers are provided access to all personally identifiable information collected about them. See 47 USC §551.

§6.15 —Computer Security and Cryptology

Page 254, note 226, at end of note add:

Passwords are considered by some to be the only cost-effective means of user authentication. See, Johnston, *Enhancing the Value of Passwords,*

32 Info Sys 44 (Nov 1985). If properly managed and maintained, passwords provide ample security. See Betts, *NBS Releases Standards for Managing Password Security*, 19 Computerworld 19 (July 15, 1985).

Page 255, text, at end of section add:

More then 10 years have passed since the Privacy Act of 1974 was enacted. Since then many states have passed similar legislation, but like the federal statute, they do not take into account the effects for the decade's technological advances. See *Privacy in the Electronic Age: U.S. Law a Decade Later*, The Scott Rep, Nov 1985, at 9.

Future Legal Trends to Protect Individual Privacy

§6.16   Legal Trends in the United States

Page 256, note 231, at end of note add:

See *U.S. International Telecommunications and Information Long-Range Policy Goals*, 6 Transnatl Data Rep 135 (Apr-May 1983) (excerpts from a report prepared by the National Telecommunications and Information Administration); *Trade Barriers to Telecommunications, Data and Information Services*, 6 Transnatl Data Rep 318 (1983); *The International Telecommunications Act of 1983: Hearings on S. 999 Before the Comm on Commerce, Science, and Transportation*, 98th Cong, 1st Sess 24 (1983); *International Telecommunications and Information Policy: Selected Issues for the 1980s: Before the Senate Comm on Foreign Relations*, 98th Cong, 1st Sess 94 (1983) (a report prepared by the Congressional Research Service, Library of Congress).

The, Electronic Communications Privacy Act of 1985, S. 1667 and HR 3378, introduced in September of 1985, would give privacy protection to electronic mail.

§6.17   Transnational Trends

Page 260, note 243, at end of note add:

Unauthorized accessing of computers, or hacking, has not been restricted to the United States. Recent breakins of the British Telecom services were accomplished by a group of four hackers. After accessing a file containing the telephone numbers of BT's technical development computers, the hackers were able to access the development minicomputers and thereby retrieve additional passwords which allowed the hackers access to any part of the Prestel system, including the electronic mail system. This breach of the system enabled the hackers to access Prince Phillip's electronic mail file. See Govt Computer News 10 (May 24, 1985).

§6.18   Attorney Ethics and Privacy (New)

Placing privileged and confidential business information in data bases raises the question as to whether the ease of accessibility to these data bases acts as a de facto waiver of the privileged status of confidential information. This confidential information could include communications occurring within a special relationship context, such as attorney-client, and thus constitute an evidentiary or testimonial privilege against disclosure. Related work product materials might also be computer-stored. Such communication or information must remain confidential. The commingling of confidential and nonconfidential information may act as a waiver of the privilege and subject the confidential information to legal discovery by opposing parties. See Soma & Youngs, *Confidential Communications and Information in a Computer Era,* (to be published in Hofstra L Rev, Fall 1984).

Computer Crime 7

§7.01 Introduction

Page 264, text, at end of section add:

The reality of computer crime is increasingly acknowledged. The American Bar Association recently conducted a survey of approximately 1,000 private organizations and public agencies concerning the nature and occurrences of computer-related crime. While there were only 283 respondents to the survey, the results provide a strong indication of the seriousness of the problem. Almost half the respondents reported experiencing a known and verified incident of computer crime during the 12-month period preceding the survey. Of the respondents reporting known and verifiable losses as a result of computer crime, the losses reported ranged from $145-$730 million. The most significant types of computer crime indicated by the survey respondents were:

1. Use of computers to steal tangible or intangible assets
2. Destruction or alteration of data
3. Use of computers to embezzle funds
4. Destruction or alteration of software
5. Use of computers to defraud consumers, investors or users

Report on Computer Crime, Task Force on Computer Crime, Section on Criminal Justice, American Bar Association (June 1984). See also Perry & Wallich, *Can Computer Crime Be Stopped?*, 21 IEEE Spectrum 34 (May 1984).

§7.02 Definition of Computer Crime

Page 264, note 13, at the end of note add:

Computer Fraud Investigators Handbook, sponsored by New Mexico Law Enforcement Academy (19   ), defines *computer crime* using five elements:

1. Intent to commit a wrongful act.
2. Disguise of purpose or intent
3. Reliance by offender on ignorance of the victim
4. Voluntary victim action to assist the offender
5. Concealment of the violation

§7.03 Targets of Computer Crime

Page 268, note 33, at end of note add:

For an explanation of how a computer crime could occur in a corporate setting, see Atkins, *Jesse James at the Terminal,* 63 Harv Bus Rev 82 (1965).

Page 268, note 34, at end of note add:

Managers are learning the benefits of joining the software industry in fighting program piracy. Mayo, *Business Battles its In-house Pirates,* 4 Bus Computer Sys 60 (1985).

Page 269, text, at end of carryover paragraph add:

The software pirate who has the industry most worried is the middle-level white-collar worker who copies expensive software programs for his or her employer's use. Bailey,*White Collar Software Piracy,* MINI, Mar 1985, at 11-12. See also Goldstein, *Study Reveals Widespread Piracy,* 224 Industry Week 51-52 (Feb 4, 1985). They typical computer criminal is a young employee working in a position of trust in a corporation. Sullivan, *Computer Criminal Profiled as a "Modern-Day" Robin Hood,* 18 Computer World 10 (1984).

Thousands of programs are duplicated each year by managers, teachers, and home users. Trigaboff, *Software Piracy,* 5 MIS Week 11 (1984). It is a corporation's own workers who pose the greatest risk to computer security. Cohen, *International Security,*Wall St J, Sept 16, 1985, at 24 But see *Secure Computing,* 1 Conscience in Computing 1 (1985). The National Center for Computer Crime Data is currently concluding a survey of more than 130 prosecuters' offices. These survey results profile the computer criminal in a different light. According to this survey, the computer criminal is not young, does not steal very much, does not have a sophisticated understanding of computers, and is not a hacker.

§7.04   Victim Unwillingness to Report Computer Crime

Page 269, note 37, at end of note add:

Computer crime is doubling every two and one-half years and no more than 15% of computer crime is officially reported, Leibholz, *Computer Criminals Can No Longer be Coddled,* 3 Govt Computer News 80 (1984).

Page 270, note 41, at end of note add:

According to the respondents of a recent ABA computer crime survey, computer crime is regarded as less important than most violent crimes, but of equal or greater importance than many other types of white collar crime, including antitrust violations, counterfeiting, consumer fraud, bank fraud and embezzlement, securities fraud, and tax fraud. In addition, of the survey respondents that had reported experiencing incidents of computer crime, approximately one third reported that none of the incidents had been reported to law enforcement authorities; one third reported that only some of the incidents had been reported; and the remaining one third indicated that most or all of the incidents had been reported. Report on Computer Crime, Task Force on Computer Crime, Section of Criminal Justice, American Bar Assn (June 1984).

§7.05   Forms of Computer Crime

Page 271, note 43, at end of note add:

The American Bar Association recently released the results of a survey on computer crime in which 48% of the respondents reported known and verifiable incidents of computer crime during the 12 months preceding the survey. The most frequently reported incidents were:

1. Unauthorized use of business computers for personal activities
2. Theft of computer software
3. Theft of tangible or intangible assets by means of a computer
4. Theft of computer hardware
5. Destruction or alteration of software and/or data

(Report on Computer Crime, Task Force on Computer Crime, Section of Criminal Justice, American Bar Assn (June 1984)).

Page 272, note 49, at end of note add:

A logic bomb placed in an IBM computer at the Los Angeles Department of Water and Power froze the internal files: the criminal remains unknown. *A Threat from Malicious Software.* Time, Nov 4, 1985, at 94.

Page 272, note 50, at end of note add:

Silicon Valley forms are hardest hit. One suspect of a seven-teenager nationwide hacker ring illicitly obtained access and service codes by creating programs that hacked the information out. Beeler, *High Tech Sting Nets Seven Teens in Nation Wide Hacker Ring,* Computerworld, Mar 17, 1986, at 10. The access to credit card numbers is also a concern. Merwin, *How Smart Crooks use Plastic,* Forbes, Sept 9, 1985, at 88.

Page 273, note 51, at end of note add:

Tapping into bank computers through phone lines is a way to launder money and points to the involvement of organized crime. Olson, *Hacking the Hacker is the Ultimate Hack,* Rocky Mountain News, Apr 20, 1986, at 78. The telephone has become an accessory to a new version of breaking and entering in the kind of computer-related crimes. Grool, *Dial-up Access is Great Accessary to Crime,* 4 Govt Computer News 46 (1985).

Page 273, text, before last paragraph insert:

Terrorism is a word that has been applied to several specific actions. A computer pirate interrupted a HBO broadcast protesting their prices. Rocky Mountain News, Apr 28, 1986, at 2. Additionally, this applies to the threat of terrorist attacks against United States data centers as the country grows more dependent on these data processing systems. Desmond, *Clear and Present Danger,* 18/19 Computerworld 15 (1985).

§7.06   Detection of Computer Crime

Page 275, text, at end of section add:

The ability to detect computer crime is dependent (outside of accidental discovery) upon formal, internal investigation and auditing techniques. Incorporating these techniques into regular business practices requires assigning computer security responsibilities to a single individual or department and implementing, *and following,* a computer security plan. See Feusse, *Computer Security: What Can We Do?,*

4 Equity 1 (May 1985). As to determining who the perpetrators of computer crime are, 39 per cent of the respondents to an ABA computer crime survey indicated that they had not been able to identify the perpetrators of known incidents of computer crime (*Report on Computer Crime,* Task Force on Computer Crime, Section of Criminal Justice, American Bar Association (June 1984)).

§7.07   Investigation of Computer Crime

Page 276, note 63, at end of note add:

In California, this problem is being countered through the District Attorney's Technology Theft Association (DATTA). DATTA, which is comprised of approximately 30 detectives from a dozen local police agencies around San Jose, California, is a new police task force trained in the sophisticated activities of "chip thieves." See Reaves, *The Chips Police,* 69 ABA J 884 (1983).

Page 276, note 64, at end of note add:

Today the FBI computer crime schools are providing the basic skills agents need to unravel complex computer crimes. Clark, *Computer-Related Crime,* 2 J Fin Software, 20 (1985).

Page 277, text, at end of section add:

The New Mexico Law Enforcement Academy, in its Computer Fraud Investigators Handbook, suggests the following methodology for a computer crime investigation:

1. Initial investigation
2. Investigation planning
3. Information gathering and analysis
4. Interviewing and interrogation
5. Technical data systems review
6. Criminalistics
7. Case presentation

§7.08   —Search and Seizure

Page 278, note 71, at end of note add:

See People v Superior Court of Santa Clara County, 104 Cal 3d 1001, 163 Cal Rptr 906 (Cal Ct App 1980), wherein the State of California appealed a lower court's ruling to suppress evidence obtained pursuant to a search warrant. The evidence involved trade secrets belonging to Intel Corporation, allegedly stolen by an Intel employee. In the affidavit on which the warrant was initially based, the affiant-police officer, averring that he could not identify the property due to its technical nature without expert assistance, requested and received authorization for such assistance (which is authorized under California's Penal Code §1530).

During the execution of the warrant, none of the officers present actually did any searching. Instead, they stood and watched while the experts searched. The latter would inform the officers when they found an item they believed to be one described in the warrant, without, however, communicating the factual basis for such belief. In addition to the items named in the warrant, one of the experts among the searchers, Dunlap, discovered other items he believed to be stolen and was directed by the officers to put such items aside, so that a second affidavit might be drawn authorizing their seizure. This was done, and later in the same day a second affidavit, incorporating the first, described the new items and recited that Dunlap had informed the affiant that he recognized such items as stolen property. The warrant was issued and executed, resulting in the seizure of a number of additional items.

In overturning the lower court's ruling, the Court of Appeals looked to the method for which the experts were used. The court stated that

> when there is a method available for identification of the specific items sought, generic description and seizure are impermissible. But patently no such method was available here. The presence, and participation, of the officer in executing the warrant cannot sensibly be understood to require knowledge which a police officer could not reasonably be expected to possess. Consequently, we think there is no requirement that such experts, prior to stating their conclusions, engage in the futile task of attempting to educate accompanying police officers in the rudiments of computer science . . . .

163 Cal Rptr at 909.

In regard to the items seized under the second warrant, the court applied a practical approach. It noted that California courts have "in effect, pragmatically accepted the 'expertise' of a dog whose sense of smell led to the detection of marijuana, and commonly informers in narcotics cases have not been required to articulate the basis upon which their belief in the narcotic nature of contraband is grounded." The court continued by stating that accepting the "probability of truth in the conclusions of trained experts in the computer field respecting the likelihood that reticles bearing the logo of other companies—in the otherwise inexplicable possession of a rival company's employee—

were stolen property, seems much less tenuous than the examples just cited." *Id* 911.

§7.09   Problems of Prosecution—21st Century Crime and the 20th Century Courts

Page 280, note 78, at end of note add:

Compex legal issues are involved in computer-assisted crime. Gish, *Computer Crime & Punishment,* 1 Info Strategy 11 (1985).

Page 280, text, at end of section add:

During the extensive research for this supplement, the author found very few cases dealing specifically with computer-related crime. This is not to say, however, that computer crime is not occurring. For example, recently TRW's Information Services Division, based in Orange County, California (which handles up to 90 million consumer credit files), found that its computer security had been breached. Rocky Mountain News, June 22, 1984, at 64, col 1.

The lack of computer-related crime cases is also due in part to the fact that it is a fairly recent phenomenon. It is the author's contention, however, that the lack of case law is the result of a combination of three factors, all of which are discussed in this chapter: (1) the unwillingness of the victim to report the crime (see §7.04); (2) the unwillingness of prosecutors to bring a case to court due to the lack of clear laws precisely defining the illegal nature of the act (see §§7.09-7.11); and (3) the inability of judges and juries to fully understand the technical complexities involved in computer-related criminal activities (see §§7.09-7.11).

The Supreme Court of Indiana refused to expand the criminal larceny statute to include use of computer time. An employee of the City of Indianapolis was using the city computer for his personal business. The computer was leased at a flat, fixed rate. The employee's use did not increase the city's cost or deny the use for city business. The problems of prosecution are continuing to occur (*State of Indiana v McGraw,* 480, NE2d 552 (Ind. 1985).

§7.10   —Prosecution Under The Federal Criminal Code

Page 280, note 81, at end of note add:

Sullivan & Shaw, *Criminal Penalities for Misappropriation of Computer Technology,* 2 Computer Law 19 (Jan 1985) (an overview of federal criminal statutes that might be used in the prosection of computer crime); George, *Contemporary Legislation Governing Computer Crimes,* 21 Criminal L Bull 389 (1985) (describes the nature of computer crime using 12 examples and then shows applicability to existing criminal doctrines).

Page 281, note 84, add to Giovengo citation:

cert denied, 450 US 1032 (1981).

Page 282, note 91, at end of note add:

United States v Computer Servs Corp was overruled by the Fourth Circuit Court of Appeals. 689 F2d 1181 (4th Cir 1982), *cert denied,* 103 S Ct 729 (1983). In concluding that dismissal of the wire fraud and mail fraud charges were in error, the court found "nothing in the statutory language itself or in the legislative history of the wire fraud, mail fraud and false claims statutes to require a determination that prosecution under one must be at the expense of prosecuting under the other. . . ." 689 F2d at 1187-88.

Page 283, text, after first full paragraph add:

The Racketeer Influenced and Corrupt Orgainizations Act (RICO) creates a strong weapon and substantial sanctions against software piracy. See Coolley, *RICO: Modern Weaponry Against Software Pirates,* 5 Computer LJ 143 (Fall 1984). Additionally, the Counterfeit Access Device and Computer Fraud Abuse Act of 1984 establishes penalties with a maxium of $5,000 or twice the value obtained or the loss created (18 USC §1030(c)(2)(A)). Penalities rise to $100,000 or twice the value obtained by the offense and a 20-year imprisonment for repeat offenses that affect interstate or foreign commerce (18 USC §1029(a), (c)). An *offense* is defined as one in which the defendant knowingly and with intent to defraud either uses or traffics in unauthorized access devices (18 USC §1029(a)(2)). For an overview of this act see Thackeray, *Computer Related Crimes,* 25 Jurimetrics J 300 (Spring 1985).

§7.11   —Prosecution Under State Statutes

Page 285, note 110, at end of note add:

To date, 38 states have addressed the issue of computer crime through statutory provisions. Thirty-four states (Alaska, Arizona, California, Colorado, Connecticut, Delaware, Florida, Georgia, Hawaii, Idaho, Illinois, Iowa, Kentucky, Louisiana, Maryland, Michigan, Minnesota, Missouri, Montana, Nevada, New Mexico, North Carolina, North Dakota, Oklahoma, Pennsylvania, Rhode Island, South Carolina, South Dakota, Tennessee, Utah, Virginia, Washington, Wisconsin, and Wyoming) have enacted some form of specific computer crime statute while four states (Alabama, Maine, Massachusetts, and Ohio) have addressed the issue through provisions incorporated into existing statutes.

The majority of the state computer crime statutes prohibit the knowing, willful and unauthorized access of a computer or computer system with or without the intent to devise or execute any scheme or artifice to defraud and the knowing, willful and unauthorized access, alteration, destruction or damage to a computer, computer system, computer program or data. (*See e.g.*, Ga Code Ann §§16-9-90 to -95 (1984).) Thirty-two of the state statutes contain antifraud provisions. Thirty-three of the statutes prohibit the destruction of computer data while thirty-two of the statutes prohibit the destruction of computer equipment. In addition, thirty of the state computer crime statutes prohibit the unauthorized access of a computer or computer system alone.

Six states (Delaware, Florida, Louisiana, Missouri, Nevada, and South Carolina) have statutes which address the issue of denying the use of computer services to authorized users or causing a degradation of such services. Three states (Connecticut, Delaware, and Virginia) provide for a private right of action by anyone damaged by a person who violates the state's computer crime statute, while three states (Connecticut, Delaware, and Wisconsin) provide for the appointment of a receiver to confiscate or restrict the use of the computer equipment of a person allegedly, or convicted of, violating the computer crime statute.

For reprints of existing and pending state computer crime statutes, see Computer Crime L Rep (JFK Library, California State University) (1984). For summaries of current and proposed state computer crime statutes, see generally Soma, Smith, & Sprague, *Legal Analysis of Electronic Bulletin Board Activities*, 7 New Eng L Rev 571 (Summer 1985).

Finally, the computer industry has drafted its own Model Computer Crime Act. It classifies computer crime into the categories of:

1. Computer fraud
2. Damage or destruction of computer property
3. Computer trespass
4. Theft of computer property
5. Wrongful acquisition or disclosure of an access device.
6. Wrongful denial of access or use of a computer

The model act also addresses the issues of:

1. Using the computer as an instrument of forgery
2. Employee authorization
3. Injunctive relief against a violator of the act

4. Civil relief for injuries sustained as a result of violations of the model act

For complete citation of state computer statutes and an overview see Thackeray, *Computer Related Crimes,* 25 Jurimetrics J 300 (Spring 1985). See also Marmaro, *Criminal Law and Technology Protection: Prosecuting a Dishonest Employee,* 2 Computer Law 15 (Dec 1985), which addresses state criminal statutes for prosecuting theft, or misappropriation of technology cases.

Page 286, at end of subsection add:

Civil remedies for computer crime are currently provided for in five states, Connecticut, Virgina, California, New Jersey, and Delaware. These civil remedies may include the right to bring a damage suit or suit for injunction as well as enforcement actions by a state attorney general, or restitution hearings. See generally Bloom Becker, *Civil Remedies for Computer Crimes,* The Scott Rep 8 (Oct 1985); *Computer Crime Update,* Computer L Strategist 2 (July 1985).

§7.12 Trial and Evidence Difficulties in Prosecuting Computer Crime

Page 289, note 124, at end of note add:

The Computer Fraud Investigators Handbook, sponsored by the New Mexico Law Enforcement Academy (1985), outlines basic procedures for maintaining computer evidence.

§7.13 —Admission of Computer-Related Evidence Under the Current Rules of Evidence

Page 291, note 132, add to Russo citation:

cert denied, 414 US 1157 (1974).

Page 291, note 132, at end of note add:

For additional cases dealing with the admissibility of computer printouts, *see also* United States v Liebert, 519 F2d 542 (3d Cir), *cert denied,* 423 US 985 (1975); United States v Fendley, 522 F2d 181 (5th Cir 1975); United States v Scholle, 553 F2d 1109 (8th Cir), *cert denied,* 434 US 940 (1977); United States v Weatherspoon, 581 F2d 595 (7th Cir 1978); United States v Vela, 673 F2d 86 (5th Cir 1982); Capital Marine Supply, Inc v M/V Roland Thomas, II, 719 F2d 104 (5th Cir 1983).

Page 291, note 133, delete note and substitute:

According to Uniform Laws Annotated, Master Edition 1984, the Uniform Business Records as Evidence Act was withdrawn by the National Conference of Commissioners on Uniform State Laws in 1966.

Page 295, note 159, at end of note add:

In addition, the Uniform Rules of Evidence, adopted by 22 states, provides in Rule 1001(3) that if data are stored in a computer or similar device, any printout or other output readable by sight, shown to reflect the data accurately, is an "original." 13 ULA 209, 350 (1980).

Some states have specifically provided for the admissibility of computer printouts as evidence. In California, for example, printed representations of computer information and computer programs will be presumed to be accurate representations of the computer information or computer programs that they purport to represent. If, however, an opposing party introduces evidence that such a printed representation is inaccurate or unreliable, the party introducing it into evidence will have the burden of proving, by a preponderance of evidence, that the printed representation is the best available evidence of the existence and content of the computer information or computer programs that it purports to represent. Cal Evid Code §1500.5 (West 1984).

§7.15   Deterrence—Security

Page 298, text, at end of carryover paragraph add:

However, executives should beware, because it has been suggested that a lack of a corporate computer security policy can serve as evidence that the executives have not been sufficiently attentive to their legal responsibilities, Sherizen, *Computer Crime Requires Preventative Action by Executives,* 18 Computerworld 11 (Oct 1984).

Page 300, text, at end of section add:

The American Bar Association recently completed a survey concerning computer crime which solicited responses from private enterprises and public organizations. The respondents to the survey ranked the means of preventing and deterring computer crime in the following order of effectiveness:

1. More comprehensive and effective self-protection by private business
2. Education of users concerning vulnerabilities of computer usage
3. More severe penalties in federal and state criminal statutes
4. Greater education of the public regarding computer crime

The survey respondents then identified the following steps which their organizations had actually taken to prevent and deter computer crime:

1. Limited access to computer programs and computer logic
2. Limited access to computer operations
3. Frequent changing of access codes
4. Limited access to input of data into computer
5. Installation of asset controls and accountability
6. Frequent security checks of computer and operations
7. Security education for employees

Report on Computer Crime, Task Force on Computer Crime, Section of Criminal Justice, American Bar Association (June 1984). See also Littman, *The Security Challenge*, PC Week, Nov 20, 1984, at 67. For additional information on various forms of security measures see Miller, *Beware of the "Hacker" Attack*, 76 Banking 50 (Nov 1984).

§7.17 —Proposed Federal Legislation

Page 301, note 185, at end of note add:

See also Wharton, *Legislative Issues in Computer Crime*, 21 Harv J on Legis 239 (1984).

Page 303, note 199, at end of note add:

To date, no federal computer crime bill has been passed. There are three computer crime bills pending in the Senate: S 1733 (Sen Paul Trible (R-Va)) would make the fraudulent or illegal use of any computer owned or operated by the United States, certain financial institutions, and entities affecting interstate commerce, a crime; S 1920 (Sen Paul Tsongas (D-Mass)) would establish a Small Business Computer Crime and Security Task Force; S 2270 (Sen William Cohen (R-Me)) would also make the fraudulent or illegal use of any computer owned or operated by the United States, certain financial institutions, and entities affecting interstate commerce, a crime. S 2270 would also punish anyone who damages, destroys, alters, or deletes any computer program or computer-stored information intentionally and without authorization. In addition, the bill would make it unlawful to intentionally buy or sell a password or access code to a computer for the purpose of executing a scheme to defraud or to obtain money, property, or services.

There are a variety of bills pending in the House: HR 1092 (Rep Bill

Nelson (D-Fla)) would make the fraudulent or illegal use of any computer owned or operated by the United States, certain financial institutions, and entities affecting interstate commerce, a crime; HR 3075 (Rep Ron Wyden (D-Or)) would establish a Small Business Computer Crime and Security Task Force; HR 3181 (Rep Hamilton Fish (R-NY)) would provide penalties for credit card counterfeiting and related fraud; HR 4301 (Rep Lawrence Coughlin (R-Pa)) would amend existing law to provide penalties for certain computer-related crimes; HR 4384 (Rep Dan Mica (D-Fla)) would establish a computer security research program and Interagency Committee on Computer Crime and Abuse, as well as provide criminal penalties for computer abuse; HR 5112 (Rep William Hughes (D-NJ)) would provide penalties for the counterfeiting of access devices, and for related fraud.

See generally *Computer Crime Bills Pending*, 22 Data Mgmt 37 (1984).

The 98th Congress enacted S 1920 and HR 3075. This amendment to the Smal Business Act established a Small Business Computer Crime and Security Task Force (Pub L No 98-362)

However, in the 99th Congress, two bills have been introduced in the Senate and two bills have been introduced in the House. In the Senate, S 2281 (Sen Paul Trible (R VA)) would provide additional penalties for fraud and related activities in connection with access devices and computers; S 1776 (Sen Patrick Leahy (D VT)) would amend little 18 U S C with respect to the interception of certain communications and other forms of surveillance. In the House, HR 3378 (Rep Robert Kastenmeier (D Wis)) is the counterpart to S 1667; HR 3381 (Rep Bell McCollum (R FL)) would enact the Federal Computers Systems Protection Act.

Page 304, text, at end of section add:

The proposed federal legislation listed in note 199, *supra*, is now useful only as a tool for tracking the legislative history of the recent Counterfeit Access Device and Computer Fraud and Abuse Act of 1984, Pub L No 98-473, 98 Stat 755, 1981 US, Code Cong & Ad News 2190 (to be codified at 18 USC §1030). The new act essentially prohibits the unauthorized access of a computer to:

1. Obtain government information considered to be protected for national defense reasons or is otherwise restricted

2. Obtain information contained in a financial record of a financial institution or consumer reporting agency

3. Knowingly use, modify, destroy, or disclose information in, or prevent authorized use of, a computer operated for or on behalf of the United States government

A close reading of the act is advised however. It does not define *access* or *use*. There is the potential, therefore, of confusion as to what exactly constitutes the unauthorized use of a computer under the act. See Tompkins & Mar, *Computer Crime Law Lacks Scope and Precision*, Legal Times, Apr 8, 1985, at 16.

The first indictment under the new act was handed down February 5, 1985 in *United States v Fadriquela*, No 85-CR-40 (D Colo 1985). The defendant, from Los Angeles, California, was charged by a grand jury of violating 18 USC §1030 (the new Computer Fraud Act), §1343 (Wire Fraud) and §1001 (Fraud).

Specifically, Fadriquela was accused of violating §1030(a)(3) and (c)(2)(A) by the following acts: the knowing and unauthorized access of a computer in the Denver, Colorado Regional Office of the United States Department of Agriculture—Forest Service, and the modification of information in said computer through which superuser passwords were created; the knowing and unauthorized access of a computer in the supervisor's office in Ft. Collins, Colorado in order to access the Forest Service computer in Denver; and the knowing and unauthorized access of the Ft. Collins computer and having data transmitted to the defendant and his having the transmission printed.

The additional charges stemmed from the defendant's alleged scheme to fraudulent access of the Tymnet and Telenet communications system by the use of access numbers not assigned to him so that he would not be billed for the services utilized. Finally, the fraud charges stemmed from the allegation that the defendant represented himself as an authorized user of the computer systems accessed in order to gain access to those systems.

The defendant was sentenced on June 14, 1985 after pleading guilty to three misdemeanor charges. He was sentenced to probation and given a $3,000 fine. In addition, the defendant was ordered to perform 200 hours of community work and pay $75 to a federal victim's compensation fund.

Throughout the case, the defendant, a computer operator, insisted he did not know he was breaking the law. Assistant United States Attorney Catherine Goodwin said that it cost between $60,000 and $100,000 to trace the defendant's path of access into the computers and to modify the systems in order to make them more secure. She stated that the federal government may seek restitution in future computer crime cases. See *Computer Hacker Given $3,000 Fine*, The Denver Post, June 15, 1985, at 15A, col 1.

See Generally, Sullivan & Shaw, *Criminal Penalties for Misappropriation of Computer Technology*, 2 Computer Law 19 (Jan 1985).

§7.17A   Recent Developments (New)

With the proliferation of the home computer, a relatively recent phenomenon has occurred—the electronic bulletin board (BBS). A conservative estimate puts the number of BBSs nationwide at over

1500. See generally Beeston & Tucker, Hooking In (1984). Other informal estimates range as high as 3500 BBSs nationwide. Little formal research has been conducted on this new development. The following information is based on the author's own informal research, accessing BBSs, and interviews conducted with BBS operators and users.

An electronic bulletin board is essentially self-explanatory—people call in via a telephone modem and read and post messages with their personal computers. Generally, BBSs specialize in certain topics, dealing exclusively, for example, with dog breeding information, real estate, or computer equipment and programming tips. A growing number of BBSs, however, are beginning to deal exclusively with illegal, or quasi-illegal, information. These boards are broken down into subclassifications dealing in specialized information for "hackers," "phreakers," and "pirates."

Originally, the term *hacker* pertained to someone who spent hours continually refining a program, constantly trying to make it a little more perfect. Today, a hacker is also someone who attempts to make an unauthorized entry into a computer system. For most hackers, the sole purpose of such entry is just to be able to outsmart the computer security system. Once inside a computer system, some hackers like to "browse through the files" or leave a message, just to let the computer analysts know the hacker was there.

A small percentage of hackers, however, are destructive. Some will vandalize a system by erasing files or by trying to make the operating system inoperative. There is also a class of hackers known as *social hackers* who disrupt the computer systems of corporations and entities whom they perceive as evil, such as defense contractors or producers of chemicals. An even smaller percentage of hackers enter computer systems for profit. They manipulate files to send out payments or merchandise to themselves under fictitious accounts.

Hacker boards are BBSs specializing in hacker information and carry information hackers share to enable others to penetrate computer systems. The information generally consists of the telephone numbers and access codes to computer systems which have telecommunication hookups.

Phreakers refers to people who specialize in using telephone services free of charge. Phreakers utilize devices known as "black boxes" and "blue boxes" which are used to bypass AT&T's and the Bell System's billing mechanisms. In addition, phreakers use unauthorized passwords to access microwave communications services such as MCI Communications. The most common use for these free long distance telephone services is to call out-of-state BBSs.

A subclass of the phreakers are the *phrackers*. Phrackers use the phreaker information to hack into out-of-state computer systems without a long distance billing record to trace back to the point of origin of the call.

Phreaker boards are BBSs which specialize in phreaker information. The information generally consists of local telephone numbers which access a telecommunications computer and a list of access codes which are valid for that number. Additional information, however, can be as complex as schematics for designing a black box.

Pirates are people who specialize in acquiring, copying, and distributing what are generally unauthorized copies of computer software. They appear to believe that all computer software should be freely available to, if not everyone, at least themselves. This includes software that is *write protected* (software which is supposedly designed to prevent copying). The pirate merely works at the software until the write protection is somehow circumvented.

Pirate boards usually trade information and services for software. Software can be *downloaded* (sent) to the BBS to be stored, or *uploaded* (received) by the caller from the BBS files. In addition, pirates share messages on instructions and documentation for the software they use and share with each other.

The difficulties in recognizing and prosecuting computer-related crime, as discussed in this chapter, are compounded by the proliferation of electronic bulletin boards. Information which previously was known only to a few people can now be shared nationwide. It is estimated that the telephone numbers and access codes to large computer systems can be posted on BBSs across the United States in a matter of days.

The first known arrest of a BBS operator (referred to as a SYSOP for Systems Operator) as a result of information posted on a board occurred in May, 1984 in Los Angeles. Pacific Bell learned of a stolen telephone charge number posted on the BBS operated by Thomas Tcimpidis. Pacific Bell notified the police, who seized Mr. Tcimpidis' computer equipment and charged him with violating the California law prohibiting the publishing of telephone credit codes. Cal Penal Code §502.7 (West Supp 1984).

The arrest immediately raised First Admendment concerns. Mr. Tcimpidis claimed from the outset that he ran a legitimate bulletin board and that the credit code had been posted without his knowledge while he was out of town. The conviction of Mr. Tcimpidis would immediately raise the issue of whether a BBS SYSOP is strictly liable for any illegal information posted on his or her BBS. The issue is still left open for consideration as the charges against Mr. Tcimpidis were dropped in February, 1985. See generally Stipp, *Computer Bulletin Boards Fret Over Liability for Stolen Data*, Wall St J, Nov 9, 1984, at 31, col 1.

The computer hackers have recently come to the attention of the national press. One immediately apparent aspect of hacker-related activities is that most of the participants, at least those catching the fancy of the press, are juveniles. This leaves prosecutorial issues subject to individual states' statutes. Congress has addressed the issue of juvenile crime. *See* 42 USC §5602.

Current federal statutes split young offenders into three groups:

1. The Young Adult Offenders Act (18 USC §4209) covers 22-26 year-olds

2. The 18-21 year-olds are covered under the Federal Youth Corrections Act (18 USC ch 402)

3. The Juvenile Delinquency Act (18 USC §5031 *et seq*)) covers offenders under 18 years of age

The primary result of these statues, however, is that offenders who are under the age of 19 are routinely turned over to the individual states, as the legislative history indicates a federal preference to individual states' juvenile systems. See 1985 US Code Cong & Ad News 3526. Only the most violent offenders are kept under the federal system.

As the press and the public have discovered the computer hacker, the hacker has begun achieving notoriety in a number of ways. Richard Sandza recently wrote an excellent article for Newsweek magazine giving a fascinating insight into the world of underground BBSs. See Sandza, *The Night of the Hackers,* Newsweek, Nov 12, 1984, at 17. Although Mr. Sandza gave a very insightful and accurate account of underground BBS activites, he raised the ire of hackers across the nation. Mr. Sandza received hundreds of harassing and threatening phone calls. The most serious consequence was, however, that his Visa account number was taken from the credit files of TRW (the nation's largest credit information operation) and posted on BBSs.

A different sort of social activity was recently performed by a 14 year-old Minneapolis computer enthusiast. A local computer programmer had been arrested on charges of sexual misconduct with a juvenile. In the suspect's home, police found floppy disks which they suspected contained incriminating evidence. The disks had, however, been locked with protective software. Enter Peter Leppik, who cracked the lock protection on the disks within 45 minutes. The contents of the disks turned out to be a diary containing sex-related material. See Elmer-DeWitt, *Triumph of a Hacker Sleuth,* Time, Jan 28, 1985, at 91; see also §7.13.

In regard to computer security, who better to give advice than a reformed hacker? Bill Landreth, a self-described master hacker, has recently published a book on computer security. In this excellent guide to computer security, Mr. Landreth discusses not only technical methods and weak points in computer security, but also the long-term perspectives and goals of computer security—all in a style that will be acceptable to both those with little or extensive technical knowledge.

Mr. Landreth also provides valuable insight into the profile and the motives of today's young hackers. See B. Landreth *Out of the Inner Circle: A Hacker's Guide to Computer Security*, (1985).

Finally, it was inevitable that the ultimate crime would be committed *by* a computer. It was difficult to ignore the screaming headline: *Jealous Computer Kills Top Scientist.* The story leads stated: " 'It was cold-blooded murder,' says grieving wife" and "Old machine electrocutes owner—after he buys a more advanced model." See 5 Weekly World News, July 10, 1984, at 5. On a more serious note, industry will have to face issues of work-related injuries and fatalities related to computer assisted machinery, such as robots. A Michigan worker, working with an automated diecasting machine, died five days after being pinned between the back of a robot and a steel pole. See 2600 (an underground phreaker's magazine), vol 2, Apr, 1985, at 2-21, citing a New York Times article.

Banking—Electronic Funds Transfer Systems   8

§8.04   —Depository Institutions

Page 313, note 22, at end of note add:

The entry of banks into the role of providing of data processing services was challenged in Association of Data Processing Serv Orgs, Inc v Board of Governors of The Fed Reserve Sys, 745 F2d 677 (DC Cir 1984). The issue arose when Citicorp sought approval to establish a subsidiary to engage in data processing services on the basis that such activities were *closely related to banking.* The Federal Reserve System's Board of Governor's decision was upheld on the basis that data processing services and turnkey product sales will be permissible as *closely related to banking activities* so long as the data involved in the proposed services is *closely related to banking activities.*

§8.11   Automated Teller Machines

Page 331, note 126, at end of note add:

For an analysis of the legal problems raised by sharing automated teller machines in an electronic funds transfer system, see Devolder, *Expansionary Possibilities for Affiliated Commercial Banks: A Current Dilemma,* 16 Pac LJ 895 (1985).

§8.14   Economics of Electronic Funds Transfer

Page 334, note 147, at end of note add:

The ability of financial instutions to use computer technology can increase competition and improve profits. See Brown, *Automation Is the Key to SouthTrust's Improved Profits,* 124 Tr & Est 40 (July 1985)

Page 335, note 150, at end of note add:

For a synopsis of current trends in electronic cash management, see *Electronic Cash Management Seen As Cost Saver for Corporations,* 59 J Accountancy 26(2) (June 1985). See also *Future of Automated Transactions Viewed In Survey of Cash Managers,* 60 J Accountancy 38(4) (Sept 1985).

Page 335, note 153, at end of note add:

Computer program failure at the Bank of New York led to a $32 billion overdraft. The bank was criticized by the United States Subcommittee on Domestic Monetary Policy, see *Software Failure Causes a $32 Billion Overdraft,* XIII EDPACS 10 (Jan 1986)

Page 335, note 157, at end of note add:

An additional factor in the cost/benefit analysis of EFT is reflected in a Banking Circular from the Comptroller of the Currency Administrator of National Banks, dated January 18, 1985 (BC-187). This circular advised national banks of the importance of performing financial reviews on their data processing service providers.

Because of their increasing dependence on computer systems, financial institutions must assure themselves of continued, uninterrupted data processing support. When, due to financial problems, data processing services have failed or have been weakened to the extend that their ability to provide dependable service was questionable, financial institutions have been unprepared. A regular review of the supplier's financial status can help reduce the impact of any problems by giving the institution ample time to arrange for alternate service.

Page 336, note 159, at end of note add:

Competition in the financial services industry is growing as financial institutions increase their use of technological advances. Computer technology has lowered the cost and increased the speed of funds transfer. See DeSanto, *Product Expansion in the Banking Industry: An Analysis and Revision of Section 4(c)(8) of the Bank Holding Company Act,* LIII Fordham L Rev 1127 (1985).

Page 336, note 164, at end of note add:

For an overview of various methods of funds transfer available to the public, see Shupack, *Cashier's Checks, Certified Checks and True Cash Equivalence,* 6 Cardozo L Rev 467 (1985).

Page 337, note 166, at end of note add:

Sears, Roebuck & Co recently began marketing the "Discover" credit card on a national scale. This expands Sears involvement in the financial services area. The Sears marketing department expects the

Discover card to become the dominant credit card in the United States. American Banker, Feb 5, 1986, at 1, col 1.

Legal Issues Surrounding Electronic Funds Transfer

§8.15 Branch Banking and Electronic Funds Transfer

Page 338, note 170, at end of note add:

See generally Ritchie, *Banks Should Be Able to Offer Financial Services Nationally,* 124 Tr & Est 18 (1985).

§8.19 Consumer Concerns: The Uniform Commercial Code and the Electronic Funds Transfer Act

Page 350, note 233, at end of note add:

For a comparison of the EFTA and the UCC as they affect bank liability, see Hewes & Preston, *Is There a Time Bomb in the Electronic Funds Transfer Act?,* 100 Banking LJ 274 (1983).

Page 351, note 235, at end of note add:

UCC Articles 3 and 4 have been found not to apply to commercial electronic fund transfers. In those situations when neither the UCC nor the EFTA apply, the courts have resorted to common law contract theory or simple negligence to allow recovery.

See Delbrueck & Co v Manufacturers Hanover Trust Co, 609 F2d 1042 (2d Cir 1979), wherein the court determined that since the UCC failed to deal specifically with the problems of EFT transactions, the UCC did not apply; Evra Corp v Swiss Bank Corp, 673 F2d 951 (7th Cir 1982), wherein the court, in adopting the reasoning of *Delbrueck,* decided that the framers of the UCC never contemplated extending the UCC to EFT transactions and, therefore, the UCC did not apply; Houston Contracting Corp v Chase Manhattan Bank, NA, 539 F Supp 247 (SDNY 1982), wherein the court found that an unsigned telex payment order is not covered by the UCC, as it could not be considered a "demand item" as required by §4-302 of the UCC. In *Houston Contracting,* the court also determined that for an item to be considered a demand item, it must be negotiable (i.e., a check or draft). 539 F Supp at 249.

See also Jetton, *Evra Corp v Swiss Bank Corp, Bank Negligence in Wire Transfers,* 9 Rut J Computers & L 374 (1983); Miller & Scott, *Commercial*

Paper, Bank Deposits and Collections, and Commercial Electronic Fund Transfers, 38 Bus L 1129 (1983).

Federal legislation and regulation have had a major impact on electronic funds transfer and bank competition. See generally Lovett, *Federalism, Boundary Conflicts and Responsible Financial Regulation,* 18 Loy LA Rev 1053 (1985).

The Permanent Editorial Board of the American Law Institute is currently developing the Uniform Payments Code (UPC). The UPC is an attempt to protect EFT transactions with regulations similar to those offered by Articles 3 and 4 of the UCC. For various interpretations of the proposed UPC, see *A Systems Approach to Payment Modes: Moving Towards a New Payments Code,* 16 UCC LJ 383 (1984); Miller, *A Report on the New Payments Code,* 39 Bus L 1215 (1984); *Overcoming the Obstacles to Implementation of Point of Sale Electronic Funds Transfer Systems; EFTA and the New Uniform Payments Code,* 69 Va L Rev 1351 (1983); Vergari, *A Critical Look at the New Uniform Payments Code,* 9 Rutgers J Computers & L 317 (1983); Geary, *One Size Doesn't Fit All: Is the New Payments Code a Good Idea,* 9 Rutgers J Computers & L 337 (1983); *Electronic Fund Transfers and the New Payments Code,* 37 Bus L 1065 (1982).

Page 352, note 240, at end of note add:

The FRB has amended this definition to cover debit card point of sale transactions that result eventually in an electronic ordering of a debit or credit to an account. Essentially the FRB is eliminating the word "initiated" from the definition as it applies to POS transactions.

The board has also narrowed the definition of an EFT by eliminating telephone transactions from coverage by the EFTA unless there is some preceding written agreement concerning telephone transactions.

The EFTA specifically gives the FRB the authority to prescribe regulations necessary to carry out the purposes of the act. 12 CFR pt 205. Concerning telephone-initiated transfers and the applicability of the EFTA, *see* Kashanchi v Texas Commerce Medical Bank, NA, 703 F2d 936 (5th Cir 1983).

Page 352, note 241, at end of note add:

For a review of unauthorized electonic funds transfer in relation to consumer liability, see Shinn, *An Overview of Unauthorized Electronic Fund Transfers; Alternatives in Reducing Consumer Liability,* 90 Com LJ 216 (1985)

Page 352, note 245, at end of note add:

The Uniform New Payment Code Draft No 3 was published June 2, 1983 by a committee created by the American Law Institute and the National Conference of Commissioners on Uniform State Laws. This codification provides a proposed framework of law that is applicable to all methods of payments including wire transfer. Designed to replace the Electronic Funds Transfer Act in areas involving electronic funds transfers, the NPC covers topics not addressed by the EFTA, such as consequential damages. See *New Uniform Payments Code,* (Permanent Editorial Board for the Uniform Commercial Code Draft No 3, 1983).

Page 352, note 246, at end of note add:

See generally Vergari, *Latent Legal Repercussions in Electronic Financial Services and Transaction,* 34 Det LJ 539 (1985).

Page 353, note 249, at end of note add:

The FRB is considering lessening the burden placed on banks by the EFTA. Among their proposals are an extended time period for POS error resolution and increasing the flexibility of the charge disclosure rules. 12 CFR pt 205.

Page 353, note 253, at end of note add:

See Judd v Citibank, 107 Misc 2d 529, 435 NYS2d 210 (1980), wherein Citibank offered only a computer printout and the nonexpert testimony of a branch manager to rebut the plaintiff's evidence that the plaintiff was at work during the time of the disputed transaction and testimony by the plaintiff that her identification number was not given to anyone else. The court refused to accept Citibank's computer printout over the credible evidence offered by the plaintiff, and, therefore, ruled in favor of the plaintiff.

Liability for losses suffered by automatic teller machine clients when they are forced to make a withdrawal is placed on the bank. The Federal Reserve Board has viewed the forced withdrawals as unauthorized transactions for which the bank is responsible for reimbursing the customer for lost funds. 70 ABA J 34 (Sept. 84). This issue was also addressed in Ognibee v Citibank NA, 112 Misc 2d 219, 446 NYS2d 845 (1981).

Page 353, note 255, at end of note add:

For proposed consumer schemes for unauthorized use of electronic funds transfer, see *Consumer Protection and Payment Systems; Regulatory Policy for the Technological Era,* 98 Harv L Rev 870 (1985). For an analysis of how to determine fault when unauthorized electronic funds tranfer occurs, see generally Norman, *Unauthorized Access to EFT Information; Who Should Be Responsible?,* 6 Computer LJ 171 (1985).

Page 354, note 261, at end of note add:

See Page, *Stop Payment in the New Uniform Payments Code,* 9 Rutgers J Computers & L 353 (1983).

Page 355, note 268, at end of note add:

For a thorough discussion of the notice requirements and error resolution procedures provided by the EFTA, see Budnitz, *Federal Regulation of Consumer Disputes in Computer Banking Transactions,* 20 Harv J Legis 31 (1983). For a detailed analysis of damages available under the EFTA, see Dow, *Damages Under the Federal Electronic Fund Transfer Act: A proposed Construction of Sections 910 and 915,* 23 Am Bus LJ 1 (1985).

§8.20 Privacy Concerns and the Electronic Funds Transfer System

Page 356, note 272, at end of note add:

See also Trubow, *Liability of a Business Computer User for Improper Disclosure of a Customers Personal Financial Information,* 17 J Mar L Rev 989 (Summer 1984). The use of telecommunication in business raises privacy and security concerns, see NYLJ, Sep 23, 1985, at 31, col 1.

Page 356, note 273, at end of note add:

The demand for information has led to a possible invasion of personal privacy. See Solomon, *Personal Privacy and the "1984" Syndrome,* 7 W New England L Rev 753 (Winter 1985).

Page 357, note 279, at end of note add:

Legislation has been introduced which would amend existing United States banking law to give Treasury Department investigators an administrative subpoena power. The 1984 Drug Money Seizure Act (S 2579) would enable the review of offshore banking transfers and would stiffen the penalty imposed against financial institutions and individuals who willfully violate the law's reporting requirements.

Page 357, note 281, at end of note add:

See also Nicewander, *Financial Record Privacy—What Are and What Should Be the Rights of the Customer of a Depository Institution,* 16 St Mary's LJ 601 (1985). For a checklist approach to electronic funds transfer liability, see Bequai, *Legal Liabilities Arising Out of EFTS: A Checklist,* 89 Com LJ 289 (1985).

Future of Electronic Funds Transfers

§8.22   Amalgamation of Interstate Banking Activities

Page 367, text, at end of section add:

The Federal Reserve Board (FRB) has recently given a boost to the computerization of banking. The FRB has altered its interpretation of the Banking Holding Company Act (12 USC §1843) to allow bank holding companies (BHCs) to engage in the selling of a far wider range of computer services than was previously permitted.

The standard, as formerly applied, permitted only services closely related to banking. (See *National Courier Association v Board of Governors of the Federal Reserve System,* 516 F2d 1229 (DC Cir 1975). The FRB, in its *Citicorp* decision (68 Fed Res Bull 505 (1982)), used the same standard as in *National Courier,* but applied it in a way so as to eliminate the "closely related to banking" requirement. See Loeb, *Approval of Citicorp's Application to Expand Data Services Activities: The Federal Reserve Board's Policies Regarding Non-Bank Activities,* 1983 Duke LJ 423 (1983).

Among the services approved by the board in *Citicorp* are timesharing, on-site data processing, and home banking. This decision should not only hasten the computerization of banking services by making larger computers economically feasible but also may allow banks and BHCs to become a force in the data processing field.

The United States Supreme Court affirmed the Federal Reserve Board's approval of applications by out-of-state companies for acquisition of bank holding companies in Massachusetts and Connecticut. The court held that the out-of-state holding company could acquire an in-state bank provided that the other state allows reciprocal privileges. This case has lifted the ban on interstate acquisitions. *Northeast Bancorp, Inc v Board of Governors of the Federal Reserve System,* 105 S Ct 2545 (1985). See Dennison, *No Questions Asked, Three Pros Wow the Court,* 7 Am Law 108 (1985). See also Wilmarth, *The Case for the Validity of State Regional Banking Laws,* 18 Loy LAL Rev 1017 (1985). See generally Note, *Banking Law Northeast Bancorp, Inc v Board of Governors of the Federal Reserve System,* 99 Harv L Rev 283 (1985); NYLJ, Jan 13, 1986, at 1, col 3; ch Daily L Bull, June 10, 1985, at 1, col 2; LA Daily J, Mar 11, 1985, at 4, col 1.

Import/Export Considerations Involving Computational Goods and Services

9

§9.01 Introduction

Page 369, note 1, at end of note add:

Government attempts to control the transfer of high technology have recently been felt in a traditionally control-free area: the university. See Alexander, *Preserving High Technology Secrets: National Security Controls on University Research and Teaching*, 15 Law & Poly Intl Bus 173 (1983). See also Zonderman, *Policing High-Tech Exports*, NY Times, Nov 27, 1983, at 100.

In 1985 foreign nations were granted protection under the Semiconductor Chip Protection Act of 1984. See *Japan and Sweden Granted Interim Protection for Mask Works; Protection Orders Pending for Netherlands, U.K., Australia, and Canada*, 2 Computer Law 27 (Aug 1985).

Page 369, note 3, at end of note add:

The growth of the international market for computer software and international licensing protection is examined in Greguras & Scott, *Licensing Software Overseas*, 4 The Scott Rep 1 (Dec 1984) and 4 The Scott Rep 3 (Jan 1985). The sale of software to a foreign buyer requires a careful examination of the proprietary rights to be protected. Export controls and technology transfer laws are only two factors to be considered when structuring a foreign contract. See Hoffman, *An Overview of International Software Protection*, 2 Computer Law 14 (Nov 1985).

Computer goods are now among the thousands of items which copy design features or otherwise infringe United States trademarks. Lanham Act jurisdiction may be found over foreign activities in some instances. See D. Harvey, *Extra-Territorial Jurisdiction Under the Lanham Trademark Act*, 2 Computer Law 5 (Nov 1985).

§9.03 —United States Antitrust Laws

Page 371, note 13, at end of note add:

For further developments of the *Timberlane* doctrine, *see* Daishowa Intl v North Coast Export Co, 1982-2 Trade Cas (CCH) ¶64,774 (ND Cal).

Page 373, text, at end of runover list add:

In 1982, Congress further codified this area by limiting application of the Sherman and Federal Trade Commission Acts to conduct which has a direct, substantial and reasonably forseeable effect. Foreign Trade Antitrust Improvement Act, 15 USC §§6(A), 45(A)(1982). The Laker litigation has resulted in several cases discussing the jurisdictional reach of the United States antitrust laws. *Laker Airways v Sabena*, 731 F2d 909 (D Colo 1984) (an excellent and exhaustive treatment of the territorial reach of the United States antitrust laws); *Laker Airways v Pan Am World Airways*, 557 F Supp 348 (D Colo 1983); *Laker Airways v Pan Am World Airways*, 559 F Supp 1124 (D Colo 1983); *Laker Airways v Pan Am World Airways*, 568 F Supp 811 (D Colo 1983). Another helpful resource is a recent article; Atwood, *Letter to Dept of Justice*, 74 Am J Intl L 667 (1980).

§9.05   Dumping

Page 382, text, at end of section add:

The International Trade Commission investigated whether Japanese dumping of 64-kilobit and 256-and-above kilobits dynamic random access memory (DRAM) semiconductors would injure United States industry. However, the Federal Trade Commission found no dumping, but rather competitive pricing. Erasable Programmable Read-Only Memories (EPROMs) made in Japan also were the subject of dumping charges brought by Intel Corp, National Semiconductor Corp, and Advanced Micro Devices. See *American Chip Manufacturers File Trade Petition Against Japanese*, 2 Computer Law 21 (Nov 1985). See also *Trade With Japan; Computer Update*, Computer L Strategist, Aug 1985, at 5; *EIAJ Disavows Responsibility for Slump in U.S. Semiconductor Industry; Micron Files Suit Against Japanese Manufacturers*, 2 Computer Law 27 (Oct 1985).

See *Kokusai Electric Co v United States*, 632 F Supp 23, which challenged the determinations of the Department of Commerce and the International Trade Commission regarding the importation of cell site transceivers from Japan for less than fair value as materially injuring the domestic industry.

§9.06   Tariff Act of 1930

Page 384, text, at end of section add:

Section 337 was recently used as authority for a general exclusion order prohibiting the entry of personal computers and components which directly infringe patents and copyrights of the complaining company. Further, microcomputers with processing hardware or chip configurations that contributed to, or induced infringement of, existing patents or copyrights were also excluded from importation by §337. The ITC ordered ROMless computers and components, which can be shown to be associated with infringing ROMs or which are intended to receive infringing ROMs in the United States, to be excluded. The commission found that there was an "industry" for purposes of §337 and found this industry to be economically and efficiently operated. The commission also found that the imports would cause injury to the industry and responded with the general exclusion order. See *Sweeping General Exclusion Order Issued in Section 337 Case,* 27 PTCJ 517 (1984). A challenge to a patent on grounds of invalidity due to obviousness fails in the Federal Circuit Court of Appeals in a §337 violation. See *SSIH Equipment SA v United States International Trade Commission,* 718 F2d 365 (1983). For a general evaluation of §337's effectiveness as a tool for combatting potentially infringing imports, see Plaia & Kaufman, *Section 337 of the Tariff Act of 1930 as Amended, Effective Protection for Changing Technology,* 10 Rutgers Corp & Tech LJ 219 (1985).

§9.07   The General Agreement on Tariffs and Trade

Page 385, note 82, at end of note add:

The GATT Government Procurement Code has been the subject of a series of meetings on the feasibility of expanding code coverage to include service contracts. See Alexander, *GATT Explores Extension of Government Procurement Code Coverage to Services,* The Scott Rep, Nov 1985 at 7

§9.09   High Technology Import/Export Considerations

Page 387, note 92, at end of note add:

See also Benson, *United States Regulation of Computer Exports,* 5 Computer L Inst, Univ S Cal L Center pt VII VII-1 *et seq* (1984); Hunt, *Multilateral Cooperation in Export Controls—The Role of COCOM,* 14 U Tol L Rev 1285

(1983); Kenfield & Woodbury, *Import-Customs Regulations of Computer Technology*, 10 NCJ Int'l Law & Com Reg 609-15 (Summer 1985). See generally Wilson, *Strategy and Tactics with the International Trade Commission, On Exclusion of Infringing Materials From the United States: Course Handbook Series Number 226*, Computer Software & Chips Protection & Marketing Program, 1986, Practicing L Inst #G4-3791, at 123-284 (discussing tariffs import trade and the *Amorphous Metals* case). See also Keplinger, *International Protection for Computer Programs and Semiconductor Chips: Course Handbook Series Number 225*, Computer Software & Chips Protection & Marketing Program, 1986, Practicing L Inst #G4-37971, at 237-402 (a look at international copyright protection for software).

Page 388, note 94, at end of note add:

See also Wilson, *The New United States and Australia Double Tax Treaty—The Taxation of Know-How and Show-How Payments*, 61 Taxes 679 (1983).

Page 391, note 112, at end of note add:

For a review of current transborder data flow problems regarding privacy and security interests, with suggestions for developing a privacy protection system, see Coombe & Kirk, *Privacy, Data Protection, and Transborder Data Flow: A Corporate Response to International Expectations*, 39 Bus Law 33 (1984). See also Hardy, *Transborder Data Flow: An Overview and Critique of Recent Concerns*, 9 Rutgers Computer & Tech LJ 247 (1983).

Page 392, note 118, at end of note add:

For a review of the effects of technology controls on the academic community, see also Alexander, *Preserving High Technology Secrets: National Security Controls on University Research and Training*, 15 Law & Poly Intl Bus 173 (1983); Zonderman, *Policing High-Tech Exports*, NY Times, Nov 27, 1983, at 100.

Page 392, text, at end of section add:

It has become apparent in the last few years that the Soviet Union is expending large amounts of time and money on acquiring the west's most advanced technology. Plousadis, *Soviet Diversion of United States Technology: The Circumvention of COCOM and U.S. Reexport Controls, and Proposed Solutions*, 7 Ford Intl LJ 561 (1984); see also L. Melvern, N. Anning, D. Hebditch, Techno Bandits (1984). It also appears that even lower level technology such as boards for personal computers are being copied by the Soviets as well. The Soviet's K580 series of circuit chips that includes a microprocessor, clock driver and interval time is almost identical to the Intel 8080 series. Hevertz, *Soviet Microprocessors and Microcomputers*, Byte 351 (April 1984). The recent introduction of a Soviet personal computer may have created quite a stir in the East but upon closer examination the computer was little more than a poor copy of the original Apple. See Bores, *AGAT, A Soviet Apple II Computer*, Byte, at 35, (Nov 1984).

It appears, at least in the production of lower level technology, that the Soviets are three to five years behind the West. That lag is substantial given the relative ease with which this lower level technology can be obtained in the West and shipped to the USSR through any number of channels. If the Soviets are unable to adequately produce the simplest of today's chips, perhaps their ability to produce higher level technology is also impaired. This lack of technical expertise certainly reinforces the need for export control.

One other approach to prevent loss of technology to the Soviet Union may be in use today and appears to be a most effective way of thwarting technology theft. French engineer and author Thierry Breton (Softwar, 1984) has accused the United States computer companies of building deliberate failures into computers that they suspect will be sent to the Soviet Union. Breton states that these software bombs were developed several years ago as a method of ensuring payment by African and South American customers. Custom engineering service is generally required to fix the flaw and none would be provided until the accounts were current or in this case if the computer was in an eastern bloc country. These defects have caused huge errors in the calculations of Soviet grain stocks and also errors in technical calculations for advanced weapons. This international defect approach may be too inconvenient for common use but it is certainly an interesting way to keep the Soviet dollars in the market without giving away the technology.

§9.10   The Export Administration Act of 1979

Page 392, note 119, at end of note add:

See also Monahan, *The Regulation of Technical Data Under the Arms Control Act of 1976 and the Export Administration Act of 1979: A Matter of Executive Discretion*, 13 GBC Intl & Comparative L Rev 169 (1983).

The Export Administration Act of 1979 expired in October of 1983. President Reagan declared an International Economic Emergency as permitted under the International Economic Emergency Powers Act (IEEPA) (50 USC §1702 (a)(1)(b)) and exercised his authority by extending the EAA.

Numerous attempts have been made to replace the EAA but the deep differences between the administration's plan, the Senate's plan, and the plan in the Congress have hampered efforts to pass a new EAA.

The administration's bill (HR 2500, 98th Cong, 1st Sess 1983) would provide for an increased allocation of resources to facilitate the upgrading of COCOM, limit the likelihood that the Department of Commerce would find foreign availability for certain products and thereby reducing the number of products that could be exported without a license. The bill would also give the President additional powers to deal with offenders.

The bill in the House would tend to restrict the scope of the President's role in export administration and give more authority to the Department of Commerce.

The bill in the Senate (S 434, 98th Cong, 1st Sess 1983) would expand the scope of the national security controls, restrict the foreign policy controls by shifting the authority to abrogate existing treaties to the IEEPA, and give the Customs Service more power to enforce the act.

The only point that they all agree on is that the current EAA does not work. See Luke, *Writing a New Export Control Law: Should the Past Be Prologue?* Fed Bar News & J, Mar 1985, at 143.

The Office of Export Administration (OEA) has taken a major step towards rationalizing their export control regulations. On December 31, 1984 the OEA issued new controls on the exports of computers and software. 49 Fed Reg 50608-32 (Dec 13, 1984). 15 CFR pt 379, 386, and 399. The regulation implements the recent strategic controls decided upon by COCOM. See the summary section in 49 Fed Reg 50608 (Dec 31, 1984).

The major purpose of the revision is to decontrol certain older, slower computers and to permit unfettered export of items that, while otherwise uncontrolled, contain certain types of microprocessors or digital computers (i.e., microwave ovens, calculators). The new regulations will also strengthen controls on more advanced technology. The regulations also provide for more detailed guidelines for the interpretation and application of the controls. See McKenzie, *Changes in Export Controls on Computers and Software,* 2 Computer Law 28 (1985) and D. Davidson & J. Davidson, Advanced Strategies for Buying and Selling Computers and Software 9-29 (1985).

Page 393, note 129, at end of note add:

See also Overly, *Regulation of Critical Technologies Under the Export Administration Act of 1979 and the Proposed Export Administration Amendments of 1985: American Business versus National Security,* 18 NCJ Int'l Law & Com Reg 425-51 (Spring 1985).

Page 394, note 135, at end of note add:

The Department of Commerce promulgated regulations identifying "low technology" goods no longer requiring a validated license to COCOM countries. The regulations established the G-Com general license to cover such exports. See Greguras & Daunt, *Export Administration Act of 1985,* The Scott Rep Aug 1985, at 4. For an analysis of both the December and April amendments and the various software categories subject to export control requirements, see McKenzie, *Recent Developments in Contracts on Software Exports* 2 Computer Law 11 (May 1985).

§9.11 —Export Trading Companies

Page 395, note 136, at end of note add:

See also Bruce & Peirce, *Understanding the Export Trading Company Act and Using (or Avoiding) its Antitrust Exemptions*, 38 Bus Law 975 (1983).

Page 395, note 138, at end of note add:

See also Seberger, *The Banking Provisions of the Export Trading Company Act of 1982*, 39 Bus Law 475 (1984).

Page 395, note 141, at end of note add:

The Office of Export Trading Company Affairs is responsible for: (1) promoting and encouraging the formation of export trading companies (ETCs); (2) providing advice and information to interested persons; and (3) acting as a referral service to facilitate contact between producers of exportable goods and services and firms offering export trade services. Intl Trade Admin, United States Dept of Commerce, The Export Trading Company Guidebook (1984). Rule, Implementation of the Export Trading Company Act of 1982, delivered to the Subcommittee on International Policy and Trade, House committee on foreign affairs, Washington, DC (Aug 1, 1984).

Page 396, text, at end of section add:

Another useful method for exporting technology is through a (DISC) Domestic International Sale Corporation. Profits earned by a Disc are not subject to taxation until distributed to shareholders. DISCs have become even more attractive since the Deficit Reduction Act of 1984. For an excellent discussion of the tax benefits of a DISC, see Falcone, *Overseas Operations of High Technology Companies After the Deficit Reduction Act of 1984*, 1 Computer Law, No 7, at 17 (Aug 1984) and Falcone, *Overseas Operations of High Technology Companies after the Deficit Reduction Act of 1984, Part II*, 1 Computer Law 1 No 8, at 22 (Sept 1984).

§9.12   United Nations Conference on Trade and Development Code of Conduct on Transfer of Technology

Page 396, note 147, at end of note add:

For an overview of the fifth session of UNCTAD Code drafting conference (October 1983), see Roffe, *UNCTAD: Transfer of Technology Code,* 18 J World Trade L 176 (1984).

Page 397, note 149, at end of note add:

Another potential weakening of protection for technology and know-how is the mandatory technology transfer provisions in the proposed Law of the Sea treaty. See Marsteller & Tucker, *Problems of the Technology Transfer Provisions in the Law of the Sea Treaty,* 24 Idea 167 (1983); Savage, *Transfer of Technology in the International Market Place,* 31 Fed Bar News & J No 1, at 13 (Jan 1984).

§9.13   The European Economic Community

Page 399, note 154, at end of note add:

For an example in the area of technology transfer, see Bessey, *Comity and Computers in the Common Market: The IBM Case,* 4 Nw J Intl Law & Bus 626 (1982). See also Wiltsie, *European Economic Community Monopoly Law: Recent Trends in the Application of Article 86 of the Treaty of Rome,* 9 Syracuse J Intl L & Com 187 (1982).

The IBM matter was finally settled when, in August of 1984, IBM and the EEC entered into an agreement which obligated IBM to disclose sufficient technical information to allow competitors to attach their own hardware to IBM equipment and to develop their own software for IBM systems.

The settlement will provide a major leg up for IBM's competitors. The result, however, was not as devastating to IBM's competitive advantage as were many of the proposed solutions. It was thought at one time during the negotiations that IBM would be required to surrender enough technical information to permit their competitors to not only produce compatible equipment, but also to reproduce equipment functionally the same as IBM's core units. This broad disclosure plan was scrapped after IBM successfully argued that the benefits of such disclosure would flow primarily to the Japanese computer manufacturers rather than to manufacturers in the EEC.

The decision appears basically sound; it grants IBM a limited competitive edge as their product will have the market to themselves for a short period before IBM's competitors can market their own goods. IBM's products may also have an initial quality edge over their competitors as IBM had a longer development period. The decision should benefit not only IBM's competitors but also the computer industry as a whole, because with the industry adopting one standard, capital and resources for research and development are able to be focused into one area rather than scattered over several incompatible systems. See NY Times, Aug 3, 1984, at Al, col 3. See also Antitrust & Trade Reg Rep (BNA) Vol 47, no 1117, at 272 (Aug 9, 1984).

There have also been rumors in the computer trade that the settlement with the EEC will allow IBM to seek a lifting of the 1956 consent decree. See **p 132** of the text for a discussion of the 1956 consent decree.

§9.15   Japan

Page 401, note 164, at end of note add:

See Bernaccni & Deffense, *Protection of Software in Japan,* Computer L Strategist, Aug 1985, at 2.

Page 402, note 166, at end of note add:

See generally Jacobson, *The U.S. & Japan Cooperating in High Technology Research and Development,* 2 Computer Law 6 (July 1985)

§9.16   Middle East & South America

Page 402, note 168, at end of note add:

See also West, *Evolving Industrial Property Law and Transfer of Technology in the Republic of Korea,* 18 Tex Intl L Rev 127 (1983); Hill, *Transfer of Technology From the United States to Nigeria: A Balancing of Legal Interests,* 6 Tex SUL Rev 380 (1981).

Page 402, note 169, at end of note add:

For an overview of current Mexican technology transfer law, see Hyde, *1981 Mexican Transfer of Technology Law,* 15 Law Am 37 (1983). For a review of old and new developments in Latin American countries regarding transfers of technology, see Radway, *Antitrust, Technology Transfers, and Joint Ventures in Latin American Development,* 15 Law Am 47 (1983). See also Baird, *The New Mexican Transfer of Technology Law,* 12 Den J Intl L & Poly 107 (1982); Jacobsen, *Mexico's Computer Decree: The Problem of Performance Requirements and a U.S. Response,* 14 L & Poly Intl Bus 1159 (1983); Correa, *Transfer of Technology in Latin America: A Decade of Control,* 15 J World Trade L 388 (1981).

India was given broader access to United States computer and semiconductor technology in exchange for India's commitment to protect the information against unauthorized diversion. See Wall St J May 28, 1985, at 16, col 3.

Page 402, text, at end of section add:

South America has adopted several tough transfer of technology laws. Brazil, in particular, has adopted a policy that they hope will allow Brazil to develop its own high technology industries. Brazil has forbidden any foreign investment at all in certain designated industries such as computers and electronic telecommunications. Further, Brazil has yet to grant software any copyright protection which forces a foreign vender into trade secret licensing agreements. The flaw with licensing nonpatented or copyrighted technology or software is that, under Brazilian law, trade secrets cannot be *leased* but only sold. Further, the term of the license can at most be five years at which point the Brazilian licensee will have the same local rights in the technology as the licensor does.

Brazil's attempt at developing an indigenous computer industry will be watched closely. Many in the business, however, feel that technology is moving too rapidly for any third world country or even a newly industrialized country to remain competitive without substantial support from the developed nations. See Bauer, *New Law Affects Brazil's Big "Informatic's" Market*, Scott Rep at 11 (Dec 1984).

§9.17   Communist Nations

Page 403, note 170, at end of note add:

See also Armstrong, *Transferring U.S. Technology to the Soviets: Some Practical Legal Problems*, 16 Intl Law 737 (1982); Zonderman, *Policing High-Tech Exports*, NY Times, Nov 27, 1983, at 100.

Yuri Gufman, head of Industrial & Scientific Part Services, Inc, pleaded guilty in federal court to exporting restricted computer parts to North Korea. See Wall St J Nov 6, 1985, at 14, col 3.

Page 403, note 171, at end of note add:

A new market with the People's Republic of China opens up as political relations with the Soviets cool down. See Meese, *Export Controls to China: An Emerging Trend for Dual-Use Exports*, 7 Intl Trade LJ 20 (1981-82); Zonderman, *Policing High-Tech Exports*, NY Times, Nov 27, 1983, at 100. See generally S. Guo, *Technology Transfer and Intellectual Property Law Development in the People's Republic of China* (Sept 16-18, 1985), International Association for the Advancement of Teaching and Research in Intellectual Property 1985 Annual Meeting; Reback, Greguras & Davidson, *China and South Asia Export License Applications*, The Scott Rep Oct 1985, at 1.

Page 403, note 172, at end of note add:

Recent amendments to the Export Administration Act of 1979 have eased the regulations controlling exports to the People's Republic of China. See Greguras, *Liberalization of COCOM Review Process for Exports to the PRC,* The Scott Rep Dec 1985, at 5.

Page 404, note 174, at end of note add:

The United Kingdom began valuing computer carrier media (storage media such as tapes and discs) as if they were blank for customs duty purposes, on May 1, 1985. New exports controls implementing COCOM revisions became effective on July 25, 1985. See Smith, *New Developments: Software in the U.K.,* Computer L Strategist, Aug 1985, at 5.

Page 404, text, at end of section add:

An important diplomatic lever used in the United States' relationship with the Soviet Union is the ability to allow the People's Republic of China greater access to high technology items while restricting Soviet and Soviet-bloc access to the same items. This advantage was applied by the Carter administration in 1980 in response to the Soviet Union's invasion of Afghanistan. The added restrictions on Soviet trade and increased access by the Chinese have opened up a new market for United States technology. This policy of favoring the People's Republic of China may be termed a "China Preferential."

The technology which has been exported to China consists mainly of selected "dual-use" items. *Dual-use* technology includes items that are primarily intended for civilian use but which have potential military applications. As relations with China improve, the possibility exists that the Chinese will be able to import United States items with military *end-use* applications. The present United States export policy towards China requires the government to show cause why the sale should not be approved. In contrast, the policy regarding the Soviet Union requires the exporter to show cause why the sale should be approved.

This situation illustrates the wide variety of treatments accorded various Communist countries, based on the current political situation, and may suggest differences in license-reviewing procedures, based on whether the foreign country is: (1) the Soviet Union; (2) an Eastern bloc country without most-favored nation status; (3) an Eastern bloc country with most-favored nation status; or (4) the People's Republic of China. The regulation of technology transfers to Communist nations will continue to shift based on the changing political climate. See Meese, *Export Controls to China: An Emerging Trend for Dual-Use Exports,* 7 Intl Trade LJ 20 (1981-82).

For an example of a technology transfer restriction with international conflicts causing problems, see Vance, *Export Controls—Challenge to the Validity of Department of Commerce Regulations Restricting the Export of Oil and Gas Equipment and Technology to the Soviet Union—Temporary Restraining Order Denied,* 18 Tex Intl L Ref 203 (1983). See also Zonderman, *Policing High-Tech Exports,* NY Times, Nov 27, 1983, at 100.

§9.19   Licensing Technology (New)

The uncertain status of software protection in many foreign countries combined with the extensive use of trade secret protection by many firms has left international software dealers with little alternative but to license the software to overseas users. The license provides numerous advantages which include controlling the user's conduct and, in some cases, allowing the licensor to retain ownership of the software. The principal problem facing many licensors is the myriad of laws that affect a licensing transaction.

The statutory barriers to writing tight licenses are particularly onerous in many third world countries with laws that can limit license terms, output restrictions, and nondisclosure clauses (see U.N. National Legislation: Regulation Relating to Transnational Corporations, Doc #ST/CTC/6 (1978).) Brazil has adopted a reverse engineering standard with regards to acceptable know-how licensing (computer programs are considered know-how) terms (Brazilian Normative Act no 015 §4.5.2 (1970)). This act plays a major role in all foreign licensing transactions while many countries including Argentina and the Philippines limit the terms of licenses to five years. One particularly problematic approach has been adopted by several lesser developed nations and France. This procedure refuses to allow the leasing of software, only the sale. A software licensee will obtain the same local rights in the software upon expiration of the term as the original licensor. See J. Delveze, *Contracts for the Transfer of Technologies* 20 (1978) and 5 D. Wise, *Trade Secret and Know-How Protection throughout the World* 7-33 (1983).

Licensing, however, is one of the most effective ways to provide an international market for your software. With certain limitations a license can protect your software in many ways that local law will not. It is important that a potential licensor be aware of the complexities of international licensing and seek informed advice before venturing into the international markets. See generally D. Davidson & J. Davidson, *Advanced Strategies for Buying and Selling Computers and Software* ch 8 (1985); Pratler, Daunt & Davidson Distribution of Computer Products to Japan and the Common Market, Fourth Computer L Inst, §X, at 23 (1983); Cubas, Certain Issues of International Distribution of Software and Hardware, Fourth Annual Computer L Inst §XI p 1 (1983); Greguras & Daunt, *Licensing Software Overseas,* Scott Rep, (Dec 1984), at 1.

Epilogue

10

§10.01 Introduction

Page 406, note 1, at end of note add:

See also R. Kanter, The Change Masters: Innovations for Productivity in the American Corporation (1983).

§10.02 Technological Revolution

Page 407, note 2, at end of note add:

See also W. Abernathy, K. Clark, & A. Kantrow, Industrial Renaissance: Producing a Competitive Future for America (1983) (contents include: Toward a Production- and Technology-based Competition; The Case of the Automobile Industry; The Possibilities of De-maturity); J. Botkin, D. Dimanecescu, R. Stata, & J. McClellan, Global Stakes: The Future of High Technology in America (1982) (outlining national policies necessary for the success of the knowledge- and capital-intensive computer, electronics, and communications industries).

Page 407, note 4, at end of note add:

See also NY Times, Jan 7, 1984, §1, at 30, col 5. (Hitachi Ltd. says it has developed the world's first one million character chip); Uttal, *Japan Inc.'s Entry In Home Computers*, Fortune, Jan 21, 1985, at 72 (discussing Japan's electronics industry entry into the United States home computer market); NY Times, June 27, 1984, §4, at 1, col 6 (Fujitsu Ltd., Japan, to export super computers to the United States in first direct challenge to American manufacturers).

See also Port, *Here Comes the Fastest Chip on Earth,* Bus Wk, Mar 4, 1985, at 205-06 (discussing a ballistic transistor that could change the way computers are designed); Wilson & Ticer, *Superchips: The New Frontier,*

Bus Wk, June 10, 1985, at 83-85 (discussing the breaking of the micron barrier and its effect on the revolutionization of electronics); NY Times, Feb 13, 1984, §1, at 1, col 6 (American scientist warns Japan has forged ahead in creation of extremely highspeed *supercomputers;*); NY Times, Jan 26, 1984, §4, at 16, col 1 (Japan to nearly double public spending, to $22 million a year, to develop computer capable of speaking in several languages).

§10.04   Foreign Technological Concerns

Page 408, note 7, at end of note add:

See also *NEC's Solo Strategy to Win the World,* Bus Week, July 5, 1982, at 79 (Nippon Electric Company, Japan's Number 3 computer maker).

See generally Aoki, *Japanese Computer-makers Strive to Penetrate the World Market,* 1982 LTCB Research 1 (1982); Lehner, *Calculated Move: Japan Electronic Firms Push into Computers,* Wall St J, Mar 8, 1983, at 201 (lagging consumer markets in world-wide recession prompt diversification); Corrigan, *The Latest Target of the Japanese: US Preeminence in Super Computers,* Nat J, Apr 2, 1983, at 688; Imai & Sakuma, *An Analysis of Japan-US Semiconductor Friction,* 4 Econ Eye 13 (1983); Takai, *Setting the Record Straight on Semiconductors,* J Japanese Trade & Industry 24 (1983) (written in response to Semiconductor Industry Association's report, *The Effect of Government Targeting on World Semiconductor Competition: A Case History on Japanese Industrial Strategy and Its Costs for America*); Pugel, *Semiconductors and Computers: Emerging Competitive Battlegrounds in the Asia-Pacific Region,* Research Intl Bus & Fin 231, pt B (1984).

Page 409, note 8, at end of note add:

See generally Gould, *Technological Change and Competition,* 4 J Bus Strategy 66 (1983) (comparing scientific and technical manpower of the United States, the USSR, and Japan).

Page 409, note 9, at end of note add:

See also Uttal, *Here Comes Computers, Inc,* 106 Fortune, Oct 4, 1982, at 82 (discussing the government-backed project to build fifth-generation machines as the Japanese strive for world leadership); Barang, *Vaulting into the Fifth Generation: Japan Goes for No. 1,* South, Sept, 1983, at 21 (examining Japanese technological innovations; economic, trade, and foreign investment trends and outlook); E. Feigenbaum & P. McCorduck, The Fifth Generation: Artificial Intelligence and Japan's Computer Challenge to the World (1983); W. Davidson, The Amazing Race: Winning the Technorivalry with Japan (1984) (examining the competition between the United States and Japan in the field of information technology); Senate Comm on Commerce, Science, and

Transportation, Subcomm on Science, Technology and Space, Role of Technology in Promoting Industrial Competitiveness, Hearings on S 428, 98th Cong, 1st Sess (1983) (Serial no 98-29) (to provide for a study on economically strategic technologies and to identify and provide for the development of such technologies).

Cases

F

Federal Republic of Germany, Visi Corp v Basic Software GMBH Sept 21, 1982 Munich Dist §2.12

G

GAF Corp v Amchem Prods, Inc, 514 F Supp 943 (ED Pa 1981) §2.05

GCA Corp v Chance, 217 USPQ 718 (ND Cal 1982) §2.12

H

Hinderliter v Humphries, 224 Va 439, 297 SE2d 684 (1982) §6.08

Honeywell, Inc v Diamond, 499 F Supp 924 (DC 1980) §2.05

Horning v Sycom, 556 F Supp 819 (ED Kan 1983) §3.10

Houston Contracting Corp v Chase Manhattan Bank, NA, 539 F Supp 247 (SDNY 1982) §8.19

I

ILC Peripherals Leasing Corp v IBM Corp, 448 F Supp 228 (ND Cal 1978), *affd per curiam sub nom* Memorex Corp v IBM Corp, 636 F Supp 1188 (9th Cir 1980), *cert denied*, 452 US 972 (1981) §2.22

Indiana v McGraw, 480 NE 2d 552 (Ind 1985) §7.09

Innovation Data Processing, Inc v IBM Corp, 585 F Supp 1470 (DNJ 1984) §4.13

J

Jefferson Parish Hosp Dist No 2 v Hyde, 104 S Ct 1551 (1984) §4.13

Judd v Citibank, 107 Misc 2d 529, 435 NYS2d 210 (1980) §8.19

K

Kashanchi v Texas Commerce Medical Bank, NA, 703 F2d 936 (5th Cir 1983) §8.19

Kokusai Elec Co v United States, 632 F Supp 23 §9.05

Krampe v Ideal Indus, [1973] Trade Cas (CCH) ¶74,439 (ND Ill 1972) §4.22

L

Laker Airways v Pan Am World Airways, 557 F Supp 348 (D Colo 1983) §9.03

Laker Airways v Pan Am World Airways, 559 F Supp 1124 (D Colo 1983) §9.03

Laker Airways v Pan Am World Airways, 568 F Supp 811 (D Colo 1983) §9.03

Laker Airways v Sabena, 731 F2d 990 (D Colo 1984) §9.03

Loctite Corp v Ultraseal Ltd, 781 F2d 861 (Fed Cir Dec 17, 1985) §4.16

M

Matsushita Elec Indus Co, Ltd v Zenith Radio Corp, 106 S Ct 1348 (1986) §4.06

M Bryce & Assocs v Gladstone, 107 Wis 2d 241, 319 NW2d

W

Whelan Assocs v Jaslow Dental
Laboratory, 609 F Supp 1325
(ED Pa 1985) 29 Pat
Trademarks & Copyright J
(BNA) 357 §2.09A

White Consol Indus v Vega
Servo-Control, Inc, 713 F2d
788 (CAFC 1983) §2.05
Williams Elect, Inc v Arctic Intl,
Inc, 685 F2d 870 (3d Cir
1982) §2.09A

Statutes

United States Code
5 USC §522 §6.07
17 USC §101 §2.09A
17 USC §901 §2.10
18 USC §1029(a) §7.10
18 USC §1029(a)(2) §7.10
18 USC §1029(c) §7.10
18 USC §1030(c)(2)(A) §7.10
18 USC §§1961-1968 §4.12
35 USC §112 §2.05

42 USC §405 §6.07
47 USC §151 §5.07
47 USC §201 §5.07
47 USC §551 §6.14

State Statutes
La Rev Stat Ann §15:1961-66
   (West 1984) §3.12

Books and Articles

A

W. Abernathy, K. Clark & A. Kantrow, Industrial Renaissance: Producing a Competitive Future for America (1983) **§10.01**

Adam, Gordon & Starr, *Contractual, Financial, and Tax Issues in Major Procurements,* 4 Computer LJ 465 (1984) **§3.28**

Adams, *Canada's Future TDF Policy: Reconciling Free Flow with National Sovereignty,* 6 Transnatl Data Rep 405 (Oct-Nov 1983) **§6.11**

A groovy way of stretching computer memories, 279 Economist 99 (1981) **§1.05**

Alessio, *Managing the Transition to Telecommunications Deregulation,* Pub Util Fort, July 7, 1983, at 21 **§5.19**

Alexander, *GATT Explores Extension of Government Procurement Code Coverage to Service,* The Scott Rep, Nov 1985, at 7 **§9.06**

Alexander, *Preserving High Technology Secrets: National Security Controls on University Research and Teaching,* 15 Law & Poly Intl Bus 173 (1983) **§9.01**

A memory that costs one-quarter cent per bit: that will happen if Ampex (corporation)'s new process for making magnetic cores proves out, Bus Week, Feb 3, 1975 at 26, **§1.05**

American Chip Manufacturers File Trade Petition Against Japanese, 2 Computer Law 21 (Nov 1985) **§9.03**

American Telephone & Telegraph: The Upcoming AT&T Divestiture and Its Implications for Investors, Sherson, Am Express (1983) **§5.01**

Andrews Publications, *Antitrust Issues: California Judge Explains Decision Allowing Apple to Terminate all Mail-Order Dealers,* Computer Industry Litigation Reporter, Jan 28, 1985, at 2,014+ **§4.23**

Aoki, *Japanese Computer-makers Strive to Penetrate the World*

Market, 1982 LTCB Research 1 (1982) **§10.04**

Appelbe & Pournelle, *Big Projects On Small Machines: Software Engineering On Microcomputers,* BYTE, Sept 1984, at 150 **§1.06**

Argy, *Legal Protection of Computer Software in Australia,* 1 J L & Info Sci 256 (1983) **§2.17**

Armstrong, *Transferring U.S. Technology to the Soviets: Some Practical Legal Problems,* 16 Intl L 737 (1982) **§9.17**

Artandi, *Computers and the Post-Industrial Society: Symbiosis or Information Tyranny?,* 33 Am Soc Info Sci J 302 (1982) **§1.01**

Arness, *Learning to Love Your Computer,* 11 Brief 32 (1982) **§1.07**

Ashman, *Software Program Can be Copyrighted,* 69 ABA J 1750 (1983) **§2.09A**

A Systems Approach to Payment Modes: Moving Towards a New Payments Code, 16 UCC LJ 383 (1984) **§8.19**

A Threat from Malicious Software, Time, Nov 4, 1985, at 94 **§7.05**

Atkins, *Jesse James at the Terminal,* 19 Computerworld, Nov 25, 1985, at 47-8 **§6.04**

Atkins, *Jesse James at the Terminal,* 63 Harv Bus Rev 82 (1965) **§7.03**

Atwood, *Letter to Dept of Justice,* 74 Am J Intl L 667 (1980) **§9.03**

J. Auer & C.E. Harris, Computer Contract Negotiations (1981) **§3.43**

J. Auer & C.E. Harris, Major Equipment Procurement (1983) **§3.06**

B

Badertschen, *An Examination of the Dynamics of Change in Information Technology as Viewed from Law Libraries and Information Centers,* 75 Law Libr J 198 (1982) **§1.01**

Baeza, *Acquisition & Exploitation of Mass—Market Software: Course Handbook Series Number 226,* Computer Software & Chips Protection & Marketing Program (1986) **§2.01**

Bailey, *White Collar Software Piracy,* MINI (Mar 1985) at 11-12 **§7.03**

Baird, *The New Mexican Transfer of Technology Law,* 12 Den J Intl L & Poly 107 (1982) **§9.16**

Baker, *Of Copyrights and Databases,* Micro Communications 34 (Aug 1984) **§2.10**

Baker & Baker, *Antitrust and Communications Deregulation,* 28 Antitrust Bull 1 (1983) **§5.17**

Banking Law: Northeast Bancorp, Inc v Board of Governors of the Federal Reserve System, 99 Harv L Rev 283 (1985) **§8.22**

Barang, *Vaulting into the Fifth Generation: Japan Goes for No 1,* South, Sept 1983, at 21 **§10.04**

Bauer, *New Law Affects Brazil's Big "Informatic's" Market,* Scott Rpt, Dec 1984, at 11 **§9.16**

Baumgarten, *Copyright and Computer Software (Including Data Bases & Chip Technology,*

Telecommunications Industry, 28
Antitrust Bull 39 (1983)
§5.17

Bessey, *Comity and Computers in
the Common Market: The IBM
Case,* 4 Nw J Intl L & Bus 626
(1982) **§9.13**

Betts, *NBS Releases Standards for
Managing Password Security,* 19
Computerworld 19 (July 15,
1985) **§6.14**

Beutel, *Government Regulation of
Diagnostics Software: A Threat to
Artificial Intelligence Software
Developers,* The Computer
Law, Feb 1985, at 22 **§1.03**

Bigelow, *The Computer and the
Tax Collector,* 30 Emory LJ
357 (1981) **§1.08**

Bing, *How to Select Add-On Main
Memory,* 14 Data Mgmt 22
(1976) **§1.05**

Bing, *New Technology and the Law:
Likely Impact and Future Trends,*
1983 Computers & Law 2
(1983) **§1.07**

Bishop, *Protection of Computer
Programs in the UK,* 5 NwJ Intl
L&B 346-55 (1982) **§2.12**

Blau, *Software for the Law Office:
Six Criteria to Evaluate It,* Trial,
Jan 1985, at 34 **§1.08**

Bloom Becker, *Civil Remedies for
Computer Crimes,* Scott Rep 8
(Oct 1985) **§7.13**

Boccardo, Alexander &
Kennedy, *How to Harness the
Information Explosion,* 18 Trial
74 (1982) **§1.08**

Boebert, Kain, & Young, *Trojan
Horse Rolls Up to DP Gate,* 19
Computerworld, Dec 2, 1985,
at 65-9 **§6.04**

Bores, *AGAT, A Soviet Apple II
Computer,* BYTE, Nov 1984, at
35 **§9.09**

Bortnick, *International Information
Flow: The Developing World
Perspective,* 14 Cornell Intl LJ
333 **§6.11**

J. Botkin, D. Dimancescu, R.
Stata & J. McClellan, Global
Stakes: The Future of High
Technology in America
(1982) **§10.01**

Brest, Brest & Horton, *Options in
Office Computer Systems,* 3 Cal
Law 34 (1983) **§1.08**

Brightman & Harris, *The
Planning and Modeling Language
Revolution: A Managerial
Perspective,* 32 Business 15
(1982) **§1.07**

K. Brimmer, Annual Review of
Information Science and
Technology (1982) **§5.18**

Brooks, *Patents, Copyrights,
Trademarks, and Literary
Property: Course Handbook Series
Number 191,* Computer L Inst,
1984, Practising L Inst
#64-3758, at 702-04 **§4.06**

Brooks, *Reverse Engineering
Computer Software: Is It Fair Use
or Plagiarism: Course Handbook
Series Number 226,* Computer
Software & Chips Protection
& Marketing Program (1986)
§2.15

Brown, *Automation Is the Key to
SouthTrust's Improved Profits,*
124 Tr & Est 40 (July, 1985)
§8.14

Brown, *Protecting a Software
Company Against a Spinoff
Formed by Departing Employees,*
5 Computer L Inst, Univ S
Cal L Center pt II II-1 (1984)
§2.12

Brownstein, *Computer
Communications Vulnerable as
Privacy Laws Lag Behind*

Think, Wall St J, Jan 6, 1983, at 1 **§1.03**

Chalton, *The U.K. Data Protection Act of 1984: A New Statutory Right to Privacy,* 4 Scott Rep 1 n 5, Feb, 1985 **§6.11**

Checklist—Acquisition Contracts for Computer Systems, 1 Computer L Monitor 16 (1983) **§3.08**

Checklist—Copyright, Patent, Trade Secret & Trademark: Some Basic Elements, 1 Computer L Monitor 64 (1984) **§2.16**

Checklist—Employment Contracts re Intellectual Property Rights, 1 Computer L Monitor 48 (1984) **§2.12**

Checklist—Service Bureau Contracts, 1 Computer L Monitor 32 (1983) **§3.15**

The chip makers' glamorous new generation: the 64K has four times the capacity of the most popular chips (semiconductor devices) now in use, Bus Week, Oct 6, 1980, at 117 **§1.05**

Clark, *Computer-Related Crime,* 2 J Fin Software 20 (1985) **§7.07**

Cohen, *International Security,* Wall St J, Sept 16, 1985, at 24 **§7.03**

Cohen & Scarborough, *The Copyrightability of Computer Programs as Literary Works: Return to a Statutory Approach,* 3 Computer Law 3, 25 (Mar 1986) **§4.19**

Cohodas, *Special Report: Technology and the Law, New Technology Puts Strain on Old Laws,* Cong Q, 135 (Jan 28, 1984) **§1.02**

Comment, *Community Television of Southern California v Gottfried: Defining the Role of the Television Industry in Serving the*

Needs of the Hearing Impaired, 19 New England L Rev 899 (Fall 1984) **§5.18**

Compendium of State Privacy & Security Legislation, 1984 Edition: Overview, Privacy & Security of Criminal History Information, NCJ-98077 (Sept 1985) **§6.08**

Computer Crime Bills Pending, 22 Data Mgmt 37 (1984) **§7.17**

Computer Fraud Investigators Handbook, sponsored by the New Mexico Law Enforcement Academy **§7.12**

Computergram International, London, No 369, Feb 10, 1986, at 1, col 1 **§4.06**

Computer Program Conversion As Possible Infringement, 5 Computer Law 199-200 (May 1986) **§2.08**

Computer Programs Are Subject to Copyright Protection in Australia, 28 PTCJ 256 (1984) **§2.17**

Computers and Law, New LJ, July 8, 1982, at 645 **§1.07**

Computers: Personal Models, Smaller and Smarter, Bus Week, Mar 28, 1983, at 134 **§1.01**

Conley & Bryan, *A Unifying Theory for the Litigation of Computer Software Copyright Cases,* 5 Computer LJ 55 (Summer 1985) **§2.16**

Conley & Bryan, *A Unifying Theory for the Litigation of Computer Software Copyright Cases,* 63 NCL Rev 563-616 (Apr 1985) **§4.19**

Consumer Protection & Payment Systems; Regulation for the Technological Era, 98 Harv L Rev 870 (1985) **§8.11**

Coolley, *RICO: Modern Weaponry Against Software Pirates,* 5

Compatibility & Copyright, 2
Computer Law 7, 11 (July
1985) **§4.19**

F. Delueze, Contracts for the
Transfer of Technologies
(1978) **§9.19**

Dennison, *No Questions Asked,*
Three Pros Wow the Court, 7
Am Law 108 (1985) **§8.22**

De Santo, *Product Expansion in*
the Banking Industry: An
Analysis and Revision of Section
4 (c)(8) of the Bank Holding
Company Act, LIII Fordham L
Rev 1127 *(1985)* **§8.14**

Desmond, *Clear and Present*
Danger, 18/19
Computerworld 15 (1985)
§7.05

Devolder, *Expansionary Possibilities*
for Affiliated Commercial Banks:
A Current Dilemma, 16 Pac LJ
895 (1985) **§8.11**

DiBernardo, *The Taxation of High*
Technology, 61 Taxes 813
(1983) **§3.28**

Discovery of Computerized
Information, 12 Cap UL Rev
71 (1982) **§1.08**

Dombroff, *Demonstrative Evidence:*
Computer Reconstruction
Techniques, 18 Trial 52 (1982)
§1.08

Dow, *Damages Under the Federal*
Electronic Fund Transfer Act: A
Proposed Construction of Sections
910 & 915, 23 AM Bus LJ 1
(1985) **§8.19**

Drater, *Trade Secret Law: An*
Impediment to Trade in Computer
Software, 1 Santa Clara
Computer & High-Tech LJ
27 (1985) **§2.11**

Dray & Menosky, *Computers and a*
New World Order: Is Adapting
Computers to the Various Cultures

of the World an Idea Whose Time
Has Come or a Pipe Dream with
Commercial Overtones?, 86 Tech
Rev 12 (1983) **§1.03**

Dunn, *Defining Scope of Copyright*
Protection for Computer Software,
38 Stanford L Rev 497 (Jan
1985) **§2.06**

Durney, *The Warranty of*
Merchantability and Computer
Software Contracts: A Square Peg
in a Round Hole, 59 Wash L
Rev 511 (1984) **§3.09**

E

Egan, *Study: Micro Privacy A*
Worry, 1984 Mgmt
Information Sys Week 14
§6.03

EIAJ Disavows Responsibility for
Slump in US Semiconductor
Industry; Micron Files Suit
Against Japanese Manufacturers,
2 Computer Law 27 (Oct
1985) **§9.03**

J. Eidenberg, The New
Telecommunications
Landscape 4 (1984) **§5.19**

Einhorn, *The Enforceability of*
"Tear-me-open" Software License
Agreements, 7 J Pat &
Trademark Off Socy 509 (Oct
1985) **§2.16A**

Einschlag & Michaelson, *Patent*
& Trade Secret Protection of
Software: Patentability of
Programs—Nature & Scope of
Trade Secret Protection: Course
Handbook Series Number 225,
Computer Software & Chips
Protection & Marketing
Program (1986) **§2.18**

Eisenstat, *Structuring Distributor*
And Dealer Agreements For
Distribution of Computer

Computer Law 10-13 (Dec 1985) §13.16

Gest, *Report on Privacy: Who is Watching You?*, 93 US News & World Rep 34, July 12, 1982 §6.04

Gilbourne, *The Grant of Marketing Rights Early in the Product Life Cycle of Hardware and Software: The Problem of Distribution Channel Lock-in*, 1 Computer Law 28 (1984) §3.04

Gilbourne, *Software Publishing: Sourcing and Distributing Microcomputer Software*, 5 Computer L Inst, Univ S Cal L Center pt VIII VIII-1 (1984) §3.04

Gilbourne, *The Use of Escrows for Source Code and Technical Design Specifications in OEM Transactions*, 1 Computer Law 1 (1984) §3.10

Gilburne, *Manufacturer's Ban on "Hardware-Only" Sales Did Not Constitute Per Se Illegal Price Fixing*, 2 Computer Law 1, 40-41 (Jan 1985) §4.09

Gilburne, *Marketing Strategies Aimed at Alleviating "Free Riding" Fears do not Constitute Sherman Act Violations*, 2 Computer Law 1, 39-40 (Jan 1985) §4.23

Gilburne, *Trade Practices - Commodore Agrees Not to Advertise Products or Products' Capabilities Unless They Exist at Time*, 1 Computer Law 7, 29-30 (Aug 1984) §4.12

Gilburne & Meyer, *Liability for Copyright Infringement Committed by Third Parties or Employees*, 2 Computer Law 1 (Apr 1985) §2.10

Gish, *Computer Crime & Punishment*, 1 Info Strategy 11 (1985) §7.09

Glasner, *Export Proposal Puts Blitz on Hi-Tech*, 1 Comp L Strategist 5 (1984) §9.10

Goldberg, *Copyright Protection for Computer Programs, Data Bases, & Related Works: Course Handbook Series Number 225*, Computer Software & Chips Protection & Manufacturing Program (1986) §2.06

Goldstein, *Study Reveals Widespread Piracy*, 224 Industry Week 51-2 (Feb 4, 1985) §7.03

Goodrich, *Hard Law for Software*, 4 Cal Law 18 (1984) §2.09A

Gordon & Milligan, *Establishing Corporate Compliance Programs to Control Unauthorized Duplication of Microcomputer Software by Employees*, 2 Computer Law 11 (Apr 1985) §2.10

Gordon & Starr, *Emerging Issues in Computer Procurements*, VI Computer/LJ Summer 1985 §3.14

Gordon & Starr, *Emerging Issues in Computer Procurements*, 5 Computer L Inst, Univ S Cal L Center pt XI XI-1 (1984) §3.05

Gould, *Technological Change and Competition*, 4 J Bus Strategy 66 (1983) §10.04

Government and Technical Progress: A Cross-Industry Analysis (R Nelson ed 1982) §1.02

Graham, *The State's Role in the New Age of Communications*, 56 Fla BJ 210 (1982) §§5.13, 55.15

Agreements, 4 Computer LJ 625 (1984) **§3.11**

Hardy, *Transborder Data Flow: An Overview and Critique of Recent Concerns,* 9 Rutgers Computer & Tech LJ 247 (1983) **§9.09**

Harlow, *Trade Secret Policy vs. Antitrust Policy: Four Lessons from the Tension,* I Trade Secret Law Rep 1, 18-23 (May 1985) **§4.09**

Harper, Computer Evidence is Coming, 70 ABA J 80 (1984) **§1.08**

Harris, *A Market-Oriented Approach to the Use of Trade Secret or Copyright Protection (or Both?) for Software,* 25 Jurimetrics J 147 (Winter 1985) **§2.12**

Harris, *Apple Computer Inc v Franklin Computer Corp—Does a ROM a Computer Make?,* 24 Jurimetrics 248 (1984) **§2.09A**

Harvey, *Extra-Territorial Jurisdiction Under the Lanham Trademark Act,* 2 Computer Law 5 (Nov 1985) **§9.01**

Hayden, *Copyright & the Right to Copy: Japan's Proposed New Legislation,* 58 Law Inst J 414 (Apr 1984) **§2.17**

Hayden, *Database Growth: 23% Annually,* Management Information Sys Week, Nov 7, 1984, at 48 **§6.02**

R. Head, Federal Information Systems Management: Issues and New Directions (1982) **§1.01**

Heintz, *Of Bits and Bytes,* 5 LA Law 43 (1982) **§1.07**

Helein, *Software Lock-in & Antitrust Tying Arrangements: The Lesson of Data General,* 5 Comp LJ 329-45 (Winter 1985) **§4.09**

Hevertz, Soviet Microprocessors and Microcomputers, BYTE, Apr 1984 **§9.09**

Hewes, *Gateways to On-Line Services,* PC World, May 1985, at 149-56 **§6.02**

Hewes & Preston, *Is There a Time Bomb in the Electronic Funds Transfer Act?,* 100 Banking LJ 274 (1983) **§8.19**

Hill, *Transfer of Technology From the United States to Nigeria: A Balancing of Legal Interests,* 6 Tex SUL Rev 380 (1981) **§9.16**

Himelson, *Frankly, Incredible: Unconscionability in Computer Contracts,* 4 Computer LJ 695 (1984) **§3.18**

Hoffman, *An Overview of International Software Protection,* 2 Computer Law 14 (Nov 1985) **§9.01**

Hoffman, *Computers for the Law Office: Some Guidelines for Coping with Rapid Marketplace Change,* 22 Law Off Econ & Mgmt 260 (1981) **§1.08**

Hoffman, *The Every Lawyer's Computer—Now and Tomorrow,* 55 NY St BJ 43 (1983) **§1.08**

P. Hoffman, Software Contract Forms (1984) **§3.11**

Hoffman, *Software Development and Services Agreements,* 24 Jurimetrics 58 (1983) **§3.11**

Hollander, *Antitrust—Tying Sale of "Initial Loading" Program to Sale of "Dump-Restore" Program,* 2 The Computer Law Monitor 2, 81-83 (Nov 1984) **§4.04**

Hollander, *Antitrust—Tying Sale of "Operating System" Program* to Sale of Central Processing Unit (CPU), 2 The Computer Law Monitor 2, 83-84 (Nov 1984) **§4.10**

Hollman, *Emerging Issues in Software License Agreements,* 5 Computer L Inst, Univ S Cal L Center pt IX IX-1 (1984) **§3.12**

Homet, *"Getting the Message": Statutory Approaches to Electronic Information Delivery & the Duty of Carriage,* 37 Federal Comms LJ 217 (1985) **§5.01**

Hopkins, *The Status of Patent Law Concerning Computer Programs: The Proper Form for Legal Protection,* 33 Drake L Rev 155 (Winter 1983-1984) **§2.05**

Horowitz, *Printed Words, Computers and Democratic Societies,* 59 Va Q Rev 620 (1983) **§1.03**

Horwitz, *Proposed Changes In Regulations Governing Deposits of Computer Programs With the Copyright Office,* 26 Jurimetrics J 305 (Spring 1986) **§2.10**

How Uncle Sam Misuses Computers, Bus Week, June 28, 1982, at 88 **§1.01**

Howard, *Vertical Integration: Should the AT&T Doctrine be Extended?* 52 Antitrust LJ 259 (1983) **§5.18**

Hunt, *Multilateral Cooperation in Export Controls—The Role of COCOM,* 14 U Tol L Rev 1285 (1983) **§9.09**

Hyde, *1981 Mexican Transfer of Technology Law,* 15 Law Am 37 (1983) **§9.16**

I

Imai & Sakuma, *An Analysis of Japan-US Semiconductor Friction,* 4 Econ Eye 13 (1983) **§10.04**

Information Flow Vital to Global Economy, 6 Transnatl Data Rep 238 (1983) **§6.09**

Information Management: Strategies for the Future, 63 Nat F 2 (1983) **§1.07**

Information Security & Privacy, 24 EDP Analyzer 1 (Feb 1986) **§6.03**

Inman, *Phone Wars: AT&T Tells Everyone Its Long-Distance Calls are Better Than MCI's,* Wall St J, Oct 27, 1983, at 1 **§5.19**

The International Telecommunications Act of 1983: Hearings on S. 999 Before the Comm on Commerce, Science, and Transportation, 98th Cong, 1st Sess 24 (1983) **§6.16**

International Telecommunications and Information Policy: Selected Issues for the 1980's: Before the Senate Comm on Foreign Relations (A Report prepared by the Congressional Research Service, Library of Congress), 98th Cong, 1st Sess 94 (1983) **§6.16**

C. Irwin, Markets Without Boundaries (1985) **§5.18**

C. Irwin, Negotiating Telecommunications Contracts: Business and Legal Aspects (1985) **§5.19**

J

Jacobsen, *Mexico's Computer Decree: The Problem of Performance Requirements and a*

in the American Corporation (1983) §10.01

Karasik, *The Computerization of an 11-Member Firm,* 69 ABA J 1236 (1983) §1.08

Karjala, *Lessons from the Computer Software Protection Debate in Japan,* 1984 Ariz St LJ 53 (Winter 1984) §2.17

Katsh, *Congress Reduces Antitrust Roadblocks for Basic and Applied R & D Joint Ventures,* 2 Computer Law 1, 32-38 (Jan 1985) §4.01

Katz & Willig, *Toward Competition in Phone Service: The Case for Freeing AT&T,* 7 Regulation 43 (1983) §§5.17, 5.19

Kayne, *Data General v Digidyne Corp: Tying the Hands of the Computer Industry,* 4 Comp L Rep 1, July 1985, at 1 §4.09

Kelman, *Computer Evidence and the Police and Criminal Evidence Bill,* New LJ, Mar 9, 1984 at 237 §1.08

Kelso & Rebey, *Problems of Interpretation Under the 1980 Computer Amendment,* 23 Santa Clara L Rev 1001 (Fall 1983) §2.08

Kemp, *Trade Secret & Copyright Protection for Mass-Marketed Computer Programs,* 90 Commercial LJ 525 (Dec 1985) §2.18

Kenfield & Woodbury, *Import-Customs Regulations of Computer Technology,* 10 NCJ Intl Law & Com Reg 609-15 (Summer 1985) §9.09

Keplinger, *International Protection for Computer Programs and Semiconductor Chips: Course Handbook Series Number 225,* Computer Software & Chip

Protection & Marketing Program (1986) §9.09

Keplinger, *Software Protection in Europe and Other Civil Law Jurisdictions,* Computer L Inst at 381 (1984) §2.12

Kesler, *The Legal Realitites of Transborder Data Flows,* Scott Rep, Aug 1985, at 8 §6.09

Kidwell, *The Day the Machine Broke Down,* 69 ABA J 50 (1983) §1.07

King, *Local Government Use of Information Technology: The Next Decade,* 42 Pub Ad Rev 25 (1982) §1.01

Kirkland, *Ma Blue: IBM's Move Into Communications,* Fortune, Oct 14, 1984, at 52 §1.01

Klasson, *Japanese Copyright Proposal Could Damage Software Trade,* 1 Computer L Strategist 3 (1984) §2.17

Kline, *Requiring an Election of Protection for Patentable-Copyrightable Computer Programs,* 67 J Pat & Trademark Off Socy 280 (June 1985) §2.06

Kneips, *Regulating by Partial Deregulation: The Case of Telecommunications,* 35 Ad L Rev 391 (1983) §5.17

Kovach, *Application of Computer-assisted Analysis Techniques to Taxation,* 15 Akron L Rev 713 (1982) §1.08

Krajewski, *Database Types,* BYTE, Oct 1985, at 137 §6.02

Kreiss, *The Theory of Overclaiming & its Applicability to Diamond v Diehr,* 5 Cardoza L Rev 97 (1983) §2.04

Kriendler, *Contracting for the Development of Customized*

Maloof, *Tax Treatment of Sale of Software*, 2 Computer Law 3 (Mar 1983) **§3.29**

E. Mansfield, A. Romeo, M. Schwartz, Z. Teece, S. Wagner & P. Brach, Technology Transfer, Productivity and Economic Policy (1982) **§1.02**

Mantle, *Trade Secret and Copyright Protection of Computer Software*, 4 Computer LJ 669 (1984) **§2.16**

Marcin, *Computer Uses in Law Libraries*, 6 ALSA F 38 (1982) **§1.01**

Markey, *State and Federal Taxation of Computer Software: A Functional Approach*, 4 Computer LJ 737 (1984) **§3.28**

Marks, *Regulations and Deregulation in The United States and Other Countries*, 25 Jurimetrics J 5 (1984) **§5.19**

Marks & Casserly, *On Introduction to the FCC's Third Computer Inquiry*, 2 Computer Law 1 (1985) **§5.07**

Marmaro, *Criminal Law and Technology Protection: Prosecuting a Dishonest Employee*, 2 Computer Law 15 (Dec 1985) **§7.11**

Marsteller & Tucker, *Problems of the Technology Transfer Provisions in the Law of the Sea Treaty*, 24 IDEA 167 (1983) **§9.12**

Matley, *Sees the Need For a National Computer Policy*, Information Sys News, July 23, 1984, at 35 **§1.02**

Matthews, *Protection of Rights of Individuals in the EEC in Relation to Automatic Processing*

of Data, Intl Bus Law 410 (Oct 1984) **§6.09**

Mayo, *Business Battles its In-house Pirates*, 4 Bus Computer Sys 60 (1985) **§§7.03, 7.04**

Mayo, Hensler, & Smith, *The AT&T Valuation Controversy*, 17 Merg & Acq 20 (1982) **§5.11**

McCoy, *Attracting and Retaining Key Employees in the Computer Industry: An Analysis of Various Strategies—Pt I*, 1 Computer Law 1 (1984) **§3.11**

McCoy, *Attracting and Retaining Key Employees in the Computer Industry: An Analysis of Various Strategies—Pt II*, 1 Computer Law 14 (1984) **§3.11**

McCoy, *Unitary Taxation: A Primer for the Expanding Technology Company*, 1 Computer Law 10 (Nov 1984) **§3.29**

McCracken, *Antitrust Issues in Structuring Joint R & D Ventures*, 5 Computer L Inst, Univ S Cal L Center pt VI VI-1 (1984) **§4.01**

McCracken, Gibson, Dunn & Crutcher, *The Vertical Restraints Guidelines: Theoretical Purpose & Practical Effects*, 2 Computer Law 8 (Aug 1985) **§4.01**

McFarlane, *Criminal Trials and the Technological Revolution*, New LJ, Apr 8, 1983, at 327 **§1.08**

McGee, *Computer Software and the Investment Tax Credit*, 5 Computer LJ 3 (Winter 1985) **§3.29**

McGee, *Computer Software and the Research Credit*, 5 Computer LJ 3 (Winter 1985) **§3.29**

McGinnins & Ackelsberg, *Effective Innovation*

Management: Missing Link in Strategic Planning?, 4 J Bus Strategy 59 (1983) **§1.07**

McGonagle, *The Electronic Law Library: The Expanding Role of Computerized Research*, 19 Trial 40 (1983) **§1.07**

McKenna, *Preemption Under the Communications Act*, 37 Federal Comms LJ 1 (1985) **§§5.02, 5.05, 5.06**

McKenzie, *Changes in Export Controls on Computers and Software*, 2 Computer Law 28 (1985) **§9.10**

McKenzie, *Recent Developments in Contracts on Software Exports*, 2 Computer Law 11 (May 1985) **§9.10**

McLellan, *Microelectronics and the Law: More than Meets the Eye*, 87 Case & Com 3 (1982) **§1.07**

Meese, *Export Controls to China: An Emerging Trend for Dual-Use Exports*, 7 Intl Trade LJ 20 (1981-82) **§9.17**

Merwin, *How Smart Crooks use Plastic*, Forbes, Sept 9, 1985, at 88 **§7.05**

Meyerson, *The Cable Communications Policy Act of 1984: A Balancing Act on the Coaxial Wires*, 19 Ga L Rev 543 (1985) **§5.02**

Mihm, *Software Piracy & the Personal Computer: Is the 1980 Copyright Act Effective?*, 4 Computer LJ 171 (Summer 1983) **§2.08**

Milgram, *Antitrust Issues In Licensing Computer Technology*, 4 Computer L Inst, Univ S Cal L Center pt III III-1 (1983) **§4.20**

Miller, *The Admissibility of Computer-Generated Evidence in Georgia*, 18 Ga St BJ 137 (1982) **§1.08**

Miller, *A Report on the New Payments Code*, 39 Bus L 1215 (1984) **§8.19**

Miller, *Beware of the "Hacker" Attack*, 76 Banking 50 (Nov 1984) **§7.15**

Miller, *Robotics: Future Factories, Future Workers*, 470 Annals Am Acad 9 (1983) **§1.01**

Miller & Scott, *Commercial Paper, Bank Deposits and Collections, and Commercial Electronic Fund Transfers*, 38 Bus L 1129 (1983) **§8.19**

Mini-symposium on Micro Computers in Local Government, 44 Pub Ad Rev 57 (1984) **§1.01**

Molnar & Babb, *The Electronic Age Challenges Education*, 16 Appalachia 1 (1982) **§1.01**

Monahan, *The Regulation of Technical Data Under the Arms Control Act of 1976 and the Export Administration Act of 1979: A Matter of Executive Discretion*, 13 GBC Intl & Comparative L Rev 169 (1983) **§9.10**

Monti, *Automating Deposition Digests: How to Develope A System*, Trial, Jan 1985, at 40 **§1.08**

Moran, *Computers for Small Cases: How Lawyers Can Set Up a Computerized System*, Trial, Jan 1985, at 20 **§1.08**

Morone & Ivins, *Problems and Opportunities in Technology Transfer from the National Laboratories to Industry*, 25 Research Mgmt 35 (1982) **§1.02**

Monitor, Nov 1985, at 164, col 2 §4.23

Note, *Teletext & the FCC: Turning The Content Regulatory Clock Backwards*, 64 BUL Rev 1057 (1984) §5.02

Note, *To Defer Or Not to Defer: The Question for The D.C. Circuit In Reviewing FCC Decisions*, 36 Federal Comms LJ 293 (1984) §5.02

Nulty, *How Personal Computers Change Manger's Lives*, Fortune, Sept 3, 1984, at 38 §1.01

O

O'Brien, *Cash Control System on the IBM Displaywriter*, 9 Legal Econ 28 (1983) §1.07

Oliver, *A Further Analysis of OFPP's Continuing Effort to Change the Competitive Forces in the Government Marketplace*, 29 Fed B News & J 317 (1982) §5.19

Olson, *Hacking the Hacker is the Ultimate Hack*, Rocky Mountain News, Apr 20, 1986, at 78 §7.05

Onove, *Using Personal Computers in Tax Practice*, 70 ABA J 96 (1984) §1.08

O'Reilly, *More Than Cheap Talk Propels MCI*, 107 Fortune, Jan 24, 1983, at 68, §5.19

Ortner, *Current Trends in Software Protection—A Litigation Perspective*, 25 Jurimetrics J 319 (1985) §§2.01, 2.16

Ortner, *The Privacy Protection Aspect of Transborder Data Flow*, 21 Intl Bus Law 171 (Apr 1984) §6.09

Osborne, *Going to Market: Tax Considerations for Inventors and Programmers In The Computer Industry*, 67 J Pat & Trademark Off Socy 149-59 (Mar 1985) §3.29

Overcoming the Obstacles to Implementation of Point of Sale Electronic Funds Transfer Systems; EFTRA and the New Uniform Payments Code, 69 Va L Rev 1351 (1983) §8.19

Overly, *Regulations of Critical Technologies Under the Export Administration Act of 1979 & the Proposed Export Administration Amendments of 1985: American Business versus National Security*, 18 NCJ Intl Law & Com Reg 425-451 (Spring 1985) §9.10

P

Page, *Stop Payment in the New Uniform Payments Code*, 9 Rutgers J Computers & L 353 (1983) §8.19

Palenski, *Computer Personnel Under The Fair Labor Standards Act*, 3 Computer Law 27 (Feb 1986) §4.22

Paperless Filing, Retrieval of Information Sought by SEC, 155 J Acct 20 (1983) §1.07

A. Pearce & P. Verveer, Some Policy-Oriented Reflections on the AT&T Antitrust Settlement (1983) §5.19

Pearson & Toedt III, *An Annotated Guide to Establishing & Registering US Computer Software Copyrights*, 3 Computer Law 22 (Feb 1986) §4.15

Pecieroni, *The Ninth Circuit has held that all Computer Programs are Copyrightable Regardless of Their Function*, 23 Duq L 457 (Winter 1985) §2.06

Pengilley, *Machine Information: Is it Hearsay?*, 13 Melb UL Rev 617 (1982) §1.08

Perry & Wallich, *Can Computer Crime be Stopped?* 21 IEEE Spectrum 34 (May 1984) §7.01

Peters, *Is the Third Time the Charm? A Comparison of the Government's Major Antitrust Settlements with AT&T this Century*, 15 Seton Hall 252 (1985) §§5.11, 5.12

Peters, *Registration of Computer Programs & Mask Works Fixed in Semiconductor Chip Products: Course Handbook Series Number 225*, Computer Software & Chips Protection & Marketing Program (1986) §2.10

Petry, *Computer Software: Course Handbook Series Number 226*, Computer Software & Chips Protection & Marketing Program (1986) §2.06

Phillips, *Cracking Down on Copycats; Fighting Counterfeiters of Trademarked Products Has Recently Became Fashionable*, 5 Cal Law 15 (1985) §4.19

N. Pilz, F. Weber & I. Gibbons, The New Telecommunications Marketplace (1983) §5.14

Piovia, A Common-Sense Guide to Law-Office Automation (1985) §1.08

Pitofsky, *A Framework For Antitrust Analysis of Joint Ventures*, 54 Antitrust LJ 3 (Nov 1985) §4.01

Plaia & Kaufman, *Section 337 of The Tariff Act of 1930 As Amended, Effective Protection For Changing Technology*, 10 Rutgers Computer & Tech LJ 219 (1985) §9.06

Plousadis, *Soviet Diversion of United States Technology: The Circumvention of COCOM and U.S. Reexport Controls, and Proposed Solutions*, 7 Fordham Intl LJ 561 (1984) §9.09

Port, *Here Comes the Fastest Chip on Earth*, Bus Week, Mar 4, 1985, at 205 §10.02

The Power of Technological Innovation, 48 Bus Q 83 (1983) §1.08

Pretty, *Harnessing a Personal Computer to Win Cases*, 69 ABA J 1438 (1983) §1.08

Price, *Counterfeiting of Computer Goods & Trademarks: Strategy & Tactics with Customs on Infringements: Course Handbook Series Number 226*, Computer Software & Chips Protection & Marketing Program (1986) §2.18

Price, *IBM Rep Denies VDT Harm From Radiation*, Govt Computer News, Mar 29, 1985 §1.08

Privacy in Peril Technology and Government Erode Protections, Law Scope, May 1983, at 565-69 §§6.04, 6.07, 6.08

Privacy in the Electronic Age: US Law a Decade Later, Scott Rep, Nov 1985, at 9 §6.14

Privacy Lost: Have Computers Already Collected More Data About Us Than Is Safe?, Student Law, Dec 1983, at 15:20 §6.03

Privacy Rights in Cordless Telephone Conversations, 18 J Marshall L Rev 1015 (Summer 1985) **§6.03**

Proceedings of the 1984 Symposium on Security and Privacy, sponsored by the Technical Committee on Security and Privacy, IEEE Computer Society, in Oakland, California, Apr 29-May 2, 1984, **§6.01**

Pugel, *Semiconductors and Computers: Emerging Competitive Battlegrounds in the Asia-Pacific Region*, Research In Intl Bus and Finance 231 pt B (1984) **§10.04**

Q

Quade, *Computers: Don't Fear Them, Lawyers Told*, 68 ABA J 253 (1982) **§1.07**

Quade, *Computing the Evidence: Technology Moves into the Courtroom*, 69 ABA J 882 (1983) **§1.08**

Quade, *Futureworld: Lawyers Become 'Computerniks'*, 68 ABA J 255 (1982) **§1.07**

R

Rabinovitz & Whalen, *Selected Problems in Taxation of Computer Software*, 4 Computer LJ 605 (1984) **§3.28**

Radway, *Antitrust, Technology Transfers, and Joint Ventures in Latin American Development*, 15 Law Am 47 (1983) **§9.16**

Rahman, *The Interaction between Science, Technology and Society: Historical and Comparative*

Perspectives, 33 Intl Soc Sci J 508 (1981) **§1.02**

Rapport, *Launching Into the Telecommunication Age: The Dawn of the Electronic Era*, 56 Fla BJ 208 (1982) **§5.05**

R. Raysman & P. Brown, Computer Law: Drafting and Negotiating Forms and Agreements (1984) **§3.03, 3.43**

Raysman & Brown, *Copyright Infringement by Nonidentical Software*, 93 NYLJ 1 (Apr 9, 1985) **§2.08**

Raysman & Brown, *Patent Protection for Software*, 190 NYLJ 1 (Nov 3, 1983) **§2.04**

Reaves, *The Chips Police*, 69 ABA J 884 (1983) **§7.07**

Reback, *Antitrust Issues in Pricing Computer Software*, 5 Computer L Inst, Univ S Cal L Center pt V V-1 (1984) **§4.01**

Reback, *Further Reflections on Data General and the Law of Pricing Unbundled Products*, 1 Computer Law 10 (Nov 1984) **§4.13**

Reback, *Of Bits, Bytes and Price Discrimination: The Robinson-Patman Act*, 1 Computer Law 7, 1-8 (Aug 1984) **§4.23**

Reback, Greguras & Davidson, *China & South Asia Export License Application*, Scott Rep, Oct 1985, at 1 **§9.17**

Reilly, *Impact of the New Patent and Trademark Fee Bill: What Hath Been Wrought?*, 65 J Pat Off Socy 166 (1983) **§4.15**

I. Reinecke, Micro Invaders: How the New World of Technology Works (1982) **§1.01**

Remer, *Goodbye Yellow Pads, Hello Computers*, 3 Cal Law 49 (1983) **§1.08**

Resale, Shared Use Regulation: Can the "Invisible Hand" Hold on to Ma Bell?, 35 Fed Com LJ 209 (1983) **§5.17**

Riccardi, *The German Federal Data Protection Act of 1977: Protecting the Right to Privacy?*, 6 B C Intl Comp L 243 (Winter 1983) **§6.11**

Rice, *Computer Products and the Federal Warranty Act*, 1 Computer Law 8 (Sept 1984) **§3.09**

Rice, *Trade Secret Clauses in Shrink-Wrap Licenses*, 2 Computer Law 17 (Feb 1985) **§2.12**

G. Ripper & J. Wanderley, The Brazilian Computer and Communications Regulatory Environment and Trans Border Data Flow Policy (1980) **§6.11**

Ritchie, *Banks Should Be Able to Offer Financial Services Nationally*, 124 Tr & Est 18 (1985) **§8.14**

Robbins, *Selecting a Law Firm's Computerized Timekeeping and Billing Systems*, 72 Ill BJ 256 (1984) **§1.08**

Robinson, *An assessment of state and federal jurisdiction to regulate access charges after the AT&T divestiture*, 1983 BYU L Rev 376 **§5.15**

Robinson, *Gallium Arsenide Chips*, BYTE, Nov 1984, at 211 **§1.05**

Roffe, *UNCTAD: Transfer of Technology Code*, 18 J World Trade L 176 (1984) **§9.12**

Rogers, *Wrap Leases*, 5 Computer L Inst, Univ S Cal L Center pt X X-1 (1984) **§3.29**

R. Romano, New Telecommunications Marketplace (1983) **§5.19**

Root, *Copyright Infringement of Computer Programs: A Modification for the Substantial Similarity Test*, 58 Minn L Rev 1284 (June 1984) **§2.08**

N. Rosenberg, Inside the Black Box: Technology and Economics (1982) **§1.02**

Roth, *FCC seeks Update of Telecom Policy*, Govt Computer News, Aug 30, 1985, at 77 **§5.07**

M. Rothenberg, The History of Science and Technology in the United States: A Critical and Selective Bibliography (1982) **§1.07**

Rubin, *Companies Benefit from Site-License Agreement*, 3 PC 60 (May 6, 1986) **§2.10**

Ruby, *Terminal Behavior*, PC Week, Nov 13, 1984, at 127 **§1.01**

Ruidl, *Investment Credit and Related Party Leases: The Impact of the Peterson Case*, 61 Taxes 238 (1983) **§3.29**

Russo & Derwin, *Copyright in the "Looks and Feel" of Computer Software*, 2 Computer Law 1 (Feb 1985) **§2.10**

Russo, Derwin & Hale, *The Impact of the Uniform Trade Secret Act on California Trade Secret Law*, 3 Computer Law 1 (Mar 1986) **§4.22**

Ryan & Schnitz, *The Justice Department's Guidelines on Vertical Restraints*, 74 Ill BJ 2 (Oct 1985) **§4.01**

Agenda, 53 Harv Educ Rev 412 (1983) §1.01

Sherizen, *Computer Crime Requires Preventive Action by Executives,* 18 Computerworld 11 (Oct 1984) §7.15

Sherman, *Special Problems in Dealing with Software Authors,* 191 Computer L Inst 337 (1984) §2.01

Shidler, *Computer Tax Research and Tax Research Sources,* 12 Colo Law 1960 (1983) §1.08

Shinn, *An Overview of Unauthorized Electronic Fund Transfers; Alternatives in Reducing Consumer Liability,* 90 Com LJ 216 (1985) §8.19

Shuey, *Legal Technology—1982 Update,* 11 Colo Law 3015 (1982) §1.08

Shupack, *Cashier's Checks, Certified Checks and True Cash Equivalence,* 6 Cardozo L Rev 467 (1985) §8.14

Simison, *R2D2 May be a Wiz, But Robots For Home Use Still Can't Do Much,* Wall St J, Apr 25, 1985, at 39 §1.01

The Smart Machine Revolution: Providing Products with Brainpower, Bus Week, July 5, 1976, at 38 §1.03

Smith, *Five Voice Synthesizers,* BYTE, Sept 1984, at 337 §1.05

Smith, *New Developments: Software in the U.K.,* Computer L Strategist, Aug 1985, at 5 §9.17

Snipes & Crook, *Introducing Computers into Local Government Administration,* 9 Current Mun Probs 66 (1982) §1.01

M. Snow, Marketplace for Telecommunications ch 4 (1986) §5.01

Sobel, *The Antitrust Interface with Patents and Innovation: Acquisition of Patents. Improvement Patents and Grant-backs, Non-Use, Fraud on the Patent Office. Development of New Products and Joint Research,* National Institute on Industrial and Intellectual Property, 53 Antitrust 3, at 681-712 §4.15

Software Failure Causes a $32 Billion Overdraft, XIII EDPACS 10 (Jan 1986) §8.14

Solomon, *The Copyrightability of Computer Software Containing Trade Secrets,* 63 Wash ULQ 131 (Spring 1985) §2.18

Solomon, *Personal Privacy & the "1984" Syndrome,* 7 W New England L Rev 753 (Winter 1985) §8.20

Soma, *Legal Analysis of Electronic Bulletin Board Activities,* 7 W New Eng LJ 571 (1985) §7.11

Soma & Youngs, *Confidential Communications and Information in a Computer Era,* (to be published in Hofstra L Rev, Fall 1984) §6.18

Sprowl, *Bridging the Gap Between Technology and Legal Protection,* 5 Computer L Inst, Univ S Cal L Center pt I I-1 (1984) §2.01

Sprowl, *New Age of Computers in the Law Office,* 71 Ill BJ 478 (1983) §1.07

Sprowl, *The New Age of Computers in the Law Office,* 24 Law Off Econ & Mgmt 223 (1983) §1.08

F. Starkey, The New
Telecommunications
Landscape (1984) §5.14

Steinberg, *Antitrust Litigation with
Competitors: Tying and
Horizontal Restraints,* 17
Computer Litigation
Resolving Computer Related
Disputes and Protecting
Proprietary Rights 725 (1983)
§4.13

I. Stelzer, The Post-decree
Telecommunications Industry
(1982) §5.19

Stern, *Another Look at Copyright
Protection of Software: Did the
1980 Act Do Anything for Object
Code?* 3 Computer LJ 1 (Fall
1981) §2.08

Stern, *Commentary on O.S.C. v.
Apple,* Computer Law Rep 81
(1983) §4.23

Stern, *Preemption and Relation of
SCPA to Other United States
Laws,* 2 Computer Law 9 (Jan
1985) §2.10

Stern, *Section 117 of Copyright
Act: Charter of the Software
Users' Rights or an Illusory
Promise?,* 7 W New England L
Rev 459 (Winter 1985) §2.08

Stipp, *Computer Bulletin Boards
Fret Over Liability for Stolen
Data,* Wall St J, Nov 9, 1984,
at 31 §7.17A

*Stipulations Speeded Trial But
Imposed Steep Costs,* Legal
Times of Wash, Jan 18, 1982,
at 1 §5.13

Stohlgren, *The Nature and
Taxability of Computer Software,*
22 Washburn LJ 103 (1982)
§3.30

Stout, *Protection of Programing in
the Aftermath of Diamond v*

Diehr, 4 Computer LJ 207
(Fall 1983) §2.04

Stover, *Copyright Protection for
Computer Programs in the United
Kingdom, West Germany & Italy:
A Comparative Overview,* 7 Loy
LA Intl & Comp LJ 279
(Spring 1984) §2.17

Strossier & Siegel, *A Computer
Sent Me to Jail,* Woman's Day
124 (Nov 1985) §6.04

Sullivan, *Computer Criminal
Profiled as a "Modern-Day"
Robin Hood,* 18
Computerworld 10 (1984)
§7.03

Sullivan & Shaw, *Criminal
Penalties for Misappropriation of
Computer Technology,* 2
Computer Law 19 (Jan 1985)
§§7.10, 7.17

Surrel, *The Treatment of Computer
Software Works Made for Hire
Under the Copyright Act of 1976,*
5 Computer LJ 579 (Spring
1985) §2.06

Swartz, *On-Line Databases: The
Legal Dilemma,* Bus Computer
Sys 28 (Jan 1985) §2.10

Swartz, Paving the Way for
Buyer Protection, Bus
Computer Sys 26 (Oct 1984)
§3.09

Swartz, *Telecommuting's Expansion
Poses Host of Legal Questions,*
Information WEEK, Apr 15,
1985, at 38 §1.01

*Sweeping General Exclusion Order
Issues in Section 337 Case,* 27
PTCJ 517 (1984) §9.06

Symposium: Computer Law, 30
Emory LJ 345 (1981) §1.01

Syrowik, *Disclosing Computer
Programs in an Application for a
United States Patent—A Trap for*

Index